S0-AHX-083

A DICTIONARY OF CHRISTIAN DENOMINATIONS

By the same author and published by Burns & Oates

THE LITURGICAL DICTIONARY OF EASTERN CHRISTIANITY
A DICTIONARY OF RELIGIOUS ORDERS

A DICTIONARY OF CHRISTIAN DENOMINATIONS

Peter Day

Continuum

The Tower Building
11 York Road, London SE1 7NX

370 Lexington Avenue
New York, NY 10017-6503

www.continuumbooks.com

First published 2003

British Library Cataloguing-in-Publication Data
A catalogue record for this book is available from the British Library.

ISBN 0–8264–5745–2

Typeset by YHT Ltd, London
Printed and bound in Great Britain by Bookcraft (Bath) Ltd, Midsomer Norton

CONTENTS

Preface and Acknowledgements vii

A-Z of Christian Denominations 1

Alternative Names 503

PREFACE AND ACKNOWLEDGEMENTS

The intended scope of this book is meant to be wide-ranging and inclusive of representative bodies from all varieties of Christian faith groups. However, as no dictionary is ever complete and considering the vast number of individual denominations, sects and cults that exist, and have existed, throughout the world, this single-volume work makes no claim to be an encyclopaedic directory, which would require many volumes to accommodate the details. Some faith groups have been included that may not be considered conventionally Christian, but their omission would have diminished the usefulness of this dictionary.

This is an easy to use, A to Z reference guide for anyone needing quick access to information about a particular Christian denomination, or faith group, whether still in existence or not, and many sects and groups from the earliest times of Christian history have been included as they have played their part in the story of man's worship in the Christian world.

The appendix lists alternative names by which a group may be more familiarly known and this can be used as a guide to the main entry in the dictionary. These entries usually give some historical background material and a brief summary of a denomination's theological standpoint, and many have their alternative names, listed after ❖, at the end of the text. Where appropriate, I have tried to supply some membership details. The statistics used have generally been taken from David B. Barrett *et al.*: World Christian Encyclopedia (2nd edition, 2001), and from J. Gordon Melton's Encyclopedia of American Religions (6th edition, 1999), as well as from denominational websites and literature. A reader wishing to have more recent membership details should seek these from the denomination itself; address details are readily available, in most cases, from Church websites. Most entries contain items printed in CAPITALS, cross-referencing to other, relevant entries in the dictionary.

None of this would have been possible without the assistance, advice and enthusiasm of Paul Burns of Burns and Oates (Continuum International Publishing Group Ltd.) and the helpful guidance of Fr David White. Philip and Rosalind Lund of Lund Theological Books in Cambridge, helped both with the supply of books and much useful information. My special thanks and gratitude for their generosity in supplying advice, essential data and, not least, some humour, go to Fr Adrian Graffy of St John's Seminary, Wonersh, Surrey and Dr Hans van der Hoeven, of the Koninklijke Bibliotheek in The Hague, Netherlands, and to Rufus Munro, who helped in a very material way.

A final, but heartfelt, tribute of thanks goes to my wife Anne, whose skills turned my work into reality and who is, in a real way, its joint author.

Peter D. Day
Cromer, Norfolk, England
January 2003

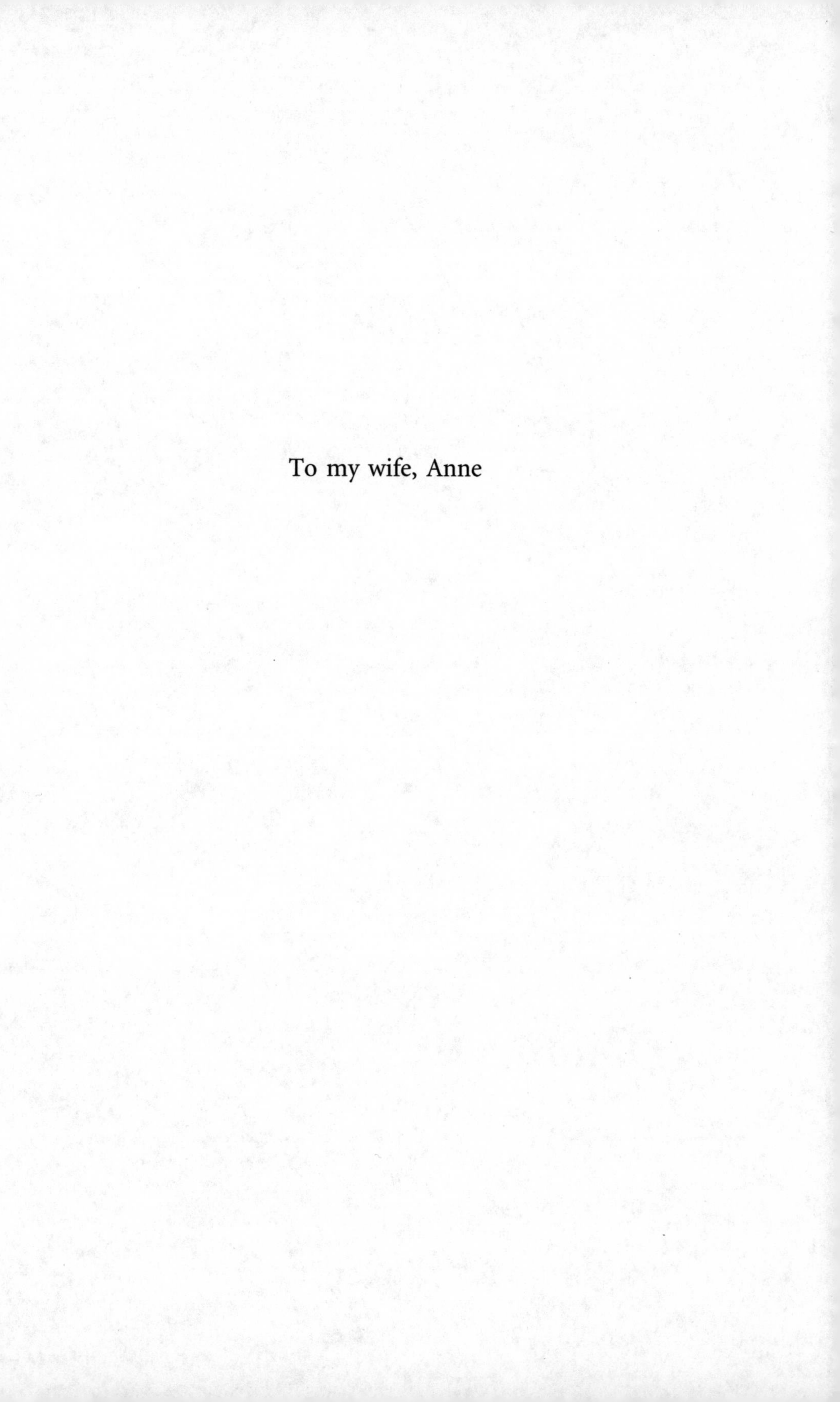

To my wife, Anne

AARONIC ORDER

Dr M. L. Glendenning, who was excommunicated from the CHURCH OF JESUS CHRIST OF LATTER-DAY SAINTS (Mormons) in the 1930s, organized this group in the USA in 1942. Believing that he had received divine revelations led Glendenning to write the *Book of Elias*, one of the major texts used by the Order, and to design the *Aaronic Wheel*, a complex chart which systematizes the full plan by which the Order is to be administered. Followers can be admitted to various types of membership. Tithing membership is a one-year period of probation during which each member gives one tenth of his/her income to the Order; consecrated membership, lasting for another probationary year, can be achieved after the year spent as a tithing member, with the members giving over to the Order all of their possessions; United Order membership, with all rights and privileges, can then be granted. The Order claims to date its history back to *c.* 1600 BC and the start of the Aaronic priesthood among the Israelites; these priests had various names in history such as the Essenes, Baptists and Levites and they entered the modern era as Christians, converting in the first century. The priesthood, they teach, continued throughout the Middle Ages in Europe and into the family of Glendenonwyn. The son of Bishop Glendenning, a Scottish forebear of Dr M. L. Glendenning, brought it to America in 1742. The Order believes in reincarnation and predestination and members hold that humans are begotten of spirits and are not the creation of God. They regard the Church of Jesus Christ of Latter Day Saints to be in a partial state of apostasy. The headquarters of the Aaronic Order is in Salt Lake City and there are members all over the USA.

ABECEDARIANS

A defunct ANABAPTIST sect founded in Wittenberg, Germany, around 1520 by the ILLUMINATI, or as Martin Luther dubbed them, the *Prophets of Zwickau* (ZWICKAU PROPHETS). Included in their number were Nicholas Storch, Thomas Drechsel and Marcus Stübner. They preached a radical Biblicism, rejecting infant baptism and learning in any form, and would not countenance a professional ministry, regarding theology as a form of idolatry. This rejection of knowledge was even extended by the more radical supporters of the sect to include an ignorance of the alphabet, which they held to be a necessary precondition for salvation, and from this extreme view the sect gained its name. One of the most enthusiastic preachers of the doctrine was Andreas Rudolf Bodenstein von Karlstadt (1477–1541), at one time professor of Thomistic philosophy at the University of Wittenberg, where he worked with Martin Luther and began by being a loyal supporter of the younger man, but he later became more extreme in his views, gaining a reputation as a radical reformer through the many pamphlets and tracts he wrote and published. Although not in holy orders, von Karlstadt held a religious service and administered holy communion to the laity on Christmas Day, 1521. The turmoil that followed caused him to denounce his university degrees and flee from Wittenberg, dressed as a barefoot peasant and known as Brother Andreas. He retired to Orlamünde where he published a string of acrimonious pamphlets filled with mystical jargon. His relationship with Martin Luther came to a head in Jena, when Luther tossed a coin at him as a token of open feud. As Luther left Jena his erstwhile friend and colleague shouted out his declamations against the background of pealing city bells. Von Karlstadt was exiled once more and it was Martin Luther who provided him with refuge in Wittenberg. Von Karlstadt's career did not end in ignominy however, for he returned to academic life, becoming professor of Old Testament theology at Basel in 1534, though remaining a controversial figure and continuing to issue his damning pamphlets. He died in Switzerland, of the plague, in 1541.

ABELITES

A fourth-century Christian sect, mentioned by St Augustine, whose members lived in North Africa. They believed that they could marry but must remain virgins, since there was no mention in the Bible of Abel, whose example they followed, having any children. To ensure that the sect survived, each husband and wife adopted a boy and a girl who were expected to follow the example of their foster-parents when they reached adulthood.

❖ Abelians; Abelonians

ABRAHAMITES

There seem to have been two unrelated sects bearing this name, both now defunct.

1 Some ninth-century Syrian heretics who were named Abrahamites after their leader, Ibrahim of Antioch; they rejected Christ's divinity.

2 A short-lived eighteenth-century Bohemian Christian-Judaizing sect which was led by John Pita, whose members claimed to practise a pre-Abrahamic religion; they believed in one God, but not in the Trinity, accepted the Lord's Prayer and the ten commandments from the Bible, but denied original sin and divine punishment. Saturday was kept as the sabbath and dietary laws precluded the eating of pork; circumcision was sometimes practised. John Pita was seized, sentenced and executed in 1748. Although there was provision granted in Bohemia in 1781 for the toleration of non-Roman Catholics, the Abrahamites were seen as heretical because they refused to describe themselves either as Jews or Christians and were banished to Transylvania in 1783. Some converted to ROMAN CATHOLICISM, but others remained with the declining sect. There have been suggestions that some remnants of the Abrahamite sect persisted in

parts of Europe into the early part of the twentieth century.

ACACIANS

Followers and supporters of Patriarch Acacius of Constantinople (*d.* 489), who was in part responsible for the Acacian schism of 484–519. This was a division between the Eastern Church and Rome, when the eastern emperor, Zeno, promulgated the *Henoticon,* a letter addressed to 'the bishops, clergy, monks and faithful of Alexandria, Libya and Pentapolis'. This made some concessions to the MONOPHYSITES, whose heresy was giving rise to much controversy, and was a form of appeasement for their opposition to the two-nature Christology of the council of Chalcedon (451).

In response to the *Henoticon*, Pope St Felix III (aka Felix II) excommunicated Acacius in 484. The document of excommunication is said to have been pinned to Acacius' vestments by some ultra-orthodox monks while he was celebrating the Divine Liturgy. In turn, Acacius removed the pope's name from the diptychs – the list of names of the living and dead for whom public prayers are offered during the liturgy.

This state of affairs prevailed during the lifetimes of several of Acacius' successors as patriarch of Constantinople and the ban of excommunication was only lifted when Patriarch Justin came to office in 518, by which time, however, the names of both Acacius and the Emperor Zeno had been dropped from the diptychs.

ACEPHALITES

The name, from the Greek '*akephalos*' – without a head – is applied to two separate groups:

1 Those faithful who would rather be without a leader, or head, than ally themselves to Peter Mongus, the MONOPHYSITE patriarch of Alexandria, (*d.* 490), also known as *the Stammerer*. Together with Acacius of Constantinople (*d.* 489), he had formulated a creed, the *Henoticon*, in which the heresiarchs Nestorius and Eutyches were both condemned but no mention was made of the other decisions taken at the council of Chalcedon (451). This new schismatic creed was an attempt to unite both orthodox and heretical believers, but it failed to attract many followers and was condemned by Pope St Felix III (aka Felix II – 483–92) who excommunicated both Mongus and Acacius. The schism it caused lasted until well into the fifth century.

2 A group of English LEVELLERS of the seventeenth century, political and religious agitators who were opposed to any sort of kingship and who demanded complete freedom of religion as well as the right to interpret the scriptures as they felt inclined.

❖ The Head-less

ADAMITES

An unorthodox group of believers established in the Near East in the second century AD, possibly by Prodicus, a son of Carpocrates, the Alexandrian GNOSTIC teacher. The followers aimed to regain Adam's innocence through the discarding of clothing in order to worship naked at gatherings called *Paradises*. The Adamites also condemned marriage, on the grounds that it was unknown in the Garden of Eden, and gained a reputation for sexual promiscuity through the male practice of sharing the women of the community. This gross behaviour came to the attention of St Irenaeus of Lyons (*c.* AD125–202), and later of Sts Epiphanius and Augustine, and their customs were condemned.

Later revivals of the Adamite tradition appeared in the Low Countries in the thirteenth century, in the communities of the BRETHREN OF THE FREE SPIRIT, and a later group was established in Bohemia in 1781, following an edict of toleration issued by King Joseph II. This latter group had to be suppressed forcefully in 1849 and it is not thought that any Adamites, as such, exist today.

ADIAPHORISTS

Members of a fifteenth-century group of German PROTESTANT reformers, the name taken from the Greek *adiaphora* (indifferent), since its adherents held to the opinion that it was a matter of indifference whether practices and doctrines which were neither commanded nor deemed permissible in the Bible were either followed or believed. Supporters of Philipp Melanchthon (1497–1560), the LUTHERAN reformer, argued that certain concessions made by protestants in the Leipzig Interim of 1548, including the sanctioning of the jurisdiction of ROMAN CATHOLIC bishops and the permitting of the rites of extreme unction and confirmation, were *adiaphora*, and therefore acceptable. This flew in the face of the more extreme protestant zealots, such as Matthias Flacius Illyricus, who claimed that these practices and beliefs had been a source of impiety and superstition. A compromise was reached in 1555 when the Lutheran Church was declared to be a legitimate religion by the Peace of Augsburg, while *Article 10* of the *Formula of Concord* of 1577 further stated that ceremonies, which were neither proscribed nor prescribed by scripture, might be altered according to the decisions of individual churches. A further controversy arose in the seventeenth century when the followers of Philip Jacob Spener (1635–1705), the founder of the German PIETISTS, held that all worldly pleasures, such as theatres and dances, were sinful, whereas the Lutherans held them to be *adiaphorous* and therefore permitted. It was through the influence of the German theologian Frederick Daniel Ernest Schleiermacher (1768–1834), that this difference of opinion was resolved by means of a compromise. While he denied the Lutheran view that worldly pleasures are a matter of indifference, he proposed that ordinary pleasures as part of the human experience have an integrity and should be pursued.

ADVENT CHRISTIAN CHURCH

A small sect founded in America *c.* 1854 under the leadership of Jonathan Cummings in the wake of the failure of William Miller's prediction of Christ's second coming (REVELATION 20). Miller (1782–1849) was an American BAPTIST preacher who had predicted the exact date of the second coming, with its spectacular fiery conflagration, which was to have taken place during the twelve-month period ending on 21 March 1844. Although Miller later revised these dates, so that the twelve-month period was to end on 22 October of the same year to coincide with the Jewish Day of Atonement, this had no discernible effect and the conclusion was swiftly reached that it had been a non-event, known thereafter as the *Great Disappointment*. This non-event had left many people deeply embarrassed, particularly those who had left mainstream Churches in their enthusiasm to follow Miller, some selling everything they owned and settling their affairs in the certainty that Miller's predictions were true. William Miller was expelled from the Baptist Church in 1845 and died a lonely death in 1849.

Believing that Miller had made a calculating error of some ten years, Cummings waited until 1854 and then gathered together other similarly disappointed Millerites and founded the Advent Christian Association, later known as the Advent Christian Church, which was established in Salem, Massachusetts, in 1860. Other frustrated Millerites went on to accept the prophetic claims of Ellen Harmon (later Ellen White) and formed the basis of the SEVENTH-DAY ADVENTISTS, while yet others remained independent and formed themselves into the American Millennial Adventists, which was later changed to the EVANGELICAL ADVENTISTS, but within 25 years these had become defunct.

In 1866, the American Advent Mission Society was organized by the Church with a principal purpose of working with the freed slaves after the American Civil War (1861–5); further missionary work followed, taking the Church to China, Japan, the Philippines, Nigeria, Mexico and India. While the early Adventists had formulated a statement of their doctrinal views at Albany, New York, in 1845, it was not until 1881 that the Advent Christian Church organized their own distinctive *Declaration of Principles,* at Worcester, Massachusetts.

In 1900, at Boston, Massachusetts, the *Ten Articles of the Declaration of Principles* was published, concisely summarizing the doctrinal position of the Church. This declaration has remained virtually unaltered except that in 1969 the article dealing with the scriptures was rewritten and an eleventh article was added, detailing the Church's position regarding war.

The Church now has 330 congregations in North America and maintains retirement homes in Vermont and Florida, and missions in many parts of the world, including inner city missions in parts of the USA.

❖ Advent Christian Association; Advent Christian General Conference of America

ADVENTISM (also ADVENTIST; ADVENTISTS)

Adventism is a belief that the second coming of Christ is imminent (REVELATION 20). The foundation of many Churches of this belief can be dated from William Miller's predictions that this return, or advent, was to occur in 1844. When this clearly did not happen, various hypotheses were proposed to explain the *Great Disappointment*, ranging from the incorrect observance of the sabbath – a reason confirmed by the visions of Ellen G. White of the SEVENTH-DAY ADVENTISTS – to the relaxation of Old Testament dietary laws, either, or both, of which were thought to have delayed Christ's predicted return. Members of these Churches continue to proselytize actively throughout the world.

AERIANS

Aerians were the followers of the fourth-century Aerius, a presbyter of Pontus, a town on the southern shore of the Black Sea. Aerius was a friend of Eustathius (300–77), later elected bishop of Sebaste in 356, who had ordained him. According to an account given by St Epiphanius in 355, Aerius had been put in charge of a hostel for the poor but was aggrieved because he saw this as a set-back, and felt that his ambition to become a bishop was thereby thwarted. He abandoned the hostel in *c.* 360, which led to a falling-out between the two men. Aerius and his followers fell into heresy, advocating that there was a parity between bishops and presbyters, and that Easter celebrations and fasts should be rejected since they belonged to the Jewish covenant and were therefore not binding upon Christians. They also denied the legitimacy and efficacy of prayers for the dead. St Epiphanius alleged that both Aerius and Eustathius were followers of the Arian heresy, in consequence of which Eustathius lost his episcopal see. Aerius' following, which was never very numerous, seems to have declined and disappeared within a year of his death.

AFRICA GOSPEL CHURCH

The Africa Gospel Church is a denomination belonging to the HOLINESS group of Churches that aim to emphasize John Wesley's teaching on holiness and Christian perfection. The Church had its origin in 1935 as the product of the work of the World Gospel Mission (WGM), whose missionaries went to Kenya. A Quaker, Willis Hotchkiss, who was also working in the same area with the Friends Industrial Mission, handed over his work to what then became known as the Christian Holiness Partnership. Members of the Church have many urban ministries and conduct missions in East and West Pokot and amongst the Masai people in South Kenya. Training is offered either through Theological Education by Extension (TEE) courses, or through attendance at the Kenya Highlands Bible College or the Kaboson Pastors' School. Medical missionary work is conducted at the Tenwek Hospital and through outreach programmes. The work of the Africa Gospel Church is further supported by means of publications, films and radio broadcasting.

AFRICA INLAND CHURCH

An interdenominational PROTESTANT Church, the largest in Kenya, which was founded in 1895 by Peter Cameron Scott, who died the following year from fever. The Africa Inland Church became autonomous in 1971. The Church is represented by over four thousand congregations and has around a million members; its clergy are offered training at Scott's Theological College in Machakos, just south of Nairobi. Over six hundred primary schools and numerous self-help schools and medical institutions come under the care of the Church, which, since 1983 and in conjunction with the REFORMED CHURCH IN AMERICA (founded 1628), has been conducting an outreach mission to the semi-nomadic Orma tribe in eastern Kenya, most of whom are Muslims, to bring much-needed education as well as a health programme and an agricultural ministry to these cattle-rearing people. Traditional music, involving the use of African drums, rattles, bugles and horns, accompanies the choirs in the worship services alongside the more usual western hymns.

AFRICAN BROTHERHOOD CHURCH

A distinctively indigenous African denomination, the African Brotherhood Church is an independent evangelical body with its headquarters in Mitaboni, Machakos, just south of Nairobi in Kenya. It is represented in 765 congregations with around 76,500 members. The Church originated in 1945 as a schism from the AFRICA INLAND CHURCH and is heavily supported amongst the Kamba speakers.

AFRICAN CHURCH

The African Church, which used to be known as the Kenya African Church, was founded in 1961 when the Kamba people, who make up about 10 per cent of the population of Kenya, parted company with the work of the Africa Inland Mission. The form of worship in this Church is within the BAPTIST tradition. The headquarters of the African Church is in Machakos, Kenya.

❖ Kenya African Church

AFRICAN INDEPENDENT CHURCHES

Small, indigenous Churches commonly found throughout southern Africa, which owe their origin to early mission initiatives from Europe and America, such as the London Missionary Society, the Glasgow Missionary Society and the American Board of Commissioners. These Churches seceded from white-dominated Christian groups in order to express their autonomy and independence; the earliest of the Independent Churches was founded in 1872. Members of the African Independent Churches are generally PENTECOSTAL in their style of worship and they place considerable emphasis upon healing and exorcism in their worship services.

AFRICAN METHODIST EPISCOPAL CHURCH

A very large and prominent black METHODIST denomination which arose at the end of the eighteenth century in Pennsylvania, USA, from the discrimination that was felt by black members of St George's Church in Philadelphia, a METHODIST EPISCOPAL CHURCH. This discrimination extended to providing separate seating arrangements for the black worshippers in galleries; in November 1787 some white members of the congregation pulled several of the black congregation away from the altar rails. As a result, many black members left the church and, with Richard Allen leading them, formed their own Church. Richard Allen, a slave from Delaware, had bought his freedom from his Methodist master and he became a successful businessman. He bought a disused blacksmith's shop that, in spite of some local opposition, was dedicated as Bethel Church by Bishop Francis Asbury (1745–1816). The bishop had been 'set apart', or consecrated, by Thomas Coke (1747–1814), himself also 'set apart' as a superintendent of the Methodist Church by John Wesley himself; both Asbury and Coke assumed the title of bishop, despite Wesley's protests. In 1799 Richard Allen was ordained as a deacon and in 1816 the courts ruled that the Bethel Church should to be allowed to retain its independence while keeping a nominal relationship with the Methodists.

In 1816 there was a call from Allen for the African-American leaders of Methodist churches from several of the mid-Atlantic states to consider the future of American Methodists of African descent and to discuss the formation of an independent body – the African Methodist Episcopal Church (AMEC). It was envisaged that the new body would adopt the discipline and order of the Methodist Episcopal Church. This proposal was accepted and Francis Asbury consecrated Richard Allen as its first bishop. The Church grew, spreading from the northern to the southern states after the American Civil War.

The Church has maintained a vigorous missionary programme since its earliest days; its first mission, to Haiti, was headed by elder Scipio Bean who had been ordained in 1827. In more recent times missions have been sent to Africa, South America and the West Indies. The Church also supports many educational institutions including Wilberforce University in Ohio, which was established in 1856, and theological seminaries in Wilberforce and Atlanta, Georgia. The AMEC opened the first African-American publishing house (AME Book Concern) in the USA in 1841, which is still in business.

AFRICAN METHODIST EPISCOPAL ZION CHURCH

The Church was founded in New York City, USA, in 1796 at the John's Street METHODIST EPISCOPAL CHURCH (MEC), when some black members of the Church approached Bishop Francis Asbury of the MEC to gain permission to hold separate meetings, as they were not allowed by the John's Street congregation either to preach, or to join the Church's conference. Permission was given and in 1801 a charter was granted which established the AFRICAN METHODIST EPISCOPAL CHURCH (AMEC), called Zion Church, of the city of New York. Having formed themselves into a separate congregation, a new home was found in an old stable in Cross Street, between Mulberry and Orange Streets and prayer services commenced, with licensed preachers coming to New York from Philadelphia. By 1820 it was decided that the new congregation should withdraw from the AMEC, although a close relationship was maintained. In 1821, together with other coloured congregations from Connecticut, New Jersey and Pennsylvania, the Zion Church held its first annual conference, represented by nineteen preachers and presided over by William Phoebus, a minister of the white MEC. The election of James Varick (1750–1828) as the first superintendent, or bishop, was made at this conference. The Church officially accepted the *Articles of Religion* as composed by John Wesley, with an episcopal polity like that of the MEC. It was not until 1848 that the name African Methodist Episcopal Zion Church (AMEZ) was officially approved. The AMEZ maintains several educational establishments, notably Livingstone College at Salisbury, North Carolina (founded 1879), and Home Missions in Louisiana, Mississippi and Oklahoma, with overseas work conducted in Liberia (1876), Ghana (1896), Nigeria (1930) and the West Indies (1965) and in some South American countries.

AFRICAN ORTHODOX AUTONOMOUS CHURCH SOUTH OF THE SAHARA

The roots of the Church lie in the action of an ANGLICAN cook in Uganda, Reuben Sabbanja Sabiminba Musaka (nicknamed Spartas) who, despite his early Christian education through the Church Missionary Society, became attracted to all things Greek (hence his nickname).

Reuben Spartas contacted Patriarch Alexander McGuire (1866–1934), an ex-Episcopalian priest in the USA who had left that Church in 1921 and received episcopal consecration from Archbishop Joseph René Vilatte, an *EPISCOPUS VAGANS*, a Frenchman who had been consecrated, irregularly, as a bishop in 1892. McGuire became head of the newly constituted AFRICAN ORTHODOX CHURCH. Spartas joined that Church and laid down foundations in Uganda for the formation of his own Church in 1929. When Bishop Daniel W. Alexander, who had been consecrated by McGuire in 1927 as primate of the province of South Africa, visited Uganda in 1931–2 he ordained Spartas as vicar apostolic.

Many converts were made, but Spartas soon became aware of the alleged heterodoxy of the African Orthodox Church and he added the term 'Greek' to the title of his Church, appealing to Meletios Metaxakis, the Greek Orthodox Patriarch of Alexandria, who was sympathetic to Spartas' cause, to recognize the new African Greek Orthodox Church. This was formally accepted in 1946 and when a Greek missionary archbishop for east Africa was appointed in 1959, Spartas vowed obedience to him.

Differences, however, soon arose. The Church employed young, Greek-trained priests who were not fully sympathetic to the African situation and much of the material assistance that Spartas was expecting was not forthcoming. Tensions mounted and by 1966 Spartas and his followers had seceded from the Orthodox Patriarchate of Alexandria to form the small African Orthodox Autonomous Church South of the Sahara, which retained various African practices despite observing many Eastern Orthodox customs, such as the wearing of Orthodox vestments and the use of icons in churches. Most members of this new Church, including Spartas, returned to the African Greek Orthodox Church in 1972.

AFRICAN ORTHODOX CHURCH

The African Orthodox Church was founded in the USA in 1921 by George Alexander McGuire (1866–1934), a doctor, who had also trained for the ministry in the MORAVIAN CHURCH in the West Indies, eventually joining the Protestant Episcopal Church. He found himself at variance with the white dominance he saw in the Protestant Episcopal Church, and was impressed by his experiences on the island of Antigua, where he had seen at first hand the work of Marcus Garvey's *United Negro Improvement Association of the World*, which had been founded there in 1914. The movement spread throughout America where there was a growing awareness of racial identity.

McGuire formed his own African Orthodox Church and was elected as its first bishop, receiving episcopal consecration in 1921 in Chicago from Archbishop Joseph René Vilatte, an *EPISCOPUS VAGANS*, and Bishop Carl Nybladh, assuming the title of Patriarch Alexander of the African Orthodox Church of the World, a year later. Archbishop McGuire consecrated several bishops and established an order of deaconesses. The path ahead was not always smooth and schisms arose, leading, for example, to the founding of the Afro-American Catholic Church in 1938.

Doctrinally, the Church accepts the seven ecumenical councils and rejects the *filioque* clause in its creed. The liturgy, which was compiled by McGuire himself, is a mixture taken from ANGLICAN, ROMAN CATHOLIC and GREEK ORTHODOX CHURCH forms, with the use of western-style vestments and *Hymns Ancient & Modern*; the traditional seven sacraments are all recognized.

Government of the Church is by means of a general synod, composed of the archbishops, bishops, priests and representatives of the laity, presided over by the presiding bishop, who is elected for life and who exercises jurisdiction over the whole Church. The headquarters of the Church is in New York.

❖ The Independent Episcopal Church

AFRICAN UNION FIRST COLORED METHODIST PROTESTANT CHURCH

The Church came about in 1866, arising from both the African Union Church, also known as the African Union Methodist Church, which derived from secessions amongst black independent METHODISTS from the Asbury Methodist Church in Wilmington, Delaware, and the First Colored Methodist Protestant Church, which arose in 1865 through a schism within the AFRICAN METHODIST EPISCOPAL CHURCH. The breakaway Methodists of the African Union Church seceded from the METHODIST EPISCOPAL CHURCH because they wanted greater lay participation in the Church as well as the elimination of episcopal polity. Following discussions in 1865 with representatives of the First Colored Methodist Protestant Church, the African Union First Colored Methodist Protestant Church came into existence. Soon afterwards, in 1866, the first edition of the *Doctrine and Discipline* of this new Church was published and the question of administrative style was agreed upon. There would be a hierarchy of president, vice-presidents, elders, deacons, licensed preachers and exhorters, the latter authorized to hold prayer meetings and to exhort the faithful to pray. The president would be expected to serve a four-year term of office and would be eligible for re-election by the Church conference.

By 1966 the need for episcopal oversight became apparent and the conference, at the annual session of 1967, held in Norristown, Pennsylvania, voted to elect and consecrate two bishops, Reese C. Scott as senior bishop and Robert F. Walters as junior bishop; these titles were later modified.

The Church does not maintain a foreign missionary programme but instead provides back-up and support for a home mission programme under the direction of a group of women members known as the *Grandbody*. The 1500 black adult members of the Church are to be found in some 30 congregations throughout the USA.

❖ African Union and First Colored Methodist Protestant Church of America or Elsewhere; African Union Methodist Protestant Church

AFRICAN UNIVERSAL CHURCH

This is a small American PENTECOSTAL-style Church that was organized in 1927 in Jacksonville, Florida, by Archbishop Clarence C. Addison. The origins of the Church lie in the then British colony of the African Gold Coast, now Ghana, through the actions of some tribal chiefs, whose aim it was to help repatriate African-Americans back to their homeland. There was a merger of the African Universal Church with the Primitive Apostolic African Church, which had originated in Ghana in 1926, founded by Kwamin Ntsetse Bresi-Ando, who became its supreme pontiff. In 1932, Bresi-Ando, who had been resident in the USA, returned to Ghana and with the help of his half-brother, Ernest, created a Ghanaian branch of the African Universal Church in Apam. The repatriation programme failed to develop, but several parishes and schools were established. This Ghanaian branch eventually became part of the EASTERN ORTHODOX CHURCH under the patriarchate of Alexandria. The African Universal Church continued in the USA, with a missionary presence maintained in Ghana. It is organized along episcopal lines with the chief governing body, the general assembly, meeting every four years. There is provision for deaconesses, called parish mothers, who are under the direction of senior and district mothers. Being pentecostal, the members of the Church believe in four experiences – justification, sanctification, baptism of the Holy Ghost and baptism with fire, which is discernible only to the believer (believer's baptism). Wine is not used in the celebration of the Lord's Supper. The African Universal Church also practises spiritual healing. One of the African tribal chiefs, Princess Laura Adanka (or Adorkor) Koffey, was assassinated in 1928 in Miama, Florida.

❖ The African Universal Church and Commercial League

AGAPEMONITES

A fanatical sect of men and women in nineteenth-century England, followers of Henry James Prince (1811–99), curate of Charlynch, Somerset and Samuel Starky, his rector, who left the CHURCH OF ENGLAND to pursue their vision; the name of the sect is taken from the Greek *agape*-love and *mone*-dwelling. Prince and Starky established a communal abode of love for their followers, who regarded Prince as a divine figure, at Spaxton, Somerset, in 1849; this was poorly regarded by the authorities on the grounds of giving scandal through licentious conduct, and met with opposition that closed it down.

The movement was revived in Clapton, London, in the 1890s by a priest, John Hugh Smyth-Pigott, under the name of *The Children of the Resurrection*, but met with even less success. Smyth-Pigott was unfrocked in 1909 after having declared himself to be Jesus Christ, the Messiah and God, on Sunday, 7 September 1902, upon which occasion he also promised to return the following Sunday to demonstrate his ability to walk on water. This event was aborted, and when he arrived Smyth-Pigott was greeted by catcalls and jeers from some onlookers and was forced to beat a very hasty retreat. Two children resulted from his marriage to a follower, Sister Ruth: a boy named Glory and a girl named Comet, the latter in honour of Halley's Comet that appeared at the time of her birth; (she was later renamed 'Life'). Smyth-Pigott died, a disappointed man, in 1927 at the age of 75. Until her death Sister Ruth confidently expected her husband to rise from the dead, but was to be equally disappointed. Although the sect dwindled after Smyth-Pigott's death, various followers remained faithful to his vision until well into the mid-twentieth century. No attempts at another revival seem to have been made.

❖ Church of the Agapemone; Starkyites

AGAPETAE

A term, from the Greek '*agape*' – pure, or brotherly love – which refers to a custom condemned by ecclesiastical canons which dealt with the behaviour of clergy during the early fourth century. The objects of their condemnation were those men and women who, despite being under vows of continence, chose to live together in a state they described as a *spiritual marriage*.

The term is also applied to later fourth-century GNOSTICS who proposed that such relations between the sexes were cleansed of any suggestion of impropriety if their minds were pure. St John Chrysostom (354–407) repeatedly censured this practice.

AGNOETAE

A sixth-century sect of MONOPHYSITES, named from the Greek '*agnoetae*' – without knowledge or ignorant – founded by Themestius, or Themistus, who was a deacon of Alexandria. He and his followers believed that according to biblical evidence, in Mark 13:32 and John 11:34, Jesus Christ had limited omniscience because of the limitations of his human nature, which gave him only an incomplete knowledge of the present and the future. Patriarch St Eulogius of Alexandria attacked their teaching (in *c.* 598).

The term was previously used of fourth-century Eunomian heretics who denied God's omniscience.

❖ Themistians

ALADURA INTERNATIONAL CHURCH, UK AND OVERSEAS

The Aladura Church started in Africa as an important indigenous religious movement among Yoruba-speaking people in western Nigeria. Its establishment dates from *c.* 1918, when some young members of ANGLICAN groups expressed their dissatisfaction with the western emphasis in Church life and wanted to explore divine healing. In this enterprise they were encouraged by the American-based Faith Tabernacle, from Philadelphia, where divine healing is strongly emphasized. A prayer and healing group was formed among the lay Yoruba Christians at Ijebu-Ode in the face of the virulent influenza epidemic of 1918, against which the western Churches seemed to be impotent. From this group emerged the Aladura movement, under the leadership of the prophet-healer Joseph Bablola (1906–59). It underwent great expansion in the 1930s on account of its mass divine-healing meetings. The movement took on a PENTECOSTAL flavour and, in the face of official opposition from the government and established Churches, the leaders appealed to the Pentecostal Apostolic Church in Great Britain, which responded by sending missionaries to Nigeria. In the event, the result was far from satisfactory as the missionaries did not hesitate to use western medicine rather than divine healing, excluded polygamy and wanted to dominate the new Church. In 1942 Joseph Bablola and Isaac Akinyele led a group of those who were dissatisfied with this development and they formed their own CHRIST APOSTOLIC CHURCH, from which further schisms grew, notably the Christ Apostolic Mission Church, founded in 1952, and the Christ Apostolic Universal Church, founded ten years later. At present there is a council of Churches, called the Nigeria Association of Aladura Churches, founded in 1960, with over two hundred indigenous denominational members. The Aladura International Church has spread throughout Nigeria and into Ghana and Sierra Leone, New York and London, but there have been many schisms.

❖ Church of the Lord (Aladura, or Praying)

ALBANIAN EASTERN RITE CATHOLICS

The first Byzantine Catholic community amongst Albanians was a small mission that was established along the coast of Epirus, which lasted from 1628–1765; a further attempt to establish an Eastern-rite mission, in Elbasen, was started by a former Albanian Orthodox priest, Fr George Germanos, in 1900. The work was supplemented by the arrival, in 1938, of some monks from the Italo-Albanian monastery at Grottaferrata, Italy.

Growth was slow and the community came to an end in 1967, when Albania was declared officially to be an atheist state. The remaining Albanian Catholics are largely of the Latin rite. It was revealed in 1998 that there were no parishes, or priests, to care for the small, remaining groups of Byzantine-rite Catholic Albanians who, despite everything, had persevered in their faith as EASTERN CATHOLICS.

ALBANIAN ORTHODOX CHURCH

Christianity came to the Albanians, who peopled the Balkans from before the fourth century AD, through two main branches of evangelization: the Latin Catholics from the north, and the Orthodox from the south. Later, as a result of Turkish conquest in the fifteenth century, most of the population became Muslim, with the rest remaining either as Latin Christians (in the north), or Orthodox Christians (in the south), the latter under the jurisdiction of the patriarch of Constantinople. Albania became independent after the Balkan Wars of 1911–13, and the Albanian Orthodox Church sought independence.

A leading player in this movement was an Albanian immigrant priest from the USA, Fr Theofan (Fan) S. Noli (1881–1965), who had been ordained in Boston in 1908 by Metropolitan Platon of the RUSSIAN ORTHODOX CHURCH. Fr Noli returned to Albania in 1920 and was consecrated as bishop three years later. His political activities remained unaltered, earning him the nickname of the *red bishop*. Following the forced departure of the Albanian king, Zog, in 1924 Noli formed a government and tried to establish constitutional rule, but this was short-lived, lasting only seven months. Noli, by now archbishop, returned to America and established a see in Boston, organizing the Albanian Orthodox Archdiocese in America. After many years of struggle, the patriarch of Constantinople recognized the autocephaly of the Albanian Orthodox Church in 1937.

With the success of communism in Albania, the religious groups were subjected to considerable persecution during the 1940s, and by 1951 all Orthodox bishops had either been executed or had been replaced by *acceptable* men. This persecution continued under the communist leader Enver Hoxha (1908–85), who had proclaimed Albania to be the first truly atheistic state in the world. Clergy of all ranks fled, or were sent into exile, and the faithful were forbidden the outward signs of their faith, not allowed to make the sign of the cross, display icons in their houses, or even decorate eggs at Easter. By 1991, when religion began to reappear, the Church had no bishops and the mere handful of clergy who had survived were too old to set about resuscitating the Church. A compromise was made between the Ecumenical Patriarch, the Albanian Orthodox Church and the government, resulting in the establishment, in 1998, of a holy synod, with newly elected bishops, which would govern the Church. The present archbishop and metropolitan of Tirana now heads the Church. The Albanian Orthodox Church holds true to Orthodox doctrine and discipline, and the Divine Liturgy is celebrated in either Greek or Latin, according to a congregation's needs.

ALBIGENSIANS

The Albigensians were a twelfth–thirteenth-century group of MANICHAEANS that flourished in southern France and northern Italy. The name *Albigensian* is derived from the French city of Albi in Languedoc, north-east of Toulouse, where their persecution started. The Manichaean heresy had originated in the third century in Persia and takes its name from Mani, whose teachings spread into Asia Minor, through the Balkans and, following the trade routes, into northern Italy and southern France. His teachings proposed that there was a god of light equivalent to the God of the New Testament, and a god of darkness, or error, who represented the God of the Old Testament. Earthly life was understood in terms of a struggle between these two gods and their forces, spirit and matter, and to lead a good life man had gradually to be purified from matter. Albigensians (aka Cathars) therefore held that marriage, reproduction and the eating of food were to be condemned and, because they also considered that corruption was to be found in every state, the members refused to take oaths and were considered subversive.

The believers could belong to either of two groups, the *perfecti* or the *credenti*. In keeping with their beliefs, the *perfecti* were obliged to maintain a very ascetic lifestyle; they were expected to forgo sexual intercourse, and by extension avoid meat, eggs and cheese, as these are either directly or indirectly the result of such intercourse. They were also forbidden to lie, cheat, kill or take oaths. The *credenti* could become *perfecti* by receiving the *consolamentum*, a type of compound rite of baptism–penance–ordination, in which a candidate requested a blessing from one of the *perfecti*, made three prostrations, or genuflections, and asked for forgiveness of sins. Many of the believers promised to receive the *consolamentum* when in danger of death; should they then recover they would be obliged to live their lives as *perfecti*, or die at their own hands by *endura*, a form of self-starvation. Monthly worship services, or *apparellamenta*, were held when sins were confessed and absolution given by the *perfecti* of the congregation. A distinctive feature of Albigensian ritual was their method of reciting the Lord's Prayer. This could be said in multiples of two, called a *double*, or six, accompanied by genuflections and the substitution of the words 'Give us this Day our Supersubstantial Bread', since they interpreted here the word *bread* to mean divine love, as earthly bread was just matter. Doctrinally, the Albigensians denied the Trinity, Christ's resurrection, hell, purgatory and the resurrection of the body, since by nature all flesh is evil. They taught instead that the souls of those who were not saved would transmigrate into the bodies of lower animals.

Contemporary clerical behaviour was not noted for its universal piety and much of this lax behaviour contrasted greatly with the austerities of the *perfecti*. This sharply drawn difference recommended the Albigensians to the common people and drew many converts, despite condemnation from the Councils of Rheims (1148), Verona (1184) and the Fourth Lateran (1215). When attempts at conversion back into the ROMAN CATHOLIC CHURCH failed, the sect was mercilessly persecuted and thousands of believers went to the stake. In the city of Béziers alone, some fifteen to twenty thousand men, women and children were killed during the Albigensian Crusade, raised by Pope Innocent III (1198–1216). That many of them were not even members of the sect made little difference. The extermination continued for some twenty years, until the heresy was exterminated. *Pope*

Innocent III is said to have congratulated the Crusaders and justified the slaughter of the innocents, claiming that they had gained their salvation through the Crusaders' actions.

Another group holding very similar beliefs were the BOGOMILS, who originated in Bulgaria in the tenth century.

❖ Albigenses; Cathars

ALBRIGHT BRETHREN

An American denomination founded by a brick-maker, Jacob Albright (1759–1808), born into an immigrant German family living near Pottstown, Pennsylvania, who were members of the LUTHERAN CHURCH. Following the death of several of his children Albright had a conversion experience and in 1790 he left the Lutheran Church to become a lay-preacher in the METHODIST CHURCH. He took up itinerant preaching in the German language throughout East Pennsylvania and maintained friendly relations with the English-speaking Methodists, who were at that time led by Bishop Francis Asbury, a pivotal figure in American Methodism. The language differences made it necessary that an independent organization should be formed and the First Evangelical Council was held in 1803, from which the Evangelical Association was formed, with Albright ordained as an elder by his congregation. This Association and its descendants worked within the PIETIST-Methodist tradition. Four years later the first annual conference of preachers was held and Jacob Albright was elected as a bishop. *The Book of Discipline*, in German, was published in 1809 but Albright did not live to see this publication. His followers became known as the *So-Called Albright People* and remained as such until 1816 when the first general conference was held and the title 'Evangelical Association' was adopted. In time, English replaced the German language and missionary work in the USA, Canada, Europe and the Far East was undertaken. The history of the Church is not without incidents. Accusations of usurpation of power and violation of the discipline by some bishops and district superintendents caused a temporary schism in 1894, with the formation of the United Evangelical Church, but a reunion took place in 1922 from which the Evangelical Church was formed to work specifically among those of German descent in the USA. The reunion had its dissenters and some remained outside the merger. Court cases were instigated to settle matters of the loss and gain of real estate between the two groups. Those remaining outside the merger continued as the Evangelical Congregational Church. In 1946 another merger, this time with the United Brethren in Christ, resulted in the formation of the EVANGELICAL UNITED BRETHREN CHURCH; this new Church was merged with the Methodist Church in 1968 to form the UNITED METHODIST CHURCH (USA).

ALL-ONE-FAITH-IN-ONE-GOD-STATE, INC

A brainchild of the Reverend Henry Corey, an ex-US marine, and Dr Emmanuel H. Bonner, manufacturer of a liquid soap, Dr Bronner's (*sic*) Magic Soap, which is alleged to cleanse both body and soul and can be used for brushing teeth, bathing (*There's Nothing like an Ice-cold Bath with Dr Bronner's Peppermint Soap!* goes one advertisement), shaving, massaging, shampooing, cleaning clothes, swabbing decks and wiping walls, and more, as it is described as having eighteen uses. The soap, which is a mixture of coconut oil, olive oil and pure peppermint oil, is available through various health-food store outlets and by mail order in the USA.

Dr Bonner enjoyed the soubriquet of Rabbi-Pope. When the Dead Sea scrolls were discovered in 1947, Bonner took them to be evidence of the imminent second coming of Christ (REVELATION 20), and the basis for his creation of his All-One-Faith-in-One-God State (founded 1959), which has four centres, three in California and one in Indiana. He taught a form of process theology in which God, who is understood to be constantly recreating himself, wants all nations and religions to unite on Spaceship Earth. To effect this union, Bonner's approach was syncretistic, following certain precepts from such diverse sources as Confucius, Hippocrates and the eighteenth-century political philosopher Thomas Paine. The State is now known as All-One-God-Faith, Inc.

❖ All-One-God-Faith, Inc.

ALLEGHENY WESLEYAN METHODIST CONNECTION

Originally known as the Allegheny Conference of the WESLEYAN METHODIST CHURCH, which was established in the USA in 1843, the Church changed its name to the present one in 1966 when greater cooperation between the groups was desired. It is found largely in the eastern states, its members distributed between some 120 congregations. The Church maintains a mission among American Indians and supports a Bible school in Alberton, Montana.

❖ Allegheny Conference

ALOGI

The Alogi were members of an heretical sect that arose in Asia Minor towards the end of the second century. St Epiphanius called them Alogi, or deniers of the word, because, since they rejected the gospel of St John, they also rejected the *Logos* (or word) revealed in that gospel, as well as in the Book of Revelation. They seem to have been opponents of the MONTANISTS and may also have denied the divinity of Jesus Christ and his eternal generation.

The Alogi are said to have attributed the authorship of both the Gospel of St John and the Book of Revelation to Cerinthus, a GNOSTIC writer of the first century. What is perplexing is that Cerinthus taught that Christ was a mere man, whereas in St John's Gospel there is a clear affirmation of Christ's divinity. This makes Cerinthus' attributed authorship of St John's Gospel seem very odd indeed.

❖ Alogians

ALUMBRADOS

Although the alternative name for this group is given as ILLUMINATI, the Alumbrados must not be confused with the secret society of that name founded in 1776 in Bavaria by Adam Weishaupt.

A mystical sect that arose in Spain in the sixteenth century, whose members might well have been described as *alumbrado* – enlightened or illuminated. The group had its origins with some Jesuits and Reformed Franciscans and was a movement that emphasized a passive surrender to, and sinless unity with, God as the object of spiritual life. Some of the more excitable members of the sect, who were given to visions and prophecies, exercised an unhealthy control over those who were more impressionable. Although many seem to have been unbalanced, other followers were decidedly saintly. The Inquisition dealt harshly with this group.

❖ Illuminati

AMALRICIANS

A twelfth-century heretical sect, founded by Amalric, who was also known as Amaury de Bene, or de Chartres, who enjoyed a reputation as a mystic and philosopher. He taught a type of pantheism, maintaining that God is all things and everything is God. The obvious consequences of this belief would be the denial of transubstantiation, the confusion of good and evil since all acts are equally of God, and a rejection of the laws of morality. They also believed that salvation depended on the service of God in the freedom of the Spirit, from which belief sprang their alternative name, BRETHREN OF THE FREE SPIRIT. Amalric's understanding of the Trinity was unusual in that he taught that those in whom the Holy Spirit had taken up his abode were to be called *The Spiritualized*, who were already enjoying the life of the resurrection. Many clergy were members of this sect and their heresy went undetected for a time, but a council of bishops and doctors of the University of Paris condemned the teaching in 1210, a few years after Amalric's death in *c.* 1207. Several of his followers went to the stake, but many of those who were deemed *ignorant converts*, which category included many women, were pardoned. Even in death, however, Amalric could not escape punishment and his bones were exhumed and thrown into an unconsecrated grave. Pope Innocent III condemned the heresy, which was described at the Fourth Lateran Council in 1215 as 'insanity rather than heresy'.

❖ Brethren of the Free Spirit

AMANA CHURCH SOCIETY

The Amana Church Society owes its origins to a group of German PIETISTS who believed that the inspiration of the apostolic age is still given to Christians. It began in 1714, in Hesse, Germany, as the *Community of True Inspiration*, under the Pietist leadership of mystics such as Johann Friedrich Rock and Eberhard Ludwig Gruber. Small prayer groups were formed, known as *inspirationist groups*, which met in members' houses. The German Pietists' rejection of LUTHERANISM was seen at that time as a threat to both the government and the Lutheran Church, as the Pietists rejected state laws which required military service and the taking of oaths and objected to church-run schools. By 1749, both Rock and Gruber were dead and enthusiasm within the group waned, but in 1817 three figures were to emerge, called the *new instruments of true inspiration.* These were Michael Krausert, a tailor from Strasbourg, Barbara Heynemann, an uneducated servant who had the gift of inspiration and stressed the importance of rebirth in Jesus Christ, and Christian Metz, a young carpenter whose parents were members of the Community of True Inspiration. Persecution of the group in Germany was inevitable and in 1842 Christian Metz led a *Committee of Four* who went to America to find a new home. Eight hundred members of the Society emigrated to America, initially settling at Ebenezer, near Buffalo, New York, where they worked a small tract of land. This was held in common, each contributing according to his ability, with all sharing equally in the rewards. The group was governed by elected elders and known as *The Ebenezer Society*. When the need for more land was coupled with trouble from the local Seneca Indians and the growth of the developing city of Buffalo, it was decided that the group would move to Iowa, where conditions were more favourable. They named their new home *Amana*, from the mountain range in Lebanon referred to in the Song of Solomon 4:8, which means *to remain true*. Five other villages were soon added, West Amana, South Amana, High Amana, East Amana and Middle Amana, which were incorporated under the Amana name in 1859. Prosperity followed, but this was to decline after the civil war and by 1932 a reorganization was considered necessary. The idea of communal property was dissolved and a corporation, called the Amana Society, was established, which development had the effect of separating the Church from temporal affairs. Each member received a number of stock certificates in proportion to their years of service.

Today the business, under the Amana trademark, makes refrigerators and other household appliances, as well as continuing with farming. The members are no longer pacifists, but they still refuse to take oaths. Amusements and entertainments, at one time considered worldly and therefore unacceptable, are now generally well received. Doctrinally, the group accepts the teaching of a holy, universal Church, and believes in the remission of sins, the communion of saints, the resurrection of the body, life everlasting and the punishment of the wicked, but it does not recognize baptism with water, only by fire and the Holy Spirit. Admission to the Church is allowed from the age of 15, when new members receive confirmation. While there is no provision for an ordained clergy, the Amana Society has a board of trustees and a council of elders who conduct services, in German and English, which consist of hymns, prayers, scripture readings and extracts from the testimonies of Rock, Metz and Heynemann, along with occasional exhortations from the elders.

❖ Amana Community of Inspirationists; Ebenezer Society

AMANAZARITES

Amanazarites are members of the Nazareth Baptist Church, an African independent Church founded in 1910 by Isaiah Shembe, who recognize Ekuphakameni as their holy city although the headquarters is currently in Inanda, South Africa. The Church evolved from an indigenous religious movement started by a Xhosa prophet, Ntikana (1780–1821), who had had no contact with any white Christians or missionaries, and this led others to believe that he had received the Christian message from God by direct revelation. His preaching predisposed many indigenous people in Africa to accept Christianity. The Church is very large and well organized, with nearly half a million members, most of whom are Zulus. It is the second largest independent African Church in South Africa.

AMBROSIANS

At the time of the Reformation in Europe a small Anabaptist group was formed, led by a man called Ambrosius. He taught the priesthood of all believers and therefore refused to recognize the need for an ordained clergy. Ambrosius also held that personal revelations he had received were of greater authority than the scriptures. The fate of the group is unknown but it seems to have been short-lived.

AMERICAN BAPTIST ASSOCIATION

This BAPTIST Church began in America as the Baptist General Association in 1905, adopting its present name in 1924. It derived from the SOUTHERN BAPTIST CONVENTION, which had been formed in 1845 as a reaction to the refusal of the American Baptist Foreign Mission Society to accept candidates as missionaries if they were slave-owners.

Dr James R. Graves, a member of the Southern Baptist Convention and editor of *The Tennessee Baptist*, called upon his fellow Baptists to reject non-Baptist denominations and their clergy in an attempt to restore what he considered was the apostolic purity of the Church, a view shared with some enthusiasm by Dr J. M. Pendleton of Bowling Green, Kentucky. Both men became leaders of what became known as the Cotton Grove Convention, which was organized in 1851 and whose *Landmarker* ideas the vast majority of members of the Southern Baptist Convention rejected. The tenets of the *Landmarkers*, or members of the present American Baptist Association, are that the local congregation, or church, is the only unit that is authorized to administer the ordinances of baptism and the Lord's Supper, and that there is no such entity as *the Church*. This means that every church, or congregation, is equal to every other church, or congregation, and therefore equal to every other such group within the association. Furthermore, valid baptism can only be conferred by a properly ordained Baptist minister.

Members of other denominations are not recognized, nor may they be allowed to receive the Lord's Supper in this Church or preach in its pulpits. Believing that they are maintaining a direct link back to New Testament times, the aim of the association is to retain the purity of what is regarded as a kind of apostolic succession. Doctrinally, there is little difference between the American Baptist Association and the Southern Baptist Convention. The Church is best described as FUNDAMENTALIST, maintaining a belief in the verbal inspiration of the scriptures, a belief in the Trinity and in the divinity of Jesus Christ, his life, death and resurrection and in his pre-millennial second coming to earth (REVELATION 20), with the wicked sent to endure eternal punishment and the saved to enjoy eternal bliss. Salvation is by grace through faith, not by the law or works, and there is an insistence on the separation of Church and state.

Polity within the group is congregational, and the association maintains a successful network of educational institutes, seminaries and Sunday schools throughout the southern states of the USA. The headquarters of the American Baptist Association is in Texarkana, on the border between Texas and Arkansas.

❖ Church Equality Baptists; Landmarker Baptists; Landmarkers; Old Landmarkers

AMERICAN BAPTIST CHURCHES IN THE USA

The name that was given in 1972 to the Church which was formerly known as the American Baptist Convention (founded 1950), which had evolved from the NORTHERN BAPTIST CONVENTION (founded 1907). The Church looks to Roger Williams (*c.* 1603–83) as the founder of the first BAPTIST Church in Providence, Rhode Island, in 1639. When he arrived in

Boston in 1634, Williams was invited by the church at Salem to become its pastor but because he preached against the authority of magistrates to interfere in matters of religion he was banished from the area in 1635 and set out for Narragansett Bay, where he bought land from the native Indians and founded the town of Providence and the colony of Rhode Island. It was in Providence in 1639 that he repudiated his own baptism in the CHURCH OF ENGLAND, received as an infant, and was baptized again by Ezekiel Holliman, a member of the Salem church. Williams then re-baptized Holliman and ten others into the first Baptist Church in the New World. The first church was established and built in Providence, the members holding true to the predestinarian teachings espoused by the CALVINISTS and the preaching of a limited atonement. More Baptist churches followed, banding together loosely into associations until, by the time of the War of Independence (1775–83), over forty such were in existence. A measure of cooperation began to bring these associations together for specific purposes early in the next century and in 1824 the triennial convention was formed, meeting to discuss and plan missionary work. Over time, the convention began to discuss other matters beside missionary work and schisms began to form. Other cooperative societies emerged, including the American Baptist Publication Society (1824), the American Baptist Home Mission Society (1832) and the American Foreign Bible Society (1837). There was a division between the Northern and Southern Baptists over the issue of slavery, and also of organizational centralization. In 1845 the Southern Baptists formed an independent organization, known as the SOUTHERN BAPTIST CONVENTION that, unlike the Northern Baptist Convention, oversaw all activities within the Church. The American Baptist Churches in the USA, which grew from the Northern Baptist Convention and is considered to be the more liberal, is heavily involved in seeking a closer working union between the various Baptist groups in a broader and more ecumenical fashion. The Southern Baptist Convention members have been described as Missionary Baptists-Calvinists, because they have supported missionary societies instead of sending missionaries from local churches. The American Baptist Churches of the USA is a member of the National Council of Churches of Christ in the USA.

The life of Roger Williams was eventful. Born in England at the beginning of the seventeenth century he graduated from Pembroke College, Cambridge, and was appointed as a private chaplain in 1626. He left for America in 1631 and became a minister at Boston, and later at Salem and Plymouth. By 1635 he had been appointed as chief teacher at Salem, but his teachings, which promoted religious freedom, proved unacceptable to the authorities and he was banned from Massachusetts for maintaining 'dangerous opinions'. Williams returned to England in 1636, where he published some writings, one of which, *The Bloudy Tenent*, was burned by the common hangman. He returned to America and was made president of Rhode Island in 1654. Even his last years were eventful, for in 1675 Williams is recorded as being a captain in the militia involved in repulsing an Indian uprising.

AMERICAN CARPATHO-RUSSIAN ORTHODOX GREEK CATHOLIC CHURCH

This Orthodox Church exists only in the USA, its members descended from

Ruthenians (UKRAINIAN CATHOLICS) from the Carpathian mountains in the former Czechoslovakia. When many of these migrated to the USA, during the nineteenth century, they brought with them their married priests which met with a considerable amount of misunderstanding and opposition from some of the local ROMAN CATHOLIC clergy. Fr Alexis Toth, a Carpatho-Ruthenian Uniat (EASTERN CATHOLIC CHURCH) priest, left the Roman Catholic Church in 1891 taking his parishioners with him. They became members of the RUSSIAN ORTHODOX CHURCH in America. The American Roman Catholic hierarchy sought clarification from Rome and an apostolic letter, *Ea Semper,* was issued in 1907 that decreed that only celibate Ruthenian priests should be admitted, or ordained, in America. This was in spite of the guarantee that had been granted to the Ruthenians and other Uniat Churches, that they would be allowed to retain their married clergy. Another decree, *Cum Data Fuerit* (1929), concerning the enforcement of the earlier apostolic letter, caused more trouble. In 1937 a public meeting was held in Pittsburgh, Pennsylvania, under the leadership of Fr Orestes P. Chornock, and it was agreed to petition the patriarch of Constantinople, Benjamin I, to receive the group into the EASTERN ORTHODOX CHURCH and to consecrate Fr Chornock as bishop, in order to form a distinct diocese. This was agreed and Chornock was consecrated in 1938, with his new diocese placed under the spiritual care of the Greek Orthodox archdiocese. The seminary of Christ the Saviour was opened in New York City, but after several transfers is now in Johnstown, Pennsylvania, where the headquarters of the Church, which is responsible for 69 parishes and 6 missions, is also located.

AMERICAN EPISCOPAL CHURCH

The American Episcopal Church was founded in Mobile, Alabama in 1968, by those members of the ANGLICAN ORTHODOX CHURCH OF NORTH AMERICA who did not accept the strong control that was exercised by the then presiding bishop, which they described as dictatorial. These disaffected people, led by James Hardin George, wanted to have a polity that was based upon a federation of autonomous parishes, with executive control in the hands of a board of lay trustees. This arrangement did not neglect the need for the creation of a hierarchy and they turned to the Most Reverend James Charles Ryan (originally Joseph Chengalvaroyan Pillai), a convert to Christianity who had become the founder and head of the Indian Orthodox Church in 1945, but who had emigrated to the USA in 1948. Archbishop Ryan consecrated James Hardin George as bishop and merged the Indian Orthodox Church with the new American Episcopal Church, becoming its primate. Bishop George succeeded on Archbishop Ryan's death in 1970. An attempt was then made at reorganization, with a view to greater centralization. The ten congregations that exist, with over five hundred members, use the *Book of Common Prayer* for their liturgical life but the *Thirty-Nine Articles* (of the CHURCH OF ENGLAND) have been replaced by a new doctrinal statement, which is decidedly conservative. The Church does not admit women to the priesthood.

AMERICAN EVANGELICAL CHRISTIAN CHURCHES

A group founded as an interdoctrinal denomination of evangelical Christian ministers in Chicago, Illinois, in 1944. The polity is congregational and it serves to charter local churches throughout the

USA as American Bible Churches. The churches are all autonomous in their management but they liaise with national headquarters in Indianapolis, Indiana. Each church member is expected to confirm acceptance of seven articles of faith, namely (a) belief in the Bible as the word of God; (b) belief in the virgin birth; (c) belief in the deity of Jesus Christ; (d) belief in man's salvation through Christ's atonement; (e) belief in the importance of prayer; (f) belief in Christ's second coming (REVELATION 20), and (g) belief in the establishment of God's kingdom on earth.

The Church operates the Evangelical Bible College in Indianapolis as an extension education college, from which four grades of church workers and clergy can receive authentication. The lowest grade is that of a certified Christian worker, essentially a lay worker called to be a helper but who may not perform any sacerdotal services. The next grade gives a student a commission to preach, and after a one year period of probation at this level a candidate who is thought suitable can proceed to qualification as a licensed minister who can fulfil most ministries, but cannot perform marriages. The last grade takes the candidate to the level of ordained minister, who receives ordination under the supervision of an appointed regional, or national, office of the Church; such a minister may then perform all sacerdotal services, including marriage.

❖ American Bible Churches; Community Churches; Evangelical Christian Churches

AMERICAN EVANGELICAL LUTHERAN CHURCH

The American Evangelical Lutheran Church was founded as the *Kirkelig Missions Forening* in 1872 for work principally among the Danish immigrants to the USA, with ministers of the LUTHERAN Church sent out from Denmark for that purpose. This small Church placed a strong emphasis on the place of the Bible in Lutheran theology and it always had a clear ecumenical basis, belonging to the World Council of Churches. The Church is no longer in existence, having united in 1962 with three other Lutheran groups, the United Lutheran Church (founded 1918), the Swedish-speaking AUGUSTANA EVANGELICAL LUTHERAN CHURCH (founded 1860) and the Finnish Evangelical Lutheran Church (founded 1890), to form (the) AMERICAN LUTHERAN CHURCH.

AMERICAN LUTHERAN CHURCH

A LUTHERAN Church that came into existence as the result of a merger of three existing Lutheran Churches; this was effected at a convention held in Minneapolis, Minnesota, in 1960. The merging Churches were:

1 The 'American Lutheran Church' (as distinct from *The* American Lutheran Church), had been formed in 1930 through a merger of four Synods: the Ohio Synod (1818), the Buffalo Synod (1845), the Texas Synod (1851) and the Iowa Synod (1854), all composed of German immigrants.

2 The Evangelical Lutheran Church, founded in 1917 from a merger of some Norwegian Churches that came to America during the nineteenth century. These included the United Norwegian Church, the Norwegian Synod and the Hauge Synod – by the

1960s this had become the largest Lutheran Church in the USA.

3 The United Evangelical Lutheran Church, which was organized in 1896 by a merger of two Synods formed by Danish immigrants: the Danish Evangelical Lutheran Association (1884) and the Danish Evangelical Lutheran Church in North America (1894).

A fourth group, the Lutheran Free Church, with a Norwegian provenance, joined the newly formed group in 1963. This Church became part of the EVANGELICAL LUTHERAN CHURCH IN AMERICA (ECLA) in 1988.

AMERICAN ORTHODOX CATHOLIC CHURCH

The American Orthodox Church, which has now merged with the APOSTOLIC CATHOLIC CHURCH OF THE AMERICAS, represented an attempt to create a Church that was at once autonomous and American, orthodox in its faith and catholic in its universality. Robert S. Zeiger founded it in 1962, following his consecration as Orthodox Bishop for the Occidentals by Bishop Peter Zurawetsky and other bishops of the NORTH AMERICAN OLD ROMAN CATHOLIC CHURCH. The doctrinal position of the Church was Orthodox and the clergy, who maintained secular occupations, were allowed to marry.

A holy synod, presided over by the prime bishop as chairman, governed the Church. Founded in California, by 1963 the Church began to establish itself in North Kentucky and its influence extended to Kansas. Bishop Zeiger retired in 1976 and the Church, led by Bishop Colin Guthrie, merged with the Apostolic Catholic Church of the Americas.

AMERICAN ORTHODOX CHURCH

Aftimios Ofiesh (1890–1971) was a monk and priest of the Orthodox Patriarchate of Antioch who had worked originally among the Lebanese and Syrians in the USA and Canada on behalf of the RUSSIAN ORTHODOX CHURCH. He was made an archimandrite in 1915, elected a bishop by the Russian holy synod and consecrated in 1917 by Archbishop Evdokim. With the approval of the Moscow patriarchate, Metropolitan Platon and various other bishops authorized Aftimios to form an American Orthodox Church, with a view to caring for American-born Orthodox Christians. It would require the cooperation of other Orthodox bishops in America, but this was not forthcoming and Bishop Aftimios was refused recognition. To make matters more difficult, the Ecumenical Patriarch in Constantinople declared the American Orthodox Church to be schismatic, and with the previous support from the Russian Orthodox Church withdrawn, Aftimios was left isolated. In 1932, having previously consecrated two bishops for work in Canada and Los Angeles, he now consecrated a colourful character, an erstwhile priest of the Protestant Episcopal Church, called William Albert Nichols. Both men were to marry in the following year, with Bishop Aftimios and his new wife retiring to live in Pennsylvania. Nichols, who has been described as 'a sporty old dog', was a veteran pressman, having been religious editor for several New York newspapers. It was alleged that he always went to work in clerical dress and spent his afternoons betting on the horses. At the end of the day he would take the ferry home to Staten Island, cheerily greeting and blessing with the sign of the cross his fellow travellers. Nichols raised one of his followers, Alexander Tyler Turner, who had previously started a quasi-religious community known as the Clerks Secular of St Basil, to the episcopate in 1939. These Basilians were later to function as the American Orthodox Church. The Church was eventually received into the Antiochian Orthodox Church in 1961 by Archbishop Antony Bashir as a western-rite vicariate.

AMERICAN RESCUE WORKERS

A HOLINESS-type denomination, which was founded in America in 1882 as a result of a disagreement that arose between William Booth, the founder of the British SALVATION ARMY and Major Thomas E. Moore, who was responsible for its American branch.

Moore and some of his fellow workers withdrew from the Salvation Army and in 1890 began to work independently, calling themselves the American Salvation Army. Before long, Moore resigned from the new group and became a minister in the BAPTIST Church. The leadership was taken over by Colonel Richard Holz who, with some others, responded to an appeal by Ballington Booth (1857–1940), the second son of William Booth, to return to the Salvation Army, for which he had taken over responsibility. Many, but not all, acceded to the request. Those who did not continued as members of the American Salvation Army. By 1913, the name had been changed to American Rescue Workers.

The work of the denomination is directed largely to home mission concerns for the deprived and homeless. The members meet regularly in mission halls and chapels where they observe the sacraments of baptism and Holy Communion, unlike their parent body. The American Rescue Workers is organized along military lines and headed by a general who, as commander-in-chief, is elected for five years and is eligible for re-election; the clergy are known as *officers*, and the laity, as *soldiers*.

AMISH

The Amish are followers of a seventeenth-century elder, or bishop, of the MENNONITE CHURCH called Jacob Ammann, who was minister of a congregation in Emmenthal, Switzerland. His teaching was considered to be very strict, insistent about adherence to the *Dordrecht Confession of Faith*, signed in 1632, which insisted that the Bible is the source of belief and that the Church is the basic society for the true Christian, and which also placed considerable importance on a believer's conversion. Other doctrines concerned the need for repentance and conversion for salvation, regarding adult baptism as a public testimony of faith and the Lord's Supper as an expression of common union and fellowship. Marriage was only allowed between those of the same faith and while respect for the civil authority was to be upheld, this did not extend to the use of armed force, as all fighting and warfare were proscribed. Ammann also insisted upon the practice of avoidance, or *shunning*, of those members who had been placed under a *ban*, or excommunicated from the Church. Even when these were family members they were to be shunned and no communication with the errant member was allowed. He introduced foot-washing as part of liturgical practice, forbade the use of buttons and hooks and eyes in clothing and insisted that men should have long hair, with untrimmed beards but no moustaches, and that women should wear bonnets and aprons.

Although most members were in agreement with Ammann's injunctions, certain difficulties and disagreements arose. Some held that the foot-washing should be performed entirely by one person, others believing that it was necessary to have two (so that one should wash while the other wiped) and there were other problems in defining articles of clothing considered by some as necessities but by others as luxuries. Simplicity was the byword, but the details could cause differences of opinion and lead to lively disparity within the Church. During Ammann's lifetime general agreement was reached in most matters, but the clause about *shunning* led to a schism that later attempts at reconciliation failed to heal. The first immigration to North America took place early in the eighteenth century. The first settlement was made at North Kill Creek, Pennsylvania, with other colonies soon developing in Ohio, Indiana, Illinois and Iowa.

The Lord's Supper is celebrated twice a year and it is now common for the foot-washing ordinance to be performed at the same time. The officials of the Church include elders, ministers and deacons who are usually self-supporting and may work in regular, secular occupations. The American communities have developed, but with some polarization between those who want to retain their old way of life with its traditional emphasis on farming and self-sufficiency, who are now organized as the OLD ORDER AMISH MENNONITE CHURCH, and others who see the need to bring the Amish into closer conformity with modern American life. Whatever their differences, the Amish people have retained a reputation for honesty and responsible farming which is without equal, and their distinctive appearance and simple, traditional way of life attracts attention from intrigued spectators.

ANABAPTIST (also ANABAPTISTS)

The name, derived from the Greek and meaning *re-baptizers*, given to various religious groups at the time of the Reformation in Europe from their practice of disallowing infant baptism; they replaced it with a baptism of believers for adults and insisted that all those who had been baptized as infants must be re-baptized when they reached adulthood. As a rule, Anabaptists held to the separation of Church and state and to the primacy of scripture. Some were millennialists (REVELATION 20) and pacifists, and most insisted upon a strict form of religious discipline in their lives. They were much persecuted at various times. Anabaptists were prominent in Switzerland, north and south Germany, Moravia and the Netherlands and were the ancestors of many groups, such as the BAPTISTS, MENNONITES and SCHWENCKFELDIANS.

ANDHRA EVANGELICAL LUTHERAN CHURCH

The Church, which was founded in 1842 at Guntur, Hyderabad, as part of the first missionary effort of the LUTHERAN Church in India, became the centre for general and higher education under Lutheran auspices, with a Bible Training School established at Rajahmundry in 1885. The founder, J. C. F. Heyer, was a member of the Ministries of Pennsylvania, the oldest Lutheran Synod in North America. The work of the Church is mainly carried out in Andhra Pradesh among the Telugu-speaking people, with evangelism through film and radio and through the access of so-called *Bible Women* who can gain entrance to Hindu and Muslim homes more readily than male missionaries. Members also provide Sunday schools and several *ashrams*, centres that give people of various castes and ethnic backgrounds the opportunity to study together. The Church has also been able to operate a college of education, some secondary and industrial schools and colleges of law and agriculture. At one time it was also responsible for the maintenance of eight hospitals, which date from 1883, but most of these have now been handed over to the government, with only two remaining in the hands of the Church. Work continues with leprosy sufferers and in the promotion of health education. The Church joined the Lutheran World Federation in 1950 and is affiliated to the World Council of Churches. The Church became part of the UNITED EVANGELICAL LUTHERAN CHURCH IN INDIA in 1975, and the first seventeen female ministers were ordained with the unanimous acceptance of the clergy in 1999, becoming the fourth of the Lutheran World Federation member Churches to ordain women.

ANGEL DANCERS

In 1890 the American sect known as the Angel Dancers was formed at Hackensack, New Jersey, by Huntsman T. Mnason (*sic*), John *the Baptist* McClintock, Daniel *Silas the Pure* Haines, Mary *Thecla* Stewart, Jane *Phoebe* Havell, and some others. Mnason had led a dissolute life until, at the age of 50, he underwent a conversion experience after attending a Methodist revival meeting in New York City. Believing that he had received a vision of heaven and hell and had seen both Christ and the devil, he felt that he was now directly in the hands of God and must do as he was bidden. Mnason dressed in messianic robes and began to preach to crowds in New Jersey, healing through the laying on of hands. His followers formed a commune, known as the *Lord's Farm* (or as the *Land of Rest and Peace*), at Hackensack where Mnason directed them. Marriage was condemned and free love practised, against a background of strict vegetarianism and pacifism. Vagrants, tramps and local outcasts were welcomed to the farm, where they were fed and clothed. Although the authorities were suspicious of what might be happening at the commune, the Angel Dancers won a good reputation locally for their charitable work. Mnason and some of his followers were arrested in 1893, charged with keeping a disorderly house. They refused to defend themselves and were sentenced, Mnason to a year's hard labour. He served his sentence and returned to Hackensack. In 1908 there were still twelve followers at the farm.

The name 'Angel Dancers' came from the frenzied dancing that preceded meals at the farm, a time when the members believed that the devil was present and had to be cast out. Following grace before meals they would whirl and jump around the room until they could leap right over the table, a sign to them that the devil had been expelled.

ANGELIC BRETHREN

The Angelic Brethren sprang from a group of SEPARATISTS, founded by John George Gichtel (1638–1710), a member of the LUTHERAN CHURCH, who had been attracted to the writings of Jacob Boehme (1575–1624). Boehme, a German shoemaker who was given to mysticism, was very critical of the PROTESTANTISM of his day, especially of the Church's emphasis on the Bible and the notion of the salvation of the *elect*. Gichtel, who also in his turn attacked the established Churches in Germany, found himself in trouble and was forced out of the country, going to live in Amsterdam. During his time there he evolved a complex message of PIETISM, theosophy and mysticism, while working on a further edition of Boehme's works. One of his distinctive ideas concerned the union between the spiritual man and divine wisdom, which he regarded as *heavenly marriage*. His followers, who came to be known as the Angelic Brethren, were expected to renounce earthly marriage. There were Angelic Brethren to be found in Germany and the Netherlands until the end of the nineteenth century.

❖ Gichtelians

ANGLICAN

As pertaining to the CHURCH OF ENGLAND.

ANGLICAN CATHOLIC CHURCH

The members of this Church had been part of the Protestant Episcopal Church of the USA until 1977. At a meeting in St Louis, Missouri, it was decided by some that there was a need for a greater emphasis on the teachings of holy scripture and that a return to Catholic worship and the promotion of traditional moral values was necessary. As a result of this meeting, a fundamental doctrinal statement for all traditional ANGLICANS in America was formulated, known as the *Affirmation of St Louis*. This resulted in the formation of the Anglican Catholic Church as a distinct body from the Protestant Episcopal Church. In order to establish a hierarchy, four bishops were consecrated in 1978, merging the episcopal successions of the CHURCH OF ENGLAND, the EPISCOPAL CHURCH IN THE USA (also Protestant Episcopal Church), the POLISH NATIONAL CATHOLIC CHURCH, the OLD CATHOLIC CHURCH and the PHILIPPINE INDEPENDENT CHURCH.

Doctrinally, the Church accepts the definitions in the Apostolic, Nicene and Athanasian creeds and recognizes the seven sacraments of baptism, penance (reconciliation), confirmation, Eucharist, ordination, marriage and anointing of the sick. *The 1928 Book of Common Prayer* is used, with the services of morning and evening prayer observed together with the main service, the Eucharist or Mass, for which vestments are worn. The Anglican Catholic Church, which is part of the CONTINUING CHURCH movement, has some fifteen dioceses in the USA as well as in Puerto Rico, Central and South America, England, New Zealand and India, with missionary dioceses in Australia, the Caribbean, New Granada and South Africa. Friendly relations exist between the Anglican Catholic Church and the ROMAN CATHOLIC CHURCH, the Polish National Catholic Church and the Continuing Catholic bodies in the USA.

ANGLICAN CHURCH IN AMERICA

The Anglican Church in America, part of the CONTINUING CHURCH MOVEMENT, was founded in 1991 as a result of a union between the AMERICAN EPISCOPAL CHURCH and a part of the ANGLICAN CATHOLIC CHURCH (ACC), led by Bishop Louis W. Falk of the Diocese of the Missouri Valley.

Bishop Falk had been elected in 1983 as the first archbishop of the Anglican Catholic Church and, following the establishment of the Anglican Church in America, he was elected, in 1992, as primate of the worldwide TRADITIONAL ANGLICAN COMMUNION, of which it is now a part.

Doctrinally, the Church follows *The 1928 Book of Common Prayer*, affirms the three traditional creeds (Apostles', Nicene and Athanasian), recognizes the first seven ecumenical councils and the *Thirty-Nine Articles of the Anglican Church*. The Church has an episcopal polity, but it is one in which clergy and laity share in the decision-making processes. Governed by a general synod, which meets twice a year, the Church has its headquarters in West Des Moines, Iowa.

ANGLICAN CHURCH OF AUSTRALIA

The ANGLICAN Church came to Australia from England with the first fleet, whose chaplain, Richard Johnson, conducted the first service on Australian soil on 3 February 1788. The first church was erected by Johnson in 1793, but was subsequently burnt down. Samuel Marsden succeeded Johnson in 1794 and it was Marsden who oversaw the rapid development of the Church in Australia and who also established a system of day schools for the children of the new colony. The first bishop of Australia, William Broughton, was consecrated in 1868; until then Australia had been an archdeaconry of the diocese of Calcutta. A second diocese was created in Tasmania, and by 1847 three more had been created. As Anglican witness throughout Australia developed, more dioceses were established and by 1872, when the first general synod was convened, they numbered ten.

Until 1961 the Church was, strictly speaking, part of the CHURCH OF ENGLAND, but on 1 January 1962 the Church of England in Australia came into existence, with its own constitution and legislative powers given to the general synod. The president of the synod, who is the primate of Australia, is selected from the diocesan bishops. The general synod is composed of equal numbers of clergy and lay representatives in proportion to the number of clergy in each diocese. In August 1981 the official name of the Church was declared to be *The Anglican Church of Australia*, and it remains part of the ANGLICAN COMMUNION.

The ordination of women priests in the Church has been accepted since 1992, but to date no decision has been made about the consecration of women priests as bishops. Female ordination prompted the departure of many congregations and clergy from the Church and most became part of the American-based ANGLICAN CATHOLIC CHURCH.

The Anglican Church of Australia has been involved in missionary outreach programmes since 1826, when the first aboriginal mission was established. Work in this field of evangelism continues, with Church sponsorship of such societies as the Australian Board of Mission, the Church Missionary Society and the South American Missionary Society. Australian Anglican missionaries work in South America, Melanesia, Polynesia and the Far East. There has always been a strong commitment to social action, notably concern for the aged, the sick and the marginalized, with a vigorous network of chaplaincies in hospitals, universities, trade and industry.

ANGLICAN COMMUNION

A composite body made up of many small, self-governing Churches in over 160 countries worldwide who are in full communion with the see of Canterbury, and therefore with the Archbishop of Canterbury. It is one of the functions of the archbishop to convene the Lambeth Conference in England every ten years, which is attended by all the bishops of the Anglican Communion. This conference has a consultative function in its direction and interpretation of current Anglican opinion. The resolutions of the Lambeth Conference are not binding on any member Churches unless they choose to modify their own canon law to be bound by them.

The Anglican Churches of England, Scotland, Ireland and Wales formed the original provinces of the Communion. In the early nineteenth century missionary initiatives led to the foundation of Anglican Churches throughout the world, as autonomous provinces of the Anglican Communion; most of these had became constitutionally independent by the end of the Second World War.

Churches within the Anglican Communion uphold and proclaim the Catholic and apostolic faith, which is presented through a shared tradition and a shared belief. The belief is based upon the Bible and the *Thirty-Nine Articles of Religion*; tradition is in part embodied in the *Book of Common Prayer*, which was first published in 1549 and revised in 1552 and 1662. Several countries now have their own Prayer Books, which borrow very heavily from the work of Archbishop Thomas Cranmer (1489–1556). Central to the Anglican Communion are the sacraments of baptism, using the Trinitarian formula, and the Eucharist, also known as the Lord's Supper, and Holy Communion, or the Mass. Other rites observed by member Churches of this Communion include confirmation, penance, ordination, marriage and the anointing of the sick. There is no central governance of the Anglican Church as each member Church and province of the Anglican Communion is governed independently, by its own canon law. Entries for many, but not all, of these can be found throughout the text.

ANGLICAN MISSION IN AMERICA

A breakaway traditional ANGLICAN group, part of the CONTINUING CHURCH movement, which was formed in July 2000 in protest against the perceived growing liberalism in both doctrine and sexual morality in the EPISCOPAL CHURCH IN THE USA.

On 24 June 2001, four new bishops for this group, named Barnum, Greene, Johnston and Weiss, were consecrated in Denver, Colorado, by the archbishops of Rwanda, Emmanuel Mbona Kolini, and of South-East Asia, Datuk Yong Ping Chung; John Rodgers and Charles Murphy had been consecrated as bishops the previous year in Singapore by Kolini and the previous Archbishop of South-East Asia, Moses Tay. These consecrations are all considered irregular. The headquarters of the Anglican Mission in America is at Pawley Island, South Carolina and there are 40 congregations with some 10,000 Church members.

ANGLICAN ORTHODOX CHURCH OF NORTH AMERICA

The Reverend James Parker Dees, who had been a priest of the EPISCOPAL CHURCH IN THE USA, founded the Anglican Orthodox Church of North America in 1963. Along with many fellow members of the Church he was concerned about changes that had been made in the celebration of the liturgy, especially by High Churchmen, the open disregard in which the *Thirty-Nine Articles* of the ANGLICAN COMMUNION were held and the liberalism that was tolerated, all of which were seen by some to be leading that Church into apostasy. James Dees belonged to the Low Church Episcopalian tradition and together with some like-minded clergy and laity left the Episcopal Church to found the Anglican Orthodox Church of North America, at Statesville, North Carolina. He established an episcopal polity and received consecration at the hands of Bishop Wasyl Sawyna, of the HOLY UKRAINIAN AUTOCEPHALIC ORTHODOX CHURCH IN EXILE and Bishop Orlando J. Woodward, of the OLD CATHOLIC CHURCH. The new Church received enthusiastic support in the southern states of the USA. Local churches are autonomous but are under the authority of their presiding bishop. The number of congregations and their members has grown and intercommunion with similar Churches in Pakistan, South India, Nigeria, Fiji, Zimbabwe, Madagascar and Colombia has been established.

ANGLICAN PROVINCE OF CHRIST THE KING

This Church began as part of the CONTINUING CHURCH MOVEMENT in the ANGLICAN COMMUNION, and formally came into being following the congress held in 1977 at St Louis, Missouri, at which traditional Anglican beliefs and practices were upheld by many concerned traditionalists, who together affirmed a doctrinal statement called the *Affirmation of St Louis*. The Anglican Province of Christ the King is one of four proposed dioceses put forward by the congress. Moves to form the ANGLICAN CATHOLIC CHURCH were put in motion and a constitution was adopted in Dallas in 1978 the aim of which was to safeguard the traditional Anglican position.

A disagreement within the Church led to the temporary and informal formation of what was called the *Anglican Church of North America* in October 1978. More internal agreements within that Church led, in 1991, to the formal establishment of the Anglican Province of Christ the King, whose congregations are now divided into three dioceses. Doctrinally, the Church upholds the *Affirmation of St Louis* and differs from the Anglican Catholic Church only in some matters of canon law and an insistence that clergy must attend a seminary to receive their training. The headquarters of this small Church is in Berkeley, California.

ANTINOMIANISM (also ANTINOMIAN)

The term, from the Greek '*anti*' – against – and '*nomos*' – the law, is applied to the heretical doctrine that holds that Christians are not bound by the moral law and have been set free by grace from obeying it. Antinomianism is linked to the GNOSTICS and the ANABAPTISTS.

APOSTOLIC CATHOLIC CHURCH OF THE AMERICAS

A Church that came into existence in the USA in 1977 through the merger of two existing groups, the Anglican Church of the Americas, and the AMERICAN ORTHODOX CHURCH. The Apostolic Church of the Americas allows its few congregations latitude in their choice of liturgical style, leaving the choice up to the congregations of whether to have a Byzantine liturgy, to follow the *Book of Common Prayer* of the Anglican tradition, or to celebrate the Tridentine Mass according to the ROMAN CATHOLIC rite.

APOSTOLIC CHRISTIAN CHURCH (NAZAREAN)

The Church has an identical history to that of the APOSTOLIC CHRISTIAN CHURCH OF AMERICA until 1907, when there was a disagreement over the use of the German language in church services and whether or not certain traditional European customs should be retained. A small group of conservative members separated from the Apostolic Christian Church of America at this point and established themselves as the Apostolic Christian Church (Nazarean). The Church is found mainly in the USA, in Illinois and Ohio, but also in some other countries. Its doctrinal position and attitude to pacifism is identical to that held by the Apostolic Christian Church of America, which remains the larger group. A further split over language differences occurred in 1930 and led to the formation of the small German Apostolic Christian Church.

APOSTOLIC CHRISTIAN CHURCHES OF AMERICA

A conversion experience in Switzerland in the 1830s led Samuel Heinrich Froehlich (1803–57), a minister, to begin to preach in his parish in the Aargau the literal translation of the Bible, meeting with great success and at the same time increasing opposition from the authorities. In 1830, largely on account of his refusal to replace the PROTESTANT *Heidelberg Catechism* of 1562 with the newly introduced catechism with its emphasis on rationalism, which he was required as a minister of the state Church to implement, Froehlich ran into serious trouble with the Church authorities and this eventually led to his excommunication. Froehlich then formed his own Church, initially known as the EVANGELICAL BAPTIST CHURCH and later as the Apostolic Christian Church, which now has congregations in 22 countries throughout the world.

Froehlich's life had many problems. In 1836 he married Suzette Brunschwiler, but their marriage was not recognized as Froehlich was no longer a member of the state Church. In 1844, after years of difficulty with the authorities over many issues, Samuel Froehlich was banished to France. Some of his followers migrated to America and established a presence there in 1847, opening churches in Lewis County, New York, and later at Sardis, in Ohio, and the movement flourished. A disagreement arose in 1907 over the retention of the use of the German language in Church services, as well as other traditional European customs that had been introduced by the immigrant congregations, and this led to the separation of a small group, calling themselves the APOSTOLIC CHRISTIAN CHURCH (NAZAREAN), from the larger group, who then became known as the Apostolic Christian Churches of America.

Doctrinally, the Church teaches complete sanctification following conversion, after which new converts give a testimony of their faith and conversion experience and receive water baptism by immersion and a laying-on of hands from an elder of the Church, which is seen as a *sealing*, or confirmation, of the presence of the Holy Spirit. The Church teaches the inspiration, inerrancy, infallibility and literal interpretation of the Bible. Members are expected to avoid oath-taking and to maintain a pacifist witness in time of war. The lifestyle of the members following conversion is expected to change. Men are required to dress in a quiet manner and keep their hair short, and women are urged to reject the wearing of jewellery and cosmetics.

The ministers pray together before a service for divine guidance from the Holy Spirit, because, unlike in most traditions, no sermon notes or selection of texts takes place. During the service the Bible is opened at random to provide the minister with material for his message. Prayer language retains the use of the words *thee* and *thou*, and in church the sexes are separated during the services, the women keeping their heads covered. All contribute to the singing of hymns in a simple *a cappella* fashion.

The ministers of the churches, who are chosen from their congregations, do not receive ministerial training and are required to serve open-ended terms. Elders, who hold a position similar to that of a bishop, are chosen by ballot and are expected to be responsible for the administration of the spiritual matters of the Church and to provide counselling for converts and members. A group of fifteen elders, all with equal status, meet together to take decisions about major Church projects and future ordinations.

Missionary work has seen the opening of many churches in the USA, in large cities as well as rural locations, with preaching on some university campuses and the provision of help for relief work; foreign missions have taken the work of the Church to Japan and India, where a medical mission has been opened.

APOSTOLIC CHURCH

The Church is known variously as the Apostolic Church of Great Britain, or of Australia and New Zealand, or simply as the Apostolic Church (as it is known in New Guinea). It arose in Wales in 1916 as a Pentecostal Church following upon the Welsh revival movement of the beginning of the twentieth century. The headquarters of the Church in the UK is at Penygroes, South Wales.

The doctrinal tenets of the Church are like those of any of the Assemblies of God, with belief in the inspiration, inerrancy and infallibility of the Bible, a traditional belief in the Trinity, the divinity of Jesus Christ and the second coming (Revelation 20). Adherents also believe in the baptism of the Holy Spirit, which is evidenced by *glossolalia*, or speaking with tongues, divine healing and the resurrection of the dead to either life eternal or everlasting damnation. Baptism is by immersion and the ordinance of the Lord's Supper is observed. All ethical, ecclesiastical and personal problems are referred to the Holy Spirit for discernment. The Church maintains a centralized structure, with a hierarchy of apostles, prophets, pastors, teachers, evangelists, elders, deacons and deaconesses, all of them appointed through the guidance of the Holy Spirit. As congregations are established, people can be called to office by the prophets and then set apart by the apostles, who exercise authority to affirm, or not, the revelations that are handed down by the prophets of the Church. There have been active missionary outreach programmes in Nigeria, Ghana and Papua New Guinea, where missionaries have been working with the people of the Western Highlands since 1954. The Apostolic Church of Australia and New Zealand was established in 1928.

APOSTOLIC CHURCH OF CHRIST

This small American Church started as a breakaway from the Church of God (Apostolic) in 1969 when two ministers, Bishop Johnnie Draft and Elder Wallace Snow, felt compelled to act upon Draft's belief that he was called upon by God to found his own Church.

While there are no doctrinal differences between the Apostolic Church of Christ and the parent Church, there was a move towards a more centralized authority in its administration. The head of the Church is known as the chief apostle, and is assisted by an executive board that is responsible for all Church property.

APOSTOLIC CHURCH OF PENTECOST IN CANADA

A Church founded in 1921 with its present headquarters in Calgary, Alberta, it represents a schism from the Pentecostal Assemblies of Canada, formed in 1910, over the issue of ONENESS teaching, which denied the Trinity and asserted the oneness of God. The Apostolic Church of Pentecost in Canada is a member of the Evangelical Fellowship of Canada and affirms belief in the Trinity, firmly rejecting the position held by the SABELLIANS. They accept the doctrine of the salvation of sinners by grace through faith alone in the perfect and sufficient work of Christ's passion and death on humanity's behalf excluding all human merit. The Church observes adult baptism by immersion and the baptism of the Holy Ghost, which is evidenced by *glossolalia*, and celebrates the Lord's Supper as a memorial for believers. Divine healing is also undertaken. The Church believes in the reality of Satan and in the second coming of Jesus Christ (REVELATION 20).

APOSTOLIC CHURCH OF QUEENSLAND

The Church was established by H. F. Niemeyer and was first known as *The Apostolic Congregations*. Niemeyer had been ordained into the General Christian Apostolic Mission in Germany, which had been formed as a schism in 1863 from the Hamburg congregation of the CATHOLIC APOSTOLIC CHURCH, and was sent to Queensland, Australia. When Niemeyer landed in Brisbane, with his wife and three children, he had one halfpenny in his pocket but he soon found employment with his father-in-law, Mr Lose, a Brisbane businessman. Niemeyer worked hard and saved money for tools to equip a farm that he planned to run at Grandchester. Many privations followed for the family in this inhospitable and dangerous area. Niemeyer was lucky to survive an encounter with a death adder, while his wife nearly perished in a house fire. The burden on Niemeyer's wife was particularly hard, with the nearest water source four miles away. While the family was still living at the farm she gave birth to their fourth child without any form of medical assistance. They were later to leave Grandchester and move across the state to Hatton Vale, near Laidley.

Niemeyer had known an apostle, or minister, of the Catholic Apostolic Church from the church in Hamburg, Fritz Krebs (1831–1905), who was credited with a reputation for discernment. He called Niemeyer back to Germany in 1886 to be ordained as an apostle. Krebs gave permission for the name of the Church in Queensland to be changed to the APOSTOLIC UNITY CHURCH. When Krebs died his replacement, the self-styled leader, or *Stamm-Apostel*, Hermann Nichaus (1848–1932) came to expect that his words should be given precedence over the scriptures and this led to much concern amongst the Catholic Apostolic Church congregations scattered around the world.

Opposition to Nichaus meant expulsion from the Church, but Niemeyer could not accept the *Stamm-Apostel*'s authority. He was expelled and his replacement sent out to Queensland in 1912, but the majority of Niemeyer's followers remained loyal to him and their Church was now re-named a second time, as the Apostolic Church of Queensland, to distinguish it from the original foundation, which came to be called the New Apostolic Church.

During the First World War, Niemeyer, as an enemy alien, was interned but later released at Dubbo, New South Wales, because of ill-health. He died there in 1920. His son, who succeeded him in the Church, appealed to the New Apostolic Church to return to scriptural tradition and to confess their sins; this they refused to do and the two bodies have remained separate ever since.

The Apostolic Church of Queensland, which is mostly concentrated around the port of Bundaberg, is very active in mission work, both in Australia and in the Philippines, South Africa and Indonesia, also sponsoring a school for the poor in India. Doctrinally, they uphold the three creeds – Apostles', Nicene and Athanasian – and are millenarians (Revelation 20). The government of the Church is in the hands of a hierarchy composed of apostles, prophets, bishops (or angels), evangelists, priests and deacons. Deacons are elected by their own congregations and can advance to the other offices, which are under the authority of the apostles. Marriage is considered indissoluble, except by death, and the sacraments of baptism, holy sealing (or laying on of hands) and Holy Communion are celebrated with considerable ritual, using vestments, incense and candles.

APOSTOLIC COMMUNITY

The Apostolic Community was founded in Germany in 1954 as a schism from the New Apostolic Church, itself a schism from the Catholic Apostolic Church. The chief apostle, or *Stamm-Apostel*, J. G. Bischoff (1871–1960) believed that he had received a private revelation that he would not die before seeing Christ's second coming (Revelation 20), and he was so convinced of the importance of this message that he insisted that it was to be preached throughout the congregations of the New Apostolic Church. Many of these congregations refused to comply and were expelled from the New Apostolic Church, and under the leadership of Peter Kuhlen they formed their own schismatic group, which they called the Apostolic Community. There are now 56 congregations of this Church, which is a member of the Union of Apostolic Christians (Switzerland), founded in 1956.

APOSTOLIC FAITH (OREGON)

This Church must not be confused with the Apostolic Faith Church (Jesus Coming Soon Church) founded in 1923.

The Apostolic Faith Mission was organized in the United States, at Portland in 1907 by a one-time preacher in the Methodist Church, the Reverend Mrs Florence L. Crawford, who had received the baptism of the Holy Spirit during a Pentecostal experience on Azusa Street, Los Angeles, California, in 1906. As part of this experience Mrs Crawford began to speak in Chinese, a language believed to be unknown to her, and her damaged eyesight was repaired. This phenomenon took place when a black preacher, W. J. Seymour, who had been barred from preaching at the city's

Nazarene Church following the hostile reception of his first sermon, went instead to preach at a house on Bonnie Brae Street. Here he preached and prayed for three days and the baptism of the Holy Spirit is said to have occurred, with the gift of tongues, or *glossolalia*, coming to the assembled people who had gathered to listen. This so captivated people's imagination that a former Methodist church on Azusa Street had to be rented to accommodate the crowds who came to witness these events. The significance of this phenomenon was given greater dramatic underlining by the San Francisco earthquake, which followed nine days after the first display of *glossolalia*. This conjunction of events received tremendous publicity and people came from all over the United States to receive the baptism of the Holy Spirit. The movement spread from the USA to Great Britain, Sweden, India and Chile.

Doctrinally the Apostolic Faith Church is FUNDAMENTALIST, Trinitarian and evangelistic, with its ARMINIAN theology stressing justification by faith; the Church also teaches the Wesleyan doctrine of entire sanctification as well as the baptism of the Holy Spirit. In addition to the usual two ordinances of baptism and the Lord's Supper, foot-washing is also observed. Whilst collections are not taken up during the services, tithing is expected from its members, to provide financial support for the work of the Church. The polity of the Church is presbyterian, with each local congregation placed under the leadership of the headquarters of the Church, which is at Portland, Oregon.

To become a member it is necessary to be *born again* and to accept the Church's doctrines. A certain change of lifestyle is expected, with an undertaking to wear sober dress and renounce smoking, the drinking of alcohol, cosmetics, and such activities as card playing and theatre attendance. Marriage with an unbeliever is not permitted.

❖ Apostolic Faith Mission of Portland, Oregon

APOSTOLIC LUTHERAN (CHURCH OF THE FIRST BORN)

This denomination is derived from the same source as the APOSTOLIC LUTHERAN CHURCH OF AMERICA, but the members look to Gallivaara (or Gallivare), in Sweden, as their Church headquarters, whose elders are consulted on important moral issues.

The Church differs from the Apostolic Lutheran Church of America in the doctrine of the fruits of faith, or manner by which sanctification may be expressed. This was initially through an emphasis upon simplicity of lifestyle and an absence of worldliness. As an example, men were not supposed to wear neckties and women were to wear headsquares, tied under the chin, rather than hats. Wall-hangings and photographs in the home were forbidden, as were floral tributes at funerals, and anything that could be considered unnecessarily decorative was proscribed. The early preachers emphasized sin in their preaching, but this has now changed.

Worship services in the Church always include a reading of a sermon written by Lars Laestadius, in addition to a normal homily. Once established in the USA, the Church quickly introduced the use of the English language into its services and began to publish books in English for its congregations. Up-to-date membership figures are difficult to access, but there are churches of the denomination in North Carolina, North Dakota, Washington and Delaware.

❖ Esikoiet; First Born Laestadians; Old Apostolic Lutheran Church; Western Laestadians

APOSTOLIC LUTHERAN CHURCH OF AMERICA

The Church derives its alternative name, Church of Laestadius, from Lars Levi Laestadius (1800–61), a pastor in the LUTHERAN CHURCH, who preached revivalism and repentance of sins, especially that of drunkenness, in northern Sweden, where he was in charge of the parish of Kaaresuvanto with responsibility for inspecting the parishes of Lapland. It is said that he had a conversion experience in 1844, through the efforts of Milla Clementsdotter (aka Lappish Mary), which led to his revivalist preaching in the years that followed. His message spread to all of northern Scandinavia, stressing the importance of the personal experience of salvation and the need for repentance and forgiveness of sins. Part of the repentance offered to people involved a public confession of sins before the assembled congregation. Laestadius sent young people as lay preachers into the vast areas of northern Scandinavia and the movement spread over much of Finland, into Russia and, through the Finnish migrants, into the USA.

Towards the end of the nineteenth century, doctrinal matters became the subject of dispute and threatened to split the movement, but it managed to stay united until the end of the century. In 1899 a schism broke out over differences of opinion concerning the understanding of righteousness, the kingdom of God and the role of the sacraments. This followed the death of Juhani Raattamaa (1811–99), a schoolmaster from Jukkasjarvi in Sweden, who had been Laestadius' student, assistant and successor, a man with natural authority who had been able to settle many of the earlier disputes and avoid schism. It was Raattamaa who introduced absolution and the laying on of hands for penitents who had made a confession of their sins. From this schism three groups emerged:

1 Apostolic Lutheran Church of America

2 First Born Laestadians (now the APOSTOLIC LUTHERAN (CHURCH OF THE FIRST BORN)

3 NEW AWAKENING

During the nineteenth century, many Finns, and other Scandinavians, became economic migrants to the USA, settling mainly in Minnesota and Michigan. Feeling insecure in their adopted country – not least because of their difficult language, which served to keep the migrant communities separate from the local people – they clung to their own familiar Finnish culture and their Church remained much as it had been back in Finland. Antti Vitikka, a preacher, gathered a Laestadian group together at Calumet, Michigan. The migrants there had been worshipping in the Lutheran church in Calumet, under a Norwegian minister, but differences between the two national groups developed and by 1872 a separate Finnish congregation asked Solomon Korteniemi, a church janitor, to be their pastor. He formed the Solomon Korteniemi Lutheran Society, but proved to be a poor leader. He was replaced by John Takkinen, a peripatetic teacher from Sweden, and the group's name was changed in 1879 to that of the Finnish Apostolic Lutheran Church of America.

This Church represented a fusion of independent Apostolic Lutheran congregations into a single national body. The foundation at Calumet was established after the fashion of the Evangelical Lutheran Church of Finland in its Sunday Worship and Communion services and other church activities. Takkinen introduced new organizational systems, including a catechetical teaching method, calling people together and then examining their ability to read the Bible and to explain doctrine.

The Apostolic Lutheran Church of America accepts the usual three Christian creeds and places great emphasis on confession of sins, absolution and regeneration. Confession can be made to any member of the congregation, since Laestadius had taught the priesthood of all believers and that all who had received the Holy Spirit were priests and had the power to absolve. If, however, a sin was public it required a public confession before the assembled congregation and absolution was given by a laying-on of hands by a Church representative. The Church adopted a constitution and set of by-laws in 1929, in which the authority of the Bible and the *Book of Concord* (1580), a collection of catechisms composed by Martin Luther, as well as articles and creedal statements, is affirmed.

There is an annual Church convention, called the *Big Meeting*, first held in 1908, at which elections of various Church officers are made. The congregations, which are self-governing, support domestic and foreign missions and maintain an overseas presence in Nigeria, Liberia and Guatemala.

❖ Church of Laestadius; Finnish Apostolic Lutheran Church of America

APOSTOLIC OVERCOMING HOLY CHURCH OF GOD

This American Church was founded as the Ethiopian Overcoming Holy Church of God in 1916 by Bishop W. T. Phillips (1893–1973), an ex-minister of the METHODIST EPISCOPAL CHURCH and the name was changed to the present one in 1927. Bishop Phillips had left the Methodist Episcopal Church because of his concern about the doctrine of HOLINESS and the process of sanctification. This PENTECOSTAL church stresses the ONENESS of God, teaching the deity of Jesus Christ and the Holy Spirit but denying a distinction between the persons; the three persons of God are thought of as modes in which God has revealed himself.

The worship services of the Church are unstructured and highly emotional assemblies, with liturgical dancing, which can be described as ecstatic, divine healing and speaking in tongues as regular features. The Bible is considered to be the inspired word of God and there is a strong emphasis upon Christ's return to earth after the millennium, when it is believed that there will be a 'white throne judgement' (REVELATION 20), followed by the destruction of the wicked. Sanctification of the person is believed to commence at rebirth, when the new member receives baptism both by immersion and the Holy Spirit. Foot-washing is also part of the Church's practice and precedes Holy Communion. Marriage to the unsaved is prohibited, along with the use of slang, loud talking, joking, tobacco, snuff and alcohol.

The Church is found throughout the USA, with missions in the West Indies and Africa, with episcopal oversight of each district in which there are congregations. These districts are managed by senior bishops assisted by an executive board composed of senior ministers of the Church. The Church is supported through tithing of its members. There is a national conference that meets annually.

❖ Ethiopian Overcoming Holy Church of God

APOSTOLIC UNITY CHURCH

A name temporarily used by a congregation of Church members of the General Christian Apostolic Mission in Germany that was established in Queensland, Australia, at the end of the nineteenth century. The founder was H. F. Niemeyer, who after his ordination as an apostle by the Hamburg CATHOLIC APOSTOLIC CHURCH wanted to change the name of the church in Queensland from APOSTOLIC CHURCH OF QUEENSLAND to the Apostolic Unity Church, for which his superior in Germany granted permission. When difficulties arose within the parent Church in Germany, resulting in Niemeyer's expulsion, his replacement set up the NEW APOSTOLIC CHURCH in Queensland. Niemeyer then changed the name of his church once again, and it then became known as the Apostolic Church of Queensland.

APOSTOLICI

This term is a generic one and was used by at least four groups of people, beginning in the third century in Syria and Asia Minor with a group of earnest, zealous Christians who tried to lead what they thought was the life of the apostles. They were given to excessive asceticism and what is now seen as a distorted notion of Christian morality, which led them to proscribe marriage. They also regarded the ownership of property as being evil, to the extent that a property owner was not to be admitted to their group. In time they lapsed into NOVATIANISM and finally became MANICHAEANS.

The second group were the New Apostolici of the twelfth century, who flourished in and around Cologne, Germany, and Périgueux, France. They rejected everything that was not to be found in the teachings of Christ and the apostles. They consequently rejected marriage, although rumours, probably calculated to scandalize, told that the women of the community were shared in common by the men. By extension, flesh meat was forbidden on the grounds that meat was the result of sexual intercourse. Infant baptism was also rejected, along with the veneration of the saints, and because they did not believe in purgatory, members neglected to recite any prayers for the dead, a most unusual omission for that period. By the reasoning of the sect those who were not members were sinners and could neither receive nor administer the sacraments. It is believed that each sect member was empowered to consecrate bread and wine at meals and through this receive Christ's body and blood. Two members of the sect were burnt at the stake, in Cologne, for heresy.

The third group known as Apostolici, also known as False Apostles, or Apostolics, existed in Italy in the thirteenth and fourteenth centuries, founded in Parma in 1260 by Gerard Segarelli, who has been described as being 'an ignorant, low class man'. He wore a white cloak and grey cinctured robe and sandals, letting his hair and beard grow unchecked. He sold his house and gave away all of his money to become an itinerant preacher, advocating penance and apostolic poverty. Many followers were gained. Their belief was that the last days before Christ's return to earth were imminent (Revelation 20), and that absolute poverty and interior obedience in imitation of the apostolic life were necessary for personal salvation. The Apostolici supported themselves by begging and receiving alms and gained a contemporary reputation for being libertines, though this may have been purely hearsay, as their behaviour did nothing to endear them to the Church authorities. The Council of Würzburg in 1287 forbade the members to continue in this way and prohibited the faithful from associating with them. Numerous members were imprisoned, but far from destroying the sect this action served to increase its membership. So serious was the situation in the eyes of the Church that two popes, Honorius IV in 1286 and Nicholas IV in 1290 condemned the movement. Segarelli went to the stake in Parma in 1300 and Fra Dulcin, or Dolcino, of Novara, who led the followers in the mountains of Vercelli, took his position as leader until 1306 when Pope Clement V organized a crusade against them. Dulcin paid for his beliefs with his life and followed Segarelli to the stake in 1307.

Some Anabaptist groups were also called *Apostolici* because of their practice of poverty and their literal interpretation of the Bible. From their practice of the washing of feet, which they regarded as an ordinance, this group also gained the soubriquet of *Pedonites*.

❖ Apostolic Brethren

APOTACTICS

The Apotactics were members of a third-century heretical sect that spread through the western and eastern parts of Asia Minor. St Epiphanius (310–403) referred to them as *Renunciators* because of their renunciation of private property, but they sometimes called themselves *Apostolics* since they tried to model their lives on those of the apostles. The members rejected marriage and refused to reconcile sinners. They did not accept holy scripture, but instead upheld writings such as the apocryphal *Acts of Andrew and Thomas*. The Apotactics received unfavourable mention by Sts Basil, Augustine and John Damascene and the sect was also condemned by the Roman Emperor Theodosius the Great (*d.* 395), who enjoyed a reputation as a formidable destroyer of heresy and paganism.

❖ Apostolics; Apotactites; Renunciators

AQUARIANS

This general term was used to describe those who used water instead of wine in the celebration of the Eucharist, a practice that was condemned by Sts Cyprian and Augustine.

It was Theodoret (*c.* 393–458) who wrote that following the death of Justin Martyr, in 165, a disciple of his, Tatian, departed into heresy by rejecting marriage and condemning the use of animal flesh and wine. Theodoret described those disciples of Tatian, who celebrated the Eucharist using water instead of wine, as Hydroparastatae; their additional rejection of meat would have identified them as being Encratites, as several early Christian groups were named, all notable for their extreme ascetic practices. St Cyprian (*c.* 200–58) also condemned the practice of replacing wine with water, which was common at the time in Africa, suggesting that it was probably done through ignorance and simplicity and therefore not intended to be heretical. St Augustine

(354–430) also condemned the practice and wrote, in his *Catalogue of Heresies*, that 'the Aquarians are so-called because in the cup of the Sacrament they offer water, not that which the whole Church offers'.

There were other Aquarians who did not reject the use of wine but used it in the Eucharist mingled with water, which prompted comments by St Cyprian (*ad Caecilium – Ep. 63*). The third Council of Carthage and the third Council of Braga also condemned the practice.

❖ Hydroparastatae

ARMENIAN APOSTOLIC CHURCH

The use of the word Apostolic *in the title is based on the legend that the holy apostles, Sts Thaddeus and Bartholomew, brought Christianity to Armenia in the first century* AD. *Despite this legend, however, the Armenians regard St Gregory the Illuminator, or Enlightener, as their national patron and saint.*

According to the many stories that abound, St Gregory was born in Armenia in AD 260, was baptized and educated in Caesarea of Cappadocia (now Kayseri in Turkey), was married and fathered two sons, Sts Aristakes and Vardanes. Gregory, who was ordained in Caesarea, returned to Armenia and was given a position at the court of King Tiridates (or Trdat III, 298–330), but he managed to annoy the king through his preaching zeal and encouragement of Christians. The king, however, was said to be suffering from lycanthropy, believing himself to be a wild beast, and when through Gregory's intervention the condition was cured, Tiridates embraced Christianity and declared it as the state religion. Gregory was consecrated bishop in Caesarea in 302 and established his see at Ashtishat. This act of consecration underlined the Church's independence of Caesarea. St Gregory died in *c.* 330 and was succeeded by his son, St Aristakes, who took part in the Council of Nicaea, returning to Armenia with the Nicene creed.

The problem of translating the scriptures into Armenian was eased with the introduction in 412 of a 36–letter alphabet. This was accomplished by St Mesrop and made the text of the Divine Liturgy using the Anaphora of St Basil accessible to the Armenian laity, who had previously been dependent on Greek and Syriac texts. The original catholicosate had been founded in 303 by St Gregory at Etchmiadzin, which means *Only-Begotten Come Down*, in obedience to a dream in which Christ reputedly told the saint to build a cathedral at this place. The catholicosate was later moved to Dvin and after many invasions was forced to relocate several times before settling in Sis, north-east of Adana in south-central Asia Minor in 1293, from where the Armenians had extensive contact with the Latin crusaders. In 1441, however, the principal see was moved back to Etchmiadzin and a monk, Kirakos, was elected catholicos of All Armenia and installed there, while the catholicos at Sis was renamed as the catholicos of Cilicia and assumed a subordinate role. The catholicos of Etchmiadzin is recognized by all Armenians as the spiritual head of the Church, which exercises jurisdiction over Armenians in the former USSR and the diaspora, including those in Europe, India, Australia and the Americas. The Supreme Patriarch and Catholicos of All Armenians resides at Etchmiadzin and is owed allegiance by the catholicos of Cilicia, who now resides at Antélias in the Lebanon and retains some administrative autonomy. Cilicia has jurisdiction in Lebanon, Syria, Cyprus, Iran, Syria and Greece. The two catholicosates are in full communion but are administratively independent while the two patriarchates listed below are dependent in spiritual matters on Etchmiadzin.

1 The patriarchate of Jerusalem, which was founded early in the fourteenth century as a result of local monastic upheaval. It now has its headquarters in St James' monastery in Jerusalem and is responsible for the holy places that belong to the Armenian Church as well as the faithful in Israel, Jordan and Palestine.
2 The patriarchate of Constantinople, which was created in 1461 by the Ottoman Sultan Mehmed II, who appointed a local bishop to be the religious leader of the Armenian community in the Ottoman empire. Today, this patriarchate has jurisdiction over Armenian faithful in Turkey and Crete.

When Soviet Armenia was formed in November 1920, and subsequently joined the USSR, the Church suffered (although not as badly as others). Following the fall of the Soviet Union, however, the new national constitution guaranteed religious freedom and now recognizes the Armenian Apostolic Church as the national Church of Armenia. In 1993 a decree was issued by the government criticizing unregistered religious groups, such as the JEHOVAH'S WITNESSES and Evangelical Christian-Baptists, as disruptive. This led to the harassment of some PROTESTANT groups as recently as 1995, a year which was also important for the elevation of the Cilician catholicos, Karekin I, to the Supreme Patriarch and Catholicos of Etchmiadzin. In order to iron out difficulties and to strengthen the unity of the Church efforts are currently being made to draft a common constitution for the Armenian Church.

Doctrinally, the Armenian Apostolic Church acknowledges the first three ecumenical Councils of Nicaea (325), Constantinople (381) and Ephesus (431) but not of Chalcedon (451). It also renounces the teachings of Nestorius and the MONOPHYSITISM of Eutyches (378–454). The Church administers the traditional seven sacraments:

1 Baptism – by immersion eight days after birth for a child or at the time of conversion for an adult;
2 Chrismation – by the anointing of the forehead, the ears, nose and mouth, palms, heart, spine and feet with holy chrism following immediately after baptism;
3 Holy Communion – the first Holy Communion follows baptism and chrismation, with a little drop of consecrated wine placed in the mouth of the child; consecrated unleavened bread and wine, without added water, are received during the Divine Liturgy, administered by intinction;
4 Penance – which is administered to the faithful before a major feast;
5 Marriage;
6 Visitation and Anointing of the Sick;
7 Ordination.

The Divine Liturgy is celebrated in the Armenian language although bi-lingual English–Armenian prayer books are available for use in English speaking countries and there is a growing trend, mainly in the USA, for the sermon and gospel to be given in English. The text of the creed used in the Divine Liturgy lacks the *filioque* clause and includes the Nicene anathemas found in the creed of St Gregory of Tours (*c.* 538–93). The creed's recital concludes with the confession of St Gregory the Illuminator, the words of which, allegedly, were said by him on hearing the decisions of the Council of Nicaea in 325.

The training of clergy takes place in one of four seminaries, including an American one, that of St Nerses, New Rochelle, New York. An ordinand may elect to be married, or to remain celibate. If he marries, however, a cleric will not be selected for elevation to the episcopate. All major holy orders involve a laying on of hands, and for the priesthood and episcopate an additional anointing with holy chrism. The outdoor dress of an Armenian celibate cleric is distinctive, consisting of a black, wide-sleeved gown and a low, conical cap over which is worn a black veil giving the characteristic pointed headdress of Armenian celibate clergy.

It may be of interest to note the special customs that are observed following a funeral. On the day of the funeral the family of the deceased invite all who were at the graveside to eat with them and the priest is expected to call at the house on eight successive days after the funeral to offer prayers for the departed and to pray for the family. On the Saturday of the week of the funeral the bereaved family will distribute special cakes amongst their friends and relatives, asking them to pray for the repose of the soul of the deceased. On the following day the family will distribute more food, and other alms, among the poor of the district.

❖ Armenian Church; Gregorian Church

ARMENIAN APOSTOLIC CHURCH OF AMERICA

The migration of many Armenians to the USA followed the Turkish persecution of Armenians in 1895/6. Upon arrival they set about creating their Church, which owed allegiance to the catholicos of Etchmiadzin. In time, difficulties broke out over the pro-Soviet bias of Etchmiadzin and the Russian dominance of Armenia, and with the arrival in the USA of the pro-Soviet Archbishop Levon Tourian (Turian), sent by Etchmiadzin, the intensity of political disagreement increased culminating in the assassination of Archbishop Tourian during the celebration of the Divine Liturgy in New York City on Christmas Eve, 1933. The Armenian Apostolic Church of America was then formed, splitting away from the jurisdiction of Etchmiadzin and being received into the catholicosate of Cilicia in 1957. During the intervening years, from 1933–57, the Church had acted without official approval. Normality was restored with the appointment of Zareh I as Catholicos of Cilicia, who gave official recognition to the Church. Doctrinally and liturgically, the Church is identical to the ARMENIAN CATHOLIC CHURCH and has dioceses in New York and Los Angeles.

ARMENIAN CATHOLIC CHURCH

Following the establishment of the ARMENIAN APOSTOLIC CHURCH, many invasions and persecutions of the Armenians, by both Persians and Arabs, led to the movement of many Armenians westward by the end of the twelfth century, to form the kingdom of Lesser Armenia. This brought them into contact with the Latin crusaders on their way to and from the Holy Land. An alliance between the crusaders and the Armenian king led to a union between the two Churches in Cilicia in 1198. This union was not accepted by the Armenians outside Cilicia and ended when the Tartars conquered the Armenian kingdom in 1375.

A decree of reunion with the Armenian Apostolic Church, *Exultate Deo*, was published at the council of Florence in 1439, and although there were no immediate results it provided the doctrinal basis for the later establishment of the Armenian Catholic Church. Armenian Roman Catholic monks, known as the Friars of Unity of St Gregory the Illuminator, or *Fratres Unitores* (approved 1356), proselytized extensively and also laid the foundations of this Armenian Catholic Church, which came under Dominican and Franciscan influences in the first half of the fifteenth century. With time, the scattered but growing Armenian Roman Catholic communities wanted a proper ecclesial structure and their own patriarch. In 1742, Pope Benedict XIV approved the establishment of a Roman Catholic patriarchal see of Cilicia and confirmed that a former Armenian Bishop of Aleppo, Abraham Ardzivian, known as Peter Abraham I (1679–1749), was to be patriarch with his see based in Lebanon; he was given authority over Armenian Catholics in the southern provinces of the Ottoman empire with Armenian Catholics in the north remaining under the spiritual care of the Latin vicar apostolic in Constantinople. The Ottoman system, however, placed the Armenian Catholics under the civil authority of the Orthodox Armenian Apostolic Patriarch in Constantinople, which led to many difficulties and even persecution for the Catholics. Matters were not resolved until 1830 when, through the good offices of the French ambassador, Count de Guilleminot, the Turks were persuaded to recognize the Catholic Armenians as a separate nation, or *millet*, with their own civil and religious head. In 1867 Pope Pius IX united the Roman Catholic sees of Constantinople and Aleppo. By 1911 there were nineteen dioceses, but during the massacres by Turks and Kurds in the First World War, several of these were abolished, leading many Armenian Catholics to emigrate.

The Divine Liturgy is celebrated in Armenian and is a translation into that language of the Liturgy of St Basil, which has undergone many modifications. The sanctuary, which is positioned at the east end of the church, contains a large curtain that is drawn across at certain points in the service. Unleavened altar bread is used, with some water added to the wine which is to be consecrated. The creed used in the Divine Liturgy includes the *filioque* clause and concludes with the same anathemas, from St Gregory of Tours' creed, as well as the confession of St Gregory the Illuminator, which are to be found in the text of the Armenian Apostolic Church's liturgy. The sign of the cross is made, by both Catholic and non-Catholic Armenians alike, from left to right.

Baptism is by immersion and followed immediately by chrismation, or confirmation, and the reception of Holy Communion, in the case of an infant by touching the lips with a drop of consecrated wine, or by signing the mouth with the reserved sacrament, known as communion of the lips. Penance is administered and the absolution is given in a form similar to that used in the West. The administration of holy orders is given in a manner similar to that of the Armenian Apostolic Church, and marriage is celebrated with a crowning of both the bride and the groom with wreaths of flowers. Visitation and anointing of the sick has now become westernized in form.

The head of the Armenian Catholic Church, who always takes the name of Peter, is styled patriarch of the Catholic Armenians and Catholicos of Cilicia, with his see at Beirut in Lebanon. There are archdioceses in Aleppo, Baghdad and Istanbul and dioceses at Alexandria (Egypt), Esfahan (Iran), and Kamichlie (Syria). Armenian Catholics in Great Britain, Australia and New Zealand are under the local Latin ordinaries, while those in the USA are under the care of a bishop in New York City.

ARMENIAN CHURCH OF NORTH AMERICA

This Church is represented throughout the USA with centres in New York, Washington and California, and was organized to provide pastoral and spiritual care for migrants who were being persecuted in Armenia by the Turks at the end of the nineteenth century. The Church owes its allegiance to the catholicos of Etchmiadzin, a city situated on the slopes of Mount Ararat in Armenia; its doctrinal and liturgical position remains unchanged. Despite its alleged pro-Soviet bias, the members of the Church have always remained loyal to the jurisdiction of Etchmiadzin. The perceived bias was a consequence of the then catholicos, Khoren Muradbekian, having to make concessions to the Soviet authorities in order to reopen some churches that had been closed by the state. This pragmatism caused a considerable amount of misunderstanding. In 1933 there was a very unpleasant incident resulting in the assassination of Archbishop Levon Tourian in New York City and a consequent schism developed when a small group of Armenians separated from the Armenian Church of North America and formed the ARMENIAN APOSTOLIC CHURCH OF AMERICA.

ARMENIAN EVANGELICAL CHURCH

In keeping with the nineteenth century spirit of enlightenment and PIETISM, there were outbreaks of evangelical fervour within the ARMENIAN APOSTOLIC CHURCH, with calls for a spiritual reform within that Church and the need for a better-educated clergy, but the Church was unprepared to meet the challenge. Religious unrest was felt even in Etchmiadzin, the spiritual centre of the Church, as well as in Jerusalem and Constantinople. As early as 1831, American missionaries in Constantinople, led by William Goodall of the American Board of Commissioners for Foreign Missions, were busy evangelizing Muslims and making contact with Armenians who were interested in Bible study. Goodall's translation of the Armenian–Turkish New Testament in 1846 encouraged the establishment of the Armenian Evangelical Church, which was founded at Pera, in modern Istanbul.

Some schools and a seminary were established under Krikor Peshimaljian, without the backing of the Armenian Apostolic Church, which excommunicated members who joined the new Church. State recognition, however, was granted in 1850, to ensure the right to trade, marry and bury the dead. The Armenian Evangelical Church increased in numbers between 1846 and 1910, most likely because of the evangelical belief in the priesthood of all believers and the use of *Bible Women*, who could more appropriately lead Bible studies groups, and cell groups, than their male counterparts in gender sensitive social situations, so introducing the new movement to a greater audience. House groups developed from these small cell groups, leading in time to the organization of functioning churches. Members of the Armenian Evangelical Church faced the Turkish massacres in 1918 and many took refuge in Lebanon and northern Syria, where their work in primary and secondary education has led to the establishment of schools and colleges.

A split within the Church came in 1920 when the Armenians in Aleppo, Syria, formed a new Church, the ARMENIAN EVANGELICAL SPIRITUAL BRETHREN, to cater for their wish for a more *Brethren* style of approach. Today, in California, there are several schools maintained by the Armenian Evangelical Church and it was their founding of the Armenian Missionary Association of America, in Worcester, Massachusetts, in 1918 that helped victims of genocide after the First World War. More recently, the Church has undertaken other humanitarian enterprises, including an outreach programme targeting young people at risk in the Los Angeles area.

The Armenian Evangelical Church can be found today in many countries throughout the world, in North and South America, Europe and Australia, where it offers evangelism through preaching, teaching and the distribution of devotional literature, and increased opportunities for women in both education and the Church, in the organization of which there is a heavy lay involvement. There have been some mergers and closures. Three churches in Los Angeles, California, merged in 1963 to form the Armenian Congregational Church of Hollywood, to serve the needs of that community, while five other churches in central California separated, to join either the First Armenian Presbyterians, or the Pilgrim Armenian Congregational Churches of Fresno. There continues to be a ministry to new immigrants and several of the churches ministering to newcomers have undergone revival and growth. Vigorous Sunday school and family life programmes have helped many families, spiritually and socially.

Members of the Church observe a ban on alcohol, tobacco, gambling and dissolute lifestyles and many are involved with missionary, charitable, educational and publishing ventures.

ARMENIAN EVANGELICAL SPIRITUAL BRETHREN

A small, evangelical church formed by a splinter group of members of the ARMENIAN EVANGELICAL CHURCH in Aleppo, Syria, in 1920, who wanted a more *Brethren*-type Church, with an emphasis on holiness and a simple lifestyle. The Church has no ordained clergy and its members actively shun worldly displays in their everyday life, with no jewellery, cosmetics, alcohol, tobacco or drugs allowed and a ban on many forms of entertainment, including the theatre. The small population of this Church is organized in Australia, Lebanon, Syria and the USA.

ARMINIAN (also ARMINIANS; ARMINIANISM)

Arminians hold to the belief and theology as taught by Jacobus Arminius, or Jacob Hermanzoon (1560–1609), a Dutch theologian and a minister of the DUTCH REFORMED CHURCH who was opposed to the Calvinist doctrine of predestination, a view that those who were to receive salvation had been chosen before Adam's fall and that therefore neither free will nor human decision could play any part in this salvation. Following his death, the followers of Arminius published *The Remonstrance* (1610), which has led to their more familiar name of the DUTCH REMONSTRANT BROTHERHOOD. The publication of this book, which contains the essential Arminian theology, was countered by an ultra-Calvinistic document, *Contra-Remonstrantie*.

Arminian theology teaches that:

1 Salvation applies to all who believe in Christ and who persevere in obedience and faith.

2 Christ died for everybody, and the notion of a limited atonement is to be rejected.

3 Mankind is not totally depraved through Adam's fall, but morality and natural evil are the consequences of his fall.

4 God's saving grace is not irresistible.

5 It is possible for a Christian to fall from grace.

The Dutch Remonstrant Brotherhood faced condemnation by the CALVINIST synod of Dordrecht in 1619 and it has been suggested that there was an agreement between the Calvinists to name the Remonstrants as enemies of their country even before the synod met and the case could be considered – the execution thereby preceding the trial. Persecution followed, with the execution, by decapitation, of one of the leading Remonstrants, Barnevelt, and imprisonment for life of another, Grotius, who evaded his fate by escaping and fleeing to France. By 1630 the heat had largely gone from the affair and Remonstrants began to be tolerated; they were finally recognized by the state in 1795.

ASSEMBLIES OF GOD

This is a large PENTECOSTAL *group of autonomous congregations, with its headquarters in the USA, in Springfield, Missouri.*

The Reverend Charles Parham, who had left the METHODIST EPISCOPAL CHURCH at the end of the nineteenth century, was so impressed with the healing work of J. A. Dowie, of Zion, Illinois, that he decided in 1898 to found a Bethel Healing Home in Topeka, Kansas. Parham went on a healing and preaching tour, taking in New York and Chicago, but on his return to Topeka he found that his work there had been taken over by others. Undaunted, he bought a building on the outskirts of the town and in 1900 established the Bethel Bible College. It was here that one of his students, Agnes Oznam, experienced *glossolalia*, the phenomenon of speaking in tongues, which was taken as evidence of the baptism of the Holy Spirit. Parham himself, along with many of his students, also experienced this baptism of the Holy Spirit. This period marks the start of the Pentecostal movement. In 1905 a Bible school was opened in Houston, Texas, at which W. J. Seymour, the founder of the CHURCH OF THE NAZARENE in Azusa Street, Los Angeles, was a student.

Parham went on to found a loosely organized fellowship in south-central America, which became known as Apostolic Faith (Kansas) and was very similar to the Assemblies of God, with a strong emphasis on divine healing. A revival movement began to spread through the United States with spontaneous outbreaks of Pentecostalism in other parts of the world. This was seen by established HOLINESS Churches to be a most unwelcome development. Participants in the new movements found themselves ostracized and made to find alternative places of worship, which led to the development of hundreds of distinct Pentecostal groups.

In December 1913, an independent Pentecostal periodical, *Word and Witness*, called for a general convention of Pentecostal saints and Churches of God in Christ; in order to gain formal recognition, establish a trained ministry and regularize the administration of the groups, it was felt that some degree of order should be imposed. The leaders of various groups realized the value of this proposal and in 1914 around three hundred preachers and laymen from twenty American states and from overseas gathered in Hot Springs, Arkansas, at the Grand Opera House and forged a cooperative fellowship which was incorporated under the name of the General Council of the Assembles of God. Most of the delegates did not want to form a new denomination or sect, but simply to rationalize their ministries and establish a legal identity. Each congregation was to remain self-governing and self-supporting, and so they remain today. By 1916 the general council had added a *Statement of Fundamental Truths* to its constitution, which provided a firm doctrinal position. This was calculated to make for a more effective preaching and missionary programme. The general council, however, retained control over missionary, educational, ministerial and publishing matters. A foreign missionary department was created in 1919 and the work of the Assemblies of God spread to many countries. A vast educational programme, involving many liberal arts colleges, some Bible colleges, a high school and several correspondence schools, has been developed in the USA, in Springfield, Missouri.

Assemblies share the same basically ARMINIAN doctrinal position as many other churches in the Pentecostal tradition. The Bible is regarded as the divinely inspired and infallible word of God and there is a strong emphasis on the baptism of the Holy Spirit, which is evidenced in *glossolalia*. The entire sanctification of the individual member is considered to be a gradual, not an instantaneous, process. Divine healing, a belief in Christ's second coming and his millennial reign (REVELATION 20), followed by eternal punishment for the wicked and eternal happiness for the believer, are characteristics of Pentecostal belief. Adults receive baptism by total immersion, are expected to observe tithing for the support of their Church and refrain from the use of alcohol and tobacco; they are also prohibited from joining secret societies. There are now many Pentecostal Churches that have evolved their doctrinal position from that adopted by the Assemblies of God.

ASSEMBLIES OF THE LORD JESUS CHRIST, INC.

This PENTECOSTAL-style Church has its headquarters in the USA, in Memphis, Tennessee, and was formed in 1952 by the merger of three Apostolic ONENESS Churches which were in the Pentecostal tradition: The Assemblies of the Church of Jesus Christ; The Jesus Only Apostolic Church of God; and The Church of the Lord Jesus Christ.

Oneness Pentecostal Churches do not affirm the traditional understanding of the Trinity and administer baptism by immersion in the name of Jesus only, in what is believed to be obedience to St Peter's command (Acts 2:38: 'be baptized every one of you in the name of Jesus Christ'), since the Holy Spirit is not thought of as a being within the Trinity but in the spirit and power of God and Christ.

As it is believed to be the direct and absolute word of God, the Bible is regarded as infallible. Justification, or conversion, is thought of as being followed by baptism of the spirit, as evidenced by *glossolalia*, or speaking with tongues. Christ's second coming is considered to be imminent and this will be followed by the millennium (REVELATION 20), after which the final judgement will save the believers but impose eternal damnation on the wicked.

Members of the Church are expected to change their lifestyle considerably, wearing modest dress at all times and eschewing tobacco, alcohol and drugs as well as the theatre and cinema; for school-age members keeping to the wearing of modest, or unrevealing, dress can present difficulties, particularly in physical education and sports classes. Membership of secret societies is not allowed, and whilst respect for civil authorities is encouraged, members are not expected to take up arms in times of war and should assume non-combatant roles.

The ordinances of the Church are baptism by immersion, foot-washing and the service of Communion and members are expected to tithe, to provide support for Church activities. Worship services involve singing and preaching and are noted for their spontaneity and the giving of witness, with opportunities for divine healing. There is a home mission programme, which concentrates on ethnic ministries, especially among Native Americans and Hispanics. The foreign missions department has recently established an educational division to provide training for members who operate in various mission stations throughout the world, the emphasis centred on Bible training courses.

ASSOCIATE PRESBYTERIAN CHURCH

Many of the Scottish Presbyterian settlers who went to America during the eighteenth century were members either of the Associate Presbyterian Church or of the Reformed Presbyterian Church and by 1782 some of these had come together to form a union, with others remaining outside. By the start of the nineteenth century this united group had become known as the Associate Synod of North America and in 1858 it joined with the ASSOCIATE REFORMED PRESBYTERIAN CHURCH to form the United Presbyterian Church of North America.

Not all newly arrived settlers wanted to join the union and they remained as the Associate Presbyterian Church of Pennsylvania, continuing an independent existence. They persevere today as a small denomination within the presbyterian tradition, affirming the *WESTMINSTER CONFESSION of Faith*.

ASSOCIATE REFORMED PRESBYTERIAN CHURCH

This American-based Church, which is still in existence, had its origins in Scotland when, after 1688, the CHURCH OF SCOTLAND had become reorganized as the established Presbyterian Church of Scotland under King William III. There was a split in 1733 when a Scottish pastor, Ebenezer Erskine (1680–1754) led a breakaway group to form an Associate

Presbytery, while others, the CAMERONIANS, created a Reformed Presbytery in 1743.

When some settlers from these presbyterian backgrounds from both Scotland and Ulster arrived in America in the mid-eighteenth century, an incomplete union between the two groups was forged. In 1782, the Associate Reformed Presbytery of the Carolinas and Georgia was formed, which, in time, divided into a General Synod and four others. One of these, the synod of the Carolinas, left the others in 1822 to pursue an independent existence as the Associate Reformed Synod of the South; in 1858, the residual synods became part of the United Presbyterian Church of North America, which is now part of the PRESBYTERIAN CHURCH (USA).

The synod of the Carolinas continued for a while as the synod of the South, dropping its title in favour of the Associate Reformed Presbyterian Church; this became a general synod in 1935, in which there are nine presbyteries. The Church affirms the *WESTMINSTER CONFESSION of Faith* (1643–6) and the *Larger* and *Small Catechisms*.

The headquarters of the Church is at Greenville, South Carolina, where supervision of its 187 congregations and 32,000 adult members is provided. Mission work, both at home and abroad, is an important part of the Church's activity, with overseas centres established in Pakistan, Mexico, Germany, Russia and the Middle East.

ASSOCIATED GOSPEL CHURCHES

This Church must not be confused with the Associated Gospel Churches (Canada), which was founded in 1922.

A merger of three American Methodist Churches took place in Kansas City, Missouri in 1939. These were the METHODIST EPISCOPAL CHURCH (North), the Methodist Episcopal Church (South) and the METHODIST PROTESTANT CHURCH. There were other Churches that were reluctant to join the union and they formed instead the American Bible Fellowship, under the leadership of Dr W. O. H. Garman, affirming a FUNDAMENTALIST tradition and observing baptism by immersion, separation from apostates and the operation of a congregational polity. This fellowship later changed its name to the Associated Gospel Churches.

The Church, which has its headquarters in Pittsburgh, Pennsylvania, is now to be found in some twenty states across the USA and also overseas, where it is represented in parts of Africa, the Far East, Europe and South America. It also acts as an agency for military chaplains, pastors and missionaries within the fundamentalist tradition.

ASSYRIAN CHURCH OF THE EAST

Nestorians, who are now known as members of the Assyrian Church of the East, are eastern Christians, descendants of the heresiarch Nestorius of Constantinople (d. *c.* 451), who taught that in Jesus Christ there were two, cojoined persons, namely God the Son (*the Word*) and the man, Jesus. Jesus was the habitation, or vesture, of the Word and it was Jesus alone who was born of the Virgin Mary, as it was Jesus, and not the Word, who died upon the cross. The controversy centred upon the use of the title *Theotokos*, or mother of God, which was used of the Virgin Mary and which Nestorius refused to recognize. Nestorius was condemned by Pope St Celestine I (422–32) and by the third ecumenical council of Ephesus in 431, a condemnation later confirmed by the council of Chalcedon in 451. The Nestorian Church, however, adopted the erroneous teaching of Nestorius.

According to tradition, Christianity was first preached in Mesopotamia, Chaldea and Persia by St Thomas the Apostle and later by Sts Addai and Mari. The Church was well established in the area by the third century and by *c.* AD300 the bishops were organized under the leadership of a catholicos who was bishop of the Persian royal capital, at Seleucia-Ctesiphon. In the fifth century, the Church of the East, as it was then called, took up the Christology of Theodore of Mopsuestia and Nestorius, and so fell out of communion with the Church in the Roman empire, declaring itself to be independent, under its own catholicos, in 424. The missionary exploits of the Church were astounding and there is evidence from a Nestorian monument found at Singan-fu (now Sian-Fu), in northwest China, suggesting that a Syrian had brought Christianity to the area in 635. This monument had been set up in 781 and provides evidence of a large, contemporary Christian population in ten Chinese provinces. Missionary work had extended Nestorian influence to both India and Arabia and a period of relative prosperity was enjoyed until, in 652, following the death of Mohammed, the Arab conquest of Persia was completed. Even so, the Nestorians continued to enjoy periods of peace with only occasional bouts of repression until the Mongol, and other, invasions of the thirteenth and fourteenth centuries. The Nestorians then underwent unwelcome domination and many suffered badly. Those who could escape went into exile and by the sixteenth century they had been reduced to a small community of Assyrians living in eastern Turkey.

Further deportations and massacres by the Turks were to follow into the twentieth century, with many survivors escaping to Iraq following the end of the First World War. The Nestorian patriarch, Mar Simon XXIII, was forced to flee to the USA, where he was assassinated in 1975. This led to the election of Mar Dinkha IV of Tehran, in 1976.

In 1994, in the light of a new understanding and interpretation of Nestorian Christology, a *Common Christological Declaration* was signed by Pope John Paul II and Mar Dinkha, affirming that ROMAN CATHOLICS and Assyrians are 'united in the confession of the same faith in the Son of God'. Foundations for future cooperation were established, especially between the Assyrian Church of the East and its Roman Catholic counterpart, the CHALDEAN CATHOLIC CHURCH and both are pledged to work towards re-integration. Although the Assyrian Church officially recognizes only the first two ecumenical councils, a conclusion was recently reached, under the auspices of the Pro Oriente foundation, that the faith of the Assyrian Church is consistent with the christological doctrines of the council of Chalcedon (AD 451).

The liturgy of the Church is that of the *Holy Apostles of Addai and Mari* and the seven sacraments observed are those of baptism, ordination, Holy Eucharist, anointing, absolution, holy leaven, called the *malca*, and the sign of the cross. The patriarch, who currently lives in Morton Grove, Illinois, USA, is known as the Catholicos-Patriarch of the Church of the

East. Church members are to be found in Iraq, Iran, Syria, Lebanon, North America, England, Sweden, Australia and India.

❖ Assyrian Church; Holy Apostolic and Catholic Church of the East; Nestorian Church

AUDIANI

The Audiani were members of a fourth-century rigorist sect reputedly founded by an ascetic deacon called Audi, or Audius, near Edessa *c.* 325 as a response to the worldliness of the Church and clergy at the time. They have been accused of holding anthropomorphic views of God, taking Genesis 1:27 literally ('so God created man in His own image. In the image of God He created him; male and female he created them'). Cyril of Alexandria, who attributed this error to ignorance when it was discovered amongst some Egyptian monks, condemned anthropomorphism. Audius left the Church that had treated him so badly and he wandered in the Near East from Antioch to Mesopotamia. The error of anthropomorphism arose again briefly in the nineteenth century, in northern Italy, but Bishop Ratherius of Verona suppressed it.

AUGUSTANA EVANGELICAL LUTHERAN CHURCH

This Church is no longer in existence. It was organized in 1860 by Swedish and Norwegian immigrants to the USA in Jefferson Prairie, Wisconsin, as the Scandinavian Augustana Evangelical Lutheran Synod, following their withdrawal from the larger LUTHERAN synod of Illinois, which had been founded in 1851 and was composed of immigrants from many different national backgrounds. By 1870 the Norwegian members had left the new Church. The word 'Scandinavian' was dropped in 1894 but the word 'Augustana', deriving from the *Augsburg Confession*, was retained. In 1962, the 600,000 members of the Augustana Church merged with the United Lutheran Church in America (founded 1918), the AMERICAN EVANGELICAL LUTHERAN CHURCH and the Finnish Evangelical Lutheran Church (Suomi synod) to form the Lutheran Church in America.

AUSTRALIAN CHURCH

The Australian Church, which was in the UNITARIAN tradition, enjoyed a short-lived existence from 1885–1955. Charles Strong, an ex-minister of the Scots Church (PRESBYTERIAN) originally organized the Church in Melbourne, Victoria. As Unitarians the members held to a belief in one God but rejected the doctrine of the Trinity, since they denied the divinity of God the Son and God the Holy Spirit.

AUTOCEPHALIC GREEK ORTHODOX CHURCH OF AMERICA AND AUSTRALIA

The migration of Greeks to the USA in the last part of the eighteenth century, with an early Greek presence established in New Smyrna, Florida, saw the formation of many GREEK ORTHODOX CHURCH parishes across America and the need was felt to organize them into an archdiocese of North and South America. This was finally done in 1918, but there were many problems and criticisms from Church members who were unhappy about the ecumenical approach to both PROTESTANT and ROMAN CATHOLIC communities, as well as the rejection by Archbishop Iakovos of the traditional

Julian calendar in favour of the Gregorian calendar in use by the non-Orthodox Churches, and other small liturgical changes. These proved to be a bitter pill for many members of the Greek Orthodox Church and they left the main Church to join a variety of schismatic bodies, of which one of the smallest is the Autocephalic Greek Orthodox Church of America, with its headquarters at Newark, New Jersey. This Church observes the Orthodox position doctrinally and liturgically and has given a greater administrative control of its affairs into the hands of the laity, with the funding of each congregation in the hands of its members.

A similar extensive migration of people from Greece and Cyprus to Australia during the 1950s and 60s, under the auspices of the Australian government immigration programme, saw a repeat of the disagreements that led to the formation of schismatic groups in the USA. By 1964 a major schism had occurred when five churches in New South Wales, four in South Australia and one in Victoria decided to ally themselves with the Autocephalic Greek Orthodox Church of America.

AVALON AND RELATED COMMUNITIES

A collection of communities in the USA that uses the media to promote its evangelism. The message, which is one of repentance and faith, prayer, witnessing and fellowship, is transmitted through publishing, a travelling rock band known as *The Peculiar People*, book stores and the maintenance of centres which give free food and clothing to those in need. Baptism of the Holy Spirit and *glossolalia*, speaking in tongues, are emphasized. The members all take part in street ministries.

B

BANGLADESH EVANGELICAL LUTHERAN CHURCH

This Church used to be known as the East Pakistan Evangelical LUTHERAN Church. It grew out of the Santal Mission of the Northern Churches that was begun in 1867, receiving support from Norwegian, Danish and American Lutheran Church Societies.

Before Pakistan was partitioned off in 1947 the Church had some 40,000 members; a large majority of these are now to be found in India under the name of the UNITED EVANGELICAL LUTHERAN CHURCH IN INDIA, which was formally organized in 1975. The Bangladesh Evangelical Lutheran Church now has around 186 congregations, with nearly 5,000 committed adult members. In 1979, Bengali and Santali speakers recognized that the cultural and linguistic differences that existed between the two communities could only be addressed by the creation of a separate Church for the Bengali speakers, and the Bengali Lutheran Church was formed, becoming a member of the Lutheran World Federation in 1986.

BANKSIA FREE CHURCH

One of many very small independent Churches of the evangelical tradition in Australia, the Banksia Free Church was organized in 1885 by ex-evangelical ANGLICANS. The principal emphasis in its doctrine is on the inerrancy and inspiration of the scriptures and a reduced concern with liturgical forms. The members of the Church stress the need for personal conversion and a change of lifestyle.

BANTU METHODIST CHURCH

An indigenous, non-white African Bantu Church founded in South Africa in 1932, which maintains a Methodist Church tradition. METHODISM was first introduced to the country with the arrival of Methodist soldiers in Cape Colony in 1806, when a small chapel was built near Table Mountain for their meetings.

❖ The Donkey Church (on account of the Church's symbol)

BANTU PRESBYTERIAN CHURCH

An all-black Church, founded in South Africa in 1820. In 1813 a PRESBYTERIAN church was built in Cape Province to serve the white population, with missionaries from the Glasgow Missionary Society arriving from Scotland in 1820. From this grew the Bantu Presbyterian

Church and the Presbyterian Church of Southern Africa, which is mainly white. Negotiations have been undertaken to unite these two Churches. The Bantu Presbyterian Church maintains a strictly PROTESTANT and PRESBYTERIAN witness.

BAPTIST BIBLE FELLOWSHIP INTERNATIONAL

A large, FUNDAMENTALIST American BAPTIST denomination founded in 1950 with its headquarters in Springfield, Missouri, USA. The modernism and rationalism of the nineteenth century were beginning to invade the various Baptist conventions and some fundamentalist Baptist ministers, such as W. B. Riley and J. Frank Norris, were not prepared to compromise on what were declared in 1909 to be the fourteen *Fundamentals*. At this time Norris was the pastor of the First Baptist Church in Fort Worth, Texas.

The *Fundamentals* were listed as follows:

1 The inspiration of holy scripture
2 Man's depravity
3 Redemption through Christ's blood
4 The true Church, made up only of believers
5 The second coming of the Lord (REVELATION 20)
6 The Trinity
7 The fall of Adam
8 The need for rebirth
9 Full deliverance from guilt, and salvation
10 Assurance of salvation
11 Centrality of Christ in the Bible
12 The role of the Holy Spirit in a believer's sanctification
13 The resurrection of believers and unbelievers
14 The preparation of the present age for the final judgement

The Baptist Bible Union was organized in 1921 by Norris, Riley and others in order to make a determined and united stand against the inroads of modernism, although there was some disagreement between them concerning the structure of the new body. In 1926 Norris was accused of killing a businessman in Fort Worth, and although he was acquitted he was expelled from the list of members of the Bible Baptist Union. He went on, with enthusiasm, to found what became the World Fundamental Baptist Missionary Fellowship in 1928, the title later changing to the World Baptist Fellowship. The following year he founded the Baptist Bible Institute, which later became the Bible Baptist Seminary, and started a publication called *The Fundamentalist*.

In 1935 Norris, who was undoubtedly the dominant leader of the World Fundamentalist Baptist Missionary Fellowship, went into an uneasy association with the Reverend G. Beauchamp Vick, who became President of the Bible Baptist Seminary in 1948, now in serious financial difficulties. Vick managed to remedy the financial situation within two years, but predictable difficulties were to arise with his dealings with Norris and he resigned his post at the seminary to found the Baptist Bible Fellowship International (BBFI) in 1950, as well as the Baptist Bible College and a new publication, *The Baptist Bible Tribune*, which is still in production.

By the start of the 1960s the BBFI had over a hundred and fifty missionaries spread between seventeen mission stations around the world and there has been a steady increase since then, in spite of the Baptist Bible College's decline in the 1980s. Today, the BBFI is the largest Baptist Mission Agency and is supported in its work by contributions from over four thousand churches worldwide. Doctrinally strongly FUNDAMENTALIST, the CALVINISM observed by this Church is not very strident, and although the members accept the notion of God's electing grace, they also believe that salvation is freely available to all who accept the gospel message. The autonomy of the local congregation is very important and a great deal of responsibility is placed upon its pastor.

BAPTIST CHURCH (also BAPTIST; BAPTISTS)

This is one of the largest of the PROTESTANT denominations, with an estimated world membership of 40 million adherents. The two main groups of Baptists – the General Baptists (GENERAL ASSOCIATION OF GENERAL BAPTISTS) and the PARTICULAR BAPTISTS – emerged in England during the seventeenth century at the time of PURITAN reform. Both groups acknowledge that only believers should be baptized, and while the General Baptists believe that atonement is available to all, the Particular Baptists recognize that atonement is only available to the predestined *elect*.

In 1813 a general union of Particular Baptists was formed in Great Britain, and in 1873 they became known as the Baptist Union of Great Britain and Ireland, which other Baptist groups joined; since 1988 this has been known as the BAPTIST UNION OF GREAT BRITAIN.

Roger Williams organized the first Baptist church in America in 1639 at Providence, Rhode Island, but progress was slow and it was only after the great *Awakening* of the mid-eighteenth century that the Baptists in America began to experience considerable growth, especially in what were then the southern colonies. By the middle of the twentieth century there were about thirty separate groups of Baptists in the USA, the largest being the SOUTHERN BAPTIST CONVENTION (15 million members), the NATIONAL BAPTIST CONVENTION OF THE USA, INC. (5.5 million members), the NATIONAL BAPTIST CONVENTION OF AMERICA (2.6 million members) and the AMERICAN BAPTIST CHURCHES IN THE USA (1.5 million members).

The first Baptist Church in mainland Europe was established in Hamburg, Germany, in 1834 by J. G. Oncken (1800–84), and the work soon spread from there into Scandinavia and parts of eastern Europe. The Church was also established in Australia and New Zealand, after an inauspicious start in Sydney, New South Wales in 1831, and by the twentieth century, through its missionary work, it was accepted in Asia, Africa and South America.

Baptists accept that doctrinal matters and practice rest with Christ and with the local congregations of baptized believers who are linked, quite loosely, to state, regional and national organizations so that their work can be coordinated efficiently. Baptists accept the congregational form of polity, with each local congregation being autonomous and their affiliation with other congregations provides for mutual support, shared advice and coordinated missionary work. Although there are similarities with the CONGREGATIONAL CHURCH, unlike

Congregationalists Baptists insist upon the separation of Church and state.

The description of Baptists as being non-creedal signifies that they assign man-made creeds to a subordinate role, below the authority of the scriptures. The first of the early Baptist declarations were the *London Confessions* (1644 and 1677), which underwent considerable revision and modification. The sacraments of baptism and the Lord's Supper are known as ordinances, because they are observed out of obedience to God's command in scriptures. Baptism is administered by immersion and the Lord's Supper is regarded as a memorial meal.

BAPTIST FEDERATION OF CANADA

This cooperative agency, with its present headquarters at Brantford, Ontario, was organized in 1944 in Saint John, New Brunswick, in an effort to coordinate the work of several Canadian BAPTIST groups.

These were:

1 The United Baptist Convention of the Maritime Provinces (now known as the United Baptist Convention of the Atlantic Provinces)
2 The Baptist Convention of Ontario and Quebec
3 The Baptist Union of Western Canada
4 The French Baptist Union (formed 1855)

The earliest Baptist Church in Canada was formed in Horton, Nova Scotia, in 1763 by the Reverend Ebenezer Moulton of New England to provide for both incomers from the USA who were fleeing the American Revolution and for settlers arriving from Scotland. In 1846, the Baptist Convention of Nova Scotia, New Brunswick and Prince Edward Island was formed, the name changing in 1879 to the Baptist Convention of the Maritimé Provinces. This group later merged with some Free Baptists in Nova Scotia and New Brunswick to form the United Baptist Convention of the Maritime Provinces that went into the formation of the original Baptist federation of Canada in 1944.

There had been a few Baptist churches in Ontario dating from the late eighteenth century, formed by migrants from the USA, England and Scotland. The Ottawa Baptist Association was formed in 1836, with other associations and mission societies following, but it was not until 1889 that many of these became consolidated into the Baptist Convention of Ontario and Quebec. Baptist missionaries from Ontario were working in eastern Canada towards the end of the nineteenth century and the congregations formed were organized into the Baptist Convention of British Columbia (1897), followed a few years later by the more inclusive Baptist Union of Western Canada (1909). There was much cooperation between the different Unions and Conventions, especially in the fields of home and foreign missions and in the opening of various educational establishments, such as Acadia University at Wolfville, Nova Scotia (founded 1838) and McMaster University, founded originally in Toronto (1887) but later moving to Hamilton, Ontario in 1930.

During the 1930s and 40s an inter-conventions committee made plans for a federation union, which was completed in 1944. Not all Baptist Churches in Canada belong to the federation.

BAPTIST GENERAL CONFERENCE

The Baptist General Conference was started in America by a Swedish teacher and lay-preacher, Gustaf Palmquist, who emigrated to the USA in 1851 in order to provide some leadership for immigrant Swedish members of the LUTHERAN CHURCH who had been influenced by the PIETIST movement, with its emphasis on personal and spiritual aspects of faith. He was rebaptized as a BAPTIST and ordained as a minister in Galesburg, Illinois. Travelling north to visit some fellow Swedes, he arrived in Rock Island on the Mississippi River where he baptized three converts. The growth of Swedish Baptist churches was rapid and they were soon established in Iowa, Maine, New York City, Illinois and Minnesota, helped initially by the American Baptist Home Mission Society and by what was then known as the NORTHERN BAPTIST CONVENTION. The Swedish Baptist General Conference, as it was initially called, was soon organized and it became self-supporting, opening a seminary in Chicago in 1871.

During these early years the foreign mission programmes were conducted through the American Baptist Foreign Mission Society, but in 1944 it became independent of this body, setting up a foreign board and conducting missions in Argentina, Brazil, Mexico, the Philippines, Ethiopia, India and Japan. Until just after the First World War the services were conducted in Swedish; English was then substituted and by 1945 the word 'Swedish' had been dropped from the title of the conference, which then became the Baptist General Conference. The work of this conference now includes home mission work in many parts of the USA and Canada, and the running of a liberal arts college, seminaries, children's homes, homes for the elderly and some media work.

Doctrinally, the members of the conference are ARMINIAN Baptists who recognize two ordinances, baptism and the Lord's Supper. Their polity is congregational and delegates from each individual church attend an annual Church meeting, presided over by a board of trustees. Their headquarters is at Arlington Heights, Illinois.

BAPTIST MISSIONARY ASSOCIATION OF AMERICA

An association of independent BAPTIST Churches that had been part of the AMERICAN BAPTIST ASSOCIATION (ABA) until 1950, when there was a protest from some of the delegates to an association meeting, which objection focused on the seating provision for messengers who were not members of the Churches which had elected them. This protest was ignored and in 1950 a protest meeting was called at Park Place and Temple Baptist churches in Little Rock, Arkansas, from which the North American Baptist Missionary Association of America was formed.

In 1969 the name was changed to its current form. The members share a FUNDAMENTALIST Christian doctrine, accepting the literal interpretation of the Bible, the imminence of Christ's return, salvation by grace through faith alone, believer's baptism by immersion, the priesthood of all believers, religious liberty for all and a separation of Church and state.

The Association maintains an active foreign mission programme and a publishing department that produces Sunday school and other religious material in English and Spanish; a radio ministry provides programmes that are received in many parts of the world. The headquarters of the Baptist Missionary Society of America is in Little Rock, Arkansas.

BAPTIST REFORMED FELLOWSHIP

A group of churches in Australia that banded together into a fellowship in 1982, all professing a Calvinist-BAPTIST doctrine. These churches hold to the belief that each local church consists of regenerated believers who received baptism following their confession of the faith. The polity of these churches is congregational, with baptism by total immersion.

Their CALVINIST theology concerns the doctrine of grace and a belief in a *particular atonement*, made for the elect alone. There are some churches that belong to the Fellowship but do not use the word 'REFORMED' in their title, such as the Bethel Baptist Church, otherwise known as the Independent Baptist Church, at Mulgrave, Victoria, and the Werrington Community Church in New South Wales.

The members of these churches are committed to a confession of faith which is compatible to the *London Confession of Faith* of 1689 as composed by the Particular Baptist Churches, as well as declaring their loyalty to one another. The *London Confession of Faith* of 1689, like its predecessor, the *London Confession of Faith* of 1644, provided for baptism by immersion and incorporated Calvinist theology with a call for religious freedom, calling for Baptists to be congregationally governed but completely separated from the state.

BAPTIST UNION OF AUSTRALIA

The BAPTIST Union of Australia, with its headquarters in Melbourne, Victoria, is a member of the Baptist World Alliance and the Asian Baptist Federation. The first Baptist service in Australia was held in Sydney, New South Wales, in 1831 by a Scotsman, the Reverend John McKeag, who had been ordained at Liverpool, in England, in 1822. After initial setbacks, a chapel was built in Bathurst Street, Sydney, in 1836 under the care of the Reverend John Saunders, who had arrived in Australia two years previously. Other Baptist foundations were made in Tasmania (1835), South Australia (1838), Victoria (1839), Queensland (1855) and Western Australia (1895).

As moves towards the federation of Australian states began there was a parallel movement towards a corresponding federation of Baptist enterprises. In 1912 an interstate Baptist convention decided on joint action in the fields of missionary work, ministerial training and publishing and a year later the State Missionary Societies combined to form the Australian Baptist Foreign Missions. The Baptist Union of Australia was inaugurated in Sydney in 1926.

Member churches of the Union profess a belief in the separation of Church and state and the independence of each local congregation, which is in the charge of a minister, usually male, assisted by deacons, male and female, who have been elected by the baptized members of the congregation. Baptism is by immersion following a confession of faith. The Lord's Supper is celebrated as a memorial and symbol of sinful mankind's fellowship in Christ's death and resurrection. Ordinary white leavened bread and unfermented grape juice are used and distributed to the congregation who remain seated in the pews. While a principle of open communion is permitted in the Union churches, which allow any Christians of good standing to receive Holy Communion in a Baptist Union church, those from the home congregation who wish to receive must be baptized members of the Church. The other services are usually non-liturgical with an emphasis on hymn singing, Bible reading and preaching. In some Baptist churches there is a strong interest in pre-millennial beliefs (REVELATION 20), but although there is some evidence of charismatic influences in the style adopted by some churches, *glossolalia*, or speaking in tongues, and spontaneous outbursts of healing are not very common.

Baptist Union Churches are heavily committed to social work, especially among retired people, in rehabilitation work, in providing children's homes and working for Native Australian welfare. In 1972, a New Settlers' Baptist association was formed, designed to help non-English speaking ethnic groups of people who had settled in Australia since the end of the Second World War. In 1913, with the establishment of the Australian Baptist Missionary Society, new missionaries were sent to Papua New Guinea, Irian Jaya, Thailand, Indonesia, Zambia and Zimbabwe.

BAPTIST UNION OF GREAT BRITAIN

A very large BAPTIST group, with its headquarters in Didcot, Oxfordshire, England, which was formed as a union of PARTICULAR BAPTISTS and New Connexion Baptists in 1891. Before 1988 the full title was the Baptist Union of Great Britain and Ireland. There are other Baptist Unions in the United Kingdom, namely those of Wales, of Scotland, and of Ireland, but the Baptist Union of Great Britain is the largest group.

BARCLAYANS

A denomination no longer in existence, which was named after its founder, John Barclay (1734–98), who had been a preacher in the CHURCH OF SCOTLAND, and was licensed to preach by the presbytery of Auchterarder in 1759. His first appointment was as an assistant to the evangelical minister, the Reverend James Jobson at Errol, where Barclay remained for four years before leaving because of some differences of opinion (he was accused of 'inculcating obnoxious doctrines').

Barclay then became an assistant to the Reverend A. Dow at Fettercairn, Kincardineshire, in 1763, but following the publication of a piece of his writing called *Rejoice Evermore, or Christ is All in All*, which attracted censure because in it he proposed the doctrine of immediate divine revelation, he was forbidden to preach again. Upon Dow's death any expectation Barclay had of succeeding him came to naught, despite a petition from the parishioners, and he was refused ordination in Scotland. Barclay went south into England and was ordained at Newcastle in 1773.

Upon his return to Scotland later that year, Barclay set up *The Berean Assembly*, so-called after the congregation of Beroeia (Acts 17:10) who were noted for their enthusiasm for the scriptures. He went again to England and in the years 1776–8 formed congregations in Bristol and London, having left the care of his Edinburgh congregation in the hands of William Nelson. Barclay returned to Scotland and died there in 1798, having opened many churches. After his death the church in Edinburgh continued to flourish for about 25 years under the leadership of James Donaldson, but after

Donaldson's death it split, and like the other Berean congregations, merged with the CONGREGATIONAL CHURCH.

Barclay taught that salvation is assured and that faith is the intellectual acceptance of biblical truths. He also questioned the value of theistic arguments.

❖ Barclayites; Bereans

BARKERS

Members of a small, fanatical nineteenth-century American group who attended revival meetings and indulged in a form of mass hysteria during which they would throw themselves around in a form of religious exercise, dancing, falling down, rolling around, jerking, shouting, and crying out with sounds that resembled barking. There were similar groups in Great Britain, such as the GLASITES.

BARROWISTS

A name by which the followers of Henry Barrow, or Barrowe (*c.* 1550–93), came to be known by 1615; before this they would have been identified as BROWNISTS, SEPARATISTS or Independents. Henry Barrow is sometimes thought of as the father of modern CONGREGATIONALISM, despite his denial of being a 'mere sectary'.

Barrow, a graduate of Clare Hall, Cambridge, and sometime member of Gray's Inn, London, had lived a promiscuous life at the court of Queen Elizabeth I, but had undergone a religious conversion in 1580, becoming a PURITAN within the tradition of Robert Browne and the Separatist Brownist movement. The early Separatists, who regarded Barrow as over radical, held the view that infant baptism should be rejected, along with tithing, and that total authority should be given to each congregation of the 'pious and devout'. Robert Browne (*c.* 1550–1633) had organized a church in Norwich, Norfolk, which was to be independent of the established CHURCH OF ENGLAND, which he regarded as being in need of instant reform. He also taught that all true Christians should withdraw from the tainted Church of England and form new congregations. For this action he was imprisoned, but was released and fled to Scotland before returning to England to be ordained in the Church of England in 1591, becoming rector of Achurch in Northamptonshire. He died in prison in Northampton in 1633, where he had been sent following an assault.

Henry Barrow was a friend of John Greenwood (1554–93), a leading Separatist, who had been ordained in the Church of England in Lincoln in 1582. In 1585 he went to London and started a small, independent congregation known as *The Ancient Church*. Guilty of the crime of conducting religious services unsanctioned by the Church of England, Greenwood was arrested and sent to prison, where Barrow visited him in 1586 and was arrested there by order of Archbishop John Whitgift on charges of producing seditious writings. Neither were to leave prison, but they continued to compose tracts defending Separatism, which were smuggled from the prison and printed and distributed in Holland. Both men were hanged for heresy at Tyburn, London, in 1593. Four years later a Statute was passed which provided for banishment, not execution, for nonconformists.

BASEL CHRISTIAN CHURCH OF MALAYSIA

The Church, which has its headquarters in Jesselton in Malaysia (formerly North

Borneo), was organized in 1882 by missionaries from the Basel Mission Society, which had been founded in Switzerland in 1815. The society attracted missionaries from Switzerland, Germany, France and Austria, who were sent to work in Africa, India and China. The British North Borneo Chartered Company brought Chinese labourers to North Borneo in 1882 and the first simple church was built at Lausan, Sabah, four years later. As more Chinese settlers followed, a second church was built in 1906 at Kudat, together with some schools. The missionary work continued and expanded, curtailed during the Japanese occupation of North Borneo between 1941–5, but has since undergone major restructuring. It is now a full member of the LUTHERAN World Federation.

The doctrine and liturgical structure of the Church reflect its origins with its Lutheran and REFORMED Church influence. The Basel Christian Church of Malaysia, together with the PROTESTANT CHURCH IN SABAH, the Lutheran Church in Malaysia, the Lutheran Church in Singapore and the Evangelical Lutheran Church in Malaysia and Singapore have formed the Federation of Evangelical Lutheran Churches in Malaysia and Singapore.

❖ Basel Church; Borneo Basel Self-Established Church; Protestant Church in Sabah

BATAK CHRISTIAN PROTESTANT CHURCH

The Church has its headquarters in Northern Sumatra, Indonesia, and is the largest Church in the LUTHERAN tradition in Asia. It was the product of the work of missionaries from the Rhenish Missionary Society, which was founded in Barmen, Germany, in 1828. A missionary team, led by Ludwig Ingwer Nommensen, who is often referred to as the apostle to the Bataks, evangelized the Batak people in Sumatra in 1862. He translated Luther's *Small Catechism*, the New Testament, a Church Order and some hymns into Batak, a written language composed of several diverse dialects; the first translation of the entire Bible into Batak was completed in 1894. The missionary work in the area concentrated on the education of local communities, and schools were set up in many villages. The Church was formally accepted into the Lutheran World Federation in 1952.

The Church is divided into districts that are overseen by superintendents who together make up the Church council, presided over by a bishop, or *ephorus*, who is elected for a specific period of time. Women play an important part in the Church, either as pastors or as *Bible Women*, in choirs and as leaders in prayer and study groups. Considerable emphasis is placed on youth ministry and a wide range of social services and health care, especially in rural areas where the majority of Church members live. There is a preparatory educational programme, teaching reading skills and the use of English to enable students to take more advanced courses, and a Theological-Education-by-Extension course, based in Pematangsiantar. The Church enjoys companion-synod status with various Evangelical Lutheran Church Synods in the USA and Chile.

❖ Batak Protestant Christian Church

BAXTERIANS

Followers of Richard Baxter (1615–91), a PURITAN, who had been ordained in the

Church of England in 1638 but who came to reject episcopal polity. Baxter served in the Free Grammar School at Bridgnorth from 1638–41 and in the parish of Kidderminster from 1641–60, but increasingly displayed what were termed Latitudinarian, or modernist, views. For some years, Baxter was part of the Parliamentary Army, leaving it in 1647. At the Savoy Conference in 1661 he produced an alternative liturgy to that contained in the *Book of Common Prayer* and this was not well received. Doctrinally, he held a theological position somewhat between Arminianism and Calvinism, for on the one hand he believed that while only a certain number of souls will be saved, he also admitted that in a certain sense Christ had died for all and that everyone had the chance to attain eternal life although many, through their own fault, would fail so to do. The 1662 Act of Uniformity deprived Baxter of his living in the Church of England. Although then excluded from the ministry he continued to preach, resulting in his imprisonment by the infamous Judge Jeffreys in 1685, on a framed charge of libelling the Church of England in his writings. Baxter endured a considerable amount of harassment and welcomed the overthrow of James II and the accession of William and Mary in 1688. He was a prolific writer, producing amongst other works the devotional classic *The Saints' Everlasting Rest* (1650) and the well known hymn, *Ye Holy Angels Bright* as well as *Paraphrase of the New Testament* for which he was imprisoned.

BEACHY AMISH MENNONITE CHURCH

This American Church represents a split from the Old Order Amish Mennonite Church and was formed in Salisbury, Pennsylvania, in 1927 by Bishop Moses M. Beachy (1874–1946), who was a leader within the Old Order Amish community from 1916–27. Beachy was always noted for his moderation especially in the application of the *Meidung*, or shunning, common in Brethren groups, which came to a head when most of his congregation wanted it to be applied to those who left the community to join a more conservative Mennonite congregation in Maryland. Finding themselves in disagreement with this, Beachy and his supporters formed a new association, the Beachy Amish Mennonite Church, which maintains the Mennonite format and whose members still wear the Old Amish dress.

The Beachy Amish developed the Amish Mission Interests Committee (MIC) in 1959. The work provides relief where it is needed and has taken members into, amongst other countries, Canada, where they give assistance in Indian schools, Germany, where workers were concerned about the plight of German Mennonites after the Second World War; Belize in 1961 in the wake of Hurricane Hatty, which left many people homeless and in need of help to rebuild their lives; and El Salvador in 1962 to provide training in agricultural skills and work in local communities.

The Church maintains a congregational polity, with a sharing of the ministry and leadership among several men. The ministers are selected by lot and the ideal ministerial team, or bench, is composed of a bishop, one or two ministers and a deacon. Congregations support Sunday schools, summer and winter Bible schools and revivalist meetings. The use of English has now replaced German in the services of most congregations.

BEHMENISTS

Followers of the teachings and writings of Jacob Boehme (1575–1624), a shepherd and shoemaker from Görlitz in eastern Germany. Boehme had a mystical experience one day while looking at the reflection of the sun in a basin of water, which he believed put him into an ecstatic state that allowed him to penetrate the deepest mysteries of God, man and nature. Although Boehme's formal education was very meagre, he nevertheless felt enabled, through divine inspiration, to write his first book *The Beginning of Dawn* (1612), which contained the insights he believed he had received. This so angered the local Lutheran pastor, Gregorius Richter, that he felt compelled to prevail upon the civic authorities to stop Boehme from writing. Boehme, however, was undaunted by this reaction, and continued to write, producing some devotional material under the title *The Way to Christ* (1623). Pastor Richter once again raised his objections and Boehme was obliged to leave Görlitz in 1624, returning there only to die later that year.

Boehme's other writings, concerning baptism, the Eucharist, the essence of God and an allegorical retelling of the *Book of Genesis*, were published posthumously. He proposed a mystical pantheism that taught that the external revelation of God in the Bible could be recognized only through an internal light, or illumination, such as he had experienced. His influence was considerable, not only in Germany within the PIETIST, romantic and idealist movements, but also in England amongst the Cambridge Platonists with other followers of Boehme, known as Behmenists, finding a spiritual home with the QUAKERS. Some of Boehme's ideas were appropriated by the secret society known as the Rosicrucians, named after their supposed founder Christian Rosenkreuz, the spurious author of some satirical writings. Rosenkreuz is now supposed to have been a pseudonym of the LUTHERAN pastor J. V. Andreae, but the writings were taken seriously and gave birth to several sects and secret societies that dabbled in alchemy and esoteric doctrines.

BELARUSIAN AUTOCEPHALIC ORTHODOX CHURCH

(The former Byelo-Russia achieved independence in 1991 and changed its name to Belarus.)

The Church owes its origin to the immigration of refugees and immigrants from the Byelo-Russia War following the Second World War (1939–45). In 1948, refugees organized a Byelo-Russian Autocephalic Church in Exile at a conference of bishops in West Germany. As a result of this, dioceses were established in Europe, North and South America and Australia. The Belarusians who are served by this Church were opposed to communism. While the Church is undergoing growth in Australia and Canada, it is experiencing a decline in the USA.

❖ Byelo-Russian Autocephalic Orthodox Church

BELARUSIAN ORTHODOX CHURCH

(The former Byelo-Russia achieved independence in 1991 and changed its name to Belarus.)

Belarus, formerly Byelo-Russia, is a territory that lies to the east of Poland and north of Ukraine. Since 1291 the Orthodox presence has been under both Greek, but latterly Russian, jurisdiction. The Christian history of the area has included periods of ROMAN CATHOLICISM, during the Polish-Lithuanian occupation that began in the thirteenth century, with the establishment in 1596 of the Belarusian Byzantine Catholic Church. With the partition of Poland in 1793 Belarus once again came under Russian control and by 1840 Orthodoxy had been imposed on the area by Tsar Nicholas I.

A schism developed in 1922 when Metropolitan Melchizedek and some of his clergy and faithful held what has become known as the Minsk Council of Clergy and Laity, which decided to form an autonomous Church that would not be under the control of the Moscow patriarchate. The outcome was tragic for the people concerned, with the Metropolitan and three of his bishops tortured to death and many of the others sent into exile in Siberia. There was a further attempt to make the Belorussian Orthodox Church independent of Moscow during the Second World War (1939–45) when the Russians lost control of the area and the Belorussian Autocephalous Orthodox Church was formed, but it later returned to the control of Moscow in 1946 during a staged event styled as the Reunion Council. In 1990 the Moscow patriarchate granted the status of an exarchate to the Belarusian Orthodox Church, which still allowed some measure of control from Moscow. By 1995 a seminary, a monastery and several convents, and a theological academy had been established.

❖ Byelo-Russian Orthodox Church

BELARUSIAN UNIAT CATHOLIC CHURCH

(The former Byelo-Russia achieved independence in 1991 and changed its name to Belarus.)

In mid-sixteenth century Poland, Jesuits attempted to encourage some Orthodox bishops to unite with Rome and by 1596, at a council held at Brest-Litovsk, most had agreed to this; these participating bishops were derisively described as Uniats, or Uniates, by the few remaining Orthodox opponents of the Union of Brest-Litovsk. The Belarusian Uniat Catholic Church officially came into existence, then, after the Council of Brest (1595–6). It maintained its Orthodox liturgical rites and language while at the same time recognizing the supremacy of the pope and Rome's doctrinal position. The Uniat Church grew steadily over the years, but in 1839 Tsar Nicholas I of Russia suppressed the Belarussian Uniat Church along with the UKRAINIAN CATHOLIC CHURCH, and many Belarussians returned to the UKRAINIAN ORTHODOX CHURCH. From 1920–39, Belarus territory in the west, near the Polish border, came under Polish control and a community of about 30,000 Belarussian Eastern-rite Catholics flourished there with an apostolic visitor, and later an exarch, appointed by Rome to care for this large group. This territory later came under Soviet control, through the Molotov-Ribbentrop Agreement of 1939. In 1946 the Belarusian Uniat Church was once again suppressed and its members were counted among the RUSSIAN ORTHODOX faithful. Rome affirmed the lawfulness of the Church in 1980, and with the collapse of communism, and subsequent independence in 1991, the Uniat Catholic Church re-emerged, its Orthodox liturgical rites and language still intact. Since then, it can be seen from surveys carried out in 1992 and 1995 that there has been a decline in numbers, with most of those who profess to be Eastern-rite Catholics now worshipping in Latin-rite parishes.

❖ Belarusian Greek Catholics; Belarusian Catholics; Byelo-Russian Byzantine Catholic Church

BEREAN FUNDAMENTAL CHURCHES

A small American denomination with its headquarters in Lincoln, Minnesota, which was founded in the early 1930s by Dr Ivan E. Olsen as a FUNDAMENTALIST, evangelical and conservative Church.

Its central organization is based on each congregation sending a clerical and a lay delegate to a convened Church council. At present there are about 64 congregations and the Church as a whole has a rising membership, mainly centred in the Midwestern part of the USA and affiliated to two congregations in Canada.

BETHEL BAPTIST ASSEMBLY, INC

The Church was originally founded in the USA in 1934 as the Evangelistic Ministerial Alliance and was a fellowship of BAPTIST ministers and churches, led by the Reverend A. F. Varnell who was in charge of the Bethel Temple in Evansville, Indiana. It was incorporated under its present name in Indiana in 1960.

The Church is in the tradition of a ONENESS, or Jesus Only, PENTECOSTAL Church in its denial of the orthodox doctrine of the Trinity. Members are received into the Church through immersion in the name of Jesus, in obedience to the injunction in Acts 2:38 to 'be baptized every one of you in the name of Jesus Christ'. Whilst this is a Pentecostal Church, there is an emphasis on the gifts of the Holy Spirit, especially healing, but when *glossolalia*, or speaking in tongues, occurs it is not taken as a sign that the member is being filled with the Holy Ghost.

❖ Bethel Assembly; Bethel Ministerial Association; Evangelistic Missionary Alliance

BIBLE CHRISTIANS

The Church was organized, as an evangelical sect, in 1815 by William O'Bryan (1778–1868) amongst the agricultural workers and fishermen in the south-western English counties of Devon and Cornwall. O'Bryan, a Wesleyan convert and wandering lay preacher in the METHODIST Church, felt compelled to expand his preaching beyond his authorized circuit and for this disobedience he was expelled from his ministry. He formed a religious society, known initially as the ARMINIAN Bible Christians, in Shebbear, North Devon, where he was assisted by James Thorne (1795–1872) and several women preachers. The Church derives its name from the importance attached by its members to the scriptures in the drawing up of the rules by which the Church is governed. It was O'Bryan's original intention to have the word 'ARMINIAN' included in its title, but this was later abandoned. The important role of women preachers and the laity, and the recourse to inner illumination, reflect QUAKER influence and this gave rise to one of the alternative names by which the Society came to be known, Quaker Methodists.

By 1821 a missionary society had been formed and the work expanded into other parts of the country, into Kent, the Isle of Wight, Northumberland and the

Channel Islands. O'Bryan's autocratic and confrontational manner, however, led to disputes over the leadership, and by 1829 he had left the movement, going to America in 1831 and dying in Brooklyn in 1868. The missionary activity continued to grow, taking the movement abroad in 1831, beginning with the first Bible Christian Church in Australia, founded at Burra, north of Adelaide, in 1849 under the leadership of the Reverend James Way. The work prospered, with further expansion to Melbourne and into Queensland by 1866.

The Bible Christian Church in Great Britain united with other Methodist groups and by 1907 formed part of the UNITED METHODIST CHURCH (UK) together with the METHODIST NEW CONNEXION and the United Methodist Free Churches. In 1932 the United Methodist Church (UK) merged with the PRIMITIVE METHODIST CHURCH and Wesleyan Methodists to form the METHODIST CHURCH OF GREAT BRITAIN.

❖ Bryanites; Quaker Methodists

BIBLE FELLOWSHIP CHURCH

When some American MENNONITE congregations collectively called themselves the UNITED MISSIONARY CHURCH, thus abandoning all Mennonite connections, those congregations that refused to change organized themselves in 1947 as the Bible Fellowship Church (BFC).

The members of the BFC affirm the *Dordrecht Confession of Faith* but have added some supplementary statements. One of these concerns sanctification, which the members believe is the second blessing that follows justification and as a consequence they are expected to adopt modest and unworldly lives. The Church is thus recognizably part of the HOLINESS tradition. Sanctification is considered completed at the premillennial second coming of Christ to earth (REVELATION 20). Divine healing is also practised, and the ordinances of believer's baptism and the Lord's Supper are observed. The practice of foot-washing has, however, been dropped.

At the outset, each congregation was autonomous according to the polity that was practised at the time, but they later came under the control of a presiding elder in a modified episcopal form of polity. Today, the Bible Fellowship Churches are more presbyterial in their form of government, with congregations now directed by local elders who, together with pastors of the Church, are sent by their congregations to the annual conference.

The social work of the Church is concerned mainly with the welfare of the elderly and a new home for their care has recently been opened at Allentown, Pennsylvania. There is also activity in the field of church planting and the improvement of educational facilities for Church members. At one time the care of orphans was a concern of the BFC, but this no longer continues.

Most of the individual congregations of the BFC are in Pennsylvania, but some are now to be found in the states of Connecticut, Delaware, New Jersey, New Mexico, New York and Virginia.

BIBLE METHODIST CHURCH

A Church in the HOLINESS tradition that was founded in the USA and is marked by two principal distinctive characteristics, in both doctrine and lifestyle.

In doctrine, the holiness tradition concentrates on the *Second Blessing of Perfection*, which follows the *First Experience of Salvation*. Justification, or first experience, being born again, is also known as the *new birth* and precedes the experience of gradual growth in grace, and gradual death to sin; this in turn leads to entire sanctification effected by the baptism of the Holy Spirit.

All Holiness Churches are within the ARMINIAN, rather than the CALVINISTIC, tradition, which allows not only for the possibility of entire sanctification but also for the prospect of falling away from sanctification through sin. The lifestyle is distinctive in that members are to avoid tobacco, alcohol and drugs, and to dress in a sober fashion, in line with John Wesley's *General Rules*. Honest business practices are expected and uncharitable conversation is to be avoided. The Bible is considered to be the inspired and infallible word of God, the complete revelation of his plan for mankind. The Church holds to a Trinitarian belief and observes the ordinances of baptism and the Lord's Supper.

The Bible Methodist Church started at a meeting in Knoxville, Tennessee, in 1966, called by D. P. Denton, an editor of an independent monthly, *The Evangelist of Truth*. Those attending were opposed to the merger of the WESLEYAN METHODIST CHURCH and the PILGRIM HOLINESS CHURCH to form the Wesleyan Church, which came about in 1968. At the meeting it was decided to form a New Connection, or association of churches, and this came to be known as the Bible Methodist Connection of Tennessee, and later as the Bible Methodist Church. The polity is congregational. There were some at the meeting in Knoxville who wanted an emphasis on healing, and these eventually separated from the Bible Methodist Connection to form the Bible Holiness Church, with a small number of members in Tennessee and Virginia. Other Methodists from Alabama and Ohio, who agreed with Denton's views and opposed the 1966 merger, had formed two separate Churches, but these eventually merged and formed the Bible Methodist Connection of Churches in 1970.

A numerically small Bible Methodist Church was formed in Queensland, Australia, in 1969, led by the Reverend R. O. Johnson, who held services in his home at Ipswich, west of Brisbane. Other Australian congregations were formed, in Queensland and New South Wales. In the Australian churches there is a strong emphasis on the inerrancy of the Bible and an insistence on simplicity of lifestyle for the members, who are enjoined to avoid luxury and unnecessary worldliness.

❖ Bible Methodist Connection of Tennessee

BIBLE MISSIONARY CHURCH

A small denomination within the HOLINESS tradition, whose origins lie in the Glenn Griffith's revivals in the USA that were held in 1955 near Nampa, Idaho. Glenn Griffiths had been a minister of the CHURCH OF THE NAZARENE and so successful was his appeal for a return to the old tenets of Wesleyan holiness that many followers organized themselves into what was called the Bible Missionary Union. In a short time many congregations of this union were spread through twenty states and at the first general conference, held in Denver in 1956, the present title of the Church was adopted.

Doctrinally, the tradition is Wesleyan holiness with a strong emphasis on the premillennial return of Christ and judgement for heaven or hell (REVELATION

20). The Church is very concerned with entire sanctification and a corresponding lack of worldliness by its members is enjoined. Despite its small size, the Church has undertaken extensive foreign mission work in British Guiana, New Guinea, Japan, India and Mexico, with home missions working with the Navaho Indians at Farmington, New Mexico. The Church provides educational opportunities through the Bible Missionary Institute, which was founded in Rock Island, Illinois, and is also active in the field of publishing.

BIBLE PRESBYTERIAN CHURCH

When Carl McIntire graduated in 1931, following his studies at Princeton and the Westminster Theological Seminary in Philadelphia, Pennsylvania, USA, he was appointed as pastor of the Collingswood Presbyterian Church in New Jersey. This work, however, was short-lived and McIntire was forced to resign and suspended from the PRESBYTERIAN CHURCH, together with J. Gresham Machen, a theologian from Princeton, because of their criticism of the Church's failure to uphold the *Five Fundamentals*, which they held to be immutable.

These fundamentals were:

1 The infallibility of the scriptures
2 The virgin birth of Christ
3 Christ's atonement
4 Christ's bodily resurrection
5 Christ's miracles

Unwilling to compromise in their conservative beliefs, McIntire, Machen and others formed the ORTHODOX PRESBYTERIAN CHURCH in 1936, but within a year McIntire and Machen came to disagreement over several issues, including Machen's refusal to oppose the use of alcohol, his liberal views concerning premillennialism (REVELATION 20), and his lack of support for the Independent Board for Presbyterian Foreign Missions, which had been founded by Machen in 1933, as an agency responsible for sending out conservative missionaries. In 1938, McIntire and others formed the Bible Presbyterian Church, but McIntire was still troubled by the liberal attitudes he saw in other Churches and he enjoined his members to have nothing to do with them. He was particularly worried by modernism, communism and pacifism and in order to counter what he saw as dangerous liberalism he founded the American Council of Christian Churches (ACCC) and the International Council of Christian Churches (ICCC) in 1948, following the Amsterdam meeting of the World Council of Churches. Both the ACCC and the ICCC were criticized by some of the important Presbyterian thinkers, who ridiculed many of the plans put forward by these councils, such as the Bible Balloon Project, which was to distribute religious literature behind the Iron Curtain by floating it across the divide by balloon. In 1961 there was a split within the Bible Presbyterian Church, with the majority of its members later forming the EVANGELICAL PRESBYTERIAN CHURCH, which merged in 1965 at Lookout Mountain, Tennessee, with the REFORMED PRESBYTERIAN CHURCH IN NORTH AMERICA (GENERAL SYNOD) to form the REFORMED PRESBYTERIAN CHURCH – EVANGELICAL SYNOD. In 1982 this joined the PRESBYTERIAN CHURCH IN AMERICA.

Those who remained loyal to McIntire and his ideals declared for independence and formed the Bible Presbyterian Church, Collingwood (New Jersey). Doctrinally, the Bible Presbyterians took the *Westminster Confession of Faith* (1643–6) as its doctrinal statement, together with the *Larger* and *Small Catechisms*. The members support a strong premillennial view concerning Christ's second coming (Revelation 20) and oppose the evolution theory as well as the United Nations, ecumenism and the use of intoxicating drinks.

Schools, Bible institutes and colleges, as well as some media and publishing enterprises, have been founded in the USA and the first Bible Presbyterian Church in Australia was established in Adelaide, South Australia, in 1969 by John MacKenzie, who had been ordained in the USA. This Church now maintains the Fundamental Bible College of Australia at Magill, South Australia, that was founded in 1985. Some small Chinese groups have also been established in Australia, in Perth, Adelaide and Melbourne, through the Bible Presbyterian Church of Singapore and Malaysia, which was created by a schism in the Chinese Christian Church in 1950.

BIBLE PROTESTANT CHURCH

An American congregation of modest size which arose through a schism in the eastern conference of the Methodist Protestant Church (founded 1830), when one third of the 150 delegates withdrew in protest against the merger of their Church and the Methodist Episcopal Church, South (founded 1845). The issues at stake were the episcopal polity endorsed by the merging Churches and their modernist tendencies. This merger later resulted in the formation of the Methodist Union of 1939 and the United Methodist Church (USA). The non-merging congregations formed the Bible Protestant Church, which is in the holiness tradition, with its headquarters at Linwood, New Jersey.

The doctrinal position is conservative with an emphasis on the verbal inspiration of the Bible, an orthodox understanding of the Trinity and other articles of faith found in the creeds, such as the deity, virgin birth, resurrection and ascension of Jesus Christ. Salvation is by faith in Christ's death and resurrection. The members hold to premillennial beliefs, with eternal punishment for the wicked and joy for the believer (Revelation 20). Baptism and the Lord's Supper are considered to be divine institutions. This fellowship of self-governing churches, with each congregation enjoying autonomous status, is organized in an annual conference of both lay and clergy representatives. The sphere of influence of the Church is confined to the eastern USA, but missionary work in the Philippines, Latin America and Japan has been undertaken.

BIBLE WAY CHURCH OF OUR LORD JESUS CHRIST, WORLD WIDE, INC.

The Church, founded in 1957 in the USA, is within the Oneness-pentecostal tradition and should not be confused with the Bible Way Church World Wide.

The Church came into being when some members of the Church of Our Lord Jesus Christ of the Apostolic Faith, Inc. (founded 1919), came together under the leadership of Bishop Smallwood Edmond Williams to form a Church that was less rigidly authoritarian in its government and procedure. Bishops Winfield A. Showell of Baltimore, Maryland, McKinley Williams of

Philadelphia, Pennsylvania, Joseph Moore of Brooklyn, New York, and John Bean of Petersburg, Virginia, assisted Bishop Williams (who is often featured wearing a white biretta with a red pom-pom) in this work.

The doctrine of the Church is described as being apostolic and PENTECOSTAL, with baptism administered in the name of Jesus Christ only, coupled with the belief that the baptism of the Holy Spirit, evinced by *glossolalia*, or speaking with tongues, is essential for salvation. The Church advocates a life of humility, godliness and Bible study. Foot-washing is also practised. There is a belief in the imminent premillennial return of Christ, with a final judgement for the living and the dead (REVELATION 20). The Church holds an annual general conference and, according to available statistics, is increasing in membership.

BODY-FELT SALVATION CHURCH

Many Torres Strait islanders, who inhabit a cluster of small islands between New Guinea and Cape York Peninsula in Northern Queensland, Australia, were at one time members of the CHURCH OF JESUS CHRIST (END TIME REVIVAL) that had been founded in Sydney in the 1960s by Bruce Jamieson. Propaganda distributed by the American-founded Hall Deliverance Foundation in the 1970s persuaded some of the islanders to form a PENTECOSTAL group that rejects baptism by water but anticipates a literal second coming of Christ (REVELATION 20). The gift of the Holy Spirit is believed to be shown not only through speaking in tongues, but also through the other senses, for the faithful will hear heavenly voices, see red clouds of fire and taste the nectar of heaven. A 'sun-tan of healing', of which there is never a short supply in the islands, is also believed to be generated by a Holy Spirit fire that is held to flow from Christ's warm, glorified body. Today there are fewer than three hundred members of the sect, which is restricted to the islands of the Torres Straits.

BOGOMILS

A mediaeval heretical sect that persisted in Bulgaria from *c.* 930 until the seventeenth century, whose beliefs later played a large part in the formation of the heresy of the Cathars (ALBIGENSIANS) in the twelfth century. A village priest called Bogomil founded the sect, whose beliefs, which may have been influenced by that of the PAULICIANS, were centred on a dualistic doctrine of good and evil, holding that it was Satan who had created the world and the human body, while God created the soul. They further held the docetic (DOCETISM) view of Jesus Christ, teaching that the humanity and suffering of Christ were apparent, and not actual. The Old Testament was rejected because it was claimed that the patriarchs had been inspired by Satan, who had originally sat at the right hand of God before his expulsion from heaven. Since all material creation was regarded as evil, including the human body which at birth surrounded and imprisoned the good soul in evil matter, there was a strong attraction among the followers to eschew marriage, abstain from sexual intercourse and all meat and wine, and to deny themselves material possessions. That the sect survived, and for so long, gives witness to the thought that all did not achieve these ideals. There was no Bogomil priesthood, and no sacraments, although members confessed their failings to each other and possibly granted one another absolution from their sins.

History has not been kind to the Bogomils, who were often accused of being influenced by the heresy of the MANICHAEANS. The movement spread to Constantinople after Bulgaria's conquest in 1018 by the Byzantine Emperor Basil II the *Bulgar-Slayer*, but was condemned by the synod of Constantinople in 1140 and at subsequent synods in 1316 and 1325. Many Bogomils, who were once described as being almost completely wrapped in clothing, leaving just their eyes and noses showing and walking with a stoop, were severely and cruelly persecuted. A great number converted to Islam, following Turkish conquests of Bulgaria, and the sect diminished, but pockets of believers persisted until the seventeenth century.

BOLIVIAN BAPTIST UNION

A BAPTIST Church founded in 1898 by Canadian missionaries after their arrival in Bolivia, but without much initial success in attracting congregations since the missionaries concentrated their efforts on the development of farm projects and schools. Since 1960 there has been an increase in interest, mainly among the urban middle-class population. The headquarters is in Cochabamba, south of La Paz.

BOLIVIAN LUTHERAN CHURCH

This LUTHERAN Church was founded in 1938 and is found chiefly amongst the Aymaras people, who form the third largest ethno-linguistic population of Bolivia. The Church is a member of the World Mission Prayer League. There is also another Evangelical Lutheran Church in Bolivia, for German speakers, which was founded in 1957 for recent immigrants.

BONOSIANS

Followers of Bonosus, bishop of Naissus (present-day Nis in Serbia), a fourth-century heretic who denied the Blessed Virgin Mary's perpetual virginity by teaching that Mary had other children after the birth of Jesus, a teaching that was condemned by the Council of Capua (391). St Ambrose of Milan tried to persuade him to abandon this teaching, but without success and Bonosus continued in his heresy. Against the advice of Ambrose he also continued to ordain priests and bishops, the validity of whose ordinations were therefore called into question; this was especially true of those who had received their ordination after the council's condemnation. The validity of baptism administered by Bonosians was also considered suspect. While it is not clear whether Bonosus himself denied Christ's divinity, it is certain that many of his followers did, and it is said that they were in sympathy with the Photinians, who affirmed the adoptive divine Sonship of Christ. The dates of his life remain obscure, but it is thought that Bonosus died towards the end of the fourth or the beginning of the fifth century.

BORBORIANS

This sect of GNOSTICS of the fourth century was considered by Epiphanius to be affiliated with the OPHITES. The members enjoyed a reputation for loose living and they denied any form of final judgement for the dead. In the early fifth century the sect was forbidden to gather together in assembly and they were classified as MANICHAEANS within the Emperor Justinian's Code of AD 534, the *Corpus Juris Civilis*.

BRANCH DAVIDIANS

A splinter group of the SEVENTH-DAY ADVENTISTS which had its headquarters near Waco, Texas, USA until many of its members were killed by fire during a US government raid in 1993. Victor T. Houteff, a member of the Seventh-Day Adventist Church in Los Angeles, had started the schism. Houteff saw himself as a reforming influence and the divinely inspired messenger of God, responsible for the gathering of the 144,000 alluded to in Revelation 14. He published a book, *The Shepherd's Rod*, in 1930 outlining his ideas. In 1935, Houteff, his wife and eleven others moved to Mount Carmel Centre, near Waco. Here they had a vision of establishing the Davidic kingdom in Palestine and waiting there for Christ's second coming (REVELATION 20).

The Second World War intervened, and with it came conscription. The Seventh-Day Adventist Church, to which the members of the Waco community believed themselves to belong, refused to certify conscientious objector status or ministerial deferment for the men at Waco. Houteff immediately issued his own membership certificates and ministerial licences, so creating a formal organization with himself as leader, changing the name of the Church to the Davidian Seventh-Day Adventists. Houteff died in 1955 and his wife, Florence, succeeded him. She prophesied that there would be a fulfilment of Revelation 11 on 22 April 1959 and that the period of 1260 days would end on that date, signalling God's intervention in Palestine and the establishment of the Davidic kingdom. When this obviously proved to be incorrect, many of the followers left Waco, some to form different groups. One member, Benjamin Roden, who led a group of defectors, told his followers to 'get off the dead rod and move on to a living branch'. From this the new group took the name of Branch Davidians. Roden died in 1978 and was succeeded by his wife, Lois. In 1983, Vernon Howell, who was later to change his name to David Koresh, joined the Branch Davidians but he soon fell out with Roden's son, George, who had the idea that he was the messiah. The conflict of personalities became too great and at one point Howell was forced to leave the community at the point of a gun. In 1987, George Roden decided that as a demonstration of his powers he would resurrect a man who had been dead for many years. The police, tipped off by Howell, raided the community and a shoot-out followed. Roden was jailed and Howell moved back into Mount Carmel, taking over the leadership of the community that was largely sympathetic to his ostensibly attractive character and force of personality. It was at this point that Howell changed his name to David Koresh, after King David and, possibly, the Persian king, Cyrus, although Koresh has also been known as the surname of God. While Koresh never claimed to be God, he did lay claim to the title Lamb of God, and to an understanding of the message of the seven seals (Rev. 5 and 10) together with the power to break the seventh seal (Rev. 8:1). This was in accord with a strong end-time emphasis in his teaching.

Koresh was a registered arms dealer and legally dealt in arms to support the community. In 1993, the FBI raided the community looking for stockpiles of weapons and ammunition. A siege lasting for some 51 days resulted, culminating in the death by fire of David Koresh and eighty members of the community, of which fifteen were children. It was reported that many of his followers who escaped the flames still affirm their belief in Koresh's messianic claims and that they anticipate his imminent resurrection.

BRANHAMISM

The movement known as Branhamism was founded in America in 1946 by William Marrion Branham (1909–65) within the ONENESS and PENTECOSTAL traditions, with an emphasis on healing as well as on *deliverance* ministry concerned with the casting out of evil spirits. Branham underwent a conversion experience as a result of a series of visions and angelic visitations he believed he had received. He entered the BAPTIST ministry and in the early years of his career he came into contact with, and was attracted by, the Jesus-Only Pentecostals, who deny the traditional doctrine of the Trinity. His friends and family prevailed upon him to keep to his more conventional ministry and for a time he did so. However, when his wife, Hope, and their baby daughter died unexpectedly in 1937, Branham believed that this was because he had not pursued his association with the Pentecostal group and also because a spiritual experience had convinced him that he had been chosen to be a forerunner and end-time prophet of the second coming of Christ (REVELATION 20).

In 1946, an angelic visitation impressed on him the belief that he had been given two gifts, that of healing and of the word of knowledge. Branham's belief in his capacity as a healer was reinforced when he apparently healed a woman diagnosed with cancer and as a result of this his reputation spread, attracting followers. Branham held to a modalist heresy that taught that in the Godhead there was only one person, Jesus Christ, who went under different modes, or titles, at various times in history. Consequently, his followers were baptized only in the name of Jesus. He held to the view that Eve was seduced by the serpent in the Garden of Eden and became pregnant with Cain, whereas Seth's descendants are from God and will experience the 'rapture before the time of tribulation' referred to in Revelation; this seduction theory is known as the doctrine of the serpent's seed.

BRETHREN CHURCH (ASHLAND, OHIO)

This American Church developed from the split in 1939 that had come about within the BRETHREN CHURCH (PROGRESSIVE DUNKERS) through the action of those members who wanted a more ARMINIAN interpretation of *The Message of the Brethren Ministry*, which had been published as a statement of belief by the Progressive Dunkers in 1917. Those favouring an Arminian interpretation wanted an emphasis on free will and insisted that salvation was for all of those who chose Christ. In all other respects, including provision for an annual conference, the Ashland group might be considered to be identical in their doctrinal position to the Progressive Dunkers.

BRETHREN CHURCH (GRACE GROUP)

When some members of the BRETHREN CHURCH (PROGRESSIVE DUNKERS – founded 1882) wanted a more CALVINISTIC approach to their doctrine, while others, such as the Ashland, Ohio group (see previous entry) wanted a more ARMINIAN interpretation, a split in the late 1930s followed and the more Calvinistic group set about forming its own body – the Grace Group.

The belief of this group stressed the doctrine of predestination and held that the number of the elect, who were to be saved, had been predetermined before the world's creation – an ultra Calvinistic view. In all other respects the members of this Church hold to the doctrinal position adopted by the Brethren Church (Progressive Dunkers).

The Church retains its own conference at Winona Lake, Indiana, and it provides education for its members at the Grace Theological Seminary and at Grace College.

Officially, the Church does not encourage ecumenical contacts, but it is responsible for a widespread foreign mission programme in parts of Europe, Africa, and Central and South America. A further split came about in 1996, with the formation of the Conservative Grace Brethren International.

❖ Fellowship of Grace Brethren Churches; National Fellowship of Brethren Churches

BRETHREN CHURCH (PROGRESSIVE DUNKERS)

The Brethren, who had settled in Pennsylvania, USA, were largely agricultural workers, but by the end of the nineteenth century there was a growing realization amongst some that an educated clergy and laity was now needed and that some other reforms were also necessary. One of the more outspoken critics, Henry R. Holsinger of Berlin, Pennsylvania, was expelled, along with others, from the main Church of the Brethren for his declared objection to the authority that the annual meeting had over the annual conference and its delegates. Holsinger's expulsion led to the foundation of the Brethren Church (Progressive Dunkers) in 1882, whose members abandoned the plain dress code and pressed for educational opportunities for clergy and laity alike.

The same ordinances of the CHURCH OF THE BRETHREN were accepted. These included the believer's baptism by triple immersion, a laying on of hands, and the Lord's Supper, which involves participating in a meal as part of a Eucharistic service, preceded by foot-washing; there is also the administration of unction of the sick with oil.

The foreign mission society of the Brethren Church was formed in 1900 and by 1909 they had sent Charles Yoder to Argentina, with later missionary work extending their message into French Equatorial Africa, now known as the Central African Republic.

In 1917 *The Message of the Brethren Ministry* was published, to which all members of the Church were expected to subscribe. This doctrinal statement underlined the infallibility of scripture, the incarnation, death, atonement and resurrection of Jesus Christ. Man's fall, and his need for salvation with justification by faith, is fully stated, as well as a belief in the resurrection of the dead, the judgement of the world and the second coming of Christ (REVELATION 20).

Another split occurred within the Progressive Dunkers group in 1939, some members favouring a CALVINISTIC view and others an ARMINIAN approach. The pro-Calvinistic Brethren formed the Grace Group, also known as the National Fellowship of Brethren Churches, while those who were Arminian in ethos formed the BRETHREN CHURCH (ASHLAND, OHIO).

BRETHREN IN CHRIST CHURCH

Many European ANABAPTISTS and PIETISTS, who went to the USA in the middle of the seventeenth century, because of persecution in Europe, settled in Lancaster County, Pennsylvania, and formed various brotherhoods. One such became known from 1778 as the River Brethren, the river in question being the Susquehanna, with the group settling on the east side of the river in the town of Marietta. By the early nineteenth century the Church of the River Brethren had spread throughout the eastern and mid-western states of America. In 1843, there was the first schism in the Church, which gave birth to the OLD ORDER (YORKER) RIVER BRETHREN, with another schism in 1855 leading to the formation of the UNITED ZION CHURCH. In 1863, after many years of re-formation, which included the introduction of baptism by triple immersion, the pacifist beliefs of the River Brethren at the time of the American civil war, and with it the drafting of young men into the Union Army, forced the Church to register as a group of conscientious objectors and with this action came a change of name to the current Brethren in Christ Church. The spread of the Church continued, and today there are congregations in many parts of the USA and Canada, with overseas missions in Central America, Africa and the Far East.

The doctrinal beliefs of the Brethren in Christ Church include a conventional understanding of the Trinity, the forgiveness of sins, resurrection of the dead with heaven or hell respectively for the saved and the wicked, and Christ's second coming (REVELATION 20). The ordinances are baptism by triple immersion and the Lord's Supper, in which the bread and wine are taken to represent the body and blood of Christ. Foot-washing is also practised as an occasion for reconciliation and affirmation of one another. There is a special service for the laying on of hands and the anointing of the sick with oil for the purpose of healing. Children are dedicated to God, with the congregation offering prayerful support for the nurturing of the young. A modest lifestyle is insisted upon, and because the members recognize their loyalty to Christ as taking precedence over that owed to the state, all forms of warfare are rejected and their pacifist outlook is maintained.

❖ River Brethren

BRETHREN OF THE FREE SPIRIT

The name *Brethren of the Free Spirit* was used as a generic label by mediaeval writers to describe those members of various sects who had placed themselves outside formal ecclesiastical authority, choosing instead to live in the so-called freedom of the spirit. More specifically, the name is usually applied to the AMALRICIANS, a pantheistic sect of the twelfth and early thirteenth century.

BROWNISTS

The name of this English denomination is taken from its founder, Robert Browne (*c.* 1553–1633), often called the father of English CONGREGATIONALISM for his promotion of separatism from the CHURCH OF ENGLAND. Browne had been educated at the University of Cambridge before going to London where he preached and taught for a while at a grammar school in Southwark. Returning to Cambridge in 1579, Browne openly criticized the Church of England and refused to accept the bishop's authority on the grounds that the calling and authority of the bishop was unlawful and that true authority was vested in the gathered Church, for which opinion his license to preach was withdrawn. This opinion arose from his belief in the priesthood of all believers, which view he promoted, teaching at the same time that the people should undertake the reform of the Church and not look to the state to do this for them. In 1581, with the help and support of a friend from his student days, Robert Harrison of Norwich, Norfolk, Browne began to organize local SEPARATIST churches, which were popular with the members of the DUTCH REFORMED CHURCH who lived in and around Norwich, working in the local craft industries. The authorities seized Browne and he was imprisoned and charged with preaching without a license, by the order of the Bishop of Norwich. Upon his release in 1582, Browne, Harrison and some of their Norfolk followers went to Holland, settling in present-day Middelburg, in Zeeland, where one of Browne's tutors from Cambridge, Thomas Cartwright, had established a congregation. While there, Browne wrote his *Treatise of Reformation . . . the Book which sheweth the Life and Manners of all True Christians.* A falling-out between Browne and Harrison led to Browne's return to England, and to a new chapter in his life. In 1591 Browne was ordained to a Northamptonshire living, having persuaded Archbishop Whitgift of his willingness to conform to the established CHURCH OF ENGLAND, and he served his parish for the next 42 years. But perhaps Browne's spirit had not been totally quelled, for at the age of 83 he was sent back to prison for the civil offence of striking his godson in a very characteristic fit of rage.

❖ Independents

BRÜDERHOF

This German *Society of Brothers*, a Christian sect similar in beliefs and practices to the HUTTERITES, was founded at Sannerz, Germany, in 1920 by Eberhard Arnold (1883–1935), a one-time secretary of the German Christian Student Movement. The Brüderhof movement spread to Liechtenstein in the 1930s and, to avoid persecution by the Nazis in Germany, to Gloucester, England. To avoid internment in England during the Second World War most of the members left for Paraguay in 1941, from where some have since dispersed to other countries, going to the USA in the early 1950s and returning to England, where the Brothers established themselves in the county of Sussex, in 1971; some remained in Paraguay where there has been a gradual increase in membership which now numbers around 1200 adults distributed in six main groups.

Eberhard Arnold tried to assimilate his Brüderhof into the various Hutterite brotherhoods in Germany, which was in part successful, but because of internal struggles for dominance, the Arnold group became unpopular. There was internal dissent within the group itself when Arnold's grandson, Heini, assumed leadership in 1961. A third of the membership left, accusing Heini of totalitarianism. Lawsuits and counter litigation followed and these have resulted in two separate Brüderhof groups that have no contact with each other.

The Brüderhof men wear beards and dark-coloured trousers held up with braces, while the women wear simple dresses with long skirts and headscarves, or caps. The group maintains its own school, with heavily Bible-based education, from which children go on to secondary schools outside the community. The group supports itself through agriculture and the making of high quality wooden toys in their own workshops.

BRÜGGLERS

This small, short-lived sect was founded at Brügglen, near Berne, Switzerland, in around 1745 by two brothers, Christian (b. 1710) and Hieronymus (1712–53) Kohler. The brothers declared themselves to be the Holy Trinity, although there were only two of them. Elizabeth Kissling, a convert, filled the position of the third person of the Trinity. Their main purpose seems to have been to issue a prediction that the world would end at Christmas, 1748. When this failed to happen the three went into exile in 1749. Hieronymus was eventually arrested and tried for heresy in 1753. Found guilty, he was burnt at the stake at Berne in the same year. Their followers dispersed into the Swiss mountains and were eventually absorbed by the Antonian sect, which had been founded by Anton Unterhäher (1759–1824), who claimed to be the ruler of the world.

BUCHANITES

A short-lived sect which was confined to Scotland where it was founded in 1783 by Mrs *Luckie* Buchan, who was also known as Mother Elspeth, or *Friend Mother in the Lord.*

Elspeth, or Elspat, Buchan was born in 1738, to John and Margaret Simpson, who kept a public house at Fatmacken in Aberdeenshire, and was married, some say irregularly, to a potter named Robert Buchan by whom she had three children. The family settled in Glasgow where the Buchans became members of the Presbytery Relief sect and at a religious meeting at Irvine, on the Firth of Clyde, *Mother* Buchan suddenly arose, claiming that she was the third person in the Godhead and, at the same time 'the woman clothed with the sun' (Rev. 12:1). Claiming also that she could bestow immortality upon whomever she breathed, she further promised that such people would never die but would be bodily assumed into heaven, provided, of course, that they put their absolute and unlimited faith in her divine mission. Her life was now changed for good.

In her mission, Mrs Buchan persuaded a young minister of the church, Hugh White, that he was the *Man-Child*, referred to in the Book of Revelation 'who was to rule all the nations with a rod of iron' (Rev. 12:5) and he became her faithful disciple. By now known as *Luckie* Buchan, Elspeth gained complete control over White, his wife, and others. The behaviour of the group, which was seen as heretical, so upset the town authorities that the members were expelled by the magistrates and left Irvine to tour southern Scotland. This pilgrimage was interrupted at intervals when the little band stopped for a time to await their promised, and earnestly expected, assumption into heaven, their travels continuing when it became clear that this was perhaps neither the time nor the place. And so the small band proceeded until the natural death of Mrs Buchan in 1791. Unable to resist her own claims, but feeling that death was approaching, the pseudo-prophetess told her followers that she was not really dying, but had to visit Paradise in order to collect some spiritual objects which were necessary for their future development and that she would return to them, perhaps in a few days, or perhaps a few years, to perform miracles. After her death, the body was taken by one of the followers, Andrew Innes, who kept guard over her remains, keeping them for 54 years while he daily awaited her return to life. The body was only discovered after his death, housed in an upper room of his house that had been made into a shrine. The sect had died out by 1848.

Robert Burns wrote about the arrival of the Buchanites in southwest Scotland in 1784, in a letter to James Burness of Montrose. He confirmed that Mrs Buchan conferred the Holy Spirit upon her followers by breathing upon them and making what he further described as an 'indecent posture' at the same time. Accounts of the activities of Luckie Buchan and her group are barely credible. In 1786 the group, by now living in a barn near Dumfries, was persuaded by her to fast for forty days and nights because at the end of that period they would all ascend into heaven. The Man-Child put on clerical clothes, complete with preaching bands and white gloves, and began to walk through the fields looking for signs. The group made its way to a nearby rise, called Templand Hill, where they erected platforms. All, except Luckie Buchan, shaved their heads, leaving tufts of hair for the angels to grasp, and wore old slippers which could be easily kicked off as they rose. Luckie Buchan stood on a small platform, higher than the rest, while the assembled group sang hymns and shouted with joy. A sudden gust of wind swept across the hilltops and the light platforms, on which they were all swaying and jumping sensing that the angels were coming, collapsed and sent the Buchanites sprawling, but even so their faith in Mother and her pronouncements seems to have remained secure.

BULGARIAN CATHOLIC CHURCH

Christian communities have existed in the Balkan Peninsula from the very early centuries of the Christian era and an independent kingdom was established there during the seventh century. The country was Christianized in the ninth century, when its ruler, Prince Boris (852–907) had himself and his people baptized (possibly for political reasons) and accepted trained clergy from Constantinople to lay the foundations of Christianity in his country. Boris wanted his Church to be independent of both Rome and Constantinople because he thought that it would help to unify his people by promoting a distinctly Bulgarian culture. He tried, therefore, to play off Rome against Constantinople and began to negotiate with Rome for the acceptance of a Bulgarian patriarch. This move was not received sympathetically by Rome, Pope St Nicholas I sending two bishops and creating a metropolitan see in 872 at Okhrida, in present-day Macedonia. Unable to achieve his ambition from Rome, Boris turned to Constantinople and gave his allegiance there. In 1018 the Byzantine Emperor Basil II, the *Bulgar Slayer*, conquered the Bulgarians and the province of Okhrida became involved in the Byzantine schism with Rome in 1054.

Numerous struggles took place over the centuries, and in 1767, after four centuries of Ottoman rule that had placed the country under the direct administration of the Patriarch of Constantinople and a Greek clergy, there was a movement by some Bulgars to return to union with Rome. The first Bulgarian Catholic prelate, Joseph Sokolsky, was consecrated in 1859, but soon afterwards was abducted by the Russians, who saw themselves as the champions of the

EASTERN ORTHODOX CHURCH in the Balkans, and interned in Kiev for nearly twenty years. Despite this, the Bulgarian Catholic Church continued to grow and counted at its height some 80,000 faithful.

But the position was not maintained and by 1872, in spite of much activity from Rome to remedy the situation, three quarters of these ROMAN CATHOLIC converts had returned to Eastern Orthodoxy. The Church was persecuted during the communist years, with many clergy imprisoned and executed, but allowed to continue at a parochial level.

BULGARIAN EASTERN ORTHODOX CHURCH (DIOCESE OF NORTH AND SOUTH AMERICA)

The Bulgarian Eastern Orthodox Church came into existence in Detroit, Michigan, USA, in 1963 through a schism in the BULGARIAN ORTHODOX CHURCH in the USA. Many parish leaders, mainly from parishes that served Macedonian immigrants, refused to recognize the Patriarch of Bulgaria as head of the Church on account of the Church's sympathetic acceptance of communism. The parish leaders reconstituted themselves as the Bulgarian Eastern Orthodox Church and elected Archimandrite Cyril Yonchev, of Toledo, Ohio, as their new bishop. The RUSSIAN ORTHODOX CHURCH OUTSIDE RUSSIA obliged them by consecrating Cyril Yonchev. The headquarters of the Church is in Oregon, Ohio. The Church later took some independent groups of Bulgarians living in Melbourne, Australia, under its wing.

BULGARIAN EASTERN ORTHODOX DIOCESE OF THE USA, CANADA AND AUSTRALIA

A Church, under the jurisdiction of the Patriarch of Bulgaria, that serves immigrants of Bulgarian and Macedonian origin and has its headquarters in New York. There are many parishes in the USA and a further five in Australia, which grew from two original foundations in Melbourne, Victoria, and Adelaide, South Australia. The first Bulgarian Orthodox parish in the USA had been established in 1907 at Madison, Illinois, followed by a diocese that functioned autonomously from 1937 to the schism of 1963, which came about because some of the American parishes, which were providing for immigrants largely from Macedonia, refused to recognize the patriarch of Bulgaria as the head of the Church. This group re-formed as the BULGARIAN EASTERN ORTHODOX CHURCH (DIOCESE OF NORTH AND SOUTH AMERICA), while those parishes that accepted the Patriarch of Bulgaria as their head renamed themselves as the Bulgarian Eastern Orthodox Diocese of North and South America and Australia.

BULGARIAN ORTHODOX CHURCH

The Bulgarian Orthodox Church is one of the national Churches of the Eastern Orthodox Communion. There is evidence of Christianity near Burgas, on the Black Sea, as early as the second century, and despite many early invasions of the Balkan Peninsula, by hostile tribes such as the Goths, Huns and Slavs, Christian communities appear to have survived. Christianity became the national religion of the kingdom of Bulgaria in 865, a kingdom which at that time stretched from the Black Sea to the Adriatic, when Tsar, or Khan, Boris I was baptized by a Byzantine bishop. His attempts to establish an independent Bulgarian hierarchy were opposed by both Rome and Constantinople, from where an archbishop was sent to administer the Church in Bulgaria. When Boris I abdicated in 889, exchanging his palace for a monk's cell, his successor was his son, Symeon, who in a reversal of roles had to leave his monastery and assume the mantle of tsar. Before his abdication Boris had been working to replace Greek with Slavonic in the worship of the Church, and his son continued with this work until his death in 927. Symeon's proposal to appoint the archbishop from Constantinople as Patriarch of Bulgaria did not succeed in his lifetime, but a patriarchate was later established. In 1018 Bulgaria was attacked by Byzantium and the patriarchate destroyed. It was not until 1235, and with the aid of Rome, that it was re-established in the city of Trnovo (now Veliko Tŭrnovo) by Tsar Ivan Asen II. Trnovo fell again, to the Turks in 1393, and the patriarch, Eftimi, was sent into exile. For the next five hundred years the Turks controlled Bulgaria's civil life, with its Church life in the hands of the Greeks.

At the end of the nineteenth century a Bulgarian exarchate was established with permission from the Turkish sultan, but the path ahead was tortuous, for in 1872 the Bulgarian Church was declared schismatic by the Patriarch of Constantinople, Anthimos VI. The exarch and his followers were excommunicated and accused of phyletism, from the Greek '*phylon*', meaning 'race' – via the New Latin '*phylum*', meaning 'group' – a deviation involving the establishment of churches that admit only people of the same national group to their membership to the exclusion of all foreigners. This heresy was condemned by a synod at Constantinople in 1872 because of excessive nationalism that was growing amongst autonomous Churches within the Orthodox communion; it was particularly aimed at the Bulgars who wanted to elect only their own nationals to the episcopate.

This was the state of affairs in the Bulgarian Orthodox Church until 1945, when the Church was received back into full communion as an independent exarchate. The advent of communist rule in Bulgaria had a widespread effect on the Church. Religious instruction in schools was forbidden, civil marriages largely replaced church marriage services and while attendance at church services was not forbidden, it became difficult to practise as a Christian. The Church itself was not treated harshly, and money was provided by the state for the support of clergy and the maintenance of church buildings. Two seminaries were built during this time, at Vraca and Sofia, and priests continued to be trained.

In 1953 the patriarchate was restored by the Bulgarian Holy Synod, acting under pressure from Moscow, when they elected the Metropolitan of Plovdiv, Cyril Markov, as patriarch but without first consulting, or obtaining the approval of, the Ecumenical Patriarch of Constantinople. Official recognition was not granted until 1961. Trouble was to come again with the fall of communism in 1991, when a schism occurred in the Church, leading at one point to some unseemly episodes in the cathedral in Sofia. The problems concerned the validity of some hierarchical appointments that had been made by the state during the preceding years, but matters were resolved and now the patriarch of Constantinople and the Bulgarian state both officially recognize the Bulgarian Orthodox Church.

BWITI

Bwiti began as a form of African ancestor worship, helped by visions induced by the ritualized consumption of large amounts of the drug ibogaine, which is contained in the plant *Tabernantha iboga*. Ibogaine, which has anti-convulsant properties, affects the central nervous system and produces hallucinations. Both male and female initiates take the drug as a powder, which is placed inside bananas, and once swallowed it is said to 'break open the head', allowing the soul to leave the body through the top of the head and to travel to where the dead ancestors reside, where a *Bwiti*, or ancestor, will be seen. It is reckoned that initiates ingest nearly a hundred teaspoons of the shredded root in a single session, though it is apparently unusual for them to die as a consequence.

The Church that developed from this form of worship started in 1890 amongst the Fang of Gabon, a West African ethnolinguistic group, as a cult the purpose of which was to help people to avoid the consequences of witchcraft. It is now becoming Christianized, and puts a strong emphasis on Jesus Christ as the Divine Saviour. However, conventional baptism is replaced by initiation with the drug ibogaine, and to date there is no ecclesiastical hierarchy or sound administration for its 1200 congregations and 250,000 followers.

❖ Church of the Initiates

C

CAINITES

A small sect of GNOSTICS that regarded all those who had suffered in the Old Testament as worthy of veneration, since they had been punished and reviled by the God of the Old Testament, whom they held to be responsible for all the evil in the world and the enemy of truth whose laws should be reversed. By this topsy-turvy thinking, Cain, and not Abel, should be commended, for the good brother was now Cain, who was seen to have killed the evil one, Abel. Judas Iscariot also emerged as a hero for betraying Christ and leading to the crucifixion, resurrection and salvation of mankind. Cainites believed that Christ himself had secretly entrusted Judas with this betrayal, in order to guarantee that the crucifixion would take place in line with what the prophecies foretold, and thus lead to man's salvation. To honour Judas, the Cainites, who were also thought to have written the apocryphal Gospel of Judas Iscariot, instituted a special holiday.

An unorthodox way of regarding sexual license, which members practised, grew from their argument that they were under a holy duty to enjoy all of life's pleasures, as had the angels. Furthermore, at the same time they were to invoke the angels by name, for St Epiphanius wrote that the Cainites would say 'O, such-and-such angel, I am practising your deed'.

The sect, which was probably operating around the end of the second and start of the third century AD, was mentioned by both St Irenaeus (*c.* 130–200) and St Epiphanius (*c.* 315–403); it would appear to have died out by *c.* AD 225.

❖ Caianites

CALIXTINES

A fifteenth century Bohemian religious party of HUSSITES, who were so-named for their contention that the laity should receive communion in both kinds, both bread and wine; the name is taken from the Latin '*calix*' – a chalice. The founder of the Hussites, John Huss, had been incarcerated in prison prior to his execution in 1415 and during this time some of his followers, urged on by Jacob of Miez, began administering communion in both kinds to their parishioners, a practice with which Huss was in agreement but which he did not consider essential. After his execution the so-named Calixtines wanted to continue this practice and to make certain reforms in the Hussite movement. They formed a moderate party and affirmed before the council of Constance in 1415 their willingness to declare their loyalty and submission to the pope and to submit any differences between them and the council to arbitration by the University of Prague. This willing cooperation was met by the council's suspension of the University of Prague together with threats of action if this heresy was not brought to order and destroyed. A popular uprising followed and a new radical party of Hussites, known as the TABORITES, was formed. A short-lived union was made between the moderate Calixtines and the Taborites, which lasted until *c.* 1424.

The Calixtines, meanwhile, agreed in 1420 on what has become known as the *Four Articles of Prague*, which stated that:

1 Free preaching of the word of God could be in the vernacular.
2 Communion was to be administered in both kinds.
3 Priests were to be simple, apostolic pastors, owning no worldly possessions.
4 Public sins of priests, especially simony, were to be punished by temporal penalties.

It was believed that an agreement had been made with Rome, in the *Compacts of Prague* in 1433, over the use of the chalice in the communion of the laity, but in reality this did not have papal approval and was revoked by Pope Pius II (1458–64), in part prompting Bohemia's separation from the rest of the Church. A century later the Holy Roman Emperor Ferdinand I, who was also King of Bohemia, urged the Archbishop of Prague, Anton Brus, to attend the council of Trent (1562) as the Bohemian legate, to urge for permission for the Calixtines to receive communion under both kinds, in the hope that this would bring many of them back to the ROMAN CATHOLIC faith. Pope Pius IV granted the concession in 1564. Those who wished to receive both bread and wine were required to profess their belief in the real presence of Christ under both kinds and the priest administering communion had to use the revised formula 'The Body and Blood of Our Lord Jesus Christ', instead of the usual formula 'The Body of Our Lord Jesus Christ'. This was thought to be enough to bring to an end this long-lasting problem, but the Calixtines objected to another requirement, that their candidates for the priesthood must be examined in Roman Catholic theology. Plans to hold a synod in order to smooth over these differences and keep the Calixtines within the Roman Catholic Church were thwarted when the emperor died in 1564, to be succeeded by his son, Maximilian II, a weak man who was afraid to offend the Bohemian nobility, most of whom were PROTESTANT. The gulf between the Calixtines and the Roman Catholic Church grew wider and many Calixtines drifted into protestantism.

❖ Ultraquists; Utraquists

CALVARY HOLINESS CHURCH

The Calvary Holiness Church evolved from the International Holiness Mission, which had been founded as the Holiness Mission in London, England, in 1907 by David Thomas, a businessman and lay-preacher. With the development of missionary work in South Africa the foundation was renamed as the International Holiness Mission (IHM) in 1917. Four of its leaders, Clifford Filer, Maynard James, Leonard Ravenhill and Jack Ford, who had led an itinerant form of evangelism under the auspices of the IHM, organized congregations from amongst their converts. They formed the Calvary Holiness Church in 1934, a split they saw as inevitable because of the International Holiness Mission's refusal to allow *glossolalia*, or speaking in tongues, in the Church, although the founders themselves did not speak in tongues, or display any other charismatic gifts. The two groups remained in friendly contact with each other despite the split.

The Calvary Holiness Church was active, undertaking missionary work in Colombia, establishing a school at Oldham, Greater Manchester, and publishing a periodical, *The Flame*. In 1952 the International Holiness Mission merged with the CHURCH OF THE NAZARENE and three years later, in 1955, the Calvary Holiness Church followed their example. The merger benefited the Church of the Nazarene greatly. The International Holiness Mission brought with it some 22 congregations with over a thousand members and 36 missionaries at work in Africa, while the Calvary Holiness Church contributed a further 22 congregations, with about six hundred members.

CALVARY MISSIONARY CHURCH

The Calvary Missionary Church was formed in 1947 by George M. Lamsa, who migrated to the USA from Syria in 1917 and studied at both the Virginia Theological Seminary and the University of Pennsylvania, becoming a notable Bible translator. It was his claim that as both Jesus and the apostles spoke and wrote in Aramaic, the *Peschitta* Bible was the original version as it was written in that language, and not in Greek. He further contended that only by understanding the Aramaic language could certain idioms of the New Testament be understood. The Church, and its affiliated Aramaic Bible Society, was created to teach Lamsa's principles and distribute his many writings. His work was increasingly linked with the metaphysical movements in the USA in the 1960s.

CALVARY PENTECOSTAL CHURCH

This Church was founded in the USA, originally as a fellowship of some PENTECOSTAL ministers who were dissatisfied with the growing sectarianism of their Churches. The fellowship was established in Olympia, Washington, in 1931 and incorporated in 1932.

The clergy of the Church, both male and female, comprise ministers, elders and deacons. The polity of the Church is presbyterial, with a general meeting of all ministers and delegates from individual congregations annually. Baptism for infants is not practised, but a child may be dedicated to God and will later receive adult baptism by immersion. Home missions are undertaken, concerned particularly with the welfare of the aged, with foreign missions maintained in India and Brazil. Evangelism and the planting of new churches are ensuring a slow, but steady, growth and there are currently 25 congregations with 9000 adult members.

❖ Calvary Pentecostal Church, Inc.

CALVINIST (also CALVINISM, CALVINISTIC)

The term describes the system of beliefs or doctrines taught by John Calvin (1509–64). Calvin was born in Noyon, France, and trained as a lawyer, but through his father, a notary public employed by the Bishop of Noyon, John was given two ecclesiastical benefices. He converted to the PROTESTANT cause through his contacts with protestants in Paris, where he had gone after the death of his father in 1531. Calvin was forced to leave the city in 1533 on account of the strong anti-protestant feeling of the time and he travelled widely in France, Switzerland and Italy. By then he had resigned his ecclesiastical benefices.

Calvin arrived in Geneva in 1536, where William Farel (1489–1565), a fellow French reformer, prevailed upon him to help establish protestantism there, but both Calvin and Farel were expelled from Geneva. From then until 1538 Calvin lived in Strasbourg, where he became a pupil of Martin Bucer and pastor of a French refugee congregation in the city. Farel, following his expulsion from Geneva, moved to Neuchatel and continued to collaborate with Calvin. Eventually, with a change of government in Geneva, Calvin was able to return to that city in 1541 and he remained there for the rest of his life.

Calvin's theology and teachings, which soon spread through his writings and correspondence, were strongly based upon the Bible, which he understood to be man's infallible rule of faith and practice. His doctrinal position was Trinitarian and he declared that Adam's sin resulted in man's total depravity, which meant that man cannot do any good without God's special grace; this is given only to those elected by God to be saved. He taught, therefore, that since only the *elect* have been chosen to be saved, then the atonement by Jesus must be limited. Calvin taught that there were only two sacraments, of baptism and the Lord's Supper; he also taught that Christ was present in the sacrament of the Lord's Supper only to faith.

Calvin's doctrines were partially, and now generally felt to be inadequately, summarized as the *Five Points of Calvinism* in the *Canons of the Synod of Dort* (1618–19). These are the total depravity of man, the unconditional election of the saved, limited atonement, irresistible grace and the perseverance of saints. Calvinism spread throughout Germany, Holland, Hungary, Transylvania, France, the British Isles, America and many other parts of the world.

CAMERONIANS

A term used to describe those who rejected the 1690 settlement of the established CHURCH OF SCOTLAND in the reign of William and Mary. The name is derived from that of their former leader, Richard Cameron (*c.* 1648–80), a convert from the SCOTTISH EPISCOPAL CHURCH to the PRESBYTERIAN cause. Cameron travelled to Rotterdam in 1678, where he was ordained in a non-episcopal service the following year. He returned to Scotland and conducted an open-air style of ministry.

Together with others, Cameron composed the *Sanquhar Declaration*, which refused allegiance to Charles II and encouraged others to refuse to recognize the king. Cameron and some of his followers were ambushed and killed by royal troops at Aird's Moss in Ayrshire in 1680.

CAMISARDS

A group of fanatical French PROTESTANTS prominent in the Cévennes district of south-east France at the start of the eighteenth century. Their name probably came from the black shirt, or *camise*, worn by members of the sect as a disguise when on night raids.

The Camisards represented a revolt against the religious suppression of the time, when the *Edict of Nantes* (1685), which protected the principle of religious tolerance, was revoked by King Louis XIV. There have been several theories concerning the origins of the movement, which may have had its roots with the ALBIGENSIANS, and was certainly fuelled by the apocalyptic preaching and hysterical utterances of leaders such as Du Serre, an old CALVINIST from Dieulefit, and the writings of French Calvinists such as Peter Jurieu, who, whilst serving as minister at the Walloon Church at Rotterdam in 1681 came to believe that Calvinism would be restored in France according to his interpretation of the prophecies of the Apocalypse. As a consequence of the revocation of the Edict of Nantes and the oppression that followed, Jurieu argued that revolution against the secular power was justified because Louis XVI had used military force to coerce religious belief.

Recruitment to the sect was successful and at one time it numbered some 3000 men, divided into small bands in order to wage guerrilla warfare. The zeal of the Camisards is evident in the fact that it took an army of more than 60,000 to suppress them. Recruits were trained to be 'prophetically inspired', with four levels of enlightenment attainable. After a long period of trial, elevation to the next level of enlightenment was marked by a ceremony of exsufflation, when the candidate was breathed, or blown upon, by leaders of the group. The initiate had also to memorize long biblical tracts and practice various physical and contortionist exercises that served to induce a trance-like state.

Although the Camisards regarded themselves as being in some sort of union with the French Calvinists, they were soon to be disabused of this idea by the synod of Nîmes (1715), which made clear that Camisard teaching was at variance with that of the Calvinists. The Camisards fled to England, where they were ridiculed when they attempted to found a *mystical phalanx* in London. Some of the members separated from the main group to form the French Prophets. One of the refugees, Elie Marion, who was given to false miracles and inflammatory writings, was forced to leave England. Louis XIV declared the sect extinct in the year of his death, 1715.

❖ French Prophets

CAMPBELLITES

A nickname applied to those congregations who left the BAPTIST tradition and were gathered together by the father and son team, Thomas and Alexander Campbell, who in 1832 formed the Christian Churches, which finally became known as the CHRISTIAN CHURCH (DISCIPLES OF CHRIST).

Alexander Campbell (1788–1866) was a native of Antrim who studied in Glasgow and followed his father, Thomas, to America in 1809, where he was ordained in his father's Secessionist sect. He prospered as a farmer and is known as a writer of religious tracts. In 1841 he founded Bethany College in West Virginia.

CATHOLIC APOSTOLIC CHURCH

This denomination arose at the time of the French Revolution and the rise of Napoleon, which had created an interest in unfulfilled prophecy and the second coming of Christ (REVELATION 20). In

Scotland, in 1828, a minister of the PRESBYTERIAN Church, the Reverend John McLeod Campbell (1800–72), had become aware of a growing sequence of supernatural happenings in his parish of Rhu, north west of Helensburgh, which were followed in the early 1830s by outbreaks of the charismatic gifts of healing and *glossolalia,* or speaking in tongues, in the parish of Port Glasgow.

News of these happenings soon spread throughout the British Isles and was well received by a group composed of both clergy and laity who, since 1826, had been in the habit of meeting at the home of a wealthy banker and member of parliament, Henry Drummond of Albury Park, near Guildford, Surrey, who had founded a professorship of political economy at Oxford University in 1825. Their interest lay in the investigation of charismatic gifts and it was from this group that the early ministries of the Catholic Apostolic Church were later formed.

At the same time, Edward Irving (1792–1834), a minister of the CHURCH OF SCOTLAND in London from 1822, had become convinced that the organized Church was facing a bleak future, citing as evidence the structure of the ministry which lacked the offices of apostle, prophet and evangelist and which he regarded as a sure sign that the Holy Spirit had deserted the Church. So imbued was he with this idea that, on one occasion in 1824, Irving preached that the organized Church was Babylon. He was fortunate to have the support of an assistant probationer minister, A. J. Scott, who shared his beliefs in the restoration of the charismatic gifts of the Holy Spirit and the imminence of the second coming (REVELATION 20). For this stand, in 1831 Scott lost his licence to preach.

Irving, like John McLeod Campbell, held to the view that Christ's atonement was for everyone. When news of the Scottish charismatic happenings of 1830 reached him, Irving's millennial interests were reinforced (REVELATION 20). His preaching by now had taken him away from what was expected from one of its ministers by the Church of Scotland. Amongst other divergences, Irving preached that Christ had a corrupt human nature and was only saved from personal sin through the indwelling of the Holy Spirit. This was sufficient to warrant a warning from the general assembly of the Church of Scotland that he was in danger of being deposed and would lose his licence to preach.

There were further outbreaks of *glossolalia* in 1831 during prayer meetings at Irving's church in Regent's Square, London. When another such episode happened, this time during a public service, it aroused much bad feeling for Irving as well as a great deal of alarm in the Church. Rumours grew unchecked when further manifestations of charismatic gifts appeared, together with a suggestion about the possible raising of the dead in preparation for the second coming and the start of the millennial kingdom (REVELATION 20), and Irving was accused of teaching heresy. Together with some eight hundred followers, he left the Church.

The followers were now ready to form a new religious body, based on the early apostolic Church, with the restoration of apostles, prophets, evangelists and pastors (Eph. 4:11–14). Irving's association with the Drummond group at Albury Park now became more substantial. In 1832 two members of the group, Henry Drummond and John Bate Cardale, were designated as apostles by one of the prophets and by 1835 a full college of twelve apostles had been assembled. The apostles held their first council in London the following year and issued memoranda to the bishops of the CHURCH OF ENGLAND and to the monarch, William IV, stating their mission, which was to include missionary work in Europe and America with the apostles designated to individual areas. The Catholic Apostolic Church was born.

The doctrine of the Church was based on the Bible, which was regarded as the supreme and infallible source of God's word, the acceptance of the usual three creeds (Apostles', Athanasian and Nicene) and the seven sacraments. The members also believed in the restoration by prophecy of the fourfold ministry of apostles, prophets, evangelists and pastors, who were chosen by the Holy Spirit speaking through the prophets. The local apostle ordained the other ministers, the angels (or bishops), priests, deacons and deaconesses.

In England, a magnificent church was built in Gordon Square, London, in 1853. The development of Tractarianism in England, with its strong ROMAN CATHOLIC leanings, probably influenced the liturgical form designed by the Church which is a mixture of Roman Catholic, Eastern Orthodox and ANGLICAN styles. Lights and incense played an important part in Church services, in order to set an atmosphere conducive to the heightening of the senses. The ritual of *sealing* was included in the services, which was to ensure that those who received it would become part of the 144,000 *elect* who would not have to endure the coming tribulation (Rev. 7:3f.).

The Catholic Apostolic Church also made great advances on the continent of Europe, especially in the Netherlands and Germany, but with the death of the last apostle, in 1901, and the non-appearance of the second coming, which according to the Church's teaching would happen during the lifetime of the chosen apostles, interest seeped away. There are still adherents in the USA, and also in various parts of Europe and Australia, but with no clergy surviving the numbers are dwindling. Irving himself was never selected as an apostle, and although his name is often used as an alternative for the Catholic Apostolic Church, many members, who claimed that he was not their founder but only a forerunner, repudiated this title. Irving died in 1834, just after his deposition from the Regent's Square church.

❖ Irvingites

CATHOLIC APOSTOLIC CHURCH OF BRAZIL

The Catholic Apostolic Church of Brazil dates from 1945 when it was founded, following a schism from the ROMAN CATHOLIC CHURCH, by Bishop Carlos Duarte Costa (1881–1961); Carlos Costa had been the Roman Catholic Bishop of Botucatu, Brazil, and had retired from the Church in 1937. In 1945 he began to make a series of attacks on the papacy for its supposed alliance with fascism and this brought about his excommunication from Rome. He then founded his schismatic Church at Belo Horizonte, in Minas Gerais State.

Costa consecrated a priest, Salomão Ferraz, who had previously founded the Free Catholic Church of Brazil in 1936. Following his consecration, Ferraz was able to bring episcopal government into his Church. Ferraz was later reconciled with the Roman Catholic Church, but the Church he founded continues to develop in Brazil and now has around twenty congregations.

Bishop Costa introduced the liturgy in Portuguese into the Catholic Apostolic Church of Brazil, and abolished priestly celibacy and the sacrament of reconciliation. The Church continues to flourish, organized into 12 dioceses with some 25 bishops and in excess of 1 million adult members.

CATHOLIC CHURCH OF GOD

This small American Church owes its origin to Steven A. Kochones. Kochones was a layman who had left the GREEK ORTHODOX CHURCH to join one of the independent ASSEMBLIES OF GOD, in which he was ordained as a minister in 1956. By 1969, Kochones felt inspired to found a Church, originally PENTECOSTAL in ethos but gradually assuming elements of both Judaism and ROMAN CATHOLICISM. This was known as the Church of God in the Lord Jesus Christ, and later as the Catholic Church of God, with its headquarters in Pasadena, California. Kochones was consecrated as a bishop by Bishop Baxter of the Orthodox Church of America, a small, independent Orthodox Church, in Little Rock, Arkansas, which gave him the privilege of intercommunion with the Orthodox Church of America. One of the more distinctive features of the Catholic Church of God is the celebration of the Eucharist at sundown on Friday evenings, preceded by the lighting of lights; further services are held on Saturdays and Sundays. The Church has several hundred members and is involved in mission work in Mexico and elsewhere in the USA.

CELESTIAL CHURCH OF CHRIST

An indigenous African Church, founded in present-day Benin in 1947 by the Reverend Oshoffa, a METHODIST layman who believed that he had received the power of the Holy Ghost and had become a preacher. Oshoffa became convinced that this was followed by the vision of an angel who commanded him to go out and teach the gospel message. He took his mission of preaching and teaching to Nigeria and from there it spread, until today there are well over 1,000 congregations with nearly 2 million adult members in 20 countries.

The Celestial Church of Christ affirms the Christian creeds and believes that Jesus Christ, as the Son of God, has completed his work of redemption. They also believe in the infallibility of the scriptures and in the Holy Spirit as the enabling power of believers. There are five types of ministers in the Church, pastor, prophet, evangelist, shepherd and teacher, all of whom may conduct the worship services. These consist of prayers, hymns, Bible readings, sermons, offerings, the sacrament of Holy Communion, which is celebrated only occasionally, baptism and marriage. Converts who are in polygamous marriages are not required to abandon any of their wives, and the clergy may also be polygamous. Hymns are considered to be of great importance, since it is believed that they have been composed through inspiration by the Holy Spirit. During worship services a believer will remove his shoes, kneel and bow his head three times, touching the ground with his forehead. The use of white robes and the carrying of palm fronds distinguish the lay members of the Church; ministers wear more colourful robes.

When a believer is received into the

Church he kneels before a bucket of water, holding a candle that is lighted by the minister who says prayers of forgiveness and sanctification. The convert then bathes, using the water in the bucket, and embarks on a programme of Christian instruction. All members are baptized, which is mandatory even for those converting from another Christian faith community. Prophecy plays its part in the Church with some of the members thought to be visionaries, dreamers and hearers of divine voice who have the duty to reveal to others what is believed to be the will of God.

❖ Heavenly Christianity Church

CELTIC CHURCH

This is the Church that existed in the British Isles before St Augustine's mission to evangelize the land in 597, and was, for a while, in competition with the Anglo-Roman Catholic Church. It is almost certain that the Celtic Church was founded in the second or third century by Roman and Gallic missions which sent three bishops to the Synod of Arles (314) and representatives to the Council of Arminum (359). A Briton who is thought to have been consecrated as a bishop by Pope St Siricius (384–99), towards the end of the fourth century, went on to pursue his apostolate among the Scottish southern Picts of Galloway and may have dedicated a stone church at Whithorn, in present-day Dumfries and Galloway.

The Pelagian heresy of the fifth century infected the Celtic Church and prompted Sts Germanus of Auxerre and Lupus of Troyes to travel to England both to eradicate this heresy and also to give impetus to the development of monasticism in the west of the country, in present-day Cornwall and Wales. Celtic Christianity grew, its distinctive character finding problems in adapting to the Roman brand of Christianity introduced into the islands by St Augustine, but after the Synod of Whitby (663–4) there was a gradual acceptance of the new usages. The three principal disagreements lay with the instructions about the form of monastic tonsure to be used, the computation of Easter and some liturgical issues concerning both baptism and liturgical changes to be observed in the celebration of the Mass.

The form of tonsure, known as the St John Tonsure, favoured by the Celtic clergy could be of two styles; the first consisted of shaving the head in front along an imaginary line drawn from ear to ear with the rest of the hair allowed to grow, while the second style allowed the front of the head to be shaved back to form a semi-circular line, again from ear to ear, with the rest of the hair left to grow naturally. St Patrick is known to have opposed the Celtic styles of tonsure and the matter was settled by the Fourth Council of Toledo (633), when the Celtic styles were abolished in favour of the Roman style, of either a completely shaved head (*St Paul's Tonsure*), or a shaved circle on the top of the head (*St Peter's Tonsure*).

The date of Easter was a matter of concern. At the Council of Arles (314) it was suggested that Easter would be celebrated on the same date throughout the Church, a date usually announced annually after the reading of the gospel on the feast of the Epiphany. The Celtic Church was not willing to make such an adjustment and it was not until the Synod of Whitby (663–4) that a decision was finally reached. King Oswy, who presided over this debate, decided in favour of the Roman argument; he is reported to have said that he would rather be on good terms with 'the keeper of heaven's gate', than with the Celtic tradition. Despite this decision, however, it was several centuries before the Celtic Easter was fully abandoned.

On the matter of baptism and liturgical practice, it was felt that the Celtic Church should accept the current Roman practice of administering confirmation immediately after baptism, and any irregularities in the celebration of the Mass should be corrected.

At one time the Celtic Church extended throughout the British Isles, but the Saxon invasions in the fifth century submerged Celtic culture in England and drove it into what is known as the Celtic fringe, those parts of the islands in the west of England, and in Wales, Scotland and Ireland. Some modern Christian groups, notably the Iona community in Scotland, claim to have revived Celtic Christianity, with its strong reverence for nature; there are also neo-pagan groups that make the same claim, though these have no Christian pedigree.

CHALDEAN CATHOLIC CHURCH

The Chaldean Catholics are descendants of Nestorians (ASSYRIAN CHURCH OF THE EAST) who are now in communion with the ROMAN CATHOLIC CHURCH. This Church, whose roots lie in the Assyrian Church, is to be found predominantly in Iraq, Iran and the Lebanon. The Church was united with Rome intermittently since 1551 and more consistently since 1830, which date marks the establishment of the Chaldean Catholic patriarchate by Pope Pius VIII. George Hormizd was elected as the first Chaldean Catholic Patriarch of Babylon.

When St Thomas the Apostle embarked on his journey to India he is said to have delegated St Addai to preach at Seleucia-Ctesiphon, near present-day Baghdad, and sent St Mari, a convert from Mazdeism, to Nisibis (now Nusaybin) on the Turkish–Syrian border. St Mari appointed St Aggai as the first bishop of Seleucia-Ctesiphon, a place reputed to be the burial place of the prophet Muhammad's barber.

When the Council of Ephesus (431) condemned the Patriarch of Constantinople, Nestorius and many Persian and east Syrian Christians refused to accept the condemnation and, with protection from the Persian rulers, the heretical Nestorian Church was founded. At first this schismatic Church went from strength to strength until, at the end of the fourteenth century, the Tartars under Tamerlane (1369–1405) laid waste to Asia and with it much of the Nestorian Church.

The remnants of the Church survived, driven into the mountains of Hakkari in Turkey, and into South India. By the mid-fifteenth century the office of Nestorian patriarch had become hereditary because the practice had gradually arisen by which a nephew of the previous patriarch was appointed to his office. This practice was challenged in 1551 when a strong party within the Church, which was uneasy about the hereditary nature of the office of patriarch and challenged the automatic succession, put a monk, John Sulaka, forward as a candidate for the office. Sulaka went to Jerusalem and made his submission to the Pope, who consecrated him as a bishop in 1552 and within a year invested him as patriarch, to be known as John Simon VIII Sulaka. The Church was now split into two factions, with those Nestorians who became Catholics known as Chaldeans and others persisting as non-Catholics. There were further unions with Rome, in 1672, 1771 and 1778, and finally, in 1830 from which time the link has been unbroken.

The Chaldean Catholic Church is administered from the patriarchal Diocese of Baghdad, with four archdioceses and seven dioceses. Doctrinally, the Church ascribes fully to the Roman Catholic faith, but with some liturgical differences. In baptism the child receives two anointings, the first a pouring of water over the whole body followed by three pourings of water over the head while the child is seated in the water. This is immediately followed by confirmation, with another anointing, this time between the eyes, with chrism.

The Church has retained the ancient east Syrian Liturgy of Addai and Mari, which is celebrated in the Syriac language or in the local vernacular, and takes place in a sanctuary containing the altar set against the east wall, enclosed by high walls and with a six-feet wide, curtained door. The baptistery is usually to be found on the southern side of the sanctuary in Chaldean churches. Leavened bread, with a little added salt, is used in the liturgy and communion is given to the faithful by intinction. The clergy wear vestments consisting of an alb, cuffs, stole and girdle, and a chasuble resembling a western-style cope, with bishops adopting western-style pontificals.

CHARISMATIC EPISCOPAL CHURCH OF NORTH AMERICA

In the America of the 1970s, many clergy from different Christian traditions felt that there should be a convergence movement that would bring together liturgical and sacramental groups as well as evangelicals and charismatics. The clergy who were pressing for this convergence issued what came to be called *The Chicago Call*, which called upon Christians to rediscover their roots in historical Christianity. With this in mind, A. Randolph Adler was consecrated as the first bishop and primate, and later patriarch, of the Charismatic Episcopal Church in June 1992, by the CATHOLIC APOSTOLIC CHURCH OF BRAZIL, which had been founded as a schism from the ROMAN CATHOLIC CHURCH in 1945.

The polity of the Church is episcopal, administered by the patriarch's council and an international college of archbishops, who confer and seek consensus on denominational issues. Below this council each province operates under its own archbishop and each diocese under its own bishop, with each parish administered by a rector and his council.

The Church affirms the Apostles' and Nicene creeds and places emphasis on the evidence of the gifts of the Holy Spirit that are imparted to believers for service and witness. Liturgically, use is made of the *Book of Common Prayer* (1979) as the standard of worship, but other liturgical forms, principally Roman Catholic and Eastern Orthodox, are permitted with the diocesan bishop's approval. Open communion is allowed, but restricted to those who are baptized and who can affirm their belief in the real presence. Tithing is expected of the members. The seven sacraments are administered, with ordination restricted to men. Recognition is also made of the fivefold charismatic ministries, according to Ephesians 4:11–13, which can manifest themselves in both the clergy and the laity of every parish.

The headquarters of the Charismatic

Episcopal Church of North America is at San Clemente, California, from where the patriarch exercises authority over a growing communicant membership throughout the USA, Central America, Europe, Asia and Africa.

❖ The Charismatic Episcopal Church; The International Communion of the Charismatic Episcopal Church

CHARISMATIC MOVEMENT (also CHARISMATICS)

A late twentieth-century religious movement whose participants believe that the more spectacular gifts of the Holy Spirit, such as healing, prophecy and *glossolalia*, or speaking in tongues, have been restored to the Church, usually with end-time significance.

CHELCIC BRETHREN

The founder of the Chelcic Brethren, Peter Chelcicky (*c.* 1390–1460), was a layman who became much influenced by the Archbishop of Prague, John Rokycana, whose eloquent preaching and influence helped his nephew, Gregory 'the patriarch', establish the foundations of the Bohemian Brethren (which later became the UNITAS FRATRUM) in Kunwald, on the north-east border of Bohemia. Interestingly, the teachings and writings of John Wycliffe also had a profound impact on Chelcicky. Chelcicky preached against the secular power of the ROMAN CATHOLIC CHURCH and advocated a return to a simpler, less worldly, Christian life.

CHILDREN OF GOD

The Children of God (COG) was part of the JESUS PEOPLE movement in the USA. David Berg (aka Moses David), a one-time public relations man for the American Soul Clinic (a PENTECOSTAL missionary organization that had been founded in 1947), moved to California in 1967 as leader of a teenage fellowship group, the Light Club. This became the nucleus of the COG. Berg claimed that he had received a revelation that California would be struck by an earthquake and he and his group left the area, spending eight months wandering the south-west before settling in Los Angeles in 1970. A community was formed, ascetic in nature and governed by a strict code of discipline.

Controversy was quickly to appear. Although the COG was much criticized by other Jesus People groups some of their leaders broke away to join the new group, bringing their followers with them. Some parents, anxious that their young sons and daughters were being held against their wishes and subjected to various brainwashing and other techniques, had them kidnapped from the communes and counter-brainwashed. Several lawsuits followed. The COG, however, continued to prosper and by 1971 was established throughout the USA, with overseas communes and missions established in 72 countries.

The doctrine of the group is uncertain as it changed in line with Berg's further revelations. Worship is informal, with the sacraments administered only at odd intervals. The group has a strong belief that the end of the world is imminent and names America as the *Whore of Babylon* whose judgement is near (Rev. 17 and 18). The writings of Berg, published as the *Mo Letters*, outline some of his beliefs and show great hostility to established religion. At one time the Church allegedly used unconventional means of evangelism, but these have since been abandoned. The group is now known as *The Family*.

❖ The Family; The Family of Love

CHINESE CHRISTIAN CHURCH

A PRESBYTERIAN missionary from the London Missionary Society, which had been evangelizing in Malacca since 1814, founded the Chinese Christian Church in 1881. This missionary activity had been largely restricted to the east coast of the Malaysian peninsula where there were many immigrant Chinese workers, although many of these had already become Presbyterian before they settled in the area, having been evangelized by missionaries in their homeland since 1843.

The Church underwent a massive increase in numbers between 1960–70 and is still showing a gradual, but steady, growth. A schism within the Chinese Christian Church resulted in the emergence of the BIBLE PRESBYTERIAN CHURCH as a fully indigenous group. The Chinese Christian Church operates within the PROTESTANT and REFORMED tradition.

❖ Presbyterian Church of Singapore and Malaysia

CHINESE CHRISTIAN THREE-SELF MOVEMENT

The invasion of China by Japan in the 1930s resulted in the departure of some western missionaries from the country and those that remained there until 1941 then either left or were imprisoned by the Japanese occupation forces. With the end of the Second World War there was an influx of missionaries to China who, because of their imperialist connections, were subject to a vigorous attack by the communist regime. While the Chinese constitution of 1954 affirmed freedom of religious belief, at the same time it allowed the state to oppose religion on the grounds that it was based on class oppression. The only relief that the Churches could claim was their right to freedom, which could only be invoked if a Church freed itself of all signs of so-called imperialism.

This meant that the *Three-Selfs* had to be put into operation by the Church. These were Self-Support, Self-Government and Self-Propagation. The Three-Self Movement was led by Mr Y. T. Wu and came into being in 1950. The purpose of the movement was to enforce all non-ROMAN CATHOLIC Churches to unite in a process of cleansing which could be brought about by attendance at denunciation meetings and communist study sessions.

Those Churches and their congregations that were able to meet the criteria of the Three-Self Movement were able for a time to have Sunday morning worship sessions, but by the mid-1960s, when all seminaries were closed with the exception of one in Nanking (which was closed in 1966, the year that marked the start of the Great Proletarian Cultural Revolution), all visible forms of religion were effectively eliminated.

There was some thaw in the climate of religious intolerance in China as a result of the Nineteenth Party Congress in 1969, and with the death of Mao Tse-tung in 1976 and the end of the Cultural Revolution there has been a gradual easing of restrictions on Christians. At present the Chinese Three-Self Churches have an official figure of 27,000 congregations with an adult membership of around 4 million.

❖ Chinese Christian Three-Self Patriotic Church

CHRIST APOSTOLIC CHURCH

The origins of the Christ Apostolic Church lie in Africa, and in an independent PENTECOSTAL group formed in Nigeria in 1917–18 in the face of the virulent influenza pandemic, which lost the earlier established mission Churches in the area much of their credibility; they were seen by many Africans to be impotent and unable to save their people from the disease which was taking its heavy toll in western Africa. Yoruba speakers, who constitute a large proportion of the people of Nigeria, formed prayer and healing groups and some of these were constituted in 1920 as the Faith Tabernacle, and later, in 1947, as the Christ Apostolic Church. Another Church which emerged from these prayer and healing groups was the Cherubim and Seraphim Movement, which was later to undergo many schisms resulting in the formation of around two hundred other Churches.

The Christ Apostolic Church itself underwent several schisms, one led by a pastor of the Church, and another forming, in 1953, the Gospel Faith Mission, with its headquarters at Ibadan claiming over six hundred congregations. Some Yoruba-speaking members, feeling that they were being discriminated against, formed the African Apostolic Church of Nigeria and Benin. The Church is Pentecostal in tradition, accepting the Bible as being literally infallible and with a strong belief in the manifestations of the spirit, which are often accompanied by emotional outbursts, hand clapping, singing, jerking, trances and *glossolalia*, or speaking in tongues; there is also a strong belief in the second coming (REVELATION 20). Two ordinances are observed: baptism by immersion and the Lord's Supper. The theme of original sin and the need for man's salvation through Christ's atonement are constant elements in preaching. The Christ Apostolic Church has been present in the USA since 1985.

CHRIST CATHOLIC CHURCH (DIOCESE OF BOSTON)

This small, but growing, American denomination had its beginnings in 1965 when a disillusioned CONGREGATIONALIST minister, Karl Pruter, found that his attempt to develop a Free Catholic movement within the recently merged Evangelical and Congregational Church, with which he was associated, was not going to work.

He resigned his parish and in 1965 sought the help of Archbishop Peter Zurawetsky of the Christ Catholic Exarchate of the Americas and the Eastern Hemisphere, who ordained Pruter and encouraged him to establish a parish in Boston's Back Bay area. In 1967 Archbishop Zurawetsky consecrated Pruter as bishop of the Diocese of Boston and in 1968 this Diocese was granted independent status as the Christ Catholic Church (Diocese of Boston).

Pruter moved to New Mexico, where he worked with Native Americans and established four parishes, went on to Chicago in 1975 and finally moved to the Ozarks area in Missouri where, in his retirement, he continued to work with the rural poor.

The clergy of this denomination, who may be either married or celibate, are self-supporting and work mainly with the poor and with Native Americans, students, patients in nursing homes and those outcast from society, especially the disenfranchised.

CHRIST TRUTH LEAGUE

A popular American New Thought (NEW AGE) leader, H. B. Jeffrey, founded the Christ Truth League in the 1930s. The writer of several New Thought books, Jeffrey's beliefs were close to those of Emma Curtis Hopkins, a Christian Scientist (CHURCH OF CHRIST SCIENTIST) who had founded the Emma C. Hopkins Association and the Christian Science Theological Seminary for the training of future New Thought leaders.

CHRIST'S SANCTIFIED HOLY CHURCH

In 1887, Joseph B. Lynch, an American METHODIST lay preacher, became convinced that holiness was necessary to achieve salvation. In the HOLINESS tradition, within which the Methodist Church was found, a person who was born again was said to be justified because he had accepted Jesus as his personal saviour; that person was then thought of as growing in grace and his perfection, or holiness, was endorsed by the experience that was called the second blessing, or sanctification, after which he would remain holy as long as the faith was maintained. Joseph B. Lynch had received that second blessing and he preached about it.

The Methodists, however, were becoming divided over this issue of holiness. A schism developed in 1892 and with it the establishment of Christ's Sanctified Holy Church. Soon after its foundation, some members of the Church began to evangelize amongst the coloured people in West Lake, Louisiana, where in 1904 they organized what was subsequently called Colored Church South, soon changed to be known as Christ's Sanctified Holy Church Colored – the word 'Colored' was later removed.

To become a member of the Church it is necessary to begin as a probationer. Only when the probationer has been justified, or born again, is full membership accorded. Doctrinally, there is a traditional understanding of the Trinity and a strong emphasis on the process of sanctification. The usual ordinances of baptism and the Lord's Supper are not recognized. A modest dress code is indicated for the members, with no gold jewellery to be worn. The use of, or trading in, alcohol and tobacco is forbidden. The organization of the Church is centred on a five-member board, which ordains all clergy, male and female, as deacons, deaconesses and ministers. There is an annual conference, district conferences and an annual Sunday school convention. The Church is found in the eastern and south-eastern states of the USA.

CHRISTADELPHIANS

This declining denomination was started in America in 1844 by an English medical doctor and CONGREGATIONALIST, John Thomas (1805–71), who had been shipwrecked whilst en route to America. He vowed that, should he survive, the rest of his life would be dedicated to religion. Survive he did, and on reaching America he left the Congregational Church and joined the Disciples of Christ, also known as the CAMPBELLITES. But his study and knowledge of the Hebrew prophecies and the Book of Revelation persuaded Thomas that he should leave the Disciples of Christ and form his own Church, returning to what he regarded as original New Testament beliefs, for he regarded the mainstream forms of Christianity to be 'an apostacy'.

In 1849 John Thomas published a book, *Elphis Israel (Hope of Israel)*, in which he argued that the world had entered into the last days, before the second coming of Christ (REVELATION 20), and Israel would be restored to the Jews. Thomas returned to Britain several times, preaching and converting many people and founding groups of Christadelphians both here and in America. The name *Christadelphian* came into being at the time of the American Civil War (1861–65), when the followers of Thomas needed to organize themselves along formal lines in order to justify their objections to military service.

His Congregational heritage persuaded Thomas against setting up a central authority for his Church and he favoured instead local autonomous congregations, each responsible for its own members, with a fellowship between these congregations based on biblical faith. Doctrinally, Thomas rejected both the incarnation and the doctrine of the Trinity, for which, he claimed, there was no biblical basis at all, asserting that the doctrine was simply an invention of the fourth- and fifth-century Church Fathers. He further maintained that the Bible taught us that Jesus Christ was not God the Son, the second person of the Trinity, but the son of God, not pre-existent but born of Mary by the Holy Spirit, whom he considered to be a power through whom the Father worked and not as the third person of the Trinity. Thomas required his followers to be rebaptized, to accept the Bible as the absolute word of God and to eschew all man-made creeds.

The Christadelphians are strongly millenarianist (REVELATION 20), believing that we are in the last days, that the Jews will play an important part in the end time and that modern political events were prophesied in the Bible. As an example, the Christadelphians claim that Jeremiah 31:10 anticipates the establishment of the state of Israel in 1948, while Luke 21:24 refers to the retaking of Jerusalem by the Jews at the end of the Six Day War in 1967.

Christadelphian doctrine teaches that eternal life, for the saved and resurrected, will be spent on earth following Christ's return, for they do not believe in the immortality of the soul, nor in heaven and hell. The unsaved, and that includes the unconverted and those who are infants and imbeciles, will not be resurrected to have an existence in Christ's theocracy. The government of the world from Jerusalem and the land of Canaan will, they believe, last for a thousand years.

The polity of the Church is completely congregational, its members electing one another to serve as either managing, presiding or preaching brethren for periods of tenure normally of no more than three years. Each congregation is called an *ecclesia* and is the principal unit of government in the Church.

Members usually meet in each other's homes, or in a rented hall, with the Lord's Supper, or *Breaking of Bread*, celebrated on Sundays. Baptism, which is by immersion, is an essential requirement for membership. Women are not permitted to have a public role in the group, nor to preach. The members are pacifist, non-voting and non-political and they are not expected to serve on juries or to join trade unions; close friendship with non-members is actively discouraged.

Towards the end of the nineteenth century a dispute broke out in the UK concerning what was called resurrectional responsibility, and this led to the formation of two groups, the Amended Christadelphians, who believe that every one who has died believing in Christ, those who are called the *saved*, will be resurrected at the end time, and the Unamended Christadelphians, who believe that all will be resurrected, whether faithful to Christ or not, and all will be judged, with some of the risen, the wrong-doers, denied eternal life.

The Church now admits that premature predictions of the second coming (Revelation 20), which it claimed would take place in 1868 (later revised to 1910), were incorrect and that the exact date of the event cannot be known. The denomination is now in decline, but can still be found in many countries throughout the world.

❖ Brothers of Christ; Thomasites

CHRISTIAN AND MISSIONARY ALLIANCE

A growing denomination that was founded in the USA by a former Presbyterian minister, Albert Benjamin Simpson (1844–1919) of New York, who experienced a healing conducted by an Episcopal minister, Charles Cullis, at Old Orchard, Maine. Simpson subsequently left the Presbyterian Church, feeling that he was called to evangelize those who were outside any Church.

To this end, in 1881, he formed two societies, the Christian Alliance to serve home missions, and the International Missionary Alliance, for overseas work. These two societies merged in 1887 to form the Christian and Missionary Alliance. It was never in Simpson's mind to form a denomination, but rather an evangelistic missionary movement. He did not propose that the acceptance of a creed was necessary, but he designed a formula of belief, built on the gospel of Christ as saviour, sanctifier, healing and coming Lord. Aimée Semple McPherson, the founder of the International Church of the Foursquare Gospel, also adopted this theme although she substituted the words 'baptizer with the Holy Spirit' for his word 'sanctifier'. Simpson placed considerable emphasis on the role of spiritual healing in the Christian life, as well as separation from the world and the importance of the premillennial return of Christ (Revelation 20). Home missions are concerned with working with the down-and-outs in society and also with minority immigrant groups in some 18 districts in the USA, with foreign mission work now concentrated in 49 countries, including many in South America, Africa, the Near and Far East as well as in Papua New Guinea.

The separate congregations are self-governing and self-maintaining, with delegates sent to an annual general conference when managers of local groups are elected and the Alliance's affairs are regulated. Several colleges, a seminary, a publishing house, retirement centres and other institutions are presently maintained; the group achieved official status as a denomination in 1974.

CHRISTIAN APOSTOLIC FAITH CHURCH IN ZION

This black Church was founded in South Africa in 1942. It belongs within the Pentecostal movement, characterized by an exuberant display of charismatic gifts and with an emphasis on healing and spiritual experience, drawing upon many elements found in traditional non-Christian religious practices. The sacred robes that are worn are usually white and blue in colour, occasionally white and green. The membership of the Church is currently increasing, drawn mainly from Zulu, Sotho and Shanagaan speakers.

CHRISTIAN ASSEMBLY

This (American) Assembly should not be confused with a similar group in South Africa, which was founded in 1931 and is decidedly PENTECOSTAL *in ethos.*

William Farwell founded this small, New Thought (NEW AGE) group in San Jose, California, in 1900. The members believe that Christianity is founded upon the doctrines of Jesus Christ and the Bible, but they also hold that within the Bible there is a spiritual kernel of meaning, contained within its historical and literal sense, which can be discerned by the spirit of truth working through an individual's understanding. They maintain that God is spirit and that his kingdom is within, and that it is within this kingdom, which is expressed through works of love and faith, that the risen Christ dwells. They hold that in Jesus, whom they accept as Christ, the Son of the Living God, there is a perfect unity of the divine and the human: the two natures become one and are 'blended and confused', as in the case of MONOPHYSITISM. Christian healing is also recognized as part of the gospel message.

The sacraments of the traditional Churches are not recognized, but in outward expression of worship there is little divergence from traditional practice, with Sunday morning worship services, prayer groups and Bible classes and lectures throughout the week. For private daily devotional purposes members of the Church may make use of books such as *Life Messages* and *Through the Year with Jesus*, both written by William Farwell. Branch groups, or churches, have been set up throughout California, manned by pastors who were trained within the Assembly, which is now allied to a larger organization known as the United Church of Religious Science.

CHRISTIAN BROTHERHOOD CHURCH

An independent HOLINESS-type denomination, founded in Japan in 1946 and now found throughout that country, with its headquarters in Tokyo. It is developing slowly and currently has almost 100 congregations, with about 3,000 adult members.

❖ Kirisuto Kyodai-Dan

CHRISTIAN CATHOLIC CHURCH

A Scotsman, John Alexander Dowie (1847–1907) founded this FUNDAMENTALIST, pre-millennialist (REVELATION 20) evangelical Church in the USA in 1896; the Church emphasizes strongly the importance of spiritual healing. Dowie had lived in Adelaide, Australia, from the age of 13 before returning to Scotland where he took up studies in Edinburgh in order to enter the ministry of the CONGREGATIONAL CHURCH. After ordination in 1870 he returned to Australia as a Congregationalist minister but resigned in 1878 so that he could be free to practise divine healing and to evangelize through missions. By 1883 he had established the Independent Free Christian Church in Melbourne and this was followed a few years later by the foundation of the International Divine Healing Association, with branches throughout Australia and New Zealand.

With Dowie's departure to San Francisco in 1888 his work in Australia suffered setbacks. The healing missions were now conducted along the west coast of the USA, with headquarters established in Chicago in 1890. Here he began to publish a weekly paper, *Leaves of Healing*, and opened thirteen Healing Homes. His healing work brought Dowie into conflict with the law and he was charged with practising medicine and running hospitals without a licence. In 1895 he was charged no fewer than a hundred times but his subsequent acquittals resulted in a great increase in members.

After the formal establishment of the Church in Chicago in February 1896, Dowie bought some seven thousand acres of land in Lake County, Illinois, in the area six miles north of Waukegan, which lies halfway between Milwaukee and Chicago. There he founded a self-contained community on a six thousand-acre site, known as Zion City, with himself as its leader, calling himself Elijah the Restorer and dressing in flowing robes; he was later to consecrate himself as the First Apostle.

Dowie's main emphasis was on the healing of disease through prayer. He was implacably critical of capitalism and totally opposed to the use of alcohol, tobacco, medicine, family doctors, Masonic, or other secret, Lodges, and the press. Certain foodstuffs, including oysters, clams, pork and rabbit meat, were forbidden in Zion City, as were theatres and playing cards. It was a well-planned city, providing open green spaces, a golf course, marina and Hosea Beach for the use of its inhabitants. The *Saved* were baptized in the ten thousand-seater tabernacle, which was built in 1907 but did not survive an arson attempt in 1937; the new Christian Catholic auditorium was built in its place. Scripture is the basis of the Church's faith and practice, with a belief in repentance for sin, trust in Christ for salvation, baptism by triple immersion and tithing. Dowie always refused to accept the doctrine of eternal punishment as he found it inconsistent with belief in a loving God. His initiative and enterprise saw the development of twenty communal businesses and industries. Two of his most enduring legacies were Zion Baking, which made a wide range of pastry products including the famously popular Zion Fig Bar which was still in production until the 1950s, and Zion Candy, which produced among other sweetmeats the Fig Pie Candy Bar, the Zion Cocoaroon and the Zion Cherry Sundae. The emphasis on the fig came from Dowie's belief in its biblical provenance. The candy division closed in 1961, but the baking division of this enterprise continued until 1988. *The Zion label is still continued for biscuits, or cookies, but these are now baked in Wheeling, Illinois.*

Dowie's final years were, however, ignominious. A failed mission to New York City, where he went in the autumn of 1903 with two thousand followers, pressing tax problems, followed by a stroke in 1905 that left him paralyzed, led finally to his replacement by Wilbur Glenn Voliva.

Under Voliva's leadership the Church experienced structural and doctrinal changes, emerging as an evangelical PROTESTANT Church. Voliva visited Australia in 1901 to reorganize the work there and established centres in Sydney and Adelaide before returning to the USA; by 1917 the Church in Australia was firmly established. Since then other foundations have been made, in the Philippines, Japan, Guyana, Jamaica, India, South Africa and the UK. There have been several schisms of the Church, perhaps the most notable of which led to the formation of the Grace Missionary Church. Ministers of this denomination are trained in conventional seminaries and Bible institutes throughout the USA.

❖ The Christian Catholic Apostolic Church (original title); The Christian Community Church (since 1997)

CHRISTIAN CHURCH

The title 'Christian Church' was assumed by several American Churches in the eighteenth and nineteenth centuries in an effort to avoid sectarian labels and to underline a creedless foundation. In 1819, many of these held a conference in Portsmouth, New Hampshire and by 1833 it was felt that a firm organization was needed. A general convention was established, that gave the Christian Church a distinct identity. The Church's REFORMED theology was affirmed, in which the authority of the Bible was stressed as well as the doctrine of salvation by grace through faith. Considerable latitude in other doctrinal matters was permitted.

This Church united with the National Council of the Congregational Churches in 1931 to become the General Council of CONGREGATIONAL-CHRISTIAN CHURCHES. This left both partners of the union free to continue with their own forms of worship, follow their own polity and develop their own doctrines. In 1957, a further union was effected between the General Council of Congregational-Christian Churches and the EVANGELICAL AND REFORMED CHURCH to form the UNITED CHURCH OF CHRIST.

❖ Baptist Unitarians

CHRISTIAN CHURCH (DISCIPLES OF CHRIST)

This denomination grew out of a restoration movement in nineteenth-century America, which was an attempt to eradicate sectarian names and human creeds and to establish a union of all Christians based on the New Testament alone. The result was shown to be anything but the desired union and the outcome was an enormous growth of independent congregations with a membership in millions, distributed throughout at least 65 countries in the world.

Two of the founders of the Christian Church (Disciples of Christ) were a father and son, Thomas and Alexander Campbell. Thomas Campbell (1763–1854) had left Scotland for America in 1807 and had joined the Philadelphia Synod of the PRESBYTERIAN Church as a minister, but he was expelled the following year for practising an open Communion service with non-Presbyterians of varying beliefs. He went on to found the Christian Association of Washington County, Pennsylvania. His son, Alexander, now abandoned Scottish Presbyterianism and joined his father in America. Together, the Campbells and the Christian Association established the Brush Run Church, near Washington, Pennsylvania, which in 1815 became part of a nearby BAPTIST group, the Red Stone Baptist Association, because of their shared sympathy with adult, rather than infant, baptism by immersion.

The Campbells and their followers, who were commonly known as CAMPBELLITES, or Reformers, found that certain differences between them and the Baptists, such as the importance and proposed methods of restoring New Testament Christianity, the need for a congregational polity and the wish to extend open weekly communion to all including the unbaptized, could not be resolved. By 1830 the reformers had cut their last ties with the Baptist Association and they became known as *Disciples.*

Meanwhile, a Presbyterian minister, Barton W. Stone (1772–1844), had formed, with four other ministers, the Springfield Presbytery after leaving the Kentucky synod of the Presbyterian Church. They denounced all human creeds and appealed to the Bible as the only rule of faith and practice, emphasizing the importance of the independence of the local church, but this was not successful and by 1809 the Springfield Presbytery had been dissolved.

There had been a correspondence between Barton Stone and the Campbells since 1824 and an agreement was reached between them concerning basic beliefs and aims. After a formal handshake at Lexington, Kentucky, in 1832 a new Christian movement was initiated. No sectarian name was wanted, as they regarded themselves as societies rather than as a denomination, and called themselves variously the Christian Church, or the Disciples of Christ.

Until 1849 the growth of the movement was rapid and the first general council was held, not so much to further the work of the societies but rather to represent them. At this convention, which was held in Cincinnati, they agreed to form the American Christian Missionary Society, which focused on Church extension, foreign missions and a programme of evangelization. It was in the wake of this convention that divisions began to appear, emerging from a concern about the use, or non-use, of church music. This division led eventually to separation and to the formation of the Churches of Christ. The Disciples of Christ continued, and at the 1910 convention it was decided to form one General Convention of the Disciples in order to unify all the various boards that were beginning to be formed; by 1917 this was organized into the International Convention, a title which was replaced in 1968 at an assembly meeting in Kansas City when the current title was adopted.

The Church believes in the divine inspiration of the Bible, regarding it as their only rule of faith, and that baptism and the Lord's Supper are divine ordinances; the observance of the Lord's Day is regarded as a sacred duty. They further believe that holiness is necessary for every believer and that there is a final judgement, with the reward of heaven for the righteous, and the punishment of hell for the wicked. Their polity is congregational and each local church elects its pastors, elders and deacons. Membership is conferred by a profession of faith after which comes baptism by immersion. The Church runs various colleges and schools of religion, as well as homes for children and for the elderly.

❖ Disciples of Christ

CHRISTIAN CHURCH OF SUMBA

This Indonesian denomination is in the REFORMED tradition and was formally and independently organized in 1947, accepting the Bible and the *Heidelberg Catechism* (1563) as its doctrinal foundation. At present there are some 66 regular congregations, and about 300 unorganized, informal preaching stations, with over 61,000 adult members in total. The Church has responsibility for two hospitals and also participates in various welfare and development programmes. It facilitates entry to higher education through a network of primary and secondary schools. The central administrative authority is a synod, with its headquarters at Sumba, southern Indonesia, which meets four times each year.

CHRISTIAN CONGREGATION

The Church was founded as a fellowship of Christians, in the style of the CHRISTIAN CHURCH (DISCIPLES OF CHRIST), and began in Kokomo, Indiana (just north of Indianapolis) in 1887. The founding idea, which was based on the new commandment in John 13:34–5, was in the minds of some members of the Independent Christian Churches who wanted to form a group where the believers were bound to each other within a fellowship of love, with each congregation having complete autonomy.

The Church is non-creedal and opposes sectarianism. It has no agreed doctrinal position but a great emphasis on Bible study, which is helped by the publication of many Bible study aids and course work. The form of worship, which is fairly flexible, is based upon PRESBYTERIAN form and usage. At one time there were congregations throughout Kentucky, the Carolinas, Virginia, Pennsylvania, Ohio, Indiana and Texas, but the numbers have decreased and the Church is now largely confined to the more rural and neglected areas of North Carolina.

CHRISTIAN FELLOWSHIP CHURCH

The Church arose in 1960 through a schism from the METHODIST Church during 1959–61, in New Georgia, one of the smaller islands within the Solomon Island group in Melanesia. The *Founder-Messiah*, Silas Eto (1905–84), had been a catechist-teacher in the Methodist Church and had trained to be a pastor under the famous New Zealand missionary, J. F. Gouldie, whom he much admired, but from the 1930s Eto displayed what were termed deviationist practices that caused some concern. Eto, who had grown disillusioned with the traditional Methodist form of worship, claimed to have been inspired by revelations from both God and the now dead Gouldie, which came to him during dreams. He spoke of himself as the fourth member of the Trinity and as the messiah, adopting the title *Holy Mama* and incorporating his name into the Church's liturgy. Some of his members have described him further as having superseded God. At any rate, with his long white robes and turban Eto certainly cut a distinctive figure.

Following Eto's death the Church was placed under the authority of Sam Kuku. It continues to grow and supports a seminary, primary schools and various business interests. A model village, known as Paradise, was created and the various Church enterprises have met with a great deal of success. There are now some 49 congregations and around 3 per cent of the population of New Georgia are members of the Christian Fellowship Church, whose worship services are marked by ecstatic dancing and healing. Despite Silas Eto's assumed status as messiah, his relations with the Methodist Church, which is now part of the United Church, were generally cordial.

❖ Etoism

CHRISTIAN FOUNDATION

Tony and Susan Alamo created the Christian Foundation in the USA in 1967 and opened a ranch near Saugas, California, where followers could stay. These followers were mainly attracted to the movement through street preaching in and around Sunset Strip, Hollywood. Those interested in hearing more were taken by bus to a nightly service and, if they wished to go further, could spend time at the Saugas ranch. The Christian Foundation attracted some attention in the mid-1970s from the Californian legislature and also from the parents of some of the young members, who suspected brainwashing had taken place. A clothes store was opened by the Foundation in 1974, in Nashville, Tennessee. It is also active in media projects and other businesses.

CHRISTIAN ISRAELITE CHURCH

Following the death of the religious zealot Joanna Southcott in 1814 (see SOUTHCOTTIANS), much of her work was continued by George Turner, a prophet whose unfortunate predictions failed to materialize. Upon his death the work was taken over by John Wroe, a Yorkshire eccentric variously described as a woolcomber, farmer and collier, whose reputation had been established by some more successful prophecies. Wroe reassembled the followers of Joanna Southcott, many of whom had dispersed after her death, as the Christian Israelite Church. A Canadian, Richard Brothers, who was much given to having psychic visions, had influenced both Turner and Wroe. Brothers had settled in London in the 1780s where he laid claim to the English crown through his alleged descent from King David of the Old Testament. For this, and other eccentricities, he was sent to an asylum, but in his saner moments Brothers was an influential figure.

John Wroe established the Christian Israelite Church in England, with branches in the USA and Australia. He had made several visits to Australia between 1844–62, and died in Melbourne, in 1863. Wroe's interest in Australia came from his belief that the country was to have an important part to play during the ingathering of the 144,000 elect (Rev. 7:4), the special group of Christians who would be given redeemed bodies of flesh and blood and would form the physically-redeemed Israel. In order to attain that state, however, it was necessary for the elect to have led lives in harmony with Christ, to have obeyed his word and fulfilled the Old Testament laws, although they could be exempt from observing the laws governing sacrifice. To that end, the Christian Israelite Church observes Jewish holidays but gives them Christian meanings. On Fridays, an hour-long watch is maintained during the hours of 6 pm and 9 pm and again on Sunday mornings between 10–11 am; on Sunday evening there is a simple public service. There is a belief among members that Saturday will come to be kept as the sabbath in the times before Christ's second coming (REVELATION 20).

Some of the requirements of its members need some explaining. Clothing is to be made from only one fibre, as this is seen as symbolic of keeping the physical body pure, with no mixing of good and evil. No black-coloured garments are worn, as black is seen as the symbol of death and the elect are aspiring to live without dying. The clothing worn at the Church services is also unusual, with men wearing a collarless, knee-length frockcoat, without lapels or pockets, as well as a tall hat, long hair drawn into a knot at the back, and a full-length beard. Women wear a full-length dress with a bonnet, or cap. Some of the group practise male circumcision, in line with Jewish custom, but it is not obligatory.

Tithing is a requirement of the Church, as part of the personal covenant that a member makes with God, and this money is used for the upkeep of the Church and its meeting rooms. Non-covenanted members can become covenanted by undertaking to adhere to all the laws in the Old Testament, with the possible exception of those governing sacrifice as mentioned above, and they must therefore have no likenesses of anything that has been made by God in their lives; this proscribes all artificial flowers or plants, pictures of animals or people, or their likenesses in any form, on furniture, wallpaper, dolls, toys, books or clothes. For educational purposes, however, these images are allowed. Baptism is by full immersion in the sea, or in a river, and is administered after an act of repentance; there is no celebration of the Lord's Supper.

The members of the Church believe that God is the creator of all things and it is into this physical, God-created world that each person is born with a body and soul, enlivened by a spirit. They also believe that there will be a small number of their fellow believers who, by following God's instructions, will prove their faith and will receive redemption of body, soul and spirit. The unrighteous, they believe, will also be resurrected but will be held back for a thousand years, until Satan is finally defeated when they, too, will be welcomed into the kingdom of heaven after their repentance, though at a lower level than that attained by the righteous. They also maintain that there are promises in the Bible, made especially to Israel, and that, although Israel did not accept the challenge of being God's *peculiar*, or chosen, people, a remnant of their descendants will fulfil the obligations of the Last Days and will receive the promised rewards. It is the mission of the Christian Israelite Church to reawaken and bring together the lost ten tribes of Israel and to make them aware of their special inheritance and so prepare for Christ's return. There are several congregations of the Church in Australia, in New South Wales and Victoria, and others are to be found in the USA, in Indianapolis, Indiana, in Radom, Poland and in Murmansk, in the Russian Federation.

CHRISTIAN METHODIST EPISCOPAL CHURCH

This large American denomination arose in the years following the American Civil War (1861–5), when it was felt by members of the METHODIST EPISCOPAL CHURCH South that the request by their black members for a Church of their own should not only be granted, but that they should be given every assistance with its formation.

To this end the Colored Methodist Episcopal Church was founded in 1870, with two black bishops ordained for the purpose. The Church made astonishing progress, largely due to the work of Isaac Lane who was instrumental in establishing the Church on a firm footing within the USA at the end of the nineteenth century. He founded the Colored Methodist Episcopal High School in Jackson, Tennessee, which later became Lane College (founded 1882). Other colleges and publishing enterprises were also started and are still maintained. In 1950 the Church supported a mission to Africa.

The doctrinal position of the Church is entirely METHODIST, with various local conferences in addition to the district, annual and general conferences regulating the administration. In 1954, the Colored Methodist Episcopal Church was renamed, at the Memphis general conference, as the Christian Methodist Episcopal Church.

CHRISTIAN NATION CHURCH

This declining American denomination was incorporated in the USA, in Marion, Ohio, (north of Columbus) in 1895 by eight *Equality Evangelists*, an independent band of missioners who had begun their work of evangelization in 1892. The Church's doctrinal position is almost identical to that of the CHRISTIAN AND MISSIONARY ALLIANCE of A. B. Simpson, emphasizing justification, full atonement, divine healing and Christ's second coming (REVELATION 20). Baptism and the Lord's Supper are observed as ordinances.

The members of the Church have to observe certain strictures governing their behaviour and way of life. Large families are encouraged, but not so marriage with divorcees or with the *unsaved.* The use of tobacco, alcohol, jewellery and fashionable clothing is strictly forbidden, as is participation in 'worldly entertainments, foolish talking, joking and the singing of worldly songs'. The polity of the Church is congregational, and the government of local churches is administered through annual and district conferences which authorize the annual licensing of pastors.

CHRISTIAN REFORMED CHURCH IN NORTH AMERICA

This PROTESTANT Church has been in decline since the mid-1990s. Its origins are to be found in the Netherlands in the early nineteenth century, when the Dutch monarchy was attempting to bring the Reformed Church under its control. This, coupled with some discontent about growing modernism and doctrinal laxity in the Church, resulted in 1834 in the formation of a secession movement, or *Afscheidung*, led by Henry de Cock and others who were opposed to these changes. Members of the secession endured much persecution. Together with this difficult situation came the 1846 potato famine, which affected much of Europe, and many of the secessionists left the Netherlands for a new life in America, settling in western Michigan in 1847 with Albert van Raalte as their leader, where they formed the *Classis Holland*, which affiliated in 1850 with the Reformed Protestant Dutch Church, later known as the REFORMED CHURCH IN AMERICA, a title which is still maintained today.

One group within the *Classis Holland*, whose members were led by Gysbert Haan, reacted to the evidence that the Reformed Protestant Dutch Church tolerated open communion, neglected the preaching of the catechism, and had never believed that the formation of the secession movement in the Netherlands had ever been warranted. The members of this single group left the *Classis Holland* in January 1857 and were joined later by others. Together they formed the True Holland Reformed Church, which in 1859 became known as the DUTCH REFORMED CHURCH. Their numbers increased considerably after the arrival of more waves of immigrants from the Netherlands in 1882 and again in 1890. Some members of the Reformed Protestant Dutch Church, not accepting that Church's alleged tolerance of Freemasonry, also joined the Dutch Reformed Church. This Church later united with a group known as the True Reformed Dutch Church of New York and New Jersey, which had been founded in 1822 by disaffected members of the Reformed Protestant Dutch Church; the new title of Christian Reformed Church was adopted in 1892. From then until 1904 the Church was known as the *Christelijke Gereformeerde Kerk*, but the use of the Dutch title was gradually discontinued as English began to supplant the Dutch language.

Doctrinally, the Church subscribes to the *Belgic Confession* (1561), the *Heidelberg Catechism* (1563) and the *Canons of the Synod of Dort* (1618–19) and it accepts the three historic creeds. Government of the Church is by means of an annual general synod, made up of two ministers and two elders from each *Classis*, whose polity is presbyterial. Infant baptism is administered only to children of professing adult members of the Church, and considerable emphasis is placed on the catechetical instruction of young people. Membership of the Church is forbidden to members of secret societies, or Masonic Lodges.

English has supplanted the use of Dutch in Church services, and there has been a broadening of the earlier custom of allowing only hymns taken from the psalms. Home missions are undertaken in New York City and Chicago, and also amongst the Navajo and Zuni Indians, with foreign missions supported in Japan, South America, Nigeria, Cuba, Formosa and parts of Canada. Two other important spheres of mission work are to be found in the *Back to God Hour*, on radio and television, and in the Christian Reformed World Relief Programme, which is concerned with relief and development in some 30 countries in Asia, eastern Europe (Kosovo and Romania), and Africa.

Ministerial training is provided in the Calvin College and seminary in Grand Rapids, Michigan, where the Church's headquarters is also located, with a more general education available through a network of elementary and high schools. The Church also provides care for the elderly and the sick, with a special programme for tuberculosis sufferers.

❖ True Holland Reformed Church

CHRISTIAN REFORMED CHURCH OF BRAZIL

This Reformed Church was established in Brazil in 1932 for Hungarian immigrants who had been members of the Reformed Church of Hungary (founded 1530). The Church, which has enjoyed autonomy since 1945, affirms the doctrinal position of the Christian Reformed Church. There are 12 congregations, with about 8,500 adult members, and the headquarters is in São Paulo.

CHRISTIAN REFORMED CHURCHES IN THE NETHERLANDS

Following the introduction of a new Church Order for the Dutch Reformed Church (NHK) in 1816 by King William I (1772–1843), considerable criticism was provoked, with the result that in 1834 one of its pastors, Henry de Cock (1801–42) was suspended from the ministry and this year is usually taken as marking the Church's foundation. De Cock and his congregation, in Ulrum, were not alone in voicing their protests about the growing liberalism in the Church and the influence exercised by the state in Church matters. By 1836 more than a hundred independent congregations then operating in the country joined forces and became established as the *Reformed Church under the Cross*. In the 1840s, when the potato famine struck many parts of Europe, many secessionists left for a new life in America, where they laid the foundations of what became the CHRISTIAN REFORMED CHURCH IN NORTH AMERICA.

By 1892 most of these congregations had joined with others, and the REFORMED CHURCHES IN THE NETHERLANDS was formed. Those congregations that felt that their independence was at risk reorganized themselves and established their own *classis* (an ecclesiastical district, or governing body of a district), with quarterly synods and provision for a triennial general synod.

In 1947, the present name of the Church was adopted. The Church affirms the traditional creeds, (Apostles', Nicene and Athanasian), the *Belgic Confession* (1561), the *Heidelberg Cathechism* (1563) and the *Canons of Dort* (1618–19). Many close links with Churches in North America, Australasia and Southern Africa have since been forged. The headquarters of the Church is at Veenendaal in the Netherlands.

CHRISTIAN UNION OF AMERICA

This slowly declining religious body was founded in 1864 in Columbus, Ohio, by a group of laymen who wanted to unite all Christians on a scriptural basis. Members of the union do not subscribe to any set of creeds, but they must be able to profess and accept seven basic principles:

1 The unity of Christ's Church

2 The acknowledgement of Christ as the only head of the Church

3 The acceptance of the Bible as the only rule of faith and practice

4 The recognition that a wholesome lifestyle is the one condition of fellowship

5 The principle that the Christian Union should not be controversial

6 The acceptance that each local Church is autonomous

7 The undertaking that all partisan political preaching is to be avoided

The ordinances of baptism by immersion and the Lord's Supper are observed and administered by both male and female ministers. From the adoption of the seven principles listed above it can be seen that the polity of the Church is congregational. The Church is organized through two councils, the triennial general council and the annual state council, to both of which lay and ministerial delegates are sent.

Home missions are carried out in various parts of the USA, while foreign missions are supported in Africa, Japan, the Dominican Republic and Ethiopia.

CHRISTIAN UNITY BAPTIST ASSOCIATION

A small American denomination within the BAPTIST tradition, which was founded in 1935 and arose over the question of open or closed Communion; open Communion could be given to anyone who claimed to be a Christian, but closed Communion was restricted to Church members only.

The Christian Unity Baptist Association was formed through the work of Francis Lee Sturgill and F. Carl Sturgill, both of whom were members of the Zion Hill Baptist Church on Big Helton Creek in Ashe County, North Carolina, together with Nancy Owens, a member of a congregation known as Bethel, in Johnson County, Tennessee. After the first meeting, which was held at Zion Hill Church in 1935 at which an attempt was made to form an organizational framework, both Sturgills were elected to offices, Frank as moderator and F. Carl as clerk. Delegates from six congregations from North Carolina, Virginia and Tennessee carried out the election. The new group differed from what had gone before in admitting women as ministers; the first two women ministers, Nancy Owen and Carrie Poe, both took prominent roles as preachers. The Association also held to the view that it was possible for people to fall from grace, and that a regular acknowledgement and confession of sins was necessary in order to remain in grace. It was also willing to admit anyone who claimed to be a Christian to take Communion in the Church. Foot-washing is regarded as an ordinance in the Christian Unity Baptist Association; many other Churches in the PRIMITIVE BAPTIST tradition practise foot-washing but do not regard it as an ordinance. Congregational polity is the rule and there is an active programme of home missions and evangelism, with revival and prayer meetings and a strong Sunday school tradition.

CHURCH IN WALES

The date of the foundation of Christianity in Wales is uncertain but by the time of the Council of Arles (314) it is known that there were three bishops present, representing Britain. Certainly the efforts of Sts Illtud and Dubritus (or Dyffrig) during the first half of the sixth century led to what is sometimes called the *Age of the Saints*, when the accomplishments of Sts Deiniol of Bangor, David and his cousin, Cuby (also Cybi), are more verifiable.

Some early difficulties, including the Welsh Church's refusal to accept the Roman method of calculating the date of Easter, were resolved in 750 and the growth of the Welsh Church continued. A growing sense of frustration and irritation began to be expressed over the action of the English crown in raising money through taxation, and in the appointment of non-Welsh clergy to benefices.

The effects of the Reformation were felt gradually in Wales. The translation into the Welsh language of the *Book of Common Prayer* and the New Testament, by Richard Davies, Bishop of St Davids, and William Salesbury in 1567, and the 1588 translation of the entire Bible into Welsh by William Morgan, made the acceptance of PROTESTANTISM easier; Morgan's translation was later supplanted by a Welsh translation of the King James' version of the Bible.

By the second half of the seventeenth century the Welsh Church had fallen on hard times. The bishops of the established CHURCH OF ENGLAND were, in the main, political appointees and few took the trouble to learn Welsh. This had a demoralizing effect on the few clergy who were working in the parishes and led to a feeling of alienation from the rest of the Established Church. The climate was right for the effect of non-conformist revivals to take root in the country. The *Evangelical Revival* of 1735, which was followed by others, had a profound social and cultural effect during the eighteenth and nineteenth centuries. By the early nineteenth century, non-conformity had become the dominant force in Wales and the Established Church began a programme of reorganization. The 1835 Act of Parliament required all clergy working in Welsh parishes to develop an adequate grasp of the language and, as the century progressed, more and more Welshmen were appointed to the episcopal sees.

Disestablishment was obviously necessary, and this came about through the Welsh Church Acts of 1914 and 1919, which did not, however, come into effect until 1920 because of the intervention of the First World War. The province of Wales, as it became in 1920, currently has six dioceses headed by a primate, who is president of the governing body of the Church. This governing body, which exercises wide powers, is composed of bishops, clergy and laity and meets twice a year; matters concerning finance and church property are administered by the representative body of the Church in Wales.

CHURCH OF ASHES OF PURIFICATION

An indigenous African and marginally Christian Church, which was established in 1922 as a result of a major schism from the Roman Catholic Church amongst the Bete tribe of Seria, Ivory Coast, most of whom are still animists, although there have been many conversions to Islam.

The Church has 840 congregations with around 84,000 committed adult members. Each church building has two entrances, one on the right, which is usually used by men, with the one on the left for the use of women. A female, known as the pope, leads the Church; further details of the liturgy and doctrine of the Church are not readily available.

CHURCH OF CHRIST

An American Church that, like the Christian Church (Disciples of Christ), arose from the nineteenth-century restoration movement in America. This was an attempt to restore the primitive New Testament Church as a basis for unity amongst Christians.

One of the earliest American leaders was James O'Kelly of Virginia (1757–1826), who, with a group of Methodist ministers, sought a congregational polity and looked for freedom from episcopal control to allow itinerant preachers to determine their own itinerary. O'Kelly and his colleagues left the Methodist Church in 1793 and formed what was called the Republican Methodists, located in Virginia and North Carolina. Two Baptists, Abner Smith (1772–1841) and Elias Jones (1769–1846) began a similar movement in New Hampshire and Vermont in 1802. Their group was successful and came to be called *Christian*, or *Christian Connexion.* Other groups that played a part in the restoration movement included those begun by Thomas and Alexander Campbell, known as the Campbellites, and Barton W. Stone; these two groups merged to become the Christian Church (Disciples of Christ).

All four groups, those of O'Kelly, Smith and Jones, the Campbellites and the followers of Barton Stone, were convinced 'that nothing should be bound to Christians which is not as old as the New Testament'. In 1832 the majority of followers of these four groups united, the merger taking place at Lexington, Kentucky. It soon became apparent, however, that some of the leaders were more conservative than others and were insisting on New Testament strictures regarding worship and organization, as well as being against the use of instrumental music in worship and the formation of mission societies.

This conservative group eventually separated from the restoration movement and was listed, by the Federal Census of Religious Bodies in 1906, as the Churches of Christ (Non-Instrumental [or *a cappella*]). Baptism is by adult immersion and a weekly Communion service, with extempore prayer, is celebrated, but it is the centrality of the New Testament as the source of all faith and practices that is the most distinctive feature of the Church. They hold that the Old Testament is inspired, but of lesser authority than the New Testament. Considerable emphasis is placed on the autonomy of each congregation and there is lay leadership, based on the belief of the priesthood of all believers.

Ministers of the Church are ordained, rather than licensed, and hold their tenure of office by agreement with the local church in which they preach. Vigorous missionary activities and evangelistic outreach programmes are maintained, and support is provided for schools and colleges as well as for homes for the very young and the elderly. Extensive use is also made of most forms of media for the purpose of evangelization. The Church underwent a massive expansion in the 1920s and 30s, but this had slowed down by the 1970s and is now in slow decline.

There are some Churches of Christ that arose from a schism within the Disciples of Christ in 1935 and which permit the use of musical instruments in their services.

CHURCH OF CHRIST (BIBLE AND BOOK OF MORMON TEACHING)

Former members of the CHURCH OF CHRIST (TEMPLE LOT), who wished to move towards orthodox Christianity, were the founders of this American group. When one of the Temple Lot Sunday school teachers, Pauline Hancock, spread her belief that God the Father, Son and Holy Ghost were one person, this Trinitarian approach was at odds with the beliefs held by most Mormon (CHURCH OF JESUS CHRIST OF LATTER-DAY SAINTS) groups and she was excommunicated. In 1946 she organized the Church of Christ. Members accept the *Book of Mormon* as valid and believe that Joseph Smith, although God had specially called him, later became wicked; his teaching about polygamy is especially condemned. The Church also differs from normal Mormon practice in not practising baptism for the dead. There are members of the Church of Christ (Bible and Book of Mormon Teaching) in Michigan, Wisconsin and California, with a further congregation established in Independence, Missouri.

CHURCH OF CHRIST (FETTINGITE)

An American, Otto Fetting, who was one of the twelve apostles of the CHURCH OF CHRIST (TEMPLE LOT), claimed in 1927 to have had a vision during which John the Baptist told him to build a temple, giving Fetting explicit instructions, and to give the priesthood to black men. Other messages followed and there was a specific command that the entire membership of the Temple Lot Church must be re-baptized. While some of the other apostles agreed to this, many did not and the Church expelled Fetting and his followers. Together, they set up another Church of Christ. The messages that Otto Fetting received did not end with his expulsion from the Church of Christ (Temple Lot) and he continued to receive them until his death in 1933; there were 30 messages in all. The Church is small, and was split by a schism in 1947 over the matter of visions received by another Church member; in the mid-1960s there were about 250 members.

CHURCH OF CHRIST (HOLINESS)

In 1894, a black preacher, C. P. Jones of Selma, Alabama, left his Church since he felt that he needed a faith to make him 'like Abraham – a friend of God'. He went to live in Jackson, Mississippi, and began to recruit followers. It was initially Jones's intention that his foundation was to be interdenominational, but by 1898 it had become a full denomination.

The Church of Christ (Holiness) subscribes to the METHODIST *Twenty-five Articles of Religion*. This places the Church firmly within the HOLINESS theological tradition, which emphasizes a conversion experience followed by baptism of the Holy Spirit as bringing entire sanctification; this is commonly called the second blessing. The Church rejects the CALVINIST view of predestination. Original sin is emphasized, along with Christ's atonement and his second coming (REVELATION 20). Entry into membership of the Church is through baptism by immersion. The Lord's Supper is observed as an ordinance, preceded by foot-washing.

The polity of the Church is episcopal, under the leadership of a senior bishop and with other bishops caring for individual dioceses, but doctrinal decisions are taken at an annual convention, to which delegates from the congregations are sent. At a local level, there are bi-annual district conventions made up of elders, ministers and local church representatives. Both home and foreign missions are supported, as well as an Industrial and Missionary College in Jackson, Mississippi.

CHURCH OF CHRIST (TEMPLE LOT)

To understand the origins of the Church of Christ (Temple Lot) it is necessary to make a preliminary comment about a few differences that exist between the Utah-based CHURCH OF JESUS CHRIST OF LATTER-DAY SAINTS, *founded in 1830 and known also as the Mormons, and the* RE-ORGANIZED CHURCH OF JESUS CHRIST OF LATTER-DAY SAINTS, *based in Independence, Missouri. This latter Church was founded in 1860 as a schism from the Utah-based Church, from which it differs in its doctrine of the Godhead and in its acceptance of the notion of a hereditary president-prophet, which the Utah-based Church did not accept, and also in its rejection of polygamy, which the other Church had practised.*

There have been as many as 89 schismatic bodies formed from the Church of Jesus Christ of Latter-Day Saints since 1831, and the Church of Christ (Temple Lot) was one such, having become schismatic in 1852 when several disaffected elders and members of Latter-Day Saints groups, who had been meeting at the house of elder Granville Hedrick at Crow Creek, Illinois, received news about polygamous practices that were being upheld by the parent body in Utah. One of the twelve apostles dating from Joseph Smith's time, John E. Page, had also become worried about the Utah Church's doctrine of baptism of the dead, and he attended a meeting at Hedrick's home in 1862 and united with them. In May 1862 he ordained Hedrick and other leaders to the office of Apostle, and in 1863 Hedrick was made the Church's first president.

The group set about establishing their stand against the polygamy and baptism of the dead, which were being practised by the Utah Church, and also against the idea of a hereditary president-prophet, which was practised by the Re-organized Church of Jesus Christ of Latter-Day

Saints. The Illinois group now called itself the CHURCH OF CHRIST, upholding their belief in the *Book of Mormon* and accepting the 1835 edition of the *Doctrines and Covenants* and the King James' version of the Bible. Hedrick had a revelation in 1864 that the group should return to Independence, Missouri, from where they had been driven across the state border to Illinois in 1833, at a time when it was felt that Mormons might begin to dominate the political scene. A covered wagon train of some sixty members returned to Independence in 1867, the place declared by Joseph Smith to be the site of the temple of Zion, where Christ would live and rule for a thousand years after his second coming (REVELATION 20); it was also suggested that this was reputed to be the site of the Garden of Eden. Smith had buried an inscribed stone marking the spot that should be used as the north-east corner of the Lord's temple, when it was built. Upon their return to Independence, Hedrick and his followers began to buy up land enough for the building of this temple, a site of over 63 acres. By 1877 eight lots had been bought, including the spot where Smith had buried the inscribed stone. The stone was recovered in 1929, along with another marking the south-east corner of the proposed temple. The Re-organized Church, which was also based in Independence, took Hedrick's group to court in 1891 in an attempt to recover the *Temple Lot*, going so far as to produce false documents, or deeds, to testify to the legitimacy of their case. When these documents were shown to be false the case collapsed. Meanwhile, Hedrick's group, by now known as the Church of Christ (Temple Lot), grew and thrived. In the early 1900s a working relationship with the Re-organized Church was established bringing back some harmony between the two groups, but there were serious differences between them and any hope of sustaining the relationship dissolved.

Further growth of the Church followed, but a split occurred in 1930 when one of the apostles, Otto Fetting, revealed that he had been receiving revelations since 1927, when John the Baptist had appeared to him, telling him that it was now time to build the temple and also to extend the priesthood to black members. In 1930 came a revelation that the entire membership of the Church should be re-baptized. Fetting was expelled from the Church and set up his own, its members calling themselves the CHURCH OF CHRIST (FETTINGITE). The revelations continued until Fetting's death in 1933.

The Church of Christ (Temple Lot) believes in God the Father, his Son, Jesus Christ, and in God the Holy Ghost. They accept the need for Christ's atonement and they obey the laws and ordinances of the gospel, which include baptism by immersion for the remission of sins, the laying-on of hands for ordination, the blessing of children, confirmation, the gift of the Holy Spirit and healing. The ordinance of the Lord's Supper is observed, using bread and wine, on one Sunday each month. The Church's more usual Sunday services are composed of prayers, testimonies and preaching by an ordained minister appointed by the local pastor. Marriage is monogamous and re-marriage only allowed for an innocent party in cases of adultery. The members believe in Christ's second coming and the millennial reign (REVELATION 20), the resurrection of the dead and eternal judgement. The Bible is accepted as the word of God, while the *Book of Mormon* is seen as an added witness for Christ. Members are expected to avoid tobacco, alcohol, drugs and membership of secret societies.

The highest office in the Church is that of Apostle, of whom there are always twelve. Each local church is free to govern its own affairs and local bishops administer all local churches. The general conference of the Church is under the supervision of a council of twelve (Apostles), which administers its temporal affairs.

In 1900 a former member who had been excommunicated, because he had joined the Church of Jesus Christ of Latter-Day Saints, burnt down the church that had been built in Independence.The temple has still not been built, but despite this setback, the Church continues to progress slowly.

CHURCH OF CHRIST, SCIENTIST

The Church of Christ, Scientist, is considered to be an unconventional Christian denomination.

The Church of Christ, Scientist, was founded in the USA in 1879 by Mary Baker Eddy (1821–1910) and fifteen other like-minded people with the aim of organizing a group that would commemorate the work of Christ and so reinstate primitive Christianity and the element of healing as recorded in the New Testament.

Mary Baker Eddy had endured a sickly childhood and two marriages when she became interested in the theories and treatment of a mesmerist, Dr Phineas P. Quimby. After reading the account of the healing of a rich man suffering from palsy (Matt. 9:1–8), and following a fall on ice which caused her serious injury, Mary made a decision to regard sickness and death as only illusions and, perhaps miraculously, she began to walk again. She expressed her thoughts initially in a booklet, *The Science of Man* (1870), which later became part of her textbook *Science and Health with a Key to the Scriptures* (1875). Until this time Mary had been a member of the CONGREGATIONAL CHURCH but she now began to teach her ideas to others, although informally at this point, and in 1876 she was obliged to leave the Church and form her own organization, which she called the *Christian Science Association.*

Mrs Eddy had married, for a third time, but by 1879 she was once again widowed. She set about organizing the Church of Christ, Scientist; a final reorganization of the Church was undertaken in 1892. The production of the *Church Manual*, which set out the Church's laws, was completed in 1895 and the first Church of Christ, Scientist, was established as the Mother Church at Boston, Massachusetts. By now Mary Baker Eddy was an ordained minister of the Church.

Doctrinally, the Church claims to be founded on the Bible but it persists in denying many orthodox Christian beliefs, such as the conventional view of the Trinity and the nature and purpose of Christ's life on earth. Likewise, the death of Christ is not understood in the conventional Christian understanding as atonement, but it is claimed that he did not die at all: his later appearances, and his ascension to heaven following his crucifixion, are testimony that matter has no real existence. It is further argued that evil, sickness and death have no reality, as God did not create them and they are simply the errors of mortal minds. The purpose of man's life on earth is to eradicate these errors and by doing so to remove suffering and, ultimately, defeat the grave. The movement met with great success.

Healings are effected by harmonizing thought and action with God's purpose for human beings, and not by faith or some form of auto-suggestion, and are brought about through the gaining of a proper understanding of God. Sunday services are conducted in an identical fashion in all branch churches and take the form established in 1895 by Mrs Eddy. The service consists of her own version of the Lord's Prayer, two readings from the Bible, a period of silent prayer, three hymns, a lesson-sermon based on one of 26 subjects chosen by Mrs Eddy, some quotations from *Science and Health with a Key to the Scriptures*, and a collection for the support of the Church, which is organized around the centralized Mother Church and is governed by a five–member board of directors. Branch churches are found in about seventy countries worldwide, but the majority of these are in North America.

Neither Christmas nor Easter are observed as Church festivals, and there is no provision for a water baptism. Instead, a spiritual communion service is held twice a year, with no physical elements employed. Membership of the Church is achieved by signing a six-point statement, composed by Mrs Eddy, and payment of an annual membership fee. Members are expected to avoid alcohol, drugs, tobacco, tea and coffee. The Church employs its own Christian Science practitioners and nurses, who practice a drug-free approach to healing and work through the Church's nursing homes and nurse-visiting services. The proselytizing success of the Church is largely due to its publication of various journals and quarterlies, including the internationally renowned *Christian Science Monitor*.

Mary Baker Eddy died, from pneumonia, in 1910 at the age of 89 years and left the bulk of her considerable fortune to the Church. It has been estimated that at the time of her death in excess of 100,000 people called her *Mother*.

CHURCH OF CHRIST WITH THE ELIJAH MESSAGE (DRAVESITE)

The American denomination known as the CHURCH OF CHRIST (FETTINGITE) had broken away from the main CHURCH OF CHRIST group in the 1920s as a result of visions claimed to have been received by one of the apostles, Otto Fetting, during which John the Baptist had passed certain instructions to him. When Fetting died in 1933 the visions died with him, but in 1937 W. A. Draves, a member from Nucla, Colorado, claimed that John the Baptist was now visiting him; the messages passed to him included one that appointed Draves to the rank of apostle. The story, however, was not believed by most of the group who accused Draves of fraud, and also of living with two wives in an act of polygamy that was specifically proscribed by the Church. Undeterred, Draves established his own group, the Church of Christ with the Elijah Message, known also as *Dravesite*. Members accept a Saturday sabbath and have their own edition of the *Book of Mormon*, which they call *The Record of the Nephites*.

CHURCH OF DANIEL'S BAND

This small American METHODIST-type denomination was organized in 1893 in Maine City, Michigan, as part of an attempt to revive the spirit of Methodism. Given that intention, the members of the Church placed a strong emphasis upon evangelism, fellowship and an avoidance of any display of worldliness. In addition to the usual Wesleyan *Twenty-Five Articles of Faith* (1784), several others have been added, such as an emphasis on belief in the resurrection and judgement of the dead, divine healing and the laying on of hands for the reception of the gifts of the Holy Spirit. As part of the revival strategy for which the Church was founded, opportunities for class-meetings for Bible study, prayer and discussion were provided.

CHURCH OF DENMARK

The state Church of Denmark has its origins in the middle of the ninth century, at a time when Christianity was developing in the country through the influence of the Anglo-Saxon world and evangelization by missionaries from the south, including St Anskar (*c.* 801–65), known as the Apostle of the North, who visited Denmark as early as 826. The baptism in *c.* 960 of King Harald *Bluetooth* (936–86) gave encouragement to evangelization in Denmark, but progress was reversed in the reign of Harald's successor Svein Haraldsson *Forkbeard*, who for five weeks in the winter of 1014 was also king of England. It was his younger son, Canute, who led Denmark to become fully Christian. Canute was king of both England (from 1016–35) and Denmark (from 1019–35) and an enthusiastic Christian. He made a pilgrimage to Rome and it is said that he insisted that all his subjects were to be taught the Lord's Prayer and to go to Holy Communion at least three times a year.

LUTHERANISM began to make its presence felt in Denmark early in the sixteenth-century, when Christian III ascended the throne in 1534. The king sought Martin Luther's help in reorganizing the Church's administration. A liturgy was compiled, the Bible was translated into Danish and the *Augsburg Confession* (1530) was adopted, making Denmark fully Lutheran. Gradually the monasteries disappeared, their property passed to the Crown, and the Danish monarch became head of the national Church.

Today, the Church of Denmark has its headquarters in Copenhagen, from where it cares for around 2,200 congregations and some 3.4 million adult members. At present there are 10 dioceses in the national Church. The monarch, who is presented with a list of episcopal nominees that have been selected by the parish councils, appoints the bishops who constitute the assembly of bishops under the chairmanship of the Bishop of Copenhagen. The Church is very active in its social service commitment.

❖ Evangelical Lutheran Church in Denmark; National Church of Denmark

CHURCH OF ENGLAND

The origin of Christianity in England is difficult to pinpoint, but at the Synod of Arles in France in 314 there were three English bishops present which points to the existence of an organized Church at that time. From about 350, the Celtic Church in Britain seemed to have been cut off from the rest of the Christian world. St Augustine of Canterbury's mission from Rome, in 597, introduced problems when he insisted on the Roman mode of baptism, that Easter should be observed according to Roman usage and that some jurisdictional changes should be made. Disagreements between the Celtic Christians and the Romans persisted until the Synod of Whitby (663–4) settled those differences and placed the English Church formally under papal control, which was maintained until the English Reformation of the sixteenth century.

The marriage difficulties of Henry VIII led to the rejection of papal authority and the connection was severed, establishing a royal supremacy through the Supremacy Act of 1534 that made the monarch the head of the Church. In the same year the English Bible became available for use throughout the land, accompanied by attacks on monasteries and shrines. Under Edward VI, Archbishop Thomas Cranmer of Canterbury (1489–1556) was responsible for the production of the first and second Book[s] of Common Prayer (1549 and 1552), an English ordinal and the adoption of the basic principles of continental Reformation formulated by the king in 1553. This formulation became known as the *Forty-Two Articles of Religion*, which was later reduced to the *Thirty-Nine Articles* by the convocations of 1563 and 1571. With British colonial expansion and missionary enterprises, ANGLICANISM became established throughout the world. In time, most of these foundations became constitutionally independent following the end of the Second World War, but they have retained their connections with the mother Church through the ANGLICAN COMMUNION.

In terms of significance, the Church of England is the major Anglican Church in the world, and is divided into two provinces, Canterbury and York, with the Archbishop of Canterbury serving as the Primate of All England and recognized as the leader of the worldwide Anglican Communion.

There are three main traditions of churchmanship which support the comprehensiveness of the Church of England: (1) the Evangelicals, (2) the High Churchmen and Anglo-Catholics and (3) the Broad Churchmen. The Evangelicals, who stand in the tradition of John and Charles Wesley (see: METHODISM), emphasize historic Protestant beliefs; their services are characterized by simplicity and lack of ritual. The High Church party can trace its origins back to the Elizabethan age and on through the Oxford Movement of the nineteenth century, which was led by John Henry Newman, who later converted to Roman Catholicism and became a cardinal in that Church. Like the Anglo-Catholics, the High Church members argue for the historic apostolic succession of the Anglican episcopate and for the sacramentality of Anglican worship and life. The Anglo-Catholic form of worship, influenced by the Cambridge Movement (1839–68) led by John Mason Neale, is very elaborate and makes use of vestments, incense and candles, emphasizing its Catholic theological position. The Broad Church also takes its tradition of churchmanship from the Elizabethan age, from the Acts of Uniformity (1549) and Richard Hooker's *Laws of Ecclesiastical Polity* (1597), with its exposition on the 'Via Media' (or Middle Way). The Broad Church regards the *Book of Common Prayer* as central to its worship and is characterized by a readiness to accept new theological views, such as liberalism and the ordination and consecration of women as priests and bishops.

The Church of England accepts the two sacraments of baptism and Holy Communion, but the other five traditional sacraments of confirmation, reconciliation, marriage, ordination and anointing of the sick are not viewed as sacraments of the gospel since they were not ordained as such by Christ. The regular Lambeth Conferences, held since 1867, have been a means of consultation and are important in underlining Anglican policy on a variety of issues confronting the Church, though they lack any authority within the provinces. Although the polity of the Church of England is episcopal, all such appointments are made by the Crown through the office of the Prime Minister, just as all *Book of Common Prayer* revisions and alterations to other procedures require parliamentary approval; since there are non-Anglicans, as well as Anglicans, in parliament this has prompted regular calls for the separation of Church and state.

CHURCH OF ENGLAND IN SOUTH AFRICA

This Church must not be confused with the CHURCH OF THE PROVINCE OF SOUTHERN AFRICA.

The Church owes its origin to the work of early missionaries from England who, as members of the Society for the Propagation of the Gospel, went to Africa in 1821, following the appointment by Queen Victoria of Robert Gray (1809–72) as the first ANGLICAN Bishop of Cape Town. In 1853, John William Colenso (1814–83), a Cornishman, was consecrated as the first Bishop of Natal and made his oath of canonical obedience to Bishop Gray.

Robert Gray was a Tractarian and it was inevitable that conflict would develop between him, as an Anglo-Catholic, and those who wanted a Church within the REFORMED tradition. When Bishop Gray formally established what became the present-day Church of the Province of Southern Africa (CPSA), not all congregations were willing to join. Bishop Colenso, who had been advised in 1863 to resign on account of the fact that he found himself in conscience unable to use the baptismal and ordination services in the *Book of Common Prayer*, also found himself outside the CPSA. Eventually, the South African bishops excommunicated Colenso. In time some of his successors in Natal returned to the larger Church of England in South Africa. Colenso had worked very hard for the social and moral welfare of the Zulus, which had earned for him the title of *Father of the People* (or Sobantu). This is remembered in the alternative name for the Church. Colenso died as an excommunicate.

In 1938, Archbishop Howard W. K. Mowll, who had been appointed to the Australian Archdiocese of Sydney after serving as Bishop of Western China, came to the rescue of the small, schismatic group in South Africa who wanted to remain within the REFORMED and evangelical tradition. He helped them by drawing up a constitution, which they adopted, as the Church of England in South Africa (CESA). The constitution provided for a federal-type arrangement, with a single diocese led by a presiding bishop and helped by area, or assistant, bishops. The Church maintained its position by affirming the use of the 1662 *Book of Common Prayer* and the *Thirty-Nine Articles of Religion.* The various congregations that formed the federation were to be known as constituent Churches and to this day each congregation remains independent.

In the early years after separation from its parent Church, black churches were still regarded as mission Churches, dependent upon the white churches for financial assistance, but this has now changed and any notion of discrimination, on the basis of either race or colour, has been removed from the constitution. In the early 1960s there were a few scattered white congregations of the CESA, in Cape Town, Johannesburg, Pretoria and Pinetown, with a larger number of black congregations in Natal and some Transvaal townships. The work of the Church has now expanded and there are many congregations in the western and eastern Capes, the Free State, Gauteng and KwaZulu-Natal, and sister churches in Zimbabwe and Namibia, with great activity in educational and outreach programmes. There are now 160 congregations, caring for 68,300 adult members. The Church is not part of the ANGLICAN COMMUNION.

❖ Church of Sobantu

CHURCH OF GOD

The Church of God is a generic name that may be applied to as many as two hundred denominations. It includes many Churches with differing emphases, such as those within the PENTECOSTAL, Wesleyan and Second-Advent traditions, as well as the group known as the WORLDWIDE CHURCH OF GOD.

CHURCH OF GOD GENERAL CONFERENCE (ABRAHAMIC FAITH)

This Church, which is a schism of the SEVENTH-DAY ADVENTISTS, arose from the *Great Disappointment* that followed upon the failure of William Miller's prediction of Christ's second coming in 1843–4 (REVELATION 20). A group of disaffected Adventists were brought together as the Church of God (Abrahamic Faith) in 1888 in Oregon, Illinois, by Benjamin Wilson of Geneva, Illinois; Wilson had been baptized by John Thomas, the founder of the CHRISTADELPHIANS.

A dispute over the question of government within the Church led to the suspension of the national governing body from 1889 until 1921, when a general conference was established at Waterloo, Iowa, and a congregational polity was agreed upon. The annual general conference acts through various boards of directors who are in charge of the administration of the Oregon Bible College, where the ministers of the Church are trained. The Church is involved with youth work, mission work in India, Mexico and the Philippines, and publishing. The conference is incorporated as the Church of God (General Conference).

The Church holds to a UNITARIAN belief in God and denies the Trinity, regarding Jesus only as the son of God, who was not pre-existent but who came into existence through being born to the Virgin Mary. When Jesus returns to earth it is believed that he will establish his kingdom in Jerusalem, and Israel will then become the head of nations. To become a member of the Church a convert has to accept the doctrine of the Church, express repentance and receive baptism by immersion for the remission of sins.

The Church of God General Conference (Abrahamic Faith) and the Christadelphians hold to many of the same doctrines, but contact between the two groups has been limited until recently. Talks are now in progress in an effort to resolve small differences. Like the Christadelphians, the members of this Church try to return to the faith and practices of the early Church. They look to the Bible for the sole confirmation of their doctrines.

❖ Church of God of the Abrahamic Faith;
Church of God General Conference;
Church of God in Christ Jesus

CHURCH OF GOD (ANDERSON)

This foundation was not established as a denomination, but rather as a Christian fellowship, working as a reformation movement. The present title was accepted only for the purpose of identification.

The organization of this movement was the work of Daniel S. Warner, who had been a minister of the general eldership of the CHURCHES OF GOD GENERAL CONFERENCE (in North America). He had been influenced by the HOLINESS movement and was expelled from the general eldership of the Churches of God for preaching about sanctification. Warner, who married three times, had problems in his private life. His second wife tried to gain control over the new foundation he was forming and this ended in their divorce. In 1880, Warner and five others formed a loose organization of believers who were not bound to the acceptance of any creedal formulas; the founders saw this as a recreation of New Testament Church standard and practice.

The movement is committed to seeking Church unity and is now found in over 80 countries worldwide. The members hold that scripture is divinely inspired and that forgiveness of sins is achieved through Christ's atonement and the repentance of the believer. Although there is a belief in the second coming of Christ (REVELATION 20), this movement deviates from the norm in holding that the kingdom of God is established here and now and they do not anticipate a millennial reign of Christ (REVELATION 20). Their belief in the Trinity, in Jesus' divinity and the indwelling of the Holy Spirit is otherwise conventional.

Three ordinances are observed, baptism by immersion, foot-washing and the Lord's Supper. The observance of foot-washing may have been influenced by Daniel Warner's past membership of the general eldership of the Churches of God that had promoted this practice vigorously; it is performed on Holy Thursday. A high degree of moral behaviour is expected of the members, together with the avoidance of tobacco, alcohol, drugs and unseemly amusements.

A congregational polity is observed, but membership of the Church is otherwise quite informal. There is a general assembly, with an international convention, which meets in the Warner Auditorium in Anderson, Indiana, where the headquarters of the Church is located, as well as at Anderson College, which was founded in 1917. Missions have been established in Europe, the Near and Far East, Africa, and Central and South America. The Church makes use of an extensive network of media resources in its outreach work, but despite these efforts it is now experiencing a slow decline.

❖ Church of God Reformation Movement

CHURCH OF GOD (APOSTOLIC)

A small black American Church, originally known as the Christian Faith Band, which is within the ONENESS and PENTECOSTAL traditions, which was founded by elder Thomas J. Cox at Danville, Kentucky, in 1897. The Church was incorporated under its present title in 1919, it having been agreed in 1915 that a change of name was necessary.

The members believe that admission to the Church is only possible after repentance for sin, confession and baptism by immersion; the formula used is not Trinitarian, but in the name of Jesus only. The principal emphasis of this Church is upon sanctification and the avoidance of worldliness, in both dress and behaviour. Members observe the ordinances of the

Lord's Supper – which is celebrated monthly using unfermented grape juice and unleavened bread – and of foot-washing, which precedes their gathering at the table.

The administration of the Church is the responsibility of a board of bishops, with a senior bishop at its head. Delegates from the various congregations attend an annual general assembly when management and other issues facing the Church are discussed.

❖ Christian Faith Band

CHURCH OF GOD (CLEVELAND, TENNESSEE)

The Church began in 1886 in Monroe County, Tennessee, as a Christian fellowship known as the Christian Union of America and was led by a BAPTIST minister, Richard Spurling, Sr (1810–91). Spurling and eight others met at the Barney Creek Meeting House to discuss the problems of modernism and spiritual aridity. They wanted to effect a revival and to preach a return to the holiness of the primitive Church, as well as to bring about a union of all denominations. Shortly after the launch of the Christian Union Richard Spurling died and was succeeded by his son, Richard Green Spurling Jr, who had been ordained by his father.

Spurling Jr and two other members of the Union began to preach sanctification at Camp Creek, North Carolina, to some small, unaffiliated Baptist groups who joined forces with the Christian Union. Shortly afterwards, there was an outbreak of *glossolalia*, or speaking in tongues, within the group which was seen as an outpouring of the Holy Spirit upon the work of the Union.

Initially, worship within the group was unrestrained and disorderly and this led to criticism from the local community, in the face of which the leaders of the Union restored some order and provided for a better, but still simple, form of government. At this point the Christian Union underwent a change of name and became known at first as the Holiness Church, and from 1907, following an agreement made at the general assembly of 1906, as the Church of God. In 1903 a Quaker, Ambrose J. Tomlinson (1865–1943), who was also an agent for the American Bible Society, joined the Church at Camp Creek. Following his reception of the baptism of the Holy Spirit it is said that Tomlinson began to speak in tongues, reputedly in at least ten languages, and he was quickly promoted to be the general moderator of the Church, and later elected as general overseer for life. Tomlinson was put in complete control of the Church's finances and in 1920, when an audit revealed some financial irregularity, he was impeached and removed from office. When he left the Church Tomlinson took with him a few followers. A court order prevented this small group from identifying themselves with the Church of God and they called themselves the Tomlinson Church of God, which was later changed in 1953 to become known as the CHURCH OF GOD OF PROPHECY.

The general assembly of 1906 also pronounced on the vexed question of foot-washing as part of their services, and it was agreed that it should be observed at least annually, or more frequently, but not as part of each service. Doctrinally, the Church follows in the ARMINIAN tradition, practising baptism by immersion and observing the Lord's Supper, with or without foot-washing. It also acknowledges that a Christian will grow in sanctification after justification, although some members still hold to the idea that sanctification occurs instantaneously and is followed by baptism of the Holy Spirit, which is signalled by the phenomenon of *glossolalia*.

Their belief in the holiness of life leads the members to adopt a simple lifestyle and to prohibit all jewellery, cosmetics and fashionable clothing, including a ban on shorts or trousers for women. The use of tobacco, drugs and alcohol is also prohibited and members are not allowed to join secret societies or Lodges. The second coming of Christ, with all his saints, and his reign on earth for a thousand years, is anticipated (REVELATION 20).

The organization of the Church is centralized, with its headquarters in Cleveland, Tennessee. There is a biennial assembly, whose chairman is the general overseer, and at other times the administration is in the hands of a supreme council and an executive committee. To fund the Church, its publishing ventures, foreign missions in over one hundred countries and educational work, tithing is expected from its members.

CHURCH OF GOD (HOLINESS)

This is not to be confused with the CHURCHES OF GOD, HOLINESS.

In late nineteenth-century America many felt the need to withdraw from man-made denominations and to recreate a New Testament-style Church, headed by Jesus Christ. One of the early leaders of the movement was A. M. Kiergan, a minister of the METHODIST EPISCOPAL CHURCH, South, who, like some other ministers from his Church, had formed Holiness Associations within their various denominations.

Some clergy from Kansas, Missouri and Iowa had formed the Southwestern Holiness Association and by 1882 six of these clergymen, including Kiergan, decided to withdraw from their denominational groups; by 1888 they had formed a Church, called the Independent Holiness People, a name that was changed in 1895 to the Church of God (known as Independent Holiness People). Difficulties arose concerning the polity of this Church, with some advocating a congregational rather than a presbyterial polity, while others preferred the opposite. As a result, a short-lived schism developed but a reunion was brought about in 1922 when the present name of the Church was adopted. Doctrinally, the Church emphasizes the spiritual experiences of regeneration and entire satisfaction for its members and it preaches the second coming of Christ with an actual millennial reign to follow (REVELATION 20).

The polity of the Church is congregational. Delegates attend an annual convention when decisions are made concerning the future work of the Church. Both home and foreign missions are supported, in the USA, concerned with ethnic minority groups, the Caribbean, Mexico, South America and Nigeria. The headquarters of this small but very active Church is in Overland Park, Kansas.

CHURCH OF GOD (HOUSE OF PRAYER)

This small American Church in the PENTECOSTAL tradition, with its headquarters in Markleysburg, Pennsylvania, was a split from the CHURCH OF GOD (CLEVELAND, TENNESSEE). The schism was led by

Harrison W. Poteat, who had been an overseer for the parent Church in the north-east of the USA for twenty years and who had established churches on Prince Edward Island in Canada in 1933.

When Poteat left the Church of God (Cleveland, Tennessee) in 1939, some of the congregations followed him, bringing with them the use of their church buildings. When Poteat was later required to return the real estate to the Church of God (Cleveland, Tennessee) this cost him many followers who preferred to stay with the buildings to which they were accustomed, but the Church of God (House of Prayer) survived. The Church is presided over by a general superintendent.

❖ Church of God (Bishop Poteat)

CHURCH OF GOD (JERUSALEM ACRES)

This small, but growing, Church owes its name to the fact that its headquarters is at Jerusalem Acres, Cleveland, Tennessee. It is the result of a schism within the CHURCH OF GOD OF PROPHECY that occurred after the death of A. J. Tomlinson in 1943, though the new Church was not established until 1957. Tomlinson had appointed Grady R. Kent as general secretary of the Church of God of Prophecy Marker Association, an association which was designed to find, physically mark, and maintain locations throughout the world that were in some way connected to the Church of God of Prophecy, usually because that was where Tomlinson had had an ecstatic experience. After Tomlinson's death and the succession of his son, Milton, which led to a schism, Kent remained loyal to Milton Tomlinson until, in 1957, he disagreed with Milton's action in replacing the office of general overseer, as the highest authority in the Church, with an assembly.

Kent, and his supporters who came mostly from South Carolina, left the Church of God of Prophecy and established their own, with Kent as general overseer. He abolished feasts, such as those of Easter and Christmas, substituting instead the feast of Passover and the Feast of Lights respectively, as the early apostolic Church would have recognized these festivals – Easter and Christmas coming only as later traditions.

The Church of God (Jerusalem Acres) is now governed by a chief bishop who appoints state bishops, assisted by a chief steward, the office of four, modelled on the four cherubim in Ezekiel 1:5–10, twelve apostles, who act as executive officers, and seven overseers.

❖ Church of God of All Nations

CHURCH OF GOD (MOUNTAIN ASSEMBLY)

The Church was formed in 1895 when a HOLINESS revival mission attracted many Baptists, both lay and clerical members of the United Baptist Church, many of whom received the blessing of personal sanctification. This situation was tolerated until 1903, when several ministers who held these views about sanctification, and who had been preaching this doctrine, contrary to the BAPTIST *Articles of Faith*, had their licences to preach revoked.

These ministers were J. H. Parks, Steve Bryant, Tom Moses and William Douglas. Together with members from their various congregations, these men met at Jellico, Tennessee, in 1907 and formed a committee for the purpose of organizing a Holiness Association. This Association came to be called the Church of God, changed to include the words *Mountain Assembly* when it was realized that there were other Church of God groups. In 1944 there was a reorganization of the government of the Church, with provision now made for a full-time general overseer, with state and, later, district overseers who all work within a congregational polity and are accountable to an annual assembly. Training for the ministry is provided by a two-year college programme of biblical studies at the International Institute of Ministry, which was established in 1997 to prepare young people for the ministry.

Doctrinally, the Church is similar to the CHURCH OF GOD (CLEVELAND, TENNESSEE), and has a permanent headquarters at the Assembly tabernacle in Jellico, Tennessee, (founded 1922). Provision for Sunday schools has been encouraged since the 1920s and work with young people has been a major priority since the late 1940s when a young people's group was created; this is now known as Youth Warriors for Christ. The Church maintains a number of foreign missions, which began in Brazil in 1968 and has now extended into twenty countries of the world, now focused on Africa.

CHURCH OF GOD (NEW DUNKERS)

A defunct American denomination that was founded in 1848 as a breakaway group from the CHURCH OF THE BRETHREN; it was disbanded in 1962.

CHURCH OF GOD (SEVENTH-DAY)

There are two American Churches of the same name, one centred in Denver, Colorado and the other at Salem, West Virginia. Both of these arose from what was known as the Second Advent movement in the nineteenth century. Members of this movement, who expected the return, or second coming of Christ, subsequently became known as the Seventh-Day Adventists (REVELATION 20).

Members of the Second Advent movement based their beliefs on those of William Miller, who had predicted the second coming of Christ between 1843 and 1844; he later narrowed this prediction to 22 October 1844. When Christ failed to appear upon that date this non-event became known as the *Great Disappointment*. In an effort to ensure that the expected return could still happen, some members of the Church, Joseph Bates, and a husband and wife, James and Ellen Harmon White, argued that it was from this predicted date that Christ would examine the names in the Book of Life, and it would be at the end of this examination that he would return to earth and begin his millennial reign (REVELATION 20). This speculation was confirmed by over two hundred visions allegedly experienced by Ellen White, which ranged through a variety of subjects from biblical interpretation to diet.

Some ADVENTISTS, unconvinced by the visions, separated from the movement, formed a new group and began to publish a periodical called *The Hope of Israel* in 1863. By 1866 they had adopted the name 'Church of God' and moved their new headquarters to Stanberry, Missouri. By the start of the twentieth century the Church was known as the Church of God (Adventist). Another split occurred in 1933, from within the Stanberry group, with the splinter group setting up their headquarters in Salem, West Virginia. The remaining members of the Stanberry group relocated their headquarters to

Denver, Colorado, but maintained their publishing press at Stanberry.

The Salem group sought a more so-called apostolic form of church government in the form of a committee of twelve apostles, a council of seventy leaders and seven business executives. The leaders were selected by drawing lots, which was considered in keeping with biblical tradition. The Salem and Denver groups held discussions in 1949 at Fairview, Oklahoma, and a satisfactory polity was agreed; there was a reuniting of the groups in 1950, with the headquarters at Denver, Colorado.

The Church affirms the ten commandments and in consequence observes Saturday as the sabbath. The members do not celebrate Lent, Easter or Christmas, or engage in military service. Members are also barred from seeking divorce, and from the use of alcohol, tobacco, drugs, and the eating of unclean meat, such as pork. The Church also teaches that Jesus Christ instituted two ordinances, the Lord's Supper, which is celebrated on the fourteenth day of the Hebrew month of Adib, or Nisan (March–April) and is preceded by foot-washing, and baptism, which is by immersion. A strong emphasis is placed on tithing.

Members believe that Jesus Christ will return, upon which occasion all will be judged according to their works, and reward and punishment will be meted out. The dead are believed to remain unconscious until the second coming of Christ (REVELATION 20). The Godhead is seen as having only two persons, God the Father and his Son, Jesus Christ; the Holy Spirit is seen only as an influence that the godhead applies to human lives.

The Church is organized into separate congregations, with a general conference held every two years attended by representatives from each congregation. A ministerial council validates clergy licences and regulates their training. Missions in many countries worldwide are maintained.

CHURCH OF GOD (WORLD HEADQUARTERS)

When Ambrose J. Tomlinson, the founder of the CHURCH OF GOD OF PROPHECY, died in 1943, his sons, Milton and Homer, saw their duty as sharing the responsibility of running the Church between them and with equal status. Homer would concentrate on foreign missions and Milton would take responsibility for the day-to-day running of the Church. Things did not go smoothly between them, however, and the matter ended in litigation, with the courts deciding in favour of Milton being in sole charge. Homer left the Church to found his own, the Church of God (World Headquarters), which he led until his death in 1968. Homer Tomlinson had originally set up his headquarters in Queens Village, New York, but after his death this moved to Huntsville, Alabama.

There was a major doctrinal difference between the brothers' Churches. This concerned the replacement of the premillennial (REVELATION 20) belief of the other Churches of God with the new idea that the Church of God can establish God's kingdom on earth by setting up the sanctified members of the Church in key government positions throughout the world. A vigorous foreign mission programme was set up and Homer Tomlinson travelled widely, assuming the title *King of Nations*; affiliated Churches of God were established in Europe, Central

America, Africa, the Near East and the West Indies. There are over 2,000 congregations in the USA alone, with around 75,000 members.

❖ Church of God (Huntsville)

CHURCH OF GOD AND SAINTS OF CHRIST

This small American denomination, with its headquarters in Bellville, Virginia, is an interesting amalgam of Judaism, Christianity and black nationalism. It came into existence when a black Sante Fe Railway cook, William S. Crowdy, who was also a deacon in the BAPTIST Church, had a vision, which he believed to be from God, calling him to lead his people into what was termed the *true religion*. As *Prophet* Crowdy, he founded the sect in 1896 at Lawrence, Kansas. The headquarters was moved to Philadelphia, Pennsylvania, before he died and it was there that the first annual assembly was convened in 1900. Prophet Crowdy died in 1908, leaving behind two bishops, who did not survive him by many years, and the leadership of the Church then fell to Bishop William Plummer, who styled himself as *Grand Father Abraham*.

This group believes that all black people are descendants of the lost tribes of Israel, and that all Jews were originally black. They observe the Jewish calendar and its festivals as well as the Jewish sabbath, and believe in the literal teachings of both the Old and New Testaments as guidelines to salvation. Membership is restricted to black converts, who are received into the Church through repentance, baptism by immersion, a confession of faith in Jesus Christ and the receiving of Communion under the form of unleavened bread and water. The convert, whose feet are then washed by an elder of the Church, agrees to observe the Decalogue (the ten commandments) and recites the Lord's Prayer before being breathed upon with what is termed the *holy kiss*.

Its bishop, who as a prophet is believed to be in direct communion with God and is able to perform miracles and make prophetic announcements, rules the Church. This bishop-prophet presides over a council of twelve elders, known as the board of presbytery. Each local congregation, of which there are around two hundred in the USA, Africa and the West Indies, is catered for by four orders of ministry, bishops, missionaries, and ordained and non-ordained ministers; deacons care for the temporal administration of each church. The Church makes its decisions through district, annual and general assemblies. The Church operates several industries, an elementary school and a home for orphans and the elderly.

❖ Black Jews

CHURCH OF GOD AS ORGANIZED BY CHRIST

This group may be better described as an evangelistic association rather than as a Church, since the members do not subscribe to denominationalism, or sect-ism.

This group was founded in the US in 1886 by an ex-MENNONITE preacher, P. J. Kaufman, who left the Mennonite Church as a protest against its growing sense of having become a denomination, and also because of its failure to look to scripture alone as the source of all faith and practice. As a result of this firm view of scripture, the members oppose any creedal formulas and human traditions.

All believers have the right to membership, since there is no formal process of initiation. Ministers are licensed, but only to give them legal recognition and status;

ordination is otherwise thought of as being effected by Jesus Christ alone. The ordinances believed to have been established by Christ are observed: baptism, foot-washing and the Lord's Supper. The emphasis during church services is firmly placed on repentance and restitution.

People who regard themselves as members of the Church oppose any form of sectarianism and ecumenism, and also avoid the use of tobacco, alcohol and drugs. The dress worn is simple, unadorned by jewellery, and worldly amusements are eschewed. They also avoid secret societies, Sunday schools, and litigation.

CHURCH OF GOD BY FAITH, INC.

The foundations of this small Church were laid in Jackson, Florida, in 1914 when a group of four men in America – Crawford and John Bright, Aaron Matthews Sr and Nathaniel Scippio – felt they were called to encourage, educate, strengthen and sustain others who they felt were in need of salvation.

The members of the Church believe in the process of conversion, followed by sanctification and baptism of the Holy Spirit, with *glossolalia*, or speaking in tongues, as evidence of this baptism. They also practise a policy of shunning, or isolating, wilful sinners. The first general assembly was held at White Springs, Florida, in 1917 and it was from this assembly that missions were planned and set up. The Church was chartered in 1923. In 1941 the general assembly was relocated to Ocala, Florida, where the Matthews-Scippio Academy was established in 1963, providing education from kindergarten to high school level. In 1987 a further change of venue now has the assemblies' meeting in Atlanta, Georgia.

The polity of the Church is episcopal and its officers include a bishop, a general overseer and an executive secretary. The general assembly, to which delegates from local congregations are sent, meets three times a year. There are in excess of 7,000 members of this Church, living mainly in Florida, Georgia, Alabama, South Carolina. Maryland, New Jersey and New York.

CHURCH OF GOD IN CHRIST

A black PENTECOSTAL Church that originated within the HOLINESS movement and was established in the USA in 1895 by a black BAPTIST preacher, Charles Harrison Mason (1866–1961).

In 1893 Mason had enrolled in the Arkansas Bible College, but after three months he withdrew because he was unsatisfied with the teaching methods and with the presentation of the message of the Bible. In 1895 he met up with C. P. Jones, who the year previously had begun to lay the foundations for the CHURCH OF CHRIST (HOLINESS) and they became close companions. Joined by some others who shared their beliefs, Mason and Jones began to preach a revival mission in Jackson, Mississippi, in 1896 and made many converts. The Baptist groups in Arkansas, however, rejected both men because of what they saw as an overemphasis on holiness. The two men began to hold meetings in an abandoned warehouse in Lexington, Mississippi, and purchased some land on which they built a small hut and formed a Pentecostal body known initially as the Church of God, to which title *in Christ* was added in 1897. Mason began to place a strong emphasis on entire sanctification, and in the course of a revival meeting he received the baptism of the Holy Spirit and the gift of *glossolalia*, or speaking in tongues. This aroused considerable resentment between Mason and Jones, with Jones and some others parting company from Mason.

Mason then called a conference in Memphis, Tennessee, for all those who believed in the baptism of the Holy Spirit, and the first general assembly of the Church of God in Christ was organized in 1907, at which Charles Mason declared that the Church was to be Pentecostal. He was elected as general overseer and chief apostle of about twelve churches located mainly in Tennessee, Arkansas, Mississippi and Oklahoma. Until 1961 Mason had single-handedly supervised all the activities of the Church, but he then surrendered some authority to four assistant bishops, and later to state overseers, who directed all the local churches within a state and called for state and annual conferences.

After his death in 1961, the administration of the Church was reorganized, but not to the satisfaction of all its members and a further attempt at reorganization was made in 1968, when authority was placed in the hands of a general assembly, to be summoned every four years, and in a general board of twelve members with a presiding bishop who would be responsible for administration between the meetings of the general assembly.

The Church believes in the Trinity, with an emphasis on repentance, regeneration and sanctification, with *glossolalia* and the gift of healing following upon baptism of the Holy Spirit. They observe three ordinances, baptism by immersion, foot-washing and the Lord's Supper.

The headquarters of the Church is in Memphis, Tennessee, and has an adult membership, which is steadily growing, currently in excess of 4.5 million in the USA and elsewhere in the world. Missions have been supported in Africa, including South Africa, Botswana, Thailand, Jamaica, Haiti and Liberia.

CHURCH OF GOD IN CHRIST (MENNONITE)

An American Church that had its beginnings in a schism from the MENNONITE CHURCH in Ohio, and was led by a young Mennonite visionary, John Holdeman, who believed that he was called to preach and to demonstrate that his Church was in error.

Holdeman preached the need for the conversion of sinners and that they should be born again, through baptism of the Holy Spirit. He called for the shunning of apostates and sinners to be enforced and the growing worldliness of the Mennonite Church to be corrected. Holdeman also objected to the Mennonite tradition of selecting ministers by lots, since he felt that he had been called to his ministry in a vision. He separated from the Mennonite Church in 1859 to begin a series of meetings with small groups of followers and in a short time the Church of God in Christ (Mennonite) was established. It was with the arrival of immigrants to America, however, that the so-called *Johnny Holdeman Movement* took off, especially in Kansas and Manitoba.

The doctrine of the Church is based on the Bible as the inspired and infallible word of God, and the members believe that the 18 Articles of the *Dordrecht Confession of Faith* of 1632 should be accepted. Holdeman preached that the same confession of faith should be believed and practised by all Churches and that worldly fashions and amusements should be strictly avoided. The

Church has missions in the USA, Canada, Mexico, Nigeria, Haiti and Brazil.

CHURCH OF GOD IN CHRIST INTERNATIONAL

An American Church now in serious decline, having lost nearly a thousand congregations in the space of 25 years. It was founded in 1969 as a schism within the CHURCH OF GOD IN CHRIST over the issue of whether authority in the parent Church body should be centralized, or not. A new structure was devised in this breakaway Church, which continues to support eighteen dioceses throughout the USA. Its doctrinal position is identical to that of the Church of God in Christ.

CHURCH OF GOD OF PROPHECY

As will have been seen in the entry for CHURCH OF GOD (CLEVELAND, TENNESSEE), Ambrose J. Tomlinson, who had been elected as its general overseer and put in sole charge of its finances, later left that Church owing to a misunderstanding about the financing of mission work. He, and some followers, formed the Tomlinson Church of God, which in 1953 came to be known as the Church of God of Prophecy.

Ambrose Tomlinson held firmly to the notion that the Church established by Christ had fallen into apostasy within a few centuries of its foundation and he also believed that in 1903 he had received a revelation from God that the movement begun in North Carolina, which had prefaced the formation of the Church of God (Cleveland, Tennessee), was part of God's plan in fulfilment of the prophecy of Isaiah 60:1–5. His belief was maintained after his separation from that Church and remained unshaken. When Tomlinson died, in 1943, one of his sons, Milton, succeeded him as general overseer and this led to another split. Another of Tomlinson's sons, Homer, would not recognize his brother's promotion and he was expelled from the Church. Homer then founded his own Church, which came to be called the CHURCH OF GOD (WORLD HEADQUARTERS), which he established in Queen's Village, New York, but which moved in 1968 to Huntsville, Alabama, following Homer's death. A further schism occurred in 1957 when a small group, under the leadership of Grady R. Kent, formed the Church of God of All Nations, now known as the CHURCH OF GOD (JERUSALEM ACRES), centred in Cleveland, Tennessee.

Today the Church of God of Prophecy has in excess of two thousand congregations and many thousands of members in the USA, as well as in overseas congregations, including those in Haiti, Jamaica and the Bahamas.

CHURCH OF GOD OF THE APOSTOLIC FAITH

A small independent American PENTECOSTAL Church, founded in 1913 by four preachers, James O. McKenzie, Edwin A. Buckles, Oscar H. Myers and Joseph P. Rhoades, near Ozark in Arkansas, north-east of Fort Smith. Doctrinally, the Church is identical to that of the CHURCH OF GOD (CLEVELAND, TENNESSEE), but a presbyterial polity was adopted, in the hope of avoiding some of the problems encountered by that Church, with provision made for an annual general conference at which the presbytery would be elected, composed of seven ministers, a general overseer and two assistants. The conference has responsibility for church property, with the presbytery in charge of the conduct of the ministry within the current thirty congregations of the Church.

The headquarters, originally in Tulsa, Oklahoma, is now in Pharr, Texas, and a small mission, which was set up in Mexico, has now become so well established that the Church's seminary is located there.

CHURCH OF GOD THE ETERNAL

Raymond C. Cole, a past member of the WORLDWIDE CHURCH OF GOD, organized the Church in the USA in 1975 because he, like many others, felt that there had been a dilution of some of the doctrinal positions held by the Worldwide Church of God. That Church had been founded in 1934 by Herbert W. Armstrong, and had been known at one time as the Radio Church of God.

When the Worldwide Church of God changed to allow the remarriage of divorcees, and also moved the celebration of Pentecost to a Sunday, this was a step too far from the original position held and preached by Herbert W. Armstrong and ran against Cole's view that remarriage was not allowable in the case of divorce, and that Pentecost should always be celebrated on a Monday, since it is to be celebrated fifty days from the sabbath occurring within the Days of Unleavened Bread. Unable to accept these changes, Cole and his fellow thinkers established the Church of God the Eternal, which now has its headquarters in Eugene, Oregon.

The Church places a strong emphasis on God's law, as handed down from the Old Testament, and holds true to Armstrong's teaching that the members are the spiritual and physical descendants of Abraham, Isaac and Jacob – the House of Israel – and that what was revealed to Israel by God through Moses must be observed in the Church today. Not surprisingly, the members of this Church subscribe to the principles of British- or Anglo-Israelism, which was a belief suggested by a Scotsman, John Wilson, in 1840 that the dispersed *Lost Ten Tribes of Israel* had migrated to Europe and that the prophecies in the Bible about the tribes of Ephraim and Manasseh refer directly to Great Britain and the USA (and, more recently, to the member states of the European Union).

The Trinity is rejected, on the grounds that it was a false doctrine originating in the period between the second and fourth centuries, but the Church affirms that God is a family, consisting of the Father and his Son, Jesus; the Holy Spirit is seen as the action of God, and not as a person. Sabbath is observed from Friday sunset until sunset on Saturday, and the members keep to some of the Jewish dietary restrictions, avoiding pork and shellfish (Armstrong had further extended the restriction to duck meat). Like the parent Church, the Church of God the Eternal teaches that military service is to be avoided and that the seven annual holy days, given by God to Israel through Moses, are to be kept.

The Church recognizes the ordinances of baptism by immersion for the remission of sins following true repentance, and the Lord's Supper, which is seen as a continuation of the Jewish Passover and is to be observed at night on the anniversary of the death of Jesus Christ, on the fourteenth day of Abib, or Nisan (March–April), in the Jewish calendar.

CHURCH OF ILLUMINATION

The Church of Illumination was organized in Pennsylvania, USA, in 1908 by the Reverend R. Swinburne Clymer as an attempt to provide a means of attracting members of the public who might be interested in seeking a spiritual and hidden interpretation of basic biblical teachings. It taught, for example, that in the late nineteenth century a new era, the Manistic age, had commenced, which had followed the Egyptian and Christian ages. The name is taken from that of Manisis, the title of a new world leader, whose teachings will allow mankind to fulfil its destiny in the new age. This new age is expected to last for two thousand years during which time the secrets of the Book of Revelation will be unsealed in readiness for Armageddon.

❖ Fraternitas Rosae Crucis

CHURCH OF IRELAND

The coming of Christianity to Ireland probably predates the arrival of St Palladius at Arklow, County Wicklow, who had been sent there by Pope St Celestine I (422–32). The earlier introduction of Christianity may have been due to the influence of British and Gaulish traders and missionaries. St Patrick arrived in Ireland following the departure of St Palladius, who returned to Rome, and the foundations of the Christian Church were laid down.

Under St Patrick the Church that developed was decidedly monastic, lacking in parochial and diocesan structures. The monasteries became centres of learning and influence, seemingly independent of Rome and staunchly holding to Irish customs, an example of which can be seen in the dating of Easter in Ireland that, until 704, differed from the accepted method. The style of tonsuring of monks was also individual and the rite of baptism was described as *irregular*; the Venerable Bede left an account of St Augustine directing the Celtic Church to complete the ordinance of baptism according to the Roman rite, a theme that was later taken up by the papal legate, Bishop Gilbert of Limerick (1106–39). In the late eighth century, when the Danish invasions laid waste to Irish culture and traditions, many Irish scholars and churchmen escaped abroad and learning in Ireland went into decline. The Anglo-Norman invasions in the twelfth century saw most of the island conquered and brought into conformity with English law and customs, and there was a tendency to appoint Englishmen to Irish sees. At the time of the Reformation in the sixteenth century, the Irish Supremacy Act of 1537 asserted the English king's supremacy in both Irish and English Churches. Some suppression of Irish monasteries followed, with many of the Irish friars adopting an itinerant way of life. Most of the Irish people remained loyal to Rome and were largely unmoved by various attempts to make them accept the PROTESTANT doctrine. This resistance sprang partly from a spirit of conservatism and partly from opposition to rule from England; the ROMAN CATHOLIC CHURCH was becoming a symbol and bond of Irish nationalism.

The repression of Roman Catholics throughout the seventeenth and eighteenth centuries strengthened the determination of the Irish. With the Act of Union in 1800 uniting the parliaments of England and Ireland, the Church of Ireland, sister to the CHURCH OF ENGLAND, was established by law, and was in the ascendant, privileged and in close association with the state. A census of 1861 showed that four-fifths of the population of Ireland was still Roman Catholic and only a slim minority were members of the Church of Ireland. This imbalance led to the passing of the Irish Church Act of

Disestablishment in 1869, which became law in 1871. In 1870, a general convention was held at which the reorganization of the Church of Ireland's ecclesiastical system was made, providing for a general synod as the supreme legislative body of the Church; this now has a house of bishops with twelve members and a house of representatives made up of both clerical and lay delegates. There is also an annual diocesan synod, with parish representatives, and select vestries at parochial level, made up of clergy and lay members.

The Church of Ireland is self-governing and its members are found in both Northern Ireland and in the Irish Republic. As part of the ANGLICAN COMMUNION it is in communion with the See of Canterbury, but not under the Archbishop of Canterbury's authority. The Church is divided between two provinces, Armagh and Dublin, each with its own archbishop. The Archbishop of Armagh is the Primate of All Ireland, with the Archbishop of Dublin as the Primate of Ireland. Within these provinces there are twelve dioceses and their parishes.

CHURCH OF JESUS CHRIST (BICKERTONITE)

This American Church was formally organized in West Elizabeth, Pennsylvania, in 1862 by William Bickerton and takes its alternative name from him. It began as an earlier breakaway Mormon group, led by Sidney Rigdon, but leaving Bickerton in charge when Rigdon moved to a fresh location near Greencastle, Pennsylvania, in 1846.

The history of the Church has been fairly uneven. In 1875 Bickerton moved to establish the headquarters in a new branch settlement in Kansas, and disagreement broke out between this new group and those remaining in Pennsylvania. Bickerton also came in for personal criticism, and an accusation of adultery led to his being debarred from his own Church, although he was later able to rejoin in 1902.

Doctrinally, the Church follows in the tradition of the CHURCH OF JESUS CHRIST OF LATTER-DAY SAINTS, although polygamy has never been practised, and the Church uses a revised edition of the *Book of Mormon*. The Lord's Supper, preceded by foot-washing, is celebrated, and it is a practice in this Church that members greet one another with a holy kiss. The Church has missionary enterprises in Europe and Africa, as well as with Native Americans in the USA and Canada.

❖ Bickertonites; The Bickertonite Organization

CHURCH OF JESUS CHRIST (CUTLERITE)

Alpheus Cutler, an elder of the CHURCH OF JESUS CHRIST OF LATTER-DAY SAINTS, whose members are also known as Mormons, had been instrumental in America in the 1840s in building up the work of that Church in Nauvoo, in Hancock County, Illinois, as part of a mission to evangelize Native Americans which Cutler claimed to have been entrusted to him by Joseph Smith, the founder of the Mormons, before he died in 1844. The Mormons had settled in Nauvoo, but after the death of Joseph Smith the group moved to Salt Lake City, Utah, leaving Cutler behind with a remnant of the Church who had chosen to remain in Nauvoo. With Cutler's death, in 1864, his successor, Chauncey Whiting, tried to re-establish the community at Clitherall, Minnesota; it was claimed that the choice of site was inspired by a revelation received by Alpheus Cutler. The community, which was to be known as the United Order, was not wholly successful and in 1928 there was a split, with some members moving to Independence, Missouri, where they established the Church of Jesus Christ (Cutlerite), which continues today. The Clitherall group became defunct when the last member moved to Independence in the 1990s.

The Church of Jesus Christ (Cutlerite) believes that the Lord will reject all those Gentiles who refuse to accept Joseph Smith's message. They also hold that the days between Christmas and New Year are to be regarded as sabbath days, when no work is to be performed. The Church is presided over by a president, with a council of 48 priests administering the larger congregations.

❖ True Church of Jesus Christ (Cutlerite)

CHURCH OF JESUS CHRIST (END TIME REVIVAL)

This is, strictly speaking, not a denomination but a group that developed as a fellowship of missionaries dedicated to pioneering 'full gospel' Churches.

This Australian group owes its origins to Bruce Jamieson, a freelance preacher to the Aborigines and Torres Strait Islanders in the mid-1960s. Jamieson had been associated with the United Pentecostal Church and therefore subscribed to the belief that in the Trinity there is no distinction of persons, but rather that the members of the Trinity are as modes through which God has revealed himself. In 1970 Jamieson invited another preacher, John Hartley from Tasmania, to preach at a convention in the Fire-Baptized End Time Revival Church centre in Redfern, an inner city suburb of Sydney, and from this the fellowship developed. There were also possible links with the American-based Church of Jesus Christ, founded in 1927 by M. K. Lawson. This is a white PENTECOSTAL group, with over five hundred congregations, which places special emphasis on divine healing. It has an extensive missionary outreach into Africa, India, Mexico, Israel and Australia.

It was on account of Jamieson's connection and dependence upon America for funding that many of his fellow preachers deserted him, and Hartley took over the running of the fellowship. The members of the group subscribe to an ARMINIAN and premillennial doctrinal position (REVELATION 20).

The group maintains a part-time clergy, the ministers known as pastors, and has been active in the planting of churches both in the Torres Strait Islands and in some Sydney suburbs, mainly where there are Native Australian families living; other groups are to be found in Melbourne, Victoria, and Taree, New South Wales.

❖ Australasian Christian Fellowship of Apostolic Faith; Ministers and Churches of the Lord Jesus Christ

CHURCH OF JESUS CHRIST (STRANGITE)

When Joseph Smith, the founder of the CHURCH OF JESUS CHRIST OF LATTER-DAY SAINTS (Mormons), was killed on 27 June 1844, one of his followers, James Jesse Strang (1813–56) claimed to have received a message and been visited on the same day by an angel who said to him 'Fear God and Be Strengthened and Obey Him for Great is the Work which He Hath Required at Thy Hands'; the angel then anointed him with oil. James Strang held high office in the Church, being ordained as an elder in the Melchizedek priesthood. When he presented his claims to have been divinely elected as its leader to the Church, backing up his argument with a letter from Joseph Smith dated 18 June 1844, which named him as the successor, he was promptly excommunicated.

Strang immediately set about establishing the Church of Jesus Christ (Strangite) at Voree, Wisconsin, which he did in 1845. After much dissension, during which he lost much of his following, Strang and his remaining loyal members went to Beaver Island, Michigan, where he set up a theocracy with himself as its leader. This move, which attracted more than two thousand followers, made James Strang into a powerful figure. By 1856 the Strangites were accounted to be the largest of the Mormon groups that had left Brigham Young, but this number collapsed when, in the same year, Strang was shot, and died several weeks later, having failed to name a successor. The followers drifted away leaving behind only a small group. The remaining apostles reorganized what remained of the group and the Church barely survived.

❖ Church of Jesus Christ of Latter-Day Saints (Strangite)

CHURCH OF JESUS CHRIST OF LATTER-DAY SAINTS

This must not be confused with the Reorganized Church of Jesus Christ of Latter-Day Saints, *which is based at Independence, Missouri.*

This American denomination is not conventionally Christian, since its founder Joseph Smith (1805–44) claimed to have received, in a vision, a message telling him that the existing Christian Church was in error and that the true gospel was to be restored and revealed to him so that he could re-establish the true Church on earth.

To this end, Smith was led to discover on a hill called Cumorah, near Palmyra, New York, some golden tablets covered in hieroglyphs, which he was able to translate with the help some special spectacles and an angel, called Moroni. The *Book of Mormon* was the result. The book was not understood as supplanting, but rather providing support for, the Bible and was considered by the followers to be equal in importance to the other writings of Joseph Smith, the *Book of Doctrine and Covenants* and the *Pearl of Great Price.* John the Baptist is said to have conferred upon Smith and his companion, who had helped in the transcribing of the *Book of Mormon*, the priesthood of Aaron, with an instruction to baptize one another. Three other heavenly visitors, Peter, James and John, then conferred the priesthood of Melchizedek upon them and gave them the keys of apostleship. These remarkable events are claimed to have occurred in 1829, the year preceding the Church's foundation by Joseph Smith and some six followers.

From Fayette, New York, the group of followers, whose number had now increased, left for Kirtland, Ohio, and went from there to Independence, Missouri from where they were expelled. The group settled in Nauvoo, Illinois, where Joseph Smith was assassinated in Carthage jail in 1844. The leadership of the group was taken over by Brigham Young, who assumed the rank of president, but this prompted others in the group to refuse to recognize his leadership and they split away, leading to the formation of the Re-organized Church of Jesus Christ of Latter-Day Saints. Led by Brigham Young, the remaining *saints*, as they were called, were driven from Nauvoo in 1846 and travelling across America they found the Great Salt Lake valley, in what is now the State of Utah, and here they set up their community. Utah was declared to be a territory in 1850 and became a state in 1896. Under Young's leadership some three hundred settlements were founded, stretching from Canada to Mexico. The members held that the Christian Church had fallen into apostasy shortly after the close of the New Testament period and that it was in need of restoration.

The Church is administered internationally by the first presidency, which consists of three men (the president and two counsellors), assisted by a council of twelve apostles. This council is chosen by revelation to supervise others and work under the direction of the first presidency. Subordinate to this group are the *quorums of the seventy*, each with seven presidents of equal rank; each quorum administers one geographical area of the world.

Conventional Christians would regard the Church's doctrines of the Trinity and Christology as being flawed and unacceptable. Mormons do not believe in one God in three persons but in three Gods and hold that both the Father and the Son have material bodies, while the Holy Spirit is a 'personage of spirit'. Christ is called divine, but by this they do not believe that this is a unique divinity and it is seen as the same that any man can attain. Baptism by immersion usually takes place at 8 years of age and is essential for salvation, which cannot be achieved by faith alone but also through good works performed in this life. Baptism for the dead, and sealing in marriage, are exclusive rites of this Church. Baptism for the dead is based upon the belief than non-Mormons will have the opportunity to accept Latter-Day Saints teaching after death; living Mormons can be baptized as proxies for dead non-Mormons in a special ceremony. Marriage has two forms, that for time and that for eternity, the latter known as celestial marriage. Because of a belief that Mormon women could not reach salvation unless they were married, this led to an acceptance of plural marriages, for both time and eternity. In turn, this led to some polygamous arrangements whose legitimacy was countenanced by Brigham Young in 1852, but the practice was officially abolished in 1890 to comply with a U. S. Congress law that had been passed a few years earlier. The practice of polygamy is believed to be still fairly widespread among more fundamentalist Mormons, with estimates ranging from 30,000 to 60,000, although if caught practitioners face the prospect of excommunication.

Mormons believe in a millennial reign of Christ on earth (REVELATION 20), during which time the centre of Christ's rule will move from Jerusalem either to Salt Lake City or Independence, Missouri. While some very wicked human beings will be consigned to hell most will be placed, in their glorified bodies, in one of three heavenly kingdoms, the celestial which has God's presence and is retained for the most worthy, the terrestrial for those who have achieved some measure of goodness and faith, and the telestial, where there is remorse for wrongdoing, but no punishment.

Mormons worship in temples, rather than churches, where the congregation meets for services of prayer, readings, songs and an address. The Lord's Supper is celebrated with ordinary leavened bread and water, since the use of stimulants such as alcohol is forbidden. Divine healing is also practised with a laying-on of hands. Tithing is mandatory throughout the Church, which has missions established worldwide. The headquarters of the Church is in Salt Lake City, Utah.

❖ Mormons

CHURCH OF JESUS CHRIST ON EARTH THROUGH THE PROPHET SIMON KIMBANGU

A small African neo-charismatic Church in Congo-Zaïre and the first indigenous African Church to be accepted for membership, in 1969, into the World Council of Churches (WCC). It maintains some 12,000 congregations, catering for over 4 million members, and was founded through the efforts of a BAPTIST catechist, Simon Kimbangu, in 1921.

Simon Kimbangu (1887–1951) was educated at a Baptist mission and was baptized in 1915. He took up catechetical work and also worked as a labourer in Leopoldville (now Kinshasa). While working there he had a vision in which God gave him a command to preach and heal the sick. In 1921 he followed his promptings, holding a mission that lasted from May to September of that year, and began to preach and heal the sick; he is even reputed to have raised the dead. Kimbangu's reputation and his ministry attracted so many people that his hometown, of N'Kamba, was renamed New Jerusalem.

The authorities, however, saw nationalistic overtones in Kimbangu's missions. He was beginning to upset the mainstream Churches and even the Belgian government, which at that time had charge of the Congo. The government was provoked to act against Kimbangu, urged on by the leaders of the mainstream European Churches, who alleged that the group was generating a wave of anti-European feeling. When the mission was completed, in September 1921, an attempt was made to arrest Kimbangu. He was charged with sedition, found guilty and sentenced to death, a sentence which was commuted by King Leopold II to a flogging, with 120 lashes, and life imprisonment in the eastern Congo, a thousand miles from his home town, where he died in 1951.

It had been Kimbangu's plan that in the administration of the Church he would occupy a central position and would be assisted by twelve apostles. The members would be opposed to witchcraft, polygamy, erotic dancing and the use of dance drums and the traditional symbols of African non-Christian religion. This opposition was highly successful, fuelling jealousy in some other local religious groups. Further persecution of the followers of Kimbangu only exacerbated the problem and drove the Church underground, with Joseph Diangienda, the founder's son, as leader. In a short time Simon Kimbangu, in his absence, became the symbol for Congolese nationalism.

During the 1950s the Church of Jesus Christ on Earth through the Prophet Simon Kimbangu became very well organized under the leadership of his son, Joseph, and his two brothers. With the coming of Congo's independence in 1960 the ban on what was called Kimbanguism was lifted and the Church grew from strength to strength. President Mobutu Sese Seko, who had agreed to the legalization of the Church, granted Simon Kimbangu a posthumous amnesty in 1991 and he was awarded the national Order of the Leopard. The Church has undertaken various medical, educational, agricultural and social initiatives, as well as providing and running a seminary for the training of clergy in Kinshasa.

CHURCH OF OUR LORD JESUS CHRIST OF THE APOSTOLIC FAITH, INC.

An American PENTECOSTAL Church that lies within the ONENESS apostolic tradition, with its emphasis on a denial of the traditional doctrine of the Trinity, and with a belief that its doctrine is based on that of the apostles and prophets. It was founded in Columbus, Ohio, in 1919, by R. C. Lawson, who subsequently became its first bishop.

The Church looks to the Bible for its creed and discipline, and anticipates the imminence of a pre-millennial second coming of Christ (REVELATION 20). It also emphasizes the priesthood of all believers. The ordinances observed are those of baptism, which is administered by immersion in the name of Jesus Christ alone omitting mention of the other persons of the Trinity, and the Lord's Supper, which is preceded by foot-washing. Baptism of the Holy Spirit is considered essential for salvation.

The Church has about 150 congregations for black Pentecostals and is served by 5 apostles and over 350 clergy, including 32 bishops. Missions are maintained in the British West Indies, West Africa and the Philippines, as well as some schools, a hospital and a Bible institute.

CHURCH OF REVELATION

Founded in the USA in 1930, at Long Beach, California, by the Reverend Janet Stine Lewis, later Wolford, this small American Church has not attracted many members since its foundation. The Church teaches a single doctrine called the *Old Christian Initiate*, which is an approach to understanding natural law, and how to achieve everlasting life without death. It also aims to spread peace and fellowship and any forms of warfare are therefore shunned. There was a certain growth in the movement at one point that took it to several other centres in California, to Georgia, Arizona and Ohio, but this was not sustained. The founder died in 1957, having failed to achieve the desired result of her pursuit.

CHURCH OF SCOTLAND

This Church, which is in the REFORMED tradition, was founded by John Knox (*c.* 1513–72) and his successor, Andrew Melville (1545–1622) and was established as an evangelical witness, presbyterian in its polity. Presbyterian and episcopal polity alternated in Scotland, due to the efforts of the Stuart kings who wanted to impose a modified episcopacy, but after their deposition William III firmly established PRESBYTERIANISM as the national form of church government in 1690.

In the eighteenth century various secessions occurred, particularly when popular rights were infringed by the Patronage Act of 1712 and by the brisk growth of moderatism, whose subscribers took a critical view both of 'man-made creeds' and of those who tolerated what they called 'infidels', in contrast to the attitude taken by their opponents, the evangelicals. As the eighteenth century drew to a close, the question of state interference in the affairs of the Church came to be underlined. These concerns were raised at the general assembly of the Church of Scotland in 1842, which declared that the Church must be free to govern itself, a claim that was rejected by parliament.

In consequence, in 1843 what was known as *The Disruption* occurred when 474 ministers of the Church of Scotland (about one-third of the clergy) walked out and formed the FREE CHURCH OF SCOTLAND. Two other seceding Churches that had been formed in the eighteenth century united in 1847 to form the UNITED PRESBYTERIAN CHURCH (SCOTLAND); this merged in 1900 with the Free Church of Scotland to form the UNITED FREE CHURCH OF SCOTLAND. Other divisions and reunions followed, especially after 1929 when what remained of the Church united with the United Free Church of Scotland to form what is reputedly one of the largest PROTESTANT Churches in the English-speaking world.

The Church of Scotland is evangelical in doctrine, based upon holy scripture and the subordinate *WESTMINSTER CONFESSION of Faith*. It is fully Presbyterian in constitution, based on a hierarchy of councils of ministers and elders; since 1990 it has also included members of the diaconate. The general assembly is the supreme authority of the Church and is presided over by a moderator who is elected annually by the delegates to the assembly.

CHURCH OF SOUTH INDIA

The Church of South India is the product of a negotiated union between episcopal and non-episcopal Churches that had been going on since 1919 and which came into effect in September 1947. The uniting Churches that were involved were the four southern dioceses of what were the Church of India, Burma and Ceylon (ANGLICAN), the South India United Church and the METHODIST Church of South India. The South India United Church itself had been formed in 1908 by a union of PRESBYTERIANS, CONGREGATIONALISTS and DUTCH REFORMED CHURCH bodies and was composed of fourteen dioceses, one in Sri Lanka.

Under the terms of the union it was agreed that the ministries of each Church were to be recognized as real ministries of the word and sacrament, that every minister of each uniting Church was to be regarded as being equal, that every ordination of presbyters was to be conferred by the laying on of hands by the bishops and other presbyters, and that the consecration of all bishops was to be administered by at least three bishops who would lay their hands on the consecrand. That some opposition was to be found against these decisions was inevitable. Part of the Anglo-Catholic element, in particular, broke away at this point, together with other provinces of the ANGLICAN COMMUNION who would not enter into full communion with the Church of South India because it meant that they would have to accept non-episcopal ministers into their own ranks.

From the 1968 Lambeth Conference and the Anglican Consultative Council of 1971 an appeal was made to Anglican Churches and provinces to reassess their position with regard to the Church of South India in the hope that full communion could be achieved. Since 1955 only a limited intercommunion was said to exist between the CHURCH OF ENGLAND and the Church of South India. Since 1988 the latter Church has been a full member of the Lambeth Conference and the Anglican Consultative Council and its moderator now attends the meetings of Anglican primates.

When difficulties arose over the matter of the liturgical usage to be adopted by the uniting Churches the matter was settled by the synod liturgy committee having regard for the cultural milieu of South India as well as the heritage of the Reformation in which all the Churches stood. When it was designing its new liturgy in 1950, the Church of South India was heavily influenced by liturgical material from the different uniting Churches, for example the *Book of Common Prayer* from Anglican sources, the *Book of Common Order* from the CHURCH OF SCOTLAND, the *Liturgy of St James* from the Syrian Churches of Malabar, the Methodist *Book of Offices*, and more. The final result was an ecumenical liturgy.

The Lord's Supper, or Eucharist, is clearly divided into the three sections of preparation, the ministry of the word and the breaking of the bread. Variable collects, lessons and prefaces are retained and a Syrian form of handclasp may be used to exchange the greeting of peace. The westward, or people facing, position is recommended in the text of the liturgy. Other new forms of service have been introduced at intervals, confirmation in 1950 and baptism in 1955, the latter normally carried out by immersion, although this form is not obligatory. A covenant service was published in 1956, while the services of *Morning and Evening Prayer* and the *Ordinal* were available from 1958; this *Ordinal* owed much of its form to that used by the Church of Scotland. The completed *Book of Common Worship*, which also included new marriage and burial services, was published in 1963.

The Church of South India has some 10,000 congregations administered by 21 dioceses, whose bishops are distinctively designated as *The Right Reverend the Bishop* 'in', and not as the more familiar *Bishop* 'of'.

CHURCH OF SWEDEN

The Church of Sweden claims that its origins lie in the establishment of Christianity in the country by St Anskar (*c.* 810–65), a French Benedictine monk from Corvey monastery on the river Weser in Saxony. Anskar, having returned from a mission to Denmark (CHURCH OF DENMARK) was requested by King Björn of Sweden to introduce Christianity to his country. Anskar's mission to Sweden met with some success and upon his return to Corvey he was appointed as abbot and nominated to the See of Hamburg, from where he could organize the missions to both Sweden and Denmark. Despite his efforts, and those by English and German missionaries, Christianity was not fully adopted in Sweden until the twelfth century when, in 1164, an archbishopric was established at Uppsala and the first Swedish archbishop was appointed.

The break-up of the Kalmar Union in 1523, which had united Sweden, Denmark and Norway since 1397 as a front against threats from the German Hanseatic League, gave Sweden its independence under King Gustav I Vasa. Under the king's authority and aided by the chancellor, Laurentius Andreae and the preaching of Olaus Petri, called the *Reformer of Sweden*, the influence and importance of the ROMAN CATHOLIC CHURCH in Sweden was weakened and in 1544 LUTHERANISM became the official state religion. Petri was an accomplished and able man, serving as pastor, city council official, secretary, and eventually as chancellor to the king while at the same time able to prepare a Swedish New Testament and hymn book (1526), a church manual (1529) and a Swedish liturgy (1531). Petri collaborated with his brother and Laurentius Andreae in the translation of the Bible, which was published in 1541. In the second half of the sixteenth century attempts were made by the CALVINISTS to influence the teaching and government of the Church in Sweden but, like later attempts by the Roman Catholic Church to regain power, it was unsuccessful. PIETISM, with its stress upon personal religious experience and a renewed emphasis on the New Testament, began to affect Swedish Lutheranism, as part of a nineteenth-century spiritual revival, and the result was an increased concern for educational and social reform, and for missionary activities.

The polity of the Church is episcopal and there is an annual synod, attended by both clerical and lay delegates from the congregations. The country is divided into thirteen dioceses and is headed by the Archbishop of Uppsala, who is the presiding bishop of the Church. The clergy of a diocese provide a list of episcopal nominations, and the monarch confirms each appointment. The Church is very active ecumenically and was involved in the founding of the Lutheran World Federation in 1947; it has enjoyed intercommunion with the CHURCH OF ENGLAND since 1922. The ordination of women to the ministry of the Church was authorized in 1959. Modifications in the status of the Church have recently been introduced by the Swedish parliament, which will change the relationship that previously existed between Church and state.

CHURCH OF THE BRETHREN

There are many denominations that include the word Brethren in their title but do not claim relationship to any of the main Brethren Churches, which had their origin in the PIETIST movement that originated in seventeenth-century Germany within the German LUTHERAN Church. One important group, known as the River Brethren (BRETHREN IN CHRIST CHURCH), is unrelated to the Church of the Brethren (Dunkers) and must not be confused with it.

Alexander Mack (1679–1735), originally from Schriesheim in Germany, not far from Heidelberg, had been a companion of the Pietist, E. C. Hochmann von Hochenau. In 1708, having gone to Schwarzenau, in present-day Lower Austria, Mack underwent baptism in the Eider River together with seven other Pietists, all declaring that they were returning more fully to the spirit of the New Testament than Martin Luther or any of the reformers of the time. Together, they agreed to found what became the Church of the New Baptists, or Schwarzenau Brethren. The members of this new Church may well have been influenced by the MENNONITE Brethren who were active in that region, for the Church was clearly in sympathy with ANABAPTISTS and SEPARATISTS, as witnessed, for example, by their method of administering baptism, which led to their alternative name in German of *Dunkers* (or Tunkers). But their path was not an easy one, and persecution sent the Brethren first to Wittgenstein in Westphalia and then on to either Holland or Switzerland.

Another group, of German Brethren, from Crefeld, led by Peter Becker (1687–1758), went to America in 1719 to take up the offer of free land that had been made by William Penn, the English founder of the colony of Pennsylvania. On Christmas Day in 1723, in the icy waters of the Wissahicken Creek, a group of seven were baptized and so began the first official Church of the Brethren in

America. The group settled at Germantown, near Philadelphia, and were joined there in 1729 by Alexander Mack and some 59 families. These newcomers formed the nucleus of what were initially known as German Baptists, becoming known as the Fraternity of German Baptists in 1836 and finally as the German Baptist Brethren, or Church of the Brethren, from 1871. The Brethren spread throughout America.

Doctrinally, the Church of the Brethren emphasized practical biblical piety, with a refusal to take up military arms and an injunction to their members to embrace pacifism. This put them into jeopardy with the authorities at the time of the revolutionary and civil wars in America, with persecution and imprisonment for many Brethren following. The Brethren also observe a total abstinence from alcohol and avoid luxuries, dressing plainly and furnishing their houses in an attractive but simple manner. One of the main services of the Church is the love feast, or *agape*, which is preceded by footwashing, leading into a full meal which incorporates a celebration of the Lord's Supper, with wine and unleavened bread, and concludes with the kiss of peace. Baptism is administered with the neophyte kneeling in the water in which he is immersed three times. Anointing with oil is used for healing, and the Brethren also obey an ordinance which they believe to have been instituted by Christ, that of the laying on of hands in the ordaining, or commissioning, of Christian workers. Women are expected to keep their heads covered during all the services in church.

The administration of the Church is in the hands of a standing committee of elected lay delegates from each congregation, who, together with all the elders and ministers, attend an annual conference. A general brotherhood board controls the administration of education, finance and missionary work, the latter now taking members into Europe, India, Africa and South America. The Church is also actively involved in social action, rehabilitation and relief programmes. It runs schools and colleges, summer camps and a theological seminary as well as maintaining a substantial publishing programme.

In the 1940s, the Brethren service committee started a *Heifers for Relief* programme in which thousands of animals were donated by individuals and their churches to be sent to Europe and Asia. The animals were accompanied by what came to be known as *sea-going cowboys*, or young Brethren who were prepared to help in a programme of rural education where this was needed.

❖ Dunkers; German Baptist Brethren; Neu-Taufer; Schwarzenau Brethren; Tunkers

CHURCH OF THE BROTHERHOOD

Although holding to the doctrinal position of the HUTTERITES and bearing a strong resemblance to other Hutterite groups, this American Church has no formal, or ethnic, ties with them. Members of the group believe that their communities must retain their separateness but at the same time continue to live in the world and conduct its business ventures in the marketplace. Full members, known as disciplined members, live in community and dedicate their work and earnings to the group; they do not adopt distinctive dress, or use an outdated mode of speech. Members who live outside the community, and are known as confessional members, tithe their goods and wealth for the support of the commune. The ministers of the Church are unpaid, and continue to work in secular jobs. No special church buildings are used for the worship services, which include love feasts and foot-washing, which take place in community houses. The group has attracted many followers and has opened care centres for emotionally disturbed children, for poor families living in slums and for migrants in need. The headquarters of the Church of the Brotherhood is in Orange County, Florida.

CHURCH OF THE FOUR LEAF CLOVER

A small American Church that was founded in New York in 1925 by the Reverend M. E. Claas and is now defunct. The symbol of the four-leaved clover was adopted to signify eternal life, everlasting light, divine love and truthfulness. There was a vaguely doctrinal emphasis in the Church on the Beatitudes, from the Sermon on the Mount, on the fatherhood of God, the brotherhood of man and the ten commandments. The few members attracted to the Church believed in reincarnation and in karma.

CHURCH OF THE LIVING GOD

A black American PENTECOSTAL Church, which is currently in slow decline. It was organized in 1889 by a former slave, the Reverend William Christian of Wrightsville, Arkansas.

William Christian had been a member of the BAPTIST Church but he left because he felt that they were preaching a fairly sectarian doctrine. Christian and his wife, Ethel, had experienced certain revelations and he felt that he needed to preach what was revealed to them both, which they believed to be true messages. He had been impressed with Freemasonry and held that in his Church the first three degrees, echoing those in Freemasonry, would be baptism by immersion for believers, holy supper, which involves the use of water and unleavened bread, and foot-washing. The Church is organized along fraternal lines, with its members obliged to tithe in order to support what are called temples, rather than churches.

Despite the heavy overlay of Masonic language and forms, the doctrine of the Church is more conventionally Trinitarian and given over to Pentecostalism but with the difference that the phenomenon of *glossolalia*, or speaking in tongues, is not taken as evidence of the baptism of the Holy Spirit as it is with most Pentecostal groups; any speaking in tongues that does take place must also be in recognizable languages. It is also believed that Jesus Christ was black, reputedly on account of his lineage from David and Abraham, and ostensibly because of a reference in Psalm 119:83: 'For I have become like a wineskin in the smoke.'

There have been schisms within the Church. One such, in 1902, led to the foundation of the Church of the Living God-Apostolic Church, which later became known as the Church of the Living God, General Assembly. In 1925 the name of this group changed once more, to become The House of God, which is the Church of the Living God, the Pillar and Ground of Truth.

❖ Christian Workers for Fellowship

CHURCH OF THE LUTHERAN BRETHREN OF AMERICA

A small but growing Church that currently has an adult membership of about seven thousand, distributed between one hundred congregations in the upper Midwestern part of the USA. It was founded in 1900 as a result of a revival amongst the LUTHERANS of the Midwest in the 1890s.

The Reverend K. O. Lundeberg was the prime mover in the organization of the Church, since he, like many others, felt concerned about the ease with which membership within the Lutheran Church was granted. He argued that it should only be given to those who professed a personal conversion experience and that the unconverted should not be allowed to receive Holy Communion. Lundeberg was also uneasy about the use of fixed and elaborate liturgical forms in the order of worship, and he felt that the laity should become active participants in church services. In order to contact some other immigrant Norwegian congregations that had decided to become independent, Lundeberg published a Norwegian-language newspaper, *Broderbaandet*. The groups gathered together at a convention held in Milwaukee, Wisconsin, in 1900 and the Church of the Lutheran Brethren came into existence.

Worship is very simple in the Church; there are no altars and Holy Communion is distributed by the elders of the congregation to the people, who remain seated in the pews. Other worship services are non-liturgical, with extempore and free prayer, testimonies and lay participation. Membership is limited only to those who have had a personal conversion experience and preparation for confirmation requires a two-year period of instruction. Unlike the practice in other Lutheran Churches, no oath has to be given at the time of confirmation. The candidate, once confirmed, then waits to receive the conversion experience before progressing to full membership.

The polity of the Church is congregational, its work supervised by a synod with a president and other officers. Separate boards organize foreign and home missions; foreign missions have been maintained in Africa, Japan and the Far East. The Church has also been involved in providing homes for the elderly and supports several schools, including a Bible school and a seminary for the training of ministers. The headquarters of the Church of the Lutheran Brethren of America is at Fergus Falls, Minnesota.

CHURCH OF THE NAZARENE

The Church of the Nazarene represents the product of a number of mergers of many small sects derived from American METHODISM. These sects were generally dissatisfied with the Methodist lack of interest in, or support for, the second blessing, or sanctification, which was believed to follow upon a person's conversion. In 1895 a former Methodist minister, Phineas F. Bresee, had formed the First Church of the Nazarene in Los Angeles, California, and at about the same time, in New York, the Association of PENTECOSTAL Churches came into being; this merged in 1896 with the New England-based Central Evangelical Association. It was this Association of Pentecostal Churches that, in Chicago in 1907, merged with Bresee's First Church of the Nazarene to form the Pentecostal Church of the Nazarene; another union was made in the following year with a southern group known as the Holiness Church of Christ at a meeting at Pilot Point, Texas. The descriptive word 'Pentecostal' was later dropped in order to avoid connection with other Pentecostal groups that taught and practised *glossolalia*, or speaking in tongues, which has always been opposed by the Church of the Nazarene. Other mergers followed, including those with two English groups, the International Holiness Mission (merged 1952) and the CALVARY HOLINESS CHURCH (merged 1955).

The doctrine of the Church is overwhelmingly Methodist, with both the *General Rules* and the Wesleyan *Twenty-Five Articles of Faith* observed. The doctrine of the second blessing, or sanctification, is strongly believed and it is impossible to become either a minister, or church official, without having experienced entire sanctification. The full inspiration of the scriptures is accepted as being all that is sufficient for Christian faith and living. Two sacraments, baptism and the Lord's Supper, are administered; baptism of infants is provided for, but many members prefer a believer's baptism, which may be observed by full immersion or by sprinkling, or pouring, water over the candidate's head. The Lord's Supper is offered in each congregation on at least four occasions in the year, with many observing it more frequently. Members of the Church of the Nazarene will not work on Sundays, abstain from what they see as worldly entertainments and will not participate in secret societies, lotteries or gambling in any form.

CHURCH OF THE PROVINCE OF SOUTHERN AFRICA

This Church must not be confused with the CHURCH OF ENGLAND IN SOUTH AFRICA.

The Church of the Province of Southern Africa (CPSA) is part of the worldwide ANGLICAN COMMUNION and is the oldest English-speaking Church in South Africa. The first ANGLICAN service was held in Cape Town in 1704 and regular services were conducted there from 1806, after the British occupation of that colony. These Anglican services in Cape Town were continued in the *Groote Kerk* as a result of a friendly arrangement made between the DUTCH REFORMED CHURCH and the CHURCH OF ENGLAND, an arrangement that continued for almost thirty years.

With the arrival of British settlers, the work of the Church expanded. In 1847 Bishop Robert Gray (1809–72) was appointed as the first Bishop of Cape Town; six years later Bishops Colenso and Armstrong were appointed to the new dioceses of Natal and Grahamstown; the Church later excommunicated Colenso. With Bishop Gray's appointment by the British Crown as metropolitan, the question of the extent of his jurisdiction arose and had to be settled in the courts by the judicial committee of the privy council. The resolution was that the Church in South Africa was made independent of the state.

The work of the Church expanded considerably and in 1900 it was joined by members of the Order of Ethiopia, which had been formed when the indigenous Ethiopian Church joined with the Anglican Church. Its members, who in 1975 numbered some 50,000 committed adults who are mostly Xhosa-speakers, adhere to the Anglican liturgy, rites and discipline. When their first bishop, Sigquibo Dwane, was consecrated in 1983 he was recognized as a bishop of the Church of the Province of Southern Africa. The Order's constitution, which underlines its independence and the right to manage its own affairs, has the approval of the CPSA.

The main legislative body of the CPSA is the provincial synod, which meets triennially and to which every diocese sends lay and clerical delegates; within each diocese there are regular synods that meet more frequently. The archbishop, who oversees the work of all the dioceses, heads the Church. Activity in the Church is very vigorous, with specific missionary objectives in its support of the Department of Mission and Ministry. This arose in 1994, through the efforts of Archbishop Desmond Tutu, and is concerned with easing the community consultative process. The Anglican Students' Federation, which was started in 1960 for those involved in tertiary education, provides opportunities for students to come together for Bible study, Eucharistic services, community outreach programmes and other student projects.

In 1970, a PENTECOSTAL-type renewal was started and this gave rise to a group of charismatic Anglicans; by 1975 this had become strongly represented in Zululand, especially amongst the clergy. Three bishops from the Archdiocese of Cape Town and the dioceses of Port Elizabeth and Pretoria, have given the movement, which now has around 15,000 mainly white adult members, their support.

The CPSA, which is generally within the High Church tradition of the Anglican Communion, has an estimated adult membership of 1.2 million. The headquarters of the Church is at Cape Town, Cape Province.

CHURCH OF THE SAVIOUR

The Church of the Saviour was formed in 1946 in Washington, DC, by a group of nine people under the leadership of Gordon Crosby, a former member of the BAPTIST CHURCH. The focus of the group, which lives in a community, is on ecumenism and evangelism together with a total commitment to Jesus Christ. They see in their way of life a symbol of a new humanity, one dedicated to a life of service and the cultivation of the spirit. Members, who make a commitment to lead lives of total integrity, are trained in the School for Christian Living on a three-year course that prepares them to meet the exacting membership requirements. Various projects undertaken by the community include the Dayspring Retreat Farm and the Dag Hammarskjöld College, the latter a cross-cultural institution where people are taught leadership skills.

CHURCH OF THE TRINITY (INVISIBLE MINISTRY)

Founded in 1972 by Friend Stuart, a publisher from the west coast of the USA who had explored New Thought (NEW AGE) philosophy, this American group espouses a theology that upholds the Christian doctrine of the Trinity as the ultimate truth and teaches that all things proceed from it. They hold that the true destiny of man can only be achieved by gaining dominion, following the example of Jesus Christ in overcoming death. The full destiny of man is to free himself from disease, conflict and poverty. Members of this group are required to obey the law and be upright citizens.

CHURCH OF THE TRUTH

An American group founded by Albert C. Grier and influenced by the New Thought (NEW AGE) philosophy. Grier, who was a Universalist minister, turned to spiritual healing when he was cured of stomach ulcers, which he believed had come about after reading a New Thought book. His action was unacceptable to the Universalist Church of America and he left his ministry to found the Church of Truth at

Spokane, Washington. The work attracted others and further churches were opened in other parts of the USA. Grier moved to Pasadena, founded another church there, and then went on to New York City where his last foundation was made. The teachings of the Church are largely those of the New Thought Alliance, of which it is a member.

CHURCHES OF CHRIST

The Churches of Christ are derived from the move in early nineteenth-century America to eradicate sectarian names and human creeds and to establish a union of all Christians. The basis of the union was to be an absolute belief in the New Testament with the aim of restoring Christ's Church to its earliest form, but the result has been to create an enormous number of separate congregations, with a combined membership in the millions, spread throughout the world.

This restoration movement was begun by James O'Kelly, an ex-METHODIST EPISCOPAL CHURCH preacher from Virginia who left his Church in 1793, with several thousand followers, as a protest against the growing power of an episcopal form of church government then developing in the METHODIST CHURCH. This group organized itself as Republican Methodists, taking the Bible as the only rule and discipline. A few years later, two members of the BAPTIST CHURCH, Abner Jones and Elias Smith, left their Church to form the First Christian Church in New England, at Lyndon, Vermont, in 1801. Their dispute with the Baptist Church arose from the use of sectarian names and creeds. These two groups joined up with a preacher, Barton Stone, who had been accused of anti-PRESBYTERIAN preaching. Stone, and his followers, went on to form the Springfield Presbytery in 1804. After some time a union was formed between these three groups. Each congregation was free to follow its own form of worship and adopt its own polity and doctrine, but certain basics were held in common.

This united group was then joined by the CAMPBELLITES, but by 1870 differences of opinion had, almost inevitably, arisen and various splinter groups began to form. The controversies were specifically concerned with the scriptural authorization of both instrumental music in worship services, and the running of mission societies within the Church. The first group to break away became known as the Disciples of Christ. The forming of a second group followed, and this came to be known as the Churches of Christ.

The belief of these Churches of Christ is non-creedal, as the Bible alone is considered as sufficient and is accepted as the revelation of God's will. Members believe the Old Testament to have been inspired, but it is held as a lesser authority than the New Testament. Baptism follows a profession of faith by each adult, with the children of the group considered to be *covered*, or under the care of Christ, until they are of an age for baptism. No musical instruments are allowed in any of the churches on the grounds that there is no mention of the use of such instruments for worship in the New Testament, nor did the early Church use them. Ministers are ordained and hold their tenure by agreement with the elders of local congregations. There has been considerable fragmentation in the Churches, and new divisions have been formed, each representing a slight change in emphasis or organization. There are some Churches of Christ, which arose from a schism within the CHRISTIAN

Church (Disciples of Christ) group, that permit the use of musical instruments in their worship. The Churches of Christ in Great Britain was formed in a separate reform movement, and was organized formally in 1842.

CHURCHES OF CHRIST IN CHRISTIAN UNION

This American denomination, the Churches of Christ in Christian Union, came about through a schism. In 1909 a council of the Christian Union of America was held in Marshall, Ohio, when those who supported the holiness tradition of full salvation withdrew from the union and formed a separate group. Their first annual council was held at Jefferson, Ohio, in 1909.

Doctrinally, the Church is in the holiness tradition of Methodism, with its emphasis on sanctification following conversion, and the members maintain a very modest and unworldly lifestyle. The polity of the Church is congregational and a great emphasis is put on divine healing and the second coming of Christ (Revelation 20). The services in this Church are non-liturgical. The Reformed Methodist Church, which had been founded in 1814 as a schism from the Methodist Episcopal Church, later reorganized itself as a result of a disagreement over the unacceptability of episcopal polity and merged with the Churches of Christ in Christian Union in 1952, to form the North Eastern District of the Churches of Christ in Christian Union.

CHURCHES OF CHRIST IN GREAT BRITAIN AND IRELAND

This small denomination was formally established in 1842 as part of the restoration movement that was emerging in Great Britain in the eighteenth century amongst the Glasites, or Sandemanians, Haldanites and some Baptists. The first recorded congregation was founded at Dungannon, in Ireland, in 1804 to be followed three years later by one founded in Scotland, at Auchtermuchty. The Church opened up talks of unity with the United Reformed Church, but these failed in 1977. They were recommenced in 1979, when some other Churches of Christ joined them. Members of this denomination observe a weekly Communion service and practise believer's baptism. The polity of the Church is congregational and it participates in foreign missions, notably in India and Africa.

Another group of Churches of Christ, organized in 1945, has been growing in numbers in the UK. This group does not permit the use of musical instruments in its worship services, as scripture does not authorize them.

CHURCHES OF GOD GENERAL CONFERENCE

The American, John Winebrenner (1797–1860), was born in Maryland and was a pastor in the German Reformed Church at Harrisburg, Pennsylvania, from 1820–5. His evangelical enthusiasm, however, annoyed and even angered many in his congregation. He was forced to withdraw from the Church in 1826 and by 1830, together with six companions, Winebrenner had formed an independent Church of God in Harrisburg.

Wishing to use only a biblical name, rather than a sectarian one, Winebrenner called his foundation the Church of God, which was later expanded. By 1845 a general eldership had been organized so as to distinguish between the national body and local churches, or elderships, which had been created since 1830, and the words 'North America' were added in the same year; the word 'Church' became changed to 'Churches' in 1903.

Members of this Church accept the Bible, which they believe to be the sole rule of faith and practice, the Trinity, the office and work of the Holy Spirit, justification by faith, and the ordinances of baptism, foot-washing and the Lord's Supper. The last two are described as companion ordinances because they are celebrated together, usually on Sunday evenings. The Church emphasizes the keeping of the sabbath and affirms the resurrection of the dead and the final judgement.

Elderships and conferences meet annually and act as regional legislative bodies, with a triennial general eldership, made up of both lay and ministerial delegates, meeting to organize the Church's plans for education, missions, publications and evangelism. The Church supports Findlay College, Ohio (founded 1882), as well as the Winebrenner Theological Seminary, also in Findlay. The Church maintains missions in the Far East and in Haiti.

❖ Churches of God in North America (General Eldership); Winebrennerians

CHURCHES OF GOD, HOLINESS

This is not to be confused with the Church of God *(*Holiness*).*

K. H. (King Hezekiah) Burrus, an elder in the Church of Christ (Holiness) who had planted a congregation of that Church in Atlanta, Georgia, in 1914, and later, in Norfolk, Virginia, in 1916, was the founder of this American Church. In 1920, following the national convention held by the Church of Christ (Holiness) in Atlanta, Burrus and some others decided to withdraw from fellowship with the parent Church, one of many schisms that occurred in that Church between 1907 and 1920, and the Churches of God, Holiness, came into being.

Doctrinally, there is very little to distinguish the schismatic Church from its parent body. The scriptures are held to be the inspired word of God and the source of all faith and practice. There is a conventional belief in the Trinity, and in justification followed by sanctification. Although an emphasis is placed on divine healing, more conventional methods of medical practice are not excluded. The ordinances of baptism, foot-washing and the Lord's Supper are observed.

The administration of the Church is by means of both an annual state convention and a national convention, which is presided over by a single bishop, or president, and it is he who appoints the overseers, who are responsible for the appointment of pastors. There are currently thirty congregations of this Church, which has its headquarters in Atlanta, Georgia.

CHURCHES OF GOD IN THE BRITISH ISLES AND OVERSEAS (NEEDED TRUTH)

This denomination was part of the break-up of the Open Brethren Churches over the question of the degree to which openness was permissible. The stricter *Needed Truth* groups were first formed in England in the 1890s, later spreading across the Atlantic to America and Canada.

Within this Church a distinction was made between the *Church which is Christ's Body* to which all believers belong, and the *Church of God which is the Fellowship* (Acts 2:42). This fellowship is the body where Christ's proper authority is expressed and to which all members belong by addition.

The lifestyle of the members is fairly spartan in character, with no music used in religious services, no television allowed for entertainment and marriage to those outside the group proscribed; the members are also conscientious objectors to both military service and voting. The polity of the Church is presbyterial, with government in the hands of elders who form a united constituency, some with congregational oversight and others with regional control. The elders appoint deacons and it is from this group of deacons that future elders are selected.

A dispute in Great Britain in 1904 led to the formation of two groups, the Green Pastures Brethren, in Scotland, led by Dr Vernal and the English Brethren under the leadership of Dr Luxmore. There are now some eighty congregations in Great Britain, with around 4,500 adult members.

❖ Churches of God in the Fellowship of the Son of God, the Lord Jesus Christ; Luxmore Needed Truth

CIRCUMCELLIONS

A wandering group of fourth-century fanatics who roamed around North Africa, especially in Numidia, their name, from the Latin '*circum cellas euntes*' – roving about the houses – given to them by their Catholic opponents. The band was alleged to roam about the peasant communities endeavouring to gain adherents for the Donatist heresy. They were called Agonistics, or Warriors of Christ, by the Donatists, but could perhaps be better described as brigands who were famed for their violent way of life. Carrying no swords, which they claimed was in obedience to Christ's command to St Peter to sheath his sword at the time of his master's arrest by the Romans, they used instead clubs, which they called '*Israelites*'. With these the Circumcellions, shouting their war cry of *Laudes Deo!* (Praises to God), would batter and bruise those who would not listen and obey, leaving them for dead. So zealous were the Circumcellions that their eagerness to gain the martyr's crown led many to commit suicide, often by throwing themselves from the top of precipices and high buildings, or even by paying others to kill them; it is even reported that some aimed to gain their crown by committing crimes which warranted a judicial death penalty, so eager were they to embrace death and gain their eternal reward. Despite the condemnation of Donatist bishops, the bodily remains of Circumcellions were often honoured, or even venerated, perhaps suggesting that many of the ugly stories that surround the group came straight from the mouths of enemies and cannot be entirely trusted.

The origin of the group is obscure, but probably arose as a protest movement concerned with social and civil grievances. The alliance of this violent group with the Donatist cause was almost certainly seen as an embarrassment to the latter. Attempts by the civil authorities to subdue the group by force were unsuccessful, but the shooting Circumcellion flame would seem to have had a fairly short life, for they died out in the fifth century.

❖ Agonistici; Agonistics

CLAPHAM SECT

This name was applied in England in the mid-nineteenth century to a group of

Anglican evangelicals, many of whom lived and were active in and around the London suburb of Clapham at the end of the previous century. The members included their leader, William Wilberforce (1759–1833), Henry Thornton, a prominent city banker and philanthropist, John Venn, founder of the Church Missionary Society and rector of Clapham, Charles Grant, a director of the East India Company, and Lord Teignmouth, a Governor-General of India; other members included Hannah More, the philanthropist, and the writer Charles Simeon, a leading evangelical of his day.

The members of the Clapham Sect had a keen sense of moral and civic responsibility and they encouraged the view that religion should be manifest in good works. They were therefore active in many humanitarian projects, from the abolition of slavery to the creation of the Church Missionary Society, in 1799, and the British and Foreign Bible Society, which was founded in 1804. A strong emphasis on education for all classes led to the publication of suitable literature for this purpose and the rapid extension of the Sunday school movement that was spreading throughout the country. Though few in number, the members' individual connections with people of significant position in British society and the government gave the Clapham Sect a great deal of influence.

CLAPTON SECT

A label attached to a group of High Church Anglicans in England at the start of the nineteenth century, who were so-called because the home of Joshua Watson (1771–1855), a London wine merchant and philanthropist and leading member of the sect, was in the London suburb of Clapton. They were also known as the Hackney Phalanx because their base was in the parish of Hackney. These High Churchmen, whose number included the last Palatine Bishop of Durham, Prince Bishop William Van Mildert, who caused much irritation to the Whig government of the day, looked back for their models of churchmanship, as did others, to the great Anglican divines of the Caroline period, men such as Lancelot Andrewes, William Laud, Joseph Butler and Thomas Ken. They were much concerned with church building and education, organizing the National Society for Promoting the Education of the Poor. High Church theology was once described by Alexander Knox, an Irish wit, as being both *High and Dry*.

❖ The Hackney Phalanx

COKELERS

Cokelers was the popular name given to an English sect, founded in Loxwood, Sussex, in 1850 by John Sirgood, a London shoemaker. A disciple of the faith-healer William Bridges, who had founded the Plumstead Peculiars in 1838, Sirgood preached in London and the south-east, finding that the further he was away from the city, the greater the enthusiasm of his audience. Packing their worldly goods on to a handcart, Sirgood and his wife set out for Sussex, setting themselves down in the small, farming village of Loxwood where he began to preach in the fields. His fame spread (and increased greatly when an almost certainly false rumour went abroad that Sirgood had raised someone from the dead) and a great many of the local farming people came to hear his message. The sect was registered as the Body (or Society) of Dependants. A commune was set up at

Loxwood, and those who became members adopted a simple lifestyle, dressing plainly and mainly in black; the Bible was their only literature and members were allowed no entertainments, no music, no sport or even flowers to decorate a room. More importantly, the group remained celibate believing that marriage interfered with man's relationship with God, which came before all. Many followers, mainly farm labourers, came to listen and to join and work in the commune; their farming activities flourished and in time a chapel, a steam bakery and a large store, which could supply almost everything from provisions to bicycles, clothes and kitchen implements, and a taxi service, were opened by the group in Loxwood. This was understandably popular in the area, although not so with the local landowners who saw the sect as a threat to their ordered way of life. An attempt to prosecute Sirgood failed and the prosperity continued. More communes were established and by 1885 there were around 1,500 followers.

Despite this prosperity, however, the Cokelers at the same time failed to multiply because of their beliefs and thereby sowed the seed of their own demise. At the turn of the twentieth century the numbers had dropped to around nine hundred and by mid-century, although not quite defunct, there were little more than a few old people remaining in the sect. John Sirgood died in 1885 and is interred in the communal burial ground behind the chapel, where the burial mounds have no names, but only numbers.

The origin of their name, Cokelers, is obscure. It may have come from the area of Loxwood where the commune was established, known at one time as Cokkeg, but it is also thought that the name may have come from the copious amount of cocoa enjoyed by the members.

❖ Society of Dependants

COLLEGIANTS

A Dutch reform group, which arose during the time of the controversies surrounding the synod of Dort in 1618–19. When ministers of the Dutch Remonstrant Brotherhood were forced to leave their congregations, it was to one of these congregations, at Warmond near Leiden, that Gijsbert van der Kodde and his brothers began to preach withdrawal from the world, baptism by immersion and the idea that no formal confession of faith, or creed, was required in order to achieve salvation. The brothers taught that Christ was the messiah and that the Bible was the inspired word of God. Groups came together, whose members met as *collegia*, or prayer groups, rather than as organized churches, which were held by them as being a corruption; it was their belief that the Church should be an invisible society. The group moved to the nearby village of Rhynsberg, which became the informal headquarters of thirty or so other *collegia* that by then had been formed in many Dutch towns and villages. When members met annually at Rhynsberg, they celebrated a commemoration of the Last Supper and prayed and studied together, reading the scriptures, singing hymns and listening as those members who felt impelled to do so gave testimony, since freedom of speech was encouraged within the groups.

Benedict de Spinoza (formerly Baruch Spinoza), the seventeenth-century Dutch Jewish philosopher who had been expelled from his synagogue and forced to leave Amsterdam, may have been an influence on the sect. Spinoza lived in

Rhynsberg from 1661–4 at a time when divisions within the group emerged. The sect persisted, however, into the late eighteenth century when its members turned either to the ARMINIANS, or to the MENNONITES. It is recorded that the last meeting of the collegiants was in 1787.

❖ Rhynsbergers

COLLYRIDIANS

The unusual name of this fourth-century sect is derived from the *collyris*, a small cake, or bread roll, which was distributed by King David at a sacrifice (2 Sam. 6:19). According to St Epiphanius (*c.* 315–403), these Collyridians were women who had introduced a cult of sacrifice to the Virgin Mary. The cult was thought to have originated in Thrace, an ancient region, north-east of Macedonia, in the eastern part of the Balkan peninsula. Its practice was to offer in sacrifice some cakes, in honour of the Virgin Mary; the cakes were later eaten. Epiphanius' condemnation of the cult was proof that even before the Council of Ephesus, in AD 431, there was an enthusiastic and possibly extravagant veneration of the Virgin Mother of God.

❖ Philomarianites

CONCERNED CHRISTIANS

This organization has no connection with the Concerned Christians Growth Ministries that was founded in Australia in 1979 by a CHURCHES OF CHRIST *minister, Adrian van Leen, in the wake of the Jonestown tragedy, which had resulted in the wholesale death of members of that cult.*

The American organization known as Concerned Christians was founded in Denver, Colorado, in the early 1980s as a Christian ministry, designed to counteract the work of cults and NEW AGE movements and to expose their danger, by Monte *Kim* Miller. In a short time this movement had itself become cultic, attracting some unfavourable publicity when Miller predicted, in 1998, that the apocalypse was imminent and that an earthquake would destroy Denver on 10 October of that year. He further predicted that he himself would die in a gun battle in Jerusalem, Israel, on 31 December 1999, qualifying these prophecies by his assertion that, as one of the two end-time prophets mentioned in Revelation 11, God spoke through him.

Miller preached that Christians must be prepared for the second coming so that they will be able to assume positions of leadership throughout the world (REVELATION 20). Many of his followers, in Colorado, Kansas and Texas, immediately gave up their careers and moved from their homes, with some sixty people following Miller to Jerusalem. Their reception in Israel was not quite what they expected, and fourteen members of the group were expelled from that country because of their perceived potential for violence. They returned to Denver, Colorado, before setting off again, this time for Greece where they were again expelled; some of the followers were known to have gone to New York from where, after meeting with some of their relations, they once again disappeared on their travels. Miller, it is reported, has not been seen again.

CONFESSING CHURCH

A Church, established in Germany, which grew out of a movement for revival and evangelism amongst Christians in Germany who were actively opposed to the FAITH MOVEMENT OF GERMAN CHRISTIANS, which had been set up by Adolf Hitler; this body had been administered by Ludwig Müller, elected as *Reichsbischof* (bishop), who looked to the Nazis for support. The Church called into question the authority of the scriptures, as well as Reformation tradition, by accepting and tolerating the Nazi doctrine of Aryan racial superiority.

The movement that later became known as the Confessing Church sprang from Martin Niemöller's *Pastor's Emergency League*, which had been founded in 1933. Two synods, those of Barmen (May 1934) and Dahlem (October 1943), which rejected the cultural principles of the Faith Movement of German Christians, were instrumental in forming the theological basis for opposition to this state-sanctioned Church that distorted Christian commitment to Christ, to scripture and to each individual's confession of faith. It was at the Dahlem synod that the Confessing Church declared its emergency law, which made it clear that the true Church in Germany could be identified by its acceptance of the Barmen Declaration rejecting the insupportable cultural principles of the Faith Movement. This led to the coexistence of two PROTESTANT Churches in Germany, with the Confessing Church having no state recognition.

The Confessing Church, together with churches in Bavaria, Württemberg, Hannover and Baden that had remained independent of Nazi rule, formed the Provisional Church Administration of the German Evangelical Church, but little over a year later the unity between these groups was shattered by differences, both theological and political, and by the growing influence of the LUTHERAN council, which had been formed in 1934 by the Lutheran bishops of Hanover, Württemberg and Bavaria, all of whom had adopted a less strident opposition to the Third Reich than that taken by the Confessing Church.

What remained of the Confessing Church aimed to make its protest against euthanasia and the persecution of the Jews heard, but increased persecution and harassment by the Gestapo forced the Church to go underground. In 1937 Martin Niemöller and others were arrested and sent to concentration camps. The work of the Confessing Church was further hindered by the conscription of clergy and laity upon the outbreak of the Second World War in 1939. In 1948, when the war was over, the Confessing Church ceased to exist; its structures were reorganized and integrated into the Evangelical Church in Germany.

❖ Bekennende Kirche; Confessional Church

CONGREGATIONAL CHURCH

A group was formed in the late sixteenth century at Norwich, England, by Robert Browne, which sought to be independent of the CHURCH OF ENGLAND. Browne preached the view that reform was needed and that the key to that was his idea that all true Christians should withdraw from the Church of England and that each local church should enjoy full autonomy. Known as SEPARATISTS, Browne's followers became the antecedents of the Congregationalists.

Congregationalism was built upon several principles, one of which was the importance of the Church as a covenant of people who had responded to Christ and had covenanted with him in a specific geographical area. The second principle was that the Church was to be a state Church and that it would become the moral spokesman for society. As events turned out this ideal was not fully realized as the Church became independent of the civil authorities.

Congregational churches in Great Britain united into unions and associations and by 1832 had formed the Congregational Union of England and Wales, with each local church free to determine its own form of worship and to appoint its own minister. In 1972 the Congregational Church of England and Wales united with other Churches to form the UNITED REFORMED CHURCH (URC); those congregations that were unwilling to unite to form the URC remained as the Union of Welsh Independents and the Congregational Unions of Scotland and Ireland.

Many Separatists were forced to leave England in the early days because of persecution and they settled first in Holland before later going to America. The Pilgrim Fathers, who set off for America in 1620 from Holland by way of the English port of Plymouth aboard *The Mayflower*, landed at Cape Cod, Massachusetts, and established Congregationalism in New England. The arrival of the PURITANS some ten years later introduced some changes. While they recognized the autonomy of the local congregations, the Puritans worked to align them with the civil authorities. These churches then worked so closely with the civil governments in every colony, with the exception of Rhode Island, that no other type of Church was tolerated in the area until 1690, when the English authorities required them to tolerate other religious groups. State government support for Congregationalist churches was provided until 1818 in Connecticut and 1833–4 in Massachusetts.

Congregationalism in the USA has always been active in the field of education, establishing Harvard University, in Cambridge, Massachusetts, in 1636 and Yale University, in Newport, Connecticut, in 1701. Missionary work also became well coordinated, with the formation of the American Board of Commissioners for Foreign Missions in 1810, which took Congregationalism to the Middle East, the Far East and Africa. A need for a national organization was felt in America throughout the nineteenth century, and a national council was organized. In 1957, Congregationalists formed the United Church of Christ, a union that was completed when a constitution was adopted at Philadelphia in 1961.

Doctrinally, the Church affirms a traditional belief in the Trinity, the importance of holy scripture and the autonomy of the local church with its independence of all ecclesiastical control. The national unions and associations are seen as bodies for counsel and cooperation only, and not as a form of control. There are differences in the forms of worship employed in Great Britain and the USA, and a wide range of liturgical material from which the congregations can choose. The officers of the Church include a minister, a deacon and a church secretary, with ordination conferred by an invocation of the Holy Spirit and a laying-on of hands by the presiding minister and Church representatives. A minister is called to assume the pastoral care of a congregation by a Church Meeting, which is composed of members of that church; deacons are also elected by church members, to help with the administration and share the pastoral care of the congregation.

Congregationalism has been most prominent in the ecumenical movement throughout the world and many mergers and unions have been made between Congregational, PRESBYTERIAN and METHODIST Churches.

CONGREGATIONAL-CHRISTIAN CHURCHES

This denomination must not be confused with the National Association of Congregational-Christian Churches.

This corporate American body, which no longer exists as such, was one of the uniting bodies that, with the EVANGELICAL AND REFORMED CHURCH, formed the UNITED CHURCH OF CHRIST in 1957. It came into existence in 1931, as the General Council of Congregational-Christian Churches through a merger between the National Association of Christian Churches and the CHRISTIAN CHURCH.

Following the arrival in America of the Pilgrim Fathers, in 1620, and other groups of PURITANS, Congregationalism was soon established and local groups insisted upon their own autonomy. This spread rapidly through the New England colonies, with the exception of Rhode Island, and soon became fully established. The early CONGREGATIONALISTS became involved in initiating campaigns concerned with peace, the rights of women, children and immigrants, and the abolition of slavery. It became evident, however, that a more structured organization was needed and in the mid-nineteenth century the national council was established, with the intention of meeting every three years. At the triennial conference in 1913 a *Declaration of Faith, Polity and the Wider Fellowship* was made, in which their REFORMED theological position was reaffirmed, along with the polity of Congregationalism respecting the autonomy of the local church. In 1924, the Evangelical Protestant Church of North America was received into the National Council of Congregational Churches and, as such, merged with the Christian Church in 1931 to form the General Council of Congregational-Christian Churches.

❖ National Council of Congregational Churches

CONSERVATIVE BAPTIST ASSOCIATION OF AMERICA

When this American group was organized in 1947 in Atlantic City, New Jersey, it was never intended that it should become a denomination. Despite this early intention, it is now established as an independent, autonomous BAPTIST Church with a constitution that was adopted in Milwaukee in 1948.

The association arose from the struggle that was inevitable between FUNDAMENTALIST and modernist tensions in what was the NORTHERN BAPTIST CONVENTION with the result that a Fundamentalist Fellowship was formed within the Convention in 1920. The disagreement within the Northern Baptist Convention concerned not only the interpretation of scripture and theology. The fundamentalists also expressed concern over the sending of both modernist and conservative missionaries abroad to foreign missions, or to staff home missions. It was thought that the problem was solved when the fundamentalist fellowship set up the Conservative Baptist Foreign Mission Society, but this proved to be unacceptable to the Northern Baptist Convention; a new body, the Conservative Baptist Association of America, was created in 1947. Because this Association rejected the notion of *separateness* from other Christians, including other Baptists, it had to reject the chance of a merger with the GENERAL ASSOCIATION OF REGULAR BAPTIST CHURCHES that was offered, since this general association held to a strict principle of *separateness.*

The Conservative Baptist Association of America now has over 1,000 congregations in the USA and maintains foreign missions in 18 countries throughout the world. The members are involved in evangelism, Bible teaching, Sunday schools, church planting and a considerable publishing output of pamphlets and tracts. Doctrinally, they uphold the Bible's infallibility, the doctrine of the Trinity and an orthodox Christology. They also recognize the sinfulness of man and mankind's need for regeneration and sanctification. The two ordinances of baptism and the Lord's Supper are observed. The headquarters of the Association is in Wheaton, Illinois.

❖ (BC America)

CONSERVATIVE CONGREGATIONAL CHRISTIAN CONFERENCE

The establishment of the CONGREGATIONAL-CHRISTIAN CHURCHES in the USA in 1931, a merger between the CONGREGATIONAL CHURCH and the CHRISTIAN CHURCH, was a matter of alarm for the pastor of the First Congregational Church at Hancock, Minnesota. The Reverend Hilmer B. Sandine was moved to produce, in 1935, a small, monthly magazine, *The Congregational Beacon*, which was to be circulated amongst like-minded conservative Congregationalists.

It was felt by some that this merger represented a departure from the norms of Congregationalism and in 1945 the Conservative Congregational Christian Fellowship was established for these concerned Congregationalists and for others who, although going along with the merger, later became concerned when, in the 1940s, a plan of union was being discussed and revised between the Congregational-Christian Churches and the Evangelical Reformed Church, with a view to the ultimate formation of the UNITED CHURCH OF CHRIST. In 1948 there was a name change, to Conservative Congregational Christian Conference (CCCC).

Doctrinally, the statement of faith of the Church is evangelical and affirms belief in the infallibility and authority of the scriptures as the word of God, in the Trinity, in the birth, life, death, resurrection and ascension of Jesus Christ and his second coming (REVELATION 20). Regeneration by the Holy Spirit is expected of everyone seeking membership of the Church.

The local churches are totally autonomous, although the work of the entire Church is directed by committees which are subordinate to the executive committee, chaired by the president. There is an annual meeting of the conference where the mission of the Church is coordinated and decisions are taken. The work of the Church is wide and far-reaching and includes missions, both at home and abroad, especially in Micronesia, Brazil and Canada. The Church is also involved in publishing Sunday school material, and in church extension.

The headquarters of the Church is in St Paul, Minnesota.

CONSERVATIVE MENNONITE CONFERENCE

The OLD ORDER AMISH MENNONITE CHURCH was established in America during the first half of the eighteenth century and a more liberal wing of the Church developed from this foundation, one which wanted to separate from its more restricted and ultra-conservative MENNONITE parent.

These more liberal congregations formed a conference that met for the first time in Pigeon, Michigan, in 1910 and by 1954 the title 'Conservative Mennonite Conference' had been adopted. Members continue to subscribe to the *Dordrecht Confession of Faith* (1618–19). They gather in meeting houses – now substituting English for the original German in their worship – promote various Sunday school schemes and pursue a policy of non-resistance and non-conformity with the world around them. There are currently around a hundred congregations of this conference scattered in the American mid-west but membership growth is now very slow.

❖ Conservative Amish Mennonite Church

CONTINUING CHURCH MOVEMENTS

These occur when members of a Church find that they can no longer tolerate many of the doctrinal and liturgical changes that a Church may be proposing. In their efforts to retain a traditional approach, these disaffected members may then form a *Continuing Church*. This has occurred amongst Anglicans throughout the world as well as amongst some Congregationalists when the UNITING CHURCH OF AUSTRALIA was being formed in 1977.

CONVULSIONARIES

A term applied to some JANSENISTS who were in disagreement with the papal bull, *Unigenitus*, issued by Pope Clement XI in 1713. The bull, in condemning the 101 propositions of the French scholar Pasquier Quesnel (1634–1719), whose teachings were fundamentally Jansenist, amounted to a full denunciation of the doctrine.

The tomb of a young Jansenist cleric, François de Paris (1690–1727), in the cemetery of St Médard in Paris, became the focus for Jansenist pilgrimages and alleged miracles. Some of the pilgrims began to experience various phenomena similar to epilepsy, which many thought to be miraculous. These experiences often resulted in cures, periods of prophesying and the conversion of onlookers and were taken as justification of the Jansenist cause. Amongst the Convulsionaries were some young women who began to eat excreta and have heavy paving stones broken on their stomachs; they are also reported to have exhibited *glossolalia*, or speaking in tongues. This strengthened the resolve of many of the nuns of the Cistercian convent of Port-Royal, who were impressed by the Convulsionaries and refused to sign the papal formulary against Jansenism; the convent became a Jansenist centre. Other sources tell of the group, most of whom were women, causing themselves to be publicly scourged, throwing themselves into water and barking like dogs. One young girl decided to be crucified on Good Friday, 1758, 'a spectacle that was more than once repeated', as J. M. Neale commented in his history of the Jansenists, *A*

History of the So-called Jansenist Church of Holland, published in 1858. She remained on the cross for three hours, while another girl was crucified in the parish church of Fareins, near Toulouse, in 1787.

In 1732, when these near-hysterical scenes had become very disruptive, the cemetery was closed for a time. Undaunted by the authorities' action, believers procured earth from the graveyard and continued to display these phenomena in private houses. Young girls who experienced these convulsions, during which they appeared to be insensible to pain and bruising as they violently threw themselves around, were believed to have received the gift of healing. Instances of extreme convulsive behaviour continued until the end of the eighteenth century.

A strange incident is reported to have taken place, which concerned a Convulsionary nicknamed La Salamandre, who, despite being suspended in a sheet above a fire for many minutes, failed to catch fire, no doubt to the great satisfaction of the assembled believers.

❖ Convulsionists

COOK ISLANDS CHRISTIAN CHURCH

This is the largest PROTESTANT denomination in the Cook Islands and it belongs within the CONGREGATIONAL tradition. It was founded by missionaries from the London Missionary Society in 1823 and it has been an active, missionary-orientated Church ever since.

In the last quarter of the nineteenth century the Church was responsible for sending many missionaries to present-day Papua New Guinea, thus continuing a tradition that had begun many years before. Membership of the Church has slowly decreased. In 1901 the Cook Islands were annexed to New Zealand and many islanders left to work there. A small schism in 1941 in the Church on Aitutaki Island, one of the most northern of the Cook Islands, led to the formation of the Amuri Free Church. There are now less than one hundred congregations in the Cook Islands Christian Church, but it is still actively involved in primary education and supports several secondary and technical schools on the islands.

COONEYITES

This is a FUNDAMENTALIST *sect, whose members refer to each other as* 'Christians' *or* 'Friends', *which meets in private houses and stages annual conventions on private property. No publicity material or literature of any kind is produced, so doctrinal statements are difficult to access.*

The origins of the sect are to be found in the Faith Mission, which was founded in 1846 by John George Govan and was concerned with itinerant evangelism in rural Scotland, the mission workers setting about their evangelizing in pairs. The work soon spread to Ireland and in 1895 William Irvine (1863–1947) of Menagh, Co. Tipperary (or possibly from Kilsyth in Scotland), became the leader of the group. Irvine, despite being the leader of the sect, was not too sure about how close they were to New Testament thought and practice. He spent the years from 1897 to 1901 drawing up a fundamental rule of discipleship based on the renunciation of the world. Because of what was seen by the Faith Mission as a growing extremism, it disassociated itself from Irvine in 1900 and Irvine publicly resigned from the Faith Mission a year later, taking with him a group of followers who included

Edward Cooney, whose name was later taken by his followers, thereafter known as the Cooneyites.

Irvine and his followers set up as itinerant preachers, holding the first convention in Ireland in 1903, which was attended by at least seventy people. In the same year Irvine left for America with some fellow workers where they formed the so-called Nameless Church; other former members of the Faith Mission left Ireland to evangelize Australia, New Zealand, South Africa, China, Germany and South America. In their evangelistic work the preachers travelled in teams of two, as successors to the Apostles (Matt. 10:1–7). The movement, which had become fully established on mainland America, reached Hawaii in 1923.

A rule of celibacy and poverty had been introduced in 1903. The preachers were expected to sell all their possessions and rely on the fellowship for their needs. By 1908 William Irvine had established two classes of membership: the workers, who were also known as senior brothers or servants, were full-time ministers, and the ordinary members, who continued in their secular work, supported the workers financially. Irvine also sanctioned house meetings of upwards of twenty persons, who were presided over by a bishop, or elder. In 1913 Irvine announced his *Omega Gospel*, or *Omega Truth*, in which he stated that he had been anointed to bring the last message of Christ to the world, that the age of grace, which preceded the second coming, was nearing its end (which he named as happening in August 1914); and that after this date no additional people would be saved and the final judgement would begin (REVELATION 20). As the second witness named in Revelation 11, Irvine came to expect martyrdom in a Jerusalem street. These unpalatable beliefs led to Irvine's rejection by the other leaders of the Church and he was excommunicated in 1914 on the grounds that he had 'lost the Lord's anointing'.

At this point Edward Cooney and others took control of the group. Cooney had been a prominent member of the original Faith Mission group in Ireland, but he openly disagreed with certain of its doctrines and also with the need for holding conventions. He became a member of the new group led by Irvine but differences soon separated them. Uneasy with some of Irvine's new doctrines Cooney proposed, instead, that there should be a return to the original notion in which all the members were workers, or ministers, instead of some being ministers with others acting as their supporters, which had become general practice under Irvine. Cooney, however, did not win support and in 1928 he was ousted from the group and excommunicated.

Cooney died in America in 1961 at the age of 93. Irvine moved to Jerusalem where he died in 1947, although not through martyrdom in the street. His four hundred loyal supporters, variously called the *Little Ones*, or *Friends*, or *Message People*, believed that the apostolic age ceased in 1914 and that the work of the two-by-two, or paired, preachers was at an end. The sect still believes that pairs of ministers announced Christ's last message before the end of the apostolic age and that salvation of the unsaved is now impossible.

Whilst the doctrinal position of the Church is simple FUNDAMENTALISM, their doctrine of the Trinity is unconventional since they seem unclear as to whether Jesus is God or not and the Holy Spirit is understood to be a force emanating from God. Two ordinances are observed, those of a believer's baptism by immersion and the weekly celebration of the Lord's Supper, using ordinary bread and unfermented grape juice, known as emblems, the latter drunk from a common cup. Services are held in house churches and are simple in form, consisting of two unaccompanied hymns, extempore prayers and a brief discussion of lessons arising from individual Bible study. Members are expected to avoid the use of tobacco and alcohol, to shun worldly amusements and adopt simple, modest dress, without adornment, and with female members usually wearing their hair in a simple bun; some of these strictures have now been relaxed. Full-time ministers take vows of poverty, chastity and obedience, and donate all their goods to the organization.

Cooneyites are still to be found in house-churches throughout the USA, Canada, Australia, South Africa, Ireland and in parts of Europe. Although they insist that they have no official name, it became necessary for the group to register a name in order to gain conscientious objector status; the registered names are *The Testimony of Jesus* (UK); *Christian Conventions* (USA); *Christian Assemblies* (Australia, Canada and New Zealand).

❖ Black Stockings; Dippers; Go-Preachers; Pilgrims; Reidites; The Damnation Army; The Jesus Way; The Nameless House Church; The New Testament Church; The Non-Denominational Church; The Secret Sect; The Testimony; The Truth; The Way; Tramp Preachers; Two-by-Two Preachers (2x2 Preachers)

COPTIC EVANGELICAL CHURCH

Three American PRESBYTERIAN missionaries started this strongly PROTESTANT and REFORMED Church in 1854 in Egypt, the majority of their converts coming from amongst the Coptic Orthodox faithful. The body had been originally part of the United Presbyterian Church of North America, but has been autonomous since 1957 and now has the care of seven hundred churches and congregations throughout Egypt.

In 1869 a group of members of the Church separated and formed the Christian Brethren (Exclusive), which abandoned any American or other foreign supervision and is now largely an Egyptian-run denomination. The fast initial growth of this group has not been sustained, but the Church is still in existence.

The Coptic Evangelical Church, on the other hand, has flourished and is recognized by the Egyptian government as providing medical care through clinics attached to its churches, that are manned by medically qualified personnel. In the field of education many schools, such as the Ramses College for Girls, and various daycare centres have been established, together with a whole range of social service programmes aimed at counteracting poverty and urban decay.

❖ Evangelical Church of Egypt; Evangelical Church of Egypt, Synod of the Nile

COPTIC ORTHODOX CHURCH

The word 'Coptic' is an English form of the Arabic 'Kibt', which is derived from the modified Greek for 'Egyptians'. The Coptic language was spoken by the indigenous Egyptian peoples from about the third to the tenth century, when Arabic became the language of Egypt.

St Mark the Evangelist is credited with being the founder of the Egyptian Church in AD 42; he was martyred at Alexandria some 26 years later. The early Coptic Church had been most influential in the development of the theology of the early Church, but it was at the Council of Chalcedon (451) that the Patriarch of Alexandria, Dioscorus, defended the MONOPHYSITE heresy which led the Church formally into heresy. Dioscourus was deposed and sent into exile by the civil authorities, dying at Gangra in Paphlagonia, by the Black Sea, in 454 AD.

The century following Dioscorus' defeat at Chalcedon was a time of religious civil war, when the Byzantine emperors persecuted the Egyptians and replaced their patriarchs with Greeks (MELKITES), appointed to take their place. There was a great struggle for the Egyptian Church to preserve its identity and national culture in the face of Byzantine persecution. The Persians had dominated Egypt for a time, from 616–28, to be replaced when Arabs successfully conquered Egypt in 641. The Egyptian Church then began to enjoy some measure of religious freedom and their patriarchs started the work of restoring the churches and monasteries that had been destroyed by the Byzantines. Arab occupation was not always marked by religious toleration, however, and it is said that under the rule of the Caliph el-Hakim (996–1021) some three thousand churches were destroyed and many Coptic Christians apostatized. By the end of the Middle Ages the Coptic Christian population had shrunk from 6 million to just over 15,000.

Real freedom of worship came only under British occupation following the battle of Tel-el-Kebir (1882), but there was still uncertainty about the fate of the Copts until independence was achieved in 1922. Since 1993 there has been an increase in anti-Coptic attacks on clergy, the laity and church buildings, allegedly the work of Muslim extremists.

Within the Coptic tradition, from the earliest times, monasticism has always been at the forefront. During the Middle Ages, Coptic monasteries functioned as seats of learning and were the source of the Church's patriarchs and bishops; there is no current shortage of monastic vocations amongst young men, especially in the monasteries of Wadi Natrun, lying north-west between Cairo and Alexandria.

The Church observes the traditional seven sacraments, with baptism performed by immersion in water three times, usually within a week or two of birth; chrismation (*myron*), the equivalent to the western sacrament of confirmation, follows immediately. The Church has been organizing the running of catechetical classes for pre-school children as well as youth and adult education classes. Social and health care is provided through several clinics, hospitals, orphanages and other care facilities. Education is also cared for, at both primary and secondary level in schools and also in vocational and literacy programmes for young people. The head of the Coptic Church, elected by his fellow bishops, is known as the Pope of Alexandria and Patriarch of the See of St Mark. He oversees the work of the Church through a network of dioceses and bishops throughout the world, including North America, Africa, Australia, the Middle East, France, Germany, Italy and Great Britain; the British Orthodox Church of the British Isles recently became part of the Coptic Orthodox Patriarchate.

COUNTESS OF HUNTINGDON'S CONNEXION

Selina, and her husband Theophilus, Earl

and Countess of Huntingdon, were noted for their modest and virtuous lives at a time when the METHODIST revival, under George Whitefield and the Wesley brothers, was attracting much attention in eighteenth-century England. This religious movement had a profound effect on Selina's sister-in-law, Lady Margaret Hastings, and she introduced the countess to Methodist doctrines.

Selina, having at the time survived a dangerous illness, underwent a conversion experience and sent a message to the Wesleys, who were preaching near the Huntingdon's home, Donington Park, in Leicestershire. Her husband did not share the countess's enthusiasm for Methodism, but loyally accompanied her to the meetings of the Methodist Society. By 1720, Selina's fervour for itinerant and lay preaching soon made her an ally of George Whitefield, whom she appointed as her chaplain. Upon the death of her husband in 1746, she went to live at Ashby-de-la-Zouch, in Leicestershire, where she encouraged Whitefield in his evangelizing and preaching and set about establishing chapels throughout the country with a view to evangelizing the upper classes. She also set about exercising what she thought was her right, as a peeress, to appoint several clergymen as her chaplains and to use them publicly as itinerant ministers for her scattered congregations. Her plan was later disallowed by the consistory court of London in 1779.

In 1768 Selina bought a mansion in Talgarth, South Wales, called Trevecca House, and established a college for the provision of a free three-year course of training for intending ministers, whether they be for the CHURCH OF ENGLAND or for any other PROTESTANT Church. A difficulty arose in 1770 when the Methodist Conference affirmed that redemption was universal, a view not shared by the countess despite its being upheld by the principal of Trevecca House. The disagreement cost him his job and led to an irrevocable split between what was known, after 1777, as *Lady Huntingdon's Connexion* and the Methodist Society.

In 1779 the countess bought a disused amusement place, called the Pantheon, at Spa Fields, Clerkenwell, London, and converted it into a chapel. The local ANGLICAN vicar objected to a chapel of ease having been erected in his parish and over which he had no control. To ensure the independence of her chapels and chaplains, the countess registered the buildings as *Dissenting Places of Worship* under the Toleration Act of 1689; those of her chaplains who held English livings thereupon abandoned their chaplaincy work with the countess. In 1783 students from Trevecca went through a presbyterial ordination and Lady Huntingdon's Connexion lapsed into open schism.

Selina took an active interest in the rights of the poor and of orphans, especially those who lived in an American orphanage she sponsored for George Whitefield in Georgia; it was also in America that she helped with the founding of Dartmouth College and Princeton University. After the countess's death in 1791, the college at Trevecca moved from Wales to Hertfordshire and from there, in 1904, to Cambridge. The few remaining congregations, which are now in slow decline, have an annual conference and belong to the British Council of Churches.

COVENANT OF FREE EVANGELICAL CONGREGATIONS IN THE NETHERLANDS

This small Church was formed by a grouping-together of some of the independent congregations remaining as a result of the Separation, or *Afscheiding*, of 1834 when many congregations left the DUTCH REFORMED CHURCH in protest against the reordering of that Church some eighteen years earlier by King William I of the Netherlands. The Church itself suffered a separation in 1993, with the loss of some ten congregations, which became established as independent bodies.

Doctrinally, the Covenant of Free Evangelical Congregations in the Netherlands does not affirm any creed but it observes both infant and believer's baptism and celebrates the Lord's Supper every alternate month. Church polity is congregational and women may be ordained to the ministry, in preparation for which ordinands are trained in the Seminary of the Covenant Free Evangelical Churches (Utrecht), which is affiliated with the theological faculty of Utrecht. The membership of the Church is around 1,200, distributed in 80 congregations, with headquarters at Velp.

COVENANTERS

The name *Covenanters* was given to those, especially in Scotland, who had subscribed to the two Covenants, the National Covenant of 1638 and the Solemn League and Covenant of 1643. The purpose of these was to unite the whole nation against the attempts by the king, Charles I, to impose an episcopal system of Church government and a quasi-ROMAN CATHOLIC form of liturgy.

The *New Service Book*, prepared by the king and Archbishop Laud, lacked the approval of both parliament and the bishops as a body, and offended the Scots because it was seen as imposed from England. Riots followed the introduction of the *Scottish Prayer Book of 1637* and this prompted a move to introduce the National Covenant of 1638, which was signed widely and which led in part to the civil war and to the execution of the king in England.

During the civil war, which began in August 1642, the Scots entered into the *Solemn League and Covenant* (1643) with the English *Long Parliament*, to impose PREBYTERIANISM throughout Britain, and this brought a Scottish army to its aid against Charles; it was also responsible for the Westminster Assembly of English churchmen and Scottish commissioners that drew up the presbyterian system of Church government, the *WESTMINSTER CONFESSION* (1648) and the *Westminster Directory of Public Worship*.

With the restoration of the monarchy under Charles II, the episcopal form of Church government was imposed and this prompted vigorous resistance. The more extreme Covenanters took up arms, meeting disapproval from more moderate Presbyterians. Eventually, when James VII of Scotland (James II of England) was forced to leave Britain in 1688, Scotland joined with England in accepting William and Mary, who succeeded to the throne in 1689. The following year an act establishing the CHURCH OF SCOTLAND was passed, the laws favouring episcopacy in that kingdom were repealed and the *WESTMINSTER CONFESSION* was recognized. Some of the Covenanters, regarding William as an uncovenanted king, refused to join the Church of Scotland and formed a group known as the CAMERONIANS. When Queen Anne came to the throne in 1702 she took an oath to preserve the presbyterian form of polity and confession of faith in Scotland. The Cameronians eventually joined the FREE CHURCH OF SCOTLAND in 1876.

CUMBERLAND METHODIST CHURCH

This small, now almost defunct, American denomination arose as a schism in 1950 from the Congregational Methodist Church (founded 1852), itself a schism from the METHODIST EPISCOPAL CHURCH. The split that gave rise to the Cumberland Methodist Church was over issues of doctrine and polity. The Cumberland Methodist Church was founded in Laager, Grundy County, Tennessee, not far from Chattanooga.

CUMBERLAND PRESBYTERIAN CHURCH

The Second Great Awakening in America, a time of revival at the start of the nineteenth century, affected many young ministers in training. One such, the Reverend James McGready (*c.* 1758–1817), had a conversion experience that strengthened his fervour for evangelism. McGready was licensed and sent to Logan County, Kentucky, in 1796. During the following year his brand of revivalism spread throughout Kentucky and affected the METHODISTS, BAPTISTS and PRESBYTERIANS, climaxing in 1800 at a great outdoor camp-meeting, an innovation of his, during which he celebrated the Lord's Supper and admitted many new church members. Scenes of emotional outburst thereafter became commonplace at McGready's meetings.

With the revivalism came new practices, which were introduced in order to meet the needs of a frontier situation. At a meeting of the 1802 Presbyterian synod of Kentucky, doubts were expressed about the licensing of clergy to staff one of their foundations, the Cumberland Presbytery; these doubts mainly concerned the lack of formal educational qualifications of some of this Presbytery. The Cumberland ministers had requested that the usual high educational standards should be dispensed with for ministers working in frontier regions so that more men could answer the call and bring their message to a largely neglected area. This was disallowed and the clergy of the Cumberland Presbytery were ordered by the Kentucky synod to appear before them for re-examination; the Synod was met with a refusal and the Cumberland Presbytery was dissolved in 1806. McGready and the other ministers formed themselves into a breakaway council and refused to stop exercising their ministerial functions. When this matter was brought to the attention of the General Assembly of the Presbyterian Church, its ruling body, it was concluded that the treatment of the Cumberland Presbytery had been irregular and attempts at reconciliation were made.

After much soul-searching, the Cumberland Presbytery was re-established by its own ministers in 1810; its first synod met in 1813 at Beech Church, Sumner County, Tennessee, and its general assembly was formed in 1829. The camp-meetings and circuit preaching begun by James McGready now became the norm and the work was able to reach people who lived at great distances from urban centres. McGready himself spent the last part of his life as a pioneer missionary in southern Indiana. A Second Cumberland Presbyterian Church was organized in 1874, for black members of the Cumberland Presbyterian Church. In 1906 an incomplete merger between the PRESBY-

TERIAN CHURCH (USA) and the Cumberland Presbyterian Church was effected; in the same year women were appointed for the first time to various church offices.

The polity of the Church remains presbyterian and it continues to maintain the small Bethel College (founded 1842) in McKenzie, Tennessee, as well as engaging in various missionary activities. Work is also carried out in the production of religious educational curricular material for schools, and other media enterprises.

❖ Cumberland Presbyterian Church in America

CZECHOSLOVAK HUSSITE CHURCH

In 1890 some ROMAN CATHOLIC priests in Czechoslovakia formed an association called *Jednota* (union), as a protest against the Habsburg government which was trying to curb rising Czech nationalism by appointing and favouring those bishops who approved centralization and Germanization.

The focus of the association was not entirely political but was also concerned with appealing to the Pope to allow the use of the Czech language in the celebration of the Mass, to abolish priestly celibacy and provide greater opportunities for the laity to participate in church government. Their submissions to Rome were dismissed in 1919 and an independent meeting of about forty priests met in Prague in January 1920 to form an independent religious body, which later attracted many converts. The civil government recognized the group. A presbyterial polity was adopted, with four bishops elected but not consecrated, because at the time the Association did not subscribe to the doctrine of the apostolic succession; these bishops were expected to serve only a seven-year term of office, though this view of the apostolic succession has now changed and since 1935 the bishops have been consecrated.

The Church, originally led by Dr Karl Farsky (d. 1927), developed a liberal Christology and Eucharistic doctrine. Members originally professed no belief in original sin, purgatory or the veneration of saints, but the Church has now adopted a more Roman Catholic theological stance and would seem to regard itself as a reformed Roman Catholic Church. The Church underwent two name changes; firstly, in 1972, it was known as the Czechoslovak HUSSITE Church and from 1992 as the Hussite Church of the Czech Republic. The Church is headed by a patriarch.

❖ Czechoslovak Church; Hussite Church of the Czech Republic; National Church of Czechoslovakia

CZECHOSLOVAKIA, ORTHODOX CHURCH OF

Moravia, the eastern part of what is now the Czech Republic, was targeted by the missionaries, Sts Cyril and Methodius, in the mid-ninth century at the request of Prince Rostislav, after whose deposition there was considerable persecution by Latins of Orthodox clergy and faithful who took refuge in the Slavic countries to the south of Moravia. Orthodoxy went into serious decline and it was not until the end of the First World War in 1918, when the Austro-Hungarian empire was broken up and the independent Czechoslovakian Republic was formed, that Orthodoxy was revived. The Serbian Orthodox Patriarch of Belgrade, Dmitry, consecrated a former ROMAN CATHOLIC priest, Matej Pavlik, as Bishop Gorazd, in 1921. Pavlik was one of thousands who left the Roman Catholic Church because of Rome's refusal, in 1919, to allow the use of the vernacular in the celebration of the liturgy, to abolish priestly celibacy or to permit a greater lay participation in church government. Some of the disaffected clergy and laity formed the Czechoslovak Church, led by Dr Karl Farsky, while the rest became Orthodox Christians under Serbian jurisdiction.

Bishop Gorazd prepared a considerable quantity of liturgical material for the use of Czech speakers and organized the education of future clergy, who were sent for training to Yugoslavia. During the Second World War, when Germany occupied Czechoslovakia, the bishop would visit parishes and give moral support to the patriotic cause against the occupying army. Together with several other Orthodox clergy, he was arrested and charged with sheltering the assassins of the notorious Nazi SS leader and key player in the holocaust, Reinhard Heydrich (nicknamed *Der Henker* – the hangman), who was bombed and shot in his car by two Free Czech agents on 4 June 1942; he died later in a Prague hospital. Hundreds of Czechs were seized and executed, and in retribution for Heydrich's assassination an entire Czech village, Lidice, was wiped out. Bishop Gorazd and some of his clergy went before a firing squad in September 1942. Orthodox clergy who escaped the death sentence were deported to German labour camps and the existence of the Orthodox Church in Czechoslovakia was officially terminated: all activities, even attendance together at prayer meetings, were made punishable by death.

At the end of the Second World War the Orthodox Church, as well as the whole country and its people, was in a parlous state and an appeal was sent to the Moscow Patriarchate for help. Archbishop Elevferij (Voronov) was sent to Prague in 1946 and new dioceses were formed. Many Orthodox Czechs who had fled to Russia during the time of trouble returned home and new parishes were set up. In 1951 Patriarch Alexis of Moscow granted the Czechoslovakian Orthodox Church the right to autocephalic status. In 1966 the Church became a member of the Ecumenical Council of Czechoslovakia, and was granted permission to apply to join the World Council of Churches the following year. The Church is now known as the Orthodox Church in the Czech Lands.

In addition to the usual round of Orthodox services and the Divine Liturgy, most parishes also have weekly Bible meetings, at which members come together to study the scriptures.

D

DARBYITES

The name given to the followers of John Nelson Darby (1800–82), the founder of the EXCLUSIVE BRETHREN, a branch of the PLYMOUTH BRETHREN.

DARIUSLEUT (HUTTERITE)

An American group of HUTTERITES, which was established by Darius Walter in Silver Lake and Wolf Creek, South Dakota towards the end of the nineteenth century. Later migration established groups in Montana and Canada and by 1974 there were 77 colonies. The groups are loosely affiliated and fairly liberal in lifestyle, although the use of hooks and eyes, rather than buttons, is still required on members' clothing. It is the Dariusleut custom for the minister to enter the gathering place for worship at the head of his congregation in contrast to most other Hutterite groups, which require that the minister should be the last to enter.

DIGGERS

An agrarian communistic movement that flourished in England in 1649–50 under the leadership of Gerard Winstanley, William Everard and some twenty others. Winstanley (1609–60) had been a cloth merchant in London, but his business had failed. In the late 1640s food prices had reached record heights and Winstanley and his Diggers, as they came to be called, decided to cultivate crown and common land in and around St George's Hill, Surrey, just north of Weybridge, their purpose being the supply of food for themselves and for the poor of the area, claiming that 'the work we are going about is this ... to dig up St George's Hill and the waste ground ... and to sow corn and to eat our bread together by the sweat of our brows' (1649). The Diggers were frustrated in their work by the joint action of the landowning gentry, who had a vested interest in the production of food and were not adverse to the rising prices. These gentry hired mobs, who set upon the Diggers and held them as prisoners in Walton parish church, where they were hit and badly beaten. By 1650 their efforts ceased, having come to nothing. Winstanley laid out his principles in several tracts, in which he argued that holding land in common would be accompanied by social equality, would bring education for all and would be a preparation for the second coming (REVELATION 20), the first two being dangerous ideas to hold, and even more to publish, at this time. In

'A Declaration by the Diggers of Wellingborough' Winstanley declared 'that in the Last Days the oppressor and the proud man shall cease and God will restore the waste places of the earth to the use and comfort of man' (1650).

The Diggers called themselves the *True Levellers* because of their idealism and less compromising stand. This was in reference to the English political and religious party then active and known as the LEVELLERS, the leaders of which condemned the Diggers for their very idealistic brand of communism.

❖ True Levellers

DINGLEY UNION CHURCH

The Dingley Union Church, which is based in Melbourne, Australia, is a member of the Fellowship of Evangelical Churches of Australia, which was founded in 1956 as a conservative fellowship of independent congregations with its headquarters in Fitzroy, Melbourne, Victoria.

Four Churches in and around Melbourne concluded that forming a fellowship would strengthen their witness and evangelism. Doctrinally, their evangelicalism is based solely on scripture, and while baptism is simply affirmed, it is up to the individual Churches to decide how it is given and upon whom, whether infants or believers.

While the second coming of Christ is affirmed, a premillennial position is not insisted upon (REVELATION 20). The fellowship of 30 congregations and around 3,000 adult members to which the Dingley Union Church belongs is found in all Australian states, with the greatest number in Victoria.

DISCIPLESHIP MOVEMENT

An American movement that originated in Fort Lauderdale, Florida, in 1970 as a white-led, charismatic group that had grown out of the Shepherd's Church, also based in Fort Lauderdale.

The movement is led by officers known as shepherds, who exercise the office of overseer and whose appointment to the overall administration and direction of the 3,000 congregations is governed by the criteria suggested in Ephesians 4:12, with its reference to pastor-teachers 'for the equipment of the saints, for the work of ministry for building up the body of Christ.' The shepherds nurture disciples through a three-part programme, firstly through baptism by water, then discipleship by a man who is 'commissioned by God', and finally by acknowledging Christ's abiding presence with the shepherd, who is also often described as a 'disciple-maker'.

The members of these congregations are required to submit their tithes to the shepherds and to give obedience to the advice that they might seek from them, which can extend to issues concerning relationships between disciples. The shepherds are thought of as being spiritually mature and the evangelistic work of the movement is limited to them. This has given rise to some criticism and the suggestion that the Discipleship Movement is not operating along biblical lines. Their doctrinal position is, however, quite orthodox in matters of Christology, the Trinity, salvation and the authority of the scriptures.

❖ Christian Growth Ministries

DISSENTERS

A term applied to those Churches and their members that are not part of the Established Church.

DOCETISM

The word derives from the Greek *'dokeo'* – I seem – and concerns the heretical belief, held by some GNOSTICS and others that Jesus had no real, human body. This belief probably arose from the Gnostic aversion to matter and suffering being associated with God. The Docetai (or Docetists) thought that the crucifixion of Jesus Christ was an illusion and that, as God, he was incapable of suffering. The belief that 'the Lord's body was asserted to be but a phantom', was described by St Jerome (*c.* 341–420) as having come into being at the time of the apostles.

DOLLY POND CHURCH OF GOD WITH SIGNS FOLLOWING

An American Church founded by Thomas Harden in the early part of the twentieth century as part of a loose network of Churches in the PENTECOSTAL tradition, whose members handle snakes as part of their interpretation of the *signs* referred to by Jesus in Mark 16:17–18: 'And these signs will accompany those who believe: in my name they will cast out demons ... they will pick up serpents and if they drink any deadly thing, it will not hurt them.'

The snake-handling movement began in 1909 when a young man, George Went Hensley of Grasshopper Valley, Tennessee, took the reference in the Gospel of Mark to be a command; he took a rattlesnake to a church service at Sale Creek, Tennessee, and asked members of the congregation to handle the snake as a manifestation of their faith. This proved to be such a remarkable demonstration that Hensley's reputation and teachings soon spread. Because it was believed that if a member was filled with the Holy Spirit he or she would not be bitten, it followed that a bite from a snake during the service would be taken as evidence of backsliding. Despite this uncomfortable doctrine, the success of the movement continued to grow. Hensley took his ideas to Pine Mountain, Tennessee, which became the centre of the movement. Thomas Harden and Raymond Hays became its leaders. Hensley himself suffered a fatal snakebite in 1955.

The doctrinal position of the Church is solidly Pentecostal, with baptism of the Holy Spirit evidenced by *glossolalia*, or speaking in tongues, but also by snake handling, and even the drinking of poison, undertaken while the participants are in an ecstatic trance often referred to as 'being in the Spirit'; this is accompanied by exuberant dancing. A fatal snakebite, in 1945, prompted the state government to legislate against the practice, but it still continues. The lifestyle of the church members is plain and simple, with the Bible consulted on every issue. Congregations are still located in West Virginia, Ohio and Indiana, and along the Appalachian Mountains into the American South.

DONALD COMMUNITY CHURCH

An Australian evangelical and FUNDAMENTALIST Church which was founded at Donald, in North Central Victoria, in 1982 by some members of the UNITING CHURCH OF AUSTRALIA who, as METHODISTS, wanted to withdraw from that Church and remain as an independent Methodist-type congregation, which is their present status.

DONATISTS

A schismatic group of followers of a fourth-century bishop in Numidia, called Donatus, who challenged the validity of the election and consecration of another bishop, Caecilian, on the alleged grounds that at least one of Caecilian's consecrators was a *traditor* (one who had surrendered, or given over, the sacred books and vessels during the time of Diocletian's persecution of the Christians). As a *traditor*, the action of the consecrating bishop would, in their eyes, have been invalid and Caecilian would not have been validly consecrated. It was later decreed that the so-called *traditor* bishop had been wrongly accused and Caecilian had almost certainly been validly consecrated all along.

The Donatists held that any sacraments that were administered by an unworthy minister were invalid and also that sinners could not be members of the Church. This schism lasted for about one hundred years and was countered by the work of Sts Optatus and Augustine of Hippo.

DOUKHOBORS

An obscure Russian sect that originated in the eighteenth century in Kharkov, eastern Ukraine. Their agrarian and pacifist way of life brought the members into conflict with the authorities. With the help of both the writer Leo Tolstoy and the Quakers the members emigrated to Canada and Cyprus in 1898. In their new countries their refusal to take up weapons, register births, deaths or property did not improve the Doukhobors' lot with the authorities and there were renewed, and frequent, conflicts.

The sect members believe that the Trinity is composed of light, life and peace, linked to each man through memory (*Father*), understanding, or reason (*Son)* and will (*Holy Spirit*). Jesus Christ is not recognized as God but is regarded as a man possessing reason to the highest degree, whose life was a symbol of spiritual development capable of being experienced by anyone. Ritualism and the importance of the scriptures are rejected, and death is believed to be inconsequential since the soul is said to migrate from one body to another until it achieves purification. Doukhobors are now found in British Columbia, Canada, and in Russian Georgia.

❖ Dukhobors; Spirit Fghters

DUCK RIVER (AND KINDRED) ASSOCIATION OF BAPTISTS

An American Association of liberal-minded BAPTISTS who broke away from the more CALVINISTIC Elk River Association of Baptists in 1825. The members of the Duck River Association wanted a more liberal view taken of the atonement, believing that Christ died for everyone and not just for the saved.

Members observe the scriptural ordinances of believer's baptism, foot-washing and the Lord's Supper. The polity of the Church is congregational and is observed by over 100 congregations with around 10,000 adult members. Mission societies are supported, but the Church does not subscribe to the idea of sending missionaries out from local churches.

A schism within the Duck River Association occurred in 1843, concerning the legitimacy of missions and the support of a publication society and denominational school. Those who separated from the parent Church came to be called Missionary Baptists, also known as Separated Baptists, or the Baptist Churches of Christ.

❖ Duck River Baptists

DUNKARD BRETHREN CHURCH

A small American splinter group that broke away from the CHURCH OF THE BRETHREN in 1926 because the members felt that the parent Church was far too liberal in its ethos, was not living up to apostolic standards and was showing signs of a growing worldliness. The Church of the Brethren had originally been formed as a result of a three-way split after 1883 of the German Baptist Brethren Church.

The Dunkard Brethren Church affirms a belief in the inerrancy of the Bible as the word of God. Baptism by triple immersion is essential for the remission of sins and the newly baptized receive a laying-on of hands to receive the gifts of the Holy Spirit. The ordinances of foot-washing, the laying on of hands for the healing of the sick and the celebration of the Lord's Supper at night are all observed. Musical instruments do not accompany the services. It is also customary for women to have their heads covered during church services and all members are expected to refrain from litigation, oath taking, military service and membership of secret societies.

The congregations of the Dunkard Brethren Church are widely scattered through much of the USA and support a mission amongst the Navajo Indians in New Mexico; in 1955 the Church also opened an African Mission in Kenya.

DUTCH REFORMED CHURCH

This is the major PROTESTANT Church in the Netherlands (properly known as the *Netherlands Reformed Church* but more familiar under this title) and through its enterprising missionary outreach it has now been established in many countries, particularly in South Africa, the USA and the East and West Indies.

Historically, the liberal Low Countries, which had come under the control of the Burgundian dukes in the fifteenth century and then of the Hapsburgs, and later of Spain in 1555, was a haven for the followers of Luther, Zwingli and Calvin, providing them with a base that was safe from persecution. The CALVINISTS became the dominant protestant force in the Netherlands when it supplanted LUTHERANISM in the sixteenth century. This time was marked by the production of the *Belgic Confession* (1561), a Calvinistic document that became a doctrinal standard for the Dutch Reformed Church, which held its first general synod in 1571.

Under the Dutch king, William of Orange, the Calvinists prospered and became established in the United northern provinces, later turning their attention to ousting the DUTCH REMONSTRANT BROTHERHOOD from the Dutch Reformed Church. The Synod of Dort (1618–19), which condemned ARMINIANISM and therefore the Remonstrants, affirmed the *Belgic Confession* (1561) and a revision of the *Heidelberg Catechism* (1563), and established Calvinism in the Netherlands.

The importance of the Netherlands during the seventeenth century, both as a naval and commercial power, led to the foundation of colonies in the East Indies and in both North and South America.

This, in turn, led to the establishment of Dutch Reformed Church missions in these areas, as well as in Formosa, New York, India and South Africa (see next entry).

In the nineteenth century, after the establishment of the monarchy in the Netherlands, various tensions between the conservative and liberal modernist religious factions arose in the Dutch Reformed Church, and several splits occurred in response to the religious tolerance that the Church was displaying. A conservative wing of the Church, known as The Awakening, or *Reveil*, wanted to see a return to what has been described as heartfelt religion, and separation, or *Afscheiding*, took place in the village of Ulrum, in Groningen in 1834, when some of the more conservative-minded churchmen left the parent body. The so-called 'Free Churches' that they formed had, within two years, grown to around a hundred, which were spread throughout the country.

In 1886, the revival of Calvinistic dogmatism initiated by Abraham Kuyper (1837–1920), centred in Amsterdam and concerned with the matter of infant baptism, caused another conservative group, the *Doleantie*, to leave the Dutch Reformed Church. Uniting with some of those conservatives who had left earlier, together they formed the *Gereformeerde Kerk*, or REFORMED CHURCHES IN THE NETHERLANDS. Accusations of laxity also led to the formation of the CHRISTIAN REFORMED CHURCH IN NORTH AMERICA.

The Dutch Reformed Church is Calvinistic in its theology and Presbyterian in its polity. The central legislative body is the general synod, with various administrative functions carried out by the general secretariat. Doctrinally, the Church adheres to the *Belgic Confession*, the *Canons of the Synod of Dort* and the *Heidelberg Confession.*

This Church, which ordains both men and women, observes infant as well as believer's baptism and the Lord's Supper, which is celebrated either monthly, or quarterly. The headquarters of the Church is in Leidschendam, in the Netherlands. Despite some fall in numbers, due to a series of separations, it remains the largest protestant Church in the Netherlands, with over 2 million members.

DUTCH REFORMED CHURCH (SOUTH AFRICA)

Known in Afrikaans as the *Nederduitse Gereformeerde Kerk (NGK)*, the Church came to southern Africa with the first Dutch settlers in the mid-seventeenth century. (Two smaller denominations are sometimes classified as being Dutch Reformed Churches; these are the more liberal DUTCH REFORMED CHURCH – *Nederduits Hervormde Kerk* – and the more conservative Reformed Church of South Africa – *Gereformeerde Kerk van Suid-Afrika.*) Difficulties concerning missionary work amongst the native population led to the establishment of various daughter Churches, to serve the black, coloured and Indian peoples. Until 1986, the government policy of separateness (*apartheid*) was defended by the NGK, which had developed theological arguments supporting it. These arguments were not acceptable outside South Africa and led to the exclusion of the NGK from the World Alliance of Reformed Churches in 1982. By 1986, however, the NGK had reversed its opinion about the policy of *apartheid*, which it denounced as a sin in 1989.

The headquarters of the NGK is in Cape Town; it is governed by a general synod that meets every four years.

DUTCH REMONSTRANT BROTHERHOOD

The Dutch Remonstrant Brotherhood represents those who followed Jacobus Arminius (Jakob Hermandszoon, 1560–1609) when, after spending many years as a pastor in Amsterdam, he became convinced that human beings were created with free will and that Jesus Christ died not merely for the elect, but for all humanity. These views were at variance with the official CALVINISTIC theology of the day, which he was expected to preach. Arminius resigned his pastorate in the DUTCH REFORMED CHURCH after fifteen years of ministry and began to teach theology at the University of Leiden. A dispute between Arminius and a colleague, Francis Gomar, over the question of predestination, led to a major division within the student body of the university and also amongst the clergy of the Dutch Reformed Church.

Arminius died, from consumption, in 1609. His followers issued the *Remonstrance* in 1610, a document that sets out the tenets of what came to be known as ARMINIANISM. The tenets were set out in five points:

1 Predestination is not absolute, but depends upon man's response.

2 The offer of salvation is open to all humanity, because Christ died for all.

3 Man can exercise his free will properly only after receiving grace.

4 God's saving grace is not irresistible.

5 Believers can fall from grace.

These five points were countered by the *Contra-Remonstrance* of 1611, and the Synod of Dort, which assembled in 1618, declared the teachings of the Remonstrant clergy to be erroneous. As a result, some two hundred of them were compelled to leave their congregations; some were imprisoned, others banished for disturbing the peace on the order of Maurice, Prince of Orange (1567–1625). Following Maurice's death the Remonstrants were again tolerated and in 1634 a seminary was established in Amsterdam, which since 1873 has been part of the theological faculty of the University of Leiden.

This small denomination is made up of independent congregations with both male and female pastors who serve in full-, or part-time, ministries. The Church is concerned with interchurch aid and service to refugees, as well as participating in the Inter-church Peace Council. Meetings are held twice a year, one composed of delegates from the various congregations who meet in the general deliberative assembly, which debates controversial matters, and the other a meeting of the general administrative assembly at which decisions affecting the Remonstrant Brotherhood as a national Church are taken.

❖ Remonstrant Brotherhood; Remonstrant Reformed Congregation

E

EAST KEILOR EVANGELICAL CHURCH

A small independent Australian evangelical Church, founded at East Keilor, Victoria, by Pastor W. Jackel in 1947. It belongs within the FUNDAMENTALIST and pre-millennial (REVELATION 20) group of Christian denominations.

EASTERN CATHOLIC CHURCHES (also EASTERN CATHOLICS)

While most ROMAN CATHOLICS belong to the Latin Rite, there are 22 groups within the Roman Catholic Church whose members observe the Eastern Rite. These Eastern-rite Catholics hold to the same doctrinal beliefs as other Roman Catholics, but their laws, traditions, languages and liturgies belong to one of the five major families within which the individual Eastern-rite bodies are to be found.

These five major families are: 1) the *Alexandrian* family, consisting of the Coptic and Ethiopian Churches; 2) the *Antiochene* family, consisting of the Malankara, Maronite and Syrian Churches; 3) the *Byzantine* family, consisting of the Albanian, Bulgarian, Georgian, Greek, Hungarian, Italo-Albanian, Melkite, Romanian, Russian, Ruthenian, Slovak, Ukrainian, Belarussian and Churches of the former Yugoslavia; 4) the *Chaldean* family, consisting of the Chaldean and Malabar Churches; and 5) the *Armenian* family.

The term Uniat Church is often, some think pejoratively, applied to the Eastern-rite Catholics and was first used by Russian and Greek Orthodox opponents of the Union of Brest-Litovsk (1595–6), when Byzantine Christians in the province of Kiev adhered to the See of Rome. They are correctly known as Eastern-rite Catholics.

While both Latin- and Eastern-rite Catholics hold to the same doctrinal beliefs and recognize the authority of the Pope, there are material differences between them. The Eastern Catholic Churches celebrate a distinctive Divine Liturgy, which is not conducted in Latin, and baptize by immersion. Members, some of whom make the sign of the cross from right to left shoulder rather than from left to right as in the Latin-rite Church, receive both the bread and wine together at communion during the Divine Liturgy. The Eastern-rite Catholic Churches are independent of each other but are dependent upon the central authority of the Pope.

❖ Uniat Churches

EASTERN ORTHODOX CHURCHES

A family of self-governing Churches held together by a shared faith based on the Bible, on holy tradition and on the decrees of the seven ecumenical councils. All are in communion with the Ecumenical Patriarchate of Constantinople, who has a primacy of honour, but not of jurisdiction. This came about through the Eastern Schism (or Great Schism) of 1054 when communion was severed between those Churches under the Pope of Rome, Leo IX, and those under the Patriarch of Constantinople, Michael Cerularius. The Nicene creed is still held by all Orthodox Christians in its original form, without the *filioque* clause. They do not accept the claim of the Pope of Rome to be the sole vicar of Christ on earth, nor the doctrine of papal infallibility. The Virgin Mary is honoured as the *Theotokos*, or mother of God, but the Eastern Orthodox Church has never dogmatized about the belief in her immaculate conception. The Blessed Virgin, along with the saints of the Church and the angels, is venerated; carved representations of Jesus Christ, the Virgin Mary and the saints are rejected and veneration is given to icons, or pictures, representing them.

The seven sacraments of the Church are recognized. Baptism, of either infants or adults by triple immersion, is immediately followed by chrismation; penance and communion are received by both adults and children. Ordination, marriage and the anointing of the sick complete the sacraments. The polity of the Church is episcopal, with a council and a synod of bishops presided over by the elected archbishop, metropolitan or patriarch. The ministry has three orders – deacons, priests and bishops. The deacons, who help in the parish and assist the priests during the celebration of the Divine Liturgy, are allowed to marry, as are the priests, but they must marry before ordination and not afterwards. Bishops are chosen from amongst the male monastic clergy, all of whom, including nuns, observe the same monastic rule of St Basil the Great and are obliged to lead lives of poverty, chastity and obedience.

This family includes The Patriarchate of Jerusalem, The Patriarchate of Alexandria, The Patriarchate of Antioch, The Patriarchate of Moscow and All Russia, The Patriarchate of Georgia, The Patriarchate of Serbia, The Patriarchate of Romania, The Patriarchate of Bulgaria, The Church of Cyprus, The Church of Greece, The Polish Orthodox Church, The Autocephalous Church of Albania, The Orthodox Church of the Czech and Slovak Republics, The Orthodox Church in America and Canada, and The Church of Sinai. Four other Churches enjoy independence, although their election of a primate is dependent upon the approval of a mother Church. These are the Churches of Crete, Finland, China, Japan and Ukraine.

❖ Eastern Church; Orthodox Christian Church

EBIONITES

The name of this group is taken from the Hebrew Ebyonim – Poor Men.

The word *Ebionites* has been variously used to describe those ascetic Jewish Christians who lived in Palestine, east of the River Jordan, between the first and fourth centuries AD. Their description, as *poor men*, might refer to the poverty of their understanding, or to the poverty of the law (Jewish Torah), to which they clung tenaciously, or even to their impoverished beliefs concerning Jesus Christ, rather than poverty of goods and property. Some writers, including Tertullian, St Hippolytus and St Epiphanius, attribute the name to a founder identified as Ebion, but modern scholarship is not of the same opinion.

According to St Irenaeus (*c.* 130 – *c.* 200), Ebionite doctrines denied the divinity of Christ and his virgin birth and held that he was the human son of Joseph and Mary on whose head the Holy Spirit in the form of a dove descended at baptism. The theologian Origen (*c.* 185–254), on the other hand, contended that there were two classes of Ebionites, those who accepted and those who rejected the virgin birth of Christ; but all were in agreement in their rejection of Christ's pre-existence and divinity. Those Ebionites who accepted the virgin birth are also said to have observed both the sabbath and Sunday as days set aside for worship.

The Ebionites are also reputed to have rejected the Pauline Epistles, because they saw St Paul as an apostate from Judaism. They used only one of the four Gospels, that of St Matthew, as well as their apocryphal *Gospel of the Ebionites* which may be identical with the *Gospel of the Twelve Apostles*, referred to by Origen and was probably written in Palestine in the second half of the second century. It displays Ebionite sentiments, such as the detail of St John the Baptist eating honey, but not locusts, which is in keeping with the vegetarianism and asceticism practised by the Ebionites, and also proposes an adoptionist Christology, which is distinctly Ebionitic.

ELIM ASSEMBLIES

The Reverend and Mrs Ivan Q. Spencer started this growing American denomination in 1924 when they founded a Bible School in Endicott, New York. This school was intended as a training school for PENTECOSTAL ministers and subsequently became the Elim Bible Institute in Lima, New York, housed in the Old Genesee Wesleyan College that had been founded there by the METHODIST EPISCOPAL CHURCH.

Some of the school's first graduates formed the mission-oriented Elim Ministerial Fellowship in 1932, which they founded to provide an informal fellowship of churches and ministers who would help with various missionary endeavours. In 1947 this became known as the Elim Missionary Assemblies, and the name was changed again, in 1972, to the Elim Ministerial Fellowship because it was felt that the new name more clearly represented the mission of the Church.

This Fellowship works to help ministers, pastors and churches launch Christ-centred revivals. To this end it provides counselling services and support for local ministers. The Church maintains many missions in Europe, South America and Africa. A ministerial training school called the Elim Bible Institute aims to cut across denominational barriers and provides training for both men and women in the charismatic study of the Bible in a three-year diploma course.

❖ Elim Missionary Assemblies

ELIM PENTECOSTAL CHURCH

This Church must not be confused with the Elim Foursquare Gospel Church, which was founded in Australia in 1929 by Frederick Van Eyck, and is affiliated with the INTERNATIONAL CHURCH OF THE FOURSQUARE GOSPEL, *founded by Aimée Semple McPherson.*

The name '*Elim*' is derived from Exodus 15:27 and was a place of refreshment for the Israelites on their way to the Promised Land. The Elim Pentecostal Church began life as the Elim Evangelistic Band, founded by a Welshman, George Jeffreys, who had been much influenced by the Welsh Revival movement and by a PENTECOSTAL experience he received. Feeling that he had a call to commence evangelistic missions throughout Great Britain, Jeffreys set about his work in 1915, and by the time his mission had reached its end, in 1934, he had converted many people and been instrumental in the establishment of many churches in mainland Britain; there is even some evidence that he conducted successful healing services.

The doctrinal position of the Elim Pentecostal Church affirms the infallibility, inerrancy and inspiration of the Bible, while its Trinitarian and Christological beliefs are orthodox. The members observe the ordinances of the Lord's Supper and a believer's baptism in the Holy Spirit, with signs following, after which the baptized believer is thought to be ready to evangelize and serve in the ministry of the Church.

The Church has extensive home mission programmes that are designed to help those who are socially marginalized, and this work is carried to 35 countries, through the International Mission Board, where orphanages, hospitals and schools have been built and maintained. The governing body is a conference, which meets annually. Any problems that arise in the day-to-day administration of the Church are dealt with by the national leadership team, which is presided over by a general superintendent. This is a growing denomination with nearly 600 congregations in Great Britain, with about 43,000 committed adult members.

❖ Elim Foursquare Gospel Alliance

ELKESAITES

A Jewish-Christian sect of the late first century that originated in Palestine, east of Jordan, founded by a man known as Elkesai, or al-Khasayh. Mani (216–76), the founder of the MANICHAEANS, was probably the son of a family who were members of this sect. Both Elkasai and Mani were given to having angelic visions.

The name taken by the sect may have derived from the sacred writings, known as the *Book of Elkesai*, rather than the man; it has been said that these writings were delivered to Elkesai by an angel who was 96 miles tall. Their teachings were very similar to that of the EBIONITES. A close observance of the Mosaic Law was encouraged, the practice of sacrifice was condemned and the Epistles of Paul and other biblical writings were rejected.

The Elkesaites held to a Docetic (DOCETISM) view of Christ and believed that his sufferings were only apparent, and not real. They placed considerable emphasis on the redemptive value of baptism. Sts Hippolytus and Epiphanius both refer to the Elkesaites in their writings.

EMMANUEL HOLINESS CHURCH

This is a white-led, American PENTECOSTAL Church. When some delegates of the PENTECOSTAL FIRE-BAPTIZED HOLINESS CHURCH had come to a general conference held at Whiteville, North Carolina, in 1953 there was some serious falling-out between them over issues of polity, tithing and the mode of dress that should be worn by members. Those who disagreed strongly over the Pentecostal Fire-Baptized Holiness Church's insistence that neckties should not be worn, and who also felt that a more congregational polity should be adopted, elected one of their number, the Reverend L. O. Sellers, as their leader and formed the separate Emmanuel Holiness Church.

The very strict dress rules of the parent group were no longer adhered to, most especially in regard to men and the wearing, or not, of neck ties. Tithing was expected of all members and a congregational polity was introduced. The government of the Church is in the hands of a general assembly, presided over by an overseer, or chairman, with the ministers and delegates from each church forming the legislative body. There are now around 40 congregations in the southern USA, with nearly 4,000 members and a mission maintained in Mexico.

EMMANUEL'S FELLOWSHIP

This American Church was started in 1966 as a breakaway group from the OLD ORDER (OR YORKER) RIVER BRETHREN and was led by Paul Goodling of Greencastle, Pennsylvania. The seceding group objected to baptism by immersion, as practised by the River Brethren, as well as their acquiescence over the question of various members of that Church receiving social security benefit payments. The new group favoured baptism with the candidate standing in a body of water and having water poured over the head and body. The Church also acknowledges the need to follow a very strict code of dress, which is to be unworldly.

ENCRATITES

This generic term derives from the Greek '*enkrateia*' – self-control, or continence – and was applied to the EBIONITES as well as to some members of GNOSTIC sects by Sts Irenaeus (d. c. 200) and Hippolytus (d. 235) and by Clement of Alexandria (d. 215) on account of the sect members' excessive asceticism and exaggerated Christian morality, that they considered warranted condemnation. The believers abstained from the use of wine, which was described as 'dope of venom from the great serpent', and also from marriage, since women were thought of as the work of Satan. The eating of meat, poultry and fish was rejected on the grounds that it was the product of sexual intercourse. St Epiphanius (310–413) noted that the Encratites were numerous throughout the land of present-day Turkey, but were less numerous in Syria. By the third century they had split into several sects and seem to have disappeared by the middle of the fifth century, most likely absorbed by the MANICHAEANS.

EPHRATA SOCIETY

This now defunct communal SEVENTH-DAY BAPTIST CHURCH group was established in America in 1732 at Ephrata, Pennsylvania, just north-west of Philadelphia. The founder was John Conrad Beissel (1690–1768), who came from Eberbach in Germany where he had been a member of an ANABAPTIST group. Religious persecution in Germany had sent him to America in 1720 where he settled in the Conestoga area of Pennsylvania. Beissel came under the influence of the Seventh-Day Baptists and he was converted and baptized by Peter Becker in 1725.

By 1750 Beissel had attracted so many followers that he formed the Ephrata Society and became its leader. His personality and zeal set him apart and he soon attracted considerable criticism as well as support when he began to introduce Judaizing practices such as the elimination of pork from the diet; with the encouragement of Beissel some of the male followers even circumcised themselves. The practice of celibacy was also emphasized and this led to the breakup of some families, for although married couples could join the society they were obliged to lead celibate lives. Members of the society were also enjoined to live austere lives, observe Saturday as the sabbath, advocate pacifism and share in agricultural and other forms of labour.

After Beissel's death in 1768 the Ephrata Society went into decline. It came under the leadership of Peter Miller, was renamed as the German Religious Society of the Seventh-Day Baptists in 1814, and was finally dissolved in 1934.

EPISCOPAL CHURCH IN THE USA

This Church is not to be confused with the *Traditional Protestant Episcopal Church.*

The Protestant Episcopal Church is part of the Anglican Communion and its origin coincides with the English exploration and colonization of North America. It is claimed that the Church's origins date from 1578, when the first Anglican services were held during Martin Frobisher's Hudson Bay expedition, when the chaplain, the Reverend Wolfall, preached and administered Holy Communion on North American land. Similarly, it was at about the same time that Sir Francis Drake went ashore in California with his chaplain, Francis Fletcher, who planted a cross and read a prayer while Drake claimed the land for Queen Elizabeth I.

The first Anglican churches in America were opened in the Carolinas, Maryland and Virginia, their clergy and parishes remaining under the jurisdiction of the Bishop of London. The American Revolution broke these ties between the Church of England and the Church in the American colonies. Most Anglican clergy, who had taken an oath of loyalty to the king, fled to Canada or to England. At the end of the war, with no episcopacy left in America and the clergy scattered and totally disorganized, the remaining Anglicans elected Samuel Seabury as their bishop. He had been ordained as a priest in England by the Bishop of Lincoln in 1753, and had been sent as a missionary to New Brunswick, and later to New York. Seabury's election as Bishop of Connecticut and Rhode Island in 1783 posed a problem, since he was unable to take the required oath of allegiance to the king; in the event he was consecrated by bishops of the Episcopal Church of Scotland in Aberdeen in 1784. By an act of parliament the way was cleared for two American bishops-elect, William White and Samuel Provoost from New York and Pennsylvania, to be consecrated by the Archbishop of Canterbury in 1787; this was achieved by removing the need for an oath of allegiance to the king to be sworn by bishops of 'foreign parts'. At a convention held in Philadelphia in 1789 the constitution of the Protestant Episcopal Church was adopted and the *Book of Common Prayer* was revised. The Church then became independent and self-governing.

There was a growing tension, however, between the Low Church party, led by William White of Pennsylvania, and the

High Church party, led by Samuel Seabury of Connecticut. The basic difference between these two parties was their different approach to liturgy and to the Eucharist, with the High Churchmen favouring the use of incense, vestments and the ROMAN CATHOLIC explanation of the real presence in the consecrated elements of the Eucharist, while Low Churchmen opposed the use of ceremonies and focused most of their attention on the reading and preaching of the word of God. A Broad Church party emerged, somewhere between the polarized High and Low parties, which is best identified by its liberalism in discipline, doctrine and interpretation of the scriptures. As a result, the Protestant Episcopal Church generated a democratic government, with its highest council being its triennial general convention, composed of a house of bishops and a house of clerical and lay deputies, presided over by a bishop who is elected to the office by the convention.

A group of Low Churchmen, led by Bishop George David Cummins of Kentucky, seceded in 1873 to found the REFORMED EPISCOPAL CHURCH; the bishop and his followers objected to the use of such words as *priest*, *altar*, *sacrament* and *Holy Communion*. They revised the *Book of Common Prayer* and, in 1875, adopted their own set of *Thirty-Nine Articles*, which were meant to supplement the Church of England's *Thirty-Nine Articles of Religion*.

There had been considerable disquiet generated within the Protestant Episcopal Church, which since 1967 has also been known as the Episcopal Church, over the approval of the 1976 revision of the *Book of Common Prayer*, previously revised in 1892 and 1928. As a result, many left the Church to found their own. The consecration in 1989 of Barbara Harris as the first woman bishop prompted the formation of the Episcopal Synod of America, a dissenting group led by several bishops.

The headquarters of the Church is in New York and has responsibility for over 7,000 congregations and 1.69 million faithful distributed in 8 provinces and 109 dioceses.

EPISCOPUS VAGANS (also EPISCOPI VAGANTES)

Literally 'wandering bishop'. Men who have been consecrated as bishops in an irregular manner, but whose orders are not necessarily invalid. They are not in communion with any recognized, or major, Christian Church. Such consecrations may still be recognized as valid by the western, but not by the eastern Churches. The main sources of these irregular successions are those founded by Arnold Harris Mathew, Joseph René Vilatte and Vernon Herford.

ESTONIAN EVANGELICAL LUTHERAN CHURCH

This is the largest PROTESTANT group in Estonia and was organized formally in 1917, when the Estonian Evangelical LUTHERAN Church (EELC) held its first congress and elected its first bishop.

The invasion of Estonia by Soviet troops, which took place in 1940, effectively silenced the EELC, along with almost all Church organizations. The period of the Second World War saw the wholesale destruction of church buildings and the confiscation of all church property. Towards the end of the 1980s, when liberating changes began to take place in the Soviet Union, organized religious life in Estonia was able to develop.

The main concern of the EELC at the moment is the education and development of men and women for functioning within both the ministry of the Church and the lay leadership. Religious instruction is being fostered in schools and many opportunities for mission work are being explored. The headquarters of the EELC, which is a member of the Lutheran World Federation, is in Tallinn.

ESTONIAN EVANGELICAL LUTHERAN CHURCH IN EXILE

The Church was formed in 1944, initially as the Estonian Evangelical Lutheran Church Committee and later became known by its current, or by its alternative, title. The organization of the Church was largely the responsibility of Bishop, later Archbishop, Johan Kopp and assistant Bishop Johannes Oscar Lauri. The Church was established for the benefit of those thousands of members of the Estonian Evangelical Church who had escaped from the country at the time of the takeover by the forces of the Soviet Union in June 1940.

The principles that were laid down concerning the Church ensured that it was to be an independent and self-governing Church, which could call congregations together, ordain its pastors, hold services and carry out religious ceremonies according to the *Service Book* and the statutes. Since the end of the Second World War many Estonians have moved from Europe to both North and South America as well as to Australia, and in 1953 the congregations worldwide were organized into *deaneries*, initially in England and Sweden and later in the USA. In the 1970s further deaneries were formed in Canada, Germany and Australia. For the training of future clergy a theological institute was set up in Stockholm, but in 1978 this was transferred to Toronto, Canada; the same pattern followed the establishment of the Church's headquarters, which removed from Stockholm and is now in Toronto.

The Church, as a member of the Lutheran World Federation, is fully Lutheran in doctrine, affirming the *Book of Concord* (1580), or Concordia, which contains the traditional creeds (Apostles', Nicene and Athanasian), the *Augsburg Confession* (1530) and the *Apology* (1531), and the strongly anti-Roman Catholic *Smalcald Articles* (1537) which were drawn up by Martin Luther and to which is added Philipp Melanchthon's tract *Of the Power and Primacy of the Pope*. The Concordia also includes Luther's *Small* and *Larger Catechisms* (1529) and the *Epitome and Thorough Declaration of the Formula of Concord* (1577).

❖ Estonian Evangelical Lutheran Church Abroad

ESTONIAN ORTHODOX CHURCH

In the mid-eleventh century there was mention made of Orthodox congregations in Estonia, which had been established in the south-east of the country by Russians. The present Diocese of Tallinn was at one time part of the Pskov Diocese, which had been brought under the rule of the Prince of Kiev in 1030. When the autonomous Diocese of Riga was established in 1850, the northern part of Estland (now Estonia) was placed under the control of the Metropolitan Archbishop of St Petersburg, because of its proximity to that city, and remained under his control until 1865. During the eighteenth and nineteenth centuries, when Estonia was part of the tsarist Russian empire, there was much conversion to Russian Orthodoxy amongst its people.

In 1917 the independent Diocese of Estonia was created and the first native Estonian was consecrated as Bishop Platon (Paul Kulbush), but in 1919 he was killed, bayoneted and then shot in the head and shoulder at point blank range by the Bolsheviks. The Patriarchs of Constantinople and Moscow declared Bishop Platon to be a saint in 2000, and as a martyr his remains were placed in a tomb in the Alexander Nevsky Cathedral in Tallinn, where they may now be venerated. Following the proclamation of Estonian independence in 1918, the Estonian Orthodox Church remained in the care of Patriarch Tikhon (Belavin) of Moscow until 1923. Tikhon and the holy synod of the RUSSIAN ORTHODOX CHURCH declared in 1920 that the Estonians could use the vernacular and the new calendar (New Style calendar) in church services. Aleksander Paulus was then elected and ordained as archbishop and head of the Estonian Orthodox Church.

Archbishop Paulus asked the Ecumenical Patriarch, Meletios IV of Constantinople, to take the Church into his jurisdiction. The request was granted and in 1923 the Church was declared to be autonomous, with Archbishop Aleksander elevated to the position of Metropolitan of Tallinn and All Estonia.

In the early part of the Second World War Estonia was occupied by the Germans, but in 1944 the country, like its neighbours Latvia and Lithuania, was occupied by the Soviet army and incorporated into the Soviet Union as a Soviet republic. Metropolitan Aleksander, together with some of his clergy and around 80,000 faithful, fled to Sweden where they established a church in Stockholm. The Church in Estonia now became subordinated within the Russian Orthodox Church. The theological seminary in the Petseri monastery, and the theological faculty within the Tartu University were both closed down, religious education in schools was forbidden and many clergy were arrested and then shot, or deported to Siberia. The daily expense needed to maintain the Church's witness became unbearable and the situation could only worsen. The autonomy that had been granted in 1923 was now withdrawn.

The Church based in Stockholm remained within the Ecumenical Patriarchate and when emigration from Europe once again became possible many people left for Great Britain, Australia and the USA, taking their Orthodox faith into these countries, where they were served by priests of the Constantinopolitan Patriarchate. Metropolitan Aleksander died in 1953 and was succeeded by archpriest Juri Valbe (d. 1961), who had been working in Sweden since 1945. The Estonian parishes in Sweden were then placed under the local bishops of the Ecumenical Patriarchate.

When Soviet rule came to an end in Estonia, in 1991, the country once more became independent. By then, most of the Orthodox faithful were Russians, people who had come from the Soviet Union to live and work in the new republic. After many years of difficult discussion about the future of the Estonian Orthodox Church, which largely centred on which patriarchate it was to be placed under, in 1996 it was once more declared autonomous and Archbishop John of Finland was appointed as its temporary leader. By 1999, the Estonian Orthodox Church felt that there was a need for a resident primate; in the event there was no suitable Estonian candidate and Bishop Stephanos Nazianzus from Nice was appointed as Metropolitan of Tallinn and All Estonia, with a mandate to oversee the formation of a local Estonian episcopate. By mid-1999, 58 Estonian Orthodox parishes had joined the autonomous Church, which was registered with the government; another 30 parishes chose to remain within the Russian Orthodox Diocese of Tallinn, reflecting the ethnic make-up of the people of Estonia.

ESTONIAN ORTHODOX CHURCH IN EXILE

When Estonia was forcibly incorporated into the USSR in 1940, the primate of the ESTONIAN ORTHODOX CHURCH, Archbishop Aleksander, fled to Sweden where he was able to organize the Estonian Orthodox Church in Exile. The Church was placed under the Patriarchate of Constantinople.

Because so many Estonians had migrated to the USA and Canada in the 1940s, it was felt necessary to form a congregation of the Estonian Orthodox Church in Exile for them. The Church was organized in America by the Very Reverend Sergius Samon in Los Angeles and this has served as the headquarters of the Church ever since. Other parishes, serving some six hundred adult believers, are to be found in San Francisco, Chicago and New York, with Canadian parishes in Toronto, Montreal and Vancouver; there are several more congregations in Australia.

ETERNAL SACRED ORDER OF CHERUBIM AND SERAPHIM

This African Church, with its headquarters at Ebute-Meta, Nigeria, owes its origin in the 1920s to Moses Orimolade who, it is claimed, began to preach under the direct inspiration of the Holy Spirit following his cure from an illness, which he regarded as miraculous. At that time Orimolade had no intention of forming, or establishing, a Church. A belief in the entire teaching of the established Churches is affirmed, but there is also considerable emphasis placed upon the power of divine healing, prophecy and visions.

The organization of the Church is hierarchical and centralized, with a basic group of either 20, 50 or 100 persons forming a *Band*, for the purpose of convenient administration, spiritual teaching, counselling and prayer sessions. Seven sacraments are recognized, and members are ordained into one of five ministries that operate within the Church, those of pastor, prophet, evangelist, shepherd and teacher. Worship takes place in a cruciform temple, or main church building, which is without any form of seating for the congregation. Footwear is prohibited both in the temple, which is reserved for prayer services only, and in an adjacent church hall, which can be used for other divine services and meetings.

There are several main streams within the Cherubim and Seraphim movement and steps towards unification have been made. Some of the streams are:

1 The Eternal Sacred Order of Cherubim and Seraphim

2 The Cherubim and Seraphim Society

3 The Praying Band

4 The Eternal Sacred Order of Cherubim and Seraphim, Mt Zion

5 Holy Order of Cherubim and Seraphim Movement.

This claims to be the original main Church body, but numerous secessions and disagreements have led to the formation of some two hundred distinct denominations.

ETHIOPIAN EVANGELICAL CHURCH MEKANE YESUS

Mekane Yesus – Dwelling Place of Jesus (Amharic language)

This is a very large denomination with over 6000 congregations and 1.2 million adult members who worship within the LUTHERAN tradition in Ethiopia. It was created by a merger in 1959 of various missionary groups and Lutheran missions that had been founded in 1866 in Eritrea by Swedish missionaries, whose work was supplemented by missionaries from Germany and the USA; following the Second World War further missionaries, from Iceland, Norway and Denmark, joined them. American Lutheran efforts were increased in the 1950s and 1960s, especially through the use of radio to broadcast religious programmes into many parts of Africa.

The Ethiopian Evangelical Church Mekane Yesus provides health services in four hospitals and 24 dispensaries, screening programmes for HIV and AIDS management, child and youth care, teacher training colleges and water and rural development programmes. The Church is also heavily committed to ecumenical relationships and is a member of various interdenominational associations as well as of the World Council of Churches and the Lutheran World Federation. The headquarters of the Church is in Addis Ababa, but its main sphere of influence is in the western part of the country, with some congregations in the north.

❖ Evangelical Church Mekane Yesus

ETHIOPIAN ORTHODOX CHURCH

An autocephalous ORIENTAL ORTHODOX CHURCH(ES), being one of six ancient Eastern Churches that rejected the Chalcedonian Christological definition in AD 451 and which uses Christological terms at variance with those used by the EASTERN ORTHODOX CHURCH. It recognizes only the first three Ecumenical Councils, of Nicaea (325), Constantinople (381) and Ephesus (431). The idea that Christianity was brought to Ethiopia through the baptism of Queen Candace's eunuch by St Philip the Apostle (Acts 8:26–40), as was once thought, is not now generally accepted. The historian, Rufinus (d. 410), refers to the role of St Frumentius in converting many Ethiopians, whose action was instrumental in having Christianity declared the official religion of Ethiopia in the early part of the fourth century.

The close reliance of Ethiopia upon the Egyptian Copts in Alexandria made it inevitable that the Ethiopian Church would similarly adopt MONOPHYSITISM. Trouble with Islam, and many failed attempts at union with Rome, followed. With the liberation of Ethiopia from Italian occupation in 1941 the Church sought, and was granted, autonomy from the COPTIC ORTHODOX CHURCH, upon which it had been dependent for the supply of senior clergy. The Ethiopian patriarchate was established in 1959. The government of the Church is in the hands of the holy synod, whose chairman is the patriarch, assisted by his archbishops and bishops. Priests, who are usually married, run parishes with the assistance of deacons and lay singers, or teachers, known as *Debteras*. A minimum of two priests and three deacons is required to celebrate the Divine Liturgy. Celibate priests are monastic and are eligible to become bishops. While the Ge'ez language is used in the Divine Liturgy, the official language of Ethiopia is Amharic and the Church is now trying to introduce this into the worship. Fasting is strictly observed on seven occasions throughout the year and involves abstinence from meat and animal products and avoidance of touching food before 3 p.m. on afternoons of fast days, except at the weekends. The Church has preserved various Judaic customs, such as keeping Saturday holy as well as Sunday, circumcision and the observance of Jewish food laws.

The separation of Church and state in 1974 provided the impetus for evangelical activity and missionary work, which is now carried out in the Sudan, the West Indies, Guyana, Europe and the USA. The Church, which has its own printing presses and issues its own newspapers, is also actively involved in the World Council of Churches, especially in programmes for clergy training and parish administration, youth work and social development activities.

❖ Abyssinian Church; Ethiopian Orthodox Tewahedo Church

EUCHITES

A mid-fourth century sect, its members known also as Messalians, which survived until the seventh century, moving around Syria, Palestine and present-day Turkey; the name comes from the Greek '*euche*' – a prayer – by extension 'people of prayer'. According to St Epiphanius of Salamis (*c.* 315–403), there were two types of Euchites, the non-Christian and the Christian. The former, although they acknowledged many gods, worshipped only one, which they called the almighty. The Christian group rejected the sacraments as being valueless, and believed that it was only through prayer, and not baptism, that the evil spirit which lurks in man, a result of Adam's fall, can be expelled and replaced by the Holy Spirit, achieving union with God. Once this union was achieved it was believed that the passions that governed man would never be a problem again.

Both male and female Euchites were given to wandering through and sleeping in the streets, which led Theodoret (*c.* 393–466) to remark that they were occupied more in sleep than prayer. Many attempts were made to suppress the group. Flavian, Bishop of Antioch, drove them from his city in 376, and St Amphilochius of Iconium (now Konya, in Turkey) condemned them during the synod of Sida (388–90), a sentiment repeated at the Councils of Constantinople (426) and Ephesus (431).

Members of the sect in Mesopotamia lived in monasteries, or folds. The men wore their hair in a female style and went beardless; both males and females dressed in sackcloth. They were accused of immorality, and Letouis, Bishop of Melitene (now Malatya, in Turkey) ordered that these monasteries were to be burned down.

The Euchites soon disappeared but the Bogomils of the Middle Ages have been linked with them.

❖ Adelphians; Lampetians; Messalians

EUROPEAN FREE CHURCH MOVEMENT

The European Free Church movement began in the fifteenth century, introduced by men known as *the radical reformers*, who, unlike Martin Luther and John Calvin, wanted to see a severance of the ties between Church and state. Churches that owe their origin to the work of these radicals include the MENNONITES, AMISH, BRETHREN CHURCH(ES) and the RELIGIOUS SOCIETY OF FRIENDS (Quakers).

Outstanding leaders within the movement include Andreas Bodenstein von Carlstadt (1477–1541), who introduced a vernacular Mass and the priesthood of all believers. He influenced Thomas Müntzer (or Münzer, 1490–1525), who defined the Church as the company of true believers gathered in fraternal love. Müntzer's concern for the poor led to his involvement in the peasants' war in Germany in 1524 and to his capture and eventual execution. Hans Denck (1495–1527), who was influenced by von Carlstadt and Müntzer, and also by Balthasar Hubmaier (*c.* 1485–1528), proposed in 1526 the practice of believer's baptism, which became a central feature of ANABAPTISM, and the rebaptism in adulthood of all those who had been baptized as infants.

The Swiss Anabaptists led by Michael Satler who had been at one time a monk, became involved in the composing of the *Schleitheim Confession*, a statement which clearly set out the Anabaptist position. This called for the total rejection of a state Church and affirmed the supreme authority of the Bible, the baptism of believers who alone could receive Holy Communion, and the imposition of a ban, which was a form of excommunication passed on wayward church members. The influence of Menno Simons (1496–1561) in the Netherlands led eventually to the formation of the *Dordrecht Confession* of 1632, which not only supported the *Schleitheim Confession* but also took the ban of excommunication a further stage by introducing the idea of *shunning*, the intentional avoidance of wayward members even by their own families, which is still a feature of some Mennonite groups today.

Various Free Church groups arose in the seventeenth century, including one led by Jacob Amman and now known as the Amish. At the same time the PIETIST movement of the late seventeenth century, which emphasized personal piety over doctrinal agreement, led to the formation of the Brethren groups. The Religious Society of Friends (Quakers) also has its roots in the mid-seventeenth century, led by George Fox (1624–91), whose ideas were in sympathy with those of the radical continental reformers.

What emerged from these movements was an a-liturgical, non-creedal, lay-orientated group of Churches. Two ordinances are observed, those of baptism and Holy Communion, with baptism of believers administered by any mode and Communion, or the Lord's Supper, preceded by foot-washing. Free Churches are free of any state ties and their members retain their *separateness* as a people of God; they also reject the idea of taking up arms and the swearing of oaths.

EUTYCHIANS

The name is given to followers of Eutyches (*c.* 378–454), the head of a monastery near Constantinople. He came out of retirement to contest and oppose the errors of Nestorianism. Eutyches suggested that Jesus, in his manhood, was not fully human; this can be taken to be the foundation of MONOPHYTISM. Because of this, Eutyches earned the condemnation of Patriarch Flavian of Constantinople and also of the Synod of Constantinople in 448, which deposed him from his post on account of his heresy. Eutyches appealed to Pope Leo I, and when the erroneous *Robber* Council of Ephesus in 449 (so-named because it was dominated by Monophysites) which had been called by Theodosius II, found in his favour, Eutyches was reinstated. The Council of Chalcedon later reversed this decision in 451, and maintained that the two natures of Christ are fully God and fully man, united indivisibly and inseparably and preserved eternally in one person.

EVANGELICAL ADVENTISTS

ADVENTISM, with its emphasis on the second coming of Christ when the wicked will be destroyed and the righteous saved (REVELATION 20), was brought into prominence through the efforts of an American BAPTIST preacher, William Miller (1782–1849). Miller had read Daniel 8:14 – 'Unto 2,300 days, then shall the sanctuary be cleansed' – and he declared, at a conference in 1840, that the time of Christ's return was scheduled to occur during the year running to 21 March 1844 (the date was later revised to run to 22 October 1844). When Christ failed to return on schedule the followers of Miller, who had been fired with enthusiasm by his predictions, experienced what was known as the *Great Disappointment*, with the result that many of them were disaffected and returned to their own Churches.

A conference of some 61 delegates, representing those who decided to remain within the Adventist movement in the hope that not all was lost and perhaps the mathematics, rather than the general idea, was at fault, met in Albany, New York, in 1845 and a fairly loosely-structured Adventist organization came into being. This quickly split into several smaller groups, one of which became known as the Evangelical Adventists.

Originally identified as the American Millennial Adventists (REVELATION 20), this group attracted to its membership the greatest number of Miller's followers. It was a short-lived organization whose members believed that the dead remain conscious after separation from the body and will rise again. The righteous will reign with Christ on earth for the millennium, a thousand glorious years of peace when Satan will be locked up and unable to wreak his usual malevolent harm, after which he will be released and defeated by Christ. Then will start the judgement, with the righteous attaining heaven for all eternity. The wicked, however, will rise from their graves on the day of judgement to be condemned to everlasting hell. The Church no longer exists.

❖ American Millennial Adventists

EVANGELICAL AND REFORMED CHURCH

The Evangelical and Reformed Church, which was the product of a union between the Evangelical Synod of North America and the Reformed Church in the United States, is no longer in existence. This union came about in Cleveland, Ohio, in 1934, followed by another, in 1957, when the new body again united with the general council of Congregational-Christian Churches to emerge as the UNITED CHURCH OF CHRIST.

The Evangelical Synod of North America had its origins in the meeting of six German ministers at Gravois Settlement, near St Louis, Missouri, in 1840. This led to the founding of the Evangelical Union of the West, led by Karl Daubert, a German Reformed Missionary. This ministerial association adopted such doctrinal standards as the *Heidelberg Catechism*, Luther's *Catechisms* and the *Augsburg Confession* in its revised form. Four other groups, all with German backgrounds and with a similar belief and polity, joined the Evangelical Union, which then took the name of Evangelical Synod of North America. At the time of the 1934 merger it had a membership of around 281,000. The other partner in the union, the Reformed Church in the United States, had its origins in Switzerland and Germany.

To effect the union it was agreed that wherever doctrinal standards differed between member Churches, then it was the right of all ministers, congregations and members to act as their consciences dictated, but the final test for any doctrine, or procedure, was to be the Bible. Two sacraments were observed, infant baptism and the Lord's Supper; confirmation in the early 'teens, ordination, marriage and the burial of the dead were thought of as ordinances. The Church adopted a presbyterial polity and was administered through synods and consistories, or church councils. Each church was governed by a consistory made up of elected representatives and these local churches together formed a synod. The synods met twice a year, with each local church represented by a pastor and a lay delegate.

EVANGELICAL BAPTIST CHURCH

A small American denomination of 40 congregations and some 2,500 members that had its origins in 1935 when it was formed by members of the Free Will Baptists. It was formerly known as the Church of the Full Gospel, Inc. Paul Palmer at Perquimans, Chowan County, North Carolina, had organized the Free Will Baptists in 1712 from amongst Welsh immigrants and it held to a distinctively ARMINIAN, rather than a CALVINISTIC, view of salvation.

The members of the Evangelical Baptist Church stress spiritual gifts and healing as well as the second coming of Christ (REVELATION 20). They recognize four ordinances, baptism of believers by immersion, foot-washing, the dedication of children and tithing. The government of the Church is congregational and each local pastor is elected by the congregation; once elected he has the authority to elect all other church officers who will assist him in the management of the local church.

❖ Church of the Full Gospel, Inc.; General Conference of the Evangelical Baptist Church

EVANGELICAL BRETHREN

This American denomination, which is no longer in existence, was formed in 1922 through the reunion of the United Evangelical Church and the Evangelical Association, which was the name formally adopted by the ALBRIGHT BRETHREN in 1816; the United Evangelical Church had been established on account of internal controversies as a schismatic group of the Albright Brethren. The Church accepted ARMINIAN doctrine and has been described as being very close to the METHODIST position. There was a characteristic emphasis placed upon personal salvation and the seeking of Christian perfection, upon which was based entire sanctification. The overall administration of the Church was placed in the hands of the general conference, which was presided over by the elected bishops and delegates who met formally every four years.

The Evangelical Brethren merged with the United Brethren in Christ in 1946 to form the EVANGELICAL UNITED BRETHREN CHURCH, which in 1968 united with the Methodists to form the UNITED METHODIST CHURCH (USA).

EVANGELICAL CHURCH IN GERMANY

The initials of its German name, EKD – Die Evangelische Kirche in Deutschland, are often used when referring to this Church.

A federation of 24 regional LUTHERAN and REFORMED Churches in Germany that was organized in 1948 in a bid to create a strong PROTESTANT bloc and to resolve some of the confusing divisions which had arisen during the previous four hundred years. Preparatory planning started at the end of the Second World War, with a group of church leaders meeting in August 1945 to find a way of forming the EKD; the constitution of the Evangelical Church in Germany was accepted in July 1948, at Eisenach.

The territorial Churches that make up the membership of the EKD are involved in ecumenical work, with medical and social activities undertaken by the diaconal work of the EKD, which was founded in 1957 and whose workers have responsibility for over 300 hospitals, dispensaries and clinics as well as care homes for the elderly, orphans, alcoholics and ex-prisoners. The EKD has its headquarters in Hannover.

EVANGELICAL CHURCH OF CAMEROON

The Evangelical Church of Cameroon (EEC) was organized by the British BAPTIST Missionary Society in 1845 and is currently the largest of any PENTECOSTAL group in that country, with in excess of 543,000 adult members spread between 1,700 congregations. Cameroon became a German protectorate in 1884 and this caused the work of the Baptist Missionary Society to be shared out between the Swiss Basel Mission and the Baptist Mission of Berlin.

The Union of Baptist Churches, which had been formed by these missionary societies, joined with the Evangelical Church of Cameroon to form the Council of Baptist and Evangelical Churches of Cameroon. Both the EEC and the Union of Baptist Churches are now members of the World Council of Churches and both have their headquarters in the capital city of Cameroon, Yaoundé.

EVANGELICAL CHURCH OF CZECH BRETHREN

This very large PROTESTANT denomination is an amalgam of LUTHERAN and REFORMED Churches in Bohemia and Moravia (now Czech Republic) that merged in 1918 with many smaller protestant groups. Its origin can be traced back to the HUSSITES and to various Brethren groups.

The Czech Reformation had been very successful up until 1621, because of the presence and support of Hussite and CALVINIST kings, who were in power, but when the Austrian Catholic Hapsburgs gained control of Bohemia and Moravia this led to the rigorous and bloody suppression of protestantism. The Edict of Toleration, which was declared in 1781 by Joseph II, the Holy Roman Emperor, restored religious rights to the protestants.

Czechoslovakia was created in 1918 through the merger of Bohemia, Moravia, Slovakia and Ruthenia, and the Evangelical Church of the Czech Brethren became the leading protestant witness in the state. During both world wars, the Church and nation suffered and despite efforts to cooperate with the communists, who took control of the government in 1948, the Church fared badly until the fall of the communist regime in 1989–90.

This Church is Bible-centred and is administered by a chief elder who presides over a council of elders. During the services the preacher, who may wear a long, black gown with preaching bands, is positioned behind a lectern facing the congregation. Confirmation is recognized as an occasion when young people are formally accepted as members of a congregation. Both baptism and the Lord's Supper are celebrated as ordinances. The Church today has 600 congregations and 117,000 members and has its headquarters in Prague, Czech Republic.

❖ Evangelical Church of Bohemian Brethren

EVANGELICAL CHURCH OF FRENCH POLYNESIA

A succession of foreign missionary enterprises, begun in 1797 by the London Missionary Society and later by the Basel Mission and the Paris Missionary Society, led to the organization of this Reformed Church in French Polynesia. An elder from the London Missionary Society left the Church in the early 1820s, declaring that he was Jesus Christ, and a short-lived sect, the Mamaia, developed and flourished over the space of some thirteen years. More recently, since the end of the Second World War, some smaller Churches have been formed by seceders from the Evangelical Church of French Polynesia, most notably the Keretitiano (Christianity) which was set up in 1950, and the Autonomous Church, founded in 1954 by an ex-pastor of the Evangelical Church. Both these Churches have maintained the REFORMED tradition in their doctrine and form of worship. A third secession, by some Polynesians of Chinese descent, formed the Polynesian Pentecostal Church, which was founded in 1968.

EVANGELICAL CHURCH OF GABON

This is the largest PROTESTANT Church in Gabon, whose foundation was laid by the American Board of Commissioners for Foreign Missions in 1842. The mission was passed on to the American PRESBYTERIANS in 1870 with the insistence that French was to be the language used in all mission schools. In 1850 Gabon became a French colony and in 1892 responsibility was passed into the hands of the Paris Evangelical Missionary Society. The Church became autonomous in 1961 and presently has five hundred congregations, the overwhelming majority of whose members are Bulu Fang-speaking women.

EVANGELICAL CHURCH OF IRAN

This small Church, which operates in Iran, is in the REFORMED tradition and was founded as the result of a mission outreach by the American Board of Commissioners for Foreign Missions in 1832.

The original missionaries, Dr Julius Davies and Dr Asahel Grant, were members of the PRESBYTERIAN Church. They called themselves the *Mission to the Nestorians*, with their headquarters at

Urmi (now Orumiyeh), but their missionary efforts did not impress the Nestorians. The result was that the missionaries soon found themselves converting some of the Assyrians in the community, who were organized into the Evangelical Church of Iran.

This is the largest PROTESTANT Church in Iran, with 10 congregations and 1,650 current adult members. The Church became autonomous in 1943. At the time of an influx of Koreans, who worked in the construction and transport industries in Iran, a congregation known as the Tehran Korean Christian Church was set up by the Evangelical Church of Iran, served by a Korean pastor who was sent as a missionary by the Presbyterian Church of Korea. The Church maintains nineteen schools in the country and has a link, through its Christian Service Board, with the Nurbakhsh School for Practical Nurses.

EVANGELICAL CHURCH OF NORTH AMERICA

An American denomination, organized in 1968 at the time when a merger was finalized between the EVANGELICAL UNITED BRETHREN CHURCH and some METHODIST groups. The schism involved the rejection of the merger by some 75 Evangelical United Brethren Churches in the Montana and North West Conferences, who then formed the Evangelical Church of North America, to which the HOLINESS METHODIST CHURCHES soon wished to unite.

The members uphold the *Twenty-Five Articles of Religion* that were abridged by John Wesley from the *Thirty-Nine Articles* of the CHURCH OF ENGLAND and were printed in *The Sunday Service of the Methodists*, which was published in England in 1784.

The administration of the Church is by means of four annual conferences, which cover geographically the whole USA and are known as the Pacific, the Eastern, the Western and the North-Central conferences; overall control is in the hands of a council of superintendents. Church missions are controlled through specific mission agencies. The headquarters of the Church is in Indianapolis, Indiana.

EVANGELICAL CHURCH OF THE LUTHERAN CONFESSION IN BRAZIL

A large, PROTESTANT denomination that had its beginnings in Brazil in 1823–4, when German migrants settled in the south of the country. The first congregations were formed by teachers and other lay workers. Missionaries and pastors were then sent out from Germany to help the migrants in their work.

In 1886 four synods were formed and a schism in 1890 produced the Lutheran Evangelical Church of Brazil, which is now related to the LUTHERAN CHURCH – MISSOURI SYNOD, which had been established in America in 1847. Following the Second World War some partially successful attempts were made to unite these groups to form a single Church. This was established in 1968, adopting a common constitution and its present name.

As it is constituted today, the Evangelical Church of the Lutheran Confession (IECLB) is probably the largest LUTHERAN Church in South America. Beginning as a largely rural group serving a German migrant population, its appeal is now much wider and no longer confined to rural areas. A vigorous missionary outreach programme in the north of the country is dealing with the problems facing small farmers, dispossessed people and street children. In partnership with the ROMAN CATHOLIC CHURCH, and through the National Council of Christian Churches in Brazil, the IECLB helps to relieve suffering and is building the foundations of agrarian reform with the aim of stemming the continual migration of people from the countryside to the city.

A centre for theological education, the EST – *Escola Superior de Teologia* – has been opened at São Leopoldo, providing training from undergraduate level to doctoral research as a preparation for the training of leaders of congregations, catechists and parochial school teachers, as well as helping in the formation of church musicians. The IECLB shares its pastors with churches in Costa Rica, Nicaragua and Venezuela and there are links with the north-west synod of Wisconsin and the New England synod. These companion synods are important relationships that help to strengthen the life and mission work of the Church, enabling exchange visits and the pooling of various resources.

EVANGELICAL CONGREGATIONAL CHURCH

The Church was formed in the USA in 1922 following a special session of the east Pennsylvania conference, which had been called in an attempt to organize a merger between two existing Churches, the Evangelical Association and the United Evangelical Church, the latter the result of a schism in 1894 from the former; the Evangelical Association had originally been known as the ALBRIGHT BRETHREN. Much dissent was voiced at the conference over the loss of church buildings that the United Evangelical Church had built and that were, as a result of some unpleasant litigation, to be handed over to the Evangelical Association when the reunion was effected. The outcome was a motion against the merger and the Evangelical Congregational Church came into existence.

The Church is ARMINIAN in doctrine and METHODIST in polity, arguing against predestination and for the exercise of man's free will to accept, or reject, grace. The integrity, inspiration and inerrancy of the Bible are emphasized and the *Twenty-Five Articles of Religion*, that were adopted in 1894 by the United Evangelical Church, are upheld. Bishops, elected every four years, have very limited powers; ministers, appointed to their charges by the annual conference, are limited to an eight-year tenure.

The Church has maintained a busy foreign missionary programme in Europe, the Far East, Africa and South America. In the USA there is an active programme of home mission work that is very extensive and includes the establishment and running of an infirmary, homes for the elderly and a school of theology. The headquarters of the Church is in Myerstown, Pennsylvania.

EVANGELICAL COVENANT CHURCH OF AMERICA

There had been a PIETIST movement in nineteenth-century Sweden, formed to counter the growing rigidity of the Swedish LUTHERAN Church and to create a more Bible-centred faith that would allow for a greater freedom of religious expression.

Many Swedes who had been influenced by this revivalism migrated to America in the mid-nineteenth century and began to organize their own churches. The result was that two synods were formed. By 1885 these had merged to form the Swedish Evangelical Mission Covenant Church of America. In 1937 the word

'Swedish' was dropped from the title and the loss of the word 'Mission', in 1957, gave the Church the name it has today.

There are now over 600 churches, with 89,000 adult members. All are committed to a rule of faith, doctrine and conduct with a strongly biblical emphasis, which is given supremacy over such creedal statements as the Apostles' creed. The Church upholds the fellowship of believers, who may exercise their freedom to baptize at any age and by whichever mode is agreeable to the local congregation. The only ordinance that is recognized is that of the Lord's Supper. An elected board, which also selects its ministers, administers each local church. The churches are divided into geographical areas, with regional conferences overseen by a superintendent. Each local church sends both lay and ministerial delegates to the annual meeting, where decisions are taken and implemented by an executive board.

The scope of work of the Church is extensive and is concerned with Christian formation, growth and evangelism, women's ministries and world missions, which are maintained in Africa, the Far East and Central America. In the USA there is much active work undertaken in health care, with several hospitals and care centres under its control as well as many retirement communities that currently offer housing for 4,500 residents. The Church has its headquarters in Chicago, Illinois.

❖ Evangelical Covenant Church; Swedish Evangelical Mission Covenant Church of America

EVANGELICAL FREE CHURCH OF AMERICA

An American denomination that began in Boone, Iowa, in 1884 as a loose fellowship of *Free* congregations, made up of several groups of Swedish PIETISTS, who merged to create the Swedish Evangelical Free Mission; in 1950 they were joined by the Norwegian-Danish Evangelical Free Church Association to form the Evangelical Free Church of America. The original merger came about through the reluctance of some Swedish groups to join a union, which reluctance led to the formation of the Swedish Evangelical Mission Covenant Church of America. This Church later became the EVANGELICAL COVENANT CHURCH OF AMERICA.

At the time of the 1884 merger of the congregations any question of doctrine was left to the individual churches, but in a short time it became clear that some sort of direction was needed. A *Confession of Faith* was adopted at the time of the 1950 merger, which stressed the inspiration of the Bible and the imminence of the second coming of Christ and his reign on earth for a thousand years (REVELATION 20).

The polity of the Church is congregational, but the licensing of the clergy is authenticated by a ministerial fellowship and an annual conference orchestrates the overall coordination of the member congregations. Great attention has been paid to the provision of college and theological education in the USA and Canada, with several colleges supported by the Church. There has been much success in missionary work, with churches established in Venezuela, the Philippines, Africa, Hong Kong and Japan, which all show very strong and rapid growth.

EVANGELICAL LUTHERAN CHURCH IN AMERICA (EIELSEN SYNOD)

This Church must not be confused with the

Evangelical Lutheran Church in America.

It was mainly from Germany and Scandinavia that Lutheranism came to America, first established there in 1638 by Swedes who founded a colony at Fort Christina on the Delaware River, with the encouragement of their pastor, Reorus Torkillus; the coming to America of German Lutherans, who settled in Pennsylvania, followed soon after. With successive waves of immigrants from Europe, each linguistic group of Lutherans established its own synod, or autonomous Lutheran Church, each independent of other language groups. By 1850 there were an estimated 159 such Lutheran bodies; this number was reduced, through the merging of many of the groups, to around 20 Lutheran Churches in the USA today.

A young Norwegian lay preacher and evangelist, Ellin Eielsen (1804–83), arrived in America in 1839 and organized the building of the first house of worship for Norwegian Lutherans at Fox River, Illinois. In 1843 a Lutheran pastor, whose background is unclear and who was the first Norwegian pastor ordained in America, privately ordained Eielsen. In 1846 Eielsen and his followers formed a synod at a meeting held in Jefferson Prairie, Wisconsin, and the Evangelical Lutheran Church (Eielsen Synod) was established.

Progress was slow on account of the synod's insistence that as a prerequisite for membership a prospective member must be able to provide proof of conversion. A split in the group came about when the constitution was revised in 1876 in order to come into line with the more open acceptance of potential church members which was desired by the majority of the laity and clergy. At the same time the name was changed to Hauge's Norwegian Evangelical Synod (which later became part of the American Lutheran Church); a minority remained loyal to the Eilesen Synod.

Eilesen himself, while strictly adhering to Lutheran doctrine, emphasized congregational autonomy, repentance, conversion and preaching by both laity and ordained pastors, but he opposed ritualism, clerical dress and authority.

This Lutheran body now has 2 congregations and about 700 members, largely confined to Wisconsin and Minnesota. Administration is in the hands of male members who may vote at the annual synod's meeting, which directs a board of trustees in taking responsibility for church property; a council, also directed by the synod, decides on doctrinal matters and discipline within the Church.

EVANGELICAL LUTHERAN CHURCH IN AMERICA (ELCA)

The ELCA is the largest Lutheran denomination in the USA, numbering some 10,900 congregations with nearly 4 million adult members. It was formed on 1 January 1988, in Columbus, Ohio, as a result of a union between:

1 THE LUTHERAN CHURCH IN AMERICA (founded 1962) – which came into existence through the merger of four Lutheran bodies, the United Lutheran Church (founded 1918), the Finnish Evangelical Lutheran Church (Suomi Synod) (founded 1890), the American Evangelical Lutheran Church (founded 1872) and the Augustana Evangelical Lutheran Church (founded 1860).

This group of Lutheran Churches crosses many national boundaries: Finnish, Swedish, Norwegian and Danish.

2 THE AMERICAN LUTHERAN CHURCH – the product of two mergers, the first made in 1960 between the American Lutheran Church (German) (founded 1930), the Evangelical Lutheran Church (Norwegian) (founded 1917), the United Evangelical Lutheran Church (Danish) (founded 1896); the second merger took place in 1963 with the Lutheran Free Church (Norwegian) (founded 1897).

3 THE ASSOCIATION OF EVANGELICAL LUTHERAN CHURCHES – which arose out of a controversy in the 1970s that affected one of the more conservative Lutheran bodies in America, the LUTHERAN CHURCH – MISSOURI SYNOD (LC–MS), whose members and seminarians believed in the inerrancy of the Bible and that it is to be interpreted literally. Doubts began to be expressed in the seminaries about the validity of this viewpoint and from this difference of opinion a schism grew, which resulted in the split of some three hundred congregations away from the LC-MS; these congregations then formed the Association of Evangelical Lutheran Churches.

An agreement between these three large Churches to unite was made in 1982 and they formed a seventy–member *Commission for a New Lutheran Church*, in order to prepare and plan for the new merger. The church conventions approved these plans in 1986 and within two years the ELCA came into existence.

Doctrinally, the ELCA holds to traditional Trinitarian and Christological beliefs and recognizes the canonical scriptures of the Old and New Testaments as being the inspired word of God and the authoritative source of the Church's faith and life. The Church also accepts the formulas of the Apostles', Nicene and Athanasian creeds coupled with the unaltered *Augsburg Confession* and other writings by Luther that were gathered together in 1580 and are known as *The Book of Concord*.

This immense American denomination maintains a vigorous missionary programme of work in 45 countries worldwide as well as supporting chaplaincy work, counselling and clinical education, and with specialized ministries within the correctional, health care and solvent abuse advisory services. Many camps and retreat centres have been established for the use of church members as opportunities for revival and reflection, as well as nearly 30 colleges and seminaries and a deaconess community, together with 28 high schools and over 250 elementary schools. Attention is also given to youth ministries, outdoor preaching and publishing, especially of catechetical material. The central administration currently oversees 65 synods, located in 9 regions, each headed by a bishop.

EVANGELICAL LUTHERAN SYNOD

This modestly sized, but active American denomination had its origins in the arrival of Norwegian settlers in Wisconsin, Iowa and Minnesota during the early years of the nineteenth century. Ministers from the LUTHERAN Church came from Norway and congregations were established, with the first service held at Koshkonong, near Madison, Wisconsin.

The first church body, known as the Norwegian synod, was organized in 1853, but a difference of opinion arose within the synod in the 1880s over the doctrine of election, so much so that when, in 1917, the Evangelical Lutheran Church was formed from the merging of various of these Norwegian groups, some 40 pastors and laity who opposed this merger met at Lime Creek Lutheran Church at Lake Mills, Iowa. Their objection to the merger was because it was based on the assumption that man could, somehow, cooperate in his own conversion and therefore the belief that our own conversion is due to God's grace is compromised. The outcome was that the dissenting group decided to reorganize themselves and in 1918 they formed the Norwegian synod of the AMERICAN EVANGELICAL LUTHERAN CHURCH, which in 1958 became known as the Evangelical Lutheran Synod.

Rapid growth followed and by 1927 the Church was able to establish the Bethany Lutheran College in Mankato, Minnesota, a liberal arts college about 80 miles south-west of Minneapolis-St Paul; by 1946 this also housed the Bethany Lutheran Theological Seminary, providing a three-year academic training and a one-year internship for future clergy. In 1993 the synod joined in establishing a new alliance, the Confessional Evangelical Lutheran Conference, composed of thirteen Lutheran bodies from around the world. As recently as 1999 a joint declaration on the doctrine of justification was signed by representatives of Pope John Paul II and the Lutheran World Federation in Augsburg, but this was rejected by the Evangelical Lutheran Synod since the document, in its opinion, reached a compromised conclusion.

Doctrinally, the Church follows a conservative Lutheran approach and is congregational in its polity. The role of the synod is purely advisory, and its decisions are not binding on local congregations. The Church has around 125 congregations across the USA and maintains an active home mission programme. Foreign missions, which were started in Peru in 1968, where there are now some 27 congregations and a seminary, expanded to include work in Chile, Ukraine, the Czech Republic and Australia. Congregations have now been established in all of these countries.

❖ Norwegian Synod of the American Evangelical Lutheran Church

EVANGELICAL MENNONITE CONFERENCE

When German MENNONITE settlers faced discrimination in their own country they welcomed the offer made by Catherine the Great of Russia (1729–96) to establish their communities in southern Russia. Most of these communities were later forced to leave Russia, heading largely for America when they faced persecution under Tsar Alexander II (1818–81).

While still living in southern Russia, a schism developed amongst some of the Mennonites. The controversy centred on the question of whether, as Mennonites, they could become magistrates, but there were also questions about the growing laxity in some of the communities. This controversy was fuelled by the preaching of Klaas Reimer, who proposed a greater sense of discipline and a simpler lifestyle in the daily life of Mennonite communities. The need for a more disciplined and sober way of life was attractive to some of the groups, who began to develop in line with Reimer's proposals; these were known as the *Kleine Gemeinde*, or Little Congregations.

With immigration to North America groups of several churches were set up in 1874 on either side of the Canadian border; these congregations are much involved in missionary work and have established further communities in Paraguay, New Mexico and Nicaragua.

❖ The Little Congregation

EVANGELICAL METHODIST CHURCH (EMC)

By 1946 there was a growing disquiet felt amongst American METHODISTS concerning modernism, when questions were being raised over the Virgin Birth, Christ's deity, the inspiration of the scriptures, biblical miracles, the need for *new birth* and the doctrine of sanctification. This disquiet also concerned the autocratic style of administration that had developed within the Church and the unease came to a head at a meeting of Methodist pastors and laity in Memphis, Tennessee, in May, 1946, with a decision taken to form a new Church, the Evangelical Methodist Church.

An independent Methodist Church had been formed the previous year at Abilene, Texas, led by Dr J. H. Hamblen, and he was invited to become the first general superintendent of the EMC at their first annual conference, held in Kansas City, Missouri, in November 1946. Mergers with other groups followed. In 1957 the Mexican Evangelical Mission, led by Dr Ezequiel B. Vargas, united with the EMC and Dr Vargas was elected as the general superintendent of the first Mexican Mission conference. Two other mergers with small Churches brought in the Evangelical Church, Inc., in 1960, with the PEOPLE'S METHODIST CHURCH of North Carolina following two years later. The EMC extended its missionary outreach in 1979 with the establishment of the Bolivian Evangelistic Mission, which is involved in medical ministry and vigorous church planting. Foreign mission work is also pursued in some 20 other countries worldwide, while at home in the USA there are now congregations established and maintained in nearly 30 States. The Church has a very conservative posture that is thoroughly Wesleyan in doctrine, subscribing to Wesley's *Twenty-Five Articles of Religion.* Members acknowledge the doctrines of original sin, free will, justification by faith and the possibility of sin after justification, which can be followed by repentance. They observe only two sacraments, baptism of the young and the Lord's Supper, and deny purgatory and the phenomenon of *glossolalia*, or speaking in tongues.

The Church has a congregational polity and is governed through the conference system, with a general conference, presided over by the general superintendent, directing the work of the Church in publishing as well as in its home and foreign missionary work.

EVANGELICAL METHODIST CHURCH OF AMERICA

This Church arose in the USA in 1952 as a direct result of a schism from the EVANGELICAL METHODIST CHURCH that was caused by a protest over theological literalism, especially concerning the doctrine of holiness as put forward by Dr J. H. Hamblen, the first leader of the Evangelical Methodist Church.

The leader of the schism was the Reverend W. W. Breckbill who, like his followers, was concerned about the Evangelical Methodist Church's membership in the National Association of Evangelicals, which they regarded as over-liberal. After their separation from the parent body, the Evangelical Methodist Church of America allied itself with some extreme FUNDAMENTALIST and Methodist Churches. The Church, with its 132 congregations and nearly 9,000 adult members, has its headquarters at Altoona, Pennsylvania.

EVANGELICAL ORTHODOX (CATHOLIC) CHURCH IN AMERICA (NON-PAPAL CATHOLIC)

The Church was founded in the USA in 1938 by Bishop William Waterstraat of Santa Monica, California, and initially named as the Protestant Orthodox Western Church. When he retired, in 1940, the responsibility for the Church passed to Bishop Frederick Littler Pyman, who was consecrated bishop in 1943 by Archbishop Henry Carmel Carfora, of the NORTH AMERICAN OLD ROMAN CATHOLIC CHURCH. Pyman continued under Carfora's jurisdiction until 1948, when he withdrew and changed the name of the Church to its current form.

The doctrinal position of the Church is largely that of the OLD CATHOLIC CHURCH, but holy scripture is regarded as being the fully inspired word of God. While the members of the Church recognize the office of the Pope in Rome, they do not accept his infallibility, acknowledging that Christ alone is infallible. Clerical celibacy is optional and oral confession of sins is not required of members. The language used in the celebration of the Mass is also optional and either Latin, or the vernacular, may be used. Membership of secret societies, for example of the Freemasons, is permitted.

Bishop Pyman strove to create a Church that could serve as a bridge employed to reconcile PROTESTANT and ROMAN CATHOLIC differences. Pyman had been (allegedly) the leader of a small number of LUTHERAN Independent congregations in California before his consecration. When he retired in the 1970s the leadership passed from Pyman to Archbishop Perry R. Sills, who was consecrated in 1974. In 1984 the Church was affiliated with the patriarchal synod of the ORTHODOX CATHOLIC CHURCH OF AMERICA, which is an association of independent bishops.

In the 1970s the Church had 7 congregations with a total membership of 500, distributed between California, Arizona, Indiana, New York and Massachusetts. The headquarters of the Church is at San Jose, California.

❖ (Non-Papal Catholic) Evangelical Orthodox (Catholic) Church in America; Protestant Orthodox Western Church

EVANGELICAL PRESBYTERIAN CHURCH

This Church should not be confused with one of the same name that was founded in 1937 as an ultra-conservative breakaway from the ORTHODOX PRESBYTERIAN CHURCH (founded 1936), and which later merged with the REFORMED PRESBYTERIAN CHURCH OF NORTH AMERICA (General Synod) in 1965 to form the REFORMED PRESBYTERIAN CHURCH EVANGELICAL SYNOD.

This American Church had its beginning towards the end of 1980 and the early months of 1981, when a group of pastors and lay people from several mainstream PRESBYTERIAN Churches met in St Louis, Missouri, for future planning and prayer in the face of what they saw as a growing liberalism and laxity in their respective denominations. They were anxious to return to the zeal of their Presbyterian founders. In 1981, having adopted the name Evangelical Presbyterian Church

(EPC), 75 delegates, representing 12 churches, met to hold their first general assembly at the World Presbyterian Church near Detroit, Michigan. During this assembly a list of essential beliefs was drafted, with allowance made for freedom to be exercised over less essential matters which would allow local churches to provide their own administrative structure in order to supervise church property and also to let local congregations decide whether women could become ruling elders, or deacons.

The doctrinal base of the EPC is the WESTMINSTER CONFESSION *of Faith*, in its most recent revision, the *Larger* and *Small Catechism* and another document, called *The Essentials of Faith*, which was drafted by the Church's general assembly. The Church is fully Trinitarian and regards the Bible as infallible and fully inspired by God. The EPC supports missionary work throughout the world.

EVANGELICAL PRESBYTERIAN CHURCH OF AUSTRALIA

Originally known as the Reformed Evangelical Church, this Church was founded in Launceston, Tasmania, in 1961 by three Presbyterian ministers, the Reverends Rodman, Turnbull and McNeilly, who were ordained for service in the Church by the Presbyterian Church of Eastern Australia.

The new Church was formed by the coming together of five, previously BAPTIST, congregations which had decided to accept the REFORMED and CALVINIST doctrinal position. However, in the early years after its foundation disputes broke out concerning what was perceived as God's disposition towards those who were not of the *elect*, and schisms developed. A major rift was created in 1965 when a group from near Ulverstone, on the north coast of Tasmania, left to join the Presbyterian Church of Eastern Australia; another Tasmanian group seceded in 1986, led by two ministers, and formed its own small Church, known as the Southern Presbyterian Church.

Doctrinally, the Church officially affirms the WESTMINSTER CONFESSION *of faith* (1643–6), as well as the *Belgic Confession* (1561), the *Heidelberg Catechism* (1563) and the *Canons of the Synod of Dort* (1618/19). The Evangelical Presbyterian Church of Australia currently has 10 congregations, with around 400 adult members, divided between Tasmania and Queensland.

❖ Reformed Evangelical Church

EVANGELICAL PRESBYTERIAN CHURCH OF GHANA

The Church was formed in 1993 as a schism from an Evangelical Presbyterian Church the foundations for which had been laid in Ghana in 1847 by the Bremen Mission from northern Germany among the Ewe-speaking people in Peki (Krepi) in what was then a German colony but is now part of present-day Ghana. At the start of the First World War the missionaries were expelled from the country and the autonomy of the Evangelical Presbyterian Church was established.

The schism that created the Evangelical Presbyterian Church of Ghana arose over the seceder's insistence that the Church was for the exclusive use of Ewe members. This Church now maintains around one hundred congregations.

EVANGELICAL PRESBYTERIAN CHURCH OF PORTUGAL

Missionary work in the early nineteenth century, originating from Great Britain and Brazil, as well as the evangelistic zeal of returning emigrants led to the foundation of many PROTESTANT Churches in Portugal. The first PRESBYTERIAN Church was built in Lisbon in 1871, financed by Portuguese migrants returning home from America.

The Evangelical Presbyterian Church of Portugal observes a strict Presbyterian polity, affirms the REFORMED tradition based on the scriptures and adheres to the *WESTMINSTER CONFESSION of Faith* (1643–6). Members are involved in the Ecumenical Centre for Reconciliation (founded 1969), which provides opportunities for cooperation with the METHODIST Church and the LUSITANIAN CHURCH of Portugal. The headquarters of the Evangelical Presbyterian Church of Portugal is in Lisbon and has responsibility for 35 congregations throughout the country. The UNITED PRESBYTERIAN CHURCH IN THE USA has helped the Church, especially since the end of the Second World War, by providing educational expertise for the training of clergy at the Protestant Theological Seminary in Lisbon.

EVANGELICAL UNION

The Evangelical Union, formed in Scotland in 1843 by James Morison (1816–93), was an association of independent Churches. Morison was licensed as a minister of the UNITED SECESSION CHURCH and was placed in charge of a congregation in Kilmarnock in 1840, but he was suspended from his duties the following year because he was preaching non-CALVINISTIC views of atonement, specifically that Jesus Christ made atonement for all, and not just for the *elect*, a view that he published in a tract. His suspension, and that of other ministers who joined Morison in his work, led to the creation of the Evangelical Union in Kilmarnock in 1843, where Morison opened a theological college and became its first principal. Morison's preaching attracted such large crowds that he was forced in 1853 to move the Union's headquarters from Kilmarnock into the city of Glasgow, where it was established at the Dundas Street Church. Morison retired in 1884 and is remembered for the publication of New Testament commentaries.

Members of this denomination were often called *Morisonians.* In 1897, a few years after James Morison's death, most of the member churches of the Evangelical Union joined the Congregational Union of Scotland.

❖ Morisonians

EVANGELICAL UNITED BRETHREN CHURCH

This American Church is no longer in existence. It was formed in 1946 through the merger of the UNITED BRETHREN IN CHRIST with the Evangelical Church. Both of these uniting Churches were strongly METHODIST in doctrine and polity and both had originated amongst German speakers in Pennsylvania, Maryland and Virginia after the American Revolution.

The doctrinal position was stated in the *Confession of Faith* (1962) which was a statement compounded from the creedal statements of the two uniting Churches. It confirmed belief in the need of man for salvation because of his sinful state, and that membership of the Church was by means of baptism. The Lord's Supper was the only other ordinance recognized by the Church and was celebrated every three months.

A general conference that met every four years, to which annual and local conferences would report through its lay and ministerial delegates, oversaw the government of the Church. The Church was active in its home missions throughout the USA, and its foreign missions in Africa, the Far East, South America and Europe. In Europe the Church was responsible for maintaining several hospitals, while in the USA it supported theological seminaries and homes for both children and the elderly.

The union, in 1968, between the Evangelical United Brethren Church and the Methodist Church created the UNITED METHODIST CHURCH (USA). At the time of the merger there was no universal approval for this action, and some 75 churches decided against following their fellow church members into the union. They formed, instead, another group known as the EVANGELICAL CHURCH OF NORTH AMERICA.

EXCLUSIVE BRETHREN

The group known as the Exclusive Brethren was formed as a result of a split within the PLYMOUTH BRETHREN movement. Their leader was an Irishman, John Nelson Darby (1800–82), a former ANGLICAN priest, who joined the Plymouth Brethren and became a vigorous founder of Brethren groups, although many disliked his authoritarian manner. He fell into disagreement with another prominent leader within the movement, Benjamin Wills Newton (1807–99) over the question of church order and prophetic interpretation. A division followed, creating the OPEN BRETHREN and the Exclusive Brethren, which became permanent after an event that occurred in 1848.

A former Baptist congregation at Bristol, known as the Bethesda congregation, had joined the Plymouth Brethren *en masse*, and had welcomed some of Newton's followers to a celebration of the Lord's Supper. This raised the issue of the doctrine of separation and resulted in an irrevocable split amongst the Plymouth Brethren, when Darby and his followers, known also as Darbyites, left to form their own group. The doctrine of separation, which is maintained by the Exclusive Brethren, teaches that none should be welcomed to the Lord's Supper unless they are *True Christians*, by which is meant that they must have no association with members of any other Church.

Exclusive Brethren congregations are found throughout the English-speaking world, and in many parts of continental Europe. Foreign missionary work is actively undertaken, principally in Latin America, India and parts of Africa.

EXHORTERS

An eighteenth-century Welsh revivalist group headed by Iefan Tyclai, who, it has been said, rode around the country on a brown horse with untrimmed mane and tail, dressed in corduroy knee breeches, wooden shoes with brass buckles, coarse black silk stockings, a checked jacket and grey coat of homespun cloth. Tyclai held his meetings in dwelling houses and barns, walking around as he preached, and addressing remarks to individual members of his audience about the law of Moses and the gospels.

EXOUCONTIANS

An extreme Arian sect of the fourth century that held to the belief that Jesus Christ was created out of nothing. Because their leader was Aetius (d. c. 367) they are sometimes also known as Aetians. Aetius suffered banishment in 360 for denying that God and the Son are in any way alike, but he was recalled from exile by the Emperor Julian in 362 and was active in the formation of the Anomoeans, a sect which held a doctrine similar to the Arians and which arose at the same time. Arianism is held by the Church to be a heresy.

❖ Aetians; Anomoeans

F

FAITH MOVEMENT OF GERMAN CHRISTIANS

Jacob Wilhelm Hauer started the Faith Movement of German Christians in 1933, as a synthesis of Nazism and Christianity; the movement had the support of many theologians, including Emanuel Hirsch. The members believed that God was calling them to become the Church of the German People, running in parallel to the rising national socialism of Adolf Hitler. Confining its membership to those of Aryan descent, the German Christians condemned communism and Freemasonry and also rejected the Old Testament and any Jewish elements in Christianity, such as the Pauline letters. The Church enjoyed initial support from the Nazi party, but this waned in time.

Its most prominent member was Ludwig Müller who was elected as *Reichsbishof* in 1933. In his attempts to place the Faith Movement of German Christians at the heart of Nazi policy, Müller met considerable opposition, especially from Martin Niemöller and the developing CONFESSING CHURCH.

❖ German-Christian Church; German Christians

FAMILISTS

A communal religious group founded in Emden, Germany, *c.* 1540 by Hendrick Niclaes (or Nicolas, 1501–80), a ROMAN CATHOLIC merchant who claimed to have been chosen as a prophet through a special outpouring of the 'Spirit of the True Love of Jesus Christ'. It is possible that he was influenced by the example of the BRETHREN OF THE FREE SPIRIT, a thirteenth-century mystical sect, and also by the mysticism of David George Jorizoon, an ANABAPTIST from Delft, in the Netherlands, whose followers are sometimes known as Davidists, or Davists. The teachings of the Familists combined elements of German mysticism and Anabaptist doctrines. Niclaes made Emden his headquarters and it was here, in 1540, that he established the Family of Love (*Haus der Liebe*), which attracted many followers including the famous printer and publisher, Christopher Plantin, who was charged in 1562 with associating with the Familists and publishing some of their works. Plantin was forced to flee Antwerp, but he was later able to satisfy the authorities of his innocence and returned to Antwerp in 1563; some two centuries later it was proved that Plantin had, indeed, printed many of Niclaes' works.

From Emden, Niclaes travelled widely throughout Flanders and is reputed to have visited England. In one of his writings, *Evangelium Regni*, which was issued in England as *A Joyful Message of the Kingdom*, he invited all 'lovers of truth of what nation and religion soever they be Christian, Jews, Mahomites or Turks or heathen', to join a great fellowship of peace.

The Familists believed that the divine spirit of love existed within the Family of Love and had a transforming effect, placing them above the constraints of the Bible, the creeds, the need for liturgical worship, and even the law. Because there was no specific form of worship involved, many members, including Niclaes himself, remained in the ROMAN CATHOLIC CHURCH. There were allegations of wife-swapping and adultery inside the group and, according to some critics, the Familists were also guilty of practising the heresy of the PERFECTIONISTS, who believed that it was possible in this life to attain moral and religious perfection through divine grace. This meant that the laws of Moses, and of the state, had no validity for them because these laws no longer bound those who had attained perfection. The communities were organized along hierarchical lines and, if ever questioned, a member was bound to deny his Familist connection in order to protect the good of the community.

Familist influence may have travelled to England by way of foreign merchants coming from Antwerp during the reign of Mary I; it is known that there was Familist activity in and around Guildford, Surrey, from the 1560s as well as in Cambridge, Wisbech and Ely. An itinerant preacher and former joiner, Christopher Vittels, who was a disciple of Hendrick Niclaes, was spreading the message in the 1550s and had translated some of Niclaes' work into English; some of these translations were available in London by the 1570s. Queen Elizabeth I issued *A Proclamation against the Sectaries of the Family of Love* in 1580 and ordered their books to be burned and any Familists found to be imprisoned, with the aim of removing members of the group from East Anglia and London. An obscure sect later (*c.* 1610) appeared at Grindleton, north of Clitheroe in Lancashire, which displayed Familist tendencies. Described as the *Grindleton Familists*, the sect survived until the 1660s. Under Oliver Cromwell (1599–1658), during his time as Lord Protector, some of Niclaes' writings were republished, but the sect does not seem to have survived long in England after the restoration of the monarchy in 1660, when Charles II returned from exile. Many of the sect members are thought to have joined the RELIGIOUS SOCIETY OF FRIENDS (Quakers) and the CONGREGATIONAL CHURCH.

❖ Family of Love

FEBRONIANISM

A late eighteenth-century German-Austrian movement that was designed to try to limit the power of the papacy. The Suffragan Bishop of Trier, Germany, Johann Nikolaus von Hontheim (1701–90), had studied at the University of Louvain and may have been influenced during this time by the gallicanism of the JANSENIST canon lawyer Zeger Bernhard van Espen (1646–1728), to whose writings he had immediate access. Von Hontheim was appointed to the See of Trier at a time when there was hope for a reunion between LUTHERANISM and the

Roman Catholic Church in Germany, and he reasoned that a lessening in papal power might effect such a reconciliation.

Von Hontheim was approached by the three Archbishop-Electors of Mainz, Cologne and Trier, and asked to investigate the position of the papacy. In his book *De Statu Ecclesiae et Legitima Potestate Romani Pontificis* (Concerning the Condition of the Church and the Legitimate Power of the Pope), which he published in 1763 under the pseudonym *Justinus Febronius*, von Hontheim concluded that a general council was superior to the pope who could, therefore, be deposed by such a council; he also concluded that a general council could be summoned without papal permission and that full papal authority was given not just to the pope but to the whole Church. He further argued that the pope held a position of first among equals (*primus inter pares*) with all the other bishops and that the Church acts through general councils composed of all the bishops, who hold their office from God, and not from the pope.

As a result of its content the book was placed on the Index (of proscribed books) in 1764, having been formally condemned by Pope Clement XIII, who requested that the German bishops should outlaw this movement, known as Febronianism, in their dioceses. The response was reluctant and feeble, with only ten bishops and the Elector of Trier complying with the papal request. The Elector of Trier, Clemens Wenzeslaus, successfully prevailed upon von Hontheim to retract the work, which retraction was received in Rome on Christmas Day, 1778, but the Febronianists argued that since the retraction had been secured by means of a threat, it was valueless. In 1769 the book underwent many revisions and was translated into several languages. It received the approval of the other archbishop-electors, who drew up a list of thirty objections to the papal claims, and these they tried to assert at Bad Ems in 1786, but without success. Despite this support for his work when von Hontheim died in 1790 he expressed regret for his doctrine and was restored to full communion with the Roman Catholic Church before his death.

Febronianism paved the way for state supremacy in religious affairs in Germany, but the movement itself soon collapsed because of a lack of real and coordinated support from the German bishops.

FELLOWSHIP OF CHRISTIAN PILGRIMS

The Fellowship of Christian Pilgrims is a small Pentecostal, Jesus People group in the USA that aims to train people to serve Christ in many capacities, as pastors, teachers, evangelists and workers. The doctrine is identical to that held by the Assemblies of God. The headquarters of the Fellowship is in Kailua-Kona, Hawaii.

FELLOWSHIP OF EVANGELICAL BIBLE CHURCHES

Menno Simons (*c.* 1496–1561), a Dutchman and priest in the Roman Catholic Church, had serious doubts about transubstantiation and infant baptism. After some investigation he left the priesthood and in 1536, convinced of the theology taught by the Anabaptists, he became a member, and later a leader, of an Anabaptist community in East Friesland in the Netherlands, where the sect was tolerated. For the rest of his life Menno travelled and preached the Anabaptist doctrine in Germany and the Netherlands, basing his doctrine on scripture alone. He taught about the imminence of the second coming of Christ (REVELATION 20) and urged believers to live in communities and apart from non-believers. Menno's contemporaries gave his name to the MENNONITE movement, which spread into Germany and Switzerland.

In time, however, local rulers in these countries rescinded their earlier toleration of the Mennonites and the followers looked elsewhere for support. Catherine the Great's offer in 1763, which opened up a chance for German Mennonite settlers to occupy parts of southern Russia, was therefore welcome, but with the accession of Tsar Alexander II (1818–81) the settlers were once more made to feel unwelcome; this was expressed in tangible ways, with the speaking of German forbidden and exemption from military service, which had been granted because of their religious views, withdrawn. This situation could only be resolved by leaving Russia, and the Mennonites emigrated to America, where their future security was more certain.

Isaac Peters and Aaron Wall, two of the leaders of groups that travelled to America, settled with their communities in Nebraska and Minnesota at the end of the nineteenth century, where they formed two new congregations and new conferences. These groups joined forces in 1910 and organized their respective groups as the Defenceless Mennonite Brethren in Christ of North America. The movement grew, with fresh immigrants arriving from Russia, and new congregations were formed in other parts of the country as well as in Canada. In 1937 the movement became known as the Evangelical Mennonite Brethren Conference. Noted for its independence, the Church regarded itself as being within the Mennonite tradition but also gained a reputation of non-cooperation with other Mennonite groups.

With further expansion and growth, the name of the denomination was changed, in 1987, to the Fellowship of Evangelical Bible Churches and is now heavily committed to missionary and evangelistic work in South America.

❖ Defenseless Mennonite Brethren of Christ in North America; Evangelical Mennonite Brethren Conference; Fellowship of Evangelical Bible Christians; United Mennonite Brethren of North America

FELLOWSHIP OF EVANGELICAL CHURCHES OF AUSTRALIA

This Fellowship was organized by four evangelical churches in Melbourne, Victoria, in 1956 and now acts purely as an advisory body for 30 congregations, with a total of around 3,000 members.

Doctrinally, the Fellowship is evangelical and Bible-based. While baptism is affirmed, how it is administered, and upon whom, is up to each local congregation. The second coming of Christ is also affirmed, but a premillennial position is not insisted upon (REVELATION 20). The headquarters of the Fellowship is in Fitzroy, Victoria.

FELLOWSHIP OF INDEPENDENT EVANGELICAL CHURCHES OF AUSTRALIA

A small Fellowship that was formed in Western Australia in the 1970s by several Congregational Churches whose members did not want to join the UNITING CHURCH OF AUSTRALIA when it was formed in 1977. The Fellowship is a cooperative group of evangelical and Bible-based churches, for which it acts in an advisory capacity only.

FIFTH MONARCHY MEN

This fanatical, mid-seventeenth century English PURITAN sect took its name from its belief that the time of the fifth monarchy was at hand, according to an interpretation of Daniel 2:44, which suggests that the successive monarchies of Assyria, Persia, Greece and Rome would be followed by a fifth, which would be the time when Christ would return to reign on earth with his saints (REVELATION 20); the members numbered themselves among the saved who would reign with Christ for a thousand years, even calling themselves *saints*. Its size belies its importance, for although never commanding more than a few thousand members, the sect was nearly successful in overturning the laws and institutions of the land. For the most part the members came from the lowly, ill-educated artisan class, those who had least to lose and most to gain from the second coming of Christ, but they had powerful supporters and became influential in the English parliament, securing places on committees which would help them in their plan to overthrow the state and replace it with one acceptable, in their eyes, to the returning Christ.

Members of the sect saw the collapse of the monarchy in England, with the execution of the king, Charles I, in London on 30 January 1649 and the establishment of the commonwealth, as a signal that the time of the rule of Christ and his saints was at hand. When the protectorate was established, with Oliver Cromwell declared as Lord Protector in 1653, the Fifth Monarchy Men turned against him declaring him to be the antichrist, although Cromwell had once been friendly towards them.

A large rally held at Abingdon, in Oxfordshire, was broken up by government troops. Determined on their course, a group of London *saints* under the leadership of Thomas Venner, a cooper, prepared for a national uprising and issued a manifesto which declared that the laws of the state would soon be overthrown and replaced by a biblical rule of law. The group planned to march into East Anglia, attracting recruits as it went, but the meeting was again attacked by government troops and the leaders imprisoned. Three years later a noisy mob, led by Thomas Venner, marched through the streets of London but the authorities were quick to act. Ferocious fighting broke out and nearly 50 people were killed. Venner was arrested and executed, declaring to the end that he was the personification of Christ, which claim only served to discourage his followers. After his death the sect soon died out.

FINLAND, CHURCH OF

Christianity was introduced into Finland, during the last part of the twelfth century and the beginning of the thirteenth, through the efforts of the Swedes and, in particular, of St Henry, Bishop of Uppsala. St Henry was an Englishman who had been consecrated in 1152 by his compatriot, Nicholas Breakspear, who later became Pope Adrian IV but at the time of the consecration was papal legate to Scandinavia. An earlier attempt had been made to bring Christianity to Finland as part of a peace deal. In response to Finnish raids into Sweden, the Swedish king, St Eric IX, mounted a form of crusade against them but also offered peace on condition that the Finns converted to Christianity, an offer that was refused. The Swedes, continuing their fight, were the victors and as a result the two countries became firmly united. St Henry's role was pastoral, baptizing those Finns who wished to convert, but he was killed with an axe by one of these converts who had been excommunicated by the bishop for killing a Swedish soldier. St Henry is now regarded as the founder of Christianity in Finland.

Because of its proximity to Russia, eastern Finland began to feel the presence of Eastern Orthodoxy from the middle of the twelfth century. Åbo (now Turku) was made an episcopal see, a cathedral was built and a Finn, Magnus, was appointed as its first bishop. LUTHERANISM spread into Finland during the sixteenth century when returning Finns, who had studied and travelled in Germany, brought back the faith with them. One such, Mikael Agricola, who had studied at Wittenberg under Martin Luther, became the first Lutheran Bishop of Turku and in 1593 Lutheranism was officially adopted. The PIETISM of eighteenth-century Germany also had an impact on Finland and prompted a deeper commitment to the Lutheran Church. During the twentieth century what was known as the *fifth movement* promoted a Bible-based revivalism and faithfulness to the Lutheran Confession.

The Church of Finland is recognized today as a state Church and it is from the state that it receives financial support. The Church assembly meets every five years and is composed of both clergy and lay members. It is regarded as the highest legislative body. Any decisions taken, however, must be ratified by the Finnish parliament. The president of Finland appoints bishops of the Church, who are chosen from candidates proposed by the eight dioceses. Twice a year an 'Enlarged Bishops' Meeting', or council, is held; this consists of episcopal, clerical and lay members and is chaired by the Archbishop of Finland.

Doctrinally, the Church believes in the authority of the Bible alone, in the Apostles', Nicene and Athanasian creeds, the *Augsburg Confession* and other Lutheran *Confessions*. It affirms that Christ, by his grace, gives salvation to all who believe in him. Only two sacraments are observed, those of baptism and Holy Communion. Worldwide missionary activity is maintained by the very large Finnish Evangelical-Lutheran mission (founded 1859), and Finnchurchaid (FCA), which provides for relief and interchurch aid and development in sixty countries throughout the world.

❖ Evangelical Lutheran Church of Finland

FINNISH ORTHODOX CHURCH

The Orthodox Church in Finland can date its beginnings to the thirteenth and fourteenth centuries when Russian monks came to the south-eastern part of Finland, into the province of Karelia. Russian monasteries were founded in the Ladoga region as a political bulwark against the Swedes of western Karelia. The Orthodox monastery of Valamo (now Valaam) was founded there on an island in Lake Ladoga, reputedly by Sts Sergius and Herman (Germanus), but the date is uncertain; although there is a suggestion that it may have been as early as *c.* 973, it is more likely to have been founded in the first quarter of the fourteenth century. The monastery was founded with the view to converting to Orthodoxy those Karelians who lived along the shore of the lake. During the years 1809–1917, when Finland was a grand duchy of the Russian empire, a separate diocese was established for Orthodox parishes (1892), centred upon Vyborg. Finland's independence from Russia was declared in 1917 and the Church's administrative links with the RUSSIAN ORTHODOX CHURCH were severed soon afterwards by the Russian Patriarch Tikhon and the synod of the Moscow Patriarchate. In 1918, the Finnish government confirmed the Finnish Orthodox Church's status as the second state Church, after the LUTHERAN Church of Finland (FINLAND, CHURCH OF), which has brought with it the advantage of state support for its clergy.

When the request by the Finnish government that the Finnish Orthodox Church be granted autonomy was confirmed by the Ecumenical Patriarch in 1923, the Russian-born Archbishop Seraphim of Finland had to resign and was replaced by his Finnish auxiliary, Germanos, who had been consecrated by the Ecumenical Patriarch Meletios II in Constantinople, in 1923. The terms of the peace treaty after the Second World War meant that a large part of Karelia was lost to the Soviet Union and with it almost all Finnish Church property, but the state helped and supported the Church.

Administratively, the Church is divided into the Archdiocese of Karelia with metropolitans in charge of Helsinki and Oulu and a bishop heading the diocese of Joensuu. There is a general assembly, made up of bishops and representatives of the clergy and laity, whose decisions must be ratified by the synod of bishops and can come into force only if approved by the Finnish parliament. The Church is a member of both the World Council of Churches and the ecumenical council of Finland (founded 1950). Church numbers are currently falling but there has been a recent upsurge in interest in icon painting, with the opening of icon painting clubs that are very popular. In order to monitor the work and maintain the strict standards required for the production of icons, icon councils have been set up by the council of bishops.

FIRE-BAPTIZED HOLINESS CHURCH (WESLEYAN)

The Fire-Baptized Holiness Church (Wesleyan), a small American denomination, was organized in 1904 in southeast Kansas by a group of dissenters from various METHODIST EPISCOPAL CHURCH groups, who supported the HOLINESS tradition and held that sanctification and complete holiness followed upon justification. The original name adopted by the group was the Southeast Kansas Fire-Baptized Holiness Association, but it was changed to its present title in 1945. The Church, which has a current membership of around seven hundred members, has an episcopal polity and is Wesleyan in doctrine.

FIRE-BAPTIZED HOLINESS CHURCH OF GOD OF THE AMERICAS

William Edward Fuller (1875–1958), a young black man, was converted by the preaching of W. T. Burgess and joined the New Hope METHODIST Church in Mountville, South Carolina. A year later, at the age of 18, he was called upon and licensed to preach and this was followed by his experience of the second blessing, which he received in 1895 in a cornfield near his home; two years later he received what he believed to be the baptism of the Holy Ghost and fire.

A little earlier, in Iowa, Benjamin Hardin Irwin also experienced the baptism of fire and, despite a considerable amount of criticism, he attracted many followers. This group was organized in 1885 as the Fire-Baptized Holiness Association, whose first general convention in Anderson, South Carolina, in the summer of 1898, was attended by William Fuller. Fuller was so inspired that upon his return to Mountville he turned in his licence and resigned his membership of the New Hope Methodist Church. Joining the Fire-Baptized Holiness Association he rose, in a short time, to become its first overseer.

The association had quickly attracted a large black membership, many of whom began to feel, with Fuller, that they were being discriminated against and segregated within the group. There was a mass withdrawal of the black members who felt that they must form their own Church. They formed the Colored Fire-Baptized Holiness Church, elected William Fuller as the general overseer and held their first general council in Greer, South Carolina. From 1922–6 the Church was known as the Fire-Baptized Holiness Church of God, but underwent a final name change in 1926 to become the Fire-Baptized Holiness Church of God of the Americas, by which title it is known today.

The Church, whose membership has remained small and still numbers less than a thousand, is administered by an executive council of bishops, district elders and pastors, with a general council held every four years. The doctrinal position is best described as PENTECOSTAL but with a distinct emphasis on the third blessing, or the baptism of fire, which has been described as a 'baptism of burning love', evidenced by *glossolalia*, or speaking in tongues, with divine healing and a belief in the imminence of the premillennial second coming of Christ to earth strongly stressed (REVELATION 20). The Church also teaches that repentance, regeneration, justification and sanctification must precede the third blessing.

❖ Fire-Baptized Holiness Church of God

FIRST CONGREGATIONAL METHODIST CHURCH OF THE USA

This small American denomination believes itself to be the original group of Congregational Methodists that was organized at Forsythe, Georgia, in 1852 and arose through a disagreement with the Georgia conference of the METHODIST EPISCOPAL CHURCH – South, over its episcopal polity, which did not permit any lay input in the Church's administration. The breakaway group, led by its elected chairman, William Fambough, also wanted a reform of the circuit system used by itinerant preachers.

A conference was held in August 1852, after which the new Church prospered until 1933, when two *Articles of Religion* were proposed, concerning regeneration and sanctification; these were added to the original *Twenty-Five Articles of Religion* issued by John Wesley in 1784, together with some paragraphs concerning the collection of funds for retired pastors and work undertaken by women and the young.

After eight years of conflict the great majority of members, led by the Reverend J. A. Cook, president of the 1941 general conference, who supported the addition of these articles and supplements, withdrew, leaving behind a smaller group whose members opposed these additions to the *Twenty-Five Articles*. This smaller group adopted the name of First Congregational Methodist Church of the USA, with the larger group retaining the title of the Congregational Methodist Church.

The First Congregational Methodist Church of the USA has 70 churches and some 4,000 members and is concentrated mainly in the southern states. It is congregational in polity and conservative in its theology, with a literal understanding of the Bible and an acceptance of premillennial beliefs (REVELATION 20).

FIRST MENNONITE CHURCH OF HOPE

The MENNONITES, so-called after their leader, Menno Simons (*c.* 1496–1561), an ex-priest of the ROMAN CATHOLIC CHURCH who was born in the Netherlands, was part of the larger ANABAPTIST movement that was concerned with the rejection of the validity of infant baptism. The Mennonites, in particular, believed in a gathered Church that was separated from the world by believer's baptism and held that this separation would keep them from the influence of worldly corruption. Generally speaking, the Mennonites today hold to an evangelical position within a moderate form of ARMINIANISM, stressing the inspiration, inerrancy and infallibility of the Bible and affirming the *Dordrecht Confession* (1632), as well as laying emphasis on the believer's experience of Christ and the working of the Holy Spirit in his, or her, life.

The First Mennonite Church of Hope was organized in Australia in 1979 by Dutch immigrants, under the leadership of Pastor Foppe, at Marmong Point on the shores of Lake Macquarie, near Newcastle, New South Wales, just north of Sydney. The group numbered some 26 families, many of whom had come to settle in Australia after the Second World War. The present congregation is made up of some 45 baptized members, led by the pastor, who supports himself through secular employment. In order to retain something of their original Dutch culture the Church has organized a weekly Dutch club. Baptism of adults by immersion is observed and the Lord's Supper is celebrated twice annually, preceded by a foot-washing ceremony. The members of this Church are very active in evangelism and in issues concerning the pursuit of peace and the relief of human suffering.

FORWARD IN FAITH

A worldwide association of ANGLICANS who are concerned about, and opposed to, the ordination of women to the priesthood and their consecration as bishops. The member congregations affirm the traditional Anglican faith in scriptures and tradition, as well as the Apostles', Nicene and Athanasian creeds. The traditional sacraments of the Church are observed along with the apostolic ministry of bishops, priests and deacons.

At present there are three main coordinating groups:

1 In the United Kingdom, founded in 1992 and active throughout England, Scotland, Wales and Gibraltar;

2 In the United States, where it was founded in 1999;

3 In Australia, where, in 1999, it was represented as replacing the Association of Apostolic Ministry and the Traditional Anglicans in Queensland.

FRANKISTS

A small sect, founded in Poland by Jacob Frank (1726–91). Born as Jankiev Lebowicz, the son of a Polish rabbi, he was quite uneducated but was strongly influenced by the Turkish *Donmeh* sect, a group of Jews who had followed a false messiah known as Shabbetai Zevi (1626–76); this group later became Muslim.

Frank initially thought of himself as being not only a reincarnation of Shabbetai Zevi but also as the second person of the Trinity. He proclaimed himself to be the Messiah in 1751 and this announcement attracted followers, who were taught strange, but not original, ideas including a belief that they were above the moral law. Frank then led his followers into ROMAN CATHOLICISM following attacks upon the group by Jewish *talmudists* outraged by Frank's heresies. After a mass baptism, at which Augustus III of Poland agreed to act as his godfather, Frank still allowed himself to be worshipped by his followers as the Messiah.

The Inquisition looked askance at these claims and Frank was imprisoned in the fortress at Czestochowa in 1760, released only when Russia partitioned Poland in 1773. Jacob Frank left Poland for Austria, living for a time in Vienna before moving on to Germany, where he settled at Offenbach, south-east of Frankfurt, assuming the style and title of baron with the full support of his loyal, if misguided, followers.

The Frankists were alleged to have indulged in licentious practices, but the movement still managed to spread from Poland to Bohemia and Germany. Upon Frank's death his daughter, Eve, took up his work but the sect began to deteriorate without its leader. Most of the Frankist descendants were assimilated into the rest of the Roman Catholic population and the movement had died out by the middle of the nineteenth century.

FREE CHRISTIAN ZION CHURCH OF CHRIST

The Reverend E. D. Brown, who left the AFRICAN METHODIST EPISCOPAL ZION CHURCH, organized this small American Church in 1905 at Redemption, Arkansas. He was joined by a small group of black METHODIST and BAPTIST ministers, who all wanted to see the Church adopt a more social role in relieving poverty and need. The Church is organized along episcopal lines with the bishop, or chief pastor, overseeing the appointment of ministers, pastors and local church deacons. The Free Christian Zion Church of Christ is very active in evangelism and in poverty-relief programmes.

FREE CHURCH OF ENGLAND

This small, PROTESTANT denomination arose from a dispute between Henry Phillpotts, Bishop of Exeter (1778–1869), a zealous Tory and High Churchman much given to controversy, and a curate in his diocese, James Shore, who was unsympathetic to the Oxford Movement and the developments that were taking place within the CHURCH OF ENGLAND. James Shore was in charge of the church at Bridgetown, in the parish of Berry Pomeroy, near Totnes, in the Diocese of Exeter, which had been built in 1832 on his lands and for the use of his tenants by the Duke of Somerset. It was agreed between the duke and the bishop that the chapel, which came within the Exeter diocese, should be used exclusively for ANGLICAN services and that Shore could officiate there. This situation proceeded smoothly until the bishop fell out with the curate.

James Shore became involved with the election of a new vicar for a local parish and, realizing that he had little chance of gaining the position for himself and also thinking that one of the other candidates was unworthy, he published a handbill which urged the parishioners to vote instead for another candidate. It was not to Shore's advantage that the candidate he spoke against was the preferred choice of the bishop. Episcopal whiskers twitched and it was only a matter of time before the bishop would find reason to make life unpleasant for James Shore. The chance came when Shore's vicar was transferred to another post. Phillpotts immediately elected in his place a man he could trust to do exactly as he wished, and who shared his opinion that Shore was an unsuitable curate for Bridgetown. Shore's licence was withdrawn, ensuring that he could no longer continue as a curate, and the chapel, which had been only temporarily licensed by the bishop, was closed. The Duke of Somerset now came to Shore's aid, urged by his tenants to reopen the chapel that, by virtue of its loss of licence, was no longer required to hold exclusively Anglican services. Shore continued to conduct services in what was now regarded as a *Dissenting* chapel, and the bishop once more decided to act. Shore was arrested and called before the Court of Arches, an ecclesiastical court, to explain his actions. Canon law declared that 'once a minister, always a minister of the Church of England', leaving Shore unable to leave the Church and thus free himself from its conditions. He was unable to preach, neither as an Anglican nor as a Dissenter. Shore appealed successfully to have the court action overturned, but he spent three months in prison until his friends could raise money enough to pay both his fines and the bishop's legal costs.

But the whole business had repercussions. Troubles in other parishes led to the formation of other Free Churches and in 1863 a formal constitution of the Free Church of England was drawn up. There are still 27 churches in this denomination in Great Britain.

FREE CHURCH OF SCOTLAND

In 1842 the general assembly of the Church of Scotland called upon the British parliament to be allowed to govern its own affairs, and when the proposal was rejected it resulted in a mass revolt a year later by some 30 per cent of the ministers and laity who took this extreme decision rather than submit to what they saw as state control of their Church; this was known as *The Disruption* (1843). Thomas Chalmers (1780–1847) led the seceders, who were mostly evangelicals, and was elected as the first moderator of their newly formed group, which the members named the Free Church of Scotland. A programme of building, of colleges and manses, began which was to play an important part in the history of the Church in years to come.

Discussions were held about joining with the United Presbyterian Church (Scotland), which had been founded in 1847. The main difference between the groups was in the matter of funding for their Churches. Whilst the Free Church of Scotland had come into existence because of their rejection of what they saw as state control, its members still expected state support that the United Presbyterians had renounced in favour of *voluntaryism*, the belief that religious bodies should accept only voluntary contributions for their upkeep. Most of the members of the Free Church entered into the union in 1900 to form the United Free Church of Scotland, but a minority, known as the Wee Frees, who remained outside the union, put in a claim for payment for the real estate that had now become the property of the new body. Unable to get satisfaction in the Scottish courts, which did not decide in their favour, the members of the Free Church appealed to the House of Lords. A parliamentary commission examined the claim and it was resolved in their favour, with real estate divided between the two Churches in proportion to their numbers.

Doctrinally, the Free Church is very conservative, the members being strict CALVINISTS who stress election to salvation. The very strict observance of the sabbath is notable and has a profound effect on local communities, but it does not always go unchallenged. The influence of the Wee Frees in the Scottish islands is very powerful and persuasive, however, and change will be slow.

The services of the Free Church are distinctive in their total lack of instrumental music and their characteristic singing of the metrical psalms. The ordinances of baptism and the Lord's Supper are observed. The Church has about 230 congregations, with around 20,000 members, scattered throughout Scotland, with a further congregation in London and more in North America; it is affiliated with sister Churches founded as a result of mission work in India, Peru and South Africa. The Church is a member of the International Conference of REFORMED Churches and is involved in local projects for the homeless and for addicts.

Aka: Wee Frees

FREE EVANGELICAL LUTHERAN SYNOD IN SOUTH AFRICA

This small South African LUTHERAN Church is in decline. It began as a schism from the Hermannsburg synod by German-speaking farmers. The present 500 adult members are to be found in 10 congregations, all observing the Lutheran traditions and Confessions.

FREE METHODIST CHURCH OF JAPAN

When anti-Christian restrictions in Japan were removed, in 1878, it became possible for METHODIST missions to be created. This Church was founded in 1895 as part of the missionary work of the FREE METHODIST CHURCH OF NORTH AMERICA. Although now in slow decline, a strict adherence to the primitive Wesleyan tradition is maintained by its 2,000 adult members, distributed between 31 congregations. The headquarters of the Free Methodist Church of Japan is in Osaka.

FREE METHODIST CHURCH OF NORTH AMERICA

During the last half of the nineteenth century in America, METHODISM came into its own with increased respectability, while the growing affluence enjoyed by its members led to a more comfortable way of life, so much so that discipline began to be relaxed and the strong emphasis on HOLINESS preaching began to decline. It was in this climate that the *Nazarites*, as they were known, who were supporters of the Free Methodist Church, emerged under the leadership of a METHODIST EPISCOPAL CHURCH minister, Benjamin Titus Roberts. Roberts started to publish a small periodical called *The Northern Independent* in 1856, in which he wrote articles criticizing the Genesee conference of the Methodist Church, held in western New York State, for its adoption of modernist theology, the acceptance of the selling of pews and the building of expensive churches, as well as its growing approval of worldly contact.

Because of his criticisms, which were not well received, Roberts was initially sent to a small, rural church at Pekin, New York, and in 1858 he was expelled from the Methodist Episcopal Church. Two years later he had organized the Free Methodist Church at Pekin. By 1860 a group with similar grievances and concerns was beginning to be formed at St Charles, in northern Illinois, led by John Wesley Redfield. This group, which also chose to call itself the Free Methodist Church, merged with the Pekin group to form the Free Methodist Church of North America. The use of the word 'Free' in the title was to emphasize freedom from slavery, fashionable clothes, rented pews, membership of secret societies and worldliness in general, which were all seen as limiting.

Two schisms from the Free Methodist Church of North America occurred, the first in 1955, which resulted in the emergence of the United Holiness Church, and again in 1962, when two groups left the parent Church, one to form the Evangelical Wesleyan Church of North America and the other to organize the Midwest Holiness Association. These schisms were prompted, once more, by a wish to return to a more austere lifestyle, and away from a growing emphasis on worldliness.

Doctrinally, the Church follows a strict primitive Wesleyanism, with an emphasis on confession, forgiveness of sins and entire sanctification, which are necessary before membership can be granted. The *Twenty-Five Articles of Religion* are strictly adhered to, with an additional article on *Entire Sanctification*. The Church maintains an extensive mission programme throughout Africa, the Near and Far East and Central America.

❖ Nazarites

FREE PRESBYTERIAN CHURCH OF SCOTLAND

This small Church was founded in Scotland in 1893 by a small group of members of the FREE CHURCH OF SCOTLAND, also known as the Wee Frees, who took exception to a Declaratory Act of 1892 that, in a way, led to a more liberal doctrinal attitude towards the *WESTMINSTER CONFESSION of Faith*, as well as a softening of rigorous CALVINISM. The members wanted to preserve the principles of the Reformation, in doctrine and worship, and they therefore felt obliged to form their own separate denomination.

The Church, in its two Sunday meetings, puts considerable emphasis on the sermon, which can be as short as thirty minutes or as long as an hour; a similarly lengthy sermon may also be preached at the mid-week prayer meeting.

Even though the Free Church of Scotland repealed the Declaratory Act in 1900, this had no effect on the attitude of the Free Presbyterian Church of Scotland. There are currently 60 congregations, distributed amongst four groups, known as the Northern, Western, Southern and Outer Islands Presbyteries. The Church maintains a missionary programme in Zimbabwe.

FREE PRESBYTERIAN CHURCH OF SOUTH AUSTRALIA

This Church is related to the FREE PRESBYTERIAN CHURCH OF ULSTER and is under the aegis of that Church but not financially dependent upon it. The Church looks to the Free Presbyterian Church of Ulster for doctrinal guidance and in this matter is identical to it.

Founded in 1969 as an informal group known as the Eyre Bible Fellowship and with just eleven members, a decision was made in 1977 that it should become formally organized as the Free Presbyterian Church of South Australia. The Reverend Fred Buick, of the Ulster group, became the first pastor, and a place of worship was opened at Port Lincoln, South Australia. Another group was started in Perth, Western Australia in 1984 and the two congregations are developing and increasing their numbers. The Port Lincoln congregation has now risen to over forty members, while the Perth group numbers about thirty members.

FREE PRESBYTERIAN CHURCH OF ULSTER

This FUNDAMENTALIST Church began in 1951, when some elders of the local Presbyterian church in Crossgar, Northern Ireland, asked the church for permission to use the church hall for a gospel mission and invited the Reverend Ian Paisley, who was leader of an independent congregation in the province, to attend. Permission, however, was refused. The elders, encouraged by Paisley and a recently returned missionary from Brazil, the Reverend George Stears, seceded from the Presbyterian Church, to be later joined by members of Ian Paisley's independent congregation, and others, and together they formed the Free Presbyterian Church of Ulster.

The polity and doctrine is Presbyterian and fundamentalist, its members implacably opposed to any ecumenical dealings with the ROMAN CATHOLIC CHURCH. In their doctrine the Bible enjoys a central authority as the word of God and is regarded as verbally inspired. There is a strong emphasis on preaching and prayer as well as the two ordinances of baptism and the Lord's Supper. The mode and age at which baptism is given depends upon the individual and there is no belief in baptismal regeneration. The Lord's Supper is open to any Christian who is in good faith with his own Christian community, and is celebrated monthly, or more frequently, as the local congregation wishes. It is clear that any notion of transubstantiation or consubstantiation is forcefully rejected.

The singing of psalms and the absence of modern hymn singing is apparent in the services of these congregations. The Church subscribes to the doctrine found in the *Small*, and the *Larger Catechisms*, as well as in the *WESTMINSTER CONFESSION of Faith*. This Church currently has around sixty congregations, maintaining a presence in Ireland, Scotland, England, Germany, Australia, Canada and the USA. Missionary work is maintained in Spain, India, Africa and the West Indies.

FREE WESLEYAN CHURCH OF TONGA

Missionaries from the London Missionary Society conducted the first, unsuccessful, attempts at missionary work in the Tongan islands in 1797 and a further attempt was made in 1822, by Wesleyan missionaries; these were followed, successfully, by a well-organized mission in 1825, conducted by the Wesleyan Methodist Mission.

A few years later a movement called the *Tongan Pentecost* took place, effecting some important and influential conversions to Christianity, notably that of Taufa'ahau, a rising political star in the islands who later, as King George Tupou I (ruled 1875–93) worked to keep Tonga out of the rising struggles between the colonial powers. It was as *Tui Tonga* (King of Tonga) that he declared, in 1880, that Tonga should have an independent Church. By 1885 this was established as the Wesleyan Free Church and not as the Free Wesleyan Church, which represented the original mission body.

In 1924 the ruler, Queen Salote Tupou III who reigned for 47 years until her death in 1965, attempted to reunite the two groups of Methodists. This may have been prompted by the fact that she had married a Wesleyan High Chief, William Tupou Tungi. Some of the Free Wesleyan groups refused to unite and formed the, now declining, Free Church of Tonga, led by Jabez Watkin. This Church subsequently endured two further schisms, to form the Church of Tonga (founded 1929) and the Church of the Red Coats (founded 1962), which was also known as the Church of God and the People of Tonga.

Of the 150 islands that make up Tonga, 40 are inhabited and 40 per cent of the population belongs to the Free Wesleyan Church of Tonga, whose head is constitutionally the ruler of the islands.

The Church is totally committed to Methodist concerns, notably missionary work, education and social issues. In the field of education, the Church manages many primary and secondary schools as well as an agricultural college and a seminary. The Sabbath is strictly observed throughout Tonga and is officially declared to be *sacred* in Article 6 of the constitution. The Free Wesleyan Church of Tonga is a full member of the World Council of Churches.

❖ Aka: Methodist Church in Tonga

FRIENDS OF GOD

The Friends of God was composed of German mystics and other Christians, mainly from the educated middle class, who came together in the fourteenth century as a lay group. The members supported and strengthened each other in their search for holiness, love and devotion by means of letters, writings and visits, and were given to asceticism and self-renunciation The possible origin of this group may have been in Basle in the mid-fourteenth century, from where the movement extended along the river Rhine and into the Netherlands. The purpose of the members, apart from the pursuit of personal holiness, was to counteract the evil influences in the world and to pray for the conversion of sinners.

Prominent among their leaders were John Tauler (*c.* 1300–61) and Blessed Henry Suso (1300–65). Unfortunately, the good effects were undone by one of the members, Rulman Merswin, a merchant of Strasbourg, who claimed to be led by a mysterious guide and mentor of the spiritual life whom he identified as *The Great Friend of God*, to whom Merswin attributed revelations, prophecies and warnings of tribulations to come, as well as receiving from him a divine mission to purify the Church. This alerted the attention of the authorities. A leader of the group, Nicolas of Basle, was condemned as a heretic and burnt at the stake in Vienna in 1409; other leaders suffered the same fate, almost certainly because of their action in attacking the corruption that they saw in the western

Church. The movement died out, but in many ways was a harbinger of the Reformation.

FRIENDS OF MAN

Charles Taze Russell (1852–1916), an American haberdasher from Allegheny, Pennsylvania, was the founder of the International Bible Students' Association that later became known, from 1931, as the JEHOVAH'S WITNESSES. Russell died in 1916, in a Santa Fe Pullman carriage, allegedly dressed in a Roman toga at the time. He was succeeded by Joseph F. Rutherford, a small-town Missouri lawyer. A former member of the association, the Swiss-born F. L. Alexander Freytag (1870–1947), joined Russell and was to run the Swiss end of the organization in what was known as the *Watchtower Movement*, but he became very critical of Russell's teachings. In 1916 he left the organization and, together with a good number of Bible students, formed the *Angel of the Lord Philanthropic Association*, which was also known as the Philanthropic Association of the Friends of Man.

In 1920, after the death of Russell, Freytag distributed *The Message of Laodicea*, a work based on Revelation 3:14–20, which was intended as a critique of the Watchtower Movement that Rutherford now headed. In this publication, Freytag concentrated on the subject of death which, he stated, could be overcome by following Christ's example of sacrificial love. He argued that by following Christ's example the Church, by which he meant his own foundation which was also known as the Church of the Kingdom of God, 'makes the sacrifice which assures to the whole of mankind the imminent great awakening from the grave', that was to occur at the second coming of Christ to earth (REVELATION 20).

Branches of the Friends of Man, by which name the group was eventually known, were founded in Switzerland as the *Amis de l'Homme* in 1919 and there are now some 60 Swiss congregations, with around 30,000 adult members; a foundation was made in France in 1934 and this now has 50 congregations with around 4,000 members. After Freytag's death in 1947 there was a schism within the group, led by an ex-ROMAN CATHOLIC layman, J. B. Sayerce (1912–63), and, confusingly, some of these schismatics set up new congregations in Switzerland, Germany and France also named *Friends of Man*.

❖ Amis de l'Homme; Angel of the Lord Philanthropic Association; The Army of the Eternal; The Church of the Kingdom of God; The Philanthropic Association of the Friends of Man

FULL GOSPEL CHURCH ASSOCIATION

One of several American Full Gospel networks, the Full Gospel Church Association was organized in 1952 by the Reverend Dennis W. Thorn, at Amarillo, Texas. The purpose of the group was to provide a means of coordinating various small, independent PENTECOSTAL churches and missions in the southern and south-western parts of the USA.

Doctrinally, they are very similar to the CHURCH OF GOD (CLEVELAND, TENNESSEE), with an emphasis on healing and tithing and a belief in a literal heaven and hell. The member churches and individual members of the Association are expected to be unswervingly loyal. The polity is congregational, with a general assembly that meets regularly to provide an administrative framework for the association, which has about 80 constituent congregations with around 2,000 adult members. The association also supports mission work in Mexico, the Philippines and Africa.

FULL GOSPEL CHURCH OF GOD IN SOUTHERN AFRICA

The Church, which was founded in South Africa in 1910, is now affiliated with the CHURCH OF GOD (CLEVELAND, TENNESSEE) and like that Church also accepts the full HOLINESS and PENTECOSTAL experience of conversion, sanctification and baptism of the Holy Spirit with *glossolalia*, or speaking in tongues. It has undertaken considerable mission work amongst the Indian population and in the late 1970s enjoyed a noticeable growth in numbers, but this has now slowed down. There was a schism in the Church in 1990, when a seceding group of white church members left to establish their own group, known as the Full Gospel Church of God.

FULL GOSPEL FELLOWSHIP OF CHURCHES AND MINISTRIES

An American Fellowship formed in 1962 by the Reverend Gordon Lindsay and other ministers from various denominations to provide a means of encouraging and promoting the apostolic ministry.

Today, the Fellowship has become identified with a deliverance ministry, mostly among white congregations of which there are currently about 650 in the USA with 195,000 adult members across the country; there are a similar number of member churches in other countries worldwide, with around double the number of members. The deliverance ministry is concerned with the casting out of evil spirits and is seen as allied to divine healing.

Doctrinally, the members subscribe to the inerrancy and divine inspiration of the Bible, a belief in the one, true God and in the conviction that man's salvation and justification is given by grace through faith. The Fellowship holds that baptism and the Lord's Supper are ordinances, together with baptism of the Holy Ghost as evidenced by *glossolalia*, or speaking in tongues. The second coming of Jesus Christ and his millennial reign on earth is emphasized (REVELATION 20). The headquarters of the Fellowship is in Irving, Texas.

FUNDAMENTAL BRETHREN CHURCH

This very small American Church was a breakaway in 1962 from the CHURCH OF THE BRETHREN in North Carolina, USA. The cause of the secession was the parent Church's recognition of the National Council of Churches and its use in its services of the *Revised Standard Version of the Bible*. The members of the Fundamental Brethren Church wanted to dissociate themselves from the National Council of Churches and they insist that the *King James Version of the Bible* is the only authorized text to be used.

FUNDAMENTAL METHODIST CHURCH

Originally known as the Independent Fundamental Methodist Church, this American group was first organized in 1942 at St John's Chapel Church, Ash Grove, Missouri, by some members of the METHODIST PROTESTANT CHURCH. In 1939 a merger that resulted in the formation of the METHODIST CHURCH had left them uneasy about what they saw as the gradual erosion of Wesleyan principles and practices. The group that met at Ash Grove, led by the Reverend Roy Keith, were from the most conservative wing of the Methodist Protestant Church.

The polity of the Fundamental Methodist Church is congregational, with each congregation electing its own pastor. Administration is conducted through a general conference to which a lay delegate and a minister from each congregation are sent. This Church has no bishops, their administrative role taken by district superintendents. There are currently 12 congregations with around 650 adult members. A very limited amount of missionary work has taken members into Mexico.

FUNDAMENTALISM (also FUNDAMENTALIST)

A Christian fundamentalist is usually understood to be one who is an evangelical in the PROTESTANT tradition. A growing feeling of liberalism, or modernism, began in the late eighteenth century when evolution, biblical criticism and the study of comparative religions were represented as challenging the authority of the Bible. In response to this perceived threat, a Bible Conference was convened at Niagara Falls, on the Canadian–American border, in 1895, that established the usual five basic doctrines of fundamentalism: the inerrant verbal inspiration of the Bible, the Virgin Birth, the divinity of Jesus Christ, substitutionary atonement and Christ's resurrection. To this list are usually added the miracles of Christ and the premillennial second coming (REVELATION 20).

Lyman Stewart, an oilman from southern California, was deeply concerned about the inroads of liberalism. Inspired by the preaching of a BAPTIST pastor and evangelist, Aamzi Clarence Dixon (1854–1925), he decided to enlist the financial help of his brother, Milton Stewart, in order to publish a twelve–volume set of paperbound books of tracts, under the title of *The Fundamentals*. These tracts were the product of a committee that included the well-known evangelist and writer, Reuben Archer Torrey (1856–1928). The books dealt with the basic doctrines of fundamentalism and were distributed between 1910 and 1915, free of charge, to all theology students and Christian workers so that they might target the English-speaking world with their contents. This had the effect of polarizing the English-speaking Christian world into fundamentalists and modernists.

By 1918, the term 'fundamentalists' had become commonly used of those who were concerned only about the preservation of the central affirmations of the Christian faith. There were attempts in the mid-twentieth century to move aside the label 'fundamentalism' in favour of 'new evangelicalism', which called for a conservative Christianity that did not offend intellectual vigour and investigation.

G

GENERAL ASSOCIATION OF GENERAL BAPTISTS

Many of the first Baptists in both England and America were Arminians, believing that salvation was possible for everyone and not, as the Calvinists believed, for an *elect* who alone were predestined to receive salvation from the beginning of time.

Roger Williams, an Englishman who sought religious freedom in America, set up the first General Baptist Church at Providence, Rhode Island, in 1639 from which other churches were planted, but by the late eighteenth century a rising tide of Calvinism spread across the country and the two denominations came into conflict. This came to a head in the 1820s when Benoni Stinson, a preacher holding Arminian views, organized the New Hope Church near Evansville, Indiana, for those who shared his beliefs. This action brought him up against local Calvinist Baptists. The Arminian view was very popular, and by 1824 the members of those churches who subscribed to Stinson's opinion formed the Liberty Association of General Baptists, which soon spread in the south and west.

The General Baptists hold to a Methodist type of theology, believing the Bible to be the inspired and infallible word of God; they also believe in the fall of man and his need for salvation, regeneration, sanctification, justification and redemption through Jesus Christ, which is open to all. They observe the ordinances of baptism by immersion and the Lord's Supper, which is available for all Christians; some General Baptists also practise foot-washing. A belief in the second coming of Christ is affirmed, with bodily resurrection of the dead and with a heavenly reward for the righteous and hell for the wicked (Revelation 20).

The polity of the Church is congregational, but the ministers of an area are grouped into local bodies that examine the candidates for the ministry and diaconate. There is an active home missions programme that includes work in child-care through an adoption agency, and the running of nursing homes. Foreign missions are supported in Jamaica, Honduras, India, the Philippines and the Marianas Islands.

GENERAL ASSOCIATION OF REGULAR BAPTIST CHURCHES

Movements towards the formation of this Association of American Baptist Churches were begun in May 1922, when the Northern Baptist Convention (founded 1907) failed to adopt the *New Hampshire Confession of Faith* (1833, revised 1853) because it was seen as less CALVINISTIC than the earlier British Confessions. The protest of some 22 BAPTIST churches, led by Thomas Todhunter Shields of Toronto, was a dissent against the growth of modernist tendencies within the Baptist movement, the denial of the independence and autonomy of many local Baptist congregations and the control of missionary work by the assessment of the Convention. The withdrawal of these Baptist churches led to the formation of the Baptist Bible Union, which took the name of the General Association of Regular Baptist Churches in 1932.

The eighteen articles of the *New Hampshire Confession of Faith* were used as a template for the General Association's *Articles of Faith*, which placed a strong emphasis upon the Bible's infallibility and the premillennial return of Christ to earth (REVELATION 20). The *Articles* also affirm a belief in the Trinity, in Satan as the author of all evil and in man's creation and fall. Salvation is seen as a state of eternal happiness for the good, with an eternity of punishment for the wicked. According to Article 16 of the *New Hampshire Confession of Faith*, the civil government of the country is of divine appointment and members also have a duty to see that 'magistrates are to be prayed for, honoured and obeyed'.

The Church observes two ordinances, those of believer's baptism and the Lord's Supper. It is a requirement for membership of the Association that local churches do not participate in any cooperative activity that includes modernists; for this reason the word Regular was used in the official title. The polity of the Church is congregational, with annual meetings at a convention where the work of the various mission programmes and the social ministries are monitored. The Association also maintains several children's homes, a home for the elderly and a residential school for the mentally retarded. The Church, which is based in Chicago, Illinois, is composed of 1,582 congregations with a total membership of nearly 216,500 adult believers.

❖ Baptist Bible Union

GENERAL CHURCH OF THE NEW JERUSALEM

This Church does not hold a conventional Trinitarian view of theology.

The General Church of the New Jerusalem is one of several bodies based upon the teachings of Emanuel Swedenborg (1688–1772), a Swedish scientist, theologian and mystic who was ennobled in 1719 by Queen Ulrika Eleanora of Sweden. At the age of 55, Swedenborg claimed that he was able to live in two worlds, the material and the spiritual, and he began to describe the spirit world in detail, writing in Latin and producing 29 volumes; he also produced his own version of the Gospels. During his visits to the spirit world, Swedenborg asserted that he had met and conversed with St Paul, Martin Luther, various infidels, popes and angels and learned from them that a new Christian Church would be formed, with his writings providing the basis of its teaching. Swedenborg's writings show a great range of thought. His interpretation of the Bible stated that the traditional doctrine of the Trinity was incorrect. In his opinion the Trinity was revealed in the person of Jesus Christ alone, 'Father' was a term that described Jesus' soul, while 'Son' described his physical body and 'Holy Spirit', his activity; Jesus Christ being regarded as the one divine being, all prayers are addressed to the Lord Jesus Christ.

Swedenborg rarely attended the state (LUTHERAN) Church, claiming that when he did so the spirits kept interrupting the sermons and contradicting the minister, but despite his beliefs Swedenborg, who died in London, was buried as a Lutheran. He had not set out to found a Church and it was only after his death that the Swedenborgian movement was started, in Manchester, England, in 1782 by two ANGLICAN clergymen, Thomas Hartley and John Clowes, and Robert Hindmarsh, a printer. A formal organization of the Church was made in London in 1787 by 5 Wesleyan preachers. This became the centre for the Church of the New Jerusalem, which in 1815 became known as the General Conference of the New Jerusalem. A schism in 1897 gave rise to the General Church of the New Jerusalem and in 1937 there was a further disagreement within the Church that led to the formation of the LORD'S NEW CHURCH.

The members of the Church accept the full divine authority of Swedenborg's writings as being from the Lord alone. Because of this unorthodox view, schools were opened for the use of members, where their children could be brought up in the faith. Infant baptism is observed and church services include hymns, psalms, prayers and readings from the Bible and from Swedenborg's writings; Holy Communion is observed about once a month. Swedenborgians believe that salvation is open for all, and that immediate judgement follows death.

The first Swedenborgian Society in America was founded in Baltimore, Maryland, in 1792 and became known as the GENERAL CONVENTION OF THE NEW JERUSALEM IN THE USA in 1817.

❖ New Church; Swedenborgians

GENERAL CONFERENCE MENNONITE CHURCH

This is one of three major conferences of the MENNONITES in North America; the other two are the Mennonite Church, which represents those who went to the USA before the Civil War of the 1860s, and the Mennonite Brethren, which started as a revivalist movement from Russia in 1860.

The Church began when a young and progressive Mennonite preacher, John H. Oberholtzer, who worked in the Franconia district of Pennsylvania, queried the custom of most ministers of the day of wearing a plain and collarless jacket, and urged for a written constitution that would ensure that meetings of the Mennonite Conference in his district could be more efficiently and systematically conducted. When he received no satisfactory reply, John Oberholtzer removed himself from the Franconia district Conference, declaring that he sought a more liberal attitude that would allow open communion, sharing with Christians from other denominations, permission for Mennonites to marry non-Mennonites, a salaried ministry and a union of all Mennonite Conferences. He was not alone in his thinking. At a meeting in Wayland, Ohio, in 1860, which was attended by other ministers and congregation members, Oberholtzer was elected as chairman and the work began to organize the General Conference Mennonite Church.

Doctrinally, the members adhere to most Mennonite doctrines, but reinterpret John 13:14–15, which they do not see as a mandate to have foot-washing observed as an ordinance, and disregard the injunction of 1 Corinthians 11:4–15 obliging women to cover their heads in church. The Conference promotes a congregational polity and insists on freedom from traditional Mennonite regulations regarding the clothing to be worn by its members.

The General Conference Mennonite Church has around 227 congregations with over 33,000 adult members and supports a vigorous home mission programme devoted to charity work among children and the aged, and with an active foreign mission enterprise that undertakes work in Mexico, South America, Africa, India and Taiwan.

GENERAL CONVENTION OF THE NEW JERUSALEM IN THE USA

This Church does not hold a conventional Trinitarian view of theology.

The General Convention of the New Jerusalem in the USA was the first SWEDENBORGIAN group of believers in America, although the movement began in 1782 in Manchester, England, after the death of Emanuel Swedenborg in 1772. The Swedenborgian movement crossed the Atlantic and the first Swedenborgian Society was founded in Baltimore, Maryland, in 1792. By 1817 this had become established as the General Convention of the New Jerusalem. The members of this Convention follow Swedenborg's doctrine and teachings, believing that salvation is open to all and that on death a person passes from immediate judgement to either heaven or hell depending on the spiritual character they have acquired on earth. Baptism and the Lord's Supper are observed and, in general, the form of worship used by this group is more liturgical than that used by other Swedenborgian groups. A form of liturgy was published by the Convention in 1822 and provision was made for the use of chants in the services of worship, which usually consist of hymns, psalms and readings from the Bible and from Swedenborg's writings. A number of members of the Convention separated from the parent body in 1890 and by 1897 they had formed the GENERAL CHURCH OF THE NEW JERUSALEM.

The General Convention currently has an American and Canadian membership of over 2,500 members and it supports foreign missions in Japan, Korea and South America.

❖ Swedenborgians; The Convention

GENERAL SIX-PRINCIPLE BAPTISTS

This very small American denomination arose after Roger Williams had founded the General Baptist Church at Providence, Rhode Island, in 1639. A split occurred within the congregation in 1652 over the maintenance of the *Six Principles* that the Providence congregation had always upheld but which were beginning to be less scrupulously observed; these *Six Principles* were laid down in Hebrews 6:1–2 and were named as repentance, faith, baptism, the laying on of hands, the resurrection of the dead and a final judgement. The principle that was beginning to be neglected was that of the laying on of hands, a sign of the reception of the gift of the Holy Spirit that signalled that a person had become a member of the Church.

Those Baptists who wanted to retain all *Six Principles* formed separate congregations and maintained a congregational polity, with administration in the hands of a Conference to which delegates from the various churches would be sent.

GEORGIAN ORTHODOX CHURCH

The Georgian Orthodox Church is one of the national Churches of the Eastern Orthodox communion.

Georgia lies between Russia and Armenia, south of the Caucasus. The name is said to have derived from St George, whose alleged female relative, St Nino, arrived in Kartli, in central Georgia, from Cappadocia in the fourth century. She is said, by Rufinus, to have cured Queen Nana of an illness and converted her to Christianity, attracting many followers. The king, who was probably Mirian, was also converted and he declared Christianity to be the state religion. St Nino then took herself to a hermitage that she had erected on a mountainside at Bodbe, in Kakheti, where she eventually died and was buried. Constantine the Great, in 326, sent a bishop, John, two priests and three deacons to Georgia to organize Christianity in central Georgia.

The eastern Roman Emperor Zeno (474–91) granted the right to be autocephalous to the Georgian Church during the reign of Vakhtang Gorgaslan; until then it had been within the ecclesiastical sphere of Antioch. The head of the Church was thereafter known as the Catholicos. The independence of the Georgian Autocephalous Church was maintained until the nineteenth century, when, in 1801, the Russian Tsar Alexander I annexed the country, and in 1811 the Catholicos was forced to resign by the Russian Holy Synod. An exarch was appointed, this appointment going always to a Russian from 1817 until 1917, and Church Slavonic, the language used in the Divine Liturgy by the RUSSIAN ORTHODOX CHURCH, replaced the familiar Georgian.

During the Russian Revolution of 1917 the Georgian Church re-established its autocephalous status and Kirion Sadzaglishvili was elected Catholicos, despite Russian protests; he died two years later. Georgia fared badly under Soviet rule during the 1920s and the Church was severely persecuted; it enjoyed more favourable treatment under Stalin, a Georgian, who had at one time been a seminarian in that country.

The Russian Orthodox Church recognized the autocephaly of the Georgian Church in 1943. Attendance, which had fallen, began to revive and in 1977, with the appointment of the Catholicos-Patriarch Ilia II, new bishops filled the vacant dioceses and a seminary, located at the historical seat of the Catholicos at Mtskheta, was reorganized. Georgia's sovereignty was declared in 1989 and independence granted in 1991; a new era of freedom followed. The Catholicos-Patriarch encouraged a revival of devotion by writing a prayer book and urging the faithful to pray during the day and to set aside part of Saturday in order to engage in charitable works.

The Church is divided into fifteen dioceses, each diocese into circuits, and the circuits into parishes; the dioceses are presided over by a diocesan bishop. The Council of the Georgian Orthodox Church is the highest legislative body and is under the control of the Catholicos-Patriarch of All Georgia; it is this council that elects the Catholicos-Patriarch and is also responsible for administering the internal and external affairs of the Church.

GERMAN APOSTOLIC CHRISTIAN CHURCH

This very small American denomination was formed as a result of a schism in the 1930s within the Apostolic Christian Church of America. The schism, led by Elder Martin Steidinger, concerned the use of the German language in worship services.

Steidinger and his followers believed that the use of German helped maintain a spirit of piety and provided a barrier that created a sense of *separateness* from the rest of the world around them. Its abandonment, in favour of English, was seen as a concession to a growing liberalism in the parent Church and a move towards that worldliness which they sought to avoid.

Members of the German Apostolic Christian Church seek entire sanctification, aided by a simple form of living and behaviour. The first German-speaking congregations were organized in parts of Kansas, Oregon and Illinois, but membership has now seriously declined.

GLASITES

Taking its name from its founder, this small sect was founded in Scotland during the seventeenth century by John Glas (1695–1773), an ordained minister of the Church of Scotland, who had the care of the parish of Tealing, near Dundee. While he was lecturing about the *Small Catechism*, and in particular about Christ as king (question 26 in the *Small Catechism*), Glas came to believe that since Christ is the king of the Church then no civil authority can have any power over it. He published these views in a tract, *The Testimony of the King of Martyrs* (1727), which eventually led to his deposition in 1730.

Unabashed, Glas took to open-air preaching, moving from Dundee to Perth. It was then that he met his future son-in-law, Robert Sandeman (1718–71), who later came to the notice of the public when he attacked James Harvey and his work *Theron and Aspasio* (1755), a Calvinistic piece of writing. Sandeman taught that faith is a simple assent to divine testimony. Together, Glas and Sandeman organized a series of congregations of followers, who were known either as Glasites or Sandemanians, and the movement spread into England, through Yorkshire and on to London where a church was founded at Glover's Hall in the Barbican in 1760; Michael Faraday, the scientist, is known to have worshipped there and to have been an elder of the church. Sandeman left for America in 1764, to found churches on the other side of the Atlantic, and he died there in 1771; his work continued in America until about 1860.

Members of the Church were notable in their rejection of all creeds and catechisms, and their affirmation that the Bible was their only guide. Foot-washing and the holy kiss were regarded as mandatory, and the love-feast, or *agape*, was celebrated with the taking of broth together on Sundays between the morning and afternoon services. There was a celebration of the Lord's Supper each week, preceded by a collection of money for the relief of the poor and the support of the Church in its work. The Church insisted on certain rules for its members to follow and those found to be offending in various ways could be excommunicated. They were forbidden to eat blood, to store wealth or to support lotteries, to engage in card playing or other gambling games; the Church regarded the casting of lots as a sacred process and not to be used by its members for worldly entertainment.

The polity of the Church was congregational, with each congregation having several elders and pastors. Fasting and prayer, a laying-on of hands and an extending of 'the right hand of fellowship' preceded ordination. The elders alone were authorized to preach but this did not prevent non-ordained members of the congregation from offering prayers. The Church did not survive in Great Britain beyond 1900.

❖ Glassites; Sandemanians

GNOSTICS (also GNOSTIC; GNOSTICISM)

A variety of religious movements that declared that salvation is not achieved by faith alone but by knowledge (*gnosis*) that is not revealed to everybody but only to a few *spirituals* (or pneumatics). These movements were influenced by pre-Christian thought and contact with Judaism and the religions of Egypt and India. Several individuals and schools from the first three centuries have been labelled as being gnostic because they shared ideas, the most basic of which is that everything in the material world is evil, and that its creator, the *Demiurge*, or *creator-god*, is set antagonistically against the remote and unknowable Divine Being, from whom it was derived.

The *spirituals* possess a spark of divinity but, according to most gnostic beliefs, they are unaware of this; it was the role of Jesus Christ, as an *aeon*, or intermediary of God, who brought with him the *gnosis*, to teach humankind how to free itself from the power and control of the *Demiurge* and return to his spiritual home after death. Allied with gnosticism was the heresy of DOCETISM, which taught that Jesus only *appeared* to be human; it was argued that it would be impossible, even temporarily, for an emissary from the Divine Being to be conquered by the *Demiurge*, and to suffer and die.

Considerable information about gnosticism comes from the writings of anti-gnostics, such as Sts Irenaeus and Hippolytus, and also from Tertullian. Some outstanding gnostic teachers include the second-century writers Basilides, Bardesanes, Tatian, Marcion and Valentinus. In December 1945, a collection of thirteen papyri was discovered at Nag Hammadi, in Upper Egypt. These were Coptic codices and their discovery has greatly increased understanding of gnosticism.

GOD BLESS CHRISTIAN MARCHING CHURCH

Past members of the Soldiers of God Church, which had itself been founded from the SALVATION ARMY in 1938, inaugurated the God Bless Christian Marching Church in Zimbabwe in 1956 along Salvationist lines. The uniforms worn by women members of the Church closely resemble those worn by Salvationists; the men beat out the rhythm with maracas while the women wave their tambourines as they march in procession. The Church fulfils an important social function in offering support for the poor, the aged and the homeless. An agricultural college has also been opened for the training of young people. With its wide ecumenical contacts, the Church now has 40 congregations with around 15,000 adult members and the numbers are still growing. The headquarters of this Church is in Harare, Zimbabwe.

❖ Christian Marching Church of Central Africa

GOD'S APOSTOLIC CHURCH

A Oneness, Pentecostal Church that adopted the original title of God's Apostolic Church in 1938 when James Forsyth and Gordon Magee started to work in Belfast, Northern Ireland.

Promoting the oneness pentecostal message, they baptized only in the name of the Lord Jesus Christ, omitting both God the Father and the Holy Spirit; nevertheless, the members hold to a conventional belief in the Trinity. The Church observes the anointing of the sick with oil in the name of the Lord as an ordinance. The Church advocates a strongly Calvinistic stance in its doctrine, rejecting the Arminian tradition of salvation for all. The autonomy of local churches is respected and all churches are supported through a system of tithing.

David Magee migrated from Ireland to Australia in the 1950s, where he created a Church of God in Montmorency, Melbourne; he has since moved to Caboolture in Queensland where he has started a new Pentecostal project among some ex-Roman Catholics.

❖ Churches of God in Ireland

GOD'S MISSIONARY CHURCH

This small independent American Church, which belongs within the Holiness tradition, was founded in 1935 and now has its headquarters at Swengal, Pennsylvania. It arose as a result of a dispute between the members of the Pennsylvanian and the New Jersey district congregations of the Pilgrim Holiness Church. The Church exacts a very high standard of behaviour from its members. Missionary work is undertaken amongst Cuban refugees in Florida and on the island of Haiti. There are presently around 40 congregations with about 1,700 adult members mostly confined to the eastern and southern American states. God's Missionary Church is a member of the Interdenominational Holiness Convention.

GOSPEL FURTHERING BIBLE CHURCH

An African Church, with headquarters in Nairobi, Kenya, which is within the Baptist tradition. It was organized in 1936 by the Gospel Furthering Fellowship, which sent out a team of missionaries from the USA to establish a strong, indigenous local Church and lay down the foundations for a national leadership.

The Church believes in the divine inspiration of the Bible and has a conventional understanding of the Trinity and of Christ's life and work. It is not sympathetic to the phenomenon of *glossolalia*, or speaking in tongues. Two ordinances are accepted, those of water baptism by immersion and the Lord's Supper, neither of which is believed to have any saving merit.

The members of the Church practise *separation* from worldly interests and fashions and no ecumenical contacts are made. The Church believes in the imminent pre-tribulational and premillennial second coming of Christ, with eternal reward and happiness for the saved and damnation for the wicked (Revelation 20).

GOSPEL HARVESTER CHURCHES

There are two such Churches, both started in the USA, the first of which was founded in Atlanta, Georgia, in 1961 by Earl P. Paulk, Jr and Harry A. Muchegan; this is identified as the Harvesters Association (Atlanta). It is a white PENTECOSTAL Church, with an emphasis on healing ministry, which has some 20 congregations containing around 8,000 members.

The second Church, which is called the Gospel Harvesters Association (Buffalo), was founded in 1962 by Rose Pezzino, in Buffalo, New York. Apart from the Buffalo foundation there are also congregations in Toronto, Canada, and some individual members in the southern USA. A foreign mission programme is maintained, with members working in the Philippines and India.

❖ Gospel Harvesters Evangelical Association

GOSPEL SPREADING CHURCH

An American Church that owes its origins to the work of a black evangelist and former minister in the CHURCH OF GOD (HOLINESS), Elder Lightfoot Solomon Michaux (1885–1968). Michaux had made a personal fortune through selling fish to the United States Navy, becoming its chief purveyor. Much of this fortune Michaux gave away to help unfortunates, both black and white.

In 1922 Michaux founded an independent Church, within the HOLINESS tradition; this was initially known as the Gospel Spreading Tabernacle Association and was established in Newport News, Virginia. A move to Washington, DC, six years later saw the establishment of the Church of God and Gospel Spreading Association. Michaux made great use of the radio in his ministry, his message being one of various holiness themes mixed with positive thinking. He broadcast to some fifty radio stations inside the USA, to an estimated audience of 25 million (in 1934). Michaux's popularity declined in time, particularly during the years of the Second World War. In 1964, towards the end of his life, Michaux organized his followers once again, as the Gospel Spreading Church, but most congregations were content to call themselves the Church of God.

❖ Elder Michaux Church of God; Radio Church of God

GOSPEL STANDARD STRICT BAPTIST CHURCHES

A hyper-CALVINISTIC stream that emerged within the BAPTIST CHURCH in England and was formally organized in 1872. The Gospel Standard Strict Baptist Churches had its origins in the PARTICULAR BAPTISTS, who accepted the Calvinist view of predestination, and with the founding of a periodical, *The Gospel Standard*, produced by John Gadsby. This publication took it upon itself to denounce a controversy that was circulating amongst the Particular Baptists, which held that Jesus Christ only became the Son of God as a result of some sort of supernatural *begetting* in the womb of the Virgin Mary, a view that was countered in *The Gospel Standard*. The controversy split the Particular Baptist Church and by the 1870s those who held to the more orthodox view emerged as a distinct and markedly separate group from the Particular Baptists.

This separateness was underlined by a Church policy of observing a restricted membership and operating a *closed* communion, which limited the sacrament to its own members. Members regard the gospel, rather than the ten commandments, as the rule of life. In more recent times the Gospel Standard Strict Baptists have become known simply as the Strict Baptists. The Church can be found in England, with 156 congregations and over 6,000 adult members; in the USA, with groups in Michigan, Montana and Wisconsin, and in Australia, where there were at one time 12 congregations, though the number has now declined to 4 groups, with some 50 members, in Victoria, New South Wales and South Australia.

❖ Strict Baptists

GRACE BIBLE CHURCH

A very small Australian Church, which was founded in Maddington, Western Australia, in 1978 and now has fewer than a hundred members. The Church is best described as belonging to the independent evangelical tradition.

GRACE GOSPEL FELLOWSHIP

John Nelson Darby (1800–82), the early leader of the PLYMOUTH BRETHREN, *interpreted the Bible as being a series of seven dispensations, or periods of God's dealings with man. Ethelbert William Bullinger, an* ANGLICAN *priest, identified baptism with water, or John's baptism, as belonging to the third dispensation that includes the gospels and most of the Acts of the Apostles. Bullinger had a marked influence on Charles H. Welch, who started The Berean Expositor and wrote several books that dealt with what has been called* ultra-dispensationalism. *Bullinger argued that when St Paul, in Acts 28:25–8, directs his efforts towards the Gentiles and no longer towards the Jews, this marks the age in which the Church exists in the Dispensation of Grace, and what is known as the Grace Gospel position. In this fourth dispensation, as it was called, there was only one baptism, that of the Holy Spirit (Eph. 4:5–7) and there was therefore no need for water baptism. Bullinger also argued that in the post-Acts Church the Lord's Supper is not to be observed. Both Bullinger and Welch also proposed a belief known as 'annihilationism', or the total destruction of the wicked who do not even get sent to hell.*

Bullinger's views spread to America in the 1920s and were taken up by Pastor J. C. O'Hair of Chicago and by Pastor Harry Beltema of Muskegon, Michigan. The Grace Gospel movement spread across the USA, with many ministers and their congregations accepting the movement's conclusions. A group of pastors and laymen convened a meeting in 1938 to discuss how best to spread the message both at home and abroad, with the result that the Worldwide Grace Testimony was established and work began in Zaïre (then Belgian Congo). In 1940 a Bible Institute was successfully founded and by 1944 the Grace Gospel Fellowship was formally recognized after a meeting of pastors at Evansville, Indiana. The headquarters of the Grace Gospel Fellowship was later established at Grand Rapids, Michigan, which since 1968 has also been the site of the Grace Bible College.

The member congregations of the fellowship reject water baptism, accepting instead the baptism of the Holy Spirit, as well as the verbal inspiration of the Gospels. Some congregations observe the Lord's Supper and do not accept the belief of *annihilationism* despite the efforts and writings of Stuart Allen, who continued Welch's work as editor of the *Berean Expositor* in London. There are currently around 128 congregations in the USA with an adult membership of 45,000.

GRANT BRETHREN

The United States Bureau of the Census respected the fact that there were many different groups of PLYMOUTH BRETHREN; *because the Brethren refused to accept denominational labels, the Bureau of Census identified the groups by Roman numerals.*

Frederick W. Grant was a nineteenth-century leader amongst the EXCLUSIVE BRETHREN in north-east America. His views concerning dispensationalism did not win him many friends or support either in England or in Canada and the Montreal Assembly excommunicated him in 1885 because of his heretical views.

The excommunication and the preceding trial attracted many Exclusive Brethren followers and Grant was soon able to establish a separate branch of the Exclusive Brethren, which takes its name from him; it was identified by the Roman numeral 'I' by the Bureau of Census.

The Grant Brethren are without a creed and they believe the Bible to be the inspired word of God, and therefore inerrant. Their understanding of the Trinity is perfectly orthodox. All men are considered sinners, with salvation and justification coming through faith in Christ's redemption. They also believe that Christ rose from the dead and ascended into heaven, and that his imminent return will be premillennial, followed by the judgement of the just and the wicked, who will merit heaven and hell respectively (REVELATION 20). The polity of the Grant Brethren is congregational and the two ordinances of baptism and the Lord's Supper, which is celebrated every Sunday morning, are observed.

GREEK EASTERN-RITE CATHOLICS

Latin-rite Catholics have been a presence in Greece since the time of the Crusades, especially on the Ionian and Aegean islands, as this was where ROMAN CATHOLIC German and Venetian merchants settled. The organization of Greek Catholics of the Byzantine, or Eastern, rite was largely the work of Fr John Hyacinth Marango, a Latin-rite priest from Syra who, in 1856, had started to try and persuade Orthodox Christians in Constantinople to establish communion with Rome. The effort involved was rewarded when a small Eastern-rite Catholic group was established at Pera (now Beyoğlu, in Turkey); Fr Polycarp Anastasiadis continued this work. In 1895, Pope Leo XIII sent some French Augustinians of the Assumption to Constantinople, with a view to opening a seminary and forming some Eastern-rite parishes there.

As a result of the Graeco-Turkish war of 1921–2, Greeks in Turkey were repatriated to Greece. The Greek Catholics endured harsh treatment from their Greek Orthodox neighbours and a law was passed in 1938 that aimed to curb the work of non-Orthodox groups, especially that of Eastern-rite Catholics. By 1972 there were two Eastern-rite Catholic parishes, both in Athens, and a smaller one at Yannitsa, in Macedonia. There are also two female religious houses, the Sisters of the Theotokos Pammakaristos, who conduct a school in Athens, and the Little Sisters of Jesus, who work to establish clear lines of ecumenical communication.

❖ Greek Catholic Church

GREEK EVANGELICAL CHURCH

This is one of the two main PROTESTANT Churches in Greece and owes its origin to a young and enthusiastic convert to protestantism, Michael Kalopathakes, who started a series of Bible study groups and a newspaper, *Star of the East*, in 1858. By 1924 the number of congregations had grown sufficiently to form a synod and the group adopted its present name. The Church, which is presbyterian in structure, currently has 35 congregations divided into two regional synods, of Greece and of North America. Pastors lead the larger congregations, with the smaller, rural ones in the charge of elders.

The Church founded the Philemon Association in 1986, which helps with the rehabilitation of drug and alcohol addicts by running counselling programmes and a centre for cure and detoxification in Athens; since 1994 recovering addicts have been able to spend some time at a farm near Thebes where a programme of farm therapy has been introduced. A cautious but actively evangelistic programme has been established, with an outreach mission in Albania that plans to distribute clothing, food and medical care to the needy, particularly to the elderly and the young.

Doctrinally, the members of the Greek Evangelical Church subscribe to a modified *WESTMINSTER CONFESSION* and accept the Nicene Creed. They also accept the divine inspiration and infallibility of the scriptures, the doctrine of the Trinity, man's fall and salvation for all. Justification through faith is followed by sanctification and the two ordinances of baptism and the Lord's Supper are observed. The second coming of Christ is anticipated, with the resurrection of the dead and the judgement of man preceding his conveyance to heaven or hell (REVELATION 20).

GREEK FREE CHURCH

A small evangelical and ethnic group of churches in Australia, which is linked with the Fellowship of Free Evangelical Churches of Greece (founded 1916).

The Greek Free Church is represented in Melbourne, Sydney, Adelaide and Perth, and holds to a kenotic view of Christology, in that God the Son, in becoming man, discarded his divinity and assumed human frailties and limitations; in one sense it could be said that Christ was unaware of his divinity. The members of the Church hold to an ARMINIAN view of salvation and are premillennialists (REVELATION 20).

GREEK ORTHODOX ARCHDIOCESE OF NORTH AND SOUTH AMERICA

Early Greek immigrants to America formed a community at New Smyrna, Florida, in 1767, but the first GREEK ORTHODOX CHURCH was not founded in America until 1864, when the Church of the Holy Trinity was established in New Orleans. The necessary clergy were provided from either the holy synod of Greece or from the Ecumenical Patriarch of Constantinople and new parishes were soon established across the country. As these congregations grew, so did the need for some centralized organization and the Greek Orthodox Archdiocese of North and South America was formed in 1918. The focus of the final authority of the Church fluctuated between Athens and Constantinople, finally settling on the latter.

This is now the largest Orthodox denomination in the USA with around 1.5 million adult members divided between 15 dioceses with nearly 600 parishes. The Church, while being completely Orthodox in its doctrine and practice, has dealt with many difficulties over the years concerned with disputes over the use of the calendar. The adoption of the New Calendar in 1924 was strongly opposed by those who wanted to retain the Old Calendar, and this resulted in schisms. Training for the priesthood was established in 1937 at the Holy Cross Greek Orthodox Theology School in Brookline, Massachusetts. Other educational establishments have been opened, including a teachers' training college at Garrison, New York.

❖ Greek Archdiocese of North and South America

GREEK ORTHODOX ARCHDIOCESE OF VASILOUPOLIS

A small Greek Orthodox denomination in the USA that observes the Old Calendar, whilst tolerating New Calendar parishes within its jurisdiction. It was founded in 1968 by Metropolitan Pangratios Vrionis and has its headquarters in Woodside, New York. The Church is also nicknamed the *M & M Diocese*, on account of its emphasis on missions and monasteries. There are parishes in most American states as well as abroad.

❖ Holy Greek Orthodox Archdiocese of Vasiloupolis; Holy Orthodox Archdiocese of Vasiloupolis

GREEK ORTHODOX CHURCH

Christianity was first brought to Greece by St Paul in the first century, with Corinth as the main centre of activity. After the death of Emperor Constantine the Great (274–337), who had established his capital at Byzantium, which he renamed Constantinople (now Istanbul), this area of the empire was divided. Constantinople became the eastern capital and a new, western capital was established at Rome, each with their own religious leaders, the pope in Rome and the patriarch in Constantinople. The growth of Christianity throughout the empire continued unshaken until the *Great Schism* in the eleventh century. This concerned a disagreement over the procession of the Holy Spirit, as stated in the *filioque* clause in the Nicene Creed, and it came to a climax on 16 July 1054 when a bull of excommunication from the pope in Rome was placed on the altar of the cathedral of Hagia Sophia in Constantinople. This action separated the Churches of Rome and Constantinople and they remain apart.

During the time of the Turkish occupation of Greece in the late-fourteenth century, which was to continue until the middle of the nineteenth century, Greece was part of the Patriarchate of Constantinople. In 1821, with the start of the Greek war of independence (continuing until 1828), this began to change. The Greeks gained formal recognition of their independence from the Turks in 1832 and the Greek provisional president, Ioannis Kapodistrias, began negotiations with the Patriarch of Constantinople aimed at gaining independence for the Greek Church. King Otto I made the final decision concerning the autocephaly of the Greek Church. He was the son of King Ludwig I of Bavaria and had been given the throne of Greece; Otto was under age at the time of his succession and three Bavarian regents were appointed to rule Greece in his name. One of these regents was G. L. Maurer, a PROTESTANT, and he feared that the Turkish government might still be able to influence Greek politics through the Patriarch of Constantinople. Maurer stressed the importance of independence for the Greek Church, which was decreed by the king in 1833. Otto I, who was never accepted with much enthusiasm by the Greek people, as he had little sympathy for the country and had retained his loyalty to the ROMAN CATHOLIC CHURCH, was exiled in 1862 when the throne of Greece passed into the hands of the Danish royal family with the accession of George I.

The Church has seen other splits. In 1924, when the Greek Church changed from using the Old (Julian) Calendar to the New (Gregorian) Calendar, many clergy and laity were upset enough to leave and form a new group, the *Palaiemerologitai*, or OLD CALENDARISTS. The ultimate authority in the Greek Orthodox Church is in the hands of the holy synod, under the presidency of the Archbishop of Athens and All Greece. This body is responsible for church policy and related issues; a second synod, under the same presidency and composed of twelve bishops who serve for only one year each, is occupied with general church administration. The clergy can be either celibate or married but candidates for the priesthood who wish to marry must do so before they are ordained; only celibate clergy, who are monastics, are eligible to become bishops. Theological training is available through the Universities of Athens and Thessalonica. Monastic communities are found throughout the country. The famous monastic republic of Mt Athos, with its twenty monasteries and dwindling communities, is independent of the Greek Church. Governed by its holy community, which is made up of representatives from each of the monasteries, Mt Athos is directly dependent upon Constantinople. Doctrinally, the Greek Orthodox Church subscribes fully to the faith of the EASTERN ORTHODOX CHURCH.

❖ Church of Greece; The Greek Church

GREEN PASTURES BRETHREN

When a split developed within the OPEN BRETHREN in 1893, over the issue of the relative importance of believers as against assemblies of believers, around one hundred such assemblies in Great Britain, called the Churches of God (Needed Truth), so-named from the title of their magazine *Needed Truth*, separated from the rest.

These separated Brethren continued to have further disagreements amongst themselves over the question of which assembly of elders, local or regional, should be able to discipline an erring elder, up until 1904. The few Brethren who agreed with the publisher of the *Green Pastures* magazine and with Dr Vernal, formed the Green Pastures Brethren, while the majority remained as the Needed Truth group, which in the UK became known as the CHURCHES OF GOD IN THE BRITISH ISLES AND OVERSEAS (NEEDED TRUTH).

With Scottish migration to Australia, some of the Green Pastures Brethren settled in Victoria and a small community is maintained there today.

H

HARMONY SOCIETY

The Harmony Society was formed when a group of German PIETIST dissenters from Württemberg, led by George Rapp (1757–1847) and his adopted son, Frederick, migrated to America in 1803–4 in search of religious freedom. The group, known also as Rappites, settled first on 5,000 acres in Butler County, Pennsylvania, which they called *Harmony*. It was while they were here that George Rapp wrote the *Articles of Agreement*, in 1805, which suggest that an austere lifestyle had already been embraced by the members of the community; by 1807 the members has also agreed to accept celibacy. The equality of their lifestyle was emphasized in the uniform manner of dress adopted by the members and by the fact that their graves had no headstones and no indication of the member's individuality or standing in the community.

In a short time a thriving agricultural plant and light industry factory had been established and a considerable amount of wealth was amassed. Led by Rapp, eight hundred *Harmonists*, as members came also to be known, moved up the Wabash River in 1814–15 to found another *Harmony* on 3,000 acres bordering the river, in Posey County, Indiana. Here the group was noted for its inventiveness and industry in the distillation of whiskey and the cultivation of silk; it is also thought the Harmonists introduced the first prefabricated house and the first printing centre in the Wabash Valley region. On their land the group built a church, constructed in the shape of a Greek cross and estimated to have been 120 feet long. Prosperity was the inevitable outcome of this industry and George Rapp began to see this as a possible threat to their faith. For this reason, he sold the Posey County estate to Robert Owen, a Welshman who had been the successful manager of a mill in Scotland and who wanted to create an ideal community, which he named *New Harmony*, on the land. Sadly, after three years his venture failed.

Rapp and his community returned to Pennsylvania and created another village, called *Economy*, near Pittsburgh. In the 1820s, without consulting his community, Rapp published a second set of *Articles of Agreement*, which upset the members, although it was no more than a simple outline of the community's practices. By now, rather more disturbingly, Rapp began to believe that Napoleon Bonaparte had been born as God's ambassador, that attendance at school was wicked, and that the ordinances of baptism and the Lord's Supper were the work of the devil. In 1832 Rapp declared to the community that the second coming of Christ was imminent (REVELATION 20), and, almost on cue, a stranger appeared in the community. This was a German adventurer, called Count Leon, who claimed to be the returned Messiah, the Christ. In a very short time the Count departed from Economy, taking 250 Rappites with him. The community now suffered a grave setback with the death, in 1834, of Frederick Rapp, who had always been the financial genius behind its prosperity. Thereafter the community dwindled, badly affected by the loss of its leader when George Rapp died in 1847. By the turn of the century the membership was in single figures, a victim of its obligation to celibacy.

❖ Harmonists; Rappites

HARRIST CHURCH (IVORY COAST)

This important indigenous African Church grew out of the work of prophet William Wade Harris (1865–1929) who was born near Cape Palmas, Liberia, and, after a short period of education, worked first aboard a ship before becoming a bricklayer. Following his marriage, Harris joined the Episcopal Church in 1885 and by 1892 he had acquired enough education to become a teacher and catechist, rising to be appointed as teacher-in-charge of a school and also becoming an interpreter. In 1908 Harris went to Monrovia, the capital of Liberia, where he was accused of stirring up anti-government sympathy, for which he was jailed. While he was in jail Harris believed that he had received a *call* from the archangel Gabriel, urging him to become a prophet and to prepare the way for Jesus Christ. Upon release, he put on a white robe and turban and went barefoot around the Ivory Coast and the Gold Coast (now Ghana), preaching as he went and carrying a stave, its end fashioned into a cross, a calabash, which would be filled with water for baptism, a gourd rattle and a Bible. Two or three women, who would sing and dance, accompanied Harris, shaking the rattle to accompany his preaching. In 1913, after his tour of the Gold Coast, Harris returned to the Ivory Coast where he was reported to have converted some 100,000 followers. The French colonial power, then in charge of the country, initially viewed Harris benignly because he taught and preached the work ethic; this attitude was later to change when the French became alarmed at the movement's potential for disorder. He was expelled to Liberia in 1915, and the churches built by his followers destroyed. These followers now became the object of interest to various ROMAN CATHOLIC and PROTESTANT missionaries who tried to recruit the newly converted Christians, but with no great success. Harris continued to preach in Liberia, but he failed to attract a great following.

Harris's message emphasized the second coming of Christ (REVELATION 20) and the importance of conversion. His followers were exhorted to obey the ten commandments, keep Sunday holy and accept the authority of the Bible. Harris also preached against the fetishes of the traditional African religions and the worshipping of idols, but he did not go so far as to condemn polygamy. The Church has thrived and today has some 290 groups on the Ivory Coast.

The Harrist Church teaches that there are three sacraments: baptism, using the triune formula, Holy Communion, which is made using local ingredients for the species of water and wine and always celebrated outside the church building, and marriage. While the clergy are expected to be monogamous, any polygamous converts are not expected to divorce excess wives. Each local church has provision for a college of twelve apostles, lay people who provide local leadership. Preachers are chosen from amongst these apostles and can rise from the office of ordinary preacher to that of superior, or chief, according to the quality of the preaching. Elders are chosen from amongst the congregation and exercise an advisory role; other church officers include cantors, bell ringers, guards, cleaners and candle lighters, the latter responsible for tending the three candles, symbolizing the Trinity, which are used during worship.

The head of the Church is known as the supreme preacher. A National Harrist Committee was formed in 1960 in order to administer the Church. The Harrist Church was granted membership of the World Council of Churches in 1998.

❖ Harris Church

HARVEST HOUSE MINISTRIES

Harvest House Ministries is an American movement founded by Oliver and Mary Louise Heath in San Francisco in 1970. The original purpose of the ministry was to offer the way of Jesus to those flocking to join the popular movements of the times, which offered a palette of occult, psychic and eastern philosophies to the young people growing up in the 1960s, particularly in California. Harvest House members began to appear at some of the popular gatherings, to evangelize and offer counselling and literature. House communes were established in San Francisco, with an elder and a deacon in charge of each house. The group is PENTECOSTAL, with no specific teaching programme but a strong emphasis on individual Bible study.

HELLENIC ORTHODOX CHURCH OF AMERICA

A small American Church, within the GREEK ORTHODOX CHURCH tradition, which was founded in 1924. When Archimandrite Petros, a monk from Mt Athos in Greece, arrived in the United States he gathered around him some Orthodox followers who were unhappy about changes in the use of the calendar in the American parishes; the traditional use of the Old Calendar (Julian) had been rejected in favour of the New Calendar (Gregorian) by the GREEK ORTHODOX ARCHDIOCESE OF NORTH AND SOUTH AMERICA. Archimandrite Petros was consecrated as Bishop of Astoria, Long Island, New York in 1962 by two Russian bishops who still observed the Old Calendar, Archbishop Leontios of Chile and Bishop Seraphim of Venezuela.

Apart from adhering to the Old Calendar, the Hellenic Orthodox Church of America is totally Orthodox. There are at present 4 congregations that serve 1,000 members; the members are also provided with classes in Greek culture, language and Orthodoxy.

HENRICIANS

A mediaeval sect of the early twelfth century in France, where an itinerant preacher, Henry of Lausanne (d. after 1145), was active. His travels had taken Henry from Lausanne to Le Mans, from where he was expelled by Bishop Hildebert, later Bishop of Tours, for heretical preaching against the objective efficacy of the priesthood and the sacraments. Henry moved south and in 1119 was condemned by the Council of Toulouse. Although he was persuaded to recant his heretical views following his arrest in Arles in 1135, Henry soon returned to his old ways and attracted the attention of St Bernard of Clairvaux. St Bernard was sent to counteract this heretical preaching and regain for the Church those followers, known as Henricians, who had been influenced by the heresy. Henry's message denied the objective efficacy of the sacraments. He taught that these were invalid if administered by a priest who was not living a life of evangelical poverty. Most of Henry's preaching was aimed specifically at much of the contemporary clergy and their love of wealth and power.

HICKSITE QUAKERS

The formal organization of the Religious Society of Friends *(Quakers) is built around Meetings; these are graded as monthly, quarterly and yearly, as the local sphere of influence increases. The Meetings are responsible for the spiritual and secular concerns of the society.*

The American Hicksite Quakers arose in New York in the 1820s, as a split from the more orthodox Quakers, or members of the Religious Society of Friends, under the influence of an eloquent speaker, Elias Hicks (1748–1830). Hicks was not only a convincing preacher but was also a social critic who attacked slavery, worldliness and conventional Christology. He further contended that man was capable of saving himself, describing the Bible and church dogma as being merely functional and both lacking authority. Hicks's appeal was to those who were resisting the evangelical thrust of others of the Quaker persuasion who wanted to unite all Quaker groups and to create a written doctrine. The split, which was a likely outcome in 1823, finally materialized in 1827 when the pro-Hicks supporters, or Liberals, formed a conference that soon became organized into a separate, yearly meeting. The split from the more orthodox Quakers occurred in New York, Ohio, and throughout the eastern and mid-western states, resulting in the establishment of seven yearly meetings. By 1900, a general conference had been formed which was more of a focus of fellowship than a body exercising legislative authority. Socially, the Hicksite Quakers were very active, but they did not support any mission work.

❖ Hicksites; Religious Society of Friends (General Conference)

HINDUSTANI COVENANT CHURCH

Hindustani is the principal dialect of Western Hindi, India.

A congregational-style Church, which owes its origins to the work of the Swedish Mission Covenant Church (founded 1878). The Church is growing, with 16 congregations and around 1,700 current members, and is mainly concerned with mission work. The headquarters of the Church is in Bombay.

HINSCHITE EVANGELICAL CHURCH

A small, declining denomination with its headquarters in Nîmes, France, that was organized in 1831 by Coraly Hinsch near Montpellier for a group of dissident Calvinists. The membership, which currently stands at around a hundred, affirms a dualist theology with an emphasis on blessings that flow from the Holy Ghost. They do not observe any sacraments and have as their main emphasis a study of the Bible. Members are active in social work and have responsibility for a girls' home.

❖ Hinschites

HOLINESS (CHURCHES or TRADITION)

Churches within this tradition are concerned with sanctification and perfection. Sanctification, or second blessing, is believed to occur when the Holy Spirit cleanses the heart and enables a believer to gradually die to sin. This sanctification comes at the end of a period of growing in grace following upon justification, or being *born again*. Personal holiness is often symbolized by the observance of a strict code of behaviour and dress.

HOLINESS CHRISTIAN CHURCH

An American Church, formally organized in 1889, that grew from a street preaching team of three men and two women, known as the *Heavenly Recruits*, who were strongly revivalist in their message and so successful in attracting followers that it became necessary to provide a framework for the group. In 1894, C. W. Ruth was elected president of the group that was then known as the Heavenly Recruit Association; the name was later changed, firstly to the Holiness Christian Association, and in 1897 to the Holiness Christian Church. Many members left the Church at the start of the twentieth century as a result of the many bewildering mergers that took place. There are now some 50 congregations, with around 5,500 adult members, largely limited to the eastern states, who follow the strict requirements of the HOLINESS tradition.

HOLINESS CHURCH OF GOD

A small, black American group founded at Madison, North Carolina, in 1920. The Church, which is administered by overseers and has congregations in several areas in the southern and eastern states, lies within the HOLINESS tradition. There is an annual general assembly, presided over by an elected president.

HOLINESS METHODIST CHURCHES

There are two member Churches belonging to this American denomination, one in North Carolina and the other in North Dakota. The North Carolina group was formed in 1900 and is known as the Lumber River Annual Conference of the Holiness Methodist Church, made up of members of the METHODIST EPISCOPAL CHURCH–South, that met at Union Chapel Church in Robeson County, North Carolina. The HOLINESS movement was subject to a great deal of criticism by some traditional METHODISTS and this led its more enthusiastic advocates to form the new Church. The members placed considerable emphasis on the second blessing, or sanctification, which is effected by a baptism of the Holy Spirit. The work of the Church is directed largely at home missions and evangelism and it is totally Wesleyan in its doctrine, with considerable stress placed on atonement and the witness of the Holy Spirit, though the tradition of an itinerant ministry has been dropped. The polity is episcopal.

The other Church included in this group of holiness Methodists had its origins in North Dakota. It was formed within the context of the *Holiness Revivalism* within the Methodist Church at the end of the nineteenth century throughout the USA. Known initially as the North-western Holiness Association, this came into being in 1909, at Grand Forks, North Dakota. This large group, which was originally an informal association of several smaller groups following in the holiness tradition, came about when it was realized that a more formal degree of organization was required. The current name was adopted in 1920. In 1948, as a result of missionary work by the Holiness Methodist Church in Bolivia, the Bolivian Holiness Church was established and is still growing.

HOLY ORDER OF MANS

This Church is not conventionally Christian.

An American New Age group founded in San Francisco in 1968 by Paul (Earl) W. Blighton and made up of a synthesis of esoteric, occult, biblical, reincarnational and eastern, non-Christian religions. The name MANS is an acronym taken from the phrase *Mysterion – Agape – Nous – Sophia (Mystery – Love – Mind – Wisdom)*, its perceived meaning revealed only to those initiated into the group. New members, in line with the training system used by conventional religious orders, are admitted to a three month novitiate followed by a period of six months in first vows and, if the member wishes to proceed, by a further period of training after which second vows, which last for life, are taken. These second vows are of humility, service, obedience, purity and poverty. Full members of the Holy Order can then become either a Brown Brother of the Holy Light, or an Immaculate Sister of Mary for Missionary Training. A third option is open for those who do not want to become full members but still wish to receive the teachings; this is known as the Outer Order of Discipleship. The group is supported by donations from members of any and all earnings from their secular occupations. The philosophy of the group is centred on the belief that man can become aware of God, which they call the *golden force*, which in turn can become a force for good in his life to help him to grow, mentally, physically and spiritually. This union with the *golden force* is mainly achieved through meditation.

The ethos of the group changed after the death of Blighton and many members left to join the Eastern Orthodox Churches; those that remained with the Holy Order were then placed under the leadership of Blighton's wife, Ruth, who was called the mother of the Order. There have been many centres of the Holy Order of Mans set up in the USA, with seminaries in San Francisco, Chicago and Boston, and also in Canada, England, Germany, Spain, France, Holland and Japan.

HOLY ROLLERS

A pejorative term, sometimes used to describe Pentecostal Church members and in particular those who are given to a vigorous style of worship, often accompanied by *glossolalia*, or speaking in tongues, and various degrees of ecstatic movement, or dancing. The services can also include extempore prayer and the free use of the cry of *Amen*, whenever members feel so prompted.

HOLY UKRAINIAN AUTOCEPHALIC ORTHODOX CHURCH IN EXILE

In 1951 some members of the Ukrainian Orthodox Church of the USA withdrew over a dispute about the administration of the Church. This group of laymen and clergy, who had migrated to the USA after the Second World War, was formally organized with the help of two bishops, Palladios Rudenko and Nikolaus

Ilnyckys. The new group, with headquarters in Brooklyn, New York, was established with its own bishop, and now has 17 parishes, with around 4,000 adult members. The Divine Liturgy is celebrated in both Ukrainian and English. The doctrinal position of the Church is fully Eastern Orthodox.

HOMOEANS

Followers and disciples of Acacius, Bishop of Caesarea (d. 366), an Arian theologian who was deposed by the Council of Sardica in 343 because of the views he held. At the Council of Seleucia, in 359, Acacius opposed the insertion of the term *Homoousios* – of the same substance – into the Nicene creed. The word was used to describe the relationship between God the Father and God the Son, holding that Jesus Christ was like (Greek 'homios') the Father, but not necessarily of the same essence. After the death of Emperor Constantius II in 361, from whom he had received much support, Acacius returned to the orthodox view and accepted the Nicene creed, reverting once more, in 364, to the Arian heresy, two years before his death.

❖ Acacians

HOPKINSIANS

An American sect of independent Calvinists, followers of Samuel Hopkins (1721–1803) who was born in Waterburg, Connecticut. After graduating from Yale University in 1741 he trained as a Congregationalist minister and was ordained in 1743 as pastor of Great Barrington, Massachusetts, moving in 1770 to Rhode Island where he became pastor of the Congregationalist Church at Newport. His views, which were unorthodox and attracted a great deal of attention at the time, opposed slavery as a moral evil, a view that found little acceptance in eighteenth century America. Hopkins also had decided views about sin and rejected the role of original sin in the lives of human beings. These views, which were at variance with commonly accepted beliefs, provoked a great deal of comment and earned the sect the soubriquet of *New School Theology*.

HOUSE OF DAVID

When the founder of the Christian Israelite Church, John Wroe, died in 1863 an English leader, originally called James White but who assumed the name of James Jersham Jezreel after Hosea's son (Hos. 1:4,11), set about publishing a book, entitled *The Flying Scroll*, in which he identified the seven angels of the *Book of Revelation*. In this book, Jezreel was identified as the sixth angel, and Shiloh, the long-awaited offspring of Joanna Southcott (Southcottians), was to be the seventh angel (notwithstanding the fact that Joanna Southcott had been dead since 1814).

In his book, Jezreel drew much attention to the Great Father-Spirit, which descended upon Jesus at his baptism and left him at his crucifixion. The Mother-Spirit was also emphasized, as it was her role to help humanity to ward off Satan's attacks. Followers, who were noted for their long hair that was looped back and tucked into a velvet cap, were attracted to Jezreel's teachings and he achieved considerable success, largely through the efforts of a young female convert, Clarissa Rogers, who claimed to have heard voices telling her to go to America. Once there, she made many more converts to the cause, and returned there again in 1880 accompanied by Jezreel, a few years before his death in 1885. The English sect continued as JEZREELITES, but is now defunct.

One of the American converts, Michael Keyfor Mills, a businessman from Detroit, sold everything he owned, sent the money to England and started again as a door-to-door salesman selling copies of *The Flying Scroll.* Mills claimed to have had a spirit baptism experience in 1891 and, in a trance that followed, it is alleged that his beard fell to the ground and he regained consciousness convinced that he was the archangel Michael and was committed to gather the 144,000 in readiness for the battle of Armageddon, as told in the Book of Revelation. He gathered together the followers of Jezreel and formed them into a community, with himself at its head. Mills then announced that as Adam had seduced Eve in the Garden of Eden and made her sin, so he could seduce women as well, and return them to virtue. Not surprisingly, Mills was arrested for this pronouncement and, refusing to explain exactly what he meant, was given a four-year prison sentence.

Benjamin Purnell, having been expelled from Mill's community, took to itinerant preaching and eventually founded his own 800–acre community at Benton Harbor, south of Kalamazoo on the shores of Lake Michigan. This came to be known as the House of David and it was here that Purnell wrote *The Star of Bethlehem* and revealed, in 1903, that he was Jezreel's seventh angel. Purnell attracted many followers and formed what he called a Commonwealth, over which he was supreme leader in both spiritual and temporal matters. All members had to contribute their money and possessions to the Commonwealth, an issue that the American Supreme Court took into consideration when Purnell was indicted for rape in 1922. The court decided in Purnell's favour over the question of rape, but declared that the Commonwealth was being run purely for Purnell's benefit. The decision came too late for Purnell, who died before it was delivered.

The House of David still operates in the USA, but with very few members. In its heyday the movement was very successful and prospered through its food canning and agricultural endeavours. The remaining members still support themselves through a much reduced business enterprise, which includes the running of an amusement park. Another community, founded in Sydney, Australia, in 1913 is no longer in existence.

In their statements of belief the members of the House of David affirm that 'we believe in God and Jesus Christ and that Benjamin is the Seventh Angel of Revelation 10:1'. They also believe in the immortality of the natural body and that during the millennium, a 'perfect creation of men and women are going to inhabit the earth and bring forth a perfect creation in the image of God' (REVELATION 20). There is a strong emphasis on the overthrow of the temporal kingdoms of the wicked, the signs of which demise were believed to be cars, radios, telephones and cinema films. Members are strictly vegetarian, men unshaven and with their hair uncut and women expected to keep their heads covered at all times.

HUGUENOTS

The name is thought to be a nickname taken from a mediaeval romance about a King Hugo, but according to Henri Esti-

enne, writing in the sixteenth century, it comes from the Gate of King Hugo, in Tours, where PROTESTANTS *used to meet at night.*

The name *Huguenots*, designating French CALVINISTIC protestants, came into use in the mid-sixteenth century, while the movement itself probably dates from the early part of that century. The Protestant Church in France, which was strongly Calvinistic, came into being following the Synod of Paris in 1559. There was almost immediate conflict with the ROMAN CATHOLIC CHURCH and it was not until 1598 that full freedom of worship was granted by the Edict of Nantes. When this was revoked, in 1685, many Huguenots were forced to apostatize or to flee the country. Many chose the latter course and went into exile in England, Holland, Switzerland, Prussia and America. It was not until the time of the French Revolution that full toleration of religious worship was restored, returning to the Huguenots their civil rights. By 1802 Calvinism was recognized as an established religion in France and the denomination grew. Several schisms arose during the nineteenth century, however, especially in 1872 when a conflict between traditional evangelicals and the more liberal wing of the Church arose. In 1938 most Calvinist groups reunited to become the REFORMED CHURCH OF FRANCE.

HUNGARIAN REFORMED CHURCH IN AMERICA

The arrival in America of many Hungarian immigrants at the end of the nineteenth century, some of whom were members of the Reformed Church in Hungary, persuaded several CALVINIST groups to target these newcomers with a view to forming Hungarian Reformed congregations in the USA. By 1904 the Hungarian Reformed Church in America had been organized under the jurisdiction of the Reformed Church of Hungary.

At the time of the break-up of the Austro-Hungarian empire in 1918, the Reformed Church of Hungary surrendered the jurisdiction of its churches in the USA to the Reformed Church in the United States, which is now part of the UNITED CHURCH OF CHRIST. These changes were all effected by the Tifflin Agreement, reached in Tifflin, Ohio, in 1921. The laity in several of the congregations, however, remained less than enthusiastic about this and saw the agreement as detrimental to both their dignity and their right to self-determination. Under the leadership of Endre Sebestyan, a pastor of the church at Duquesne, Pennsylvania, the Free Magyar Reformed Church in America was organized in 1923, holding its first constitutional assembly in Duquesne. In 1958, with further congregations who were anxious to retain their Hungarian roots and traditions now part of the group, the Church was renamed as the Hungarian Reformed Church in America and has recently become a member of the World Council of Churches.

The Church affirms the *Second Helvetic Confession* of 1566, which presents Calvinism as an evangelical form of Christianity in which the tradition of the early Church is emphasized and the doctrine of election confirmed. Administratively, the polity of the Church is a mixture of episcopal and presbyterian, with a single diocese, headed by a bishop and a lay curator, overseeing three *classes*, or groups, which cover New York, the east and the west; a deacon and a layman head each *class*. The headquarters of the Church is in Poughkeepsie, New York, and has responsibility for 27 congregations and over 7,000 adult members.

HUSSITES

The followers of the Bohemian reformer John Huss (*c.* 1369–1415), who was ordained and appointed as rector and preacher of the Bethlehem Chapel, Prague. At that time, partially through the marriage of King Wenceslas IV's sister, Anne, to the English King Richard II, the writings of the English reformer John Wycliffe were circulating in Bohemia. Huss, in agreement with many of Wycliffe's teachings, began to include them in his preaching. This soon brought him into conflict with the ROMAN CATHOLIC CHURCH and when Huss began to attack the clergy for their immorality and the practice of selling indulgences he was denounced, forbidden to preach and eventually excommunicated. In order to facilitate the physical removal of this troublesome man the city was placed under an interdict by the Church, removable only when John Huss left Prague. He went into exile in southern Bohemia, where he continued to preach and to write.

In 1414 John Huss was asked to attend the Council of Constance, which was called to decide which of three claimants to the papacy was the true one, and was guaranteed safe conduct. Trusting that he would be safe, John Huss presented himself but the guarantees were not honoured. He was seized, arrested, tried for heresy and found guilty. Defrocked and dressed in an exaggerated fool's cap, covered with pictures of devils struggling for his soul and with his tonsure disfigured, John Huss was burned at the stake, his ashes thrown into the river. Those of his followers who remained loyal to him, the Hussites, established the Church of the UNITY OF THE BRETHREN, from which the MORAVIAN CHURCH emerged.

❖ Wycliffites

HUTCHINSONIANS

Two groups are known by this name:

1 The followers of Mrs Anne Hutchinson (1591–1643), an Englishwoman who migrated to America. Settling in the PURITAN colony of Massachusetts, Mrs Hutchinson founded an ANTINOMIAN sect for which she was later banished from the colony, where she was regarded as a heretic. Her teachings, that only those who had the *inner light* would be saved, gained her many followers but few true friends, not least because she spread her view that many of the Puritan leaders were not on the list of the saved. Anne was tried for heresy and banished from the colony, settling in Rhode Island. Her end was tragic, with Anne and most of her family slaughtered by Indians.

2 A small, short-lived English sect, whose members were followers of a Yorkshireman, John Hutchinson (1674–1727). Although a largely self-educated man, in 1724 he published a two-part book known as the *Moses's Principia*, in which he argued against current scientific observations, including those of Isaac Newton, and held that God communicated with man only through the Hebrew language; by his thinking, the Old Testament therefore contained all that man should know. After his death his followers were known as Hutchinsonians, but the sect was short lived.

HUTTERITES

An Anabaptist sect, organized in Moravia in 1533 by a hat maker, Jacob Hutter. Hutter's followers came from those who had taken refuge in Moravia when persecution, driven by envy of the Hutterite economic success and because of their promotion of the separation of church and state, made life impossible for them in Switzerland. The Anabaptist movement had developed very quickly in and around Zürich in the early sixteenth century, when the Swiss reformer Ulrich Zwingli (1484–1531) was active. The group practised adult baptism, communal ownership of property and pacifism. Jacob Hutter died in 1536, having been arrested, immersed in freezing water and burned.

The followers moved eventually from Moravia to Transylvania (then part of Hungary) and on to Ukraine in 1595 where they settled, later emigrating to America and Canada between 1874–9. In America they established themselves in South Dakota, but underwent further persecution for their belief in pacifism, which forced them to flee into Canada where they formed communities in Manitoba, Saskatchewan and Alberta. Other communities were later established in the USA, where colonies of Hutterites, usually of between fifty and sixty people, still operate collective farms, known as Brüderhofs. Distinctively German in their way of life, Hutterites still use the German language in their homes and churches. Children receive their early education within the colony before attending state schools from the age of 14 years. Their communal way of life is believed to be in imitation of early Christian practice. Each colony is managed by a spiritual leader working with an advisory board, comprised of a colony manager, who cares for the finances, and a farm manager, who is concerned with the distribution of work within the group; deacons are also appointed to take responsibility for various other parts of communal life.

Members observe a Bible-centred faith and their non-conformity with the world is said to recover something of the spirit and fellowship of the New Testament Church. Hutterites avoid direct contact with the community at large, refusing to play any part in local politics or community projects, and still maintain a distinctive dress code. This has led to some problems for them, with local legislation imposed in some areas with the aim of limiting the growth of Hutterite colonies. There are thought to be some 45,000 adherents in the USA and Canada today.

❖ Hutterian Brethren

HYDROPARASTATAE

Any heretical group which uses water instead of wine in the celebration of the Eucharist, such as the Aquarians.

HYPSISTARIANS

The name of this largely Jewish sect comes from the members' description of themselves as worshippers of the most high, or highest (from the Greek 'hypsistos' – highest). It was found most commonly in Asia Minor, in Cappadocia, Bithynia and Pontus, from the second century BC to the fourth/fifth century AD. St Gregory of Nazianzus (*c.* 329–89) refers to his father having been a member of the sect in his youth, but having later been converted to Christianity by his wife, Nonna, and St Gregory of Nyssa (*c.* 330–95) also alludes to it. Certain Jewish and pagan beliefs were combined, with the sect believing in one God, named as the almighty, the most high, or the creator (but never as the Father), who was symbolized by fire and light. The Jewish Sabbath was observed, as were various dietary restrictions, but circumcision was proscribed; pagan sacrifices and idols were rejected.

❖ Hypsistians

I

ICELAND, NATIONAL CHURCH OF

According to legend, monks discovered Iceland at the start of the eighth century. Norwegian settlements were first made there towards the end of the same century, their government and administration placed in the hands of an elected body, the Althing, by 930. The first native missionary was Stefnir Thorgilsson who was commissioned in 996 to spread the Christian message in Iceland by King Olaf Trygvesson of Norway, who had converted to Christianity. The endeavour met with little success, mainly because of the over-extreme methods employed by Thorgilsson, and much of the country remained pagan. For a time it was thought that civil war between the Christians and the pagans might be inevitable, but a compromise was reached by the Althing, which allowed for the pagan population to accept baptism while at the same time offering secret sacrifices to the old gods. Diehards, who still refused to accept baptism, were only to receive minor forms of punishment. With the heat taken out of the situation civil war was averted and within a few years paganism was abolished. In little more than fifty years Christianity was well enough established in the country to justify the appointment of the first Icelandic bishop, Isleifur Gissurarson, to serve as a suffragan to the Archbishop of Hamburg in Iceland, with his see at Skálholt. A further bishopric was established in 1106 at Hólar for Isleifur's son, Gissur. During the thirteenth century Iceland came under the sovereignty of Norway. Benedictine monasteries and Augustinian convents were established and with them came a flowering of Icelandic culture, with a strong emphasis on learning and literature. Iceland, however, did not escape the ravages of the Black Death that swept Europe, although it came late to the remote island, arriving in the fifteenth century. Internal unrest, earthquakes and other conflicts afflicted the country and there was a steep decline in morality, with the clergy quickly earning for themselves a reputation of great unworthiness. By 1540 the country was ready for reform. King Christian III of Denmark and Norway (1503–59) imposed LUTHERANISM upon the land, declaring it to be the state religion in 1550 after deposing the bishops of the ROMAN CATHOLIC CHURCH and seizing their property. One such bishop, Jon Aresson of Hólar, resisted the change and was supported by local nationalists, but he and members of his family were captured and beheaded.

In general, though, the uptake of Lutheranism was a peaceful process. The sees of Hólar and Skálholt were united under one Lutheran bishop, Gudbrandur Thorlaksson, who prepared a hymnal and authorized a translation into Icelandic of the entire Bible in 1584; previous to this only the New Testament had been available in the native language. The publication and distribution of various other works, such as catechisms and other Lutheran literature, ensured that Lutheranism swiftly became familiar to the people.

Iceland became an independent state in 1918, and was established as a republic in 1944. The historical relationship between state and Church has been maintained, but attendance is not high. State support is given to the Church, but there is no interference in its functioning. The Church of Iceland, to which most Icelanders belong if only nominally, is administered as a single diocese, divided into provostries, or districts, which are in turn divided into parishes.

❖ Evangelical Lutheran Church of Iceland; The People's Church

ILLUMINATI

The name *Illuminati* is applied to several groups of religious enthusiasts claiming superior enlightenment. These include the ALUMBRADOS, those also known as the Perfectibilists and the Rosicrucians.

The Alumbrados were a mystical Spanish sect of the sixteenth century, whose ethos emphasized a passive surrender to God's will and a personal, and sinless, unity with God. As this had the effect of suggesting that the usual paths to goodness, consisting of both good works and the sacraments, were unnecessary, it is not surprising that the sect was held in disfavour and condemned, in 1525, by the Inquisition. The Inquisition believed it to be allied to LUTHERANISM, and many sect members were dealt with harshly, suffering execution for their faith.

The Illuminati, also known as Perfectibilists (or Enlightened Ones) was a secret society formed in Bavaria by the Jesuit-trained canon lawyer, Adam Weishaupt (1748–1830), who proposed that man could progress to *illumination* by going through various stages of initiation in the society. Members believed that the illuminating grace of Jesus Christ resided in them and this justified a shunning of other religious groups and denominations. A subsidiary aim of the society was to establish a worldwide republic, and this led to its outlawing in 1784/5. The movement reappeared at the end of the nineteenth century but later disappeared in the face of the rise of German national socialism in the twentieth century.

The Rosicrucians were a secret society that venerated the Rose and the Cross as being symbols of Christ's resurrection and the redemption of mankind. The members were devoted to the study of the esoteric and were strongly anti-ROMAN CATHOLIC. The movement spread throughout Germany, Russia and Poland and is still present in some parts of the world, notably in the USA, where the largest Rosicrucian body, the AMORC, was founded in New York in 1915. Christian Rosenkreuz allegedly started the society in Germany in 1459, but various writings attributed to him are now thought to have been the work of a Lutheran pastor, Johann Valentia Andreae (1586–1654).

INDEPENDENT AFRICAN METHODIST EPISCOPAL CHURCH

A small American Church, which was founded as a breakaway from the AFRICAN METHODIST EPISCOPAL CHURCH in Jacksonville, Florida, in 1907 by some ministers who left that Church on account of a dispute with the district superintendents.

The ten congregations that currently comprise the Church's membership observe the traditional *Twenty-Five Articles of Religion* (1784), but they use a revised edition of the *Book of Discipline* that organizes the procedures and doctrine of the Church. Quarterly, annual and general conferences are held. New deacons are ordained at the annual conference, with the ordination of elders and bishops confined to the general conference.

INDEPENDENT ASSEMBLIES OF GOD, INTERNATIONAL

When the ASSEMBLIES OF GOD was being organized finally in 1914 in the USA, there were many independent PENTECOSTAL groups, many of Scandinavian origin, which did not want to join because they wished the work of the Church to be wholly congregational and centred upon local churches. One such group was founded in 1918 as the Scandinavian Assemblies of God in the USA, Canada and Foreign Lands, a name that persisted until 1935. At the 1935 annual conference, held in Minneapolis, Minnesota, the group merged with another, known as the Independent Pentecostal Churches, and they emerged together as the Independent Assemblies of God International.

The Church maintains an extensive mission outreach programme extending throughout the USA and abroad, including Africa, Canada, Guatemala, India, Mexico, Brazil and the Philippines. Doctrinally, members affirm that the Bible is the inspired and infallible word of God, they believe in the Trinity and in traditional Christology and hold that salvation is effected through Christ's sacrifice. Two ordinances, those of water baptism by immersion and the Lord's Supper of bread and wine as a memorial celebration, are observed. There is also a belief in divine healing and baptism in the Holy Sprit as evidenced by *glossolalia*, or speaking in tongues, as well as in sanctification, the second coming of Christ and the resurrection of the dead followed by the final judgement and the passage to heaven or hell (REVELATION 20). The Church aims to found a Bible college and training institutes as well as providing accredited correspondence courses with a view to establishing many new churches worldwide.

❖ Independent Pentecostal Churches;
Scandinavian Assemblies of God in the USA, Canada and Foreign Lands

INDEPENDENT BAPTIST CHURCH OF AMERICA

This is a very small denomination of Swedish origin, which was founded following the immigration to America of Swedish Free Baptists in the 1870s, who settled in the Midwest. The Church was formed at an annual conference at Dassel, Minnesota, under the name of the Swedish Independent Baptist Church; the name was later changed to the Scandinavian Baptist Denomination of America.

A split occurred in 1912, when one section wanted to incorporate itself as the Swedish Independent Baptist Denomination in the United States of America. Each group went its own way until 1927 when they reunited at a conference held at Garden Valley, Wisconsin, and adopted the present name.

Doctrinally, members hold to a conventional Christology with an emphasis on repentance and baptism by immersion followed by participation in the Lord's Supper. To gain membership, a potential convert has to receive a laying on of hands, as is the practice with the GENERAL SIX PRINCIPLE BAPTISTS which was founded in 1652. This practice is taken as a sign of the reception of the gifts of the Holy Spirit. Church members, who are pacifists, are expected to obey the civil authorities except in the matter of participation in war.

❖ Scandinavian Free Baptist Society; Swedish Independent Baptist Church; Scandinavian Independent Baptist Denomination in the United States of America

INDEPENDENT BRETHREN CHURCH

A very small American Church that was founded in 1972 by dissident members of the CHURCH OF THE BRETHREN at Upper Marsh Creek, Gettysburg, Pennsylvania, who left the parent body and declared themselves to be independent. The group later united with a similar Pennsylvanian dissident group, who had withdrawn from their own parent body at Blue Rock, near Waynesboro; together they formed the Independent Brethren Church. There are currently just two congregations, with a very small membership.

INDEPENDENT CHURCH

The Independent Church, which has a large following, is to be found in Johannesburg, South Africa. Although there are no church buildings, the members, who wear blue and white robes, are very visible as they hold services wherever they gather together, on street corners or in open spaces. The doctrinal position of the Independent Church is a blend of Christianity and some traditional African beliefs. Recent attempts to unite and formalize similar independent groups have not met with success and have engendered more schisms than unions.

INDEPENDENT EVANGELICAL LUTHERAN CHURCH

Formed in 1972 by the merger of many Independent Confessional Lutheran Churches throughout Germany, this Church is identified by the initials SELK. After the first merger the group was known as the Evangelical Lutheran Free Church, and after another merger in 1991 with the Evangelical (Old Lutheran) Church, which had been located in the former German democratic republic, the present name was adopted.

The doctrinal position of the Church is wholly LUTHERAN except in one respect. Members do not recognize fellowship with any other Lutheran group and for this reason the body is not a member of the Lutheran World Fellowship (LWF). The Old and New Testaments are accepted as the inspired and revealed word of God. Members accept the *Confessions of the Lutheran Church*, which consist of the three creeds (Apostles', Nicene and Athanasian), the unaltered *Augsburg Confession*, its *Apology*, the *Smalcald Articles*, Luther's *Small* and *Larger Catechism* and the *Formula of Concord*. Female ordination has been rejected.

Since the SELK is an independent Church body it does not receive any subsidies from the state and is self-financed through members' contributions. In order to educate future pastors, a seminary has been opened in Oberursel, just north of Frankfurt. The Church also maintains a mission society and provides care for the needy in hospitals and nursing homes. Congregations of the SELK are to be found throughout Germany, where there are about 26,000 members divided between about 180 congregations, with the greatest numbers in Berlin, North Rhine-Westphalia, Lower Saxony and Hesse.

INDEPENDENT FUNDAMENTAL CHURCHES OF AMERICA

Dr R. Lee Kirkland of the Lake Okoboji Community Tabernacle in Arnold's Park, Iowa, spurred on by his opposition to growing modernism, organized the American Conference of Undenominational Churches (ACUC) in 1922, gathering together other groups who were in agreement with his outlook. In 1930, when some CONGREGATIONAL Churches joined with the ACUC, together they formed the Independent Fundamental Churches of America at a meeting held at the Cicero Bible Church at Cicero, Illinois.

Doctrinally, the group affirms the inspiration of the Bible and man's sinfulness, a state that can only be redeemed through Jesus Christ. The ordinances of water baptism and the Lord's Supper are observed and there is a strong belief in the second coming of Christ (REVELATION 20).

The polity of the group is congregational, with administration in the hands of an executive committee of twelve who are elected for a period of three years. An annual convention is held, to which all local congregations, which currently number nearly 700, send their delegates. The Church maintains a Bible camp, Bible college and Bible institute, a school and children's home and some foreign missions, but will not become involved in ecumenical projects.

INDEPENDENT METHODIST CHURCH

This small English denomination must not be confused with the (American) Independent Fundamental Methodist Church that later became the FUNDAMENTAL METHODIST CHURCH.

Organized in England at the start of the nineteenth century by a chair maker and unpaid preacher, Peter Phillips of Warrington, as a secession from the METHODIST CHURCH, the Independent Methodist Church is one of only five Methodist denominations existing in the UK. The others are the Free Methodist Church, the WESLEYAN REFORM UNION, the METHODIST CHURCH IN IRELAND and the METHODIST CHURCH OF GREAT BRITAIN. Many names were used initially to identify this Church, but in 1898 at the annual meeting the present name was adopted. From the start, the members displayed a strong Quaker influence in their restrained speech and dress as well as the lack of distinction between ministers and the laity. The polity of the Church is congregational, with most of the churches located in the north of England, especially in industrial, and formerly poor, areas.

The local churches are autonomous, but those in close proximity to each other have been able to form circuits through which they can work together and provide a framework of support. Administrative control of the Church is in the hands of delegates who come together at the annual meeting. An unpaid, male ministry has always been maintained by the Church, with potential ministers nominated by their own churches; once approved the candidates undertake a course of part-time study for four years.

Doctrinally, the Church is evangelical and affirms traditional beliefs in the Trinity, in salvation for all through Jesus Christ, and in the ordinances of baptism and the Lord's Supper, to which all believers are welcome. The Bible is regarded as the inspired word of God and the authority in faith and the conduct of life. In the matter of baptism, local churches are free to decide whether this should be administered to infants or only to adults. The Church, which has recently suffered a decline in membership, has opened a retreat and conference centre in north Cheshire, and maintains its headquarters at Loughborough, Leicestershire.

❖ Independent Methodist Connexion

INDEPENDENT PRESBYTERIAN CHURCH OF BRAZIL

The migration of Europeans to Brazil during the nineteenth century brought in its wake missionaries from America, anxious to provide for their spiritual needs. Ashbel Green Simonton, a PRESBYTERIAN minister who went to Brazil in 1859, founded the first Presbyterian Church in Rio de Janeiro in 1862. From this grew the Presbyterian Church of Brazil, which convened its first synod in 1888 but was subject to a schism in 1903 when some members, in opposition to what they saw as growing modernism, left the parent Church to form the Independent Presbyterian Church of Brazil, which maintains a strong, evangelistic programme. In recent years the expansion of this group has been rapid and there are currently more than 150 community service ministries, or social projects, run by the Church. In 1986 a theological college, the Fortaleza Theological Seminary, was opened for the training of pastors and lay leaders to work in north and north-east Brazil; until 1998 the office of pastor was restricted to men, but is now open to women. The 420 congregations, with around 55,000 adult members, are administered from the Church's headquarters in Recife, in north-east Brazil.

INDIAN SHAKER CHURCH

This Church is not to be confused with the United Society of Believers in Christ's Second Coming, *which is known as the* SHAKERS.

The Indian Shaker Church began as a movement in America amongst the American Indians of the north-west. An American Indian, John Slocum, a member of the ROMAN CATHOLIC CHURCH, from Squaxin Island, Washington, was a logger who was killed in an accident at his logging camp on Skookum Inlet. His two half-brothers, paddling to Olympia, Washington, to collect a coffin for John, returned to find that he had apparently come back to life and was speaking about his death, of how he had been refused entry to heaven and had been given the choice of going either straight to hell or returning to earth to preach the message of Jesus, a choice he did not, in the event, find hard to make.

In 1882 John and his followers built a cedar and tule mat (a type of bulrush matting) church at a site known as Church Point where he began to preach and hold services, founding his Church in the following year. When John's wife, Mary, had a shaking fit during a service this was seen as a manifestation of the working of the spirit of God, and from this the name *Shaker* was applied to the movement. Many congregations were formed, which were united in the late twentieth century, by which time there were some two thousand adherents, many from the Yakima Reservation on the north-west coast of the USA. In the 1960s the movement attracted much interest among young American Indians, particularly those living in north California.

The Church places a strong emphasis on healing through dance, using the *shuffle dance* and shaking in its rituals; it has been suggested that it is the rhythmic, semi-hypnotic dancing that induces a shaking spasm. The healing ceremonies take place during the regular services and are accompanied by the ringing of hand bells. There is a conventional belief in the Trinity, but the Church observes no sacraments or Christian festivals. The original upholding of the teachings contained in the scriptures gave way in time to a belief that the group was receiving divine revelations. From this a schism occurred, one group leaving the Indian Shaker Church to join with some Bible-based evangelicals. The Church insists on its members leading upright, moral lives and lays an emphasis on the importance of honesty and sobriety.

INDONESIAN CHRISTIAN CHURCH OF CENTRAL JAVA

A Church, belonging to the LUTHERAN World Federation, which was founded in 1945. In 1962, it merged with the Indonesian Christian Churches in East and West Java. This particular Church was founded amongst Chinese immigrants but is now moving towards a greater multi-ethnicity.

INSTITUTE OF ESOTERIC TRANSCENDENTALISM

An American group that was founded in 1956, in Los Angeles, California, by Robert W. C. Burke and known at first as the Robert Burke Foundation. In 1969 it united with another group, known as *Christology*, and was renamed as the Institute of Esoteric Transcendentalism. There is no formal statement of belief and members are free to hold divergent religious beliefs. The purpose of the group is to study Christology, the science of the knowledge of Jesus Christ, which they explore through the recorded words of Jesus Christ alone. Everything else in the Bible is regarded as history, or simply as stories that guide and inspire. The members are taught that man has divine power within himself, which he mostly misuses; it is through a growing intellectual awareness, attained through study and meditation, that he can correct this by eventually gaining complete self-awareness.

INTERNATIONAL CHRISTIAN MINISTRIES

An ex-member of the ASSEMBLIES OF GOD, Duane Peterson, started this American movement in the 1970s with the distribution of ten thousand copies of a free Christian newspaper, *Hollywood Free Paper*. Circulation increased with each issue, attracting many new members, and new ministries were formed, working through Bible study groups, emergency switchboards for those in trouble and needing help, and drug counselling operations. In 1972 the movement was known as Jesus People International, later changing to its current name. The movement spread across America and affiliated groups were formed in many cities. The headquarters was in Venice, California, where the

Venice Bible Church's Chapel by the Sea was opened.

INTERNATIONAL CHURCH OF THE FOURSQUARE GOSPEL

The founder of the International Church of the Foursquare Gospel, a PENTECOSTAL group, was *Sister* Aimée Semple McPherson (1890–1944), a Canadian by birth. Her mother was a devout member of the SALVATION ARMY who wanted her daughter to join its ministry, but a Baptist minister, Robert J. Semple, whom she married in 1908, converted Aimée. They went as missionaries to China but Robert Semple died of malaria in Hong Kong. Aimée, now with a daughter of her own, returned to Canada and entered a second marriage, in 1912, to Harold McPherson, a drug store owner, but the marriage failed and they were later divorced; a third marriage, in 1931, also ended in divorce. Aimée, who kept the surnames of her first two husbands, went to Los Angeles in 1918 and began an evangelistic preaching tour of the USA, attracting much attention and not a little criticism, especially from those who did not like to see women in the pulpit. So successful was the work, however, that by 1922 Aimée's followers had financed the building of the Angelus Temple in Los Angeles, to the tune of $1.5 million. Her charismatic message attracted many listeners; some may also have come to see the performance of this flamboyant and unusual lady who was known to adopt unlikely costumes, appearing at one time dressed in football kit and riding a motorcycle. The Angelus Temple was dedicated in 1923, with a thousand-strong choir singing *Open the Gates of the Temple*. It was at the Angelus Temple that Aimée preached the *Foursquare Gospel of Jesus Christ*, making many of the same points as those made by A. B. Simpson of the CHRISTIAN AND MISSIONARY ALLIANCE. At this time the movement was known as the Evangelistic Association, taking its present name in 1927. Aimée also founded the Echo Park Evangelistic and Training Institute, to train Church leaders, and the L.I.F.E. Bible College, as well as the first Church-owned radio station in the USA, KFSG, which operated out of Los Angeles. A strong missionary programme was established, which now operates in nearly eighty countries worldwide.

Doctrinally, Aimée Semple McPherson's message must be described as FUNDAMENTALIST, ADVENTIST, PERFECTIONIST and Pentecostal, with the emphasis on Jesus Christ as saviour, as baptizer (with the Holy Spirit and the gift of tongues following), as healer and as the coming king (REVELATION 20). Baptism and the Lord's Supper are observed as ordinances and the Bible is regarded as the infallible, inerrant and inspired word of God. The Church is administered by a board of governors under the direction of a president, with an annual convention deciding on legislative matters.

After returning from a tour of the Holy Land and Great Britain, Aimée Semple McPherson died, possibly from a heart attack, although a barbiturate overdose has also been suggested as the cause of her death. In keeping with her extraordinary life, which included an alleged kidnapping in 1926, when she went missing for five weeks, and other colourful episodes that often involved legal suits against her, Aimée's funeral was less than ordinary. Twelve pall bearers took twenty minutes to move the 1200 lb bronze casket the few hundred yards to her grave in Forest Lawn Cemetery, Los Angeles, the procession passing a 600-feet floral cross. Her influential writings include *This Is That* (1923), *In the Service of the King* (1927) and *Give Me My Own God* (1936).

❖ Evangelistic Association

INTERNATIONAL CHURCHES OF CHRIST

This Church is not to be confused with the CHURCH OF CHRIST.

The International Churches of Christ, an ultra-evangelical American group, developed from a controversial campus ministry, known as the Crossroads Church of Christ, that was operating in Gainesville, Florida in the 1970s. One of the members, Kip McKean, moved to Boston in 1979 and established there the Boston Church of Christ and it was from this that the International Churches of Christ was developed. Individual churches adopt the name of their city or town, calling themselves, for example, the Boston Church of Christ.

A distinctive feature of the movement is the system of *discipling* (or shepherding) that is employed, each *discipler* responsible for helping members from a lower level move up through the Church hierarchy; the discipler has considerable authority over the disciple, which extends as far as examining the disciple's lifestyle and personal relationships. Some members choose to live in a communal house and can be encouraged to mix only with other Church members, a matter which has given rise to controversy. Methods of recruitment are described as over-aggressive and pervasive and have led to the Church being banned from some university campuses.

The doctrine of the International Churches of Christ, which believes itself to be the only true Church, is evangelical with a strong emphasis on faith, obedience, confession, repentance and baptism; all new recruits are baptized, whether or not they come to the group as baptized Christians. Confession of sins, which is made to the discipler, or to another member, is not regarded as secret and individual sins are sometimes written on a *sin list*, which can be seen by the community. The movement claims some 110,000 committed members worldwide, distributed among 113 countries.

INTERNATIONAL PENTECOSTAL CHURCH OF CHRIST

This American Church belongs to the PENTECOSTAL tradition and has its present headquarters in London, Ohio. It was formed in 1976 as a result of a merger of the International Pentecostal Assembles (formed 1936) and the Pentecostal Church of Christ (PCC; founded 1917). The International Pentecostal Assemblies came about through the union of two earlier Pentecostal groups, which had been founded in 1914 and 1921.

The founding bishop of the PCC was John Stroup who, in South Solon, Ohio, in 1908, underwent a baptism of the Holy Spirit with *glossolalia*, or speaking in tongues. This young evangelist preached in south-east Ohio, Kentucky and West Virginia, organizing many congregations in the course of his itinerant ministry. In 1917, at Advance, Kentucky, some Pentecostal ministers met and decided to found the Pentecostal Church of Christ, appointing John Stroup to be its leader and bishop. The Church was incorporated at Portsmouth, Ohio, ten years later.

Doctrinally, the Church places a strong emphasis upon divine healing, the premillennial return of Christ to earth (REVELATION 20) and the observance of Sunday as the sabbath. Two ordinances are recognized, those of baptism and the Lord's Supper, with foot-washing performed as an option. There are congregations in eleven states in the USA.

The polity of the Church is congregational and its work is coordinated by a general overseer, whose election is for a period of two years. Like the merging bodies, this Church is heavily committed to missionary work and currently maintains missions in Mexico, Brazil, India, Kenya, the Philippines and Uruguay.

INTERNATIONAL PENTECOSTAL HOLINESS CHURCH

A movement started by Benjamin Hardin Irwin, an American who had experienced sanctification through the, largely METHODIST, Iowa Holiness Association, which had been formed in 1879. He became interested in the 'baptism of burning love' that had been described in the writings of John Fletcher, the noted eighteenth-century divine.

Irwin claimed that he had received the baptism of Fire, or the third blessing, about which he began to teach and preach, attracting considerable controversy and criticism. The movement began to spread through the mid-west and southern parts of America, and by 1895 Irwin had formed the Fire-Baptized Holiness Association (National), with Irwin elected as its general overseer.

The following year, four missionaries from the association went to Cuba to begin the Church's missionary activity and in the same year the first women from this movement were ordained. As new state-wide organizations followed, Irwin was able to supervise the convening of the first general convention of the Fire-Baptized Holiness Association in 1898, at Anderson, South Carolina. In the meantime a Methodist minister, A. B. Crumpler from North Carolina, received the second blessing, or sanctification experience, through the ministry of Beverly Carradine, a Southern Methodist preacher, and was persuaded to leave the Methodist Church in 1899. The following year he formed the Pentecostal Holiness Church at Fayetville, North Carolina.

In 1902 the Fire-Baptized Holiness Association changed its name, dropping Association and substituting Church in its place. At this point Irwin left the Church and handed over its organization and running to another former Methodist minister, J. H. King. In 1907 King was introduced to PENTECOSTAL revivalism, including *glossolalia*, or speaking in tongues, and this experience, despite its controversial nature, was accepted by the FIRE-BAPTIZED HOLINESS CHURCH (WESLEYAN) a year later. The Fire-Baptized and the Pentecost Holiness Churches merged in 1911, retaining the name of the latter, and were joined in 1915 by the Tabernacle Pentecostal Church from Georgia. It was not until 1975 that the Church adopted the present full title of International Pentecostal Holiness Church.

The Church insists that the baptism of the Holy Spirit, signified by speaking in tongues, is a third blessing and is therefore available only to those who have undergone the other two blessings of justification and sanctification. Directly derived from the HOLINESS movement, the Independent Pentecostal Holiness Church retains its Methodist heritage, with its doctrinal position based upon the Methodist *Articles of Religion* (1784). The

Church puts an emphasis on divine healing, but does not prevent a member from seeking conventional medical attention; there is also an emphasis upon the second coming of Christ (REVELATION 20).

The polity of the Church is based upon the Methodist pattern, with a four-yearly general conference and a series of annual conferences; there are also regional judicatories, or conferences, held in North America, Europe, Africa, Australasia and Latin America. Missions are maintained in many countries throughout the world, providing evangelism, health, nutrition and education. In North America the Church runs the Falcon Children's Home, an Alternative to Abortion ministry for girls and women in crisis pregnancies and the New Life Adoption ministry. Older people in need are catered for at Carmen House in Oklahoma. Educational institutions have been opened to provide a full network of undergraduate and graduate accredited courses. The headquarters of the Church, which was at Franklin Springs, Georgia, moved to Oklahoma City in 1974.

ITALO-ALBANIAN CATHOLIC CHURCH

This Eastern, or Byzantine-rite, Church has been under the jurisdiction of Rome since the sixth century, except for a four hundred–year period from 731. Greek colonies had for many years before the birth of Christ been established in Sicily and southern Italy; the provinces of Calabria and Apulia were known historically as Magna Graecia. Members of this Church may be descendants of Greek colonists in southern Italy and Sicily from the fifteenth and sixteenth centuries, as well as of Albanian refugees who migrated to southern Italy to escape the Turkish invasion of the Balkan lands and who maintained their own rites, language and customs. In 1742 Pope Benedict XIV issued the constitution *Etsi Pastoralis*, asserting the validity of the ancient Italo-Greek-Albanian rite and declaring that the Latin rite should not be thought of as taking precedence over the Byzantine. In 1919, Pope Benedict XV constituted a separate eparchy for the Byzantines of Calabria, with its see at Lungro, near Cosenza. A further, separate, eparchy was set up in 1937 at Piana degli Albanesi, near Palermo, Sicily. These two eparchies, or provinces, constitute the Italo-Albanian Catholic Church, while the monastery of Santa Maria at Grottaferrata, which was established by St Nilus of Rossano (*c.* 908–1004) and is the only Italo-Greek monastery to have survived of some three hundred founded, was given the status of a territorial abbey whose abbot may exercise jurisdiction like that of a diocesan bishop. The abbey attracts many vocations from the Italian-Albanian community.

The Italo-Albanian Catholic Church has no parishes in the English-speaking world, but the identity of the small, immigrant communities in these areas has been preserved by such groups as the Italo-Albanian-Byzantine Rite Society of Our Lady of Grace which was founded in 1947 and is based on Staten Island, New York. The purpose of this society was to establish the Italo-Greek-Albanian rite in the USA and it sponsors the celebration of the Divine Liturgy in various churches within the metropolitan district of New York. The liturgical language used in the celebration of the Divine Liturgy is Greek and there is provision for a *low*, or recited, celebration.

❖ Italo-Greek Church; Italo-Greek-Albanian Church

J

JACOBITES

The name, Jacobites, was given to a group of Syrian MONOPHYSITES for the first time by the Second Council of Nicaea (787), naming them after Jacob, bishop of Edessa (nicknamed Baradaeus, meaning 'clothed in rags', from his ragged appearance), who died in 578. Jacob had been born near Antioch into a priestly family and was consecrated clandestinely as bishop in *c.* 542, with the encouragement of the Empress Theodora who was sympathetic to the Monophysite cause he espoused. With the aim of avoiding the attention of the imperial forces and the wrath of the Emperor Justinian, who opposed this teaching, Jacob adopted the torn and ragged dress of a poor beggar as he wandered throughout the Middle East, spreading the Monophysite heresy with enthusiasm. This came at a time when Monophysitism, whose followers rejected the conclusion of the Council of Chalcedon (451) concerning the two natures of Jesus Christ, was not prospering, mainly because of internal wrangling but also because of the recent death of their leader, Severus (*c.* 465–538). Following the Arab invasion of Syria in the mid-seventh century, many Monophysites converted to Islam and when the ROMAN CATHOLIC CHURCH was established in Syria, during the seventeenth century, yet more chose to become Roman Catholics. The word 'Jacobite' is also used to describe Monophysite Christians in Egypt.

JANSENISM (also JANSENIST; JANSENISTS)

The Jansenists were followers of Cornelius Otto Jansen (1585–1638), Bishop of Ypres from 1636, who studied at the Universities of Louvain and Paris where he met Jean du Vergier de Haranne who became Abbot of Saint-Cyran. Jansen immersed himself in the works of St Augustine and both he and the abbot saw that their mission in life was to reshape ROMAN CATHOLICISM through the teaching of St Augustine. Jansen's work produced a treatise *Augustinus*, which effectively undercut the sacramental and hierarchical claims of the counter-Reformation Church. His propositions resembled CALVINISM with its views on free will, predestination, moral asceticism, the sacraments, hierarchy and the mission of the Church. Jansen attracted many followers, including Angelique Arnauld, the Abbess of the Cistercian convent of Port Royal, which had been founded in 1204 south-west of Paris, and the convent became a Jansenist centre. The abbess's brother, Antoine, succeeded as Abbot of

Saint-Cyran in 1643 and he became a spokesman for Jansenism.

The moral impact of Jansen's ideas was felt strongly in a corrupt age, and his propositions were subjected to the scrutiny of scholars at the Sorbonne University in Paris. In 1649, the university issued a censure of Jansen's propositions and sent them to Rome where Pope Innocent X condemned them in his Bull *Cum Occasione.* Jansen's ideas continued to be condemned, notably by Pope Clement XI in 1713, in his decree *Unigenitus,* which was directed at over a hundred propositions made by Pasquier Quesnel, a Jansenist leader. Jansenists were persecuted throughout France, with many fleeing to Holland where their ideas were tolerated. The Dutch Jansenists nominated as their archbishop the schismatic, Old Catholic (Church) Bishop of Utrecht, Cornelius van Steenoven, who was consecrated in 1724 but died the following year. Jansenism also flourished in Tuscany, Italy, where it was supported by the strongly anti-papal climate encouraged by Grand Duke Leopold.

❖ Cyranists

JAPAN COVENANT CHRISTIAN CHURCH

The Church originated from a mission established in the USA in 1885 by the Swedish Mission Covenant Church, which had been founded in Sweden in 1878. Missionaries from the American Church were sent to Japan after the Second World War and the first product of their work in Tokyo was the establishment, in 1952, of the Covenant Seminary; a vigorous programme of church planting in Tokyo, Kanagawa, Gunma and Niigata followed. At the outset there were two groups running in parallel, with one led by American missionaries and the other by Japanese pastors, and in 1967 they merged to form the Japanese Covenant Christian Church, the work largely centred in the Kanto area.

The polity and doctrinal position of the Church is best described as congregational. It is responsible for the Odawara Christian Centre, located in Odawara City, where Bible courses are taught in both Japanese and English and worship services are conducted in English. The Akagi Bible Camp, located on top of Mt Akagi in Gunma and available for people of all ages in the summer months, is also in the care of the Church. The Covenant Seminary offers both night and part-time courses as well as full-time day classes, designed to provide education for lay leadership and also ministerial training; in addition there is a two-year research programme for continuing theological education.

JAPAN EVANGELICAL LUTHERAN CHURCH

Some missionaries from an American Lutheran group, the United Synod of the South (formed 1865), were sent to Japan in the latter part of the nineteenth century. Two of these missionaries, James A. B. Scherer and R. B. Peery, held the first worship service in the city of Saga, Kyushu, during Easter 1893, assisted by a local co-worker, Ryohei Yamanuchi. The advent of the Second World War sent western missionaries from the country, but they returned in force during the period after the war, leading to a great flowering of Christian denominations in Japan. In 1963, two of the Lutheran groups joined with six established missions to form the Japan Evangelical Lutheran Church (JELC), with other Lutheran groups continuing their independent existence.

The JELC has a small membership of around 7,000 adult believers in 155 congregations, but despite the low numbers the Church has sent missionaries to serve amongst Japanese expatriates in Brazil and the USA. The pastors are trained at the Lutheran Seminary in Tokyo. Education has always been a matter of concern to the JELC and in 1911 it established the Kyushu Gakuin High School, originally established for the education of boys but now co-educational, where the education is aimed at providing future pastors and lay workers for the Church. A girls' school, the Kyushu Jogakuin High School, was opened in 1925 and the Kyushu Lutheran College, accredited for the granting of degrees, in 1997.

The Church has established two pioneer institutions in the field of social welfare, a House of Mercy in Kumamoto and the Tokyo House for the Elderly. Members also work in the provision of childcare, learning and community projects, including help for those living in slum conditions. Workers in these sensitive fields train at the Japan Lutheran Theological College in Tokyo. The JELC and the Evangelical Lutheran Church of America exchange personnel and visits, and a companion synod has been established between the JELC and the Evangelical Lutheran Church of America (South Carolina Synod) that forges a strong relationship between the two countries. This is designed to strengthen the mutual work of the member Churches through prayer, study, communication and the exchange of pastors, leaders and resources.

JAPAN LUTHERAN CHURCH – MISSOURI SYNOD

This Church, whose initials are NRK (corresponding to its name in Japanese) should not be confused with the Japan Evangelical Lutheran Church.

The Church was begun by the Japan Mission of the American Lutheran Church-Missouri Synod in 1948 and from its inception was intended to be self-governing. It was not until 1970, however, that it finally achieved this status and it took a further six years before it was able to be self-supporting. Its determination to become independent of the missionaries was underlined when, in the 1970s, the Japan Mission suffered a serious internal conflict which affected the NRK and resulted in the withdrawal of the missionaries; it was feared that the NRK would disband as a result. The withdrawal of these missionaries resulted in the closure of three churches in Niigata and the shrinking of three congregations in Sapparo and Hokkaido into one.

About half the congregations are fully self-supporting with the others, mainly small rural churches, helped by the NRK headquarters. The Tokyo Seminary in Mitaka, which is run jointly by the Japan Evangelical Lutheran Church and the Japan Lutheran Church, provides theological education.

JAPAN ORTHODOX CHURCH

This Church arose in Japan through the early missionary efforts of a priest of the Russian Orthodox Church, Fr (later St) Nicholas Kasatkin, who brought the Orthodox faith to Hakodate in 1861, where he had been appointed chaplain to the Russian consulate. While he was there, Kasatkin mastered the Japanese language and translated scriptures and liturgical books into the vernacular. From Hakodate, Kasatkin moved around the country, taking the Orthodox faith to Senclai, Tokyo, Kansai, Kyoto, Osaka,

Kobe and finally to Kyushu. By the time of the outbreak of the Russo-Japanese war in 1904 there was an Orthodox following of some 28,000 laity with 39 clergy, all but three of whom were Japanese. Kasatkin was created Archbishop of Tokyo in 1906 and died there in 1912; he was later *glorified*, or canonized, as St Nicholas Kasatkin Equal to the Apostles.

Kasatkin's successor, Metropolitan Sergei Tiklomiroff, set about consolidating the foundation laid by the archbishop, but the Church began to suffer from political and economic problems as well as both internal and external difficulties that arose from the 1917 Russian Revolution and the effect which that had on the Russian Orthodox Church. Metropolitan Sergei died in 1945, but not before signing over the property of the Russian mission into Japanese hands and appointing the archpriest, Heikichi Ivazava, as administrator of the Church. At the end of the Second World War the clergy and faithful established a relationship with the Russian Orthodox Metropolia, or ORTHODOX CHURCH IN AMERICA as it has been called since 1970.

The first Japanese Archbishop of Tokyo, John Ono, was appointed in 1941. His wife, the daughter of the first Japanese Orthodox priest, Paul Savabe, wanted to become a nun and husband and wife received the monastic habit together on the same day. The Church was granted autonomy in 1970, although the choice of metropolitan is still confirmed by the Patriarch of Moscow. There are three dioceses, the eastern Diocese of Sendai, the Archdiocese of Tokyo and the western Diocese of Kyoto. The head of the Japanese Orthodox Church, who resides in Tokyo, is known as His Eminence, the Archbishop of Tokyo, Metropolitan of All Japan.

❖ Holy Orthodox Church of Japan;
Orthodox Church in Japan

JEHOVAH'S WITNESSES

This Church is not regarded as conventionally Christian.

The name by which this group is now known was assumed in 1931 by the members of the Watch Tower Bible and Tract Society and the International Bible Students Association, both founded by Charles Taze Russell (1852–1916), the son of a clothing store chain owner in America. Russell was born in Pittsburgh, Pennsylvania, of Scottish-Irish Presbyterians and in 1870 he joined an ADVENTIST group led by Jonas Wendell, who had predicted that Christ would return to earth in 1874 (REVELATION 20). The failure of this prediction led Russell to reassess his beliefs and he organized this sect, which is millennialist and is based upon biblical literalism. It denies the divinity of Jesus Christ and traditional Trinitarian doctrines and cannot therefore properly be described as Christian. Russell affirmed the imminent end of the world for all, relying on data for his calculations not only from biblical evidence, as he understood it, but also from the internal measurements of the passageways in the great pyramid at Giza, Egypt. The *elect of Jehovah* (the 144,000 saved) were expected to survive to inherit the messianic kingdom.

The sect had its beginnings in Allegheny, Pennsylvania, as the Bible Students' Association. For a short time, in 1879, it was known as Zion's Watch Tower before it changed its name to the Watch Tower and Tract Society. This was not intended as a central organization for all the small congregations of Bible Students, since they were self-governing; the Society saw its function simply as a coordinating body. Charles Taze Russell died in 1916 and was succeeded as leader by James Franklin Rutherford (1869–1942), a Missouri circuit judge who, during the space of some twenty years, had written and published a considerable output of material that revised many of Russell's doctrines. He replaced the congregational structure with a less hierarchical organization in which all members were to sell and distribute, as door-to-door salesmen, Watch Tower literature; the profits were all to go into purchasing Kingdom Halls, in which the congregations of Witnesses gathered. Rutherford predicted that Abraham, Isaac and Jacob, together with the faithful prophets of old, would return physically to earth in 1925, before the battle of Armageddon, and in readiness for that event he purchased luxurious accommodation for them, known as Beth Sarim, in San Diego, California. In the interim it seemed only wise to Rutherford that he should live there when he was not at the Brooklyn headquarters in New York.

It was in 1931, at a convention in Columbus, Ohio, that the present title of the sect, Jehovah's Witnesses, was adopted. The rejection of Christ's divinity was replaced by a belief that he was originally Michael the archangel, born on 1 October 2 BC, and that he had lived and died as a mortal but is now an exalted figure. The Witnesses do not have a separate clergy, since all members are thought of as ministers and are expected to give personal witness and to distribute tracts and literature, such as the magazines *Awake* and *The Watch Tower*, from door-to-door. Members are pacifists and will not salute the national flag of any country, arguing that their membership of the theocratic kingdom precludes their allegiance to any country; this led to their suppression in Australia and New Zealand during the Second World War. They also refuse blood transfusions, although more recently the sect's attitude to these and to vaccinations has changed several times and any decision is now largely left to the individual.

The Witnesses observe mass baptism by immersion and there is provision for a springtime Lord's Supper, at which only the *elect* may receive Communion. Abstention from alcohol, dances, cinemas and theatres is expected of each member. Each country, or area, is overseen by a branch office and each branch is divided into districts and then into circuits; each circuit is made up of around twenty congregations. There is provision for two assemblies to be held annually for each circuit. An overseer is appointed whose duty it is to visit each congregation in his circuit at least twice a year. Members of a congregation are assigned to territories, which they are expected to visit regularly to bear witness and to sell their publications. The headquarters of the Jehovah's Witnesses is in Brooklyn, New York. Missions have been established in England, Germany, Africa, the Philippines and South America.

❖ Millennial Dawnists and International Bible Students; Russellites; Watch Tower and Tract Society; Zion's Watch Tower

JESUS FELLOWSHIP CHURCH

This evangelical, REFORMED and charismatic Church originated within the Baptist tradition. It was organized in England in 1969 by a Baptist minister,

Noel Stanton, and some fellow Baptists in Bugbrooke, south-west of Northampton. They had all received the baptism of the Holy Spirit and were speaking in tongues (*glossolalia*), healing and preaching charismatically, all of which persuaded them to organize themselves into a charismatic fellowship. This brought the men into conflict with the BAPTIST CHURCH and the group was expelled from the Baptist Union of Great Britain, later resigning, in 1986, from the Evangelical Alliance of Great Britain. Despite this, the theology of the group remains entirely orthodox, affirming a belief in the Trinity and in Christ's divinity and upholding the historical creeds.

As a result of their evangelism, the founders attracted many followers who brought with them money enough to purchase buildings and a farm, the *New Creation Farm*, which allowed the community to flourish. The leaders have been accused of *shepherding*, or appointing mentors to guide and direct other members of the community in every aspect of their lives. Up to one third of the members, who currently number around 2,500, live in community, where their incomes are pooled in a common purse. A part of this money is donated to a community trust fund, and is returnable, usually with interest, if a member leaves the group.

Life in the community can be seen as austere, since there is no television or radio, only Christian music played and only a few toys are provided for the children, who are subjected to a regime of strict discipline. Popular Christian festivals, like Easter and Christmas, are not celebrated, as these occasions are considered to be thinly disguised pagan festivals. People joining the group as members must be over 21 years of age and must spend two years as a probationer before entering the community permanently. The work of the Church is best described as aggressive evangelism, but there is also work undertaken amongst the homeless, with drug and alcohol addicts, and with prisoners and ex-prisoners.

❖ Jesus Army; Jesus Fellowship Army

JESUS MOVEMENT

A totally disorganized American movement that arose spontaneously in California in the hippie and flower power culture of the 1960s. House fellowships are formed and although the members are generally distrustful of organized Christianity, these may be loosely attached to a local evangelical church.

Early converts to the movement were expected to read a pamphlet called *The Four Spiritual Laws*, and having read it they were urged to accept its logic and sign in the appropriate space on the back page. This was taken as confirmation that the person was a Christian and was eligible to join the group. The style of preaching is loosely in the PENTECOSTAL, millennialist tradition (REVELATION 20). The CHILDREN OF GOD, a controversial sect with many followers in Europe and the USA, arose from the Jesus Movement.

❖ Jesus Freaks; Jesus Revolution

JESUS PEOPLE

The movement known as the Jesus People arose in America in the late 1960s, following hard on the era of hippiedom and flower power that began in California and spread widely. The movement began as a street ministry, offering people an alternative to the myriad eastern and occult groups that had arisen at that time, most of which were heavily involved with the drug culture that was attracting many young people. The simple messages broadcast by the Jesus People were instantly understandable. Activities that were guaranteed to appeal to the young, a mixture of rock festivals, rap sessions and preaching, brought in many converts and communes were set up. The message preached was one of hope for those who turned their backs on the evil world, ready to repent and accept the gifts of the Holy Spirit and the doctrine of the second coming (REVELATION 20). The movement spawned its imitators, such as the CHILDREN OF GOD, who are considered heretical by the Jesus People, and the CHRISTIAN FOUNDATION.

JESUS PEOPLE USA

The Jesus People USA was formed in 1969 by John and Dawn Herven as a JESUS PEOPLE group that would use the road network to carry the ministry throughout the country. The mobile ministry, which included a rock band called *Resurrection*, travelled from location to location, preaching and holding evening meetings wherever they stopped. The preaching was accompanied by dramatic offerings from the Holy Ghost Players.

JEZREELITES

A small English sect founded in Gillingham, Kent, in 1875 by James White (1849–85), a private soldier in the British Army who later changed his name to James Jershom Jezreel. He preached the view that Christ would redeem only souls, since the body is saved only by a belief in the law of God as given in the Old Testament. Members of the group aspired to become part of the 144,000 *elect* who, according to Revelation 7:4, would be given immortal bodies at the last judgement (REVELATION 20).

Thinking that Christ's return to earth was imminent, the Jezreelites believed that they would ascend to the New Jerusalem by an edifice they built for that purpose. This was known as the tower of Jezreel and was a familiar sight in Gillingham; in later years, long after the Church of the Jezreelites had become defunct, it served as a bus terminal.

An American continuation of the sect was founded in the late nineteenth century, known as the HOUSE OF DAVID. This is still in existence, but now has very few members.

❖ The New and Latter House of Israel

JUDAIZERS

A section of Jewish Christians in the early Church who insisted on the acceptance and observance of the Old Testament Levitical laws as necessary for salvation and believed that they should be imposed on any Gentile convert. Their insistence upon circumcision and the distinction between clean and unclean meat, for example, was refuted by St Paul, as evidenced in his writings.

JUMPERS

A nickname given to WELSH CALVINIST METHODISTS in the nineteenth century who were noted for their frenzied response to revivalist preaching. Members of the congregation would jump about, shouting *Amen* and *Glory*, or *Gogoniant*, before falling down exhausted. They cited biblical evidence for this behaviour by quoting 2 Samuel 6:16 and Luke 6:23. The name was also given to another nineteenth-century group, the WALWORTH JUMPERS, and to a group of Russian schismatics, the MOLOKAN SPIRITUAL CHRISTIANS.

K

KEHUKEE ASSOCIATION OF NORTH CAROLINA

At one of the regular meetings of the members of the Association of American BAPTISTS, which was held at Fishing Creek, North Carolina, in 1826, a Baptist elder, Martin Ross, proposed that they should support the General Missionary Convention of the Baptist Denomination in the United States for Foreign Missions (founded 1814). Most Baptists favoured the work of the missionary societies and boards but Joshua Lawrence, of the Kehukee (Baptist) Association, published a *Declaration of Principles*, arguing against this work. The result, after some debate, was that it was agreed that the Kehukee Association would have nothing to do with missionary societies, Bible societies or theological seminaries and would not give them their financial support.

There was considerable readjustment amongst those churches that supported a missionary cause, both inside and outside the Kehukee Association. Several supported the Kehukee position and a new body, the Contentea Association, was formed around the Kehukee position. In time those congregations that were opposed to the missionary societies and their support arrived at the conviction that they were the *true*, or *primitive*, Baptists. This marked the start of the Primitive Baptist Associations that by the 1840s had spread throughout America.

KENTUCKY MOUNTAIN HOLINESS ASSOCIATION

The Association was organized in the USA in 1925 by a deaconess of the METHODIST EPISCOPAL CHURCH, Lela G. McConnell, who began her ministry in the mountains of eastern Kentucky. McConnell's preaching emphasized sanctification, as a follow-on from justification, or being *born again*, as part of the HOLINESS tradition; her theology was otherwise entirely that outlined in the Methodist *Twenty-Five Articles of Religion* of 1784.

The Association has been very successful and has maintained missions in many countries. A summer camp is held annually at Camp Lewis, Kentucky, for a week following 4 July. In 1931, the Kentucky Mountain Bible College was founded, receiving its accreditation in 1990 and now offering a four-year bachelor of arts programme and a two-year associate of arts course which provides training opportunities for future ministers, missionaries and lay leaders.

KINKI EVANGELICAL LUTHERAN CHURCH

This Japanese Church, with its headquarters in Osaka, is a member of the Lutheran World Federation and was started in 1951 by the Norwegian Missionary Society (NMS) and the Lutheran Free Church of Norway (LFCN), which was forced out of China by the communists in 1950. Both the NMS and the LFCN began their work in the Kinki area, in south-eastern Japan, during the 1950s when they managed some fourteen congregations, but difficulties soon developed for both Norwegian missions in supporting missionaries in the Far East and soon moves for self-government and self-support for the Kinki Evangelical Lutheran Church (KELC) began. By the end of 1995 one of the Church's ventures, the Kinki Radio Ministry, called *The Lutheran Hour*, was forced to close because of financial difficulties.

The KELC has tried to encourage women to become pastors in spite of opposition from the Norwegian missions. Although church growth has been poor in recent years, there is now hope that new mission stations at Mie and Osaka will become established as congregations. Work with youth, and support for a kindergarten of the Evangelical Lutheran Church of Hong Kong continues, as does the Kairos Communication Service that broadcasts to mainland China and to Japanese laity working in Norway, and which is used as a means of extending the influence of this small LUTHERAN CHURCH. There are currently around 1,100 adult members distributed in 31 congregations.

KIRIBATI PROTESTANT CHURCH

The headquarters of this large CONGREGATIONALIST Church in the now-independent republic of Kiribati (formerly the Gilbert Islands, part of the British Crown colony of the Gilbert and Ellice Islands) is at Tangintebu, Tarawa.

The first wave of missionary work in the islands was undertaken by Hiram Bingham of the American Board of Commissioners for Foreign Missions (ABCFM) when a mission station was opened at Abaiang in 1856. Missionary work in the Ellice Islands had also been undertaken by Samoan missionaries and with the aid of J. S. White of the London Missionary Society (LMS). In 1917, the ABCFM formally handed over their area of control to the LMS. After certain ethnic tensions caused a split in the Church, two autonomous Churches emerged in 1968, one serving the Gilbert Islands (now Kiribati) and known as the Kiribati Protestant Church, and the other providing for the Ellice Islands (now Tuvalu) and called the Tuvalu Church. The Kiribati Protestant Church applied successfully to join the World Council of Churches in 1972.

The early educational and medical work undertaken by the LMS has been continued by the government of Kiribati, leaving only one primary Church school and a teacher training college still under Church control.

KNIPPERDOLLINGS

The name of this German sect comes from that of its leader, Bernard Knipperdolling, or Knipperdollinck (1490–1536), a cloth merchant who joined the ANABAPTISTS in Münster in 1533/4 along with Bernard Rothmann, a LUTHERAN Their decision to join was prompted by the arrival in Münster of some of the disciples of the widely travelled and influential Melchior Hofmann who had been responsible for the spread of

Anabaptist teachings in Lower Germany and the Netherlands. Münster at that time was also the home of two prominent Anabaptist citizens, Jan Matthys (or Matthiessen), a former baker, and John Bockelsohn (or Bockold), a Dutch tailor who was also known as John of Leyden.

Knipperdolling was elected as *Bürgermeister* at the start of 1534 and the city soon found itself under the control of the Anabaptists. Knipperdolling and his followers made Münster the centre for the founding of the *New Jerusalem*, which called for the reconstruction of society, both ecclesiastical and civil. As a result, there followed the wholesale destruction of art and literature and wild rumours circulated in the city telling of orgies and polygamy, particularly targeted at Bernard Rothmann and Jan Bockelsohn, who were both said to have many wives, four in the case of Rothmann and an amazing sixteen for Bockelsohn. The Bishop of Münster, Francis of Waldeck, who was also temporal lord of the city, laid siege in 1534 and Münster fell to him in 1535. Knipperdolling, Jan Bockelsohn and another city official, Krechting, were arrested, imprisoned and tortured with red-hot pincers before being executed, their bodies suspended in iron cages from the tower of the church of St Lambert.

KODESH CHURCH OF IMMANUEL

This small American Church, in the HOLINESS tradition, was intended to be an inter-racial Church, but most of its 600 members, distributed between 10 churches, are black.

The Reverend Frank Russell Killingworth of the AFRICAN METHODIST EPISCOPAL CHURCH founded the Church in 1929. With around 120 others, most of whom were members, Killingworth later seceded to form another Church. Doctrinally, the group is Wesleyan and ARMINIAN, stressing entire sanctification with baptism of the Holy Spirit and premillennialism (REVELATION 20). Divine healing plays an important part in the life of the Church, although conventional medical aid is not proscribed.

Being within the HOLINESS tradition, members are expected to abstain from alcohol, drugs, tobacco, membership of secret societies, fashionable dress, dancing and theatrical performances that might be described as *dubious*. Members also avoid working on the sabbath. Divorce is recognized in cases involving adultery. Water baptism is observed, but the mode of administration is left for the individual, or family, to decide. Although the Church members are few in number they support a missionary station in Liberia, West Africa that was opened in 1956 and is still flourishing. The churches of this denomination, which are found in Pittsburgh and Philadelphia, are under the care of ministers who are elected and ordained by annual assemblies; ministers and their congregations are supervised by elders who are elected and consecrated by the quadrennial general assemblies, which are responsible for directing the Church in its various undertakings. In 1934 there was a merger with the Christian Tabernacle Union of Pittsburgh.

KOINONIA PARTNERS

The group began as an experiment in communal living on a four hundred-acre farm, called Koinonia, in Georgia, USA. Clarence and Florence Jordan, together with another couple, started the commune in 1942, with an emphasis on brotherhood and peace. Their aim was also to introduce modern farming methods to the local farming community, but it was not long before they faced much hostility from the farmers, not least because the Koinonia commune included black members who were allowed the full rights of all other members at a time when the southern states of the USA found this unacceptable. Violence erupted in the 1950s, with scenes of beatings and bombings, and the farm commune was forced to rethink its role.

In 1968 the Koinonia Partnership was created. After the death of Clarence Jordan in 1969, a collective leadership was established and a new phase of growth then focused on communicating its message to a larger, worldwide audience. Its message is contained in the *Cotton Patch Version of the New Testament*, which was published as separate pamphlets and is an attempt at retelling the New Testament in the modern idiom. The farm, which grows and markets pecan nuts, is also supported through the production of handicrafts, books and tapes. Most of the resident members work on the farm and the profits that come through their efforts are channelled into charitable operations that help with low cost housing, job creation and support for the poor.

KOREA, ANGLICAN CHURCH OF

The only specifically ANGLICAN missionary work in Korea, prior to the arrival in 1890 of Charles John Corfe who had been consecrated in Westminster Abbey in London in 1889 as the first diocesan Bishop of Chosun (Korea), had been run by two Chinese lay evangelists who had arrived in the country in 1880. When the bishop arrived, together with several others, he immediately began his work in the Seoul area and in the provinces of Kyung-gi and Chung-cheong. Under his direction, and that of his successors, a number of educational institutions, medical facilities and social work centres were opened. These included the Shinmyoung (Faith and Enlightenment) Schools as well as hospitals and orphanages and St Michael's Theological Institute for the training of local clergy, which later became the Songgonghoe (Anglican) University, was fully accredited in 1982 and has now been expanded and upgraded.

Korea was occupied by the Japanese from 1910 to 1945 and missionary work during this period was very slow, but following independence the work continued and in 1965 the first native Korean bishop was consecrated. The original mission diocese was divided into two, that of Seoul, under the control of the first Korean bishop, and Taejon, which was administered by the last English bishop; in 1974 a further diocese, Pusan, was created, by which time all the bishops were Korean. There was a rapid expansion of the Church's work during the 1970s and there are now around 100 parishes and mission churches with about 50,000 adult members. Religious communities have also been established, the Society of the Holy Cross at Seoul (1925), the Benedictine Sisters at Pusan (1993) and the Korean Franciscan Brotherhood at Inchon (1994). In 1993 the Archbishop of Canterbury installed Simon S. Kim as primate, having approved the provisional constitution of the Anglican Church of Korea six months previously.

KOREAN CHRISTIAN CHURCH IN JAPAN

The Church, which is doctrinally and organizationally in the PRESBYTERIAN tradition, was started by the Young Men's

Christian Association (YMCA) in 1908 at a time when that association had a mission relationship with the Presbyterian Church in Canada (PCC) and with other Churches in Korea including the KOREAN METHODIST CHURCH.

At the time of the Japanese takeover of Korea in 1910, many Koreans went to Japan and by the 1920s were to be found in such numbers in most major Japanese cities that the formation and organization of congregations was needed. A Canadian couple, Luther and Miriam Young, who were fluent in the language having worked for some years in Korea, undertook this task. In 1927, the Federal Council of Churches and Missions in Korea asked the PCC to appoint the Youngs as overseers of this work in Japan. The growth of the work was considerable, but in time a more structured organization was needed and this was achieved by the gathering together of the many congregations into the Independent Korean Church of Japan, with churches in Tokyo, Osaka and Kobe. The pastors and missionaries still included many Canadians and these were expelled from the country during the Second World War. The Japanese imperial government insisted that the smaller PROTESTANT Churches should then either unite, or be disbanded, with the result that the Korean Christian Church in Japan merged with others to become the UNITED CHURCH OF CHRIST. The use of the Korean language, in church services and preaching, was forbidden upon pain of arrest.

The Korean congregations withdrew from this imposed merger once the war was over, reorganized as the Korean Christian Church in Japan (KCCJ) and resumed its association with the PCC. The Youngs were invited to return to Japan, but under hard conditions. As the Church was regarded as foreign, no government money was available for the restoration of church buildings and the Board of World Mission of the PCC, and the Women's Missionary Society, had to come to the rescue and provide what was needed.

The Church flourished, now has 73 congregations with around 4,000 adult members and is found throughout Japan. It is deeply involved in human rights issues, adult, child and kindergarten education centres and courses teaching the Korean language for the many people of Korean descent in the country. The Church has established the Korean Rainbow House, just south of Osaka, the Seniors' Centre and the Nagamine Group House, the latter for the care of adults with developmental problems. The headquarters of the Korean Christian Church in Japan is in Tokyo; it is a member of the World Council of Churches and the World Alliance of Reformed Churches.

KOREAN METHODIST CHURCH

First introduced to Korea by Japanese Christians, who came to the country as part of an invading force in the late sixteenth century, Christianity at first made little impact in the country and very few converts. It was not until the end of the nineteenth century, after the declaration of religious freedom, that missionaries arrived in Korea. The first PROTESTANT missionary, Suh Sang-Yun, was a Korean who had been converted by PROTESTANT Scots in Manchuria and he began to gather together the first group of worshippers. A METHODIST mission was organized by two American Methodist

Societies, working independently, and the first protestant school was opened in 1886; further waves of missionary work followed and between 1906 and 1910 there was a large increase in conversions, possibly due to a revivalist movement that had started in Wonson in 1903 and continued in Pyongyang in 1907. The missionaries organized Bible classes to train the laity so that they could help to spread the faith.

The PRESBYTERIANS and Methodists were in close cooperation until, in 1907, the Presbyterians established themselves as an independent body. The two Methodist Societies united to form the autonomous Korean Methodist Church in 1930, despite the hostile attitude of the Japanese authorities that had annexed Korea in 1910. The Reverend Yang Yu-Sam was elected as first general superintendent, a position similar to bishop, at the first general conference. Under his guidance the Church steered a careful course through the many difficulties and persecutions imposed on them by the authorities; revival meetings also helped to sustain the members through the difficult years of the 1930s. Liberation from Japanese control was achieved in 1945, at the end of the Second World War, but matters for the Church worsened, rather than improved, because of internal divisions. These were healed and by 1949 the Korean Methodist Church had reunited. The Korean war, in 1950, led to further hardships; many of the leaders were kidnapped and some executed by the North Korean army and many church buildings were destroyed. Today, the Korean Methodist Church sends missionaries throughout the world and aims to have a thousand such working in many countries by 2008. It is also actively involved in social reform and human rights, medical facilities and educational opportunities including literacy programmes. Aid is also given to rural agricultural workers and land reform and reclamation and there is support for those marginalized by society.

L

LABADISTS

Followers of Jean de Labadie (1610–74), a Frenchman born at Bourg, near Bordeaux, who was educated by the Jesuits, later joined the Order (the Society of Jesus) in 1625 and was ordained as a priest in 1635.

Labadie claimed to be possessed by the spirit of John the Baptist and, in imitation of him, would eat wild herbs and tried, for a time, to live in a wilderness until his health failed and he was obliged to leave the Jesuits in 1639. He became a secular priest and travelled widely, preaching in Paris, Bordeaux and Amiens. In 1644 Labadie founded the first of several small societies whose members were dedicated to living pious and devout lives; these societies can best be described as PIETIST on account of their emphasis on godliness. Finding himself in conflict with both the ecclesiastical and civil authorities, who did not relish the effect his words had on the population, Labadie withdrew for a time to a Carmelite monastery but his preaching, especially on mental prayer, attracted more attention. By now, Labadie was claiming to have been commanded by Jesus Christ directly and was ordered to change his name to Jean de Jésus-Christ. His preaching now included prophecies about the coming millennium, which he foretold would happen in 1666 (REVELATION 20). Now in even worse trouble with the authorities, Labadie was forced to flee to Montauban, in the south-west of France, in 1650 where he joined the Reformed Church and took up pastoral work before accepting a call to go to Flanders and to the Walloon church at Middleburg, in Zeeland. His stay there was short. Labadie refused to subscribe to the *Belgic Confession*, or to recognize the authority of the Reformed Church, and he was forced to leave the city. He went to the Netherlands, arriving in Amsterdam in 1669 in company with several followers. Here they formed a community of disciples dedicated to leading a communal life of purity, humility and penance, sharing their temporal goods and living in union of spirit. Members joining the group sold their properties, often abandoning their families as it was a stricture of the community that a marriage was not recognized unless both spouses became members. Many of Labadie's principles are outlined in a book, *Eucleria*, written by Anna Maria von Schurman, an artist especially well regarded for her glass decoration, who met Labadie while he was living in Amsterdam. In 1670, with some 55 followers, Labadie moved to

Herford in Westphalia but was once again forced by the authorities to withdraw. In 1672 he moved for the last time, going to Altona, near Hamburg, where he died in 1674.

The next year some 160 of his followers moved to West Friesland, where many new converts were made, increasing their number to about 400 and attracting attention and financial support. This reversal of fortune persuaded the group to expand into the missionary field and they sent members to Surinam, in South America, though their efforts there were fruitless. Two members, Jasper Dankers and Peter Sluyter, were sent to America to try to establish communities there in New York and New Jersey and as far south as Chesapeake in Virginia. In 1683, a community of about 100 people was started in Maryland, where the Labadists had received a grant of some 4,000 acres; this was known as Bohemia Manor and was for a time successful, before it disbanded in 1722 following the death of Peter Sluyter. The lifestyle of this community was reputed to have been harsh, the members living separately in unheated cells, with husbands and wives forbidden any display of affection between each other, and all meals eaten in silence. Members supported themselves by manual labour, growing the crops needed for their sustenance.

Labadists stressed the necessity of interior illumination by the Holy Ghost for the understanding of the Bible. The group was regarded as a community of holy persons who were *born again* free from sin and who alone could receive the sacraments. Infant baptism was not approved of and the Lord's Supper was celebrated very infrequently. Strangely, perhaps, their observance of the sabbath was very lax indeed.

LATTER HOUSE OF THE LORD FOR ALL PEOPLE AND THE CHURCH OF THE MOUNTAIN

An American sect founded in 1936 by a black, former BAPTIST, preacher from Cincinnati, Bishop L. W. Williams, following a spiritual experience. This persuaded Williams to found a Church that combined CALVINISTIC doctrine and PENTECOSTALISM.

At the celebration of the Lord's Supper water is used, instead of wine. Members of the Church are pacifists and are under the direction of the chief overseer, or bishop, who is elected for life.

LATTER RAIN MOVEMENT

A Canadian PENTECOSTAL movement that was started in North Battleford, Saskatchewan, after the end of the Second World War and was led by two ex-ASSEMBLIES OF GOD ministers, Hawtin and Hunt, and a former minister of the INTERNATIONAL CHURCH OF THE FOURSQUARE GOSPEL, Herrick Holt. In 1948, some students at a college in North Battleford were led by these men to experience a spiritual revival, in which the gifts of the Holy Spirit, which included prophecy and divine healing, were manifest. Several features of this revival caused some consternation amongst the leaders of the Assemblies of God; these included the use of laying on of hands to impart the gifts of the Holy Spirit and the rise of individual charismatic leaders through the phenomena of healing. The Assemblies of God also expressed concern about how the scriptures were being manipulated, with the extraction of parts of the text that were not acceptable. In 1949 the general council of the Assemblies of God was prompted to issue a resolution that condemned the movement.

The Pentecostal Assemblies of Canada and the Assemblies of God began to suffer defections of many pastors and their congregations as the Latter Rain movement gained in strength, Stretching out from central Canada to British Columbia in the west, and from Portland, Oregon, the movement soon consolidated across the USA.

LATVIA, EVANGELICAL LUTHERAN CHURCH OF

This Church, which is now a member of the World Council of Churches and the LUTHERAN World Federation, currently enjoys a committed membership of some 300,000, distributed within almost 300 congregations. Its membership in the late 1950s, of 600,000, fell sharply due to persecution at the time of the Soviet occupation. This pattern of persecution was similar to that employed at the time of the Second World War, when many congregations lost leaders, who were either executed or deported.

In 1987, many young and trained Lutheran theologians started the *Rebirth and Renewal Movement*, which was aimed at restoring parish life, and in 1985 the opportunity was seized to vote out the existing leadership of the Church and replace it with a more vigorous group of leaders recruited from this movement.

With the fall of communism, the Evangelical Lutheran Church of Latvia took advantage of the situation and started to rebuild its destroyed church buildings, establish mission centres and restore Sunday schools; the Church also urged the education authorities to introduce Christian education as part of the school curriculum.

The Church is now governed by a consistory made up of clergy and laity, elected by the synod, over which the archbishop acts as president. Clergy training is now undertaken at the recently established seminary, the Luther Academy, and in the theology faculty of the University of Latvia.

LATVIAN EVANGELICAL LUTHERAN CHURCH IN AMERICA

This Church emerged officially as a distinct denomination in 1975, having previously existed as the Federation of Latvian Evangelical Lutheran Churches in America since 1955. Its aim is to encourage the perseverance in the Lutheran faith of its 13,000 committed members, who are mostly Latvian refugees from the Soviet Union and their descendants. To that end, the Church emphasizes the importance of the holy scriptures, and the affirmation of the three creeds (Apostles', Nicene and Athanasian), and the unaltered *Augsburg Confession* and the *Small* and *Larger Catechisms* of Luther.

The Church is presided over by a synod, or general assembly with an executive board, and district conferences, which regulate church life locally. The headquarters of the Church is at Golden Valley, Minnesota. It has been a member of the Lutheran Council in the USA since 1982.

❖ Federation of Latvian Evangelical Lutheran Church in America

LATVIAN ORTHODOX CHURCH

Latvia, a country formerly known as Livonia, or Livland, came into contact with Orthodoxy through trade links with Kiev, capital of Ukraine. It is probable that the first Orthodox church in Latvia was established in the first half of the twelfth century, in a small town called Jersika (Gercike) from which a local ruler, Visivalois, controlled the area. Orthodoxy spread throughout the country, most likely with the help of missionaries from Pskov and other Christian centres. Late in the twelfth century an army from Germany vanquished the country and forced the inhabitants to adopt the faith of the ROMAN CATHOLIC CHURCH; this conversion was complete by 1215. With the establishment of trade links with Russia, merchants brought the Orthodox faith back to the area, and churches were opened in the great trading centres such as Riga, Jakobstad and Ilukste. The Russian tsar, Ivan IV, sent an Orthodox bishop to the country in *c.* 1474, to be responsible for the Orthodox faithful there.

Despite various military occupations, by Russians, German, Swedes, Poles, Lithuanians and others, the Orthodox faith survived and by the mid-nineteenth century there were around thirty parishes, using service books and catechisms which had been translated into Latvian. A theological seminary was established at Riga under Bishop Philaret (1805–66) and the progress of Orthodoxy was so rapid that by 1890 the number of churches had grown to 124. By 1920, after Latvia's independence had been proclaimed, the Church was granted autonomous status as the Latvian Orthodox Church, but under the jurisdiction of the Moscow patriarchate of the RUSSIAN ORTHODOX CHURCH.

Latvia suffered badly during both world wars, suffering a considerable loss of Church personnel and property. With the communist takeover after 1945 the Church was again targeted. The teaching of religion in schools was forbidden and the Orthodox cathedral in Riga was converted into a planetarium and coffee shop. By 1989 all church property had been appropriated by the state. Since 1991, when Latvia's independence was once more declared, the Church has been able to grow once more and has fully regained its independent status. There are now 110 active and major parish churches and cathedrals, with around 200,000 faithful members, and new parishes are being established in Ogre and Dagda, with others under construction. The head of the Latvian Orthodox Church, who is styled the Archbishop of Riga and All Latvia, has his headquarters in Riga.

LAY METHODIST CHURCH

A unique METHODIST group, formed in the Newcastle area of New South Wales, Australia, towards the end of the nineteenth century. The Church, which had no ordained ministers, was concerned with the many social issues of the time and placed considerable emphasis on the fight to combat the problems of drinking, gambling, dancing and the 'misuse' of Sunday. In an industrial centre like Newcastle, this presented the members with quite a challenge, but much good work went on. The Church lasted until the early 1950s.

LEHRERLEUT

The Lehrerleut grew from a group of American HUTTERITES who migrated to Parkston, South Dakota, in 1877, where they lived communally under the leadership of Jacob Wipf, an accomplished teacher, or *Lehrer*, from which the group's name is derived. The community slowly expanded into Montana, and later into Alberta in Canada. This is one of the more liberal of the Hutterite communities; buttons are used on clothing, which is forbidden in some other communities, but a link with German heritage is still maintained through the use of the High German language in preference to English. A Lehrerleut minister follows his congregation into the gathering place at the beginning of the service of worship.

LESOTHO EVANGELICAL CHURCH

An African Church, which owes its foundation, within the PROTESTANT and REFORMED tradition, to the arrival in 1833 of missionaries sent by the Paris Evangelical Missionary Society. The Church now has an affiliation with the UNITED CHURCH OF CANADA.

The Church has a clear ecumenical outlook and is a member of several alliances and councils, including the World Council of Churches. It is also heavily involved in providing education through primary, secondary and vocational training schools and it supports teacher training colleges, hospitals and a dispensary. The Church's autonomy was recognized in 1964, two years before Lesotho achieved its independence. There are at present around 100 congregations, catering for about 67,500 adult members. The headquarters of the Church is in the capital, Maseru.

❖ Fora

LEVELLERS

A defunct political and religious party in seventeenth-century England, which vigorously opposed the monarchy and argued that the powers held by monarchs should be transferred to the House of Commons. The members called for religious freedom and a wider extension of suffrage, which at the time was available to few. Their prominent leader was J. Lilburne (*c.* 1614–57) who was able to muster some support from the army. In 1647 Lilburne published *The Case of the Army Truly Stated*, a document that called for the dissolution of parliament and its re-establishment along democratic, or more level, lines. (Members of the group subsequently became known as Levellers.) This led to a debate in Putney, London, on October 1647 between the Levellers and General Henry Ireton, a supporter of the status quo; the result was a draw.

After the execution of Charles I in 1649, the Levellers continued to agitate on behalf of their cause, arousing the suspicion of Oliver Cromwell. Lilburne was banished from the country in 1652. He chose to return to England and was arrested, tried and imprisoned; released in 1655, he apparently changed his religious position and became converted to Quakerism (RELIGIOUS SOCIETY OF FRIENDS). The Levellers lasted for some time but seem to have disappeared by the time of the restoration of the monarchy in 1660.

LIBERAL CATHOLIC CHURCH

The Liberal Catholic Church has its origins in an English branch of the OLD CATHOLIC CHURCH.

An Englishman, Arnold Harris Mathew, was consecrated as the Old Catholic bishop for Great Britain and Ireland. In 1908 he knowingly ordained priests who were involved with the Theosophical Society and raised one such, Frederick Samuel Willoughby, to the episcopate in 1914. Mathew then urged all clergy who were still connected with the Theosophical Society to resign from that group, but this was met with a good deal of disagreement and led to a schism. Bishop

Willoughby then consecrated as bishop two of Mathew's priests, Bernard Edward R. Gauntlett, a theosophist, and Robert King, a professional psychic. In 1916 these three bishops consecrated James Ingall Wedgwood as presiding bishop. Almost immediately Wedgwood set out on a world tour, during which, in Sydney, Australia, he consecrated as bishop an ex-ANGLICAN minister, Charles Webster Leadbeater, who had been a member of the Old Catholic Church. Two priests whom he had only recently ordained assisted Wedgwood at this consecration, which was effected using the *Roman Pontifical*. When Wedgwood returned to England in late 1917 he called a synod of the Church and it was decided to give the theosophical section of the Church the official title of the *Liberal Christian Church (Old Catholic)*; in the following year this was changed to the present title.

Leadbeater was a close friend of Annie Besant, the leader of the Theosophical Society from whose ranks many laity and future Liberal Catholic clergy were recruited. Together, Wedgwood and Leadbeater worked to produce a new liturgy based on a Tridentine model used by the Roman Catholic Church, which first appeared in 1918 and was later enlarged in 1924. Wedgwood resigned in 1933 and was succeeded by Leadbeater as presiding bishop of the Church. During his world tour, Wedgwood also established a regionary bishop for the USA and ordained some priests, including Charles Hampton who, in 1935, succeeded the first regionary bishop, Irving Steiger Cooper.

It was not long before schisms appeared in the American branch of what had become the Liberal Catholic Church, culminating in a bitter and litigious dispute that broke out in the 1940s between the American clergy and the presiding bishop, Frank Waters Pigott of London, who had suspended the American regionary bishop, Charles Hampton, and all those clergy who supported him. This led to a battle within the Liberal Catholic Church, between the American province and the rest of the Church throughout the world, resulting in a division. The two Churches which emerged from the split are the Liberal Catholic Church International (LCCI), with its headquarters at San Diego, California, which employs a more Roman Catholic approach, and the more theosophically based Liberal Catholic Church – Province of the United States (LCC), with its headquarters at Ojai, California. American clergy are trained at either the St Alban's theological seminary, established in California for the LCCI in 1923, or through the Liberal Catholic Institute of Studies, which was launched in the 1980s for the LCC. The organization of both Churches is hierarchical, with supreme authority vested in the General Episcopal Synod under the chairmanship of the Presiding Bishop. The Synod also has authority to make liturgical changes and amend canon law.

The Liberal Catholic Church is represented throughout the world, present in some 33 countries. During the celebration of the Divine Liturgy it is believed that a great, spiritual power sweeps over the congregation and through them to the world at large. There is no strict requirement of submission to any creed, scripture or tradition and, in consequence, no one is barred from receiving Holy Communion. Liberal Catholic clergy are free to marry.

LIBERAL CATHOLIC CHURCH, ORDER OF ST GERMAIN

A small Church organized in 1969 in the

USA by James A. J. Taylor (aka James Matthews) under the original name of the *Order of St Germain*, but which adopted its present name some two years later. There are no lay members of this Church since all members are classified as either *clerical*, or as *practitioners*.

Doctrinally, the Church in general observes the LIBERAL CATHOLIC (CHURCH) approach and it sees its purpose as forwarding the work of *The Masters* (or Christs) in the world. It does not oblige any member to affirm acceptance of a detailed statement of belief. The head of the Church is the archbishop; he is assisted by bishops who are in charge of the work in those states where the Order is represented, namely Texas, Colorado, Oklahoma and California.

❖ Order of St Germain; Order of St Germain Ecclesia Catholica Liberalis

LIFE AND ADVENT UNION

An American sect that arose in the mid-nineteenth century in America in the aftermath of the *Great Disappointment* that followed the non-appearance of the second coming of Christ as predicted by William Miller (MILLERITES; REVELATION 20). This was supposed to have happened in 1844 and a great many people were left embarrassed and frustrated when it did not happen. New sects were formed, with many Millerites joining the ADVENT CHRISTIAN CHURCH. It was a member of this Church, George Storrs, who left the sect and joined with John T. Walsh, who was preaching that the wicked-dead would not be resurrected and that the millennium had already started and would result in the second coming, but with no certain date predicted. Together, Walsh and Storrs formed the Life and Advent Union in the 1860s, a Church that was largely confined to a few congregations in New England. In 1964 this merged with the Advent Christian Church.

LING LIANG CHINESE CHURCH

Until the outbreak of the Second World War, evangelization and church activity in China had been in the hands of missionaries from the West and their various mission societies. In 1942, the Reverend Timothy Dzao, concerned that the country had a need for a self-supporting and self-governing Chinese evangelizing force, set up the first Ling Liang Church in Shanghai. ('Ling Liang' translates as 'Food to Nourish Our Spirit'.)

In spite of the war, many Ling Liang churches were established throughout China, but following the political changes that began in China in 1949, Dzao and his family moved to Hong Kong and there, in the space of three months, he conducted a massive campaign of evangelism and revival camp meetings. The Ling Liang Church was formally organized in Hong Kong in 1950, with its headquarters in Kowloon. There is a strong bilingual tradition in these Hong Kong congregations, with the use of Cantonese (the dialect used in South China) and Putonghua, or Mandarin (the official dialect of China, based on that used in North China), employed in church services.

By means of the Ling Liang Worldwide Evangelistic Mission from Hong Kong, new churches have been established for Chinese immigrants in Taiwan (The Spiritual Food Church), Indonesia (The Spiritual Food Church of Indonesia) and in India, Australia, the Philippines, Malaysia and throughout North America.

❖ The Spiritual Food Church; The Spiritual Food Church of Indonesia; The Spiritual Food Worldwide Evangelical Mission

LITHUANIAN NATIONAL CATHOLIC CHURCH

This short-lived Church was organized by Bishop Francis Hodur of the POLISH NATIONAL CATHOLIC CHURCH of America (PNCC) in 1914, for the care of those Lithuanian immigrants to America who wished to retain their national identity and to practise a form of ROMAN CATHOLICISM that reflected their national ethos. For a time the Church remained independent, but in 1964 it merged with the Polish National Catholic Church.

In both doctrine and practice the Church was thoroughly Catholic, but like the PNCC, which is OLD CATHOLIC (CHURCH) in origin, the Divine Liturgy was celebrated in the vernacular and its clergy were allowed to marry

LIVING WATERS CHRISTIAN FELLOWSHIP

A small Japanese Church founded in 1930 by the Japan Evangelistic Board and lying within the PENTECOSTAL tradition. The Church has a membership of 1,500, currently distributed between 12 congregations, though its numbers are now in decline. The Church's headquarters are in Odawara, on Surgura Bay.

❖ Living Water Christian Church (sic)

LOLLARDS

The name, possibly a term of abuse, given to followers of John Wycliffe (*c.* 1329–84) and probably derived from the Dutch *lollen* (to mutter); the term was used by Archbishop William Courtenay (1342–96), who condemned Wycliffe's teachings. When Courtenay became Archbishop of Canterbury he held a synod to condemn *Lollardy* in 1382 and urged his bishops to imprison heretics, including the Lollards.

The Lollard movement developed through two main phases. The first phase involved its penetration of institutions of learning. It had appeal for Oxford scholars led by Nicholas of Hereford (d. 1420), an ardent supporter of Wycliffe and preacher of his doctrines. He was excommunicated and twice imprisoned for this action. Nicholas became the leader of the Lollards in the west of England, but was later captured and tortured, leading to an apparent recantation of his views; this did not, however, deter him from translating the Old Testament in its first Wycliffite version.

From Oxford, Lollard ideas spread to Leicester where the movement entered its second phase, becoming more generally popular and with its social teaching receiving greater emphasis. Many were attracted to these ideals, from all classes of society, with some followers ready to achieve their aims through active revolt. Parliament passed a statute in 1401 'On the Burning of a Heretic', aimed at the Lollards, but despite this, and the very vigorous opposition posed by Thomas Arundel (1353–1414) who had been elected Archbishop of Canterbury in 1396, the perseverance of the Lollards remained unswerving. A Lollard march on London, led by Sir John Oldcastle (later Lord Cobham), was a disaster. Rather than amassing an expected crowd of several thousand Lollards, only a few hundred turned up; most of these were arrested, tried and executed. Oldcastle escaped and went on the run, but was eventually caught and executed in 1417. The Lollard movement went underground. As a warning to would-be heretics John Wycliffe's body, which had been buried some 44 years previously, was exhumed and burnt as a heretic. Another attempt to achieve its aims was made by the Lollards in 1431, this time planning to overthrow the government and disendow the Church, but it was thwarted.

Doctrinally the Lollards expressed themselves in the *Twelve Conclusions*, which had been assembled for parliament's approval in 1395; in this statement the Lollards expressed their disapproval of the church's hierarchy, as well as of the doctrine of transubstantiation, clerical celibacy, the temporal power of the church, prayers for the dead, pilgrimages, images of war and the use of art in churches. Although not mentioned in the *Twelve Conclusions*, the Lollards asserted their belief that the main purpose of priests was to preach and that the validity of a priest's action was determined by his moral behaviour. They also contended that the Bible should be in the vernacular, to be understood by all, and must be regarded as the sole authority in religion. All people, they contended, had the right to read and interpret the scriptures for themselves. These aims could only meet with hostility from the church.

A brief Lollard revival occurred in the early sixteenth century, in London, East Anglia and in the area of the Chiltern Hills, west of the capital. However, by 1530 the movement had gradually merged into the broad spectrum of PROTESTANTISM, with its sympathetic climate of dissent and anticlericalism.

LORD'S NEW CHURCH, THE

This is a Church in the SWEDENBORGIAN tradition, formed in 1937 as a split from within the GENERAL CHURCH OF THE NEW JERUSALEM. The schism was prompted by a series of articles, coming out of the Netherlands, in which the writings of Emanuel Swedenborg were reassessed and declared as originating in the Lord, and were not to be thought of as being of human origin. It was consequently concluded that as the inner meaning of Swedenborg's writings is unravelled, and as the Church follows the Lord, the evolution of these ideas will grow into eternity.

These conclusions were not acceptable to all members of the General Church of the New Jerusalem and several breakaway congregations were formed in the USA, in Bryn Athyn in Pennsylvania and in New York City. There are now several small congregations of The Lord's New Church in the Netherlands, Sweden. Japan and South Africa, as well as in the USA.

❖ Lord's New Church Which is Nova Hierosolyma

LUMPA CHURCH

The prophetess Alice Lenshina Mulenga Mubisha founded this independent religious movement in Zambia in 1954, initially in order to combat witchcraft and sorcery that were both practised widely. She was given to having visions and claimed to have been taken to heaven, where she received a divine message directing her to work to destroy these practices. This prompted Alice to found the *Lumpa* movement, a name that in Bemba, the dialect spoken by about 20 per cent of the population, means 'better than all others'. The movement was started in a town that Alice renamed Zion. She was nevertheless baptized into the PRESBYTERIAN CHURCH; this had the effect of intensifying the visions and led to both Alice and her husband being expelled from the Presbyterian Church in 1955.

As a result of her preaching, Alice attracted many adherents and by 1959 it has been estimated that approaching 100,000 people had joined the movement, mostly converting from either ROMAN CATHOLICISM, or from the PRESBYTERIAN CHURCH. Doctrinally, the Church is basically Christian, but observes only one ordinance, that of baptism, which takes the form of a special ceremony administered by Alice herself. The attacks against witchcraft and sorcery were extended to include a zealous campaign against the use of alcohol and the practice of polygamy. Members are instructed to live purified lives in readiness for the second coming (REVELATION 20); a cathedral, which Alice had erected at Zion in 1958, included a tall pillar on which Christ was expected to descend at this time.

Alice's work brought her into opposition with the authorities and in 1958 she ignored an instruction to register her Church as an approved organization and mounted what was perceived to have been a challenge to the United National Independence Party (UNIP), the winner of the 1961 elections. When Zambia became independent in 1964 the Lumpa Church remained in open defiance of the new government and as a result suffered from conflicts with the police and army. The Lumpa followers fortified their villages, but the outcome was inevitable, and during the three–month long conflict around seven hundred members were killed. The Church was then banned and Alice arrested. She was subsequently released and rearrested in the mid-1970s on the grounds that she continued to hold church services. By 1975 the Lumpa Church was virtually defunct with many of its members having been converted to Roman Catholicism and other Christian denominations; only a few congregations remain, composed mainly of Bemba and Senga speakers.

❖ Lumpa (Visible Salvation) Church

LUSITANIAN CHURCH

A breakaway group of Portuguese priests and laity left the ROMAN CATHOLIC CHURCH in 1880 because they could not accept the decision of Vatican Council I in 1870 concerning the universal authority of the pope. The disaffected clergy formed a synod, presided over by Bishop Henry Chauncey Riley, who had been consecrated as a bishop for Mexico in 1874 by the AMERICAN EPISCOPAL CHURCH. Congregations were formed in and around Lisbon, using a Portuguese translation of the *1662 English Prayer Book* in their services. A constitution was drawn up, suitable for a Church in which the principles of the Roman Catholic Church tradition were to be maintained and local ecclesiastical authority respected. The synod did not have its own bishop, and the disestablished CHURCH OF IRELAND offered its support. This came in the form of a group of three bishops who formed a council of bishops and supplied the necessary episcopal ministries, like confirmation and ordination. The CHURCH OF ENGLAND felt that it could not offer support because of its established status and also because the British government was reluctant to offend the Roman Catholic Church, which was, and still is, the established Church in Portugal.

In the late 1950s the American Episcopal Church consecrated a bishop for the Lusitanian Church, as did the bishops of the Union of Utrecht (OLD CATHOLIC CHURCH) together with some ANGLICAN bishops, in 1958. Several years later the American Episcopal Church, and some other Churches in the ANGLICAN COMMUNION, issued a concordat of full communion with the Lusitanian Church. Full integration into the Anglican Communion came in 1980, when the Lusitanian Church became an extraordinary diocese under the metropolitan authority of the Archbishop of Canterbury.

The Lusitanian Church is small, with 176 congregations and just under 5,000 adult members.

❖ Portuguese Episcopal Church; The Lusitanian Church, Catholic, Apostolic, Evangelical

LUTHERAN BRETHREN OF AMERICA, CHURCH OF THE

The Church is an independent LUTHERAN group that was formed in 1900 in Milwaukee, Wisconsin, when five independent Lutheran congregations gathered together and agreed to unite and adopt a constitution.

The merging congregations were concerned about several issues, and decided together on the following standards:

1 Holy Communion is restricted to those members who have had a personal experience of salvation. In its form of worship the Church avoids the use of liturgical vestments, does not use an altar and serves Holy Communion to members of the congregation in their pews. Worship services are mainly composed of hymn singing, preaching and readings from the scriptures.

2 Admission to full membership and communion is granted only to those who have been confirmed, which follows upon a two-year period of instruction; an individual who has received the conversion experience may then be admitted to membership privileges.

3 The polity of the Church is a matter of concern and although each congregation is to be regarded as autonomous it falls to the synod to advise and to coordinate the administration of the Church.

Doctrinally, the Church affirms the three creeds (Apostles', Nicene and Athanasian), the *Augsburg Confession* (1530) and Luther's *Small Catechism* (1529). The Church is much concerned with missions, both at home and abroad. The home mission work is involved in church planting in both the USA and Canada. Education is also a major concern and is catered for by the Church's three campuses, a Bible college, a seminary and an academy, all of which are located at Fergus Falls, Minnesota, alongside the administrative headquarters of the Church. In addition, the Church is involved in maintaining homes for the aged and infirm as well as conducting a flourishing publishing business. The foreign mission work is currently restricted to Africa and the Far East.

LUTHERAN CHURCH

This worldwide Church is based on the work of Martin Luther (1483–1546), an ex-Augustinian German priest whose

Ninety-Five Theses, allegedly nailed to the door of Wittenberg Castle church on 31 October 1517, were an attack on various contemporary Roman Catholic ecclesiastical abuses. Some have suggested that this marked the date on which LUTHERANISM, and possibly the Reformation, began.

Luther had endured a long period of religious doubt and became convinced that the righteous are such by grace and through faith in the merit of Christ alone (*Sola Fides*) and not so with the help of any preparatory or other supplementary effort, either of their own or another's on their behalf. For Luther the righteousness of Christ alone would suffice to pay the price for sin; only if that righteousness could be imputed (or transferred) to the believer might he be spared its penalty. This is called the doctrine of justification by faith alone and it ran counter to the Roman Catholic practice of indulgences, or remission of the temporal penalties of sin. Luther also concluded that all doctrine must be authorized by scripture alone (*sola scriptura*).

Luther wrote prolifically and his works included hymns, two catechisms and comments on various parts of the Bible. He limited the sacraments to two, those of baptism and the Lord's Supper. Baptism was understood to be the means of regeneration, especially in infants, and he held that the Lord's Supper was not to be thought of as a memorial meal, because in the bread and wine of the sacrament the body and blood of Christ are present by a process called *consubstantiation*. By this was meant that after consecration, the substances of both the body and blood of Christ and those of the bread and wine co-exist in union with each other.

Lutheranism's doctrinal position is declared in the assembled *Book of Concord* (1580), or Concordia, which includes the three ancient creeds, the Apostles', Nicene and Athanasian, and the *Augsburg Confession*, which had been prepared by Philipp Melanchthon (1497–1560) at Luther's behest. The *Book of Concord* also contains the *Apology for the Augsburg Confession* (1531) and the *Smalcald Articles* (1537), which were drawn up by Luther at the request of Frederick the Wise, Elector of Saxony, the *Small* and *Larger Catechism* (1529) and the *Formula of Concord* (1577), which was designed to settle many disputes that had arisen since the deaths of both Luther and Melanchthon and was supported by strict Lutherans who resisted the making of any concessions.

Luther had developed a *Formula of Mass and Communion for the Church at Wittenberg* (1523) and went on to produce the *Deutsche Messe* (1525); the latter, though following the Roman liturgical form, made provision for the use of the vernacular and for access by the laity to the chalice during Holy Communion. The role of the sermon in the liturgy received an emphasis that, together with hymns, came to be an important feature of the Lutheran Church tradition. The use of candles and vestments remained optional.

The Lutheran movement, which was a central element of the PROTESTANT Reformation, spread throughout Germany and Scandinavia, where today the greatest concentration of Lutherans is found. There are now about 9 million Lutherans in the USA, and smaller Lutheran populations in many parts of the world. All Lutherans subscribe to the *Augsburg Confession* and Luther's *Small Catechism*, but only a few now accept the

Formula of Concord. There is, consequently, no complete unity of doctrine, polity or church structure amongst the Lutherans.

The Lutheran World Federation (LWF) was organized at Lund, in Sweden, in 1947 as the ecumenical voice of international Lutheranism. It is designed to create a sense of unity among Lutherans throughout the world. The headquarters of the LWF is in Geneva, Switzerland. The recent signing of the Joint Declaration of the Doctrine of Justification, at Augsburg (October, 1999) was made between representatives of the LWF and the ROMAN CATHOLIC CHURCH, but despite this apparent consensus serious theological differences persist between Lutherans and Roman Catholics.

LUTHERAN CHURCH – MISSOURI SYNOD

This is the second largest LUTHERAN body in the USA, surpassed only in membership by the EVANGELICAL LUTHERAN CHURCH IN AMERICA. It owes its origin to the arrival in Perry County, south of St Louis, Missouri, of 750 immigrants from Germany in 1839. In 1847, twelve congregations and their pastors signed a Constitution, establishing the *German Evangelical Lutheran Synod of Missouri, Ohio and Other States* (the current name was only adopted a century later); other congregations, who had not at first voted to join the synod, signed up only as advisory members. Carl Ferdinand Walther, a young minister, was elected as the first president at the first convention, held in Chicago in 1847.

A period of sustained growth followed, which has only recently slowed. Schisms along the way were inevitable. In 1956 a group separated to form the Concordia Lutheran Conference and another split occurred in 1964, with the separating group forming the Lutheran Church of the Reformation. The most serious schism was in 1976 when 100,000 liberal-minded Church members formed the Association of Evangelical Lutheran Churches (AELC), separating from the parent body over the question of congregational, as against synodical autonomy and the Church's mission. The new denomination also decided to ordain women to the ministry, which the Missouri Synod would not. In 1982 the AELC voted to merge with two other Lutheran bodies and by 1988 the Evangelical Lutheran Church in America had been formed.

Doctrinally, the Lutheran Church – Missouri Synod emphasizes a strict interpretation of the Bible and affirms the three traditional creeds (Apostles', Nicene and Athanasian) and the six Lutheran Confessions (the *Augsburg Confession*, the *Apology of the Augsburg Confession*, the *Smalcald Articles*, the *Formula of Concord* and Luther's *Small* and *Larger Catechisms*). In 1982 the synod published *Lutheran Worship*, a new hymnal.

The polity of the Church is congregational, with the synod exercising a purely advisory role through the biennial general convention. The Church evangelizes through all forms of the media, provides a library for the blind and is involved with hospitals and children's homes. It places a strong emphasis upon social issues, providing pro-life, anti-euthanasia and anti-racism support and a ministry to homosexuals. The Church's foreign activity has always been ambitious and has grown steadily from its first mission, in 1894, until, today, when missions are maintained in some fifty countries around the world. The Church, which has its headquarters in St Louis, Missouri, is a member of the International Lutheran Council

LUTHERAN CHURCH OF AUSTRALIA

The Lutheran Church of Australia was recently formed, in 1966, and is a union between the Evangelical Lutheran Church of Australia (ELCA) and the United Episcopal Lutheran Church in Australia (UELCA). Both of these distinct LUTHERAN groups were derived from Prussian Lutheran immigrants to South Australia at the start of the nineteenth century. Two groups had been formed because of differences of opinion about premillennialism (REVELATION 20).

The ELCA, which favoured the rejection of premillennialism, later formed a link with the LUTHERAN CHURCH – MISSOURI SYNOD. It also promoted a view of the inerrancy of the scriptures in all matters. Whilst the UELCA regarded scripture as inerrant in matters of salvation, it was not too concerned about inerrancy in some more minor matters and, furthermore, the Church supported premillennialism. The UELCA allied itself to the American Lutheran Church and joined the Lutheran World Federation at its creation in 1947. The two groups settled their differences in 1966, both separating from their American alliances.

The union that was formed is now represented by 649 congregations, with over 197,000 adult members, divided into autonomous districts, each with its own annual conference. A triennial general synod is convened to which delegated representatives from the congregations are sent; it is the duty of the synod to elect the president, who oversees the work of the Church for a six–year term of office. Doctrinally, the Church affirms the contents of the *Book of Concord* (1580) and it places great stress upon unity of doctrine.

LUTHERAN CHURCH OF OLDENBURG

This independent LUTHERAN CHURCH in Germany, which currently has 124 congregations, was started in Oldenburg in the sixteenth century by some pastors who had accepted the Lutheran faith during the PROTESTANT Reformation. By 1573, these pastors and their congregations were satisfied fully with the Lutheran *Confessions*, which they adopted. The Church remained under the control of the head of state until the time of the First World War, but in 1919 it became disestablished and the method of church government was reviewed.

There was an unsuccessful attempt by the state authorities to regain control of the Church during the Second World War, but this was resisted and the Church experienced a period of growth and renewal. The Lutheran Church of Oldenburg belongs to the Lutheran World Council and is presided over by a bishop, with all the congregations arranged into districts, each of which is headed by a superintendent. It is also a member of the EVANGELICAL CHURCH IN GERMANY, which is a federation of Lutheran, Reformed and other Churches, but it is not part of the United Evangelical Lutheran Church of Germany, which was formed in 1948 as a union of Lutheran churches.

❖ Evangelical Lutheran Church in Oldenburg

LUTHERANISM (also LUTHERAN)

The doctrinal position inspired by the writings and teachings of Martin Luther (1483–1546) and held, for the most part by most Lutherans. The definitive doctrinal position of the LUTHERAN CHURCH is contained in a composite book called the *Book of Concord* (1580), also known as the Concordia.

LYGON STREET CHURCH OF CHRIST

A small, independent Australian Church which has retained the title of Church of Christ, *even though the congregation withdrew from the official* Churches of Christ Conference *in 1979.*

The members of this congregation began meeting for worship in the Mechanics Institute, Collins Street, Melbourne, in May 1854. After some ten years these meetings were moved to St George's Hall, Bourke Street, in the same city and this became the site of the evangelizing ministry of an American preacher, H. S. Earl, as a result of which many were baptized into the Church. Land was purchased in Lygon Street and the foundation stone for a new church building was laid in 1865; within six months the first church services were held there. It was not long before a Bible school, which had been started in 1862, moved to the Lygon Street premises and in 1889 a programme of building expansion began to accommodate the requirements of the growing congregation.

The congregation's concern for those less fortunate than themselves was demonstrated during the economic depressions and the troubled times of the two world wars. The Church's lecture hall was used to provide billets for troops on leave, with twenty-four–hour canteens and members enthusiastically helping to pack food parcels to be sent to Britain, which were so welcome at this bleak period.

Because of the size and location of the Lygon Street Church it was used for a time as a centre for Churches of Christ Conference activities, but in 1979, on account of a new ecumenical approach to the ROMAN CATHOLIC CHURCH made by the Churches of Christ Conference, which the home congregation rejected, the Lygon Street Church became independent. The Church retains its independence and has become a member of the Carlton Overseas Christian Fellowship. The members have a special ministry to foreign students coming to live in the Melbourne area, an association that has continued since the first mission, to the Chinese, was set up in 1893.

MAADI COMMUNITY CHURCH

This is an international, interdenominational Church that has served the English-speaking community of south Cairo, Egypt, since 1947. A temporary building was erected by the Church Army in 1920 and dedicated initially to St John of the Wilderness; it was later renamed as the Episcopal (ANGLICAN) Church of St John the Baptist. This church served as a focus for many Americans in Cairo, who would attend the Sunday morning community service; from this fellowship grew the Maadi Community Church.

The only statement of faith observed by the Maadi Church is the Apostles' creed. A constitution, drawn up in 1955, was adopted in 1956. By 1989 it had become obvious that the arrangement between the Anglican diocese and the Maadi Community Church needed to be placed on a more formal footing and as a result it was agreed that the Maadi Community Church should take responsibility for its own administration. This is now in the hands of an elected fifteen-member church council that is responsible for overseeing such work as Christian education, the care of the needy, local ministries, property management, financial matters, outreach missions, worship and youth concerns. As a concession to the Islamic weekend, services are held on Fridays and on Sundays, while Holy Communion is celebrated on the first full weekend of each month. The Maadi Community Church is a member of the Association of International Churches in Europe and the Middle East (AICEME).

MACEDONIAN ORTHODOX CHURCH

The Macedonian Orthodox Church belongs to a proud tradition, since it was the apostle, St Paul, who introduced Christianity to the country during his journeys through Europe and Asia (1 Tim. 1:3). As a result of the early Christianization of the region during the first three centuries AD, it was to be expected that its hierarchy was in position at a very early date, and by the fifth century Thessalonica was established as a papal vicariate. The Slavic colonization of Macedonia was undertaken in the seventh century and in time the Slavs became assimilated with the native Macedonians. It was through the efforts of the *holy brothers*, Sts Cyril (827–69) and Methodius (815–84), that the southern Slavs were Christianized and Slavic literary culture was developed from the glagolitic script that St Cyril is reputed to have created and from which the cyrillic script finally emerged. The work was continued by Sts Clement and Naum after the death of the two saints, and Ochrida (now Ochrid), in south-west Macedonia, was established as the patriarchate of an autocephalous Church. Following the overthrow of the Bulgarian kingdom in 1018 the city lost its patriarchal status, reduced to the rank of an archbishopric by the Byzantine emperor, Basil II, although it was allowed to preserve its former status within the autocephalous Church. The Turkish Sultan Mustapha III abolished the archbishopric in 1767 and its territories were annexed to the Patriarchate of Constantinople.

After many centuries of struggle a Board called the First Church Popular Congress was formed in 1944, which resolved to organize the Macedonian Orthodox Church. This decision was submitted to the United Church of the Serbs, Croats and Slovenians, later called the SERBIAN ORTHODOX CHURCH (SOC), for its approval; several Macedonian bishoprics were integrated into the SOC from 1919. The SOC, however, rejected this resolution. In 1958 the proposal for the establishment of an autonomous Macedonian Orthodox Church was finally agreed, but it had to remain in canonical unity with the SOC and under the jurisdiction of the Serbian Orthodox patriarch.

The Macedonian Orthodox Church was later able to form its own Holy Synod and in 1967 its autonomy was proclaimed. Training facilities for future clergy were established, initially at Banyanid, near Skopje, but this has now moved to Drachevo, where the students pursue a five-year course before continuing their studies in the faculty of theology at the university in Skopje, or abroad. Today, the Church has 300 priests and monks with about 100 active churches and two overseas eparchies, the Canadian–American and the Australian. The creation of a Macedonian eparchy for western Europe is currently under consideration.

MACEDONIANS

The name given to an heretical sect, originating in Asia Minor in the fourth century. Macedonius, from whom the sect takes its name, was introduced to the See of Constantinople by Arians in 342, and enthroned by Constantius, the Eastern Roman emperor.

Macedonius' enthusiasm for the faith was characterized by considerable aggression; unbaptized women and children were forced to accept baptism, and those who were unwilling to enter into communion with Macedonius were imprisoned and tortured. His cruelty provoked an uprising amongst the NOVATIANS in Paphlagonia (northern Anatolia), bordering on the Black Sea, and many soldiers in the imperial army were killed. His career came to an abrupt end after Macedonius ordered the disinterment of the body of Constantine the Great without first seeking permission from the Emperor Constantius. Deposition followed, not for doctrinal reasons alone but mainly because of the bloodshed he had caused, and he was replaced by Eudoxius in 360.

It is believed that it was during his early retirement that Macedonius formed his notions regarding the divinity of the Holy Spirit; at this time he seems to have insisted that the Spirit was on a level with the angels and was to be thought of as a minister and a servant, although he later denied this. Macedonius died *c.* 362 and his followers soon dispersed. It is thought, however, that some Macedonians may have joined up with the PNEUMATOMACHI, or Spirit Fighters, a group that also denied the divinity of the Holy Spirit.

The sect was anathematized in May 381, at the First Council of Constantinople (the Second General Council) and had disappeared by 383 as a result of the anti-heresy enactments of the Emperor Theodosius I *the Great* (379–95).

MACMILLANITES

Members of a Scottish group that seceded from the CAMERONIANS in 1743 and were so-called after their leader, John Macmillan (1670–1753). They were seeking a stricter observance of the principles of the Reformation in Scotland. In 1743, when the group acquired the services of a second minister, it was able to establish a presbytery, which grew to become a synod in 1811.

The form of worship is simple, and psalms are sung without musical accompaniment. Doctrinally, the Church affirms the *WESTMINSTER CONFESSION of Faith* (1643–6) and the *Larger* and *Small Catechisms*. The Church currently has 4 congregations, with nearly 300 members.

❖ Reformed Presbyterian Church

MAI CHAZA'S CHURCH

An indigenous African Church, founded amongst the Shona-speaking Manyika people in Zimbabwe in 1952 by Mai (Shona for 'Mother') Chaza, a METHODIST laywoman. Methodism had been taken to Zimbabwe from Great Britain in 1890, when the country was colonized as a British South Africa Company possession.

Mai Chaza (d. 1960) went into a coma during the 1950s, during which she claimed to have had a mystical experience of death and resurrection. Her Church, though developing initially in the early 1950s within the Methodist tradition, became independent in 1955. It was centred upon a village called Guta Ra Jehovah (City of Jehovah), created by Mai Chaza as part of her intention to establish a series of holy cities that were to be given over to faith healing and, in particular, to the treatment of barren women.

This Church is vigorously opposed to ancestor worship, magic and both traditional African and western medicine. Its members are expected to observe monogamy and to avoid the use of drugs, alcohol and tobacco. The only ordinance observed by the Church is that of infant baptism. Mai Chaza produced a collection of her works and teachings that have been gathered together as the *Guta Ra Jehovah Bible*, which is used by the 160 congregations now in existence. These currently have nearly 34,000 members and are centred in *Jehovah's Cities* in many parts of Zimbabwe. The Church services are characterized by much singing and dancing, usually accompanied by the rhythmical use of maracas.

MALABAR INDEPENDENT SYRIAN CHURCH

The Malabar Independent Syrian Church is one of several different groups of Syrian Churches in the state of Kerala in south-west India. The headquarters of the Church is in Thozhiyur, a small village in the Thrissur district.

According to tradition, Christianity came to India in AD 52, when St Thomas went to Kerala and founded seven churches there; he died in Myalopore, near Madras, in *c.* AD 72. The early Christians in Kerala were probably of East Syrian, or Chaldean, origin and maintained a link with Syriac-speaking groups in Mesopotamia from the fourth century. A number of carved crosses with Pahlavi inscriptions, which are said to date from the eighth and ninth centuries, suggest a Persian origin and probably confirm the Church's East Syrian Catholic linkage.

After the landing of Vasco da Gama in India in 1498, the Portuguese missionaries who followed in his wake were amazed to find Christians already in the area, using East Syrian prayers in the Syriac language in their worship services. In time these Malabarese Christians began to be lose their Chaldean bearings largely because the Portuguese, who had settled in the area, were unable to accept that anything other than the Latin way could be truly ROMAN CATHOLIC and the Eastern Catholic Rite, as observed by the Indians, was not acceptable to them.

When the last Chaldean bishop died, the Catholic Archbishop of Goa, Alexis de Menezes, who was also an Augustinian friar, tried to bring the indigenous Church under Latin rule by the Synod of Diamper (1599); this saw the destruction of the existing service books that were considered by Menezes to be heretical. A Latin hierarchy was imposed by abolishing the jurisdiction in India of the Chaldean patriarch and replacing the Syrian episcopate with Portuguese Latin-rite bishops. Roman vestments were introduced and Holy Communion under one kind only was imposed, along with the practice of clerical celibacy. A group within the Christian community, which wanted to be independent of foreign missionaries (and Jesuits, in particular), took an oath, known as the Coonen (or Koonen) Cross Oath, in a cemetery at Mattancherry, near Cochin, in 1653; it is said that the oath-takers each held on to ropes tied to a stone cross. Most of these Christians, or their descendants, returned in time to the Roman Catholic Church. Those who remained independent and opposed to Rome elected an archdeacon, Thomas, as their bishop and consecrated him, albeit irregularly as there was no presiding bishop, by the laying on of hands by twelve priests; he was then known as Mar Thoma I. The Church eventually became part of the Syrian Patriarchate of Antioch.

Today, the Church provides health care, education for the poor and Sunday schools. It has links with both ANGLICAN and LUTHERAN Churches. There are now about 10,000 faithful distributed between 20 parishes and chapels, with a cathedral at Thozhiyur, near Kunnamkulam.

MALAGASY LUTHERAN CHURCH

Norwegian LUTHERAN missionaries started an inland mission in the island of Madagascar in 1866, and in 1888 an American Lutheran pastor, John P. Hogstad, and his wife, Lena, arrived at Fort Dauphin in the south of the island. They came there from the Augsburg Seminary in the USA to commence their missionary work and were joined the following year by another missionary couple, the Reverend Erik Tou and his wife Caroline. The missionaries suffered many hardships and setbacks. Madagascar became a French colony in 1896 and the French colonial government proved to be very unco-operative.

The Norwegian and American missionaries continued their separate activities until 1950, when they united to form the Malagasy Lutheran Church, which joined the Lutheran World Fellowship in the same year. At the time of this unification there were 1,800 congregations with around 180,000 members; these numbers thereafter rose steadily, and in 2001 the membership stood at 1.5 million divided into 13 synods, cared for by 1,000 pastors and a slightly greater number of catechists.

A seminary established by the Norwegian missionaries at Ivory, Fianarantsoa, has now become the Malagasy Lutheran Church seminary and provides a strict academic course in theology. There is also a network of regional seminaries for the training of priests at a less demanding academic standard. The Church places considerable emphasis upon evangelism and the development of future congregational leaders, but also pays much attention to spiritual and physical health care programmes, with nine hospitals and thirteen dispensaries opened and maintained by the Lutheran Church. It is also concerned with the care of those individuals who are perceived to be suffering from mental illness, depression and demonic oppression. A school of nursing is provided, with courses for child survival, family planning, AIDS prevention and other areas of importance in the community. Considerable effort has also been put into agricultural and development programmes.

As part of the evangelization programme, revival meetings have been a feature of Christian life in Madagascar, and one held at Soatanana in 1895 led to some internal dispute in the Church. In 1955 many committed Lutherans finally left the Malagasy Lutheran Church to form the Disciples of the Lord, which is strongly PENTECOSTAL in its approach. Another schism led to the formation of the Malagasy Spiritual Church of the Revival in 1958, following another revivalist rally. Both of these schisms are experiencing a healthy pattern of growth, with around three or four hundred congregations between them today.

MALANKARA ORTHODOX SYRIAN CHURCH

This Church must not be confused with the MALANKARA SYRIAN ORTHODOX CHURCH (see next entry) or the SYRO-MALANKARESE CHURCH, which was formed when a group of Oriental Orthodox West Syrians, under Bishop Ivanios, joined the ROMAN CATHOLIC CHURCH in 1930.

St Thomas, who died as a martyr in Mylapore, near Madras in *c.* AD 72, is alleged to have landed in Kerala, in south-west India, where he evangelized the district and established some seven churches. Accounts by early travellers, such as Cosmas who had come to India from Alexandria *c.* 520–5, record that there was a Church in India that was supervised by a bishop from Persia (Iran). Cosmas was also known as the 'Indian Sailor' and was the author of *Christian Topography*. Other observers, including Marco Polo, who was in India in 1288 and 1292, support the existence of such a Church. In the early fourteenth century the Pope mandated the French Dominican, Jourdain de Severac, to work in Kerala and to encourage the Syrian Christians there to submit to Rome.

The Portuguese discovery of the Cape route to India in 1498 and their seizure of and settlement at Goa in 1510 had a profound effect on the subsequent history of this area. Missionaries from Portugal, who found local Orthodox Christians using the Syrian language and reciting East Syrian prayers, were eager to convert these *heretics*, as they saw them, and even prevented a Persian bishop from landing in India. A Roman Catholic archbishopric was founded at Goa in 1557 and by 1599, as a result of the Synod of Diamper, it was demanded that the Syrian Christians had to be *romanized*, Some resisted the call to convert to Rome and took an oath, known as the Coonen Cross Oath, to that effect at Mattancherry, near Cochin.

The Portuguese were forced out by the arrival of the PROTESTANT Dutch who conquered the towns of Quilon, Craganore and Cochin in 1661–3. The presence of the Dutch was a factor that led to the formation of the Malabar Independent Syrian Church. The subsequent arrival of the British in the eighteenth century ended Dutch occupation; this, in turn, was instrumental in the formation of the MAR THOMA SYRIAN CHURCH. Those who had not seceded from the Orthodox faith throughout all these trials then had to contend with disputes about patriarchal jurisdiction. Only after extensive litigation was an autonomous and autocephalous Church, with its own catholicos, established in Malankara in 1912; this is now known as the Malankara Orthodox Syrian Church (of India) and has its headquarters in Devalokam, a suburb of Kottayam.

The synod of the Church is presided over by the catholicos and lay participation in the management of the Church is encouraged. Education is provided through the Mar Dionysios Seminary and High School, which were established in 1893, as well as through 17 church colleges, several teacher training institutes, industrial training centres and more than 200 schools. The Church is also responsible for 16 orphanages, which accept children from any religious background, and institutions for the mentally retarded and the blind; it also runs over 20 hospitals and medical care facilities and several social welfare programmes.

Doctrinally and liturgically the Malankara Orthodox Syrian Church is within the West Syrian tradition of Antioch, with the Divine Liturgy celebrated in Malayalam, the vernacular language of Kerala, as well as in Hindi, Tamil and, occasionally, English. There is an extensive network of provision for Sunday schools, and associations exist to provide for youth training for leadership. Opportunities are also provided for men and women to live a monastic life that closely follows ANGLICAN and Roman Catholic models.

❖ Indian Orthodox Church; Malankara Orthodox Syrian Church – Catholicate of the East; Oriental Malankara Orthodox Syrian Church of India; Orthodox Syrian Church of the East

MALANKARA SYRIAN ORTHODOX CHURCH

The Malankara Syrian Orthodox Church came into formal existence in 1975 with the consecration of Metropolitan Mar Philoxenos as Catholicos, or head of the Church, by the Syrian Orthodox Patriarch of Antioch. Mar Philoxenos was then replaced by Mar Mathews (*sic*) Athanasius. The Church now has around 300,000 members.

The headquarters of the Church is at Vetikel, east of Cochin, India. It is strongly ecumenical and provides a great number of training opportunities for young people of both sexes to enable them to prepare for future leadership roles. The Church is also deeply involved in social concerns and publishing, maintaining several hospitals, schools and colleges as well as monasteries and convents for those attracted to the religious life.

❖ Syrian Indian Church of the Patriarch of

Antioch; Syrian Orthodox Church of the Patriarch of Antioch

MAMMILLARIANS

An ANABAPTIST sect of uncertain date, but whose origin was at Haarlem, in the Netherlands. The name derived from a young man's indiscreet and affectionate touching of his bride-to-be's breast, an act of tenderness that became voiced abroad among members of the sect. This elicited great disapproval amongst some of the members and they urged in favour of the young man's excommunication, while others took a more tolerant view. A split occurred in the sect, with those who were willing to overlook the display of affection, who subsequently became known as Mammillarians, separating from the hardliners.

MANDAEANS

This group must not be confused with the Sabian Assembly, a group given to occultism, NEW AGE, theosophy, kabbalism and spiritualism, which was founded in the USA in 1922.

This small, GNOSTIC sect still survives in parts of southern Iraq, Iran, Europe, the USA and Australia, with a membership thought to number no more than 100,000 worldwide. Its date of origin is difficult to pinpoint, but it has been suggested by some authorities that it arose in the second century, and sprang from the land that lies east of the River Jordan. The doctrine held by the sect is monotheistic, the members holding to a mixture of biblical notions intermingled with astrology, Iranian dualism and a legendary account of St John the Baptist, which probably accounts for one of their alternative names, the *Christians of St John*, which was given to the sect in 1652, erroneously, by a Carmelite priest who was impressed with their veneration of St John the Baptist coupled with the similarities of their rituals to those of more conventional Christian usage. This led the priest to conclude that the members were descendants of those Christians who had received the baptism of St John.

Mandaean doctrine can be studied from the *Holy Books*, which were written originally in the Mandaean language, a dialect of eastern Aramaic derived from the Semitic family of languages. The Mandaean alphabet has 24 letters, starting and ending with the letter '*a*' (*aleph*), as it is believed that all things return to their origins and beginnings; many Mandaean sacred writings have now been translated into several languages.

Ritual washing, or baptizing 'in the name of Life and the knowledge of Life' (synonyms for God), occupies an important and frequent part of the rituals observed by the Mandaeans, the ceremony accompanied by an anointing with oil and followed by a sacramental meal of bread and holy water. To observe the rituals it is essential that the believer, whether priest or layman, faces north, which is believed to be where paradise lies and where the souls of the dead enjoy immortality with God, wearing a ritual costume made from white cotton or muslin, occasionally of white silk, which is called a *Rasta* and is said to symbolize the heavenly dress of light which is believed to be worn by the angels and all pure souls. This garment may never be washed with soap. A new *Rasta* may be worn for a wedding, for the ordination of a priest, on certain feast days and when a person is near to death.

Mandaeans, who are also known as

Nasoreans or Sabians, are expected to give alms and to practise exacting fasts. They observe many prohibitions, which include the familiar ban on murder, adultery, abortion, divorce (with some exceptions) and suicide, but there are also bans on the practice of magic and witchcraft, crying over the dead, eating dead animals and blood products, and self-mutilation.

❖ Christians of St John; Nasoreans; Sabians

MANICHAEANS

A sect founded by Mani, also known as Manichaeus (*c.* 215–76), the self-styled *Apostle of Jesus Christ*. He was born into a wealthy, aristocratic family in Seleucia-Ctesiphon in Persia (Iran) and between the ages of 12 and 24 received revelations that persuaded him to leave his home and community. His first vision was of an angelic being who prophesied this departure would happen; a second vision from the same angel, called *al-Tawm* (the Twin) because his physical appearance seemed to mirror Mani himself, told when the time for this departure had arrived.

Afer a period of study, Mani began to preach the truth as it had been revealed to him. Mani devised a doctrine that held that there were two eternal principles, God, the cause of all good, and Matter, the cause of all evil, with both God and Matter seen as equals. In time, the world of Matter began to penetrate the world of God, or Light, and particles of light were imprisoned by Satan, the prince of darkness, in man. Adam's creation was a counterplot to retain the imprisoned Light, through reproduction, and it was the role of Jesus Christ, the Buddha and Mani to release the particles of Light. Mani saw Christ's role as that of a redeemer, whose work was to teach men to control their desires and so return to their true home, the kingdom of Light. At Jesus' second coming, and with the millennial reign, the elect will be reunited with Light and the earthly creation will be destroyed (REVELATION 20).

Mani taught that man's liberation could be achieved over a period of time by following an ascetic way of life and abstaining from meat, eggs, milk and wine, as well as accepting celibacy. A hierarchy of membership was formed, depending on the degree of asceticism practised, forming two main groups, the *elect* and the *hearers*. The *hearers* could gather the vegetables and prepare them for their own consumption and for the *elect*, who would take the food from their hands; the *elect* were expected to observe the Manichaean doctrines and disciplines rigidly. All Manichaeans were expected to fast for up to thirty days each year, leading up to a special festival that was held at the spring equinox. This fasting was observed on Sundays. Prayers were to be recited at four regular intervals each day. Doctrinally, the sect rejected the Old Testament but accepted the New Testament in so far as it supported their position. The support of the clergy came from a system of tithing.

Despite his legendary sickliness and lameness, Mani travelled widely throughout the Persian Empire and India. He later returned to Persia, encouraged by the support of the newly enthroned King Shapur I, and began to preach and write; his six books and various letters make up the *Manichaean Canon*. This period of support ended with the accession of King Bahram I, when Mani fell out of favour. At the insistence of Karter, a Zoroastrian high priest, he was imprisoned and executed.

Manichaeism became quite widespread and was established in Egypt before the end of the third century and in Rome by the early fourth century. According to documents discovered at Turfan (now Sinkiang) and elsewhere in Chinese Turkestan in 1904–5, the sect may have persisted in the area into the thirteenth century. St Augustine of Hippo was a *hearer* for nine years, but following his conversion to Christianity he derided Manichaean beliefs in his *Confessions.*

MAR THOMA SYRIAN CHURCH

The Syrian Orthodox Church in Malabar at the end of the eighteenth and the start of the nineteenth century was in a state of confusion and decline. The English had displaced the Dutch from Cochin in 1795, and with their arrival the East India Company, under which the English operated in India, appointed two resident governors, one for Cochin and the other for Travancore (now Kerala).

These resident governors, Colonel Macaulay and Colonel John Monroe (or Munro), wanted to help the Syrian Christians and assisted in the production of a special report by Claudius Buchanan (1766–1815), an ANGLICAN priest and principal of Fort William College in Calcutta who, because of his duties with the East India Company, was prevented from ministering to the local Indian community. During Buchanan's visit to Malabar in 1806–7 he met with Mar Dionysios I, who had earlier made some unsuccessful attempts at union with the ROMAN CATHOLIC CHURCH. Dionysios talked of a possible union between the Syrian Church and the CHURCH OF ENGLAND and Buchanan was able to argue the case of the Syrian Christians upon his return to England. As a result, four missionaries, the Reverends Thomas Norton, Benjamin Bailey, Joseph Fenn and Henry Baker, all of the Church Missionary Society (CMS) and under the auspices of the Church of England, started work in Kerala in 1816. In consequence of this a number of disaffected Jacobites came under their influence. A reform group within the Syrian Church in India was established under the leadership of two professors from the Syrian seminary at Kottayam. One of these, Abraham Malpan, was excommunicated because of his proposed reforms and he decided to send his nephew to the Patriarch of Antioch to explain the situation. The nephew returned home as Mar Athanasios, having been consecrated by the Patriarch of Antioch in 1842–3 and, as metropolitan, he assumed the leadership of the reform group.

Lengthy legal battles followed, and in 1875 Mar Athanasios was deposed by Ignatius Mar Peter IV, then Patriarch of Antioch, and all property rights were lost. In 1889, with the help of the CMS, the Mar Thoma Syrian Church was organized. Since 1961 the Church has been in full communion with the Church of India, Pakistan, Burma and Ceylon, and, since 1974, with the Church of England.

The Mar Thoma Syrian Church, which successfully blends both Orthodox features and Reformation ideals, is headed by a metropolitan who presides over the general assembly, which is composed of bishops, clergy and elected representatives from the parishes. There are around 1,000 parishes and over 0.5 million adult members distributed within 6 dioceses.

❖ Mar Thoma Syrian Church of Malabar

MARA EVANGELICAL CHURCH

The Mara, formerly known as the Lakher, is an ethnic group, at one time allegedly given to headhunting, which lives along the border between India and Myanmar (formerly Burma). Evangelization was started in the area in 1907 by a British missionary couple and by 1960 almost the entire Mara people are said to have been converted to Christianity. Because of the geographical dispersal of the Mara, two Church groups were formed, the Evangelical Church of Maraland on the Indian side of the border, and the Mara Independent Church in Burma on the Burmese side. This latter Church developed a further division in 1970 that lasted some sixteen years, with the break finally healed in 1987. This was achieved with the help of the Myanmar Council of Churches and the new name of the Mara Evangelical Church was adopted to underline the union.

This is an evangelical Church holding to a conventional Christianity and committed to a holistic ministry. The Church, which currently has several thousand members served by some fifty pastors, is very busy maintaining evangelists who work amongst neighbouring ethnic groups. The polity of the Church is presbyterian and until recently the roles of pastor and elder were restricted to men alone, but there is now an intention to encourage women to assume these leadership positions. The Church is thoroughly ecumenical and is a member of the Myanmar Council of Churches, of the Christian Conference of Asia and the World Alliance of Reformed Churches. It is currently seeking membership of the World Council of Churches.

❖ Lakher Independent Evangelical Church

MARCIONITES

Followers of a heretic, Marcion, a son of a Christian bishop, who was born at Sinope on the Black Sea towards the end of the first century AD. He appears to have been a wealthy ship owner who, according to Tertullian, settled with a Christian congregation in Rome in *c.* 138–9, to whom he gave generous donations of money. Marcion had trouble in reconciling the Old and New Testaments and concluded that there must be two Gods, the one of the Old Testament, who is the creator of the world and is the God of Judaism, the Demiurge (who was held by the GNOSTICS to be an inferior deity who created the material universe), and the other God, the God of the New Testament who is a God of love and was made known for the first time by Jesus Christ. Marcion taught that Christ was the messenger of this supreme God, who had come down from heaven to preach deliverance from the rule of the Demiurge, whose followers he believed had crucified Christ. These and other views that he preached in Rome led Marcion to reject the Old Testament; he was ultimately expelled from the Church in AD 144 and his generous donations were returned to him.

Marcion was prompted by St Paul's outspoken views of the law of the Old Testament to examine the Pauline literature from the collection of available Christian writings. He sought to purge them of any Judaizing passages, or those parts which spoke of the Father as the creator, which identified the God of the New Testament with the Demiurge. This left him with a shortened Gospel of St Luke, from which the birth of Christ narratives were omitted, and only ten of the Pauline Epistles, parts of which were also omitted. Marcion called the edited version of St Luke the *Evangelicon*, and that of the the Pauline Epistles became the *Apostolikon*.

Marcion's negative attitude towards the body and the physical world was very Gnostic, as was his emphasis on asceticism and his docetic (DOCETISM) Christology. His views on marriage, which he rejected because he thought that it contributed to the further imprisonment of souls in the material world, required of a married couple who sought baptism in Marcion's Church that they first separate. Rules concerning food and drink, which had to be accepted by the followers, were very detailed.

Expulsion from the ROMAN CATHOLIC CHURCH left Marcion and his followers to form their own, separate Church and this he organized from Rome. Tertullian, St Irenaeus, St Clement of Alexandria and Origen all attacked Marcion's theology. According to Tertullian, writing in *c.* 207, Marcion professed penitence and accepted as a condition of his readmission to the Roman Catholic Church that he would bring back those he had led away from the Church, but his death intervened.

The Marcionites, who spread throughout Europe, persisted well into the fourth and even fifth centuries; there is evidence that they were refuted in the fifth century by an Armenian archpriest, Eznic, but by then most of the Marcionites had been absorbed by MANICHAEISM. There has been a suggestion that Manichaeism lasted until the tenth century in Syria.

MARCOSIANS

Followers of an Alexandrian GNOSTIC leader called Marcus, who might himself have been a disciple of the second century Gnostic, Valentinus. Marcus was condemned in *c.* 175 by St Irenaeus, Bishop of Lyons (*c.* 125 – *c.* 202), who wrote of him as of one who was alive at the time of writing.

Marcus put considerable emphasis on both numerology and prophecy and taught that by calculating the numerical value of God's names all manner of hidden wisdom could be deduced. He encouraged women, especially those of wealth and fine appearance, to become prophetesses and it has been alleged that their incoherent babblings were said to be the voice of God. Irenaeus also claimed in his writings that Marcus had a sexual relationship with these women and condemned him as a self-proclaimed prophet and magician whose sole aim was to lead a dissolute life.

The followers, both male and female, celebrated a form of Eucharist, during which the celebrant, after reciting the words of consecration, would pour wine into a large vessel into which some purple liquid, known as the 'Blood of Grace' had been introduced previously but whose composition was, by all accounts, unsavoury. The final result was a remarkable colour change, as well as a change in volume, which had a marked effect on the assembly.

This sect employed a strange rite, a combined form of the usual Christian baptism and confirmation. The candidate had a mixture of oil and water poured over his head with the following formula recited at the same time 'In the Name of the Unknown Father of all, in the Truth, the Mother of All, in Him who came down on Jesus'. The scriptural basis of Marcosian teaching was the apocryphal *Acts of Thomas*, in which Thomas is depicted as Christ's twin and the recipient of 114 secret teachings of Jesus; other apocryphal works may also have been used. Marcosians flourished in the mid-second century in the Rhône Valley and possibly survived until well into the fourth century.

MARIA LEGIO OF AFRICA

This is a schismatic Church, formed in Kenya by a very large number of former Roman Catholics who seceded from their Church in 1962. The Maria Legio Church has a presence in neighbouring Tanzania, having been established there by immigrants from Kenya in 1963; it was also founded in Uganda in 1968, though later banned during Idi Amin's purge of various religious organizations.

Since this Church was formed as a schism from the ROMAN CATHOLIC CHURCH it is not surprising that much of the structure and liturgical form of that Church has been adopted, such as the offices of a pope, cardinals and diocesan bishops. The Church makes use of vestments and written liturgies, which is somewhat untypical of the usage in many African indigenous Churches. Incongruously, the Church betrays its African origins by employing sniffers, or *Juchekos*, who literally sniff at newcomers to discern whether their intentions are evil or not. At present the Church is growing in strength and there are now nearly a thousand congregations in Kenya alone, with around 130,000 adult members. The same pattern of growth is repeated in Uganda and Tanzania.

MARIAVITES

This is a general term used to cover two distinct Churches, with a common origin in 1906 when the group was founded by a Third Order Franciscan Sister, Maria Frances Kozlowska and a Roman Catholic priest from Warsaw, Jan Kowalski. These are the Catholic Mariavite Church and the Old Catholic Mariavite Church (in Poland). The name 'Mariavite' *was adopted to emphasize the members' devotion to the Blessed Virgin Mary.*

Both Maria Kozlowska, also known as Little Mother, and Jan Kowalski were excommunicated from the ROMAN CATHOLIC CHURCH in 1906, in part because of their refusal to deny the divine revelations that they were allegedly receiving and which the Church authorities had declared to be hallucinatory, and partly because they refused to accede to Rome's demand that the community of men and women, called Mariavites, which the two had been instrumental in assembling together, should be disbanded. This opposition had been directed at Kozlowska and Kowalski largely by Polish Jesuits. The formal condemnation of the Mariavites was declared in *Tribus Circiter (On the Mariavites, or Mystic Priests of Poland)*, which was issued by Pope St Pius X in April 1906, and the excommunication of all Mariavites was declared in December of that year.

A period of bitter persecution and physical attacks followed and several church buildings were burnt down. It became clear that there was a need for overall episcopal administration and the OLD CATHOLIC CHURCH of Utrecht, in the Netherlands, was approached. Jan Kowalski and two of his community were sent to the Old Catholic Congress in Vienna in 1909 where they met the Russian theologian, General Alexander Kireef, who lent them his support. The Old Catholic bishops consecrated Jan

Kowalski as brother-bishop in October 1909.

In 1921, after the death of Maria Kozlowska, news that *mystical marriages* between cohabiting Mariavite priests and nuns were being tolerated reached the Old Catholic authorities. The children born to these irregular couples were thought of as 'being born without original sin' and were declared to be the first born of a new and sinless humanity. This resulted in the expulsion of the Mariavites from the Old Catholic communion.

The ordination of women was authorized by Kowalski in 1930, followed by the inauguration of the notion of a universal priesthood, or a priesthood of believers. This meant that every Mariavite could celebrate a *People's Mass*, as it was called. This lasted for around ten minutes and could be celebrated in the home by any Mariavite to whom permission had been granted by a Mariavite bishop. A major schism occurred in 1936, led by one of Kowalski's bishops. This group was accepted back into the Old Catholic communion in 1973 and is now known as the Old Catholic Church of the Mariavites, with a more regular ecclesial structure, several convents and training opportunities for future priests at a seminary in Plock, Poland. There are currently 194 congregations serving the needs of some 15,500 members.

At the time of the 1936 split those Mariavites who did not join the group which later rejoined the Old Catholic Church formed the Catholic Mariavite Church, also known as the Mariavite Church of Ancient Catholic Rite. This Church has its headquarters at Felicianow, Poland, with 31 congregations and a total current membership of 3,450, but it is experiencing little growth.

MARONITES

Maronites are members of an Eastern Catholic Churches, found mainly in Lebanon, Syria, Cyprus, Egypt and North and South America. Controversy surrounds the origin of the name. It is alleged that a hermit, St Maro, a contemporary of St John Chrysostom (*c.* 347–407), lived near Cyrrhus (now Cyr) in Syria and that after his death in 410 a monastery was founded at Beit-Marum, in the Apamée region of Syria and near to the source of the River Orontes. This is claimed by some Maronites to be their origin and St Maro is venerated as their founder.

The Maronites became a separate body in the seventh century when, as a group, they adopted Monothelitism, for which they were excommunicated at the Third Council of Constantinople, held in 680–81. The monastery at Beit-Marum was destroyed by Arabs in the tenth century and another was founded at Kefr-Nay, in the Botyrs district of Syria, where the head of St Maro is enshrined. In 1182, as a result of the crusades, some 40,000 Maronites converted to Roman Catholicism and have remained as Eastern-rite Catholics ever since. The Maronites prospered under Rome, but in the mid-nineteenth century thousands of them were massacred by the Turks; Pope Pius XI beatified some of these martyrs in 1926. Further massacres followed during the First World War and this prompted many Maronites to flee the country. Of those who remained behind, many became involved in the fighting in Lebanon in the 1980s.

The Maronites are headed by a patriarch

who lives in Lebanon, at Bekorki (now Bkerke). There are also dioceses for Maronites in France, the USA, Brazil, Argentina, Egypt, Cyprus, Syria and Australia. The Divine Liturgy used is that of the Antiochene rite, with Latin modifications such as the use of Latin-style Mass vestments and unleavened hosts as well as the form of distribution of Holy Communion. The Maronite Mass is celebrated in Syriac-Aramaic and Arabic, the present-day vernacular of the Maronite people.

MARSFIELD COMMUNITY CHURCH

A small, Australian independent evangelical Church formed in Marsfield, a northern suburb of Sydney, New South Wales, in 1933 as a BAPTIST/METHODIST Sunday school. It attracted enough local interest that in 1978 it was more formally organized as a Church. The doctrinal position is Bible-centred and baptism is affirmed. There is also an emphasis on Christ's second coming (REVELATION 20).

MEGIDDO CHURCH

This small American Church, currently based in Rochester, New York, derives its name from a Mississippi river steamer which was launched at the start of the twentieth century to operate as a floating evangelizing centre; in 1903, two years after its launch, the *Megiddo* was sold and the members of the Church opened a land-based community at Rochester. The founder, the Reverend L. T. Nichols (1844–1912) was a keen Bible student.

It is said that during a Christmas party when Nichols was 10 years old he saw the facemask slip from Santa Claus, revealing that of a neighbour and, presumably appalled at discovering this deception, he thereafter questioned closely everything he came across in life; it is also said that, as a teenager, Nichols would carry a Bible with him at all times and was given to conducting courses in Bible study for his fellow students during school breaks, earning himself the soubriquet of *Elder Joe*. This incident seems to have influenced his thinking greatly.

After his marriage Nichols set out upon evangelizing trips to Oregon, Illinois, Indiana, Ohio and Texas. He established a church at Barry, Illinois, and placed it under the care of an ex-ROMAN CATHOLIC follower, Maud Hembree. Throughout these journeys Nichols preached a distinctive message based on his *discovery* that there was no original sin through Adam's fall, but that all people are responsible for their own sins. The way to salvation was to follow Christ, whose imminent return to earth was expected. It was Nichols' idea to spread his evangelical gospel more effectively by using a river boat and this led to the launching of the *Megiddo*, which was also used to house 90 of his followers, people who had sold up their property to live on board and act as missionaries. The group evangelized the towns along the Mississippi and Ohio rivers and their tributaries. After the sale of the boat and the removal of the members to their shore-based church, Maud Hembree carried on the river-evangelization. After the death of Nichols, she took over the leadership of the group and perpetuated his idea of a roving ministry by making use of several more boats, which plied the Great Lakes spreading the message. The community based in Rochester continued its work and is now largely concerned with providing publications concerned with Bible study and the end of time.

The members of this Church believe that the signal for Christ's return to earth will be the reappearance of the prophet Elijah, with other indications such as the growth of rampant hedonism, political corruption, an acceleration of the arms race and the growth of peace movements. Once Christ has returned, they teach, the battle of Armageddon will commence and at its conclusion the millennial reign of Christ will begin (REVELATION 20). Doctrinally, the Church does not profess a belief in the Trinity, but its members clearly acknowledge that Jesus Christ is God's Son. The Holy Spirit is considered to be a divine power, but not a person. Man's earthly mortality is accepted and it is believed that immortality can only be achieved after a righteous life on earth; if man chooses to live a wicked life, however, there will be no eternal punishment in hell but that individual's existence will terminate with death.

❖ Megiddo Mission

MELCHIORITES

The name given to followers of Melchior Hofmann (*c.* 1500–43), a German ANABAPTIST furrier and leather worker who lived in Livonia (part of present day Latvia). He became a LUTHERAN, rising to the office of lay preacher in 1523, but soon came into conflict with the authorities. Hofmann moved to Sweden, settling in Stockholm in 1526 where his interest in eschatology, the theology of *last things*, flourished until he felt confident enough to predict the imminent end of the world. His preaching took Hofmann into Germany where, in Flensburg (Holstein), in 1529, he argued against the Lutheran belief concerning the Eucharist, which he declared to be purely a sign, or symbol. Joining other groups of Anabaptists in Strasbourg, Hofmann and his companions travelled and preached throughout Friesland and Holland from 1530–3.

Apart from his eschatological views, Hofmann held to the believer's baptism, which he argued was a covenant, and advocated the principle of non-resistance and rejection of oaths as well as the separation of church and state. In 1533, upon his return to Strasbourg, Hofmann was arrested and imprisoned. During his incarceration he predicted that after his death, which event he placed some six months into the future, he would return with Christ in glory and that the city of Strasbourg would become the New Jerusalem (REVELATION 20); in the event he died in prison, but not until 1543. After Hofmann's imprisonment some Melchiorites, led by Jan Matthys, a baker, and *King* Jan van Leyden (who was also known as Jan Bockelsohn), a tailor from Haarlem, declared that Münster, in Germany, was to replace Strasbourg as the New Jerusalem. Rumours of polygamy and orgies spread during the following period of anarchy and destruction in Münster, when the civil authority of the bishop, Francis of Waldeck, was lost. Determined to regain his authority, Bishop Francis formed an alliance with Philip of Hesse and the town of Münster was laid siege to in 1535, falling after sixteen months; the Melchiorite leaders were executed. The anarchistic reputation that the Anabaptist movement earned through the violent behaviour of the Melchiorites did not persist and the good example and preaching of Anabaptists such as Menno Simons, whose followers, the MENNONITES, are still in existence, far outweighed the excesses of the Melchiorites in Münster.

❖ Brethren of the Covenant; Covenanters

MELKITES

Members of Eastern and Byzantine-rite Churches who accepted the decrees of the Council of Chalcedon (451), thereby rejecting MONOPHYSITISM. The Melkites, or *King's Men* (from the Syrian '*melcho*'– king) are so called because they followed the lead given by the Eastern Roman Emperor, Marcion of Constantinople (450–7), in the rejection of Monophysitism, a heresy that asserted that the two natures became 'blended and confused' in the one person of Christ.

Although the name can apply to those Catholics who follow the Byzantine rite and remain in communion with Rome, as well as to those Orthodox Christians who followed Constantinople into schism from Rome after 1054, it is now more properly applied to the Byzantine-rite Catholics of Syria, Palestine, Egypt, the Lebanon, Israel, Jordan, North and South America and Australia. Like the MARONITES and the SYRIAN CATHOLIC CHURCH, the Melkite community has its own hierarchy and its own Byzantine rite, which is almost always celebrated in the vernacular except for a few versicles and exclamations in Greek; on solemn occasions the entire Divine Liturgy may be celebrated in Greek.

The head of the Melkite Church, who remains under the authority of the Pope in Rome, is styled as the Patriarch of Antioch and all the East, of Alexandria and of Jerusalem. He is elected by the bishops of the Church who present their chosen candidate's name to Rome for approval. It is the patriarch, who lives in Damascus, who confirms the election and consecration of all bishops within his jurisdiction.

Celibate priests, who may not necessarily be monks, are eligible to become bishops while those priests who wish to marry must do so before they are ordained. Seminaries in Harissa and Beirut provide training for the priesthood, and those faithful who may have a religious vocation may enter monasteries and convents observing the Basilian rule.

❖ Melchites

MENNONITE BRETHREN CHURCH OF NORTH AMERICA

There were small colonies of MENNONITE Germans living in Russia in the mid-nineteenth century who were seeking a greater religious experience than existed in their group at the time. Influenced by an evangelical preacher, Pastor Edward Wuest, their frustration grew and they demanded a separate Communion service because of their self-perceived spirituality. In addition, the members wanted a greater amount of Bible study and more frequent prayer services. When the request for separate Communion services was not granted, the members began to hold their own, resulting finally in the establishment of a separate Mennonite Brethren group, the *Mennoniten Brüdergemeinde*, in 1860. The first members of the group to emigrate to the USA went there in 1874 and under the influence of Elder Abraham Schellenberg this American congregation grew in number, size and influence, spreading throughout America and into Canada.

In 1869 Jacob Wiebe had organized the Crimean Brethren in Russia, which later became known as the Krimmer Mennonite Brethren Church, members of which also emigrated to the USA in 1874, settling in Kansas. With them they brought their very rigid way of life, in which worldly amusements are forbidden. In 1960 the Krimmer Mennonite Brethren

Church merged with the Mennonite Brethren Church, the formal ceremony taking place in Reedly, California, after discussions and proposals that had lasted for nearly a century. Other changes followed, and seminaries and colleges were opened. By the mid-1980s the Church was supporting 137 missionaries in 23 countries. As new members from different cultural and ethnic backgrounds, including Chinese, French Canadians, Hispanics and Vietnamese, have found their way into Mennonite congregations, there has been a corresponding breakdown of the original cultural structure. Nevertheless, the Mennonite Brethren Church of North America, with its 134 congregations, is still growing.

The Canadian Mennonite Brethren Churches experienced a great increase in membership at the time of the ending of the Second World War and this led to a need for greater independence for the Canadian Church with the result that area conferences were established to manage administration in Canada.

❖ Brüdergemeinde; General Conference of Mennonite Brethren Churches

MENNONITE CHURCH (also MENNONITE; MENNONITES)

In post-Reformation Europe there were many Christian groups that sought a return to an early, or primitive, expression of Christianity. One such group included the ANABAPTISTS, who insisted that infant baptism could not be scripturally justified with the result that those adults who had been baptized as infants were seen as in need of re-baptism.

Menno Simons (1496–1561), who is acknowledged as the founder of the MENNONITES, was born in Friesland and was ordained in 1524 as a priest in the ROMAN CATHOLIC CHURCH. The execution of an Anabaptist in Friesland in 1531 deeply shocked him and although he was still acting as a priest, Simons came to the conclusion that infant baptism was wrong and that only a believer's baptism was scripturally sound. Becoming convinced of the Anabaptist cause by 1536, Menno Simons joined an Anabaptist group in the Netherlands that was led by Obbe Philips (*c.* 1500–68). Philips baptized and ordained Simons, who undertook extensive missionary journeys throughout the Netherlands and Germany, aware of the threat of persecution facing him from Roman Catholics and LUTHERANS alike. He settled in Holstein, Denmark, from where he would set out on further missionary excursions, and was soon recognized as the leader of the Anabaptists in the Netherlands and North Germany, Philips meanwhile having withdrawn from the scene.

Some of Simon's Dutch followers settled around Danzig (now Gdansk, Poland) in the 1540s, from where some went to Russia in the last half of the eighteenth century, drawn there by the religious toleration extended by Catherine the Great to the German settlers who were populating parts of the country. Some Mennonites left Europe and settled in America as early as the 1640s, but the first permanent American Mennonite settlement, at Germantown near Philadelphia, was not founded until 1683.

A serious split in the Church occurred in 1693, when Jacob Ammann, a leader of the Swiss Mennonites, called for a return to a strict form of discipline which was to include the avoidance of those members who had erred, which is also known as *shunning*. This led to a division, with some members following Ammann and separating themselves from their erstwhile fellows. This group became known as the AMISH. Ammann's followers imposed a stern discipline on themselves, to the extent of condemning the use of buttons. Broad brimmed hats for men, together with the mandatory wearing of beards, were also introduced, the women adopting the use of demure bonnets and aprons with their plain dresses. Waves of immigrants followed the early settlers and made their way to America, founding groups in Pennsylvania, Virginia and Ohio. This later extended westwards and into Canada, where settlements were made in Ontario. At the end of the nineteenth century and during the first half of the twentieth century, waves of Russian Mennonites arrived in North America, settling in Manitoba and Kansas, while others went to South America, settling in Paraguay and Brazil.

Menno Simons had placed a great emphasis upon a literal interpretation of the Bible, prayer and holiness as well as withdrawal from the world and its pursuits, and much the same is expected of present-day Mennonites who are still accustomed to the wearing of plain clothes and the avoidance of jewellery and all unnecessary decoration. Simons, as already mentioned, had also called for the strict use of *shunning*, which involves the imposition of the *ban*, as a way in which the Church could be kept free from the taint of corrupt movements, and had insisted that even family members should shun those who had received the *ban*, refusing even to eat with them. This shunning of a person who is seen as living in error is based on 1 Corinthians 5:11, but the practice has been modified in recent years.

The doctrinal stand of the Church was set out in the *Dordrecht Confession* of 1632, which acknowledges the Trinity, and the life, death and resurrection of Jesus Christ and affirms that baptism is for repentant adult believers. Although infants are not baptized, they are thought of as *saved* and a dedicatory service is conducted to ask a blessing upon the newborn child and its parents. Baptism is usually administered to candidates in their teens and is given by pouring water over the recipient. The Lord's Supper is celebrated as an ordinance, very solemnly, twice a year and is preceded by a foot-washing ceremony. This practice was the cause of another split within the Church, when some members could not agree whether it takes two to perform the ceremony, one to wash the feet and the other to wipe them, or whether the entire ceremony is best performed by a single person.

Pacifism is insisted upon, and both oath-taking and military service are generally forbidden to Mennonites. The congregations are autonomous, with a general conference meeting every two years and acting as an advisory body for the whole Church, which is now heavily involved in mission outreach programmes and various other ministries, in education, church development and the media. Some 300 workers are involved in foreign missions, currently in over 50 countries; home missions and charitable efforts are directed to various ethnic and disadvantaged groups such as the Native Americans, African Americans, Hispanics and Asian refugees. The Church also maintains various colleges and seminaries.

MESERETE KRISTOS CHURCH

A Church organized in Ethiopia during the 1940s by MENNONITE missionaries from America, who had gone to the country as part of a relief agency following the Second World War, but who sought permission to evangelize soon afterwards.

This is one of two Churches that emerged from the Mennonite mission; the other is the Full Gospel Church, which is also known as the Full Gospel Believers' Church (founded *c.* 1960). The Ethiopian government later outlawed the latter Church, which must not be confused with American-based foundations with a similar name, and three hundred of its members were imprisoned on charges of treason and immorality. Some members of the Church went underground, while others joined the Meserete Kristos Church (MKC). The PENTECOSTAL spirit of the Full Gospel Church soon spread to the MKC, and a considerable emphasis was placed on faith healing, exorcism and *glossolalia*, or speaking in tongues.

With the coming to power of a pro-Marxist military junta in the 1970s, the MKC and its members were persecuted for nearly nine years, and with the collapse of this regime in 1991 religious freedom was re-established and the remnants of the Church began a programme of reorganization. This resulted in a tenfold increase in membership and the Church currently enjoys an annual growth rate of nearly 20 per cent.

The MKC has developed an extensive theological educational programme, which includes a series of six-week courses and a two-year Bible school course which is designed to prepare the future leadership of the Church. Many new places of worship are being opened to provide for the 600 congregations, which now provide for over 100,000 adult members.

❖ Christ Foundation Church; Christ is the Foundation Church

METHODISM (also METHODIST)

The beliefs and organization of those Churches founded by John and Charles Wesley, and their followers. For an outline of Methodism, see METHODIST CHURCH OF GREAT BRITAIN.

METHODIST CHURCH

This must not be confused with either the Methodist Church of Great Britain, or the Methodist Church in Ireland.

This American Church, which is no longer in existence, was formed in 1939 in Kansas City by the merger of three Methodist Churches; these were the METHODIST EPISCOPAL CHURCH (North), the Methodist Episcopal Church (South) and the METHODIST PROTESTANT CHURCH.

Organizationally, the Church was governed through a system of annual conferences, whose work was supplemented by jurisdictional conferences that met every four years. One of the functions of the annual conference was to elect bishops to join the council of bishops, which had responsibility for the temporal and spiritual welfare of the Church. The general conference was attended by an equal number of lay and clerical delegates. Any matters arising that needed to be decided by a higher body would be referred to a judicial conference, composed of five ministers and four laymen, whose decision was final.

The Methodist Church, which placed a heavy emphasis upon foreign missions, education, health and social welfare, especially for the elderly, ceased to exist *per se* in 1968 when it was agreed that it should merge with the EVANGELICAL UNITED BRETHREN CHURCH to form the UNITED METHODIST CHURCH (USA).

METHODIST CHURCH IN IRELAND

Methodism came to Ireland in the last half of the eighteenth century and was considered to be such an evangelistic movement within the established CHURCH OF ENGLAND that separation was inevitable. This separation was achieved in 1878 since when the Methodist Church in Ireland has been very active in providing support for various charitable causes, particularly with the poor, the elderly and with orphaned children. Education has not been neglected, and the Wesley College in Dublin, the Methodist College in Belfast and the Gurteen Agricultural College in north Tipperary were established.

Organizationally, the members are distributed in congregations, six or seven of which constitute a circuit; each circuit is directed by a quarterly board, comprising a senior minister, the circuit superintendent, who is assisted by other ministers and lay preachers together with delegated leaders from individual congregations. These circuits are collectively grouped into districts and delegates from the congregations attend an annual conference. There are currently nearly 200 congregations, with an adult membership of about 43,000 adult members, with the headquarters of the Church in Belfast, Northern Ireland.

METHODIST CHURCH OF GREAT BRITAIN

All members of the World Methodist Council, of which the Methodist Church of Great Britain is one, are derived from the work of John Wesley (1703–91), and his brother, Charles (1707–88) who, with others, met in Oxford and formed the *Holy Club*, whose members were derisively called *Methodists* because of their strict, methodical routine in following a spiritual and charitable rule of life.

The Wesley brothers left Oxford University in 1736 and went to America where John took up missionary work amongst the American Indians in Georgia, a venture that failed, while Charles became secretary to General Oglethorpe. John Wesley had met up with a group of members of the MORAVIAN CHURCH and upon his return to England he attended a Moravian meeting at a gathering in London, in 1738, where he underwent a conversion experience that led him to form the United Societies, simple groups of dedicated, evangelizing Christians who still regarded themselves as being within the CHURCH OF ENGLAND.

The first Methodist Society was attached to a Moravian congregation in Fetter Lane, London, in 1739; this later moved to its own quarters in an old, abandoned government building known as The Foundry. Within three years the first *classes*, or weekly meetings of converts, were formed and by 1743 the rules of the society had been drawn up. In the following year the first conference was convened; by 1746 the societies had become organized within set geographical boundaries, known as *circuits*. A society was thought of in terms of a gathering of people rather than a specific place; there was a considerable amount of outdoor, or field, preaching that made use of lay preachers.

In 1784 John Wesley named, in a deed of

declaration made in the Court of Chancery, a hundred of his preachers as a self-perpetuating body known as the *Legal Hundred*, whose mandate was to direct the movement. Until the nineteenth century this group was composed only of ordained clerics, giving legal status to the yearly Methodist conference. In the same year Wesley published his *Twenty-Five Articles of Religion* based upon the Church of England's *Thirty-Nine Articles*. Wesley's *Articles* excluded those dealing with hell, the creeds, predestination, bishops, excommunication and the authority of the Church. The Methodist societies did not regard themselves as a separate denomination until after the death of John Wesley in 1791 and many continued to receive the sacraments in the Church of England. Wesley, himself, never doubted that he was a member of the Church of England. This was changed in 1795, by which time separation from the state Church had been effected. The *Plan of Pacification* was drawn up which allowed for the administration of the sacraments, the celebration of marriage and the conducting of funerals in Methodist chapels. Admission to the ministry of the Church was at first validly achieved simply through being in *full connexion with the Conference*, but by 1836 ordination through the traditional laying on of hands had become the norm.

Following Wesley's death several secessions from the Church occurred over disputes concerning polity, rather than doctrine, and by the start of the twentieth century many of these small, seceded groups had reunited to form the UNITED METHODIST CHURCH (UK) (1907); this Church, together with two small seceded Methodist groups, the Wesleyan Methodist Church and the PRIMITIVE METHODIST CHURCH, united in 1932 to form the Methodist Church of Great Britain.

Even before Wesley's death there had been a strong missionary emphasis in the group. In 1769 Richard Boardman and Joseph Pilmoor volunteered to undertake missionary work in America, and other missions followed shortly afterwards, to Nova Scotia, Antigua and Newfoundland and over the years other missions were set up in the West Indies, Africa and throughout Asia.

The doctrinal position of the Church is traditionally Christian and based upon the Apostles', Nicene and Athanasian creeds. The Church affirms the vital role of scripture, the sacraments of infant baptism (usually by sprinkling, although pouring is permitted), the Lord's Supper, the Trinity and a strict ARMINIAN view that salvation is available for all, and that each person is not inherently sinful and is free to accept, or reject, opportunities for salvation. The Church also accepts the possibility of Christian perfection (PERFECTIONISM), which implies that a Christian can experience a second moment of spiritual assurance of their conversion, and this enables them to live a life of true holiness; this second experience was never claimed by John Wesley.

Autonomous Methodist Churches were established in Australia (these are now part of the UNITING CHURCH OF AUSTRALIA), in North America, New Zealand, South Africa and Europe, many of which have now undergone unions with other PROTESTANT Churches. Today, the Methodist Church of Great Britain has over 400,000 members distributed amongst 6,452 churches with over 3,000 ministers and nearly 11,000 lay preachers.

The headquarters of the Church in Great Britain is in London.

In 2001, Methodists became involved in formal conversations about the question of unity with the Anglicans. A draft report is to be produced and this was considered by the Methodist Conference in June 2002, and by the General Synod of the Church of England in the following month.

METHODIST EPISCOPAL CHURCH

METHODISM arose as an evangelical movement within the CHURCH OF ENGLAND in the early eighteenth century, when Charles Wesley, George Whitefield and some others formed a small group of students at Oxford University who gave set periods of time to prayer, Bible study and charitable work. John Wesley, the elder of the two Wesley brothers, had been ordained as a priest in the Church of England in 1728. He joined the *Holy Club* that his younger brother, Charles, and the others, had formed and soon took over its leadership. The group attracted a variety of nicknames, some deprecating such as *Bible Bigots* and *Bible Moths*, but the one that was to remain with them was *Methodists*, as the group was seen to be methodically religious in the working out of salvation, in line with their claim that just as justification required decision, this process (sanctification) required effort and a Christian's life should be virtuous and concerned with those less fortunate than himself.

The Methodists were given to open-air preaching and attracted a large following, so much so that it became necessary to organize the converts into societies. Between 1739–46, an organizational pattern was arranged with lay preachers appointed (in 1741) and *classes*, or weekly meetings, held for converts (in 1742). By 1746 the societies within a geographical area had become known as *circuits.*

Methodism was introduced into the USA through the work of unofficial lay preachers such as Philip Embury, who preached the first sermon to four people in his own house in New York in 1766. This proved instrumental in encouraging a spread of interest and many people, much encouraged by the preaching of a British Army officer, Captain Thomas Webb, were converted to Methodism. The movement soon spread into Pennsylvania, Delaware, Virginia and New Jersey. Amongst the early missionaries sent to America by John Wesley was Francis Asbury. He arrived there in 1771 and became the leading light of American Methodism. The first conference was convened at St George's Church in Philadelphia in 1773, when John Wesley's authority was affirmed and the conclusion reached that the preachers were not, unlike priests, authorized to administer Holy Communion. The American Revolution intervened and the Methodist missionaries, with the exception of Asbury, returned to England. Wesley, himself, had spoken against the independence of colonies in one of his pamphlets. At the war's end it was clear that the American Church now needed separate organization. Wesley ordained two preachers, Whatcoat and Wasey, as elders, and Dr Thomas Coke as superintendent for America.

The 'Christmas Conference', as it has become known, was convened in 1784 in Baltimore, Maryland, establishing the Methodist Episcopal Church as an autonomous denomination. Thomas Coke had brought with him to America Wesley's plans, his *Twenty-Five Articles of Faith* and *The Sunday Service* (an abridged version of the *Book of Common*

Prayer), as well as *Discipline* (the law and practice of the Church). These were all adopted and Asbury was ordained deacon, elder and joint superintendent, upon successive days, by Thomas Coke, whose own appointment as superintendent was confirmed; the title of superintendent was later changed to bishop, despite John Wesley's opposition.

Since the early days of the METHODIST CHURCH in America there was some friction between the black and white members of the congregations, especially in Philadelphia and Baltimore. In 1844 a split came about when a slave-owning bishop, James Andrew of Georgia, found himself unable, despite his wishes, to free his slaves under the laws of Georgia. The 1844 general conference in New York ordered James Andrew to cease acting as a bishop until he freed his slaves, but this decision upset delegates from the southern states, who formed a plan of separation. They organized their own Church, the Methodist Episcopal Church (South) in 1845. The schism was not healed until 1939, with the formation of the Methodist Church. This later became a partner in the 1968 merger that created the UNITED METHODIST CHURCH (USA).

METHODIST NEW CONNEXION

Towards the close of the eighteenth century, many METHODIST laity were agitating for a formal separation of the Methodists from the CHURCH OF ENGLAND, and one of the most vigorous supporters of this separation was Alexander Kilham (1762–98), an Englishman, who was born into a METHODIST family and at the age of 23 became a preacher in that Church. Many of the laity felt strongly that they should be able to receive Communion from their own preachers and this was even more strongly argued after Wesley's death. Kilham further pressed for a greater lay participation in the Church's administration. His argument for separation was reinforced by the publication of several booklets, especially by the preface to *The Life of Mr Alexander Kilham*, in which he exposed what he saw as abuse of the system as it existed. In consequence, Kilham was expelled from the Methodist Conference in 1796. The following year he summoned a convention, in which he continued to argue with the conference in support of his radical democracy, but he was unsuccessful. Kilham responded by forming the Methodist New Connexion in 1797, a year before his untimely death at the age of 36.

Despite the loss of its leader and the poverty of the new group, the New Connexion managed to survive and by the end of the nineteenth century had a membership of around 30,000 with its greatest support in Ireland. In 1907 the Church merged with the UNITED FREE METHODIST CHURCHES and the BIBLE CHRISTIANS to form the UNITED METHODIST CHURCH (UK), which in 1932 was amalgamated with the Wesleyan Church and the PRIMITIVE METHODIST CHURCH to form the METHODIST CHURCH OF GREAT BRITAIN.

❖ Kilhamites; The New Itinerancy; The New Methodists

METHODIST PROTESTANT CHURCH

The Methodist Protestant Church, which arose briefly in North America, is no longer in existence as such but merged with others within the METHODIST tradition. It came into existence in New England and some western states in the early part of the nineteenth century, mainly in rural areas, as a result of agitation for the rights of laity in the METHODIST EPISCOPAL CHURCH. It was felt strongly by some that there should be lay representation at conferences and with the appointment of ministers. In 1828 this protest for reform led to schisms when lay representation at the general conference of the Methodist Episcopal Church was denied; by 1830 the dissidents had organized themselves as the Methodist Protestant Church at Baltimore, Maryland, with around five thousand members in, as they said, 'a Church without a bishop for a land without a king'. The Church was so organized that its lay members at conference were able to assign the ministers to their congregations, a privilege that had been the responsibility of the bishop in the Methodist Episcopal Church. The Methodist Protestant Church recognized that women should be ordained for the pastoral ministry and by the latter part of the nineteenth century this had been achieved. The Church was initially concentrated in rural areas and small towns, mainly because of a lack of education in its clergy that was thought necessary for ministries in the more sophisticated urban areas. The Church was enthusiastic in its support for the social issues of the times, which included movements for the abolition of slavery, the encouragement of temperance and the avoidance of membership of oath-taking secret societies.

Other schisms within the Methodist Episcopal Church developed as a result of controversies concerning the issues of slavery and episcopal polity, resulting in the formation of two more Churches, the Methodist Episcopal Church (North) and the Methodist Episcopal Church (South). The strong anti-episcopal stance adopted by the Methodist Protestant Church was modified in time, allowing an important merger to take place in 1939 when the Methodist Episcopal Church (North) and the Methodist Episcopal Church (South) merged to form the METHODIST CHURCH. This union had the beneficial effect of bringing into the Church many who had contributed greatly to the careful preservation of the Wesleyan-ARMINIAN theology. A final merger was made with the Evangelical United Brethren in 1968, which resulted in the formation of the UNITED METHODIST CHURCH (USA).

METROPOLITAN CHURCH ASSOCIATION – USA

This American Church, which is within the HOLINESS tradition, broke away from the METHODIST EPISCOPAL CHURCH in Chicago in 1894, adopting the name of Metropolitan Holiness Church; it was subsequently renamed as the Metropolitan Church Association (MCA) in 1899. There was a brief period of cooperation with another breakaway holiness group, the Pentecostal Union, which was renamed after 1917 as the PILLAR OF FIRE.

Doctrinally, there is an emphasis not only upon justification, or being born again, but following conversion there is the hope of the second blessing, or sanctification. Members of the Church do not accept the creeds, regarding the scriptures as sufficient for the living of a Christian life in keeping with the holiness tradition. The worship services have a reputation for being occasions for enthusiastic and emotional outbursts. Members are expected to avoid expensive clothing and maintain a simple lifestyle. Extensive foreign missions have been established and the Church now maintains a presence in India (since 1904), South Africa (since 1930) and Swaziland (since 1936), with further missions in Mexico and the Virgin Islands. There are currently 20 congregations in the USA, serving a committed membership of 600, and the headquarters of the Church is at Lake Geneva, Wisconsin.

METROPOLITAN COMMUNITY CHURCH

This Church is part of the Universal Fellowship of Metropolitan Community Churches (UFMCC) and has observer status at the World Council of Churches (WCC). A defrocked minister of the CHURCH OF GOD OF PROPHECY, Troy D. Perry, founded the group at Santa Ana, California, in 1968. Perry had been defrocked when it was revealed that he was homosexual. He attempted suicide, but having survived, felt inspired to found a Church that would be able to offer a ministry to gay men, lesbians, bisexuals and the transgendered, as well as to any who felt discriminated against by their communities. The first service, which marked the foundation of the Metropolitan Community Church, was held in Los Angeles on 6 October 1968, led by Perry and attended by eleven men and one woman.

The Church recognizes two sacraments, baptism and Holy Communion, as well as six rites, which include membership, holy union (or matrimony, between people of the same sex), funeral (or memorial) services, laying on of hands, blessing and ordination. With many priests and clergy from other denominations joining the Church, its doctrinal position is very wide, extending from the liberal to the conservative, but there is a great emphasis on the development of a theology of love that teaches that God accepts everyone regardless of their sexual orientation. During the 1990s the Church achieved prominence through its advocacy for an end to the ban on lesbians in the US military services and its fight to develop AIDS awareness, for which a network of care, education and hope for HIV sufferers was established; provision was also made for the collection of resource material to help in the ministry among AIDS sufferers and the promotion of a public policy for an understanding health care system.

The Church actively promotes the ministry of female clergy and the priesthood of all believers, with lay people ministering at all levels. Training facilities operate through a network of both correspondence and taught courses that are available through the Samaritan Colleges, which are to be found in the USA, Canada, Australia and Europe. Administration is managed through an annual general conference, presided over by the moderator, which elects a board of seven elders. Because of the controversial nature of the Church it has been targeted by arson attacks and fire bombings. Church buildings in Los Angeles were also destroyed during the Northridge earthquake in 1994 and a new building programme has begun in West Hollywood, which will be both the site of a local church and also house the world headquarters of the UFMCC; this now has responsibility for over 300 churches around the world with an estimated committed membership of 40,000 people.

METROPOLITAN SPIRITUAL CHURCHES OF CHRIST

In 1925, Bishop Frank Taylor and Leviticus Lee Boswell founded this largely black American Church, which has its headquarters in Baltimore, Maryland. The Church acknowledges the Trinity, but it employs the unusual formula of baptism using the words 'in the Name of Jesus and in the Name of the Father and the Son'. The text of the Apostles' creed is altered by the omission of the word 'Catholic' for which the word 'universal' is substituted. Healing is practised and the doctrine of reincarnation is taught. There are around 100 congregations, with some 12,000 adult members, distributed mainly along the eastern side of the country, and the Church also supports overseas missions in Ghana and Liberia.

MIDDLE EAST EVANGELICAL CHURCH

This very small independent Church, based in Sydney, Australia, is evangelical in doctrine and practice and caters for Arabic speakers. It affirms that the Bible alone is sufficient for all doctrine and there is a stress on the need for a personal experience of being justified, or *born again*.

MILLENARIANISM

See REVELATION 20.

MILLENNIAL DAWNISTS

The Millennial Dawnists were the early followers of Charles Taze Russell (1852–1916), of *Watch Tower* (JEHOVAH'S WITNESSES) fame, who helped their founder in the spread of his message. Russell believed in the establishment of God's direct rule on earth and the glorification of the saints, scheduled to take place in 1914, though subsequently revised to 1918.

Russell taught that the period 1874–1914 was the *millennial dawn*, a period of forty years which would be the time during which the Jews would return to Palestine and the Gentile nations would be overthrown. The coincidence of this date of 1914 with the onset of the First World War was taken as a sign of God's direct intervention in man's affairs and a sign of the beginning of the world's end (REVELATION 20). With Russell's death in 1916 an organization was left behind that was later to become the Jehovah's Witnesses.

❖ Millennial Dawn Students

MILLERITES

The name given to followers of William Miller (1782–1849), an American BAPTIST preacher who was much given to the predicting of the date of Christ's return to earth (REVELATION 20). This was initially set at a date in the twelve months leading up to 21 March 1844, and when nothing happened Miller adjusted his mathematics and recast the date as 22 October of the same year. When the scheduled event again failed to take place, to the dejection of the Millerites, this became known as the *Great Disappointment.*

Most of Miller's followers adopted the name of American Millennial Adventists and later became known as EVANGELICAL ADVENTISTS, which group eventually became defunct. There were, however, some Millerites who came to accept the alternative views offered by Ellen Gould Harmon (1827–1915), later known as Ellen G. White, who was given to having visions that supported some modified Millerite ideas. This group formed the SEVENTH-DAY ADVENTIST CHURCH, which can be said to have started following a conference of independent Adventist congregations at Battle Creek, Michigan, in 1860 and was formally organized as a Church in 1863.

The change of name to Seventh-Day Adventist Church was not unanimously agreed upon by the congregations, some of which preferred to be called the Church of God and were officially named as the CHURCH OF GOD (SEVENTH DAY) in 1884. This group retained Saturday worship and rejected most of Mrs White's theology.

MISSIONARY CHURCH

The Missionary Church came about through a merger, in the USA, between the MISSIONARY CHURCH ASSOCIATION and the UNITED MISSIONARY CHURCH in 1969 and has its headquarters in Fort Wayne, Indiana. As the name implies, the Church is involved in missionary work and supports some 100 missionaries in over 20 countries around the world.

The members uphold the importance and value of the scriptures as the primary source of doctrine, obey Christian principles for living and emphasize the four-fold view of Jesus Christ as saviour, sanctifier, healer and coming king. They affirm man's original sin and need for redemption through Jesus Christ. Their concern for the community and for brotherhood has impelled the members to provide nursing and retirement home facilities for the elderly, resources for education and ministries for family life, youth and children's work. The Church also maintains Bethel College in Mishawaka, north of Fort Wayne, Indiana.

MISSIONARY CHURCH ASSOCIATION

J. E. Ramseyer founded this Church in 1898 in Berne, Indiana; it later merged with the UNITED MISSIONARY CHURCH in 1969 to form the MISSIONARY CHURCH. The Church emerged as a result of a schism within the AMISH people of Indiana, some of whom formed the Missionary Church Association, which was organized on the basis of a firm belief that the contents of the Acts of the Apostles and the New Testament epistles had relevance for the daily practice of a Christian life and was the basis of their faith.

The members of the Association firmly believed that the Bible was the fully inspired word of God, and they accepted the Virgin Birth and Christ's divinity, atonement and resurrection. The group practised divine healing and were pre-millenialists (REVELATION 20) with a belief in eternal life for the just and everlasting punishment for the wicked. Baptism was administered by immersion and a policy of open communion was the norm.

The local churches of the Missionary Church Association enjoyed autonomy, but were formally organized under a general conference of clergy and laity that met biennially. As the name suggests, the Church was very active in its foreign missions, which were conducted in Haiti (established 1900), the Dominican Republic (established 1945), Ecuador (established 1945), Sierra Leone (established 1945) and Jamaica (established 1949).

MISSIONARY METHODIST CHURCH OF AMERICA

The Reverend H. C. Sisk and four others founded this American Church in Forest City, North Carolina, in 1913, as a secession from the WESLEYAN METHODIST CHURCH. The Church, which stands within the HOLINESS tradition, was initially to be called the Holiness Methodist Church, but when it was discovered that this title was already in use, the present name was adopted. The reason for the secession was the objection by some members of the Wesleyan Methodist Church to the vast number of rules and regulations that were being adopted by that Church.

The members of the Missionary Methodist Church of America hold to regeneration, or conversion, followed by sanctification. To prevent themselves from falling from grace members avoid all forms of worldliness in their lifestyles. They affirm belief in a personal devil and an actual, flame-filled, hell; they also anticipate the premillennial return of Christ to earth (REVELATION 20). The Church has some nine hundred members and seems to be experiencing a slow decline in growth.

MOLOKAN SPIRITUAL CHRISTIANS

The Molokans are *raskolniks*, or Russian schismatics, originating in the Caucasus mountain region, whose name is derived from their practice of drinking milk (Russian '*moloko*') on most days during the Great Lent and Holy Week in defiance of the fasting regulations of the RUSSIAN ORTHODOX CHURCH. The name was first applied to a group of these schismatics in the Tambov province of Voronezh Guberniia in *c.* 1765.

The origin of the group can be traced back to a seventeenth-century movement, known as Spiritual Christianity, which arose amongst the Russian peasantry as a move away from the tsarist-dominated Russian Orthodox Church. Molokanism spread to central and southern Russia, but in fear of religious intolerance and the enforcement of military service that ran counter to their religious beliefs, the Molokans left these areas and settled in the Far East, Ukraine and the Caucasus. With the conquering of the Caucasus area, which included Georgia, Armenia and Azerbaijan, by Russia at the start of the nineteenth century many resettled in undeveloped areas of Transcaucasia where they remained as a group for a century before migrating to the USA between 1905–12, settling in Los Angeles, California. There are around 200 Molokan communities worldwide, 150 of which are in Russia. Following the era of *glasnost* in the late twentieth century, they formed the Society of Spiritual Christian Molokans. There are another 30 Molokan communities in the western USA and 7 in Australia.

The Molokans in the USA are divided into two groups, the Steadfast (*Postoiannye*), or Constant, who are settled around Potrero Hill, San Francisco, and the Jumpers (*Pryguny*), also known as the Prancers, Dancers, Leapers or Skippers, who are to be found in Los Angeles and central California. The two groups differ in doctrine, customs and ritual; the Steadfast group are the greater in number.

Services, or gatherings (*Sobraniia*) are not held in recognizable church buildings but usually in unremarkable halls or in private houses, with the room arranged with a table in one corner and wooden benches running parallel to two sides of it. The Sunday service is arranged in two parts, the first part concerned with the chanting of verses of scripture and the sharing of religious thoughts, with the congregation seated. The second part sees the benches moved away and the congregation, now standing, reciting prayers and singing songs. Within the congregation the women are separated from the men. In the Steadfast group there are four groups of office holders (five for the Jumpers): the *Presviter*, or presiding elder who faces the congregation from one side of the table, the *Besedniki*, or speakers; the *Pevetsy*, or singers; and the *Skazateli*, or readers; the Jumpers have a fifth office of *Proroki*, or prophets.

On the table are placed the books that will be needed for the service, which include the Bible and Apocrypha, a collection of song texts and a book of prayers. Jumper congregations have, in addition, a collection of prophetic writings known as *The Spirit and Life*. The *Presviter*, or presiding elder, co-ordinates the services and recites the prayers but rarely does he give a sermon as this is prepared by one of the *Besedniki*, or speakers, the subject usually being a biblical theme. The normal language used is Russian, but English is now becoming more common in the diaspora.

The Jumpers get their name from the custom of members, moved by the Spirit, who jump around, leap, dance or skip; others may want to speak 'in the Spirit', but *glossolalia*, or speaking in tongues, is less frequent. The Steadfast group is less overt.

Food is provided after the Sunday service; work groups gather early in the morning to produce four-course meals in the congregation's kitchen which is attached to their place of worship. The four courses include *Chai*, tea with sweets and pastries, *Borscht* (beetroot soup) or *Lapsha* (noodle soup), *Miasmo*, a meat dish usually of boiled kosher beef or chicken, and *Kompot*, a stewed fruit course. Both groups follow the Jewish dietary laws and eat only kosher meat; during the meat course the Jumpers sometimes listen to a message from one of the Proroki, or prophets. In their daily lives the Molokans are urged to observe the Mosaic dietary laws and buy only kosher food.

Jumpers tend to wear traditional Russian peasant clothes at their services, but the Steadfast group have now adopted more conventional clothing although the women still keep their heads covered. Upon entering a gathering place the elder will enter first, and it is usual for a woman to be escorted by a man. The Steadfast group are especially noted for their cordiality towards outsiders, but the Jumpers are seen as more reserved.

❖ Dancers; Jumpers; Leapers; Skippers; Steadfast, or Constant Molokans

MOLUCCAN EVANGELICAL CHURCH

In 1951 some 12,500 Moluccans, who belonged to the Moluccan Protestant Church in Indonesia – arguably the oldest PROTESTANT Church in Asia – arrived in the Netherlands; this was some 6 years after Indonesia's independence was gained. The immigrants were determined to promote the cause for an independent Moluccan state, an idea that was incompatible with the policies of either Indonesia or the Netherlands.

Many secessionist movements occurred in the Moluccan REFORMED community in the Netherlands, one of which was the Moluccan Evangelical Church (GIM), whose members had been unsuccessful in their attempt to form a *classis*, or district division, of their parent Church, the Moluccan Protestant Church of Indonesia (founded 1534).

At present the Church has a total membership of some 29,000 adults, distributed between 85 congregations. Both infants and adults may be baptized and the Lord's Supper is celebrated, but only twice a year. The doctrinal basis of the Church, in which women may now be ordained, is limited to the Apostles' creed. The headquarters of the Church is in Houten, in the Netherlands.

MONARCHIANS

A second- and third-century religious movement centred in Asia Minor and Rome, but commonly followed elsewhere. The term *monarchiani* was first coined by Tertullian in the third century and was used to describe those who, in general, held to a unipersonal, rather than a Trinitarian view of God.

There were two Monarchian parties:

1. The earlier Dynamic Monarchians, also known as Adoptionists.
2. The Patripassians, also known as SABELLIANS, or Modalists.

The Dynamic Monarchians held to a view taught by Theodotus, a learned leather-seller from Byzantium who went to Rome at the time of the pontificate of Pope St Victor (189–98). Theodotus taught that Jesus was only a man who, until his baptism, had lived the life of an ordinary, but most virtuous human, his virgin birth notwithstanding. At Jesus' baptism the 'Christ' descended upon him from God the father and this filled him with a divine power, or *dynamis* (Greek 'power'). As a result, he was able to work miracles but without becoming divine himself. Some of Theodotus' followers further believed that Jesus' deification followed only after his resurrection. Pope St Victor excommunicated Theodotus, but his ideas were perpetuated by another man, a banker or moneychanger also named Theodotus, and by Artemon, or Artemas, who lived in Rome during the latter part of the third century.

The Patripassians, also known as Sabellians or Modalists, held to a heresy that developed during the first three centuries. The Patripassian view, which arose during the middle of the second century, concerned the notion that God the Father became incarnate as the human person Jesus, and so must also have experienced the suffering as the Son. The Modalist view was that God the Father, God the Son and God the Holy Spirit were the same person appearing in three different *modes* of existence. Modalism is usually associated with the writings of Praxeas that date from the early third century and were criticized by Tertullian (*c.* 160–225). The first to state the Monarchian position was Noetus of Smyrna, who was condemned by an assembly of presbyters at Smyrna in *c.* 200. His views were revised by Sabellius who went to Rome towards the end of the pontificate of Pope St Zephyrinus (198–217). Sabellius was attacked by St Hippolytus and was eventually excommunicated by Pope St Callistus (217–22).

The Monarchian heresy did not persist beyond the third century, although it is possible that some Spanish clergy at the time of the early Middle Ages may have taken up Adoptionist views, for which they were condemned by Charlemagne (*c.* 742–814) in the year 794.

❖ Adoptionists; Modalists; Patripassians; Sabellians

MONOPHYSITES (also MONOPHYSITISM)

Holders of the heretical view that after the incarnation Jesus Christ had only one nature – the divine. In 451 the Council of Chalcedon condemned this heresy and asserted that following the incarnation Christ had two natures, divine and human.

MONOTHELITISM

A seventh-century heresy which proposed that, as Christ had two natures, the divine and human, but in one single person, it must follow that he had only one will. The Synod of Rome condemned the heresy in 649 and the Third General, or Sixth Ecumenical, Council of Constantinople subsequently upheld this in 680–1, asserting that Christ had two wills, divine and human.

❖ Monotheletism

MONTANISM (also MONTANISTS)

A mid-second-century apocalyptic movement, which attracted many followers. It was led by Montanus, a Christian convert, in Phrygia (now part of modern Turkey) who proclaimed the imminence of the second coming of Christ (REVELATION 20). Montanus preached in the village of Ardabau, where he was given to uttering ecstatic prophecies, spreading his views that the signal of the second coming and the era of the New Jerusalem would be felt by an outpouring of the Holy Spirit and that the event would take place near Pepuza, a small village in the same region. Convinced that he was the appointed prophet of God, Montanus believed that he had received some special knowledge from the Holy Ghost directly, knowledge that had not even been vouchsafed to the apostles.

Associated with Montanus were two women prophets, Priscia (or Priscilla) and Maximilla (or Maximilia), who led the movement after the death of Montanus. In readiness for the prophesied events, the two women set up their headquarters in the village of Pepuza. They were later denounced by one of their contemporaries, St Hippolytus.

To prepare for the second coming, Montanus taught that it was necessary for his followers to adopt an ascetic lifestyle, avoid marriage, separate from a pre-existing spouse and observe severe rules of fasting. Followers were further enjoined to withdraw from the world and to expect persecution from non-believers, which was to be faced and endured. Tertullian (*c.* 160 – *c.* 225) was much taken with Montanism, which spread quickly through the African Churches; it seems to have been unopposed by Pope St Eleutherius (*c.* 174–89), but the Montanists were virtually excommunicated by the Synod of Iconium (*c.* 230), which declared that their practice of baptism was invalid.

Some strange customs have been alleged of the Montanists. It was believed that the prophetess Priscilla, in a dream, received a revelation from Jesus concerning Pepuza, the site of the forthcoming second coming and the New Jerusalem; this was a *holy place* and many Montanists were persuaded to go to the village in order to fall asleep in the hope of having a similar experience. The Montanists also acquired a nickname, *Tascodrugitae*, from the Phrygian words meaning 'peg' and 'nose', because they were said to put their forefinger, or perhaps a stick, or rod, up their noses when praying 'so as to appear dejected and pious' (Epiphanius). Other rumours and wild stories circulated for many years, but the sect went underground and died out during the mid-fifth century. Montanus' bones were exhumed in 860, but of their fate nothing is known.

❖ Cataphrygians; Pepuzians; Phrygians

MORAVIAN CHURCH

The Moravian Church was in reality a PIETISTIC renewal of the UNITAS FRATRUM, a group that had been started in the fourteenth century by the followers of John Huss (1373–1415) in the Bohemian and Moravian areas of the former Czechoslovakia.

John Huss, a priest of the ROMAN CATHOLIC CHURCH, was upset by the corruption of his Church, with the selling of indulgences and denial of Communion under both kinds to the laity, as well as the clearly evident moral turpitude of the papacy and much of the clergy at the time. Huss's brave views were only to earn him a defrocking and led finally to his execution at the stake on 6 July 1415. Huss's followers, doubting that they would ever be able to affect a change in the Roman Catholic Church, formed themselves into the Unitas Fratrum and set about finding a means of preserving an apostolic succession for their clergy; this came about through the offices of the WALDENSIAN CHURCH. The movement grew, but under persecution during the time of the Reformation it suffered a decline, especially after the PROTESTANT defeat at the battle of the White Mountain in 1620.

The relocation in 1722 of three hundred members of the Unitas Fratrum, under the leadership of Christian David, to the estate of Count Nicholas Zinzendorf (1700–60) at Berthelsdorf in northern Germany allowed them to develop a wild, uncultivated spot that was eventually to become the home of the community of Herrnhut. Some German Pietists joined the community and it was agreed that they should form a Church that was to be constituted along the lines of the old Unitas Fratrum. In 1727, during a communion service, there was a remarkable 'outpouring of the power of God', and this is accepted as the foundation date of the Renewed Church of the Brethren, or the MORAVIAN CHURCH. Count Zinzendorf set about trying to organize the group and to regularize the ordination of its clergy. The first bishop of the Renewed Church, David Nitschmann, was ordained in 1735 by a bishop of the last-remaining Bohemian Brethren group in Poland, and another bishop from Berlin. Zinzendorf introduced liturgical changes, with the inclusion of an *agape*, or love feast, which consisted of a light meal, singing and a talk that together comprised an informal service of Holy Communion. The use of a litany was introduced in 1731, together with the practice of the use of the *Watchword*, or *Daily Texts*, a collection of Old and New Testament texts with a verse of a hymn chosen to expound upon the texts. In 1732 David Nitschmann and Johann Dober were sent to the Virgin Islands to minister to the inhabitants of St Thomas but this mission met with little success; others followed, including a mission to Greenland in 1733.

The first Moravian settlers in North America, who formed the MORAVIAN CHURCH IN AMERICA led by Bishop August Gottlieb Spangenberg, travelled to a piece of land on the Savannah River in Georgia in 1734. The settlement was seen as a security measure for members of the Church remaining in Europe should religious persecution again arise, as well as a place where a mission to the Native Americans could be established. Almost at once, the chosen land in Georgia became far from secure when it was caught up in the war between the British in Georgia and the Spanish in Florida and the situation brought with it the possibility that the members, vowed to pacifism, might be required to enter the army. The group relocated to Pennsylvania, where they founded the communities of Nazareth and Bethlehem. Meanwhile, back in Europe, Count Zinzendorf had been sent into exile by the King of Saxony, August III, at the behest of the imperial government in Vienna. During his exile, between the years 1737–47, Zinzendorf founded congregations in the Netherlands, England and Ireland. The British government recognized the Moravian Church as 'an Ancient Protestant Episcopal Church' in 1749 and allowed members to settle both in Great Britain and its colonies.

Further persecution in Germany during the eighteenth century led to more migration to America and by 1776 a permanent settlement had been made at Bethania, later called Salem (now Winston Salem), in North Carolina. One of the major emphases of the Church is missionary work, and missions were set up in South America and Lapland (in 1735), South Africa (in 1736), Labrador (in 1771), amongst Australian aborigines (in 1850) and in Tibet (in the mid-nineteenth century).

The Church, with its threefold ministry, is an episcopal Church with a presbyterian polity that recognizes the *Augsburg Confession* but remains fairly liberal about the interpretation of what are considered to be non-essentials. The Bible is taken as the sole arbiter of faith and conduct, with a great emphasis laid on Bible reading, prayer and the turning away from worldly activities.

The Church is divided into provinces, each headed by a bishop and a synod. Local churches have a council of elders to deal with the spiritual affairs of the congregation, and trustees to handle the temporal administration. The headquarters of the Moravian Church is at Herrnhut, Germany.

❖ Moravian Brethren; Renewed Church of the Brethren; Renewed Unitas Fratrum

MORAVIAN CHURCH IN AMERICA

The Moravian Church in America dates from the arrival in Georgia from Germany of Bishop August Gottlieb Spangenberg in 1734, where he came with the intention of evangelizing the Native Americans. Because of political unrest in Georgia the group moved to Pennsylvania, establishing the colonies of Nazareth, Bethlehem and Lilitz; further foundations were made in North Carolina (1752). The headquarters of the Church is at Winston Salem, North Carolina. In order to finance its ambitious missionary and publishing programmes, Spangenberg started a plan, called *Economy*, for the Church by which members provided their abilities, time and effort free of charge in return for food, accommodation and clothing. This scheme, although initially successful, had been abandoned by the mid-nineteenth century.

Doctrinally, the Moravians regard the Bible as the inspired word of God and sufficient for a believer's faith and practice. They affirm man's depravity, his need for reconciliation and justification, and the fellowship of believers; their belief in the divinity of Jesus Christ and in his second coming is conventional (REVELATION 20). Infant baptism by aspersion is practised and admission to Holy Communion comes only after confirmation. Holy Communion is celebrated at least six times a year, together with the *agape*, or love feast, a light meal accompanied by singing and prayer, which was first introduced in the early days of the Church's beginning in Herrnhut, Germany, in the mid-eighteenth century.

The major feast of the liturgical year is Easter and there is a special Moravian Easter Sunrise Service. Christmas is celebrated with a characteristic liturgy that involves the use of a distinctive, multi-pointed star and the *Putz*, a decorative representation of the Nativity.

There are currently 153 congregations of the Church, with 43,500 adult members divided between three groupings, the southern, northern and Alaskan provinces. A provincial synod, made up of a bishop and a council of clergy and laity, directs the missionary, educational and publishing programmes and administers each province.

MORAVIAN CHURCH IN GREAT BRITAIN AND IRELAND

The preparation for the Moravian Church in Great Britain and Ireland started with the formation of a vestry society, which was a group of individual members of the CHURCH OF ENGLAND who gathered together for mutual help, prayers and a reading from the scriptures. James Hutton, a London bookseller and contemporary and friend of John Wesley and his brother at the university of Oxford, formed one such society. Like the Wesleys, Hutton had become most impressed by some MORAVIANS when he met them at Gravesend, Kent, from where they sailed, with the Wesley brothers, for America in 1735.

James Hutton's vestry society met at his home, where Peter Boehler preached to the members. Boehler was a Moravian missionary and was in London en route to South Carolina, having been recently ordained, and it was agreed by the members that Boehler should compose a set of rules for the society that would incorporate Moravian precepts. These included an agreement that the members would meet once a week, confess their faults to one another, pray together and observe definite periods of fasting and retreat from the world. Hutton and his fellow members founded the *Great Meeting House* in London's Fetter Lane, made famous by a spiritual experience received there by both John and Charles Wesley. It was not long before the members of the vestry society were ostracized by the established Church of England. In 1742, when August Gottlieb Spangenberg arrived from Germany, he admitted the vestry society as a full congregation of the Moravian Brethren.

The vestry society was then known as the London Church, or as 'a Moravian Congregation in Union with the Church of England'. It was very active in setting up Moravian congregations in Britain, especially in Yorkshire, but the law did not recognize them. To rectify this, an appeal was made to the British government to bring in a Bill (aka The Bill for Encouraging the People known by the Name of the UNITAS FRATRUM, or United Brethren, to Settle in His Majesty's Colonies); this was passed by the House of Commons with only one opposing vote and was unopposed in the Upper Chamber. From 12 May 1749 the Church had full legal status in Great Britain and Ireland.

The Church now has around 2,500 adult members, of which around 15 per cent are of West Indian origin, gathered into 44 congregations which are divided into 5 districts.

MORAVIAN CHURCH OF NICARAGUA

A missionary from Germany called Pfeiffer, through whose efforts one of the earliest PROTESTANT missions in Central America became fully organized, established the Moravian Church in Nicaragua in 1849. Today, the Moravian congregations are found mostly along the extensive east coast of Nicaragua, especially amongst the Miskito Indians, some of whom have now been ordained as ministers of the Church, and some of the English-speaking black population. The Moravian Church of Nicaragua supports a Bible institute and various grade schools for up to 2400 students.

MT ZION SPIRITUAL TEMPLE

This black American PENTECOSTAL Church was founded by a notable Blues singer, *King* Louis H. Narcisse (1921–89), a one-time shipyard worker and bank janitor who had been baptized in Mt Zion Baptist Church. Little in his early life gave a hint of the flamboyant future that lay ahead.

In 1945 Narcisse had a vision that led him to form a prayer group that grew to such a size that he felt justified to found a Church, now known as the Mt Zion Spiritual Temple. This was established at Oakland, California, and attracted a great membership in part due to a series of radio programmes. These were called *Moments of Meditation* and proved to be a wonderful vehicle for Narcisse's colourful and persuasive manner and style. He also made use of a theme song and a motto, *It's Nice to be Nice*, which became identified with the Church. In his earlier, pre-Second World War days, Narcisse had won several radio auditions as a singer and this ability was now put to use in producing recordings with titles such as *Jesus, I Can't Forget You.*

The Church flourished and new centres and temples were established, in California, Michigan, Texas, Florida, Washington DC, and New York City. In 1955 Narcisse was crowned, at a public meeting in the municipal auditorium at Oakland, California, by Bishop Frank Rancifer, receiving the style and title of *His Grace, the King of Spiritual Church of the West Coast*. To give substance to his status, Narcisse thereafter wore a crown and many diamond rings during his public appearances; it is said that he was driven around in a Rolls Royce that rode on a red carpet which unrolled before it, a remarkable feat of logistics in itself. A large home, known as *The Lamp on the Hill* was built at Oakland and here Narcisse would receive guests in his throne room. Narcisse always claimed that his extravagant way of life was intended to attract followers and it is known that he was very generous in his support for the needs of the local community, financing many projects that the Mt Zion Spiritual Temple still maintains through its support for a food bank distribution programme in Oakland, which is the headquarters of the Church.

MUGGLETONIANS

This denomination, which became extinct in the late nineteenth century but whose last surviving member is said to have died in the middle of the twentieth century, was named after one of its founders, Ludowicke Muggleton (1609–98). Muggleton, and his cousin John Reeve (1608–58) declared themselves to be the *True Witnesses* (Rev. 11:3).

Muggleton and Reeve believed that their duty was to preach to an ungodly world in preparation for the beginning of the final days that were to precede the second coming (REVELATION 20). The impetus to found the movement came to Muggleton, a tailor who later turned pawnbroker, through visions he claimed to have received in April 1651 and which were to last until January 1652. John Reeve, also a tailor, received similar visions in the space of a fortnight, during the early part of 1652, and claimed that he had received 'a commission from God' to be his appointed last prophet; Muggleton was to be the appointed voice of the last prophet of God.

Reeve's teachings were published in various tracts and he enjoyed a growing reputation as 'a prophet that damns people'. The contents of the tracts encompassed many of the views held by the RANTERS and FAMILISTS and placed considerable emphasis on predestinarianism. Reeve's authority as the prophet of God went largely unchallenged, since his followers feared condemnation. This fear was based on their belief that Reeve had been enlightened by God and was able to discern who would, and who would not, be saved. Both men were imprisoned for their beliefs in the Old Bridewell prison in London during 1653 and further spells of imprisonment followed over the succeeding years.

The common themes in their preaching included disillusionment with the monarchy, nobility and the CHURCH OF ENGLAND. Although the men did not embark on an active campaign to enlist members, their message attracted a good following. The early death of John Reeve in 1658 left Muggleton in charge of the movement and, despite many challenges for his position, he survived.

Muggleton's preaching affirmed that God took no notice of his creation and that it was, therefore, pointless either to pray or to worship him. Strongly anti-Trinitarian, to a point that bordered on UNITARIANISM, Muggleton asserted that Jesus was the true God come down to earth, leaving Elijah, and just possibly Moses as well, to see to the government of heaven. The unforgivable sin, he taught, was to disbelieve the two *True Witnesses*, themselves.

The services held by the group were informal and mostly took place at private gatherings in an inn for a couple of readings from the Bible and the singing of a few *Divine Songs* to traditional tunes; in 1829 a 620–page publication appeared called *The Divine Songs of the Muggletonians*. These informal meetings were accompanied by the drinking of a few beers, both to satisfy the innkeeper and, quite possibly, to attract new followers; women were encouraged to play an active part in the proceedings.

The Muggletonians found some local support at grass roots level in English society, with centres created in London, Derbyshire, the south and the midlands.

N

NAASSENES

Members of a Christian-GNOSTIC sect, whose name is derived from the Hebrew '*nahas*' – a serpent. They were so-named because of their reputation for worshipping the serpent (Gen. 3:1ff) as the symbol of wisdom, which they believed was concealed from mankind by the God of the Jews. In their worship of the serpent the Naassenes were unlike the OPHITES, who recognized the serpent only as a symbol of divine wisdom. St Hippolytus, in his *Refutation of All the Heresies*, cites a Naassene hymn.

NATIONAL ASSOCIATION OF CONGREGATIONAL-CHRISTIAN CHURCHES

This is a voluntary association of free Churches, found especially throughout the USA and Canada. It was formed in 1955 in Detroit, Michigan, by some of those Churches whose members wished to remain congregational and did not want to participate in the union with the EVANGELICAL AND REFORMED CHURCH that was going to form the future UNITED CHURCH OF CHRIST in 1957 because they recognized that the polity of this Church was going to be presbyterian, rather than congregational.

The National Association places considerable emphasis upon the autonomy of local churches and provides for an annual meeting, held each year in a different city. It is involved in programmes for welfare, education, church development and employment issues. Home missions in the USA and Canada are complemented by missionary work in twelve overseas countries. There is a membership of about 79,000 distributed between 399 churches, with headquarters in Oak Creek, Wisconsin.

NATIONAL ASSOCIATION OF FREE WILL BAPTISTS

A group of American BAPTISTS that originated from Welsh immigrants who travelled to the New World in 1701, settling in Pennsylvania. By 1717 they had been organized as a group by Paul Palmer in North Carolina, with another group gathered together in 1787 in New England by Benjamin Randall. In 1916 the General Association of Free Will Baptists was formed, but this was subject to a schism in 1921 when some of the member Churches left to form the Eastern General Conference. By 1935 these differences had been resolved and the majority was able to come together again to form the National Association of Free Will Baptists while the small number of groups that decided to stay outside this union formed themselves into the General Conference of the Original Free Will Baptist Church.

Free Will Baptists hold to the ARMINIAN, or Free Will, doctrine which teaches that salvation is available for all, and not just for those predestined to be saved, as is the CALVINIST belief. Baptism by immersion is practised and the group observes a policy of open communion, preceded by foot-washing. The National Association operates a congregational polity and its administrative headquarters is in Nashville, Tennessee, where a Free Will Baptist College is maintained. There are over 2,400 congregations with almost 250,000 adult members. Home and foreign missions have taken the work throughout the USA and into Africa, the Far East and Central and South America. In 1972 the Free Will Baptists left the National Association of Evangelicals, an inter-denominational co-ordinating body.

❖ Free Will Baptists

NATIONAL BAPTIST CONVENTION OF AMERICA

British colonists and slave holders who moved to the southern parts of America during the eighteenth century were often anxious to provide places of worship for their slaves, who were otherwise obliged to sit in the gallery in a white church. This was the situation until the first black BAPTIST church was formed, at Silver Bluff, South Carolina, in the mid-1770s. The first congregation was led by Brother Palmer, and the Reverends David George and George Lisle. This foundation was followed by the organization of a second and third black Baptist church in 1785, one at Williamsburg, Virginia, and the other at Savannah, Georgia; other such Baptist churches followed.

In 1880, in Montgomery, Alabama, the Foreign Mission Baptist Convention of the USA was formed, under the guidance of the Reverend W. W. Colley. There were two independent bodies inside this group, the American National Baptist Convention, formed in St Louis in 1886, and the Baptist National Educational Convention, formed in 1893 in the District of Columbia. In 1895 the Foreign Mission Baptist Convention merged with these two bodies in Atlanta, Georgia, to form the NATIONAL BAPTIST CONVENTION OF THE USA, INC. (NBCUSA). An internal dispute arose in 1915, concerning the ownership of the publishing arm of the Church and a clarification was needed to settle the problems that had arisen from alleged mismanagement of the proceeds of the operation that should have been available to fund the NBCUSA's various programmes. In response, the publishing wing withdrew from the convention's control, marking the starting point of the National Baptist Convention of America (NBCA).

The NBCA, with its headquarters in Dallas, Texas, now has responsibility for 3.5 million adult members who attend nearly 20,000 churches throughout the USA. At the height of its missionary outreach work the Church maintained missions in Jamaica, Panama and Africa.

NATIONAL BAPTIST CONVENTION OF THE USA, INC.

This black BAPTIST Church dates its foundation from the first black Baptist Church that was organized at Silver Bluff, South Carolina, in 1773 under the leadership of Brother Palmer and the Reverends David George and George Lisle. In 1783 George Lisle went to Jamaica and established there a congregation that developed into the Jamaica Baptist Union.

The National Baptist Convention of the USA, Inc (NBCUSA) came into existence in Alabama, Georgia, following the merger of some Baptist groups in 1895, led by the Reverend E. C. Morris and Lewis G. Jordan. In polity and doctrine the Church is indistinguishable from the white Baptist groups but in its form of worship tends to be a little more exuberant and spontaneous. A schism occurred at the end of the nineteenth century when a group of black Baptists formed an independent missionary group, known as the Lott Carey Foreign Mission Convention. In 1915 an important dispute led to another split, when the publishing arm of the Church separated from the Convention and formed the NATIONAL BAPTIST CONVENTION OF AMERICA.

The NBCUSA, which has its headquarters in Nashville, Tennessee, supports an extensive foreign mission programme, with members working in Africa and the West Indies.

NATIONAL BAPTIST EVANGELICAL LIFE AND SOUL SAVING ASSEMBLY OF THE USA

A. A. Banks founded this black Baptist Assembly in 1920 in Kansas City, Missouri, as a city mission and evangelical outreach ministry. The movement was initially conducted under the auspices of the NATIONAL BAPTIST CONVENTION OF AMERICA, but in 1936, in Birmingham, Alabama, a move was made for independence. The Church is indistinguishable doctrinally from its parent body. Most of its work is concentrated upon relief work, charity and evangelism in cities across the USA. There are currently 270 congregations and some 60,000 adult members.

NATIONAL DAVID SPIRITUAL TEMPLE OF CHRIST CHURCH UNION (INC.) USA

One of the three merging Churches that formed the UNIVERSAL CHRISTIAN SPIRITUAL FAITH AND CHURCHES OF ALL NATIONS in 1952. The National David Spiritual Temple of Christ Church Union was founded in 1932 by an ex-BAPTIST minister, David Williams Short, who could not condone denominational Churches as such, and considered that they had been founded in error and not in keeping with the paradigm laid out in the New Testament (1 Cor. 12:1–31). He further taught that baptism of the Holy Ghost is accompanied by *glossolalia*, or speaking in tongues, as well as evidence of other gifts of the Holy Ghost. In keeping with his proposed model of the Church the members included pastors, prophets and prophetesses, archbishops, bishops, elders, overseers, healers, deacons and missionaries.

Before its merger with the St Paul Spiritual Church Convocation and with King David's Spiritual Temple of Truth Association in 1952, the Church managed to provide support for a hospital and nursing home; it also published some evangelical material from a publishing centre in Kansas City, Missouri.

NATIONAL EVANGELICAL CHURCH IN KUWAIT

This PROTESTANT Church was organized in 1903 by Samuel Zwemer of the REFORMED CHURCH IN AMERICA (founded 1628), as part of that Church's missionary outreach. The National Evangelical Church in Kuwait has only two churches, the first of which was built in 1931, catering for nearly 300 worshippers. The members are drawn mainly from the Arabic, English and Indian Christian communities. Each community has its own resident pastor.

NATIONAL EVANGELICAL SYNOD OF SYRIA AND LEBANON

This Church traces its origins to work that had been undertaken in Syria, beginning in 1823, by the missionaries of the American Board of Commissioners for Foreign Missions (ABCFM), an interdenominational organization which was organized in 1810 for both home and mission work and staffed by CONGREGATIONALISTS, PRESBYTERIANS and members of the DUTCH REFORMED CHURCH. Their mission work was largely concerned with humanitarian and educational concerns. In 1848 the work of the ABCFM in Syria was extended to Beirut, Lebanon. Responsibility for this mission was later deputed to the PRESBYTERIAN CHURCH (USA). Other missionary groups merged to form the, now-autonomous, National Evangelical Synod of Syria and Lebanon that was finally formed in 1920. There was a failed attempt in 1958 to unite with the National Evangelical Church in Beirut, and more recently fresh talks about such a union were recommenced in 1973.

The organization of the Church is presbyterian in polity, caring for 38 congregations and for more than 4,500 communicant members and although this membership is currently in slow decline, largely through emigration, the Church still sponsors two hospitals, some primary and secondary schools and the Beirut University College for Women. The headquarters of the Church is in Beirut, Lebanon.

NATIONAL EVANGELICAL UNION OF LEBANON

A PROTESTANT Church, which was founded in 1950 and has its parish centre in Beirut, that is small in size but very influential. Apart from the city parish two more churches have been opened in mountain villages, all providing services within the REFORMED tradition for around one thousand members. In 1958 the Church rejected the opportunity to join the NATIONAL EVANGELICAL SYNOD OF SYRIA AND THE LEBANON.

NATIONAL PRESBYTERIAN CHURCH

The National Presbyterian Church was formed in the USA in 1973 at a constitutional assembly of delegates representing some 260 Presbyterian congregations who were on the point of leaving the Presbyterian Church in the United States (Southern) on account of what they saw as a growing liberalism, with the deity of Jesus Christ denied and the meaning and authority of the Bible slowly eroded. The pastor of the Briarwood Presbyterian Church in Birmingham, Alabama, Frank Barker, convened this assembly and the new body was known as the National Presbyterian Church; the name was changed in 1974 to the PRESBYTERIAN CHURCH IN AMERICA.

NATIONAL PRIMITIVE BAPTIST CONVENTION

Until the time of the American Civil War black BAPTISTS had worshipped in white Baptist churches, but from 1865 they were encouraged to have their own places of worship. Eventually, these black Baptist churches were sufficient in number to warrant the establishment of associations, which represented small groups of separate congregations, usually no more than five in number. These associations became known collectively as the Black, or Colored, Primitive Baptists. In 1906 some black Baptist elders, Clarence F. Sams, George S. Crawford and James H. Carey, together with some others, proposed to call a meeting at Saint Barley Primitive Baptist Church at Huntsville, Alabama, in order to discuss the organization of a national conference. This idea did not meet with unquestioned approval, as some thought that such a move would run counter to the Primitive Baptist notion that the Church should be a loose organization of associations. A year later saw a positive response from some 88 elders from seven southern States and the National Primitive Baptist Convention was established. James Carey of North Carolina was elected as president and George Crawford, of Virginia, as vice-president.

The Bible is held to be the only rule of faith and practice and the polity of the Church is congregational. Baptism is by immersion; the Lord's Supper, and the following act of foot-washing, are both regarded as sacraments. At a local level, the pastor or elder is usually assisted by a deacon, or deaconess. The upkeep of local churches is provided through a system of tithes and offerings. The Church has its own publishing house and supports many enterprises, including a youth camp, a nursing home, a Bible institute and several educational academies. The Church, which has its headquarters in Tallahassee, Florida, has 1,520 congregations and around 1 million adult members.

NAVIGATORS

This informal organization was formed in the USA in the 1930s by a Californian, Dawson Trotman, as a means of fostering Christian fellowship, witness, Bible study and memorization. The organization takes its name from the fact that Trotman's first convert was Les Spencer, an American sailor who became his disciple through a discussion of 2 Timothy 2:2. Trotman was inspired to organize the Navigators and he incorporated the movement in 1943. In 1948 the first band of missionaries belonging to the group set out for China.

The members subscribe to the belief that both the Old and New Testaments were inspired by God and that therefore the Bible is inerrant and is the supreme authority in matters of faith. They affirm a belief in the Trinity, in the divinity of Jesus Christ, in his rising from the dead and ascension into heaven and in man's atonement through him. They also accept the anticipated second coming of Christ, the bodily resurrection of the dead and the reward of everlasting happiness for the saved and eternal punishment for the wicked (REVELATION 20).

The Navigators are active in their various ministries, which are numerous and take the members into college campuses, youth camps, prisons and inner city missions. They are also active in working with the ethnic minority communities and in evangelizing new believers, working with them individually, or in small groups in which the Bible is studied systematically and sections are memorized. Trotman died in 1956, during his attempt to save someone from drowning in Schroon Lake, New York.

The headquarters of the Navigators is in Colorado Springs, where they maintain the Glen Eyrie Conference Center and a publishing house called Navpress.

NETHERLANDS REFORMED CHURCHES

This is a comparatively small Church in the Netherlands, which was formed in 1965 as a split from the REFORMED CHURCHES (LIBERATED). The seceding group was initially known as the Reformed Church (Liberated), but the current, slightly different, name was adopted in 1969.

Although not providing formal theological education for its own ordinands, the Church is able to send students to the Theological University of the Christian Reformed Churches in the Netherlands, which is in Apeldoorn; some informal training is also provided by Church clergy in Hellevoetsluis.

The members of the Church subscribe to the *Belgic Confession* (1561), the *Heidelberg Catechism* (1563) and the *Canons of the Synod of Dort* (1618–19), as well as the Apostle's, Nicene and Athanasian creeds. Both infants and believers are baptized and the Lord's Supper is celebrated every alternate month. Women may be ordained in this Church, which provides care for some 18,000 committed members who are distributed in around 100 congregations. The headquarters of the Church is at Badhoevedorp in the Netherlands, from where it is administered through a series of regional assemblies and a triennial national assembly. The Church has maintained close relations with other REFORMED Churches.

❖ Netherlands Free Reformed Churches

NEW AGE (also NEW THOUGHT)

A belief that every good thing is possible through a right relationship with what is called 'the ultimate power of the universe', whether that be identified as God, love, life, power or beauty. Believers in the New Age also believe that the universe is the body of God, that human beings are invisible spiritual beings only inhabiting bodies and that as human beings we continue to change and develop after death. Many cults were built around these beliefs during the twentieth century.

NEW APOSTOLIC CHURCH

This Church began in Germany, following the death of the last apostle of the CATHOLIC APOSTOLIC CHURCH (CAC). In the face of opposition from the United Kingdom, where a decision had been made to appoint no new apostles, a prophet from Berlin, Heinrich Geyer, was inspired to call two men to the apostleship and they were appointed as coadjutors of the CAC in Germany. Prophet Geyer went on to appoint yet another apostle, an action which received the approval of angel (*bishop*) F. W. Schwarz of Hamburg. This resulted in the excommunication of both men. Undeterred, Geyer was inspired to designate Schwartz to become an apostle, an action rejected by the remaining British apostles with the further effect that some 4,500 members of the Hamburg CAC withdrew from the Church. The foundation was laid for the establishment of a schismatic Church, known until 1906 as the General Christian Apostolic Mission and thereafter as the New Apostolic Church.

Schwarz went to the Netherlands, where he led congregations that had been constituted as the RESTORED APOSTOLIC MISSIONARY CHURCH. A further foundation, called the Apostolic Congregations, was made in Queensland, Australia, in 1883 by H. F. Niemeyer and this, in turn, established a foundation in

1903 in South Africa known as the Apostolic Unity Church. A schism occurred in the Australian Church in 1912, which led to the formation of the Apostolic Church of Queensland; those who did not join the schism formed the New Apostolic Church.

Doctrinally, the New Apostolic Church was at first similar to the original CAC but in time has become more Protestant, and less Catholic, with its emphasis upon the gifts of the Holy Spirit, prophecy, healing and *glossolalia*, or speaking in tongues. Three sacraments, baptism by aspersion of both children and adults, Holy Communion celebrated weekly, and a type of confirmation, known as *Holy Sealing*, are recognized. This last sacrament is administered by prayers and a laying on of hands through which the candidate receives the Holy Spirit; the *Holy Sealing* of a member ensures participation in Christ's rule on earth for the millennium following the second coming (Revelation 20).

The Church is administered by a hierarchy made up of the chief apostle, aided by district apostles who are the heads of the different regional churches. The chief apostle is credited with semi-papal powers and is recognized as the source of all the ministries in the Church, which include those of bishop, district elder, pastor and evangelist. His headquarters is in Zürich, Switzerland. Every three years the apostles gather together to form an International General Assembly. In January 2001 the chief apostle, Richard Fehr, published a new guideline, *Serving and Leading the New Apostolic Church*. The publication of this document is remarkable because the Church, which always relied for its evangelization on word of mouth, has never produced very much literature.

By the late twentieth century the New Apostolic Church had in excess of 2 million members, mostly in Germany, with other congregations in France, Switzerland, the USA, South Africa, Indonesia and Australia.

NEW AWAKENING

The New Awakening is the smallest branch of the Church of Laestadius, or Apostolic Lutheran Church of America, and was formed by some Pietists in Finland who sent Mijkko Saarenpaa and Juho Pyorre to the USA in the mid-nineteenth century.

Members of the Church observe the ten commandments as well as two *laws of love*, as revealed by Jesus Christ, the love of God and the love of one's neighbour. Following conversion, members of this branch of the Church accept the second experience, or *circumcision of the heart*, a term that describes how a believer comes to a fuller understanding of Christ's redemption and of his own personal sanctification.

NEW BEGINNINGS

An American Church that was started in the mid-1960s as a syncretistic movement combining Pentecostalism and British-Israel identity teachings. Eldon Purvis, the editor of the Pentecostal-charismatic magazine *New Wine*, which was based at Fort Lauderdale, Florida, founded the Church. In the early 1960s Purvis fell out with those who led the *New Wine* ministry over the question of a policy of *shepherding*, by which a more senior member would take responsibility and care of a younger, or more recent, convert over all issues concerning his life.

This falling out was a two-way affair as many of the leaders of this movement disagreed with Purvis, who taught that modern Anglo-Saxons identify with the ancient Israelites.

Eldon Purvis was also associated with the Pentecostal movement, known as *Latter-Day*, which had originated in Canada during the 1940s. One of its principal emphases was the ordering of Church life after the *Ephesian* pattern, so-called because the early Church in Ephesus was seen as illustrating the divine pattern. With this idea went the proposal that there should be only one church organized for each city, or geographical area, each functioning under the guidance of the Holy Spirit through a body of elders who worked as a single, presbyterian unit. Members believed that God was preparing for Christ's second coming through the *Latter-Day* movement and had endowed its members with gifts of prophecy and healing (REVELATION 20).

After his disagreement with *New Wine*, Purvis left this ministry to establish the Holy Spirit Teaching Ministry; by 1981 he had laid the foundations for the New Beginnings Church of Jesus Christ, which today has its headquarters in Waynesville, North Carolina, and over 30 congregations catering for some 2,000 followers in the USA and Europe. True to its British-Israel roots, members of the Church maintain an annual celebration of the Jewish feast of Tabernacles and are encouraged to gather together at the feasts of Passover and Pentecost (the Jewish feast of the Weeks), the latter observed fifty days after the second day of Passover.

❖ New Beginnings Church of Jesus Christ; New Beginnings Fellowship

NEW CHURCH OF SOUTHERN AFRICA

David Mooki founded this small and slowly declining Church in South Africa in 1911. Mooki, who was born in 1876 in the Transvaal, lived near Krugersdorp and was a member of the African Catholic Church, which had been founded by John Lelepo Molife in 1908. Mooki was very impressed and influenced by Emanuel Swedenborg's work, *The True Christian Religion*, which he had come across in a Johannesburg bookshop. With the support of his wife, Emmie, he set about trying to find members of Swedenborg's New Jerusalem Church (SWEDENBORGIANS) in South Africa, with a view to founding a new branch.

In 1911, Mooki organized the New Church of Africa and by 1917, had established links with Swedenborgians overseas. The British General Conference of the Church of New Jerusalem was very supportive and encouraging. Having brought his Church under the control of The Foreign and Colonial Mission Committee it was renamed as The New Church (Native) Mission in South Africa.

Two years later James Buss, a minister of the Church of New Jerusalem, was sent to South Africa and immediately set about instructing the members of Mooki's Church in Swedenborgian doctrine. David Mooki was ordained by Buss in June 1921. Mooki died in 1927, his work eventually taken over by his son, Obed Simon David Mooki (1919–90), when his education had been completed. Under Obed's leadership the New Church prospered and the Mooki Memorial Church and College were established in Soweto. In 1961 the Church merged with the Ethiopian Catholic Church in Zion, which had been founded in 1904 by Samuel Brander but which was then under threat of closure by the government.

The New Church of Southern Africa, as it was renamed, has a declining presence today, with only 100 congregations and about 8,000 adult members remaining. Doctrinally, the New Church does not subscribe to the orthodox view of the Trinity, believing instead that the Trinity was revealed in the person of Jesus Christ, with the term 'Father' describing his soul, the term 'Son' describing his body and the term 'Holy Spirit' describing his activity. Jesus Christ in his risen person is believed to be the one divine being, and therefore all prayers in the New Church are addressed to the 'Lord Jesus Christ'. Sunday services of worship include hymn singing, the recitation of some psalms, and a sermon with readings from the Bible and the writings of Swedenborg. The monthly 'Holy Supper' and infant baptism are observed as ordinances. The New Church was taken to Basutoland (now Lesotho) through the work of Buss and Mooki and still retains a small presence there.

NEW CONGREGATIONAL METHODIST CHURCH

An American Church that arose as a result of a disagreement within the Georgia Conference of the METHODIST EPISCOPAL CHURCH (South) concerning the consolidation of certain rural properties in the southern part of the state. As a result, a secession movement by members of the Waresboro Mission took place in 1881 at Waycross, Georgia, and the group adopted the Constitution of the Congregational Methodist Church (founded 1852).

The Church adopted a mixed polity of both METHODIST and CONGREGATIONAL Churches and rejected the system of annual conference assessments. Some of the congregations that had initially joined later withdrew and united with the Congregational Methodist Church and this led to a rather poor growth of congregations and membership.

The Church observes baptism by immersion and authorizes foot-washing at the celebration of the Lord's Supper. The headquarters are in Jacksonville, Florida.

NEW COVENANT APOSTOLIC ORDER

The New Covenant Apostolic Order (NCAO) was formed in the USA in 1973, when some staff members of the Campus Crusade for Christ ministry, an evangelical ministry that operated on many American university and college campuses, resigned to follow a more independent course. Seven of them decided to merge their ministries and form the NCAO, which was designed to work through a system of house churches scattered throughout the country. The founders were of the opinion that the Church of the first century had become corrupted away from its original mission and this was now being restored by the work of evangelical Christians. The leaders met in Chicago in 1979 and announced the formation of the Evangelical Orthodox Church (EOC), which was to succeed the NCAO.

The Church, which was remarkable for the importance that ritual played in its style of worship (an emphasis that had been largely ignored by other evangelical Christians), also practised healing, *glossolalia*, or speaking in tongues, and deliverance ministry for those considered to be possessed by malign spirits. The leaders of the EOC, who were styled as bishops of the Church, realized that for their style of worship to have any sound basis, validity of holy orders was needed. To remedy this defect, they turned to the Antiochian Orthodox Church and were re-ordained under Metropolitan Philip Saliba, renouncing their previous titles, as these did not exist in that Church. In 1987, most of the 1,800 members of the EOC joined the Antiochian Orthodox Church (of North America) and formed the Antiochian Evangelical Orthodox Mission (AEOM).

By 1995 the leaders of the AEOM and of the Antiochian Orthodox Church realized that it was impractical to continue as separate groups. This led to a split within the AEOM in 1998, when the majority in the parish of Ss Peter and Paul in Ben Lomond, California, left the Church to form the Orthodox Christian Brotherhood (OCB) under the leadership of Weldon (John) Hardenbrook. Those members of the AEOM not joining the schism were absorbed into the Antiochian Orthodox Church.

NEW TESTAMENT ASSOCIATION OF INDEPENDENT BAPTIST CHURCHES

The association dates back to 1964 when some members of the CONSERVATIVE BAPTIST ASSOCIATION OF AMERICA (CBA) met to consider adopting a more premillennialist (REVELATION 20) and separatist stance than that held by the CBA. In the following year 27 groups were affiliated at a founding meeting held in Denver, Colorado, during which Richard V. Clearwaters, of the Minnesota Baptist Convention (MBC), took a leading role.

The polity of the association is loosely congregational, with provision for an annual meeting to be attended by a pastor and five delegates from each congregation. The meeting has the authority to elect a president and other executive officers, as well as a board of trustees. Doctrinally, the *New Hampshire Confession of Faith* (1833) was adopted and modified with a stronger emphasis put upon the separation of church and state, and premillennialism. The headquarters of the Association is at Rochelle, Illinois.

NEW TESTAMENT CHURCH OF GOD

Founded in 1942 as a schismatic movement from the CHURCH OF GOD (ANDERSON), by G. W. and Martha Pendleton together with some like-minded ex-members of the CHURCH OF GOD, this American Church has its headquarters at Mountain Home, Arizona. The schism had come about because of an objection to the parent Church's co-operation with and support of the National Council of Churches. There are presently some 850 congregations of the New Testament Church of God, with an adult membership of around 9,000. State and regional conventions are held, as well as camp meetings and the Church supports foreign missions in eight Latin American countries, Asia and Africa.

NEW ZEALAND, ANGLICAN CHURCH IN

Aotearoa is the Maori name for New Zealand.

The Reverend Samuel Marsden (1764–1838), a Yorkshireman who had accepted the challenge of becoming a chaplain in *His Majesty's Territory of New South Wales*, was ordained in 1793 and settled in Paramatta, west of Sydney, in the following year. While returning from a visit to England, Marsden met up with a

Maori chief, Ruatara, who was best described as sickly and emaciated. The chaplain took him under his wing, taking the man to live with him in Paramatta where he was nursed back to health. Evangelized, as well as healed, Ruatara then returned to New Zealand, having promised protection from his people for Marsden and a group of lay missionaries and their wives who were being sent to the country by the Church Missionary Society (CMS). A vessel, the *Active*, was hired, together with a motley crew, and the party set sail for New Zealand, whose native population had a fearful reputation for cannibalism. They disembarked at Whangaroa, in the Bay of Islands, on Christmas Day 1814. There Marsden preached his first sermon and celebrated the first Christian service in the country (see below). During his remaining years, Marsden made many journeys to New Zealand and recruited many Maoris. These were taken to New South Wales for Christian instruction and training before being returned to their homes in order to evangelize their own people.

A possibly apocryphal story has been told of this journey. When the party arrived in the Bay of Islands, Ruatara tried to persuade Marsden not to land. The party aboard came face to face with naked warriors, all wearing necklaces made from human teeth and brandishing spears, who seemed to be executing a war dance; this, it was said, was a dance of welcome, although it was not easy for the newcomers to accept this explanation. Fearing for his life, but intent upon landing, the unbowed Marsden left the ship astride a horse, presumably thinking that it would give him some sort of chance against the unmounted warriors. The effect on the Maori warriors was electric, as horses were unknown to them. Marsden spent his first night ashore, sleeping peacefully on the beach, and had no further confrontations to endure.

The work of the CMS in New Zealand was led by the Reverend Henry Williams from 1823 onwards, but their work was to fail during the Maori uprisings of the 1860s, which were concerned with land arrangements that had been made by the Treaty of Waitangi (1840), the spirit of which had been broken by the colonists when many of them began to cheat the Maoris over the price in land sales. It was with the advent of organized European settlement after 1840, which had come mainly from England and Scotland, that the formation of the ANGLICAN Church began. A prime mover in this was Bishop George Augustus Selwyn, who arrived in the country in 1842 as a bishop of the United Church of England and Ireland. Bishop Selwyn established his headquarters at Waemate North, about 150 miles north of Auckland, and it was here that he opened the country's first theological college. By 1851, some British colonists, who were mainly Anglicans, had established a Christian church on the South Island. The work of the CMS was largely over by 1883 and the missionaries were withdrawn, leaving the work of the Church in the hands of the Church of New Zealand. A general conference was assembled in Auckland in 1857 and a constitution was agreed upon, making the Church of New Zealand an autonomous province of the CHURCH OF ENGLAND. Bishop Selwyn's original diocese of New Zealand underwent some divisions in 1856, and again in 1858, and further dioceses were created, including those of Christchurch, Waiapu, Wellington, Nelson, Auckland, Dunedin and Waikato. Towards the end of the nineteenth century, the Church was concerned with establishing parishes and building churches. In the early part of the twentieth century the focus was turned towards the area of social concern, particularly among young people. This concern with social matters continues today and is reflected in the Church's decision to permit the remarriage of divorced people in church, the ordination of women priests (in 1997) and the consecration of the first woman diocesan bishop, Dr Penelope Bansall Jamieson (in 1990), as Bishop of Dunedin.

For the celebration of Holy Communion, and other ceremonies, the Church produced its own revised prayer book, called *The New Zealand Prayer Book: He Karakia Mihinare o Aotearoa.* A revised constitution was adopted in 1992 that provided an opportunity for the three cultural streams within the Anglican Church to be able to express opinions in the decision-making process of the general synod. These three streams are the Tikanga Maori – Aotearoa, the Tikanga Pakeha – New Zealand, and the Tikanga Pasifika – Polynesia. With the adoption of this latest constitution the Church of (the Province of) New Zealand has now become the Anglican Church in Aotearoa, New Zealand and Polynesia, with its headquarters in the capital, Wellington.

The Pacific Islands had always been included as part of the Church, but in 1975 Melanesia was formed into a separate province, with its headquarters in the Solomon Islands. The Anglican Church in the islands of Polynesia (Fiji, Tonga and Western Samoa) became a diocese in its own right in 1990 and is known as the Diocese of Polynesia.

❖ Anglican Church in Aotearoa, New Zealand and Polynesia

NIAS CHRISTIAN PROTESTANT CHURCH

This Church is one of the largest PROTESTANT denominations in Indonesia and belongs within the LUTHERAN tradition, having been organized in 1865 by members of the Rhenish Missionary Society (founded 1828) as part of its mission outreach programme from Germany. The Church achieved autonomy in 1940 and currently has 53 indigenous clergy caring for about 141,000 committed members.

❖ Nias Protestant Christian Church

NICOLAITANS

A sect originating in the early Church at Ephesus and Pergamum (now Bergama in Turkey), which was condemned by St John (Rev. 2:6 and 2:14f.). According to St Irenaeus (*Adv. Haereses*), Nicolaitans 'led lives of unrestrained indulgence', and were under the leadership of Nicholas of Antioch, who is referred to by St Hippolytus (*c.* 170 – *c.* 236) as a deacon and founder of a sect, although Hippolytus based his opinion on that of Irenaeus.

The meagre facts concerning the sect are difficult to assess, but it would seem that they enjoyed a reputation for pagan morals and idolatrous worship, becoming defunct by the second century. St Clement of Alexandria (*c.* 150–215) attempted to exonerate Nicholas and suggested that all the reports concerning the promiscuity of the sect members were a distortion. It is also possible that the sect, as such, did not exist. During the Middle Ages the same name was sometimes used in a deprecating manner by upholders of clerical celibacy when referring to married priests.

❖ Nicolaites

NONJURORS

This term is applied to those ANGLICAN clergy and laity in England, Scotland and Ireland who refused to take the oath of allegiance to William III in 1689, on the grounds that they were still bound by their former oath to James II 'his heirs and lawful successors'. This refusal to recognize the new king resulted in the removal from office of the clergy involved. Included in their number were some 9 bishops and 400 priests as well as prominent laymen. In Scotland, when the Episcopal Church was disestablished in 1690 in favour of PRESBYTERIANISM, the majority of the clergy became Nonjurors.

It was required that the new oath of allegiance be taken by the beginning of August 1689, with failure to do so resulting in suspension of those refusing to comply, although a six-month period following this date was allowed before the suspension was to come into force. The party of bishops who refused to take the oath was led by the Archbishop of Canterbury, William Sancroft, and included Thomas Ken (1637–1711), the Bishop of Bath and Wells. A noted scholar and hymn writer, Ken was also a man of forthright opinions. As chaplain to King Charles II he once refused to allow Nell Gwyn, the king's mistress, the use of his prebendal house when the court went to Winchester. The group also included one Irish bishop and all the Scottish clergy, bishops and priests. Together, they created a type of High Church non-conformity, separate from the national Church but claiming to be the true, historical CHURCH OF ENGLAND. As such they held their own services privately and consecrated two bishops, Wagstaffe of Ipswich and Hickes of Thetford, to safeguard the succession; Bishop Hickes later consecrated three more bishops 'not as diocesan, but as Catholic successors'.

An initiative towards unity with the Eastern Church was made over a period of nine years, but difficulties broke out concerning liturgical matters, commonly known as *Usages*. In 1732, these issues were settled allowing for *Prayers for the Dead*, for the *Invocation of the Holy Spirit*, *Prayers of Oblation* and the use of a mixed chalice, where a little water could be added to the wine before it was placed on the altar.

The movement had died out by the start of the nineteenth century, with the last congregation becoming defunct, and the last bishop, Charles Booth of Long Millgate, Manchester, retiring to Ireland where he died in 1805. It has been suggested that in trying to preserve the Catholic tradition, the Nonjurors might be thought of as precursors of the Oxford movement.

NORTH AMERICAN BAPTIST CONFERENCE

The Church was started among German-speaking American BAPTISTS in the early nineteenth century, an initiative that was encouraged by English-speaking Baptists. Although many earlier attempts to form such a group had been made, the German Baptists regard Konrad Anton Fleishmann as the first to form a successful German Baptist Church. Fleishmann, a Bavarian who had emigrated to America, had become pastor of a German-Protestant church in Newark, New Jersey, but he had been asked to leave this post because of his refusal to baptize infants. In October 1839 he baptized three people and sent them to an English Baptist church; he also started an itinerant ministry throughout Pennsylvania, where many Germans has settled, and in New

York state, with the aim of consolidating small German Baptist groups and organizing preaching stations. By 1843 he felt it timely to draw up a series of *Articles*, for use at the German Baptist foundation he had made in Philadelphia.

The German Baptists, who had been aided in their work by the American Baptist Home Missionary Society, organized their first eastern conference in 1851, at which 8 churches, and over 400 members, of the eastern American congregations were represented. Other local conferences were established along geographical lines so that by 1865 joint meetings of eastern and western conferences, designated then as a general conference, could be held. These general conferences now meet every three years, attended by clergy and laity from the local conferences, which are held annually.

Doctrinally, members of the Church affirm the *New Hampshire Confession* of 1833 (amended 1853), in which the supreme authority of the scriptures is stressed, together with a belief in God's revelation in Christ and in the need for regeneration, believers' baptism by immersion and the separation of church and state. The polity of the Church is congregational and the strong tradition of foreign missions is seen in its work in Mexico, Eastern Europe, Cameroon, Nigeria, the Philippines, Japan and Brazil. Home missions, especially to Spanish speakers in Colorado and Texas, as well as to other cultural and ethnic groups, are also maintained. Clergy training for the Church is provided through the North American Baptist Seminary at Sioux Falls, South Dakota, with facilities available in Canada at the North American Divinity School and the North American Baptist College, both situated in Edmonton, Alberta. The current headquarters of the Church is at Oakbrook Terrace, Illinois, and it is from there that the co-ordination of media coverage, publishing, education and missionary work is undertaken.

❖ North American Baptist General Conference

NORTH AMERICAN OLD ROMAN CATHOLIC CHURCH

The foundation of the North American Old Catholic Church can be dated to either October 1916, with the consecration of its first primate, Henry Carmel Carfora, at Waukegan, Illinois, from the hands of Prince-Bishop de Landas Berghes et de Rache, or to an earlier consecration that Carfora is thought to have received in 1912 from Bishop Paola Miraglia Gulotti, who was in the line of succession through Archbishop René Vilatte. The prince-bishop, consecrated by Archbishop Mathew in the OLD CATHOLIC CHURCH succession, had fled to the USA during the First World War in order to escape internment in England.

As a priest of the ROMAN CATHOLIC CHURCH, born in Naples, Italy, Henry Carfora had been sent to work among immigrant Italian workers in West Virginia. Falling out with his bishop, and thereby earning himself a reprimand from the apostolic delegate, Mgr Falconio, Carfora left the Roman Catholic Church in 1911. By 1923, Carfora had both received episcopal consecration and fallen out once more with his superior and he left the Old Catholic Church to begin an independent Church, for which he drew up the *General Constitution and Bye-Laws*, stating that he was to be recognized as the supreme primate of the new Church, with an implied infallibility; following Carfora's removal to Chicago,

Illinois, this was established as the North American Old Roman Catholic Church. Carfora now bestowed upon himself a new title, that of *Most Illustrious Lord, the Supreme Primate of the North American Old Roman Catholic Church*. Before his death, in 1958, Carfora had consecrated many bishops; many of these subsequently left his jurisdiction to found a plethora of new jurisdictions of their own.

Carfora's consecration of a black bishop, Hubert A. Rogers (d. 1976), antagonized many white clergy and laity who withdrew from the Church to join other jurisdictions. Hubert Rogers, later styled archbishop, was succeeded by his son, James, who is currently head of the Church.

In most respects the North American Old Roman Catholic Church follows the doctrine of the Roman Catholic Church as it was before the changes introduced following the First Vatican Council of 1869–70, with the exception that it permits the marriage of clergy at every level. The current headquarters of the Church is at St Albans, New York.

NORTH INDIA, CHURCH OF

The Church of North India, which is in full communion with the ANGLICAN COMMUNION, was formed in 1970 as a result of a union between Anglicans and Christians of other traditions. This union avoided having a *mixed* ministry, with some clergy episcopally ordained and others not, by using a representative act of unification of the ministry when the Church was inaugurated. Three ministers of the Church, one a bishop, had hands laid on them by ten other ministers, six of whom were representatives of the uniting Churches and four of whom were ministers from outside the Church; these four included two bishops who were understood to be in the historic episcopate. The ten conferring clergy then laid hands on the three ministers in silence, and the three then laid hands on the representative ministers of the uniting Churches.

The uniting Church included The Church of India, Pakistan, Burma and Ceylon (Anglican), The United Church of Northern India (Presbyterian and Congregational), The Council of the Baptist Churches in Northern India, The Church of the Brethren, The Methodist Church (British and Australasian Conferences) and the Disciples of Christ. Despite this show of unity and concord not all BAPTISTS OR PRESBYTERIANS wanted to join the union and some chose to remain outside and independent (see below).

To overcome the problem of whether there should be infant, or believer's baptism, it was decided that both forms should be permitted. Where there was to be no infant baptism, there would instead be a service of infant dedication followed, in time, by a believer's baptism which could be by immersion, sprinkling or affusion; this was then to be followed by a service that admitted a believer to full, communicant membership and this would involve a laying on of hands, similar in style to a conventional confirmation service.

Moves towards the final union were started as early as 1924, with the merger of the Presbyterian and Congregational Churches, and this trend towards unity was further extended, in 1929, when further denominations joined the union. In 1951, a draft plan for the future of the union was drawn up and submitted for consideration by a committee of delegates. This plan was finally approved in 1965 and formally inaugurated in 1970.

The Church is currently responsible for many medical and health care programmes and also provides education, poor relief and care for the orphaned, widowed, disabled and aged in the community. The headquarters of the Church, the principal officer of which is an Anglican bishop styled as the moderator, is in New Delhi. There are negotiations now in hand, aimed at seeking a merger between those Baptists and Presbyterians who did not join the union, to form a Church of North East India. These include the Council of Baptist Churches in North East India and the Presbyterian Church in North East India.

NORTHERN BAPTIST CONVENTION

After the foundation of the earliest BAPTIST Churches in America by Roger Williams at Providence, Rhode Island, in 1639 and by John Clark, at Newport, Rhode Island, in 1648, the American Baptists began to form associations for the sake of evangelism. Two early examples are the Philadelphia Baptist Association (formed 1707) and the Charleston Baptist Association (formed 1751), after which there was a great upsurge in interest especially during the time known as the *Great Awakening* during the last half of the eighteenth century.

Two CONGREGATIONALIST missionaries, Adoniram Judson (1788–1850), and his wife, Ann (1789–1826, also known as Nancy), had set out for India from Salem, Massachusetts, aboard the brig *Caravan*. During the voyage both Judsons were converted to the Baptist view and upon arrival in Calcutta they were baptized by William Ward, travelling on to Rangoon, Burma, as Baptist missionaries. Here, Adoniram translated the Bible into the Burmese language. He was imprisoned by the British for over a year, a victim of the British-Burmese conflict of 1824–5.

The Judsons continued in their work, now with the support of the Baptists in America and a more formal organization was formed, known as the General Missionary Convention of the Baptist Denomination. This Convention, which was also known as the *Triennial Convention* because it met every three years, was composed of groups concerned with missionary enterprises. As these several groups all needed to raise money for their various objectives, this led to inefficiency and confusion. Meanwhile, more difficulties arose among the General Baptist congregations, when some members began to feel uneasy about this wealth of missionary activity and wished to distance themselves from it. These became known as the Primitive Baptists.

In 1840, the American Anti-Slavery Convention was formed and this caused a split in the following year between the abolitionists and the pro-slavery Southerners; the latter argued that while slavery was an evil, it had not been condemned in the Bible as a sin. By 1844 it had become evident that the Board of Foreign Missions could not accept slaveholders as missionaries, a position which was further clouded by the question of organizational structure. The Southerners developed a fully integrated and cohesive organization, whereas those Baptists under northern leadership found that what was left of their denomination was composed of many different organizations and this made for a fractured structure. The Southerners withdrew in 1845 and formed the SOUTHERN BAPTIST CONVENTION, leaving the remaining Baptist agencies, or societies, to consolidate and form the Northern Baptist Convention, organized formally in 1907 at the Calvary Baptist Church building in Washington, D.C.

In the period between the two world wars the Northern Baptists were faced with a growing disagreement between the supporters of liberal theology and those who upheld FUNDAMENTALISM and many conservative members left the Church over this dispute The Church favoured a move away from its earlier belief in predestination and the introduction of a less strict adherence to confessional statements, such as the *New Hampshire Confession*.

From 1950 to 1973 there were two name changes, the first in 1950 when the Church became the American Baptist Convention, and later, in the early 1970s, when it was changed again to become the AMERICAN BAPTIST CHURCHES IN THE USA (ABC in the USA). Unlike its southern counterpart, the Church is noted for being liberal and ecumenical in outlook. The Church observes a congregational polity, with biennial meetings of delegates. The headquarters of the Church is at Valley Forge, Pennsylvania, and membership currently stands at over 1.5 million adult believers divided between 5,800 congregations.

NORWEGIAN–DANISH EVANGELICAL FREE CHURCH ASSOCIATION

This American Church was established in 1909 through a merger of what was the Western Evangelical Free Church Association and the Eastern Evangelical Free Church Association, both founded in 1891. These Associations had been formed by PIETIST immigrants to America from Norway and Denmark, many of whom had been members of the Mission Covenant Church of Norway, which had been founded by the Reverend Frederick Franson (1852–1908) of the Bethlehem Church, Oslo.

These immigrants were aiming to break away from a state-dominated Church and were seeking autonomy for their local churches. The established state Churches in their home countries were seen by many as being dead and formalized. The immigrants wanted greater involvement of all church members in the organization and life of their local churches, and they also saw a great need for more missionary work. When some people who held these opinions organized informal groups within the state Churches they were told to either stop their activities, or leave. Many chose the latter course of action and emigrated to America, where religious freedom was tolerated.

In 1909, the Eastern and Western Evangelical Free Church Association merged and became the Norwegian–Danish Evangelical Free Church Association. A similar growth of Swedish Pietist groups in America led to a merger in 1884, forming the Swedish Evangelical Free Mission, later known as the Swedish Evangelical Free Church.

A merger conference was held in 1950 at the Medicine Lake Conference Grounds near Minneapolis, Minnesota, when the Swedish Evangelical Free Church and the Norwegian-Danish Evangelical Free Church Association merged to form the EVANGELICAL FREE CHURCH OF AMERICA, which aims to incorporate over 1,250 autonomous Churches throughout the USA and around the world as part of its missionary outreach programme.

NOVATIANS (also NOVATIANISM; NOVATIONIST)

Followers of the third-century presbyter, Novatian of Rome, who opposed leniency for those Christians who had apostatized during the persecutions of the Emperor Decius in AD 250 and later sought readmission to the Church. Novatian had been ordained priest at Pope St Fabian's (236–50) behest, despite protests that he had only received a clinical baptism (i.e. he was baptized in his bed when he was thought to be dying) and no confirmation, which prompted St Cornelius to remark 'how then can he have received the Holy Ghost?' St Cornelius was elected Pope in 251, when the persecutions were relaxing, and he was prepared to readmit these apostates. Novatian was elected as a rival Bishop of Rome by those who shared his extreme views and was consecrated by three bishops whom he had summoned to Rome to ordain him. As St Cyprian wrote, Novatian 'assumed the primacy'.

St Cornelius and Novatian set out their respective claims to the Church. Novatian received support from the African episcopate after an investigation had been made by the Council of Carthage, and he also had the benefit of St Dionysius of Alexandria's support. These supporters formed themselves into their own party, under strict discipline. Although Novatian was the author of an orthodox work on the doctrine of the Trinity, yet he and his followers persisted in their error that the Church had no power to grant absolution in certain cases.

The followers, who called themselves *katharoi* – the pure ones – were plentiful in number and were distributed widely throughout the empire. Where Novatian had refused absolution to *idolaters*, his followers extended this refusal to those who were in mortal sin acquired through acts of murder, adultery and fornication. Novatian suffered martyrdom during the Valerian persecutions (257–8), but the sect persisted in Rome until the fifth century, and a little longer in Constantinople.

It may be no more than malicious gossip put out by his enemies, but a story persists that Pope St Cornelius (251–3), writing about Novatian who was poised against him as an anti-pope, sent a letter to Fabius of Antioch commenting that while Novatian was a catechumen he was, for a while, possessed by Satan and in need of exorcism. After his deliverance he fell into a sickness and was baptized by affusion as he lay in his bed, and did not receive confirmation. As far as Novatian's ordination to the priesthood is concerned, Pope St Fabian (236–50), who authorized it, was thought to have flown in the face of opposition because of this clinical baptism and lack of subsequent confirmation.

O

OLD BELIEVERS

Patriarch Nikon (1605–81) of the Russian Orthodox Church rose from monastic obscurity to become patriarch because he found favour with the tsar, but Nikon, from peasant stock, was not noted for his tact. In 1652–3 he introduced changes and reforms in the liturgical practice of the Russian Orthodox Church, in imitation of the usage of the Greek Orthodox Church. Nikon, who had always been an admirer of all things Greek, remarked 'I am a Russian and the son of a Russian, but my faith and my religion are Greek'. Amongst other changes, he insisted that the sign of the cross was to be made with three fingers, rather than the traditional two used in the Russian Church, and that during the Divine Liturgy the *Alleluia* was to be sung twice during Lent, and not, as was usual, three times. He further prohibited the use of mirrors by the priests, insisted that five loaves, and not the usual seven, must be used during the celebration of the Divine Liturgy and commanded that some modifications that he wished to be introduced into the text of the Apostles' creed must be accepted.

This all met with stiff resistance from many clergy and much of the laity, led by Archpriest John Neronov and Avvakum Petrovitch, who defended the old Russian ways and refused to accept the new service books which Nikon had issued. Disagreement and opposition were not tolerated by Nikon and the full weight and support of the civil authorities was brought to bear on the dissidents. Neronov capitulated, but Avvakum Petrovitch refused to comply and was sent into exile for ten years, then imprisoned for another twenty years, twelve of which were spent in an underground hut, before being finally executed, by burning at the stake, in 1682.

Those dissidents who persisted in their refusal to conform united themselves to become a sect, or *Raskol*, and were known as the Old Believers, or Old Ritualists. In time, the *Raskol* split into two groups, the *Popovtsy*, or priestly sect, and the *Bezpopovtsy*, or priestless sect. Since no Orthodox bishop had seceded with them, the dissenters could not establish a hierarchy and further splits developed. The *Raskolniki*, or sect members, continued to suffer persecution at the hands of the Russian tsars throughout the eighteenth century, with the exception of Peter III.

The *Popovtsy* sought to establish a Church that was based upon a priestly hierarchy and was dependent upon the ministrations of discontented Orthodox priests until 1846, when a deposed bishop, Metropolitan Ambrose of Sarajevo (Bosnia), consecrated two bishops for the group at Bielo-Krinitz in the Austrian empire, forming the Old Ritualist Church Belokrinitsa Concord. An *Edict of Toleration*, issued by Tsar Nicholas II in 1905, allowed the Old Believers to function freely in Russia, and in 1971 the Russian Orthodox Church finally lifted the anathemas pronounced against the sect. Metropolitan Alimpyj of Moscow and All Russia currently heads the Popovtsy Old Believers, with his headquarters in Moscow. The Church has 120 parishes in Russia and 4 dioceses, in Kestroma, Siberia, Ukraine and Moldova; in 1996 a seminary was opened for the training of clergy.

Another group of *Popovtsy*, known as the *Yedinovertsy*, had come to an understanding with the Russian Orthodox Church at the start of the nineteenth century. In 1918 Patriarch Tikhon (1866–1925) agreed to consecrate a bishop for them. The communists killed both this bishop and his successor, but the Church continues. A third, and smaller, group of *Popovtsy* formed the *Beglopopovtsy*, or Church of Fugitive Priests, which gained its own episcopal hierarchy after the Second World War. The members of this Church are also known as the Old Ritualist Ancient Orthodox Christians and have their current archbishop based in Kuibyshev, south-east of Moscow.

When the *Bezpopovtsy* was formed by the *Raskolniki* they argued for a priestless Church. These dissenters are scattered throughout the far north of Russia, from Karelia in the east to the Urals in the west, at one time numbering as many as 46 factions. Most groups now limit their sacraments to baptism and absolution, arguing that Holy Communion need not be regarded as a sacrament as any meal eaten in the right spirit constitutes communion with Christ. Marriage of members is simply blessed by a community elder. The *Bezpopovtsy* can also be found in Romania, the Baltic regions and Belarus.

With legal recognition now granted to all factions of Old Believers their numbers have grown and a recent estimate puts their collective membership at about 1 million. Parishes and a hierarchy have been established abroad. In 1966 the hierarch Bishop Safrony was elected and is based in the USA, in Gervais, Oregon, where he is responsible for several thousand faithful who live in the USA, Canada and Australasia.

❖ Old Ritualists

OLD CALENDARISTS

Following the First World War many Orthodox Churches began to abandon the Julian in favour of the Gregorian calendar, which is thirteen days ahead. This move was seen by some Orthodox Christians to be an attempt at ecumenism, to which they were opposed.

In 1932, the Ecumenical Patriarch of Constantinople summoned an inter-Orthodox congress to meet in that city and one of the many items on the agenda concerned the introduction of the New (Gregorian) Calendar. Many of the lower ranking clergy and much of the laity were of the opinion that the decision to accept or reject the change of calendar could only be taken by an ecumenical council, as not all of the Orthodox Churches agreed to the change. Determined opposition to the reform broke out in Romania, Bulgaria and Greece. The opposition came from a group known as the Old

Calendarists, who formed themselves into a separate body. This group was met by violence, death and exile, in which state authorities were called upon to play a role. Metropolitan Chrysostomos of Florina led the Old Calendarists, who were known in Greece as the Church of True Orthodox Christians, in the early years. Schisms developed within the Greek Old Calendarist movement, resulting in the formation of rival synods, which were formed in 1979 and 1984.

Meanwhile, in Romania, a parallel Old Calendarist movement had begun in 1924 when Patriarch Miron Criatea introduced the Gregorian calendar. This was opposed by a hieromonk named Glicherii, who in the space of 12 years went on to establish 40 churches, most of which were in Moldavia; these were later suppressed by the Romanian civil authorities. By the end of the Second World War nearly all of these had been re-opened and a hierarchy established. This Church is now known as the Old Rite Romanian Orthodox Church and has its headquarters at Suceava, north of Bucharest. A splinter group was organized in 1934 and is variously known as the Traditional Orthodox Church, or the Traditional Christian Church. Hieromonk Glicherii died in 1985 and was canonized by his Church in 1999.

The adoption of the New Calendar by the Bulgarian Orthodox Church was delayed until the 1960s. Only after the fall of communism, which had been implicated in the persecution of the Old Calendarists, did it emerge to become a viable community with its headquarters at Sofia.

The Old Calendarists in Greece today function freely. The hierarchy is responsible for about 250 priests, 81 monasteries and convents and many thousands of faithful, both at home and abroad.

❖ Palaioemerologitai

OLD CATHOLIC CHURCH

The flight and plight of Jansenist refugees from France to the Netherlands, pursued by Jesuits, aroused the attention of the Roman Catholic Church in the Netherlands and of Peter Codde (d. 1710), a Roman Catholic priest who had been consecrated in 1689 by the Bishops of Mechlin, Antwerp and Namur, for the See of Utrecht. Codde wanted to enter into some sort of dialogue with the Jansenists, but Rome asked him to desist from any dealings with this group. When Codde refused to comply he was accused of Jansenism himself, on the evidence of some anonymous accusers. Codde was eventually acquitted, but suspended from his office for the rest of his life. Upon his death, Rome refused to approve the consecration of a new bishop for Utrecht and declared that it had the authority to abolish that see.

This created the problem of finding an ordaining bishop for the churches in the See of Utrecht, but a solution was found in the person of Bishop Luke Fagan of Meath, in Ireland, who obligingly, and in secret, carried out the ordination of twelve men. Rumours of this reached Rome, but came with no details of who had *obliged* Utrecht. By this time Fagan had become Archbishop of Dublin and he was ordered by the Holy See to find out the name of the ordaining bishop, who was rumoured to have been an Irishman. Fagan duly carried out an investigation and reported back to Rome. With a clear conscience his somewhat Jesuitical conclusion was that nobody of whom he had enquired had ever held such ordinations.

In 1719 the appointed Roman Catholic Bishop of Babylon, Dominique Marie Varlet, arrived in Amsterdam en route to Persia where he was to take up his duties. In April of that year, Varlet was prevailed upon to administer confirmation to some 604 children of the See of Utrecht. When he reached Persia, in October 1719, Varlet received notice of his suspension from office because of this action and some other, possibly trumped up, administrative errors. He returned to Amsterdam where he was persuaded to consecrate Cornelius Steenoven as Archbishop of Utrecht in October 1724. When Steenoven died the following year Varlet consecrated his successor, Cornelius Johann Barchman Wuytiers. Rome, informed of these actions, declared the consecrations to be illicit, but not invalid. Undaunted, Varlet went on to consecrate more bishops, for the Dutch Sees of Haarlem and Deventer. For the next 150 years the Church of Utrecht, commonly called the Old Catholic Church, remained separated from Rome over the issue of episcopal supervision.

When, in 1870, the First Vatican Council promulgated the declaration of papal infallibility this was understood by many members of the Roman Catholic Church, especially those from parts of German-speaking Europe, to be a deviation from tradition and this led many to leave the Church. A congress was convened in Munich in 1871 by around three hundred clergy who considered the dogma to be of recent origin and unacceptable to them. By the end of that year as many as 23 congregations in Germany and Austria, who were in sympathy with the Old Catholic position, had been established. The perceived aim of the congress was to perpetuate true Roman Catholicism and it was ready to elect a bishop. The choice fell upon a church historian, Joseph Hubert Reinkens (1821–96), and he was consecrated as Bishop of Bonn by an obliging independent Dutch bishop, Herman Heykamp, at Deventer. The Dutch, having realized that any hope of reconciliation with Rome was out of the question, joined forces with the German and Austrian seceders. Bismarck's *Kulturkampf* movement in Germany provided support for the Old Catholics, as part of its anti-Rome stance, by supplying them with church buildings and subsidies.

The Old Catholic movement now gathered momentum and began to spread throughout Europe. In 1889 it issued the *Declaration of Utrecht*, which set out the principles of the Church, upon which the Old Catholic bishops had reached agreement. The declaration affirmed the decisions and creeds of the seven ecumenical councils before the schism of 1054, and accepted that the Pope, as Bishop of Rome, was historically *primus inter pares* (first among equals), but roundly rejected the dogma of the Immaculate Conception as promulgated by Pope Pius IX in 1854, as well as the encyclical *Unigenitus* (1714) against Jansenism, the *Syllabus of Errors* (1864) and the decrees of the Council of Trent on matters of discipline. Other points of difference with Roman usage concerned the election of bishops, which the *Declaration* decreed was to be in the hands of synods, upon which clergy and laity were able to sit with equal status. It was also stated that parishes could elect their own priests, all clergy were free to marry and provision was to be made for the liturgy to be celebrated in the vernacular, with auricular confession not obligatory.

Other autonomous Churches which have affiliated with the Old Catholic Church include the POLISH NATIONAL CATHOLIC CHURCH, founded in Scranton, Pennsylvania, USA, in 1897, the Yugoslav Old Catholics and the PHILIPPINE INDEPENDENT CHURCH, who all established sacramental communion with the Old Catholics in 1965.

The validity of ordinations in the ANGLICAN Church were recognized by the Old Catholics in 1925 and full intercommunion was achieved in 1932. Today, the Old Catholic Church is a recognized presence in the Netherlands, Germany, Switzerland, Austria, Poland and North America.

OLD CATHOLIC CHURCH (ANGLICAN RITE)

The Old Catholic Church (Anglican Rite) was founded in the USA in 1951 by an ex-priest of the LIBERAL CATHOLIC CHURCH, Jay Davis Kirby (d. 1989), who wanted a Church that would be, in his opinion, free of theosophy, parapsychology, homosexuality and female clergy. Curiously, Archbishop Herman Adrian Spruit of the Church of Antioch who, until his resignation in 1991 and subsequent death, had headed a Church noted for its Gnostic-Christian and liberal theology, consecrated Kirby. Even more surprisingly, the same archbishop had consecrated a woman bishop in 1976.

The Church is affiliated with the Old Catholic Order of Christ the King, which had been founded in England by Fr Alban Cockeram of Leeds and introduced to California by Bishop Kirby. The Old Catholic Order of Christ the King, whose members provide a ministry of social service in hospitals and other care-providing institutions, was designed to be flexible enough to permit its members to belong to jurisdictions of a similar nature.

The headquarters of the Old Catholic Church (Anglican Rite) is at Laguna Beach, California, from where it supervises an adult membership of around 600, distributed through 6 congregations, two of which are in Mexico. Archbishop Kirby resigned from the Church in 1988 and died the following year, having previously consecrated a suffragan bishop in 1978.

❖ Old Catholic Episcopal Church

OLD CATHOLIC ORTHODOX CHURCH

This defunct sect, originally called the Independent Catholic Church, was founded by the Most Reverend James Bartholomew Banks, affectionately know to his friends as *Piggy* on account of the happy conjunction of his vast inherited wealth with his surname. The Church's foundation followed upon Banks' ordination and subsequent consecration as bishop, which derived from an OLD CATHOLIC CHURCH source. The church itself was situated in London, just off the Strand, and changed its name several times in the course of its short history. It began in 1922 as the Church of the Great Sacrifice, an allusion to the memory of the fallen troops of the First World War. In 1924, Banks declared that he was thenceforth to be known as the Patriarch of Windsor and the Church was renamed as the Old Catholic Orthodox Church (Apostolic Service Church). Banks took up residence in a large house at East Molesey, Surrey, complete with a fifteen-foot flagpole from which was flown a standard bearing his arms, decorated with fleurs-de-lis, and founded the Priory Church of St Michael and All Angels in a building adjacent to the patriarchal residence. The Church was to be governed by a sacred senate under the direction of the *Sovereign Primate with Universal Jurisdiction* (Banks, who thereafter wore a white stock to signify this), with provision made in the constitutions for a panoply of church officials and a curia; the clergy were largely recruited from amongst ex-servicemen and serving members of the armed forces. Trafalgar Day, Anzac Day and Armistice Day were included in the church calendar, each commemoration granted its own *Proper* for use during the Divine Liturgy, all with individual prefaces. The military tone was maintained during the service of Benediction of the Blessed Sacrament, when a hymn was sung which referred to 'Our Loved Ones marching on ... their long way to Tipperary'. All baptized Christians were welcome to receive Holy Communion and to participate in the spiritual healing services. The text of the creed used in the liturgy affirmed Banks' belief in reincarnation, the text concluding with the words 'And I look through reincarnation to the perfection of all men and the life of the world to come. Amen'. The liturgy contained certain portions of the LIBERAL CATHOLIC CHURCH rite, and many of their hymns were used, which Banks acknowledged in the preface of his book *The Holy Liturgy and other Rites* (1954). The number of church members was never very great and the Old Catholic Orthodox Church disappeared after the death of *Piggy* Banks.

❖ The Apostolic Service Church

OLD GERMAN BAPTIST BRETHREN (OLD ORDER DUNKERS)

The Church of the Old German Baptist Brethren was founded in the USA in 1881 by arch-conservatives who left the CHURCH OF THE BRETHREN on account of its perceived liberality. This matter had gradually come to a head with the establishment of Sunday schools, missions, higher education for its members and the founding of various church societies. These activities were thought, by some, to taint the purity of the Brethren movement.

The Church, the members of which are now spread amongst some 55 congregations across the USA, still maintains its ultra-conservative manner of life. The discipline of wearing only plain and simple clothing is insisted upon, as well as abstention from alcohol and what are described as worldly amusements. Members may not take oaths in court, but must simply affirm, and they are not expected to undertake litigation or participate in any military activity. Members believe in the literal interpretation of the scriptures and observe a closed communion in their celebration of the Lord's Supper, which they achieve by excluding from the service anyone who is not a member of the church. Children are not allowed to attend Sunday schools, but they may attend church services from the age of 10 and are now no longer discouraged from seeking education at every level.

❖ Old Order Dunkers

OLD ORDER AMISH MENNONITE CHURCH

The Amish movement within the ranks of the MENNONITES takes its name from Jacob Ammann, a minister in the Emmenthal congregation of Swiss Mennonites in the late seventeenth century, promoted a strict interpretation of the writings of Menno Simons (1496–1561), the Dutch ANABAPTIST leader who, with his followers, had fled to Switzerland in the wake of severe persecutions. Menno Simons' writings put a heavy emphasis on the practices of *avoidance* (or shunning, based on Matt. 18:15–17) and of foot-washing, which were not acceptable to the larger group and led to a split within the Mennonite group that was never healed. Those who separated, in 1693, became known as the AMISH.

In the early years of the eighteenth century the Amish from Switzerland began to migrate to America, settling in eastern Pennsylvania, Ohio, Indiana, Illinois and Iowa. In time, they found themselves having to face various issues that were considered liberal. At first concerned with matters such as schooling and the decision as to whether Amish children should be educated with others in schools, or be schooled in their own communities, in time the decisions to be made widened to include farming regulations, the use of cars and farm motor vehicles and the attitude towards tourists who came to observe what was increasingly seen as a *quaint* way of life. Because there was often little agreement on new issues, schisms were inevitable. Attempts were made to arrive at a consensus through general conferences, the first such held at Wayne County, Ohio, in 1865. The conclusions of these conferences persuaded some conservative Amish to break away and organize themselves separately. These became incorporated as the Old Order Amish Mennonite Church.

The members of the Church are noted for their plain clothing and agricultural lifestyle. The men cultivate beards, but no moustaches, wear broad-brimmed black, or straw, hats, black trousers and lapelless coats, without a necktie except on their wedding day. No buttons are allowed on clothing, other than on men's coats and trousers, and alternative methods are used instead. The women wear long dresses, aprons and capes, with a white cap or bonnet, the clothing fastened with straight pins or press-studs (snaps). The cutting of female hair is forbidden and their long hair is gathered into a simple bun. No jewellery is allowed. The people live without electricity, telephones, radio or television and use horse-drawn buggies instead of cars, which are forbidden.

The engagement and marriage of couples, which is only permitted between Amish believers, is marked by certain traditions. Instead of the giving of an engagement ring, the man will present his fiancée with a piece of china, or perhaps a clock, and their marriage intentions will be kept secret for a while, until the woman decides the time is right to tell her family, which is usually done in July or August. The careful dating of these occasions is dictated by the farming year and all neatly tucked in to those times of the year when the whole community is free to attend the celebrations. The marriage plans, therefore, will normally be announced in late October, at a Sunday service, and the marriage will take place in November or December, after the harvest is in. By tradition, the bride makes her own wedding dress and that of her attendants, or *Newehockers* (Pennsylvanian Dutch for 'side-sitters'). Her bridal dress is made from either blue or purple material and will be fashioned in a simple style, mid-calf length and unadorned; this subsequently becomes the bride's Sunday dress, and may be the one in which she is buried. The bride and her attendants wear capes and aprons over their dresses and in place of a veil the bride will wear a black prayer head covering, instead of her daily white cap or bonnet. For his marriage, the groom will wear a black suit, with a white shirt and a bow tie, and a broad-brimmed black hat. The marriage service, which can last for three hours, is followed by a reception at which the seating plan is highly formalized. Marriages are usually celebrated on either Tuesdays or Thursdays.

The Old Order Amish are FUNDAMENTALIST to the extent that they accept the literal interpretation of the Bible and foster separateness from the world. They also acknowledge *Ordnung*, the oral tradition that regulates the Amish way of life, and they never proselytize to attract members. Little value is placed on schooling and since 1972 the communities have been exempted by an American Supreme Court decision from compulsory school attendance laws. Instead, Amish children attend their own, usually one-room, schoolhouses where a female member of the group teaches them. In their early teens the young people turn to training in either agriculture or in the family business, which is generally connected with farming. It is estimated that Old Order Amish communities exist now in about 20 states in the USA and in one Canadian province, with an adult membership in the region of 56,000. This figure is increasing, possibly because of the Amish ban on contraception and the very low infant mortality rate that has been observed amongst them.

OLD ORDER (HORNING) MENNONITES – WEAVERLAND CONFERENCE

This modestly-sized American Church, which is found largely in south-east Pennsylvania, was organized by Bishop Moses Horning (1870–1955) as a liberal branch of the OLD ORDER (WISLER) MENNONITE CHURCH. This group allows the ownership and use of motor vehicles, but, in order to allay any suspicion of ostentation, the cars must always be black and any chrome trim has to be painted the same colour.

❖ Old Order (Black Bumper) Mennonites – Weaverland Conference

OLD ORDER (REIDENBACH) MENNONITES

Among some of the American Old Order MENNONITE groups there was an understanding that the response of their young men to military call-up during the Second World War should be to accept imprisonment as conscientious objectors. A small group of OLD ORDER (WENGER) MENNONITES voiced the opinion that any of their young men accepting one of the alternative forms of service, offered by the government to those who would not take up arms for ethical and religious reasons at time of war, should be excommunicated as a punishment. The members established their own, separate meeting house at the settlement of Reidenbach's Store (population currently 79), in Lancaster County, south-east Pennsylvania, where their conservativeness and separateness from the world is underlined by their use of candles for lighting, and their resistance to the use of manure spreaders on their fields, or rubber tyres on their carriage wheels.

OLD ORDER (WENGER) MENNONITES

This small group of American MENNONITES is found in south-east Pennsylvania and represents a breakaway group, seceding from the OLD ORDER (WISLER) MENNONITES, which was led by Bishop Joseph Wenger in the 1930s.

The cause for the secession concerned confrontation with change, in this case precipitated by the issue of whether cars could be used for occupational purposes, or for easing the journey to church. Bishop Wenger, unlike Bishop Horning of the OLD ORDER (HORNING) MENNONITES – WEAVERLAND CONFERENCE, argued that the use of cars could not be tolerated. Those who agreed with Wenger formed themselves into a small and very conservative group, whose ideas even extended to insisting that only the German language could be used as a medium for preaching and that young men must be prepared to accept imprisonment in time of war rather than volunteering for any form of alternative service offered to them.

OLD ORDER (WISLER) MENNONITE CHURCH

A split in the MENNONITE congregation at Yellow Creek, near Elkhart, Indiana, occurred in the 1860s because of opposition to the introduction of innovations such as preaching in English, and the use of Sunday schools for the children. Jacob Wisler, who organized a new congregation in 1870, led this ultra-conservative faction.

Other like-minded groups, from Pennsylvania, Virginia and Canada, joined Wisler's Church between 1886 and 1901. One such group had used as their reason for leaving their home group their opposition to the introduction of a new pulpit in their church, which they considered unnecessary.

The Old Order (Wisler) Mennonite Church does not undertake any missionary work. It currently has 19 bishops, 49 congregations and over 10,000 adult members in Ohio, Pennsylvania, Virginia and Ontario, Canada. This very conservative group resembles the AMISH people, but the men are not required to wear beards and the congregations worship in a church building rather than in private homes.

OLD ORDER (YORKER) RIVER BRETHREN

One of the smallest American denominations within the Brethren in Christ movement, the Old Order (Yorker) River Brethren derives its name through the attempts of its members to keep the old Brethren traditions alive and also maintain a separate existence in York County, Pennsylvania.

Under the leadership of Bishop Jacob Strickler, the group separated from the parent body in 1843 as a protest against what they saw as over-relaxed attitudes. There have been many splits over the years, often resulting from arguments concerning which means of transport should be permitted – a matter of great contention as modern vehicles supplanted the old horse-drawn carts and carriages throughout the country. The members do not erect church buildings, but meet for services in each other's homes.

OLD REFORMED CONGREGATIONS IN THE NETHERLANDS

Following the 1834 *Afscheiding*, or separation, from the DUTCH REFORMED CHURCH, the efforts of two pastors, L. G. C. Ledeboer and G. H. Kersten, to form unions of all those independent congregations that had been formed were not totally successful. Some who persisted in their independence established their own ultra-conservative Church, which they named the Old Reformed Congregations in the Netherlands (OGG), under the leadership of Pastor L. Boone (1860–1935).

This is a very small Church, with a total

membership of about 58,000, with congregations all in the Netherlands apart from one, an English-speaking congregation, in Salford, Canada. The Church follows a congregational type of polity and does not ordain women to the ministry. It follows the *Heidelberg Catechism* (1563) and the *Canons of the Synod of Dort* (1618–19). There is collaboration with the FREE PRESBYTERIAN CHURCH OF SCOTLAND for work in the mission field. The headquarters of the Church is at Barneveld in the Netherlands.

OLD ROMAN CATHOLIC CHURCH OF GREAT BRITAIN

Following the declaration of papal infallibility by the ROMAN CATHOLIC CHURCH in 1870, the OLD CATHOLIC CHURCH in the Netherlands was determined to pursue an independent existence and found sympathizers in Germany, Switzerland, Poland and the USA.

In England, Arnold Harris Mathew, a former Roman Catholic priest, informed Bishop Edward Herzog, the Old Catholic Bishop of Switzerland, and the Dutch Old Catholic authorities that many Anglo-Catholics might welcome the establishment of an Old Catholic Church in England and that such a Church might be a haven for many disaffected Roman Catholic clergy.

Mathew's case was received sympathetically by the Dutch Old Catholics, who consecrated him in 1908 as the first Old Catholic bishop for England. However, Bishop Mathew seems to have been deceived and he had overestimated the support he expected to follow. Although Mathew was diligent in informing the Old Catholics in Utrecht about this shortfall, he failed to consult the continental Old Catholic bishops when he consecrated two excommunicated former Roman Catholic priests as bishops and thereby created a storm within the movement, which was fast to point out to Mathew that he had broken the *Declaration of Utrecht* that had been drawn up in 1889. This prompted Mathew to issue his own *Declaration of Autonomy and Independence*, which was printed in the Manchester Guardian newspaper on 6 January 1911. This formalized the separation of the Old Catholic Church of England from its Utrecht forbears. Consequently, a title for the new Church was sought, and it became known as the *English Catholic Church*. In the same year a union was also arranged with the Patriarch of Antioch.

With the reception into the English Catholic Church of Prince de Landas Berghes et de Rache, and his subsequent ordination in 1912 and consecration in 1913, the way was paved for the establishment of the Mathew Old Catholic succession in the USA (NORTH AMERICAN OLD ROMAN CATHOLIC CHURCH). A former ANGLICAN priest, Frederick Samuel Willoughby, joined the Church and was raised to the episcopate in 1914, to be Mathew's coadjutor bishop; this action laid yet another foundation, this time for the LIBERAL CATHOLIC CHURCH.

In 1915, Archbishop Mathew (he had raised his clerical status in the meantime) changed the name of his Church again, and it was now known as the Old Roman Catholic Church. The Church, whose clergy are non-stipendiary, celebrates the Tridentine Mass, affirms the Apostles', Nicene and Athanasian creeds and administers the seven sacraments. The Church, which is now headed by a primate, approached the Roman Catholic

Church in 1982, seeking unity. It has not so far received a reply.

ONEIDA COMMUNITY

This now-defunct American community was organized by John Humphrey Noyes (1811–66), who was born in Brattleboro, Vermont, and graduated from Dartmouth College. Noyes underwent a conversion experience during a revival meeting in 1830 and took up studies for the CONGREGATIONAL CHURCH ministry at Andover Theological Seminary and Yale Divinity School. Even before he could be ordained, however, Noyes had come to the view that Christ had made perfection humanly possible and that as part of that scheme of perfection there was no reason to observe earthly laws. These views caused the Congregational Church to reconsider his suitability for ordination, especially after Noyes had publicly declared that he was sinless, and he was duly turned down.

Over the next few years Noyes, with some followers, moved around the country, visiting Vermont and New York State. By 1837, an informal Bible study group had been formed in Putney, Vermont. One of the disciplines which Noyes introduced into the group was that of mutual criticism sessions, also known as *cures*, a practice he had brought with him from the seminary and which was thought to be a good way for individuals to overcome their shortcomings. After the community had become more formally organized, these criticism sessions became a means of ensuring social cohesion and an instrument of control amongst the members. These sessions, which could be regarded harmful, were as nothing compared with Noyes' alarming proposals, later implemented by the community, regarding sexual relations. These he justified by his opinion that monogamy was not going to be relevant in heaven, whereas sexual relations would continue after death. He devised a system of complex 'marriage', whereby men and women in the community constantly changed their partners. Even this, however, was not by random whim, for the partners were chosen for the younger women by the older women of the group, usually on a monthly basis. In 1847 Noyes declared that the spirit of Christ had returned to earth, earlier than expected, and had entered the Putney community.

This behaviour aroused indignation in the local area and Noyes moved his community to Oneida, New York, where it flourished. Until the time of this move the community had supported itself through farming and logging, but it now turned to a new venture. A new member introduced them to working in steel, producing the Oneida Trap that he had invented and which proved to be a great commercial success. Other initiatives were introduced, including the making of silverware and silk embroidery and the canning of fruit.

The complex marriage arrangements, unorthodox as they may have been, were also successful and very few unplanned pregnancies resulted. A eugenics programme was introduced by which selected members were chosen to be parents, and set aside from community work so that they could reproduce efficiently. As a result, 51 children were born, each regarded as having ideal qualities. This outraged the residents of Oneida and the community was forced to abandon the marriage system and undergo some reorganization. Noyes and a few followers moved away from the community in

1876, going into Canada to live at Niagara Falls, Ontario, where he died ten years later. As a religious group the community ceased to exist.

The work of the Oneida Community carried on as a joint stock company, incorporated in New York in 1880 as the Oneida Community Ltd (later as Oneida Ltd). Today it is known for its stainless steel and silver-plated ware, china, crystal and glassware, a successful company with outlets worldwide.

❖ Bible Communists; Perfectionists

ONENESS

A form of PENTECOSTAL belief in which the deity of Jesus Christ and the Holy Spirit are affirmed but not distinguished as separate persons, as in the orthodox view of the Trinity.

OPEN BIBLE CHURCH OF GOD

This small PENTECOSTAL Church is affiliated with the United Full Gospel Ministers and Churches (incorporated 1951) and was founded by Willis M. Clay. The Church provides support for some 15 congregations and about 500 members in the Nilgiri and Coimbatore districts of southern India. From its headquarters in Tatabad, village evangelism within the Pentecostal tradition is organized.

OPEN BIBLE STANDARD CHURCHES, INC.

This white-led, American PENTECOSTAL Church was founded in 1935 through the merging of two revival movements. One of these was the Bible Standard, Inc. that had been founded in Eugene, Oregon, in 1919 by Fred Hornshuh. The other partner in the merger was the Open Bible Evangelistic Association, founded by John R. Richey in Des Moines, Iowa, in 1932. The two merging movements established headquarters at Des Moines, taking the combined name of Open Bible Standard Churches, Inc.

The doctrine of the Church can best be described as FUNDAMENTALIST, affirming the Trinity, Christ's divinity, divine healing, baptism of the Holy Spirit, as evidenced through *glossolalia*, or speaking in tongues, baptism by immersion, personal holiness, and the premillennial return of Jesus Christ (REVELATION 20); the Bible is regarded as the infallible word of God.

The Church maintains 368 congregations in the USA and has missions in 30 countries, which inclusively represent over 700 congregations. Each individual church is congregationally governed and locally owned. The administration is directed through a biennial convention, to which lay delegates from all the churches meet with all the licensed and ordained ministers, when a national board of directors is elected. A Bible college has been opened at Eugene, Oregon, and the Church also publishes a monthly periodical, *The Message of the Open Bible*, as well as producing books and material for the convention.

OPEN BRETHREN

John Nelson Darby (1800–82), an Irish ex-ANGLICAN priest who was ordained in 1826, came to reject the state Church and withdrew from it in 1827, expressing concern about the low spiritual state of denominational Christianity. With others, he sought to establish groups of like-minded people seeking a non-denominational approach to church life. The group, which accepted no name for itself, wished to be known simply as

Christians, but from its earliest days the name *Brethren* began to be used. One of the earliest of such groups met at Plymouth, Devon, and the unofficial title PLYMOUTH BRETHREN became commonplace. The movement spread to the United States, where the United States Bureau of the Census designated them with Roman numerals (Plymouth Brethren I, Plymouth Brethren V, etc.).

A serious split began to develop during the 1840s when a member of the group, Benjamin W. Newton, came to differ from Darby on many important issues concerning eschatology, the doctrine of the Last Things. Newton wanted each local group to be autonomous, and argued that they should accept Christians from other Churches, whereas it was Darby's view that the movement should remain united. A division was effected in 1848, when the Plymouth Brethren split into the Exclusive, and the Open, Brethren. The basis of the division concerned the question of *separation*. The EXCLUSIVE BRETHREN, following J. N. Darby's opinion, refused to join with anyone at the Lord's Table who was not a *full* Christian in the true sense. A *full* Christian was judged to be a member of a fully separated assembly, or group, who associated only with other Brethren, and not with people from other Christian Churches.

The Open Brethren followed Benjamin W. Newton's stance and accepted other Christians even if, in their opinion, these other Churches taught a false doctrine. With the passage of time, numerous subgroups appeared within these two major initial divisions.

OPHITES

The Ophites were members of a second-century heretical GNOSTIC sect, written about by St Irenaeus (*c.* 130–200), Origen (*c.* 185–*c.* 254) and others. Their name was taken from the word '*ophis*' (Greek for 'serpent'), the tempter of Eve, who was seen by the sect as a liberator since it had taught men to rebel against Jehovah and to search for the knowledge of the true and unknown God.

The Ophite belief was based on the heretical teachings of Marcion, taken to an extreme degree. Marcion suggested that the Jehovah of the Old Testament was the Demiurge, or subordinate, deity who had created the world and that hostilities between Jehovah and the God of the New Testament were inevitable. Ophites regarded man's fall as progress from ignorance to truth and knowledge, since the serpent in Genesis 3 enables mankind to acquire the knowledge of good and evil that Jehovah had withheld from them. They saw Christ as a spiritual figure who, because of his union with Jesus *the man*, had taught saving knowledge, or *gnosis*. It was because the serpent was regarded as the first liberator that the Ophites worshipped it. Whether live serpents were used, or not, in their rituals is conjectural, but according to some accounts a snake was used to consecrate the loaves of bread, which were used in a kind of Eucharist, by being released from a chest and allowed to move through the loaves that were set out on a table.

The Ophites were also given to representing their cosmology in the form of diagrams filled with mathematical shapes, such as circles, squares and lines. Conjecturally, it has been suggested that these *ophitic* diagrams also played a part in Ophite rituals. Other ancient sects, such as the NAASSENES, have also been linked with serpents, and snakes still play a part in the American DOLLY POND CHURCH OF GOD WITH SIGNS FOLLOWING.

ORIENTAL MISSIONARY SOCIETY HOLINESS CHURCH OF NORTH AMERICA

This Church began as an informal prayer group at Trinity Mission Church in Hollywood, California, which was formed by six Japanese seminarians studying in Los Angeles in the 1920s. The group then set about the task of evangelizing Japanese-Americans in Los Angeles, holding street meetings on Sunday afternoons at the corner of East First Street and San Pedro Street and inviting people to attend Trinity Mission Church. As a result of their activities, the men were able to found the Los Angeles Holiness Church in 1921. The evangelizing fervour then spread throughout California and into Hawaii, where many Japanese-Americans were living.

In an effort to coordinate the work it was decided in 1934 to formalize the organization by forming the Oriental Missionary Conference of North America. However, internment of Japanese residents during the Second World War halted this work until the war was ended. The Church was finally established and now has responsibility for a group of nineteen churches throughout north and south California, Arizona and Hawaii. Members affirm belief in the Trinity, the divinity of Jesus Christ, his birth, life, death, the resurrection and second coming (Revelation 20). Salvation is believed to be a gift of God, received by accepting Jesus Christ as the lord and saviour. The Bible is regarded as the infallible and inspired word of God. Two sacraments are observed, those of baptism by immersion or sprinkling, and Holy Communion, with access to the Lord's Supper open to all Christians. The Church has its headquarters in Los Angeles, California.

ORIENTAL ORTHODOX CHURCHES

There are five ancient Eastern Churches, each being fully independent. These are the Coptic Orthodox Church, the Ethiopian Orthodox Church, the Armenian Apostolic Church, the Syrian Orthodox Church and the Malankara Orthodox Syrian Church.

The Assyrian Church of the East, which is also known as the Nestorian Church, was formed after the Council of Ephesus (431) had declared Nestorius to be a heretic; the other Churches were formed as a consequence of their rejection of the christological definition declared by the Council of Chalcedon (451).

❖ Ancient Oriental Churches; Lesser Eastern Churches; Non-Chalcedonian Churches

(ORIGINAL) CHURCH OF GOD, INC.

This Church sets its foundation date at 1886, which is the foundation date of the Church of God (Cleveland, Tennessee) from which it split in 1917. A Church of God pastor, Joseph L. Scott, led the schism at Chattanooga and the seceding Church has maintained its headquarters in that city; it was incorporated in 1922 and upholds the Pentecostal tradition. The disagreement with its parent Church concerned the issue of local church autonomy and the question of tithing and whether it should be obligatory, or not.

In practice, the Church recognizes five ordinances, baptism by immersion, tithing, foot-washing, the Lord's Supper and biblical church government. Through the latter ordinance each church takes its name from the locality, for example the 'Church of God at Chattanooga', in imitation of the Church of God at Corinth, and the pattern of Church ministries follows that laid down in Ephesians 4:11–14; these comprise orders of ministers, apostles, deacons, exhorters, evangelists, bishops and teachers. A presbytery regulates the ministry of the Church.

The Church does not recognize the historical creeds as binding, since these cannot be justified by reference to scripture. It does, however, recognize repentance, justification or rebirth, sanctification and divine healing as well as accepting the experience of *glossolalia*, or speaking in tongues, as evidence of the baptism of the Holy Spirit. Members anticipate Christ's second coming and the judgement of all, with eternal reward for the righteous and eternal punishment for the wicked (Revelation 20). The Church currently has 70 congregations, with around 12,000 adult members and is mainly concentrated in the eastern and south-eastern parts of the USA.

ORIGINAL FREE WILL BAPTIST CHURCH, NORTH CAROLINA STATE CONVENTION

An American Baptist Church, which originated from immigrant Baptists who left Britain to settle along the Delaware River in north Pennsylvania during the eighteenth century. It was here that Paul Palmer was baptized and by 1720 was pursuing a ministry of preaching and evangelizing in New Jersey and Maryland. He established a Baptist congregation in North Carolina, at Perquimans, Chowan County, but this was disbanded in 1732 when its first pastor, Joseph Parker, moved to another part of the country. Other congregations were established by Paul Palmer in North Carolina during the 1720s, at Pasquotank and New River, and grew significantly in size over the next hundred years until it was possible to form a general conference in 1827 and in the following year the name Free Will Baptists was formally adopted; eventually, this group became part of the National Association of Free Will Baptists.

In 1913, the North Carolina state convention was formed, allowing the Church to support a Free Will Baptist Press, a college and seminary and an assembly site. In the meantime other Free Will Baptist groups had been growing and by 1935 the National Association of Free Will Baptists was formed at Nashville, Tennessee. With the passage of time dissension broke out when it was perceived that Nashville was fast becoming the epicentre of the movement, and the North Carolina State Convention withdrew from the National Association in 1961, becoming independent and adopting its current title.

Doctrinally, the Church is Arminian, affirming that every human being has free will and, as such, is free to yield to the Spirit or to resist and perish. Salvation, which is available to all, is believed to depend upon repentance of sin, faith in Jesus Christ as saviour, and perseverance in that faith until death. Three ordinances are accepted, those of baptism of believers by immersion, foot-washing and the Lord's Supper. The Bible is believed to be the inspired and infallible word of God, from which all their doctrine is derived; this includes an orthodox view of the Trinity and of Jesus Christ's incarnation, death and resurrection, ascension and second coming (Revelation 20).

In their lifestyle, members are expected to abstain from alcohol and worldly amusements and to observe honesty in all their dealings. The polity of the Church is congregational, with all local churches belonging to the conferences. These, in turn, compose the state convention, which is the final arbiter of disputes and the administrative centre of the Church. The convention provides not only for the Mount Olive College at Mount Olive, North Carolina, (chartered 1951) but also supports a children's home and the Free Will Baptist Press, which publishes the periodical *The Free Will Baptist*. Foreign missions are maintained in Austria, Mexico, the Philippines and India, with home missions concerned with Laotian refugees throughout North America and with Hispanic communities in Florida. These missions are under the control of a board of missions, answerable to the state convention at Ayden, North Carolina.

ORIGINAL SECESSION CHURCH

There was a secession from the CHURCH OF SCOTLAND in 1733, over the issue of patronage, or the right of a patron to nominate someone for appointment to an ecclesiastical benefice, or to administer it. Attempts were made to try and bring about reconciliation over this issue by the general assemblies of the Church in the following years, but to no avail. Ebenezer Erskine (1680–1754), a minister in the Church of Scotland, together with others, formed a presbytery in 1737; Erskine's brother and some other sympathizers joined them. The Church of Scotland was left with no alternative but to formally depose the men, which they did in 1740.

Some seven years later, the seceders split into two groups over the issue of whether it was lawful, or not, for members to take an oath, known also as the Burgher's Oath, required of the burgesses of certain cities. This required those qualified to swear the oath, which was publicly preached throughout Scotland and was legally authorized, to acknowledge the true religion. The seceders, according to the action they took, were thereafter known as *Burghers*, who regarded the taking of the oath to be lawful, or *Anti-burghers*, who were those who regarded the action as sinful.

Towards the close of the eighteenth century and the start of the nineteenth, both the Burghers and the Anti-burghers split into two groups, known in both cases as the *Auld Lichts* and the *New Lichts*. The split concerned differences of opinion over the WESTMINSTER CONFESSION *of Faith* (1643–6) and whether, according to its dictates, a civil magistrate had a duty to impose the true faith on the people; this view was opposed by both New Lichts groups but supported by the Auld Lichts groups. Both groups of New Lichts were united in 1820 to form the UNITED SECESSION CHURCH and most of the Auld Licht Anti-burghers joined the FREE CHURCH OF SCOTLAND in 1852, with the rest continuing as the Original Secession Church, which now has around three thousand members. The Auld Licht Burgers reunited with the Church of Scotland in 1839.

❖ Synod of United Original Seceders

ORIGINAL UNITED HOLY CHURCH INTERNATIONAL

This American Church, which functions within the PENTECOSTAL tradition, was formed in 1977 when Bishop James Alexander Forbes and some congregations of the UNITED HOLY CHURCH OF AMERICA, INC, parted company. From its headquarters in Durham, North Carolina, the Church has responsibility for some 220 congregations, most of which are found along the Atlantic seaboard, with others in Texas, Kentucky and California. The Church also actively supports a mission in Liberia.

Doctrinally in accord with its parent Church, an agreement was made in 1979 to affiliate with the INTERNATIONAL PENTECOSTAL HOLINESS CHURCH at Wilmington, North Carolina.

ORTHODOX CATHOLIC CHURCH OF AMERICA

Bishop George Augustine Hyde, a man with an interesting clerical background, founded this American Church. Hyde was consecrated by Archbishop Cyril Clement Sherwood (1895–1969), who had founded the American Holy Orthodox Catholic Apostolic Eastern Church in 1933; his own holy orders derived from Archbishop Joseph René Vilatte, an *EPISCOPUS VAGANS*. Bishop Hyde, feeling that Sherwood was too eastern in his liturgical practices and theology, left his jurisdiction in 1960 to found a group that would be more appealing to western converts. This was the Orthodox Catholic Church of America.

Doctrinally, the Church accepts the seven ecumenical councils, but it rejects papal infallibility, purgatory, the Immaculate Conception and clerical celibacy. Ordination within the Church is available for both sexes. A ministry to the gay community is provided, which offers an opportunity for the celebration of the Holy Union to take place 'between persons committed to one another in the love of God'; the usual sacraments are also celebrated, using eastern and western rites.

The Church has its present headquarters at Angola, Indiana, where the Metropolitan Archbishop of the Archdiocese of North America currently resides. A presence is maintained in around twenty American states and also in Canada. A synod of bishops comprises the principal authority of the Church. All clergy come together every four years to attend a national synod, where future plans for the Church are discussed.

ORTHODOX CHURCH, ARCHDIOCESE OF FRANCE AND WESTERN EUROPE

The Patriarch of Russia, Tikhon, was aware of the potential danger that communism posed for the RUSSIAN ORTHODOX CHURCH and as a result he issued a decree, in 1920, that authorized the Russian bishops to set up temporary independent organizations of their own should the normal relations within the patriarchate become impossible. Consequently, in 1921, the Patriarch of Serbia assisted in the formation of a synod, known as the Karlovtzy Synod, which met in Sremski-Karlovci (then known as Karlovtzy), for the purpose of setting up a temporary ecclesiastical framework for those members of the Church who were then in exile.

In 1922, Patriarch Tikhon issued another decree abolishing this administrative board set up by the Karlovtzy Synod and ordering the Metropolitan of Paris, Evlogy, to prepare a new approach for the Russian Orthodox Church Outside Russia. To what extent Tikhon was under the influence of the communist government is hard to determine, but a new administrative programme was devised. By 1926, Metropolitan Evlogy had ceased attending the annual meeting of the synod and in 1931 he was finally separated from the Russian Orthodox Church because of his insistence that prayers should be said for those Christians who were being persecuted in Russia, a fact that the newly-elected Russian patriarch, Sergius, wanted to repudiate. Evlogy then placed himself and his parishes under the jurisdiction of the Ecumenical Patriarch in Constantinople.

Evlogy attempted reconciliation with the Karlovtzy Synod in 1935 and just before his death, in 1946, he was reconciled with the Moscow Patriarchate. This move, however, was one that many of his parishioners were unable to make and they chose to remain under the jurisdiction of the Ecumenical Patriarch.

❖ Russian Exarchate in Western Europe

ORTHODOX CHURCH IN AMERICA

This Church is not to be confused with the much smaller Orthodox Church of *America.*

From the start, Orthodoxy in America was a missionary endeavour from Russia, first to the people of Alaska following its discovery by the Russians in 1741, and then to the waves of immigrants from Europe. The Orthodox presence started with the arrival in 1794 on Kodiak Island, Alaska, of eight monks and two novices from Valaam, on Lake Ladoga, just north of St Petersburg. Here, the Russian missionaries followed up the initial evangelization that had been done by Russian laity in Alaska soon after its discovery. As a result, within two years it is claimed that some 12,000 native inhabitants, mainly Inuit and American Indian, were baptized.

St Herman of Alaska was a notable missionary in these early years, as was Fr John Veniaminov, a married priest. After the death of his wife, Veniaminov was consecrated as Bishop Innocent and founded the first missionary diocese in Alaska with its first cathedral and seminary at Sitka, on the west coast. Prior to his recall to Moscow, Bishop Innocent translated St Matthew's Gospel, the text of the Divine Liturgy and the catechism into Aleutian; he was later canonized, in 1977.

After Alaska's purchase by the Americans in 1867, the Alaskan missionary diocese was moved to San Francisco. Five years later this became known as the Russian Orthodox Church, Diocese of the Aleutian Islands and North America, and an expansion of the missionary work was undertaken, in Canada and the eastern USA. The diocesan see was elevated to the rank of archdiocese in 1904 and was moved to New York a year later. Until 1914, the RUSSIAN ORTHODOX CHURCH in Russia had jurisdiction over all Orthodox Christians in the USA and Canada.

The Russian Revolution had many effects on the Church, one of the most important of which was the drying up of funds from Russia that were necessary to support the archdiocese and the waves of Russian immigrants who were fleeing to the USA. The arrest of the Patriarch of Moscow by the Soviet authorities in 1922 contributed to a split that then developed within the Russian Church in America.

There were those who still wanted to remain loyal to the Moscow-based Church, identified as belonging to the Living Church, and those who refused to accept the Soviet-controlled Church. A *Sobor*, or convention, was held in Detroit, Michigan, in 1924 and those who asserted their independence from Russia rejected the Living Church. They formed the Russian Orthodox Greek Catholic Church, or Metropolia. The remaining segment of the Living Church was led by an American-born Russian Orthodox bishop, John Kedrowsky, who laid successful legal claims to St Nicholas' Cathedral in New York in 1926 (see below).

A synod of the Russian Orthodox Greek Catholic Church was called at Cleveland, Ohio, in 1946 at which four bishops, together with many parish delegates, opted to submit to the Patriarch of Moscow in return for recognition of their autonomy. Patriarch Alexis of Moscow, however, made impossible demands at first, but in 1970 agreed to the requested administrative autonomy and the Church was renamed as the ORTHODOX CHURCH IN AMERICA (OCA). Other non-Russian Orthodox Churches that had been formed in the USA did not feel able to unite with the Russians and remained outside the OCA, whose jurisdiction now extends throughout the USA and Canada and to an exarchate in Mexico.

Some of the parishes that wished to remain directly under the jurisdiction of the Patriarch of Moscow, and therefore outside the OCA, were organized as the Patriarchal Parishes of the Russian Orthodox Church in the United States and Canada, *with a bishop appointed to care for some forty parishes. The Cathedral of St Nicholas in New York became its headquarters; some of these parishes, however, have transferred subsequently to the OCA.*

❖ Metropolia; Russian Greek Catholic Church

ORTHODOX CHURCH IN GHANA

This Church, which is now part of the Greek Orthodox Patriarchate of Alexandria, was founded by Kwamin Ntsetse Bresi-Ando in Apam, Gold Coast (now Ghana). It began as an all-African-run PROTESTANT group known as the AFRICAN UNIVERSAL CHURCH. The membership was largely composed of ex-METHODISTS, and Bresi-Ando had himself been ordained as a minister in that Church, leaving it in 1926 when he went to Nigeria for a brief spell and founded there an independent PROTESTANT Church, called the United Free Church of Africa, before returning to the Gold Coast in 1932. Bresi-Ando, who sometimes used the name Ebenezer Johnson Anderson, went to England and lived for a time in Hornsey, north London. While there, he came into contact with Archbishop Churchill Sibley, an *EPISCOPUS VAGANS* who consecrated Bresi-Ando in London in 1935. Taking the episcopal style and title of Mar Kwamin I, Bresi-Ando returned to the Gold Coast and renamed his Church as the African Universal Church. The Church grew slowly during the late 1930s, but deteriorated after Bresi-Ando left for another spell in Nigeria, and many schisms were formed. In 1951 the title of the Church was changed again, now becoming the Orthodox Catholic Church, with its members convinced that they were truly Orthodox. When Bresi-Ando died, in 1970, a search for true Orthodoxy began, as it had become clear to its members that the Church was not part of the canonical Orthodox Church. The Orthodox Youth Organization (OYO) was formed, in 1971, with the aim of resuscitating the floundering Church and bringing it into the true Orthodox Church. In 1974 two OYO leaders, Kwame Labi and Godfried Mantey, hearing that some Orthodox clergy were to attend a WCC meeting at a university campus at Legon, made contact with the visiting clergy and arranged for some youth leaders to study Orthodox theology at St Vladimir's Orthodox Seminary in New York and at the University of Athens, Greece, in preparation for future ordination as Orthodox priests.

Kwami Labi, having graduated from St Vladimir's Seminary, returned to Ghana in 1982 where he was given the task of preparing the Ghanaian communities for reception into canonical Orthodoxy. This reception took place through holy baptism and chrismation in September of the same year and four priests and three deacons were ordained in the town of Larteh, where around 1,500 people were baptized; over the next few years many more Ghanaians were received into the Church, bringing the current total to nearly 3,000.

ORTHODOX CHURCH OF CYPRUS

The apostolic Church of Cyprus was founded by Ss Paul and Barnabas (Acts 13:4–13) and because of its apostolic origin and geographical position the early Church tried to proclaim its independence from any patriarchal see. The Church of Cyprus' autocephalous, or self-governing, status was confirmed by the Council of Ephesus (431) and further confirmation of the Church's status was upheld by Acacius in 488, the Eastern Roman Emperor Zeno (474–91), and the Council of Trullo (692).

From the mid-seventh to the mid-tenth century, the island suffered frequent attacks from the Arabs, which caused major devastation. Because of this situation and in the teeth of threats of further trouble, the Byzantine Emperor Justinian II (685–95) moved the Christian population of Cyprus, from 688 onwards, settling them in a new city on the Dardanelles called Nea Justiniana; during this exodus many people died from shipwreck or disease and most returned to Cyprus after a short while. A peaceful period of history for the island began in the tenth century, which saw the building of monasteries and churches, and the Church flourished.

The island was conquered by King Richard I of England *the Lionheart* in 1191 and sold to the Knights Templar and then to Guy de Lusignan, the exiled king of the Crusader state of Jerusalem. He established a western feudal society in Cyprus and a dynasty that was to last for three centuries, and this imposed a Latin hierarchy on the Cypriot Church. By 1260, Orthodox monasteries were made subject to Latin bishops and the number of Orthodox bishops was reduced from fifteen to four, all of whom were under the jurisdiction of the new Latin Archbishop of Cyprus.

The Venetians seized the island in 1489 and it was again taken, by Ottoman Turks, in 1571. The existing western feudal system was ended and the Latin hierarchy banished. The Ottoman Turks recognized the status of the Orthodox bishops, who then became the civil, as well as spiritual, leaders of their people according to the *millet* system introduced by the Turks (*millets* were religious nations existing within the Ottoman Turkish Empire). When the Greek Revolution came, in 1821, the bishops and clergy of the Cypriot Church were thought to be sympathetic to the Greeks and were suspected of giving their help to the cause. The archbishop, Cyprian, and the remaining bishops and senior clergy were summoned to the governor's palace, the gates were closed behind them, and they were all summarily executed with great barbarity by order of the governor, Kuchuk Mehmed. At the same time the governor confiscated much of the wealth of the Church.

It was not until Great Britain leased the island from the Turks in 1878 that some measure of peace was established. After the First World War many Cypriot Orthodox people backed the *Enosis* movement, which wanted to bring the island into union with Greece. The leaders of the Cypriot Orthodox Church were heavily implicated in this movement. Two bishops of the Church, Nicodemus of Larnaka and Makarios of Kyrenia, led insurrections and were deported and put under a decree of banishment by the British; the island retained only one bishop, that of the See of Paphos.

Britain granted independence to Cyprus in 1960 and Archbishop Makarios III was elected as its first president; his appointment was challenged by the three metropolitans of the island but these men were deposed by a synod (1973), representing the Patriarchates of Antioch, Alexandria and Jerusalem, and the Church of Greece, and other bishops were appointed in their place. Further clashes between the Turkish and Greek communities culminated in 1974 with a Turkish invasion of the island and the establishment of the Turkish republic of Northern Cyprus. With this came the destruction of many monasteries and churches in the north of the island.

In 1978 Archbishop Makarios III reopened the seminary of St Barnabas. The seminary had been built by the Kykkos monastery in 1950, on its own land and at its own expense, and had operated for 27 years before being closed, at the time of the Turkish invasion, because of economic difficulties. Makarios III baptized thousands of converts in Kenya and built schools, orphanages and homes for the elderly.

The head of the Cypriot Church has the style of His Beatitude, Archbishop of Nea Justiniana and All Cyprus, and lives in Nicosia. Currently, all of the island's convents and two of the monasteries are cenobitic, the monks and nuns living in religious communities rather than as hermits. Sunday schools and Bible study groups provided by the Church are proving very popular throughout the Orthodox community.

ORTHODOX PRESBYTERIAN CHURCH

By affirming the WESTMINSTER CONFESSION *of Faith* and the *Small* and *Larger Catechisms*, which were the result of the convening of the Westminster assembly by order of the English parliament in 1643, this Church places itself firmly in the REFORMED, or CALVINIST, tradition, employing a Presbyterian polity throughout the Church.

With immigration to America from England, Ireland and Scotland, it was not long before PRESBYTERIANISM became established in the New World. During the nineteenth and early twentieth centuries, the Presbyterian Church was affected by the growth of liberalism. In 1924 matters came to a head with the signing of the Auburn Affirmation by liberal-minded leaders, in which the inerrancy of the Bible and other fundamental beliefs were impugned. The loss to the Princeton Theological Seminary of some of its conservative-minded professors, following a reorganization of its board in 1929, led to the establishment of the Westminster Theological Seminary in Philadelphia by four of these professors, where a less radical and biblically based theology could be taught.

One of the leading opponents of liberalism was J. Gresham Machen, a Presbyterian minister and professor at Princeton and in 1932, with some others, he charged the board of foreign missions with sending out missionaries who did not preach that Jesus Christ was the exclusive way of salvation. In 1933, they created the Independent Board for Presbyterian Foreign Missions, an action that precipitated the suspension of Machen and others from the ministry. Machen, who was tried and found guilty of insubordination in 1935 together with some of his followers, formally founded the Orthodox Presbyterian Church in the following year, when some 34 ministers, 17 ruling elders and 79 laymen met in Philadelphia.

Initially, the new Church was known as the Presbyterian Church of America but this was later changed, in 1939, to its current style following legal action by the existing Presbyterian Church in the USA, with which it could be easily confused. The anticipated rush to join the new Church failed to materialize, and some of the ultra-FUNDAMENTALIST and evangelical members, led by Cornelius van Til and John Murray, left the new body to form the BIBLE PRESBYTERIAN CHURCH in 1937, the year of Machen's death; the split had much to do with the organization of foreign missions, which could not be resolved.

Through its presbyterian polity each congregation is part of a regional Church, governed by a presbytery, consisting of all the ministers and commissioned ruling elders, which meets several times each year. This body is responsible for the health and well-being of the local churches and may be called upon to resolve conflicts, supervise ministers and prepare ministerial candidates. An annual general assembly, which oversees the ministry of the Church, is responsible for missionary activity as well as for resolving difficulties that arise. As an example, the assembly decided to uphold the use of alcohol as being a matter for individual consciences, but condemned Freemasonry, voluntary abortion, homosexuality and the teaching of evolutionary views. Today the Church sends missionaries to work in China, Eritrea, Ethiopia, Japan, Korea, Kenya, the Middle East, Surinam and Uganda.

ORTLIBARII

The name given to followers of a thirteenth-century heretic, Ortlieb of Strasbourg, who advocated an ascetic regime that involved abstention from all material things. He preached against the Roman Catholic Church, identifying both it and the Pope as the harlot of the Apocalypse. Ortlieb's followers believed that they should rely on the inner authority of the Spirit and they rejected the authority of the Church and its sacraments. The Ortlibarii also held some unorthodox views about the creation, the Trinity and Christ's incarnation and were consequently condemned by Pope Innocent III (1198–1216). The sect was short-lived.

❖ Ortlibenses; Ortlibians

P

PAKISTAN, CHURCH OF

This Church, which is part of the ANGLICAN COMMUNION, was formed in 1970 as the result of a union between Anglicans, METHODISTS, LUTHERANS and Sialkot Presbyterians (SIALKOT CHURCH COUNCIL).

According to tradition, Christianity first reached India with St Thomas the Apostle and in the late sixteenth and early seventeenth centuries missionaries from Rome, mostly Jesuits, Carmelites and Augustinians went there to proselytize among the Hindus, Sikhs and Muslims. The Anglicans, through the Church Missionary Society, began their work in the Kushtia district in 1821 and following a severe famine in the area it is alleged that some five thousand Indians were baptized into the Anglican faith; other missions followed and in 1877 the Anglican Diocese of Lahore (now in north-east Pakistan) was established.

The appearance of American Methodists in Karachi can be pinpointed to 1873, with their missionaries working in central Punjab among Hindu outcasts. At the time of the 1970 union the Indus River and Karachi Conferences contributed about 60,000 members.

Another denomination contributing to the 1970 union was the Lutheran Church, a presence made possible through the missionary efforts of the Danish Pathan Mission (aka the Tent Mission), which began work in what is now north-west Pakistan in 1903 with the assistance of the Finnish Missionary Society and the American World Mission Prayer League. The Danish Pathan Mission, however, decided to remain outside the union.

A Presbyterian presence was established when the CHURCH OF SCOTLAND sent the Reverend Thomas Hunter and his family to Sialkot in 1857, where the Sialkot Church Council, later to join the union, was established. Other PRESBYTERIAN groups that were established, such as the Lahore Church Council and the United Presbyterian Church of Pakistan, chose to remain outside the union. In 1968 a schism in the United Presbyterian Church resulted in the formation of the United Presbyterian Church in Pakistan.

The synod of the Church of Pakistan, which is headed by a moderator, currently oversees the work of eight dioceses. In addition to various development projects the Church is deeply involved in education and the provision of social workers, teachers and medical personnel. In 1972, following a government decision, denominational schools and colleges in the country were nationalized, but the Church of Pakistan still maintains two theological seminaries, two colleges and a hospital. The headquarters of the Church of Pakistan is in Sialkot, and has an adult membership of some 500,000.

PAPUA NEW GUINEA, ANGLICAN PROVINCE OF

This Church is part of the ANGLICAN COMMUNION and forms an autonomous province of Papua New Guinea, which is divided into five dioceses currently containing 667 congregations with around 163,000 committed members.

The Anglican presence in Papua New Guinea began at Dogura, in east Papua, in 1892. It was founded by the Reverend Albert MacLaren, who came to New Guinea in 1890 and stayed for six months before returning to Australia to raise funds and recruit missionary volunteers. MacLaren returned to Papua New Guinea in August 1891 together with another priest, Copland King. The missionary band landed at Bartle Bay, where many became ill with a fever. MacLaren died within a few months of their arrival and the mission continued under the leadership of Copland King. The general synod of the Anglican Church elected and consecrated (Montague) John Stone-Wigg as the first Bishop of New Guinea in 1898.

From Dogura, mission stations were set up at Taupola, Wamira, and Menapi but the malaria-infested environment was hostile to the foreign missionaries and many became ill. Although some expansion was made under the leadership of John Stone-Wigg, it was a hard life and he was forced to resign after ten years, to be succeeded by Gerald Sharpe, who was consecrated in Brisbane in 1910. It was Bishop Sharpe who ordained the first native clergy as deacons, and by the time of his departure, to become Archbishop of Brisbane, many more had been ordained as deacons and priests and a large number of Papuans had been established as teachers in the villages. A secondary boarding school, a technical school for teaching trades and a training college for teachers and candidates for the ministry were opened and maintained at Dogura.

Throughout the history of the Church in Papua New Guinea there had been a growing awareness of the need for the Church to be self-supporting and self-propagating. The Diocese of Papua New Guinea, which was established in 1898, remained as a missionary diocese of the Church of England in Australia until its autonomy was granted in 1977.

❖ Anglican Church of Papua New Guinea

PARTICULAR BAPTISTS

The BAPTIST CHURCH in England was founded in Newgate Street, London, in 1612. The congregation was composed mainly of those who had fled to Amsterdam in search of religious freedom and who had returned to London under the leadership of Thomas Helwys. In London they were organized by John Smyth who through his book, *Mistery of Iniquity*, pleaded for religious freedom. Smyth, his congregation and their successors became known as the GENERAL ASSOCIATION OF GENERAL BAPTISTS, ARMINIAN in their theology and independent in their organization.

The Particular Baptists emerged from this association in 1633, as a distinctive group which had gradually adopted an ultra-CALVINISTIC theology. By 1644 they had issued the *First London Baptist Confession of Faith* with 52 Articles. A second edition followed in 1689 and revisions have been made from time to time, the most recent of which was published in 1966. Where the General Baptists hold the view that salvation of the soul is the responsibility of the individual, the Particular Baptists follow Calvin and believe in predestination and redemption only for the *elect*. Additionally, the Particular Baptists put considerable store by independent, or congregational polity.

A *New Connexion* of the more evangelical General Baptists was formed in 1770; in 1891, led by John Clifford (1836–1923), they merged with the Particular Baptists to form the Baptist Union of Great Britain and Ireland; in 1988 this became the BAPTIST UNION OF GREAT BRITAIN.

The Particular Baptists pride themselves in believing and preaching a theology within the principles known as the *Doctrines of Grace*. The Lord's Supper is served only within the congregation of saved, immersed believers. There are no centralized headquarters, president or committees, with members meeting in buildings known now more usually as chapels, rather than meeting-houses as was once the custom. The clergy are not ordained by any denominational organization, but are called to the ministry by their own congregations, neither do they use the title of 'Reverend', or wear clerical collars. Funds are gathered to provide for the poor and for the old who are in need, and can also be used to help with property maintenance, publishing and other media enterprises.

PATARINES

The name given to a reform movement directed against the contemporary moral poverty of the clergy in the eleventh century and centred in northern Italy. It was headed by a priest, Anselmo da Baiggio, later Bishop of Lucca, and by a deacon from Milan, Arialdus (later St). The name of the group is said to derive either from the term *rag picker*, used of people from the lowest class, or from the *pataria* quarter of Milan where the reforming fellowship held their meetings.

The morality of contemporary Italian clergy at this time was very lax, with simony commonplace and celibacy often ignored. The reformers were not only targeting the Archbishop of Milan and many of his clergy, but their action was also directed at some members of the upper class laity who had begun to enjoy certain privileges acquired by unethical means and usually restricted to the religious. The reformers used both argument and demonstration to voice their dispute, and did not stop at that, bringing in physical force in an effort to make erring clergy comply with the rules of celibacy and to force others to leave those benefices that they had obtained through simony. They were encouraged in their efforts by two eleventh-century Popes, Stephen IX (X) (see below) and Alexander II, and became allies of Pope Gregory VII in the whole issue of papal prohibition of lay investiture, which came to a head when the Emperor Henry IV, in 1071, wanted to invest the new Archbishop of Milan; the Patarines, siding with the Pope, called for free canonical elections. Despite their influence the Patarines had died out before the end of the eleventh century, although their name was sometimes applied a century later to the heretical CATHARS, and during the thirteenth and fourteenth centuries became a label for heretics in general.

Pope Stephen IX (X) is styled in this way because of the election of an earlier Pope,

Stephen II, a priest who died four days after his election in 752 and whose name initially was omitted from the list of popes because his consecration to the episcopacy had not been effected before his death; this consequently altered the designations of subsequent Popes taking the name of Stephen.

❖ Patarelli; Patarins

PAULIANISTS

Followers of Paul of Samosata, a third century Bishop of Antioch who was consecrated to that see in 260 but, on account of his heretical views, was deposed eight years later. He appears to have denied the divinity of Christ and was also thought to have been guilty of introducing a defective form of baptism. Paul appears to have taught that the divine Word of God was to be distinguished from the human being, Jesus, and that during the incarnation the Word descended upon the human being. His followers also held a dualistic doctrine, in which the *Good God* was believed to have created both heaven and the human soul, while the *Evil God* was responsible for creating the material world; their theology also seemed unable to distinguish between the persons of the Trinity.

PAULICIANS

Members of a dualistic Christian sect originating in Armenia in the mid-seventh century. Its founder was probably Constantine-Sylvanus of Mananali, a MANICHAEAN village near Samosata. The sect seems to have arisen from a political and military rebellion, which prompted Emperors Constantine III and Justinian II to send expeditions to suppress it between the years 668 and 698. A community, which may have been founded by Constantine-Sylvanus, was established at Kibossa (now Cibossa) in Armenia. Constantine-Sylvanus was stoned to death under Emperor Constantius II in *c.* 684. Ironically, his persecutor, Simeon, was also martyred, burnt at the stake some six years later.

The Council of Dvin, in 719, brought a new wave of persecution for the Paulicians in Armenia but through the kindness of the permissive Isaurian emperors they were allowed to settle in Thrace. The sect also, albeit briefly, enjoyed the protection of the Byzantine Emperor Constantine V Copronymus (740–75) during the middle years of the eighth century, but a further period of persecution in the ninth century led to their dispersal; they maintained a presence in Armenia, Asia Minor and the Balkans at least until the twelfth century and it is even suggested that a colony of people professing Paulician beliefs settled in Russian Armenia in 1828.

The fundamental Paulician doctrine was that there were two principles: an *Evil God* who created the material world and was its ruler, and a *Good God*, who is the ruler of the world to come. They argued against the divinity of Jesus and considered his role to be that of a teacher, rather than a redeemer. They rejected the sacraments, the hierarchy of the Church and icons and honoured the Gospel of Luke and the Pauline Epistles but rejected the Old Testament and the Epistles of Peter.

The sect was organized into four grades: apostles, prophets, itinerants and copyists. These were later reduced to two grades, itinerants and copyists, the former superior to the latter, whose job it was to transcribe the sacred books and to maintain order in church.

PEACE MISSION MOVEMENT

This remarkable movement was organized in New York in the 1920s by Father Major Jealous Divine (1880–1965), who had been an assistant of the itinerant preacher, Samuel Morris, also known as Father Jehovah; it has been suggested that Father Divine's real name was George Baker.

Father Divine left Brooklyn and moved to Stayville, New York, where he met his first wife, Sister Penny, later known as Mother Peninniah Divine, who bought a house for them both there. This house soon became known as 'The Rescue Home for the Poor Only', because Father Divine's reputation for 'sensible' charity had spread, attracting the poor, the unemployed and the needy. Before long many followers, most of whom were black, gave their help to the cause. The presence of these visitors in town created a situation that led to the arrest of Father Divine in November 1931, charged with causing a disturbance of the peace; he was tried, fined $500 and jailed. This affair, with its perceived racial overtones, attracted worldwide publicity. Following his release in 1932 Father Divine and his wife moved to Harlem, New York, where he felt he could appeal to more of those in need.

Once there, the Divines bought up many cheap hotels and converted them into Peace Mission Heavens, which were to provide cheap food (15cent. meals), job opportunities, accommodation at $1 a week and practical help for people wishing to reform their lives. New members had to pledge that they would undertake to pay all their debts, cancel all insurances, return all stolen money and pay cash for everything.

In 1946, after the death of his first wife, Father Divine was married for the second time, to Edna Rose Ritchings, a white Canadian. They moved to Pennsylvania, where they went to live at Woodmont Estate, situated on the highest point in Montgomery County and it was here that Father Divine died, in 1965, and where his body is enshrined. His widowed wife, who was also known as Sweet Angel, or Mother Divine, took over the leadership of the Peace Movement.

The members of the Peace Movement believed that Father Divine had fulfilled all the scriptural promise of Christ's second coming (REVELATION 20) and of the coming Jewish Messiah, although he never claimed that for himself. They also believed that the policies adopted under Father Divine's leadership would eventually usher in the Kingdom of God on earth. Woodmont was seen by some to be the Mount of the House of the Lord (Mic. 4:1–2 and Isa. 2:2–3) from where the law will go to all nations. The Mission accepts the ten commandments and the Sermon on the Mount and has developed its social, economic and political programmes from this religious perspective.

The Peace Movement regards all men as equal in the sight of God and any form of discrimination is strictly prohibited. The members live communally, with strict separation of the sexes extended to married couples, and all possessions owned corporately. There is no financial compensation for any work undertaken by the members, because room, board and a small allowance for incidentals are provided in exchange for such work in any Peace Mission-owned business. Father Divine's International Modesty Code requires that there must be 'No Smoking, no Vulgarity, no Profanity, no Undue Mixing of Sexes, no Receiving of Gifts, Presents, Tips or Bribes.'

The Movement has three categories of membership:

1. *Rosebuds* – for women of young to middle age, who wear a distinctive red jacket with the letter 'V' (for virtue) over the heart, with a navy blue blouse and skirt. *Rosebuds* may be called upon to assist at worship services and to act in theatrical dramas.
2. *Lily-buds* – for older women, who wear dark green jackets trimmed with white and who lead in music and reading at worship services.
3. *Crusaders* – for men.

The Church services include hymn singing, readings from the scriptures and from Father Divine's writings, listening to tapes of Father Divine's sermons and Holy Communion, to which all are welcome. The Peace Mission Movement has branches in many parts of the USA, with others in several parts of Europe, Australia, Canada, Nigeria and South America.

PELAGIANS

Followers of the heretical British monk, Pelagius, who went to Rome at the end of the fourth century, during the pontificate of Pope St Anastasius I (399–401), where he was scandalized by the immorality of its citizens. Pelagius and his friend and supporter Caelestius, most likely an Irishman, who was described as a man of 'incredible loquacity', travelled to North Africa following the capture of Rome by Alaric the Visigoth in 410, where they encountered St Augustine of Hippo's opposition to their ideas. Pelagius and his followers denied the doctrine of original sin and claimed that all human beings have power of themselves to either receive, or reject, the gospel. St Augustine's opposition to Pelagianism was based on his argument that humans could not attain righteousness through their own efforts but only through the grace of God.

Pelagius stayed for a short time in Carthage before moving east, leaving his ally, Caelestius, behind. Caelestius applied for ordination in 412, but was refused on account of his heretical teachings, which included his belief that Adam's fall injured himself only and did not affect the whole human race. Undaunted, Caelestius also travelled east and was eventually ordained priest at Ephesus. Pelagius, by then living in Jerusalem, aroused the hostility of St Jerome (345–420) and of Orosius, a young Spanish priest and disciple of St Augustine. But, despite this, in 415, Pelagius was exonerated by a synod at Jerusalem, and by another held at Diospolis (now Lod, in Israel); he was, however, condemned by two councils held at Carthage and at Mileve, in Numidia, in 416, a finding confirmed by Pope St Innocent I. Following the death of Pope St Innocent, in 417, Pelagius appealed to his successor, St Zozimus (417–18), and was declared to be blameless; this opinion was reversed the following year, a decision that was reinforced by a council at Carthage in 418. Thereafter, Pelagius seems to have faded from the scene and it is thought that he died in Palestine. Caelestius continued to preach, in Sicily and Asia Minor, where he sought the support of Nestorius, then Bishop of Constantinople.

Pelagianism was adopted in Britain, much to the chagrin of orthodox British bishops who called for the assistance of St Germanus of Auxerre and St Louis of Troyes in mounting their opposition to the heresy. A public debate was held at St

Albans and the Pelagian argument was roundly defeated. The Ecumenical Council held at Ephesus in 431 condemned both Nestorianism and Pelagianism. The heresy and its supporters seem to have survived until about the second half of the sixth century.

PENTECOSTAL (also PENTECOSTALISM)

This Christian tradition, which affirms the infallibility of the Bible, holds to the belief that all Christians should seek a post-conversion religious experience called baptism with, or in, the Holy Spirit. This baptism heralds the indwelling of the Holy Spirit in an individual believer. As a result of this experience the believer may exhibit one or more supernatural gifts; these gifts were known to the early Church. The gifts may include sanctification, which can be instantaneous, ability to prophesy, divine healing, *glossolalia* or speaking in tongues, and the interpretation of these tongues.

There are different types of Pentecostals, such as the baptistic Pentecostals, also known as Keswick Pentecostals, who hold to a two-crisis spiritual experience, of conversion and baptism of the Spirit. This is the most numerous group, with an estimated 47.7 million members in 380 countries, the greatest concentration in Brazil with an estimated 22.6 million members. There are also the Holiness Pentecostals, who anticipate a three-crisis religious experience, of conversion, sanctification and baptism of the Spirit. This group is present in 233 countries worldwide and has a membership in the region of 5.6 million. There are many other groups that can be identified as being in the same tradition, such as the Assemblies of God, the Church of God in Christ, the International Church of the Foursquare Gospel and the United Pentecostal Church International.

The Oneness Pentecostals, who are also known as Apostolic Pentecostals, Unitarian Pentecostals or Jesus-Only Pentecostals, are so called because of their insistence that baptism, which they regard as essential for salvation, should be administered in the name of Jesus only, quoting Acts 2:38, and other references, as sufficient authority for their practice. These Pentecostals do not consider the Holy Spirit to be a third person of the Trinity, but as the spirit and power of God and Christ.

PENTECOSTAL ASSEMBLIES OF THE WORLD, INC

In America in 1906, following an outbreak of *glossolalia*, or speaking in tongues, which was witnessed in Azusa Street, Los Angeles, prompting a period of Pentecostal revivalism, a loosely formed body of Trinitarian Pentecostals began to be organized. Difficulties arose some years later, mainly concerning the *Jesus-Only* controversy, which prompted some members to leave the organization. This controversy concerned the denial of the standard Pentecostal belief in the Trinity of the Father, Son and Holy Spirit, and the taking up of what has been dubbed 'Apostolic Theology', which identifies Jesus with Jehovah in the Old Testament and denies the Trinity. A more formal organization was established, originally as an inter-racial body, but in 1924 many white members withdrew to form the Pentecostal Church, Inc, which subsequently became part of the United Pentecostal Church International.

The remaining members, who were mostly black, elected a bishop, Garfield Thomas Hayward (1880–1931), and organized their Church along similar lines to that of the Methodists, having adopted the name of Pentecostal Assemblies of the World, Inc.

Doctrinally, the Church regards the Bible as the inspired and infallible word of God, but it does not recognize the Trinity in a conventional sense, baptizing only in the name of Jesus Christ and not employing the Trinitarian formula. Footwashing, the Lord's Supper and divine healing are all observed, as is the anticipation of the *Rapture – the glorious catching away of the saints when Jesus returns to take his people to heaven.* Members of the Church are expected to be pacifists and to observe a strict code of dress and behaviour. Divorce and remarriage are permitted under certain circumstances, for example, when, in a mixed-faith marriage the unbelieving partner contracts a divorce the believing partner may then re-marry.

There is provision for a general assembly, responsible for the election of the bishops and the general secretary. The Church is divided into districts, or dioceses, presided over by a bishop and maintains a missionary overseas board to oversee the extensive mission outreach programme that takes workers into outreach centres in many parts of the world. At present, missionary activity is taking place in Africa, Asia and the Caribbean. In 1969 a mission group was sent from St Kitts, Jamaica, to work in England.

PENTECOSTAL CHURCH OF GOD

This Church must not be confused with the PENTECOSTAL CHURCH OF GOD (OF AMERICA)*, which was founded in 1919.*

Apostle Willie James Peterson, who was born in the USA in 1921 and brought up as a BAPTIST (although never baptized in that faith), founded this black PENTECOSTAL Church. In his early adult years Peterson had a dream in which he saw himself in the presence of God and the angels, an experience that inspired him to pray and to meditate upon his future, which he believed must be spent as an independent preacher-evangelist.

Peterson adopted the apostolic ONENESS position, which had been introduced by R. E. McAllister in Los Angeles in 1913 and which held to the view that baptism should not be administered in the name of the Trinity, but in the name of Jesus only. Stress was laid upon the oneness of God, with Jesus Christ identified with God the Father, but the Holy Spirit not considered as the third person of the Trinity but only as the spirit and power of God and Christ.

Water baptism by immersion is administered in the name of Jesus only, while salvation is said to be achieved through repentance. Peterson, who preached this message in and around Meridian, Mississippi, was held in high esteem and thought of as an apostle despite his very strong and bitter anti-ROMAN CATHOLIC and anti-PROTESTANT message.

The members of the Church, who are pacifists, refuse to salute the national flag and do not vote or celebrate the traditional feasts of Christmas and Easter. Peterson died in 1969, but his Church continues under the administration of its bishops.

PENTECOSTAL CHURCH OF GOD (OF AMERICA)

Some PENTECOSTAL leaders, who chose the Reverend John C. Sinclair as their first moderator, organized this American PROTESTANT denomination in Chicago in

1919. The title adopted by the Church has undergone a few changes, beginning as the Pentecostal Assemblies of the USA (1919), then becoming the Pentecostal Church of God (1922), the Pentecostal Church of God of America (1936) and finally the Pentecostal Church of God (of America) in 1979.

The Church is typically pentecostal in its faith, with insistence on the verbal inspiration of the Bible, and on regeneration, sanctification and baptism of the Holy Spirit, with *glossolalia*, or speaking in tongues, regarded as physical evidence of faith. Members express a conventional belief in the Trinity, in the life, death, resurrection, ascension and premillennial second coming of Jesus Christ, with judgement following, which will lead to eternal life for the saved and eternal damnation for the unsaved (REVELATION 20). Three ordinances are observed, those of baptism of believers by immersion, the Lord's Supper and foot-washing, although the latter is optional and not observed by all congregations. Divine healing is practised. In contrast to the custom observed by many Pentecostal groups, this Church does not insist upon pacifism, but, like others, it advocates tithing for its members.

The members are very active in home missions, where they are involved in providing shelter, re-location homes and feeding and clothing the needy. Foreign missions are maintained in 32 countries and a strong missionary force is provided. The Church is headed by a general superintendent who is assisted by a general secretary and various directors of specific areas of activity. Each congregation, of which there are more than 1,100 with around 40,000 committed members, belongs to a district, presided over by a district superintendent, presbyters and other church officials. A district convention is held annually and a general convention every two years. The headquarters of the Church, and its publishing house, are in Joplin, Missouri.

❖ Pentecostal Church of God International

PENTECOSTAL CHURCH OF GOD, NATIONAL AND INTERNATIONAL

This very small American PROTESTANT denomination was founded at Riddle, Oregon, in 1960 but now seems to be in serious decline. While holding to the same beliefs as the ASSEMBLIES OF GOD, it ordains women to the ministry and is administered by an annual general convention.

PENTECOSTAL FIRE-BAPTIZED HOLINESS CHURCH

The Church was formed in the USA in 1918 by members of the Pentecostal Holiness Church (PHC), which had itself been formed as a result of a merger in 1911 between two other PENTECOSTAL groups.

Those members of the PHC who went into schism in 1918 did so over their perceived need for the observance of stricter standards concerning matters of dress, the use of both alcohol and tobacco, attendance at various forms of amusement and the keeping of company by their young men and women. This had a marked effect, particularly on the appearance of the women of the group who were expected to wear their uncut hair in a bun, wear no jewellery and dress in simple, inexpensive, mid-calf length frocks. Men had fewer restrictions, but were not permitted to wear neckties; both genders were forbidden to attend swimming pools, fairs and concerts. Some members of other independent Pentecostal groups joined the Church, including the entire membership of the North Carolina Conference of the PENTECOSTAL FREE WILL BAPTIST CHURCH, which went over as a body in 1921.

Doctrinally, the Church is strongly premillennialist (REVELATION 20) and their services marked by spontaneous crying and hand clapping accompanied by shouts of joy. The government of the Church is by means of a biennial general convention, during which an election of a seven-member board of missions, which currently oversees the mission work in Haiti and Mexico, is held. The headquarters of the Church is at Toccoa Falls, Georgia, where a printing press produces a periodical called *Faith and Truth*. At present the Church has around two hundred members.

PENTECOSTAL FREE WILL BAPTIST CHURCH

The American PENTECOSTAL evangelist, G. B. Cashwell, conducted a revival mission to the Free Will Baptists at their 1907 Cape Fear Conference in Dunn, North Carolina. He introduced Pentecostal teachings to the gathering, and the Conference members accepted these. Between 1907 and 1912, the Cape Fear conference was the parent body that gave rise to four smaller conferences. By 1943, representatives from each of these had tried to form a general conference, but this proved to be unworkable. A decision was taken, in 1959, to organize themselves as the Pentecostal Free Will Baptist Church, a white-led Pentecostal group.

Doctrinally, the Church teaches an amalgam of Pentecostal and Baptist beliefs, which include the three experiences of grace, that of regeneration, or rebirth through faith in Christ's atonement, sanctification and the Pentecostal Baptism, by immersion, in the Holy Spirit. Foot-washing is observed, as a preliminary to the ordinance of the Lord's Supper, divine healing is sought and premillennialism is anticipated (REVELATION 20).

The Church observes a congregational polity and has its headquarters at Dunn, North Carolina, with most of its current 141 congregations, and in excess of 11,500 committed members, distributed in parishes in the Carolinas, Virginia, Georgia and Florida. Foreign missions are carried out in Costa Rica, Puerto Rico, Mexico, Nicaragua, Venezuela and the Philippines.

❖ Pentecostal Free Will Baptist Church, Inc.

PEOPLE OF THE LIVING GOD

Harry Miller, a former minister of the ASSEMBLIES OF GOD, and his father-in-law, who had been a minister of the PRESBYTERIAN CHURCH, formed the movement known as the People of the Living God, in the USA in 1932. They opened a Bible school in Los Angeles, where they taught that sectarianism was wrong and where they trained non-sectarian ministers. Many years were spent carrying the message throughout Kentucky and in the mountain areas of Tennessee before the group settled in New Orleans.

In its doctrinal beliefs the group closely resembles the Assemblies of God. Members believe that *glossolalia*, or speaking in tongues, is a sign of baptism of the Holy Spirit. A very simple lifestyle is maintained, with members working outside the group and returning their earnings to a common purse. This allows a large amount of money to be used to support various activities, as well as the overseas missionaries. Much of the literature produced by this group is considered by some to be controversial.

PEOPLE'S METHODIST CHURCH

This small, American METHODIST group of congregations was organized in North Carolina at the time of the Methodist merger of 1939, which involved the uniting of the METHODIST EPISCOPAL CHURCH (South) with the Methodist Episcopal Church and the Protestant Methodist Church. Within the Methodist tradition, the Church holds conservative views concerning the inspiration of the Bible, the Trinity, the divinity of Jesus Christ, his life, death, resurrection, ascension and second coming (REVELATION 20). Two sacraments are observed, those of baptism of both infants and adults by sprinkling, and the Lord's Supper. This Church stresses the importance of the second blessing, which is taken as an indication of a member's perfection in holiness.

PERFECTED CHURCH OF JESUS CHRIST IMMACULATE LATTER DAY SAINTS

William C. Conway was the founder of the Perfected Church, which arose in the USA at the end of the nineteenth century and can be classed as one of the most unusual of the polygamy-practising groups, of which the CHURCH OF JESUS CHRIST OF LATTER-DAY SAINTS (LDS) was once the best known. Conway claimed that he was 'the scribe and goodwill ambassador' for the 500,000 American Indians he counted as members of his Church. The story is a strange one, of visions and dreams directing several hundred Indians to go to Walker Lake, Nevada, in 1890. Here Jesus, having abandoned the LDS when its members rejected the six commandments concerning plural marriage given to Joseph Smith, re-established the Kingdom as it was in pre-Eden days, giving the authority to Eachta Eacha, a young Indian from Yu-ka-tan. The late Joseph Smith, now reincarnated, and the angel Moroni then joined Eachta Eacha, who was identified as the 'One Mighty and Strong' mentioned in the *Book of Mormon*. The angel Moroni, it is claimed, 'succeeded in perfecting a plan of instruction that abolished menstruation among women folk', under direct guidance from Jesus, who had 'explained the technique for immaculate conception. Babies conceived immaculately stay for twelve months in the womb and are immune to all diseases.'

Meanwhile in 1886, before the publication of a manifesto prohibiting plural marriage, which was issued by the president of the LDS, Wilford Woodruff, in 1890, a previous president, John Taylor, claimed to have spent a night in deep conversation with the deceased Joseph Smith and the Lord, and after this he came to the conclusion that plural marriage should be allowed. As a result of this conversation, Taylor allegedly gave a copy of the Lord's revelation to Lorin Woolley and four other men, all of whom were given authority by Taylor to permit the covenant (i.e. plural marriage). This authority was, again allegedly, transferred to the Perfected Church of Jesus Christ Immaculate Latter-Day Saints. The Church is now defunct.

PERFECTIONISM (also PERFECTIONIST; PERFECTIONISTS)

The teaching that moral or religious perfection is attainable in this life, and is not just the goal towards which man strives. One of John Wesley's teachings about the possibility of achieving perfection instantaneously by faith gave rise to the American HOLINESS movement from which developed the traditions of the CHURCH OF THE NAZARENE and some forms of PENTECOSTALISM.

PETITE ÉGLISE

Prior to Napoleon Bonaparte's concordat with the Vatican in 1801, the Constitutional Church that had been formed in France in 1790 caused many bishops and priests, and much of the laity, to leave the country and go into exile. It was after the signing of the concordat that twelve of these *Constitutional* bishops were allowed to remain in their sees, having submitted to Pope Pius VII. Those clergy and laity who refused to accept the concordat formed the Petite Église.

The concordat, which recognized ROMAN CATHOLICISM as the religion of the majority in France, provided for the return of confiscated property to the Church and stated that bishops who had been appointed by the pope after being nominated by the state, and those of the lower clergy who had been appointed by diocesan bishops, could still have their appointments vetoed by the French state, especially since all clergy were to be paid for by the state.

With Napoleon's downfall in 1815 and the restoration of the Bourbon monarchy most of the bishops and clergy still in exile were reconciled with the papacy. Three bishops, however, refused to obey Pope Pius VII. These were de Courcey of La Rochelle, de Themines of Blois and Seignelay de Colbert of Rodez who, with other clergy and laity, remained with the Petite Église. Members of the sect, who met in private houses for worship, regarded Bishop Themines of Blois as their primate. Themines died in 1829, without having consecrated a successor. When their last priest, the Abbé Ozouf, died in 1847 the membership of the sect declined rapidly. It is said that they persevered by having lay-led services and went to great pains to ensure that any children were baptized in a valid manner by a layman. It is on record that there are about 10 groups of sect members, with a total membership of about 1,000, still in existence, although a few returned to the Roman Catholic Church in 1963–4.

The real name of the Bishop of Rodez was Traill and he was the younger son of the laird of Castlehill in Caithness, Scotland. He was sent to France, where he trained as a priest, following in the footsteps of his uncle who had been educated at the Scots College in Paris. Following his ordination, Traill was appointed Vicar-general of Toulouse and consecrated as Bishop of Rodez in 1781. Having become a member of the Petite Église, Traill left France and never returned, spending the rest of his life either in London or staying with his wealthy relations in Scotland. During his time in France he had been elected as Grand Master of the Order of St Thomas of Acre, a chivalric Order that had been revived in the early eighteenth century in Jacobite circles and placed under the protection of the exiled Stuarts in France.

❖ Clementines; Filochois; Illumines; Louisets; Stevenists

PETROBRUSIANS

Followers of Peter de Bruys (d. *c.* 1140), who, following his ordination as a priest, preached heresy in and around the Dioceses of Embrun, Die and Gap in south-east France between the years 1117–20;

his work is mentioned by Abélard (1079–1142) and by Peter the Venerable (1092–1156).

Bishops of those dioceses suppressed the heresy, but de Bruys gained followers in Narbonne, Toulouse and Gascony. He declared that the only doctrinal authority was the Gospels, in their literal interpretation, and that all other Old and New Testament writings, as well as the writings of the Church Fathers, were useless.

De Bruys held the Church in contempt and preached and taught about the rightness of physical violence against the clergy and all church buildings. He totally disregarded all ceremonies of the Church and regarded the Mass and Holy Communion as being without value. His reasoning was that Jesus Christ had given his body and blood to his disciples but once, and that repetition of this act is impossible. Although de Bruys recognized that baptism was essential for salvation, he claimed that it should be preceded by personal faith and so should be a believer's baptism, thus denying the validity of infant baptism. The dead, he argued, could not benefit from the good works of the living and the cross should not be venerated, as it was the instrument of Christ's death. He went further, destroying crosses by publicly burning them. Given to burning any crucifix he came across, it is said that on one occasion a large bonfire was made from them upon which de Bruys roasted meat and distributed it to the people around him. The people of St Gilles, near Nîmes, exasperated by this burning of crosses, which they held dear, threw de Bruys into the flames, where he perished. The heresies were condemned by the Second Lateran Council (1139), along with the teachings of one of de Bruy's followers, Henry of Lausanne, the founder of the HENRICIANS.

Henry was somewhat more fortunate than de Bruys in that he probably escaped a violent death, languishing in a prison in Toulouse after being condemned as a heretic in 1145, and dying soon after his incarceration.

PHILADELPHIANS

A seventeenth-century sect, originating in England when the ANGLICAN rector of Bradfield in Berkshire, John Pordage (1575–1624), who was also an astrologer and mystic, became impressed with the writings of Jacob Boehme (1575–1624), a German LUTHERAN mystic. His interest attracted the attention of the Triers, a body of lay and clerical commissioners who had been appointed by Oliver Cromwell (1599–1658) to affirm a preacher's orthodoxy. Deciding that John Pordage did not measure up to the required standard, the Triers had him ejected from his parish in 1655, having described him as 'ignorant and insufficient', his Cambridge MA and his medical degree from Leiden University notwithstanding. He was reinstated in 1660.

Pordage's enthusiasm for the works of Boehme was undiminished and in a short while a group was organized which, in 1670, adopted the name of *The Philadelphian Society for the Advancement of Piety and Divine Philosophy*. The body was formed as a society to enable members to maintain their respective church loyalties.

Members of the society professed a belief in a kind of nature-pantheism and held that their souls were immediately imbued with the Holy Spirit. One such member, Mrs Jane Leads (1623–1704), who had been having visions since childhood, kept a diary from 1670, which she called *A Fountain of Gardens*, in which she recorded these visions. She took over the affairs of the society when John Pordage was no longer able. The society went into a swift decline after Jane Leads' death, despite the efforts of Francis Lee (1661–1719), a surgeon and enthusiastic member, who, like Pordage, had studied medicine at Leiden University; Lee tried to spread the Society's beliefs on the Continent but without great success.

❖ Behmenists; Philadelphists

PHILIPPINE INDEPENDENT CHURCH

Spanish influence began in the Philippine Islands in 1521 and although by the start of the seventeenth century most of the islands had become colonies of Spain, little had been done to prepare the population for either political or ecclesiastical independence. Politics, land ownership and church life were in the hands of the Spanish bishops and clergy, including members of the main religious orders such as the Augustinians, Franciscans, Dominicans and Jesuits. In time, native clergy were trained to minister to their congregations, but the Church remained under the control of Spain.

An anti-Spanish uprising in 1872 met with vicious suppression. The execution of three of these native priests consolidated the patriotic and enthusiastic members of the Young Philippine Party. The balance between the colonists and the indigenous population was destroyed and the Spanish were overthrown by the end of the nineteenth century, with a declaration of independence for the new republic of the Philippines made in 1898.

The foundations for an anti-Spanish Church had begun in 1890, through the efforts of Isabelo de los Reyes, a future politician, and a priest, Gregório Aglipay, together with some other secular clergy. By 1902, the Church became formally organized as a breakaway Church from that of Rome and was to be known as the Philippine Independent Church (PIC). Gregório Aglipay was asked by de los Reyes to become the supreme bishop of the PIC, which he did in 1903, accepting consecration, irregularly, at the hands of his fellow priests. Aglipay knew that consecration other than by a bishop was highly irregular but he justified it by arguing that the FINNISH ORTHODOX CHURCH was known to have used this method when no bishop was available. The PIC attracted many followers, including priests and around half of the Roman Catholic laity. In 1906, a setback came with a ruling of the supreme court in Manila ordering the return to the Roman Catholic Church of any property seized by the PIC; many of those who had left the ROMAN CATHOLIC CHURCH now returned to it.

Aglipay, meanwhile, was courting the favour and wealth of the Freemasons and was becoming influenced by the UNITARIAN(S). This made his negotiations with ANGLICAN and OLD CATHOLIC CHURCH sources, which he needed in order to establish a recognized succession of Orders for the PIC, rather difficult. The Unitarians invited Aglipay and some of his senior clergy to attend Unitarian conventions, held in the USA, at Boston, Massachusetts, and also in Denmark, further compromising his position. Then, in 1940, Aglipay died.

The Unitarian faction that had developed within the PIC left, and the position of supreme bishop passed to Isabelo de los Reyes, Jnr, the son of the founder, who had been ordained by Aglipay and four other bishops. In 1947, de los Reyes issued a *Declaration of Faith and Articles of Religion*, of which there were 21, all completely Trinitarian. De los Reyes and his clergy officially renounced Unitarianism and declared their acceptance of the theology of the then Protestant Episcopal Church (PEC).

After requesting valid Anglican orders from the PEC, this was provided in 1948 by Norman S. Binstead, American Episcopalian bishop of the missionary district of the Philippines, and two other bishops, at the pro-Cathedral Church of St Luke in Manila, when three bishops of the PIC were consecrated. Thereafter PIC clergy, who are free to marry, were ordained according to the Anglican rite. Until very recently the PIC had a completely male priesthood, but in 1997 the first female priest was ordained.

In 1961 the PIC was accepted into full communion with the Church of England and the Old Catholic Church. The liturgy used by the PIC is an adaptation of the Roman rite in the vernacular and with additions from the American edition of the *Book of Common Prayer*. The PIC began to conduct missions for Filipino-Americans in 1959 and several parishes have been established in the USA. Today, the PIC has the responsibility for about four million faithful worldwide.

❖ Aglipayan Church

PHILIPPINO ASSEMBLIES OF THE FIRST BORN

This small, Pentecostal denomination was founded in the USA in 1933, at Stockton, California, by the Reverend Julian Barnes for immigrants from the Philippines. The doctrine and practices of the Church are those of the Assemblies of God, but most of the services and preaching are in the Filipino language. There are currently 50 congregations and a total membership of 5,000.

❖ Filipino Assemblies of God

PHILIPPISTS

The name given to followers of Philipp Melanchthon (1497–1560), a Lutheran scholar and reformer whose real name was George Schwarzerd but who had been given the name Melanchthon by his great-uncle, Johannes Reuchlin, a German humanist; despite the fact that Melanchthon was his nephew, Reuchlin never adopted the Lutheran cause.

Melanchthon was more conciliatory towards the Roman Catholic Church than Martin Luther and advocated a softening of the latter's dogmatism on the subject of the real presence in the Eucharist.

❖ Crypto-Calvinists; Synergists

PICARDS

An extremist sect of Adamites that appeared in Bohemia in the fifteenth century, possibly as a revival of a similar group that had been active in the area during the thirteenth century. They were given to communal love and nakedness, claiming that as such they were enjoying the state of innocence existing before the fall of Adam. In an effort to emphasize this innocence, members would dance naked around an open fire to the accompaniment of hymn singing. The name of the sect possibly derives from that of their reputed leader, Picard of Flanders, who called himself the *New Adam*. The group was pursued by the

Bohemian HUSSITE leader, John Zizka (*c.* 1370–1424) and took refuge, in 1421, on an island in the River Nezarka, just west of Brno in the present-day Czech Republic. The *Pikarti*, as they were also known, were also ultra-anarchistic murderers. They barricaded themselves on the island where, despite their efforts, all except one were killed. The survivor was *persuaded* to give an account of the group's doctrines and practices and having done so, he was burnt at the stake and his ashes were thrown into the river.

Another group of Adamites emerged in Bohemia in the late eighteenth century and is believed to have been successfully suppressed by the mid-nineteenth century.

❖ Pikarti

PIETISM (also PIETIST; PIETISTS)

A reform movement, rather than a denomination, which began in the state LUTHERAN and REFORMED Churches in Germany in the late seventeenth century, introduced by P. J. Spener, who organized prayer and Bible study sessions in an effort to revitalize the Church. Spener ran against church authorities when he declared the universal priesthood of all believers, and acrimony followed. The movement was popular in its day and received much support.

PILGRIM HOLINESS CHURCH

Almost sixty years after the founding of the METHODIST EPISCOPAL CHURCH in America in 1784, a group of clergy and laity left that denomination because of their strong anti-slavery convictions, their preference for a more democratic form of church government and the need, as they saw it, for a greater emphasis on various forms of piety. In total some 22 ministers and 6,000 laity left to form the WESLEYAN METHODIST CHURCH in America.

In 1897 another group of ministers, encouraged by the Reverend Martin Walls Knapp and other clergy members, decided to form the International Holiness Union and Prayer League, at Knapp's home in Cincinnati, Ohio. This was intended to be an interdenominational fellowship, not a separate Church, with an emphasis on seeking the evangelization of the world, the regeneration of sinners, the entire sanctification of believers and the stimulation of interest in the imminence of the premillennial second coming of Christ (REVELATION 20). To accomplish these ends they embarked upon a programme of city missions and established rescue homes and camp meetings. In 1900 the name changed to become *The International Apostolic Holiness Union* and at the same time a programme of foreign missions was started, taking the work to South Africa, India, Japan, the West Indies and South America.

A series of mergers resulted in several more name changes until 1922, when the present name was adopted. The result of these many mergers was a great growth in ministries throughout the USA and Canada, and an increase in missionary work which extended the field of operation into South Africa, several other African countries, the Philippines, the Caribbean, Guyana and England.

Doctrinally, the Church was ARMINIAN-Methodist, with a polity that was a mixture of episcopal and congregational. It affirmed the Trinity, regeneration, sanctification, divine healing and premillennialism (REVELATION 20), calling upon the infallible authority of the Bible to justify its doctrinal position. Two sacraments, those of baptism and the Lord's Supper, were observed, with the method employed to administer baptism being completely optional. Both men and women could be ministers and a church board, made up of a pastor, elders, deacons and other officials, governed each local church. Representatives of local churches elected district councils and these met annually; an international council, with responsibility to co-ordinate the extensive foreign and domestic missionary work, met every four years. In 1968, the Wesleyan Methodist Church and the Pilgrim Holiness Church merged to form the WESLEYAN CHURCH.

PILGRIM HOLINESS CHURCH OF NEW YORK

This small American Church was founded originally in 1897 in Binghamton, New York, as the Pentecostal Rescue Mission, which had affiliated with the International Holiness Church; in 1922 the name PILGRIM HOLINESS CHURCH was adopted. Because of disagreements that arose in the 1960s, when preparations were in place for the merger of the Pilgrim Holiness Church with the WESLEYAN METHODIST CHURCH, the New York group declared its autonomy as the Pilgrim Holiness Church of New York. The Church now maintains missions in Brazil, Haiti and Canada. The headquarters is currently in Albany, New York.

PILGRIMS

This now defunct group originated in Quebec, Canada, a little way north of the border with Vermont in 1816 and was brought together by Isaac Bullard, who preached a return to a form of primitive Christianity, with goods held in common. The members of the group were expected to spend most of each day in prayer and fasting. Their desire to return to a primitive form of life was realized when the followers adopted the wearing of clothes fashioned from animal skins. This, allied with a refusal to wash or take baths, resulted in a collective body odour that made their very presence obnoxious.

In 1817 Bullard was inspired to move his group to the south-western states of America, in search of the Promised Land. He, and his wife, their son, who was named *Christ*, and about fifty followers travelled the area for almost a year. During the course of their travels the group was heard, or perhaps misheard, to mutter the following prayer from time to time: 'My God, My God. What wouldst't Thou have me do? Mummyjum, Mummyjum'; this last part of the incantation earned the group the nickname 'the Mummyjums'.

At their journey's end, in Arkansas, only a handful of the group had survived intact, the rest having left on account of illness or disillusionment, or having deserted to join the group known as the SHAKERS. The ten survivors took up residence on a small island and nothing more was heard of the movement after the early part of the nineteenth century.

❖ Mummyjums

PILLAR OF FIRE

A Church within the HOLINESS tradition, which was founded in 1901 in the USA as the Pentecostal Union, and incorporated as such the following year. The title was changed to Pillar of Fire in 1917 by its founder, Mrs Alma White (1862–1946), the wife of a minister of the METHODIST EPISCOPAL CHURCH in Colorado.

In the face of opposition from officials of the Methodist Church, Mrs White used to preach from her husband's pulpit, and at revival meetings. She was an ardent supporter of women's rights, an alleged supporter of the Ku Klux Klan in the 1920s, and an advocate for vegetarianism. Having been forced to stop preaching, Mrs White began to form small, independent missions along the lines of the early Methodist societies within the CHURCH OF ENGLAND in the eighteenth century.

The Church has an episcopal polity, and Mrs White was its first bishop. Upon her death the leadership passed in turn to her two sons, Ray B. White and Arthur K. White, the latter leading the Church for a period of thirty years. After Arthur White's death the leadership passed to Dr Donald J. Wolfram, who became its bishop and general superintendent.

Affirming a modified version of John Wesley's *Twenty-Five Articles of Religion*, the Church also recognizes the legitimacy of divine healing, preaches premillennialism (REVELATION 20), regeneration and the second blessing; it also condemns modernism. Its doctrine is based upon the belief that the scriptures are divinely inspired and inerrant. The sacraments of baptism and the Lord's Supper are observed, and marriage is regarded as a divine institution. Members of the Church are expected to adopt a pacifist attitude to warfare.

The clergy includes bishops, deacons, deaconesses, ministers of both sexes, presiding elders, who may also be known as district superintendents, licensed preachers and missionaries. It is administered from its headquarters at Zarephath, near Bound Brook, New Jersey, and has other important centres in Colorado, Ohio, Florida, California and London, England. Schools, radio stations and a publishing house are all maintained and active missions have been undertaken in Great Britain (since 1922), in Liberia (since 1961) and in India, Malawi, Nigeria, the Philippines and former Yugoslavia.

PLUMSTEAD PECULIARS

The name of this sect, which was started by William Bridges in England in 1838, has nothing to do with strange, or odd, but takes the meaning of *idiosyncratic*, something which belongs to an individual and is distinctly his or hers.

Bridges was a hat-block maker and with his friend, John Banyard, he preached in the southern counties of Sussex and Essex, attracting many followers especially from amongst the poor. Their message was one of total acceptance of the literal truth of the Bible, simple living and faith healing, which had undeniable appeal at a time when only the wealthy could afford a doctor's fee for his services. Bridges taught that medical aid was unnecessary and that anointing with oil accompanied by prayer would heal the sick. Public attention was drawn to the sect when some of the followers' children died from diseases that could be cured by medical intervention, and clashes with the law put some members of the sect in court. The group survived these problems and by 1903 there were five meeting houses, all in the poorer districts of London and all well attended. It is estimated that in 1934 there were around six thousand Peculiars in existence.

The members were noted for their sombre clothes and their small clapboard chapels to which they processed as a group, fervently singing hymns and anthems without music and all the time calling out religious exhortations and praises.

❖ Peculiars; The Peculiar People

PLYMOUTH BRETHREN

A denomination that combines CALVINISM, PIETISM and millennial beliefs (REVELATION 20) with an overall puritanical moral outlook. The name derives from a group that was established in 1831 in Plymouth, England, by an ex-Anglican priest and barrister, J. N. Darby (1800–82). This English group was in sympathy with a small FUNDAMENTALIST group to which Darby had belonged in Dublin, Ireland, in 1828. The members felt that there was a need to return to apostolic simplicity in terms of worship and doctrine. Darby set up many Brethren groups in Great Britain and continental Europe, especially in French Switzerland.

In the course of its history there have been many splits. Nineteenth-century breakaway groups included the OPEN BRETHREN (or Neutral Brethren), who favoured a more congregational form of church government, and the EXCLUSIVE BRETHREN, or DARBYITES, led by J. N. Darby himself, who preferred a federalist form of church government, which group subsequently underwent further splits.

The Brethren are Trinitarian, fundamentalist, creedless and committed to believing in the sole authority of the Bible as inerrant and verbally inspired by God. They hold that the Church of the New Testament, intended for the righteous alone, has become corrupt through its admittance of both *good* and *bad* members and by having an ordained ministry, thus denying the priesthood of all believers and rejecting the guidance of the Holy Spirit. On both counts such a corrupt Church is seen by the Brethren as condemned to extinction, and separation from other Christian Churches that are tainted by the same corruption is thought necessary.

Whilst there are no clergy as such, the Brethren recognize that some members have been given special gifts that qualify them to teach and preach. The Lord's Supper is observed every Sunday. The Exclusive Brethren baptize infants, but with the Open Brethren this is reserved for adult believers only. Brethren congregations are to be found in Great Britain, Europe and the USA, with missions in Africa and Peru.

❖ Believers; Christians; Saints

PNEUMATOMACHI

A heretical sect, whose name means 'against the spirit', that flourished in the fourth century in the area we now know as the Dardanelles. The heresy concerned the divinity of the Holy Spirit, which they denied.

The sect may have been led by Eustathius of Sebaste (*c.* 300 – *c.* 377) and was anathematized, along with other heretical sects, at the Council of Constantinople in 381, having been previously condemned by Pope St Damasus in 374. There is no mention of the sect surviving beyond the end of the fourth century.

Members of the sect are sometimes called Marathonians, because it was said that Bishop Marathonius of Nicomedia owed the possession of his see to their influence. In the writings of Ss Jerome, Augustine, Damasus and Rufinus, the Pneumatomachi are more commonly referred to as MACEDONIANS, but there is no established connection between the two sects.

❖ Macedonians; Marathonians; Spirit Fighters

POLISH NATIONAL CATHOLIC CHURCH

Polish immigration to America led to the concentration of many Polish families in the industrial states of the north-east and the northern mid-west, where they settled in Massachusetts, Connecticut, New York, New Jersey, Pennsylvania, Ohio, Michigan, Illinois and Wisconsin. Many of these immigrants gradually found themselves dissatisfied with the ROMAN CATHOLIC CHURCH authorities in the USA, who would not accede to their request for a bishop of Polish birth, or origin, or for Polish pastors. Furthermore, they were unhappy about the ruling of the third plenary Council of Baltimore (1884) that the title to all church real estate was to be signed over to the diocese, meaning that even after building and financing a church for themselves the laity had no right to act as trustees of that property.

An important move towards independence was made at Scranton, Pennsylvania, in 1896–7, a parish made up largely of coal miners and factory workers who had contributed to the building of a new church whose clergy, although Polish, were under the jurisdiction of an Irish bishop, Mgr O'Hara. Lay members of the parish asked to be represented in the management of parish affairs and made a request for the Polish language and culture to be taught in parish schools, but these appeals were all curtly rejected. Fights broke out in front of the church building and 52 people were arrested, with severe sentences handed down to them; earlier moves towards independence had been made in Chicago under Fr Anthony Kozlowski.

Fr Francis Hodur, a Polish priest born into a poor, rural family at Zarka, six miles from Krakow, had gone to the USA after his ordination in 1893 and become an assistant priest at Scranton, where he became well known to the people of the parish. In 1895, he was approached by some of the dissatisfied members for his assistance. He advised them to build a church and refuse to hand over to the bishop its deeds and title. Hodur took charge of the parish and celebrated Mass in the new church, dedicated to St Stanislaus, in March 1897. A congregational meeting was held, composed of members of the 250 families who had joined the church building scheme. Despite appeals to Rome to recognize this parish, Hodur and the participating families were excommunicated in October 1898. The document of excommunication was burnt in front of the congregation and its ashes were taken and thrown into a nearby brook. In an act of defiance, the whole parish refused to recognize the authority of Rome. Mass, in Polish, continued to be celebrated there and by 1904, together with members of other seceded and independent congregations, the first synod met, made up of 147 clerical and lay delegates representing some 24 parishes and 20,000 adherents in the five states of Pennsylvania, New Jersey, Maryland, Connecticut and Massachusetts. The synod adopted a constitution and elected a lay-clerical supreme council, with Francis Hodur as bishop. He was consecrated in 1907, in Utrecht, in the Netherlands, by the OLD CATHOLIC (CHURCH) Archbishop of Utrecht assisted by the Bishops of Haarlem and Deventer.

Further decisions were taken, to reprint the Latin service books in Polish, establish a theological seminary in Scranton for the training of clergy, and found a mutual benefits society, named *Spujnia*, which would serve the material needs of the faithful. Two large farms were bought, and set up as vacation camps, and homes for the elderly and the disabled were opened. A printing press was developed in Scranton, for the publishing of church materials.

Doctrinally and liturgically, the Polish National Catholic Church has adopted a modified Roman Catholic approach, substituting the *Credo* instead of the Nicene creed in the celebration of the Mass, and expanding the *Kyrie* into a litany. Other changes include the introduction of some distinctive and non-Roman feasts, such as the Feast of the Poor Shepherds and the Feast of the Christian Family. Doctrinal statements include the *Credo*, drawn up by Francis Hodur and adopted officially in 1913; this was later expanded into the *Eleven Great Principles* (1923), *The Short Catechism* (1936) and the *Declaration Made by Those About to be Confirmed*. Masses in English have been permitted since 1958 and have been adopted by some parishes. Clerical celibacy has been abolished, along with auricular confession for adults, although it is still maintained for children. Baptism and confirmation are regarded as a single sacrament but the remaining sacraments are the usual, traditional ones; a second sacrament is taught, this being 'the Word of God, read, expounded or listened to'.

The congregation has control of its local church property and a say in the appointment of a priest. The Church is currently organized in four American dioceses and one Canadian see, in Toronto, Ontario. An active mission to Poland was begun in 1920, following the First World War and by 1922 the Polish National Catholic Church was formally recognized there. There are now three dioceses in the country, at Warsaw, Krakow and Wroclaw.

The headquarters of the Church is at Scranton. Synods are called every four years, bringing together both clerical and lay delegates. The executive power of the Church rests with the prime bishop and the supreme council, which is made up of clerical and lay representatives from all the dioceses.

❖ Polish National Catholic Church of America and Poland

POLISH ORTHODOX CHURCH

Poland became a republic after the First World War, acquiring territory from Ukraine and with it some four million Orthodox Ukrainians, Russians and Byelorussians, together with their own bishops. These now came under the jurisdiction of Metropolitan Deonisey of Warsaw. The Polish government of the time, wishing to sever connections with communist Russia (which was antagonistic to the Church), approached Patriarch Meletios II of Constantinople to request autonomy for the Orthodox Church in Poland and this was agreed. The autocephaly of the Church was granted in 1925, after the death of Patriarch Meletios II, by the Ecumenical Patriarch of Constantinople Gregorius III at the request of the synod of bishops and the Polish government, despite the protests of Patriarch Tikhon of Moscow. It was now placed under the metropolitanate of Warsaw and Poland.

Most of those areas of land previously

granted to Poland were returned to the Soviet Union following the Second World War and the bishops returned to the jurisdiction of Moscow, leaving less than 400,000 Orthodox faithful on Polish territory. In 1948, Patriarch Alexis of the RUSSIAN ORTHODOX CHURCH granted autocephaly to the Polish Orthodox Church. The head of the Polish Orthodox Church is styled as His Beatitude the Metropolitan of Warsaw and All Poland, with additional responsibility for the dioceses of Bialystok, Łódź, Przemsyl, Wroclaw and Lublin.

The work of the Church continues, with particular emphasis on outreach to young people in schools and colleges. This is achieved through the organization of various youth services, discussion groups, social gatherings and the provision of catechesis through parish centres. Much attention has also been paid to the importance of the lay influence in the Church.

❖ Autocephalous Orthodox Church of Poland; Orthodox Church of Poland

POOR PREACHERS

The Poor Preachers, itinerant teachers who had been introduced by John Wycliffe (*c.* 1330–84) as part of his apostolate to carry the Christian message throughout Britain, used his vernacular translations of the Bible extensively. Wycliffe felt strongly that the scriptures were the supreme authority under God and that no-one, whatever their learning or lack of it, should be excluded from hearing the scriptures and being able to understand them. The preachers wore a recognizable garment, a plain russet cloth gown that reached to their bare feet, and they carried long staves. So equipped, they would preach in churches, in market places and on village greens, taking whatever sustenance and shelter the people might offer. The Poor Preachers taught the Lord's Prayer, the ten commandments and the seven deadly sins in the vernacular, so that all could understand them, and were also given to denunciation of the papacy and clergy for their perceived errors.

To help the preachers, Wycliffe wrote tracts, sermon outlines and paraphrases of the Bible that they could use. At its outset only clergy and some well-positioned laity were to be found amongst their ranks, but in time the movement began to attract the interest of people of poorer means. This was especially the position after 1400, when the LOLLARDS' social teaching became more prominent. These itinerant preachers were accused of causing trouble and it was alleged that they would not obey any summons from local bishops. These bishops, authorizing the sheriffs to imprison any of the Poor Preachers they named, issued commissions to this end, a course of action that did not meet with wholehearted approval from parliament.

The Poor Preachers and their work did not survive the condemnation of Thomas Arundel, Archbishop of Canterbury, who spoke out against Wycliffe's doctrines and his unauthorized translations of the Bible. There were further persecutions of the group under both Henry IV and Henry V.

POTTER'S HOUSE

This American Bible-based FUNDAMENTALIST Church was founded in 1970 by Wayman Mitchell in Prescott, Arizona. Mitchell recognized the need for a return to a New Testament-style Church, from which trained workers would emerge to evangelize and plant similar churches throughout the world. He planned meticulously the training of young men to become pastors, ensuring that they would be well disciplined and equipped to evangelize; it was expected of these young men that they would marry before leaving for their foreign missions.

Doctrinally, the Church accepts the verbal inspiration of the scriptures and believes in the Trinity and the deity of Jesus Christ, in the resurrection of the body and in a final judgement, when the good will be rewarded with heaven and the wicked will go to eternal punishment. It recognizes man's depravity and need for atonement, with salvation by grace through faith and not by works. Divine healing and baptism of the Holy Spirit are seen as following upon regeneration and water baptism of believers, and the Lord's Supper is open to all. The Church practises tithing and anticipates the pre-millennial return of Jesus Christ to earth (REVELATION 20).

Its active missionary programme has taken the Church into some 73 countries throughout the world. Twice a year a large, week-long, conference is assembled at Cape Cod, Massachusetts.

❖ La Puerta; Praise Chapel, Grace Chapel; The Door; Victory Chapel, The Christian Fellowship

PRESBYTERIAN CHURCH (USA)

The Presbyterian Church (USA) was formed in 1983 by a union between the UNITED PRESBYTERIAN CHURCH IN THE UNITED STATES OF AMERICA (founded 1958) and the PRESBYTERIAN CHURCH IN THE UNITED STATES (founded 1861).

The Church takes its doctrinal position from that of the United Presbyterian Church in the United States of America. This is published in a *Book of Confessions*, together with the texts of the usual, traditional creeds, the *Reformed Confessions*, which include the *First Helvetic Confession* (1536), the *Belgic Confession* (1561), the *Second Helvetic Confession* (1566), the *Canons of the Synod of Dort* (1618–19) and the *Westminister Confession of Faith* (1647) as well as the *Small Catechism*. For the purpose of directing liturgical ceremonies, the *Book of Worship* provides the format suggested for use in the Church's worship.

The Presbyterian Church (USA), with its headquarters at Louisville, Kentucky, has responsibility for 11,433 congregations caring for about 2.8 million adult members. The Church has established partnerships with others in mission fields in a further 63 nations worldwide.

PRESBYTERIAN CHURCH IN AMERICA

The Church was originally formed as the NATIONAL PRESBYTERIAN CHURCH in 1973 but shortly afterwards the name was changed to the current one. It had come about through a schism in the Presbyterian Church (USA – Southern) because of a perceived growing liberalism in that body. The 1965 merger of two further Presbyterian Churches resulted in the formation of the REFORMED PRESBYTERIAN CHURCH – EVANGELICAL SYNOD, and in 1982 this group also joined the Presbyterian Church in America.

Doctrinally, the Church holds to the *WESTMINSTER CONFESSION of Faith* and the catechisms produced in England in the 1640s, in which the infallibility and unique authority of the Bible is affirmed together with a belief in man's total depravity. This renders him incapable of reaching out to God and only capable of achieving this relationship through the irresistible grace of God and the perseverance of the saints, which will enable him to be saved. The polity of the Church is presbyterian, as set out in the *Book of Church Order*. The presbyters and elders operate through graded assemblies, or courts, of which there are three types: 1) sessions that govern the Church at local level; 2) the presbytery, which governs regional matters; and 3) the general assembly, which governs and administers nationally.

The Presbyterian Church in America co-ordinates its various ministries throughout the world through its foreign missions, which extend into 60 nations and support many hundreds of missionaries. Mission work is also maintained in the military field, in prison welfare, in hospitals and on many university and college campuses. The Church, which has the care of more than 1,450 congregations, has its headquarters in Atlanta, Georgia.

PRESBYTERIAN CHURCH IN THE UNITED STATES

After the outbreak of the Civil War in America (1861–65), the general assembly of the Presbyterian Church in the United States of America met in Philadelphia. Without the presence of any delegates from the south, a unilateral decision was taken to declare the assembly's loyalty to the United States. Subsequently, the southern presbyteries withdrew and at the end of 1861 they organized themselves as the Presbyterian Church in the Confederate States of America, which later became the Presbyterian Church in the United States. The first assembly of the Church was held in Augusta, Georgia, where its headquarters was also established. Doctrinally, the Church was CALVINISTIC, with ministers, elders and deacons appointed to minister to the laity; women were excluded from joining their ranks. The polity of the Church was presbyterian. There was much concentration on home mission work amongst various ethnic groups in the southern states and a vigorous foreign mission programme in Central and South America, the Far East, Iraq and Portugal.

The Church was a partner in the 1983 union with the UNITED PRESBYTERIAN CHURCH IN THE UNITED STATES OF AMERICA, when the PRESBYTERIAN CHURCH (USA) was established.

PRESBYTERIAN REFORMED CHURCH IN CUBA

The foundation of this small Presbyterian presence in Cuba was made in 1884 and augmented by missionaries sent from the USA in 1898. It is the only PROTESTANT Church in Cuba that opens its doors daily to provide a counselling service, an enterprise called the *Opened Temple*. The Church is also involved in providing health professionals to give advice about alcoholism, sexually transmitted diseases and stress management, through a family-oriented care centre. Home mission work was attempted in 1996 when a new centre was opened in Marianao, an area of Havana City.

Clergy-in-training attend courses at the Union Theological Seminary. This was opened in Matanzas in 1947 and offers training to seminarians from other traditions, including BAPTISTS and Episcopalians. At present the headquarters in Havana administers 63 congregations and oversees work carried out amongst some 7,000 faithful.

PRESBYTERIANISM (also PRESBYTERIAN CHURCH; PRESBYTERIANS)

The term 'Presbyterian' is usually given to identify those English-speaking REFORMED Churches professing various shades of CALVINISM, which emerged from the Reformation in Europe.

When a Church's polity, or form of government, is described as presbyterian, it refers to a Church that is governed by presbyters, or elders, some of whom are pastors or ministers but who can also be from the laity; all are of equal status. Deacons in a community are expected to manage the temporal affairs of the church. The presiding minister and elders form a session, or consistory, which is the first step in the hierarchy of the courts of the Church, and since the ministers and the elders are elected by the congregation, the presbyterian polity is directed by that congregation. The next highest court, the presbytery, or colloquy, which is composed of equal numbers of ministers and lay elders, may receive appeals from the session. Its concern is with the administration of church property and it confirms a minister's appointment within the Church. The synod, which is made up of ministers and elders from a determined number of presbyteries, has the authority to exercise a limited supervision over both presbyters and congregations. The final authority within the Church rests with the general assembly, which is made up of equal numbers of lay and clerical representatives meeting annually, which has responsibility for overseeing the work of the entire Church.

The first complete statement of the Presbyterian doctrinal position came from the Westminster Assembly of Divines (1643–9), which prepared the *WESTMINSTER CONFESSION of Faith*, the *Larger* and *Small Catechisms*, a *Directory of Worship* and *The Form of Church Government*. This doctrinal standard was adopted by the CHURCH OF SCOTLAND by a special act in 1647 and has been the doctrinal foundation of the Presbyterian Church throughout the English-speaking world ever since.

This Reformed faith holds to the inspired nature of the Bible as the infallible rule of faith and practice, which is expressed in the Apostles', Nicene and Athanasian creeds. In accord with its Calvinistic theology, it upholds the doctrine of limited atonement and salvation for the *elect*; traditionally, the *elect* were regarded as few in number, but now the opposite is held to be true by many Calvinist theologians. The sacraments of baptism, of both infants and believers, and the Lord's Supper are observed and are regarded as signs and seals of God's covenant of grace and benefit, whenever they are received as such by faith.

The Presbyterian Church, as a Reformed Church, was not founded by John Calvin, but rather he laid the foundations upon which it was constructed in Switzerland, the Netherlands, France, England, Scotland and Ireland. It was Calvin's inspiration that fired John Knox and the COVENANTERS of Scotland and made that country PROTESTANT and Presbyterian. Following Oliver Cromwell's Commonwealth and the restoration of the monarchy in England in the mid-seventeenth century, persecution forced many Presbyterians to flee to America with the PURITANS. Attempts to establish the episcopate in Scotland after 1662 resulted in others leaving for Ireland, and from there many more went on to America. Presbyterian congregations had been formed in America as early as 1611, in Virginia, and 1630, in Massachusetts and Connecticut, followed some ten years later by others on Long Island and in New York, well before the arrival, between 1710 and 1750, of the Scottish and Irish Presbyterians.

There are now large numbers of Presbyterians and Reformed congregations in Scotland, the Netherlands, Hungary, South Africa, the USA, Australasia and South Korea, with small groups in over one hundred other countries. The Reformed and Presbyterian Church lends itself to constant division and this, in turn, has led to a myriad of different denominations, many of which lie outside the scope of this book. Despite this diversity, however, many alliances have been made, one of the most important of which was a merger that resulted in the establishment of the World Alliance of Reformed Churches (Presbyterian and Congregational), with its headquarters in Geneva, Switzerland. This merger acknowledges the common heritage of the Reformed, Presbyterian and Congregational Churches in the Reformation theology of John Calvin and Ulrich Zwingli.

PRESBYTERY OF LIBERIA IN WEST AFRICA

Missionaries from the PRESBYTERIAN CHURCH IN AMERICA founded this small but growing Church in Liberia in 1831. At present there are 15 congregations and about 1,500 faithful. The Church has been autonomous since 1890. The clergy are mostly male, but there are some female ministers and evangelists active in the Church.

❖ Presbyterian Church in Liberia

PRIESTLY UNION OF ST JOHN MARY BAPTIST VIANNEY

A traditionalist ROMAN CATHOLIC group, which went into schism in the 1990s inspired by the ideals of the late Archbishop Marcel Lefebvre (1905–91) and the SOCIETY OF ST PIUS X. The Church has a bishop, some 25 priests and about 28,000 lay members in Campos, Brazil.

The Priestly Union, currently under the leadership of Bishop Licino Rangel, who was consecrated by Lefebvrist bishops in 1991, rejects most of the conclusions of the Second Vatican Council, especially in liturgical matters. In 1991 the group was excommunicated by the Vatican, which later made a move, in January 2002, to lift this ban. The Vatican proposed that the Priestly Union could be given the status of an *Apostolic Administration* directly dependent upon the Apostolic See, and its permanence guaranteed. This reconciliation with Rome was entrusted to the Pontifical Commission *Ecclesia Dei*, under the presidency of Cardinal Darío Castrillón Hoyos. While the group will be able to continue with its celebration of the Divine Liturgy using the pre-Vatican II rite, there has been some disquiet expressed by other Lefebvrists in Europe, who have condemned the agreement, especially if it means accepting some of the other changes introduced by Vatican II.

PRIMITIVE ADVENT CHRISTIAN CHURCH

This small, and slowly declining, American Church was founded in 1930 in protest against the preaching of the Reverend Whitman, a minister of the ADVENT CHRISTIAN CHURCH in Charleston, West Virginia. The protest was over Whitman's proposal that foot-washing and the re-baptizing of those who had left the Church and wanted to return should be discontinued. A group of Whitman's congregation found itself at odds with their pastor's views and left to found the Primitive Advent Christian Church, which retains both foot-washing and re-baptism. This now has 19 congregations with around 340 committed adult members.

Each congregation sends delegates to an annual conference, which is responsible for coordinating the work of the local churches. A congregation is presided over by its pastor, ordained by the authority of the annual conference, assisted by deacons and elders. Doctrinally, the Church does not differ in any other respects from its parent Church. The headquarters of the Primitive Advent Christian Church is in Sissonville, West Virginia.

PRIMITIVE BAPTISTS – ABSOLUTE PREDESTINARIANS

A small faction within the Primitive Baptist movement in the USA, numbering in the region of 8,500 adult members distributed in around 50 associations and found mostly in Texas, Alabama, North Carolina, Virginia and the north-east of the USA.

The members of the Church hold to the doctrinal views of the Primitive Baptists, but their belief extends beyond simple election by asserting that not only are the saved pre-selected, but so is every event that occurs in the world. Other doctrinal beliefs extend to an affirmation of natural man's depravity and to a special atonement, which teaches that salvation was intended for the elect alone; this is tied to a belief in irresistible grace, by which each of the elect will be quickened by the spirit of God at some point in the course of their natural lives. The Primitive Baptists also hold to what is called the perseverance of the saints, which refers to a belief that every member of the elect will finally be saved. The Holy Spirit is believed to operate on man directly and independently and the scriptures are held to bring all those quickened by the Holy Spirit to the 'discovery of life and to transform them thereby'.

Their church buildings, as in all Primitive Baptist churches, are very simple with plain glass windows and an interior marked, again, by its simplicity. No religious signs or symbols adorn the walls and an unadorned bookstand is placed, slightly elevated, at one end of the worship area from which the elder of the congregation will read the Bible and direct the worship service with its unaccompanied singing of hymns. At one time there was a separation of the sexes during services of worship, but this has been modified in recent years with a view to keeping families together when they worship.

PRIMITIVE BAPTISTS – MODERATES

An American group of BAPTISTS that prefers not to be known as a denomination, believing that each church should govern itself, denying the authority of any minister, association or convention, and without a centralized administration. The group is also known as the Anti-Mission Baptists, because of the belief that mission and benevolent societies have no place in their community on the grounds that they did not exist at the time of the apostles; for similar reasons Sunday schools are not allowed. The firm opposition to missionary work, which was outlined in a *Declaration of Principles*, written down in 1827 during the Kehukee association in North Carolina, is justified because it is seen as contrary to Christ's teachings.

Doctrinally, the Primitive Baptists are strongly CALVINISTIC, holding that man is depraved and that salvation will only come to those elected by God before the foundation of the world. There are two ordinances, those of baptism of believers by immersion, and the Lord's Supper, but some groups also practise foot-washing as an ordinance. Members believe in the second coming of Christ, when the dead will be raised to face their judgement, the righteous receiving their heavenly reward and the wicked their punishment (REVELATION 20). The Bible is regarded as the verbally inspired and infallible word of God. Elders and deacons run the local churches, the elders receiving their calling from God with a laying on of hands. Deacons, who have not usually received theological training and who retain their normal occupations, are responsible for the temporal affairs of the congregation. Divine services are not accompanied by instrumental music but by a form of *a cappella* singing known as *Sacred Harp Singing*, which resembles eighteenth-century folk music. Sermons are delivered in a distinctive, extempore fashion that has sometimes been described as *sing-song*.

❖ Anti-Mission Baptists; Hard Shell Baptists; Old School Baptists; Primitive Baptists – Regular

PRIMITIVE BAPTISTS – PROGRESSIVES

A faction of the Primitive Baptist Church in the USA, with a doctrinal position similar to that of the other Baptist Churches. In their congregational life these BAPTISTS are noted for their innovativeness, which is expressed through their organization of youth fellowships, camps and Bible study classes, as well as the formation of men's brotherhoods and women's societies. This Church is much more outgoing than the others belonging to this tradition. Members in Georgia have, for example, undertaken work with the elderly in Bethany Homes, and a radio ministry, known as *The Lighthouse*, which is broadcast throughout Georgia and most of Alabama. Projects involving church building and planting are also undertaken, by the Primitive Baptist Builders.

The membership of the Church is calculated to be about 7,600 adult members in some 128 churches, which are located chiefly in Georgia and in the mid-western and southern states of the USA.

PRIMITIVE CHURCH OF JESUS CHRIST (BICKERTONITE)

In 1914 a split occurred in the CHURCH OF JESUS CHRIST (BICKERTONITE), led by James Caldwell, and this resulted in the founding of a new group, the Primitive Church of Jesus Christ (Bickertonite) at Washington, DC. Another of the schismatic Bickertonite groups, known as the Reorganized Church (formed 1907), joined them shortly afterwards. The form and practice of the Primitive Church, which represents a reform of the original Bickertonite Church, is still very similar to that of the parent group. Members do not approve of, or practise, polygamy or baptism of the dead. The Church has a very small membership but still maintains a headquarters in Erie, Pennsylvania.

PRIMITIVE METHODIST CHURCH

This Church began as an unofficial movement for outdoor evangelism by a

METHODIST minister, Hugh Bourne (1772–1852), in and around Mow Cop, a folly north of Newcastle-under-Lyme, England. Fortuitously, Lorenzo Dow, an American camp meeting revivalist, came to England in 1807 and introduced his methods to Bourne and to another Methodist minister, William Clowes, who was evangelizing in a neighbouring area. The preachers took up Dow's ideas and camp meetings were held in the open, designed to attract converts. The Wesleyan conference in Liverpool considered these meetings to be both improper and likely to be the cause of considerable mischief, but neither preacher was willing to desist and for this refusal both men were dismissed from the Wesleyan Church and their converts were made unwelcome in any Wesleyan establishment. Upon Bourne's dismissal, in 1810 he founded the Camp Meeting Methodists. A year later, following Clowes's dismissal, the two groups of followers united, adopting the name of the Primitive Methodist Church in 1812. Within two years a set of rules, or *Discipline*, had been drawn up, but persecutions and a lack of internal organization led the group into serious decline between 1825–8. Bourne tried to introduce a more centralized administration, with a consequent loss of autonomy. In 1932, the Primitive Methodist Church in the UK united with the Wesleyan Church and the United Methodists to form the METHODIST CHURCH OF GREAT BRITAIN.

Some English and Welsh Primitive Methodists who had settled in America began to ask for Primitive Methodist ministers to be sent out from their homeland. Four missionaries, William Summersides, Thomas Morris, Ruth Watkins and William Knowles, were sent to work in New Jersey, New York, Pennsylvania and Connecticut in 1829. A break had been made from the British parent body by 1840, when the American Primitive Methodist Church was established. Autonomous conferences were soon established and today the administration of the Church is under the control of an annual conference, presided over by a president who is elected for four years. The Church also conducts missionary initiatives.

From the 1840s missionaries became active elsewhere in the world, forming Primitive Methodist societies in many parts of Australia and New Zealand and towards the end of the nineteenth century extending into Africa. In 1977, the Australian Methodists became part of the UNITING CHURCH OF AUSTRALIA after its union with the CONGREGATIONALISTS and PRESBYTERIANS.

The headquarters of the Primitive Methodists in America is in Wilkes-Barre, Pennsylvania. The Church has the care of 81 congregations with over 5,500 adult members.

❖ Ranters

PRISCILLIANISTS

Followers of a fourth-century Spanish bishop, who was declared to be a heretic and who had the dubious distinction of being the first such executed for his teachings. Priscillian (*c.* 340–85) was from a noble Spanish family and was noted for his learning and asceticism. He had been introduced to GNOSTIC heresy through the influence of an Egyptian from Memphis, called Marcus.

The doctrine taught by Priscillian attracted many followers, including several bishops and a great number of women, and these followers began to form a group, which was seen by some as an oath-bound society. It attracted the attention of Hyginus, the Bishop of Córdoba, and Hydatius, the Bishop of Mérida, who consulted with other bishops with the result that a synod was held in Saragossa in 380 to address the problem. Although Priscillian and his followers were not present, a sentence of excommunication was passed on them all. In defiance of the synod, Priscillian was ordained and consecrated, and appointed as Bishop of Ávila by his episcopal supporters, Instantius and Salvian. But, by the order of the Emperor Gratian and issued at the insistence of Priscillian's opponents, he was sent into exile. Priscillian appealed against the order to Rome and to St Ambrose of Milan, but without success.

The decree of exile was eventually lifted and Priscillian returned to Ávila. The murder of the Emperor Gratian followed shortly afterwards and Priscillian's position changed yet again. Gratian's successor, the usurper Maximus, anxious to replenish the imperial coffers and to court favour with the bishops, ordered a synod to be held at Bordeaux in 384. One of Priscillian's supporters, Instantius, was sentenced to be deposed; charges were again levelled at Priscillian, and once more appealed against, with St Martin of Tours intervening on Priscillian's behalf. The appeal was initially granted, but the case eventually went against Priscillian, who was found guilty of witchcraft and beheaded at Trier, together with six of his followers. The sect flourished until well into the sixth century, when the Council of Braga definitively condemned it in 563. *In the event, the fate of the usurper Maximus was no less bloody, for he was defeated by Theodosius and executed at Aquileia in 388.*

Priscillianism has been described as a form of MANICHAEAN dualism in that it held to the existence of two kingdoms, of light and darkness. Human souls were intended to conquer the kingdom of darkness, but they fell and were imprisoned in material bodies. They believed that man's salvation consisted in his release from the domination of matter, for which purpose Jesus Christ came to earth in a heavenly body that only *appeared* to be like that of other men, and through his *apparent* death released the souls of men from the influence of the material world. Since the material body was seen as the creation of the devil, who was not held to be a fallen angel, then marriage and procreation, together with the eating of flesh meat, were forbidden; it is probable that free love was permitted.

PROGRESSIVE NATIONAL BAPTIST CONVENTION, INC.

This black American BAPTIST Church arose in 1961 from a dispute concerning the tenure of the presidency of the NATIONAL BAPTIST CONVENTION OF THE USA, INC. (founded 1895). It had been argued at the 1960 meeting of the convention that the then president, Dr J. H. Jackson, who had been elected in 1953, should step down, as the right to life tenure of any church office did not exist within the constitution of the Church. The attempt to remove Dr Jackson from office failed.

Those members opposed to Dr Jackson left the Church in 1961, forming the Progressive National Baptist Convention and electing their own president. The first national convention of the new Church was held the following year, when it was agreed that the maximum tenure for holding office in the Church should be limited to two years and that there should be equality of access to office, the fullest freedom of opportunity to seek any office and the broadest possible participation in the life and work of the Church by all of its members.

Doctrinally, the Church is in full agreement with the position held by its parent body. There is an annual session of the convention, held in August, and a midwinter session, held in January. The headquarters, in Washington, DC, is responsible for over 1,800 congregations and nearly 2.5 million committed believers who are cared for by over 850 ministers. The Church actively supported the campaigns of Martin Luther King and the Civil Rights movement of the 1960s.

PROTESTANT (also PROTESTANTISM; PROTESTANTS)

Used either of a Church, or a member of a Church, that has accepted the beliefs and practices preached by such sixteenth-century reformers as Martin Luther, John Calvin and Ulrich Zwingli.

PROTESTANT CHRISTIAN CHURCH OF BALI

Despite the changes wrought throughout the East Indies by the colonialism of the Portuguese, followed by the Dutch, and the impact that European missionary work had brought, Bali remained resolutely Hindu throughout the nineteenth century and into the twentieth. It had been Dutch colonial policy to preserve the indigenous Hindu-rooted faith and culture and Christian missions into the area were disallowed; Christian mission work amongst the Chinese community in Bali was, however, tolerated. In the 1930s, when the first Balinese Hindus began to convert to Christianity, missionary work in the area was expanded, and the Dutch colonial officials evicted many of the early missionaries, who were negative in their attitude towards Hindu culture.

Bishop Wayan Mastra, who became the principal architect of the Protestant Christian Church in Bali (GKPB – founded 1932), was born into a Hindu family in the village of Sibetan, in eastern Bali, and after his conversion and ordination he became prominent throughout the Balinese Christian community. Bishop Mastra tried to promote integration of Balinese cultural forms into the Church, which was entirely European in tradition and form. He chaired the so-called *watershed* synod in 1972, when it was agreed that Dutch colonial influence should be erased and a truly Balinese Church should be created. The synod resolved, among other things, to draw up a building programme for the creation of a cultural and training centre, which was to be known as the *Dhyana Pura*, in Denpasar. The purpose of the centre was to proclaim the Gospel of Jesus Christ in a way that was relevant to the Balinese people and to help Balinese Christians appreciate more soundly their cultural heritage within the context of their Christian faith and to find ways of expressing that faith within their culture. This interplay of faith and culture was to be underlined by making greater use of the distinctive Balinese architecture in giving witness to Christianity in Bali.

The Church, which has its headquarters at Denpasar, is made up of some 48 congregations, with about 3,700 committed members, most of whom are ex-Hindus, cared for by 25 indigenous clergy. It retains links with the Evangelical Missionary Society (EMS), which was founded in 1972 as a platform for the exchange of ideas and initiatives about missionary and ecumenical issues.

❖ Bali Christian Protestant Church

PROTESTANT CHURCH IN ALGERIA

The Protestant Church in Algeria was formed through the union of the METHODIST and the French Reformed Churches, the MENNONITES, the ASSEMBLIES OF GOD and the SALVATION ARMY in 1972–3.

A PROTESTANT witness was first established in Algeria in the 1830s, with the coming of the French McCall Mission, and later with the arrival of the Basel Mission from Switzerland, but the work failed. The Methodist presence came originally from the USA, whose missionaries worked amongst young people in particular and opened a dispensary at Les Ouauhias and a hospital at Il-Maten. There are now only 13 congregations belonging to the United Church, with some 300 adult believers and the numbers are declining. The headquarters of the Protestant Church in Algeria is in Algiers.

PROTESTANT CHURCH IN ARUBA

The Protestant Church in Aruba is one of three constituent Churches that make up the UNITED PROTESTANT CHURCH OF THE NETHERLANDS ANTILLES. The Church was established in Aruba in 1822, for PROTESTANTS of the REFORMED and LUTHERAN traditions (some 80 per cent of the islanders are ROMAN CATHOLIC). The two protestant traditions on the island united in 1825, but Aruba only occasionally benefited from the visit of a protestant pastor, who had to travel from the island of Curaçao; the first full-time pastor was appointed in 1858. The Church now has several clergy and helpers who minister to three congregations and a total membership of over a thousand believers. The headquarters of the Church is in Oranjestad, Aruba.

PROTESTANT CHURCH IN BONAIRE

One of the three constituent Churches that now make up the UNITED PROTESTANT CHURCH OF NETHERLANDS ANTILLES. The first PROTESTANT service was conducted there in 1843, following which a church was built some four years later. In the early days, in the absence of a pastor, it was once the custom for laity to read sermons approved by the DUTCH REFORMED CHURCH. Two worship services in the Church are now conducted in Dutch, English and Papiamento, a mixture of Portuguese, Dutch, English and Spanish. The headquarters of the Church is in Kralendijk, Bonaire.

PROTESTANT CHURCH IN INDONESIA

This is the largest PROTESTANT Church in Indonesia, currently maintaining over 4,400 congregations with nearly 2.6 million members. The Church serves as a general synod, comprised of eight other smaller component Churches, all following the REFORMED tradition of Christian doctrine and practice.

Portuguese colonialism had extended to the Moluccas and Celebes by 1522, and with it came extensive ROMAN CATHOLIC missionary activity, conducted especially by the Jesuits who, it has been estimated, had the care of 80,000 Christians by 1569. This activity ceased when the Portuguese were ousted by the Dutch at the start of the seventeenth century. The Dutch established themselves at Batavia, on the island of Java, leaving Roman Catholic communities to remain on part of the island of Timor. Dutch interests were managed by the East India Company, which supported pastors of the DUTCH REFORMED CHURCH. At this point, some 30,000 Indonesian Christians were received into this protestant Church, following the faith of their new colonial masters.

By the start of the nineteenth century a determined programme of evangelism, financed and supported from Europe, began and many of the indigenous populations were able to hear the scriptures in their own languages through the efforts of the missionaries. Education came to be seen as a more fruitful way of evangelizing than previous methods had supplied. Inevitably, many of the mission Churches grew to independence from European and other foreign control.

The Protestant Church in Indonesia (GPI) is responsible for a wide range of support services in education, social service and health. Schools and colleges, from kindergarten to university, are maintained and health work is provided through a network of dispensaries, health centres, family planning clinics, hospitals and leprosy centres. In some parts of Indonesia the Church is heavily involved in agricultural projects concerned with irrigation, rice cultivation, fisheries and lumbering and it has also taken some responsibility for road and bridge building.

PROTESTANT CHURCH IN SABAH (MALAYSIA)

This Church, which is within the LUTHERAN tradition, can date its foundation from 1882 when the Basel Mission from Switzerland began to work amongst the Chinese Hakka families in northern Borneo. The congregations have expanded ever since, mainly because of Chinese immigration but also through conversions within the local communities and a population increase.

From 1952 work was continued amongst the Rungus and Dusun tribes in north Sabah. The Church, which became autonomous in 1967, has over 300 congregations and some 15,000 committed members who are in the care of 64 indigenous clergy. The Church has been a member of the Lutheran World Federation since 1995 and is a member of the World Council of Churches. Together with the Basel Christian Church in Malaysia, the Lutheran Church in Singapore and the Evangelical Lutheran Church in Malaysia, it is now part of the Federation of Evangelical Churches in Malaysia and Singapore.

PROTESTANT METHODIST CHURCH IN THE IVORY COAST

Workers from the METHODIST Missionary Society first arrived in the Ivory Coast of Africa in 1924. Their work was soon augmented by members from the Christian and Missionary Alliance, who organized the HOLINESS-type Church, known as the Evangelical Protestant Church of the Central Ivory Coast, in 1930. Members from the World Evangelization Crusade arrived in the area in 1934 to establish a PROTESTANT Church amongst other linguistic groups in the central coastal region of the country.

An understanding was reached by these various protestant organizations, with the result that the Methodists agreed to concentrate their efforts in the south-east of the country, amongst the Alagya, Attie, Avikam and Dida linguistic groups, and matters were so arranged to ensure that the missionary outreach programmes of other groups did not overlap.

The headquarters of this Church is in Abidjan, with responsibility for 750 congregations with over 72,000 committed members. A coup in the Ivory Coast in 1999 ended some thirty years of ethnic and religious harmony and caused the violent death of many. The president of the Protestant Methodist Church in the Ivory Coast, the Reverend Benjamin Boni, spoke out against the situation; some measure of civilian rule was restored under President Laurent Gbagbo.

PROTESTANT METHODIST CHURCH OF BENIN

This African METHODIST group was founded in 1843 with the arrival in Abomey (a large city of Benin, previously Dahomey), of Methodist missionaries from Great Britain. They concentrated their attention on the Gun, an ethnolinguistic group in the south of the country. The Paris Evangelical Mission Society and the *Action Apostolique Commune* have recently started a missionary enterprise amongst the Fon people in and around Abomey, who form about 25 per cent of the population of Benin.

The Church survived the time of the revolutionary military government that created a tense situation for the various religious groups in Benin from 1971–91, when the country was a communist state. This was a time when all denominational schools were nationalized and lost their state subsidies, a situation that has now eased. Benin has been a republic since 1990. The headquarters of the Church is at Cotonou, Benin's largest city.

PROTESTANT REFORMED CHURCHES IN AMERICA

The REFORMED tradition, in which this Church stands, is to be distinguished from the LUTHERAN tradition in that it originated in Switzerland under the Reformers Ulrich Zwingli (1484–1531), John Calvin (1509–64) and Philipp Melanchthon (1497–1560); members of these Churches emigrated to America and it was one of these groups which eventually became organized as the Christian Reformed Church (CRC).

It was from the Christian Reformed Church (CRC) that three clergymen, Herman Hoeksema, Henry Danhof and George Ophoff were deposed because they could not accept the ARMINIAN doctrine that was being preached in their churches and advocated, instead, the CALVINISTIC view that grace was for the *elect* alone. The consequence of the deposition was the founding of the Protestant Reformed Churches in America, which began in 1926 with three congregations. Today the number of congregations has risen to 35, with around 3,100 adult believers. The polity of the Church is presbyterian and provision is made for an annual synod.

Doctrinally, the Church affirms the Reformed confessions, including the *Heidelberg Catechism* (1563), the *Belgic Confession of Faith* (1561) and the *Canons of the Synod of Dordrecht* (1618–19). The so-called *Five Points of Calvinism* are also affirmed; these are a belief in man's total depravity and unconditional election, Christ's limited atonement, the irresistible grace of God and the final perseverance of the saints.

The Church pursues an active mission programme, both within the USA and Canada as well as overseas, in Jamaica, Singapore, the UK, Ghana and the Philippines.

PURITAN (also PURITANISM; PURITANS)

An important, extreme PROTESTANT religious movement, or its members, that arose in England during the sixteenth century and influenced the formation of many denominations in later years.

Puritanism was most active during the period from the reign of Queen Elizabeth I (1533–1603) to the restoration of the monarchy in 1660. The aim of its adherents was to purify the Church, which they saw as tainted by corrupt practices, removing anything they considered to be unwarranted by scripture. This extended to details of public worship, especially with regard to the use of ornaments, vestments, the sign of the cross and the employment of organs in church music. The Puritans' CALVINISTIC theology had been brought back to England by many of the prominent Puritans of the day, who had studied in Holland and at Geneva. Puritans practised an extreme form of scrupulosity with regards to dress and the avoidance of amusements and dancing. A strict observance of Sunday was of paramount importance.

The merchant class in English society readily adopted Puritanism, and it became an active force during the sixteenth century. In 1603, on the accession of James I, the Puritans presented him with the *Millenary Petition* containing some demands for reform in the Church, which led to the Hampton Court Conference of 1604. In the event, little was achieved beyond some small changes in the *Book of Common Prayer*.

Q

QUAKERS

A popular name given to members of the Religious Society of Friends.

QUIETISM (also QUIETISTS)

A late seventeenth-century system of spirituality, which dispersed through Christendom and was spread by its advocates, such as Miguel de Molinos (*c.* 1640–97), François de Salignac de La Mothe Fénelon (1651–1715) and Madame Jeanne-Marie Guyon (1648–1717). Quietism insists that once the soul is surrendered to God in one decisive act, despite all temptations it will enjoy an unbreakable union with the divine. The Roman Catholic Church condemned Quietism because of anti-ecclesiastical implications that can be drawn from it. It has been seen as the logical outcome of the Reformation.

De Molinos, a Spanish-born Roman Catholic priest, held that perfection consisted in the complete passivity of the soul. Although he was a friend of Pope Blessed Innocent XI, the Pope condemned de Molinos's work, at the insistence of the Jesuits. On the orders of Louis XIV of France, de Molinos was arrested and imprisoned, dying in captivity.

Fénelon, the Roman Catholic Archbishop of Cambrai, became acquainted with Madame Guyon (see below) in 1688. Although attracted to her views, Fénelon at one point condemned Quietism, but later wrote in its defence, so surrounding himself with controversy and censure.

Madame Guyon has been described as a neurotic woman who claimed to be able to preach and write with ease the words given to her from above, and to perform miracles, read people's minds and have absolute power over their wills and bodies. She came under the influence of de Molinos and went around France, accompanied by a Barnabite friar, preaching Quietist views. They were both arrested in 1687. Madame Guyon spent two periods in prison for heresy and suspected immorality, and was eventually released from the Bastille in Paris in 1702. Her mystical teachings attracted the attention of Fénelon.

QUINTILIANS

A heretical sect of Montanists, named after Quintilia, a female companion of Montanus who has been identified with Priscilla, or Prisca. The sect is said to have given thanks to Eve for eating the fruit of the tree of knowledge and to have ordained and consecrated women in her honour. It has also been claimed that the sect used bread and cheese as the elements in their Eucharist.

R

RANTERS

The term is used to describe an English radical group that was especially prominent in the period 1649–54. Ranters were said to be imbued with the heresy of the free spirit, as affirmed by the BRETHREN OF THE FREE SPIRIT, also known as *Beghards*, a fourteenth-century heretical group holding that each member had attained a perfection so absolute that he was incapable of sin, with the consequent repudiation of moral norms which we know as ANTINOMIANISM, a view held by various GNOSTIC sects. The *perfect man* could always conclude that it was not only permissible for him, but also even required of him, to do whatever was commonly thought of as being taboo.

This attitude led Gerrard Winstanley (1609–60), the founder of the DIGGERS at St George's Hill, near Weybridge in Surrey, to declare that Ranting principles denoted a general lack of moral values, or restraint in worldly pleasures, underlining the fact that the most usual Ranter venue was the alehouse. English Ranter activity was centred mainly in London, but there was some spread throughout the rest of the country.

Ranter belief argued furthermore that since man had the Spirit within him, there was no need for a risen Saviour and for this reason all outward forms of religious worship were rejected and the acceptance of the Bible, as the word of God, denied. The movement was also quasi-millennial in outlook (REVELATION 20). The Ranters had faded from the scene by the middle of the seventeenth century.

Notable Ranters included some prominent men of their day. Laurence Claxson (or Clarkson, 1615–67) was the Ranter leader in Cambridge, whose publication *A Single Eye, All Light, No Darkness* (1650), landed him in prison; in 1658 Claxson joined the MUGGLETONIANS. Another outstanding member was Abiezer Coppe (1619–72), whose writings were most influential but also earned for him a spell in Newgate Prison; he pleaded insanity and was released in 1651. The antinomian views of both men were so forcefully stated that parliament, fearing a breakdown in law and order, became deeply agitated.

George Fox, the founder of the RELIGIOUS SOCIETY OF FRIENDS, commonly called Quakers, observed of the Ranters that 'they were very rude ... that they sang, whistled and danced; but the Lord's power so confounded them that many of them came to be convinced and were converted' (to Quakerism). For this reason, Quakers were sometimes mistaken for Ranters. In the nineteenth century members of the Primitive Methodist Church were sometimes also called Ranters, but only on account of their wild arm movements and the shouting that ministers of the Church employed in order to make themselves, and their message, heard and understood.

❖ High Attainers; Religious Libertines

RASKOLNIKI

A blanket-term for Russian schismatic groups that is applied to those who refused to accept the reforms of Patriarch Nikon (1605–81) following his election as Patriarch of Moscow in 1651. Nikon's reforms met with considerable opposition, but they were confirmed at a council held in 1667 and the opposition parties were excommunicated. The schismatics became a sect, or Raskol, and were known as the Old Believers.

RATANA CHURCH

An indigenous Church in New Zealand, which arose after a Maori Methodist wheat farmer felt inspired to urge his fellow Maoris to leave their superstitions behind and to be confident that God will send his angels to help them.

The farmer, Takapotiki (or Tahupotiki) Wiremu Ratana (1873–1939), gained a reputation as a visionary and faith healer. Ratana had experienced several visions, but these were overshadowed by one that happened on 8 November 1918, when he had what he described as a visitation in which he was aware of the presence of the Holy Spirit. The archangel Michael spoke to him, telling him to unite the Maori tribes under one God. Ratana soon attracted wide attention and many, both Maoris and whites, came to hear him preach a doctrine of moral reform under the one God of the Old and New Testaments. Aiming to express the teachings of Jesus Christ through traditional Maori religious and cultural forms, Ratana achieved a great measure of success. Many Maoris came to accept his teachings and many were cured of alcoholism and other illnesses.

By 1920 an interdenominational Church had been founded and in 1925 a separate temple for the *Morehu* (or Remnants, the name given to Ratana's followers) was established at his home village, Ratana Pa. Maori schools, a Maori bank and a welfare league were opened as part of the socio-economic dimension of the Church's message, while sporting and social activities were organized for the young. This was at a time when there was much disquiet amongst the Maoris, who felt aggrieved by the actions and disregard of the New Zealand government, especially because of its non-implementation of the land promises that had been provided by the Treaty of Waitangi (1840). Among the terms of this treaty, and in return for the recognition of British sovereignty, the Maoris had been promised continued possession of their land. The uprisings that followed, during 1845–8 and 1860–70, gave the colonists much cause for concern.

Ratana travelled throughout New Zealand and collected many signatures for a petition seeking the redress of the treaty's violations. Together with his companions he went to England to present the petition to George V but was unable to gain access to the king. The group returned to New Zealand by way of Japan and Australia. Ratana, who was also known as the *Mangai* (mouthpiece), enjoyed a warm welcome in Japan where he received the support of Juji Nakada, a bishop of the METHODIST EPISCOPAL CHURCH; his welcome in Australia was also cordial and he was assured of encouragement and support. From 1922, the Ratana Church began to move into the political arena and took to sponsoring candidates for the national legislature, but it took nine years before a candidate was elected. By 1931, in an effort to improve the social conditions of the Maori community, the Church had aligned itself with the reformist New Zealand Labour Party. During the years 1943–63 followers of Ratana took all four available Maori seats in the House of Representatives.

Other Christian groups had at first co-operated with the Ratana Church, but this stopped when an amalgam of various beliefs and unusual rituals began to be adopted, with Ratana himself glorified in prayers as being God's *Mangai*, or mouthpiece. A hierarchy of church officials, some of whom were known as apostles, was created. Doctrinally, the creed of the Ratana Church is an unconventional version of the Apostles' creed. It recognizes the Trinity, the fall of mankind, the redemptive work of Jesus Christ and the work of the Holy Spirit, but places an emphasis upon the work of the angels, who are seen as doing God's will, and holds that Ratana is his mouthpiece. In this respect, Ratana is seen as one in a line of Maori prophets; others include Aperhama Taoniu, Tawhiao, Te Kooti and Te Whiti. Their central prayer of enlightenment, or *Whetumarama*, is 'Father, Son, Holy Spirit and the Mangai, forever and ever, Amen'.

The Church's *symbol of enlightenment* is a star beneath a crescent moon, a badge that may also be worn by members of the Church. The star, or *Whetu*, and the moon, or *Marama*, are carved into the ends of each pew in Morehu's temple, and each of these pews is decorated either in white, blue, purple or gold, the colours representing the Father, the Son, the Holy Spirit and the Mangai respectively. The Church services, known as *Whakamoemiti* (Thanksgiving), are not formalized, but there are opportunities for confession, repentance, contrition, prayer for guidance, a sermon and words of thanksgiving. Feast days, such as Easter and Ratana's birthday (25 January) and the feasts commemorating Ratana's mystical visitation on 8 November, are observed.

In 1980, the government of New Zealand formally established a Waitangi tribunal and this is seen as a step towards Maori-Pakeha (White) reconciliation. The Church now has about 140 congregations, with a membership in excess of 28,000, and is to be found not only in New Zealand but also in the Australian cities of Sydney, Melbourne and Brisbane.

REBA PLACE FELLOWSHIP AND ASSOCIATED COMMUNITIES

Mennonite students at Goshen College, Indiana, founded this American fellowship in the mid-1960s, as an off-campus ministry. The members, reacting against what they saw as a growing lack of dynamism in the Church, wanted to establish a disciplined brotherhood that would be divided into small, consensual communities. In 1967 the group moved to Reba Place, Evanston, Illinois, where the first commune was organized. A few years later the Plow Creek Fellowship was opened as a rural counterpart of the Reba Place commune; other communes followed. Membership requires a commitment to Jesus and to his teaching, a renunciation of property and an acceptance that anger, violence and war are all wrong. The MENNONITE theology is strongly maintained, but there are differences in the way of worship. The Fellowship allows the use of guitars, folk music and emotional outpourings in its worship services. Members support their communities by working locally, their incomes pooled and each individual member, or family group, receiving an allowance.

REFORMED (also REFORMED CHURCH)

A term used to describe those PROTESTANT Churches that hold to the theological views expressed by John Calvin (CALVINISM), as against those proposed by Martin Luther (LUTHERANISM).

REFORMED APOSTOLIC COMMUNITY

This small German denomination was formed in 1921 when two *apostles* of the NEW APOSTOLIC CHURCH (NAC), Ecke and Brueckner, were expelled from that organization; the NAC had been formed as a result of a schism from the CATHOLIC APOSTOLIC CHURCH in 1863. The reason for the expulsion of both men was their opposition to Herman Niehaus (1848–1932), the chief apostle, who claimed quasi-papal authority and regarded himself as the 'Jesus revelation for all time'. The source of all ministries within the Church, he further claimed, must come from him. A less radical chief apostle succeeded Niehaus.

This split was not an isolated one, and there has been an attempt in recent years to unite these schismatic groups. For that purpose, the Union of Apostolic Christians was formed in Switzerland in 1954.

REFORMED CATHOLIC CHURCH (UTRECHT CONFESSION)

A small, independent and obscure American Church, its headquarters believed to be in Los Angeles, California, with a current clergy of 15 serving a membership of 800. It is difficult to determine when and where this Church was started, but it claims an apostolic succession, derived from both Roman and Eastern Catholic sources. This suggests that its orders derive from a seventeenth-century Dutch succession and, according to the Church's statement, it is a member of a group of Reformed Catholic Churches that can trace its ancestry back to that time. However, what little is certain is that there was a connection with the now-defunct Old Catholic Evangelical Church of God (OCECG), whose founder, Matthew Cooper, may have been consecrated in 1924 by Patriarch Banks of the OLD CATHOLIC ORTHODOX CHURCH. The OCEC gave rise to a daughter Church, the Old Holy Catholic Church, one of whose priests, Dr Pitt-Kethley, later became the administrator of the Reformed Catholic Church (Utrecht Confession) in Great Britain; other provinces of this Church were established in France and Germany but it is not certain that they still exist.

The Church affirms the Nicene Creed and the canons of the first seven ecumenical councils, but of its work little is known with any certainty.

REFORMED CHURCH IN AMERICA

Calvinism took root early in the Netherlands and with the arrival of the Dutch settlers in New Amsterdam (later New York) in the seventeenth century, accompanied by Pastor Jonas Michaelius, came the organization of the collegiate church of that city in 1628. The change to English rule in the colony in 1664 had little effect on the Church, which was given assurances that it would still be able to enjoy freedom from English control and could continue under the ecclesiastical jurisdiction of the governing body, or *Classis*, of Amsterdam.

The estimated 8,000 Dutch men and women in America held their services in Dutch and were led either by Dutch pastors or by young native-born men who were sent to Holland for training and ordination. This proved expensive and permission was given in 1766 for the foundation of a college and seminary at New Brunswick, New Jersey, to be known as Queen's College (and from 1924 as Rutgers University). This need for training and ordination in America was advocated by the outstanding Dutch Calvinist, Theodore Jacobus Frelinghuysen (1691–1747), who had emigrated to New Jersey in his late twenties.

The Dutch Churches in America achieved their independence in 1770 as a result of a dispute concerning the authority of the *Classis* in Amsterdam. A constitution was drawn up in 1792 and in 1819 the Church was incorporated as the Reformed Dutch Protestant Church, taking its present name in 1867. The Church grew and spread through the states of New York and New Jersey and by the middle of the nineteenth century, with the arrival of a new wave of Dutch immigrants, expanded into other areas including Michigan, Iowa and South Dakota.

Doctrinally, the Church, which is best described as being conservative, affirms the *Belgic Confession* (1561), the *Heidelberg Catechism* (1563) and the *Canons of the Synod of Dort* (1618–19). The polity of the Church is presbyterian, with the highest authority being the annual general synod with a 62-member executive committee functioning between successive synods. These synods receive delegates from all of the subsidiary local governing bodies and these are distributed amongst some eight regional synods and made up of both lay and clerical representatives. Each local church's governing body is the consistory, made up of elders, deacons and a pastor, the latter always acting as the president of his local consistory.

The Church, with its headquarters in New York, is very active in mission work amongst Native American communities and in providing social services, especially amongst the urban poor and immigrant peoples throughout the USA. It is also heavily committed to a foreign mission programme, which extends to the Far East, the Middle East and Africa, as well as throughout Central America and parts of South America, particularly Venezuela and Ecuador.

REFORMED CHURCH IN HUNGARY

Following the defeat of the Hungarians by the Turks at the battle of Mohacs in 1526 many important and influential ROMAN CATHOLIC clergy, along with the king, were killed and the Roman Catholic inhabitants in Hungary became leaderless. The occupying Turks favoured the protestants against the Roman Catholics and PROTESTANT influence made itself felt in the country, in the form of LUTHERANISM. At the start of the sixteenth century, Hungarian theology students returning from their studies in Wittenberg brought Luther's teachings with them; foremost amongst these was Matthias Biro of Deva, known as Devay, called the *Hungarian Luther*, and Stephen Kis of Szeged. In the wake of their return the writings of Martin Luther became influential.

Towards the end of the sixteenth century, the Reformation movement in Hungary gained momentum, following the acceptance of the *Augsburg Confession* (1545), the *Lutheran Catechism* (1550) and the *Second Helvetic Confession* (1567). By the end of that century most Hungarians were protestant, mostly members of the REFORMED faith; the Jesuits later effected only a partial re-conversion of the population to Roman Catholicism. The development of protestantism in Hungary and Transylvania was divided along racial lines, with Lutheranism being adopted by the German, Slavic and some Magyar peoples; whilst other Magyars espoused the Reformed faith. By the close of the eighteenth century, with the protestant population of Hungary reduced to around one-third of the total, both the Lutheran and the Reformed Churches were reorganized, with the laity assuming control.

In worship, members of the Church may attend services in both the morning and evening. Two ordinances are observed, those of baptism, for both infants and adults, and the Lord's Supper. The presbytery and pastors of a local church are elected by its congregation and these local churches are divided into dioceses on a regional basis and led by curators to form a church district, presided over by a bishop and the church district curator. Every pastor, male or female, is eligible to be elected to the post of bishop after ten years of service. A synod meets annually and is the principal legislative and executive body of the Church, controlling dogma, the establishment of new church districts, the constitution and governing rules of the Church.

Education for future pastors is provided through a six-year course in Budapest, interspersed with practical experience in a congregation. Charitable institutions have been set up, which are concerned with the welfare of the handicapped, the aged, pensioners and single-parent families, together with social services that care for the deaf, the blind and those suffering from leprosy; the Church also provides marriage and family counselling and a prison mission.

The headquarters of the Reformed Church of Hungary is in Budapest, from where it serves 1,133 congregations with around 1.6 million members. Close fraternal relationships are maintained with co-religionists living abroad.

REFORMED CHURCH IN ZAMBIA

Formed in (present-day) Zambia in 1899, this Church now cares for around 250,000 members, most of whom are members of the Chewa or Nyanja-speaking people, from its headquarters in Lusaka. The Church has provision for one synod meeting every four years, with six delegates attending from each of the eleven presbyteries into which the local congregations are divided. Doctrinally, the Church has affirmed the *Belgic Confession* (1561), the *Heidelberg Catechism* (1563) and the *Canons of the Synod of Dort* (1618–19).

In association with the DUTCH REFORMED CHURCH Missions of South Africa, the Reformed Church in Zambia is involved in a programme to improve the basic education of rural children through a system of community-managed primary schools that provide opportunities for children without access to the normal government education services. Training for future clergy is provided at the Justo Mwale Theological College in Lusaka. Until August 2000 the Church ordained only men, but the provision of women ministers has now been accepted.

REFORMED CHURCH IN ZIMBABWE

This Church, which is within the REFORMED tradition, was founded in 1891. From its headquarters in Masvingo, due east from Bulawayo, it supervises the work of its ministers and evangelists, who serve an adult membership of about 85,000. Doctrinally, the Church adheres to the *Belgic Confession* (1561), the *Heidelberg Catechism* (1563) and the *Canons of the Synod of Dort of* (1618–19). Ministerial training is provided at the Murray Training College in Masvingo.

Delegates from both clergy and the laity meet in a synod that is held every two years. The main focus of the Church's work at present is concerned with church growth. In 1995 a new centre was opened in Dete, south of Victoria Falls, with another opening the following year in Binga, amongst the Tonga people, and there are plans to evangelize amongst the Shonganese and Vhenda people in the south of the country.

❖ African Reformed Church in Zimbabwe

REFORMED CHURCH OF CHRIST IN NIGERIA

This Church, which functions within the REFORMED tradition, evolved from the Christian Reformed Church of Nigeria when a group of believers from the Kuteb tribe left that Church; the parent Church had been organized by the Sudan United Missions and was founded in 1951.

The Reformed Church of Christ in Nigeria (RCCV) was formed in 1973 and from its headquarters in Takim, Taraba state, it provides leadership for its 277,000 adult members with the primary concern of combating the poverty of the people. A general church council meets regularly twice a year to legislate and approve various outreach programmes. Doctrinally, the Church has adopted the *Belgic Confession* (1561), the *Heidelberg Catechism* (1563) and the *Canons of the Synod of Dort* (1618–19), as well as the texts of the Nicene and Athanasian Creeds. Ministerial training is provided in the Veenstra Bible College – Lupwe, at Takum, north-east of Enugu and near Nigeria's border with Cameroon.

REFORMED CHURCH OF FRANCE

The Reformed Church of France was organized in 1938 through the merger of several REFORMED groups that had developed in the country during and after the Protestant Reformation in the sixteenth century. During the early part of that century, LUTHERANISM and CALVINISM were growing in a country that was ready for, and receptive to new ideas. The French Humanists had expressed an interest in, and enthusiasm for, biblical studies and the mathematician and priest, Lefèvre d'Étaples (1455–1536), favoured by both kings Louis XII (1498–1515) and Francis I (1515–47), had urged that religion should be brought back to its primitive purity.

Lefèvre and others, who had Lutheran and Humanist tendencies, were teaching at Meaux, where Bishop Guillaume Briconnet (1470–1534) had created an atmosphere that was sympathetic to Humanist and mystical ideas. They also had the support of Francis I's sister, Margaret of Valois, who was strongly impressed by both Luther and Calvin, although she remained a member of the ROMAN CATHOLIC CHURCH. Francis I's attitude to the PROTESTANTS depended upon his mercurial international policy and although he was ready to persecute them when the time was thought expedient, the king became more moderate in his dealings with them when he wanted to gain the friendship of the German princes.

In 1555, after a period of considerable repression by the authorities, Calvinists were able to organize themselves in protestant congregations throughout France. A national synod of Reformed Churches was created in Paris in 1559, by which time there were some 72 Reformed Churches in France, a number which had swelled to 2,000 two years later. The wars of religion between the HUGUENOTS and Roman Catholics were to follow, during which time the St Bartholomew's Day massacre (1572) occurred, leading to further war. In 1589, with the accession of the Huguenot leader, Henry of Navarre, as Henry IV of France, whose mother, Margaret of Valois, had shown great sympathy with the protestant position, matters came before Pope Sixtus V. The Pope declared that if he remained a protestant, Henry would never reign in France but, if he abjured his heresy, he could reign as a Roman Catholic monarch. Henry accepted, observing that 'Paris was worth a Mass'. Henry promulgated the Edict of Nantes in 1598, which guaranteed freedom of religion to all protestants, but this respite was short-lived. Louis XIV (1643–1715) revoked the Edict of Nantes in 1685 and severe restrictions were again imposed and followed by a further period of repression. This encouraged mass emigration, with thousands of French protestants going to Germany, Holland, England, Switzerland and America.

Protestants remained a persecuted minority in the country until the French Revolution of 1789, which saw the restoration of full rights to protestant communities. By 1801, Napoleon had negotiated a concordat with the Vatican that recognized Roman Catholicism as the religion of the majority in France, and the following year this recognition was extended to the Lutheran and Reformed Churches. Schisms broke out between the different factions of the protestant Church after 1848, with some insisting upon loyalty to the traditional confessions of faith and others arguing for a more liberal approach, resentful of the imposition of these confessions.

For protestants, as well as for Roman Catholics, there was a separation of church and state in 1905. As a result, all Churches had to provide for their own support and efforts were made to unite the Reformed Churches. After some negotiations between the different synods a common declaration of faith was voted for in 1936 and the Reformed Church of France was organized in 1938.

The Reformed and Lutheran Churches of Alsace-Lorraine remain a special case and are supported by the French state. At the time of the 1905 regulation concerning the separation of church and state, the territory of Alsace-Lorraine was annexed to Germany and the laws did not apply. The area was returned to France in 1918.

REFORMED CHURCHES (LIBERATED)

During the Second World War a schism, known as *Vrijmaking*, or Liberation, broke out in the Reformed Churches in the Netherlands (GKN) concerning several doctrinal issues including the nature of grace and baptismal regeneration. The GKN aimed to settle these questions by resorting to making and issuing doctrinal statements.

This solution did not appeal to many members of the Church and several congregations followed a church minister, Professor K. Schilder (1890–1952) in making their objections heard. Consequently Schilder was suspended from the ministry of the GKN. The congregations, seeking to liberate themselves from what were termed 'synodal power structures', re-formed themselves in 1944 as the Reformed Churches (Liberated), or the (GK(V).

In 1965 this Church also endured its own schism on account of what was perceived as its insistence that it was the only true Church in the Netherlands, as well as its strict insistence on the affirmation of the confessional statements of the Church. Objections were also voiced concerning the Church's support of its own political party. The schism resulted in the formation of the Netherlands Reformed Churches (NGK).

The Church is administered through a general synod, which meets triennially, and a series of interim provincial synods, classes and communities. The Church practises both infant and believer's baptism and celebrates the Lord's Supper four times a year. Women are not ordained to the ministry in this Church. The Church has 270 congregations and an adult membership of some 62,000, with headquarters at Zwolle. It works in close collaboration with other Reformed Churches and is involved in missionary work in Indonesia, South Africa, Brazil and Ukraine.

REFORMED CHURCHES IN THE NETHERLANDS

Formed in 1892 in Amsterdam as a result of schisms, the Reformed Churches in the Netherlands (GKN) was established through division from the Dutch Reformed Church (NHL). This schism was led by Abraham Kuyper (1837–1920), who had started the Doleantie congregations which united with most of those independent congregations that did not want to form the union that later became the Christian Reformed Churches in the Netherlands (CGKN). The future was not peaceful and the Church itself suffered from two schisms, the first in 1926 over the interpretation of Genesis 2 and 3; this led to a group of congregations becoming independent before uniting with the Netherlands Reformed Church in 1945. The second schism took place in 1944 and was led by Professor K. Schilder. This resulted in the formation of the Reformed Churches (Liberated). There was further discontent in the years following the Second World War over the growing liberalism within the Church and, to counter these influences from within, two groups were formed, Scripture and Witness and Confessional Reformed Consultation. Moves towards restoring a union with the Netherlands Reformed Church (NHK) were started in 1973 when a joint synod was held and this resulted in a merging process, starting in 1995, to form part of what will in the future become the United Protestant Church in the Netherlands.

Doctrinally, the Church affirms the three early Christian creeds, Apostles', Nicene and Athanasian, as well as the *Belgic Confession* (1561), the *Heidelberg Catechism* (1563) and the *Canons of the Synod of Dort* (1618–19). There is both infant and adult baptism and the Lord's Supper is celebrated either weekly, or six times a year. Women may be ordained to the ministry of this Church, whose ordinands receive their training at the Theological University at Kamper and in the theological faculty of the Free University of Amsterdam. The headquarters of the Church is at Leusden.

REFORMED CONGREGATIONS

There were some congregations in the Netherlands that remained independent following the 1834 *Afscheiding*, or Separation, from the DUTCH REFORMED CHURCH. Led by Pastor L. G. C. Ledeboer they came to be known as Ledeboer Congregations, or the Reformed Congregations under the Cross. It was not until 1907 that the Reverend G. H. Kersten (1892–1948) was able to unite 35 of these independent congregations into what came to be known as the Reformed Congregations (CG).

The Church places considerable emphasis upon personal conversion and affirms the three early Christian creeds, the Apostles', Nicene and Athanasian, the *Belgic Confession* (1561), the *Heidelberg Catechism* (1563) and the *Canons of the Synod of Dort* (1618–19). Church polity is congregational and the Church practises baptism of both infants and adults, and celebrates the Lord's Supper four times a year. Women are not ordained to the ministry in this Church, which has its headquarters at Woerden.

REFORMED EPISCOPAL CHURCH

The Reformed Episcopal Church arose in the USA in 1873 through a schism from the Protestant Episcopal Church when its Assistant Bishop of Kentucky, George David Cummins (1822–75), resigned his post as a protest against what he saw as the growing ritualism of the Church and in the face of criticism that he received when he participated in a Communion service with the Presbyterians in New York.

The growth of ritualist tendencies in the Protestant Episcopal Church had followed in the wake of the bishop of North Carolina's defection to the ROMAN CATHOLIC CHURCH, which signalled a similar move by many clergy and laity and left behind some High Churchmen whose influence began to grow. This led to the discomfort of some evangelical churchmen, who followed Bishop Cummins into the Reformed Episcopal Church; the name was chosen by the founder members who desired that the Church should 'reform itself around the Protestant principles of Sola Scriptura and Sole Fide'.

An initial 8 clergy and 20 laity formed the new denomination adopting the 1785 Prayer Book, a revision of the *Book of Common Prayer* for use in English colonies. A declaration of principles, formulated by the Reverend William Muhlenberg who was not himself a member of the group, was presented by Bishop Cummins to the founding members of the Church for adoption. Its four principles, which outline the theological position of the Reformed Episcopal Church, are:

1 A statement concerning the supreme authority of holy scripture, the Apostles' creed, in which the Nicene and Athanasian creeds both find their àffirmations, the recognition of the sacraments of baptism and the Lord's Supper, and the Church's doctrine of grace as set out in the *Thirty-Nine Articles of Religion*.

2 A declaration about church government, especially the role of the episcopate that is strongly reminiscent of the pronouncements of Richard Hooker (1554–1600).

3 A statement about liturgical worship and the use of the distinctively American 1785 Prayer Book, which did not provide for prayers for the British monarch.

4 A statement that identifies those beliefs and practices considered contrary to God's word; this leads to the rejection of the belief that the sacraments, in and of themselves, convey salvation apart from faith.

The principles reject the view that the Communion table is an altar, that Christ is present in the elements of the bread and wine in the Communion service and that regeneration is inseparably connected with baptism. The Church recognizes the episcopal ordering of clergy by a laying on of hands. While rejecting the doctrine of apostolic succession, it accepts historic succession and affirms the priesthood of all believers.

The Reformed Episcopal Church currently conducts foreign missions in India, Brazil, Uganda and Germany and has parishes throughout the USA as well as in Canada and England. Its clergy are trained in the USA, at seminaries in Philadelphia and South Carolina.

REFORMED MENNONITE CHURCH

A small American Church founded in 1812 and at one time led by Francis Herr, who had been expelled from the Mennonite Church, and subsequently by his son, John. John Herr vigorously attacked what he saw as the corruption of the Mennonite Church by the outside world and insisted upon a stricter enforcement of Mennonite discipline. The Reformed Mennonite Church rigidly observes the *ban* on those who violate its discipline, and members practice avoidance, or *shunning*, a discontinuation of fellowship, and even of conversation, with erring members who have been excommunicated by the Church, even when these are family members.

Church members wear simple, plain clothing and insist on the same plain surroundings in their daily lives. They are pacifist in their attitude to war and do not take part in any missionary or educational work. The church groups are to be found mainly in south-eastern Pennsylvania, but there are a few hundred members living in Canada.

REFORMED METHODIST CHURCH

A now-defunct American Church, since it merged with the Churches of Christ in Christian Union of Circleville, Ohio, in 1952 and became that Church's north-eastern district. The Reformed Methodist Church broke away from the Methodist Episcopal Church (MEC) in 1814 when a group of Methodists in Readsborough, Vermont, led by a local preacher named Pliny Brett, objected to the episcopal polity of the MEC; they formed their first conference in 1814 when they accepted the Wesleyan *Twenty-Five Articles of Religion* (published in 1784) and opted for a more democratic form of church government. The conference finally decided in favour of a congregational polity, with its focus upon the local church, which was to have the authority to ordain its own elders and select its own ministers.

REFORMED METHODIST UNION EPISCOPAL CHURCH

This American Church, with its headquarters in Charleston, South Carolina, was organized in 1885 by members of the AFRICAN METHODIST EPISCOPAL CHURCH who were dissatisfied about the selection of ministerial delegates for the general conference of the Church.

The Reverend William E. Johnson was elected as the first president of the new Church. It was apparent from the beginning that their conference did not at first approve of an episcopal polity, but this disapproval gradually reversed and by the time of the death of William Johnson the Church had agreed upon this form of government. This was put into operation by inviting Bishop Peter F. Stevens, of the REFORMED EPISCOPAL CHURCH, to consecrate E. Russell Middleton as the Church's first bishop. Bishop Middleton did not consecrate a successor and upon his death the next bishop was consecrated by the laying on of hands of seven elders of the Church.

The doctrinal stand adopted by the Church is fully within the Methodist Episcopal tradition. Members meet regularly for classes, which are small gatherings for discussion, prayer and Bible study. The Church also makes use of *Love Feasts*, informal gatherings centred on the service of the Lord's Supper that include a light meal, some singing and a talk by the celebrating minister. The Church remains small in number, with some 3,500 members distributed between 17 congregations.

REFORMED PRESBYTERIAN CHURCH – EVANGELICAL SYNOD

The Reformed Presbyterian Church – Evangelical Synod, came into existence in 1965 as a result of a union between the EVANGELICAL PRESBYTERIAN CHURCH and the REFORMED PRESBYTERIAN CHURCH IN NORTH AMERICA (GENERAL SYNOD), the latter derived from the *New Lights* group of the Reformed Presbyterian Church. The Church, which was strongly opposed to modernism and worldliness, had a missionary outreach programme known as the World Presbyterian Missions. In 1967 it was approached for support by a female missionary who was working amongst the Noongar Aborigines in the Brookton area of Perth, Western Australia. The Church sent missionaries into the area and before long several congregations had been formed and a presbytery established; missionary work in Australia was also undertaken in Brisbane, Queensland, and more recently, under its new identity, in the western suburbs of Sydney, New South Wales, where more congregations have been formed. These congregations, originally dominated by American ministers, are now mostly run by Australian clergy who have organized themselves and their congregations as the Westminster Presbyterian Church. Missionary work was also undertaken in India. In 1982 this Church merged with the PRESBYTERIAN CHURCH IN AMERICA and does not now exist under this title.

REFORMED PRESBYTERIAN CHURCH IN NORTH AMERICA (GENERAL SYNOD)

This Church must not be confused with the REFORMED PRESBYTERIAN CHURCH OF NORTH AMERICA.

When the Reformed Presbyterian Church was split, in 1833, into the New Lights and the Old Lights, over the issue of whether members could participate in civic affairs, one of the seceding groups adopted the title of the Reformed Presbyterian Church in North America (General Synod). Members of this group were permitted to take part in civic affairs, to vote and hold office. The Church held to the WESTMINSTER CONFESSION *of Faith* and the *Small* and *Larger Catechisms*, and allowed the use of instrumental music in the singing of hymns and psalms. There was a merger between the Church and the EVANGELICAL PRESBYTERIAN CHURCH which formed the REFORMED PRESBYTERIAN CHURCH – EVANGELICAL SYNOD and this took part in the 1982 merger which formed the PRESBYTERIAN CHURCH IN AMERICA.

Those who opposed participation in civic affairs at the time of the 1833 split formed the Reformed Presbyterian Church of North America.

REFORMED PRESBYTERIAN CHURCH OF IRELAND

The origins of the Reformed Presbyterian Church of Ireland are to be found in the seventeenth century with the coming to Ulster of the Scottish COVENANTERS. Covenanters were those Scottish Presbyterians who had signed covenants that defended the REFORMED faith and rejected the imposition of episcopacy; of particular importance were those covenants signed in 1638, and the *Solemn League and Covenant* of 1643. A century later, in 1763, a Reformed Presbytery was established, and a synod of the Church was eventually formed in 1811.

The distribution of the population of Reformed Presbyterians, who are still often known as Covenanters, had generally followed the pattern of the original Scottish settlements, with most congregations to be found in the counties of Antrim, Londonderry and Down. The members of the Church are largely from rural areas, but there has been a recent development amongst the urban dwellers of greater Belfast that has resulted in the formation of new congregations. Today, there are 40 congregations, with over 2,500 members, distributed not only in Northern Ireland but also in the counties of Monaghan and Donegal in the Republic of Ireland.

The doctrinal position of the Church is based upon the Bible, which is believed to be the inspired and inerrant word of God. Members also affirm the *WESTMINSTER CONFESSION of Faith*, the *Larger* and *Small Catechisms* and *The Testimony*, a more recent document that expands the Church's teachings. Two sacraments, those of baptism and the Lord's Supper, are recognized. Baptism is administered to an adult, or to a believer's child, by pouring, immersion or aspersion of water. The Lord's Supper may be celebrated from two to four times a year. Open Communion is practised, allowing Christians from other denominations that are known to the presiding elder, to be admitted.

The service of worship usually takes the form of preaching and reading from the Bible, with psalms sung according to the *Scottish Metrical Psalter*, unaccompanied by any form of musical instrument since it is believed that nothing should be introduced into the service that has not been authorized by the Bible. This Psalter is currently under revision.

The polity of the Church is presbyterian, with each congregation led by an elder. Elders are chosen for this work by the laity and together form a session, which sends delegates to the regular meetings of the highest court of the Church, the presbytery; these presbyteries, in turn, meet together in a synod. Evangelism in the immediate community and abroad is encouraged, as are close relations with the Reformed Presbyterian Churches in Scotland, North America, Australia, Japan and Cyprus. The Church is a constituent member of the International Conference of Reformed Churches. Ecumenical contact with ROMAN CATHOLICS, however, is actively boycotted and discouraged.

REFORMED PRESBYTERIAN CHURCH OF NORTH AMERICA

COVENANTERS from Scotland who, by 1782, had formed a union with some immigrant Scottish Seceders, who had earlier formed themselves into the Associate Presbyterian Church, established this Church in America. The result of this union was the establishment of the Associate Reformed Presbyterian Church, but some of the members of the Reformed Presbyterian Church would not join the union. They reorganized themselves under the name of the Reformed Presbytery and by 1809 had formed a synod; by 1833 this had split into two major groups, the *New Lights* and the *Old Lights*. The issue at question was whether members should vote, or take part in public affairs. The *Old Lights* group was opposed to such participation, but the *New Lights* were in favour of it. The Reformed Presbyterian Church of North America is the descendant of the *Old Lights* group.

The polity of the Church is presbyterian and there is provision for an annual synod. The *WESTMINSTER CONFESSION of Faith* is subscribed to and worship is restricted to readings from the Bible and sermons, which may arise from these readings, extempore prayers and hymns, the latter restricted to the singing of unaccompanied psalms. A policy of closed communion is observed and members may not join any secret societies. Foreign mission work is carried on in Cyprus and Japan. The headquarters of the Church, which is in Pittsburgh, Pennsylvania, oversees the work of 68 congregations and a membership of nearly 4,000 adult believers.

REFORMED PRESBYTERIAN CHURCH OF SCOTLAND

This small body of PRESBYTERIANS at present has 4 congregations and around 200 committed members. The Church, which had its origins in Scotland and derives from the COVENANTERS, includes those Presbyterians who were unwilling to accept the settlement of 1600, which established the CHURCH OF SCOTLAND. The Reverend John MacMillan was the only minister until 1706, but the arrival of a second minister in 1743 enabled the group to constitute a presbytery. There was then an increase in numbers and in 1811 this allowed the group to form a synod. A split developed within the Church in 1863, and in 1876 a large proportion of the membership left to join the FREE CHURCH OF SCOTLAND.

The Church holds to a simple form of worship with psalms sung without any musical accompaniment. Participation in any political activity is shunned and the joining of any secret societies prohibited. Doctrinally, the members affirm the *WESTMINSTER CONFESSION of Faith* and the *Larger* and *Small Catechisms*; the polity of the Church is presbyterian.

The Reformed Presbyterian Churches of both Scotland and Ireland united for missionary work, which began in Syria in

1871 and since 1963 has been concentrated mainly in Ethiopia.

REFORMED PRESBYTERIAN CHURCH OF SOUTH AFRICA

The Reformed Presbyterian Church of South Africa, whose congregation is entirely black and composed of Xhosa, Zulu and Sotho people, was formerly known as the BANTU PRESBYTERIAN CHURCH.

The PRESBYTERIAN presence started in the country as a CALVINIST Society that had been formed by Presbyterian soldiers of the Argyll and Sutherland Highlanders Regiment who were stationed in Cape Town as an occupying force in 1806. The first minister of the Church, George Thom, arrived in Cape Town from Scotland in 1812, while he was en route to India. Thom decided to spend some time ministering to the troops and a congregation was established. Two years later the Regiment left Cape Town, seriously reducing the congregation. George Thom resigned to return to his original mission. The Glasgow Missionary Society (GMS) then sent two of its workers, led by John Bennie and William Thomson, to the eastern frontier and by 1824 a mission station, Loverdale, had been established at Incehra. The mission station was to gain a fine reputation for its extensive educational and community development programmes, which aimed to create a homogenous society. Growing numbers of Presbyterians now entering the country re-established the Cape Town congregation and in 1827 the first church, St Andrew's, was built and received its first minister, John Adamson, from Scotland, who was to work there until 1841.

There was a division within the GMS in 1837 over the issue of whether the funding of its work should be sought from the state or from voluntary sources. Further divisions followed and by the close of the nineteenth century some of the presbyteries came under the control of the FREE CHURCH OF SCOTLAND, while others became the responsibility of the UNITED PRESBYTERIAN CHURCH (SCOTLAND). A proposed union, which had been first planned in 1895, brought some, but not all, of the divided presbyteries into the General Assembly of the Presbyterian Church of South [later Southern] Africa (PCSA) and the Reverend John Smith was elected as its moderator in Durban. The change of name in the Church's title, from *South* to *Southern*, was motivated by the expansion of the work the Church had undertaken, which extended into countries north of the South African border.

A merger of those remaining presbyteries that had not become part of the PCSA led to the formation, in August 1923, of the Bantu Presbyterian Church of South Africa. In 1978, in line with changes that had occurred in South Africa, the name *Bantu* was dropped in favour of *Reformed*, giving the Church its present title. In 1994 the Church started unity talks with the PCSA and a draft *Basis of Union* was adopted in 1998. The first assembly was held in Port Elizabeth in September 1999 when the new Uniting Presbyterian Church of South Africa was formed.

Doctrinally, the Church affirms the Trinity, the scriptures as the word of God, the texts of the Apostles' and Nicene Creeds, the *WESTMINSTER CONFESSION of Faith* and the *Twenty-Four Articles of the Faith* of the Presbyterian Church in Southern Africa, with its appendix. The Church also affirms the *Declaration of*

Faith for the Church in South Africa of the PCSA.

REFORMED ZION UNION APOSTOLIC CHURCH

This American Church, which was formerly known as the Zion Union Apostolic Church, came into existence as a black METHODIST Church at Boydton, Virginia, in 1869, formed by those who were unhappy about the discrimination they felt they were subjected to by fellow Methodists in white congregations and who wanted to form a religious organization that was dedicated to effecting Christian unity.

In this aim they were encouraged by Elder John Howell of the AFRICAN METHODIST EPISCOPAL ZION CHURCH of New York, who was elected as the first president of the new Church, then known as the Zion Union Apostolic Church, but in 1874 dissatisfaction and disruption occurred over the issue of Howell's election as bishop-for-life. In 1881–2, the Church was reorganized under its present name and a presidency of four years' tenure was agreed upon; in the meantime, John Howell had resigned from the Church.

The doctrinal position is fully Methodist and the legislative authority of the Church is based in the general conference, which meets every four years. In recent times there has been a move to revive the idea of lifelong tenure for bishops of the Church. The headquarters of the Church is in South Hill, Virginia, from where it oversees 40 congregations, with some 8,000 adult members.

REGULAR BAPTISTS

Baptists first went from England to America in the mid-seventeenth century and some of the first churches were formed in Rhode Island; before the end of the century the Pennepack church in Philadelphia had been opened. By the start of the eighteenth century, the first Baptist Association, known as the Philadelphia Association, had been formed, whose task it was to act as a disciplining body for the regulation of the clergy. This association adopted the *London Confession of Particular Baptists* (1644). The PARTICULAR BAPTISTS were CALVINISTIC in their theology, insisting upon adult baptism by immersion and calling for complete church freedom from the state.

The revivalism associated with the *Great Awakening* in America, a series of revival programmes instituted between 1725 and 1760, introduced one of the outstanding evangelists of the time, George Whitefield (1714–70). Whitefield travelled from England to conduct a tour of the American colonies that was to create divisions in the ranks of Presbyterians and Baptists alike. The Baptists divided into the Separate and the Regular Baptists. The Regular Baptists, who were also known as the *Old Lights*, were very distrustful of this revivalism and its emotional fervour. The Separate Baptists, who were also known as *New Lights*, insisted, on the other hand, that anyone seeking membership of their body must have been *born again*, or regenerated in the faith.

Doctrinally, the Regular Baptists do not insist upon an overall *Confession of Faith* for all, but many hold to a view of salvation that is generally ARMINIAN, believing that salvation is open to all who accept the gospel and its message by exercise of their own free will; some hold to a more Calvinistic position that suggests that the number and identity of those who will be saved, the *elect*, have been predetermined. In 1894 there was a dispute over predestination that led to secession by church members, some of whom formed an association which holds firmly to the Calvinist view and these are now known as Regular Baptists (Predestinarian).

Regular Baptists affirm the Trinity and accept the Bible as the word of God. They practice the two ordinances of believer's baptism, by immersion, and the Lord's Supper, which is closed to non-church members. The polity of the Church is ultra-congregational to the extent that there is no central headquarters and local churches organize the work of their congregations. The Church is well represented in North Carolina, Virginia, West Virginia and Kentucky but is also to be found distributed elsewhere in the USA.

RELIEF CHURCH

This Church, which no longer exists, was founded in Scotland in 1761 by Thomas Gillespie (1708–74). Gillespie was a minister of the parish of Inverkeithing, on the Firth of Forth just north of the present Forth road bridge, but he was deposed by the general assembly of the CHURCH OF SCOTLAND because he supported the town council, the Kirk Session and members of his parish in their protest against the patron's choice and imposition of a minister contrary to the wish of the parish.

As a result, Gillespie, his congregation and two other ministers left the Church and founded the Relief Church, which took a keen interest in missionary work. It observed a policy of open communion with all Christians who presented themselves. By 1847, the Relief Church agreed to form a union with the UNITED SECESSION CHURCH to form the United Presbyterian Church (UPC). In 1900, the UPC joined with the FREE CHURCH OF SCOTLAND to form the UNITED FREE CHURCH OF SCOTLAND.

RELIGIOUS SOCIETY OF FRIENDS

The Religious Society of Friends, better known to many as the Quakers, is a body of PROTESTANT Christians that originated in England in the seventeenth century under the leadership of George Fox (1624–91). Fox had started his working life apprenticed at age 12 to a shoemaker, but disillusioned with his religious life and that of his PURITAN neighbours, he gave up worldly concerns in search of enlightenment. It was not until 1646 that he discovered the Inner Voice (or Life), based upon the description given in John 1:9: 'the true light that enlightens every man was coming into the world', which George Fox believed was available to all, regardless of creed.

Fox began to preach and to teach this view as he travelled on foot around northern England, soon attracting followers who were known as *Children of Truth* or *Children of Light*. His followers were also called *Friends*, the name deriving from John 15:14: 'You are my friends if you do what I command you.' Fox's followers not only refused to attend church, but also insisted on freedom of speech, assembly and worship. They also refused to take oaths in law courts, or go to war, and did not recognize any distinction between the genders, or the social classes. Fox maintained that intermediaries, such as priests and the sacraments, interrupted the direct relationship that should exist between Christ and his followers. By 1667 the group had become organized into a system of monthly, quarterly and yearly meetings. As a result of what were regarded by some as negative attitudes to church custom, George Fox became the object of public hostility. He was arrested and imprisoned on no fewer than eight occasions between 1649 and 1673, but was not stopped in his endeavour. He travelled widely, to Ireland, North America and the Caribbean colonies as well as to the Netherlands and other parts of northern Europe. In the colonies of America the first groups of Quakers were organized in Rhode Island, North Carolina, Pennsylvania and New Jersey. Their resistance to the religious laws of the sixteenth century in Europe had led many to emigrate to the American colonies where a Quaker, William Penn (1644–1718), had founded Pennsylvania as a 'holy experiment in religious toleration'. Penn had become a Quaker after meeting George Fox and being impressed by the latter's determination in the face of persecution.

Members of the Religious Society of Friends believe that the Bible is not the only source of revelation, which is continued between the believer and the divine Spirit, but it is viewed as the source-book of the Quaker faith. In general, Quakers do not observe a fixed, or programmed, form of worship, although there are many who do so and conduct worship services using hymns, extempore prayers, Bible readings and a sermon given by the minister. The unprogrammed services consist in the group sitting quietly until the Spirit moves a member to speak. It is not unusual in these services for none to be so called and the members just to sit quietly, intent on their own meditations. Quakers hold to a belief in the Trinity, salvation by faith and baptism of the Holy Spirit.

The group is served by various church officers, including elders and ministers, who are chosen for their ability to lead in spiritual matters, but this in no way diminishes the Quaker belief in the priesthood of all believers. The original pattern of monthly, quarterly and yearly meetings is maintained. Quakers enjoy a fine reputation for their humanitarian aid, especially in war zones and disaster areas. In times of war, despite the fact that most are pacifists, many Quakers have volunteered to serve in the ambulance corps and provide relief services by way of gifts of money, clothing, bedding and any other material support that may be needed.

There have been some important divisions within the group. The HICKSITE QUAKERS in America, led by Elias Hicks (1748–1830), separated in 1827 and are now known as The Friends General Conference. Another schismatic group was the Wilburites, or Conservative Friends, led by the evangelical Quaker minister John Gurney (1788–1847), the brother of the prison reformer Elizabeth Fry, and John Wilbur from Rhode Island, which separated in 1845. There was also another group, now defunct, known as the Primitives, which separated in 1861.

The term 'Quaker' was applied to the group from 1650, when George Fox told a certain Justice Bennet to 'tremble at the Lord's Name', to which the Justice replied derisively, calling Fox a *quaker*. The name is also an old term applied to those given to religious ecstasy. Notable Quakers have included John Woolman (1720–72), who was committed to the abolition of slavery, Lucretia Mott (1793–1880) and Susan Anthony (1820–1906), who were both concerned with the question of female suffrage, and Elizabeth

Fry (1780–1845), renowned for her work in prison reform.

❖ Quakers; Society of Friends; The Friends

RENOVATED CHURCH

Strictly speaking, the Renovated Church is not a denomination but was a federation of several reformist groups in Russia that took over the central administration of the RUSSIAN ORTHODOX CHURCH *in 1922 and controlled many of the religious institutions of the Soviet Union for some twenty years.*

After the advent of the 1917 Russian Revolution, the Russian Orthodox Church felt confident that many long-overdue reforms could be introduced. The patriarchate, that since the time of Peter the Great had been abolished, could now be restored because the dominance of the Tsar over the Church had been removed. It was restored by the Church Council, or *Great Sobor*, in Moscow on 15 August 1917, with Tikhon elected as patriarch. He adopted a policy of total independence, but by 1922 the communist government had unilaterally decided to confiscate all church property.

The patriarch raised an objection, for which he was put under arrest and his offices closed. This was an opportunity for some married priests, led by Alexander Vvedensky and Vladimir Krasnitsky, to organize what was called a Temporary Higher Church Administration that could bring in many changes, particularly for the clergy. This was popular amongst the married clergy whose promotion to the episcopate was until then blocked by canon law that forbade bishops to be married; support was also forthcoming from the Russian intelligentsia and the movement, in turn, received governmental sympathy.

The Renovated Church, having deposed Patriarch Tikhon, was able to establish a synod of bishops, priests and laity and to introduce many reforms, but the Church was in league with the Soviet government and, allegedly, many pro-Tikhon clergy were arrested and executed as counter-revolutionaries. Tikhon was released from his imprisonment after signing a confession that clearly takes a non-political stand. The Renovated Church continued to survive, mainly because of government support. Tikhon died, some say mysteriously, in April 1925. A year earlier the Ecumenical Patriarch of Constantinople had recognized the Church, named as the *Living Church*, as the legal ecclesiastical authority in the Soviet Union.

The activities of this schismatic movement ceased during the Second World War. In September 1943 Stalin permitted the election of Metropolitan Sergius (Starogorodsky) of Nizhni-Novgorod to succeed Patriarch Tikhon. Sergius died the following year and was succeeded, in 1945, by Alexis (Shimansky), Metropolitan of Leningrad. With the exception of Alexander Vvedensky, the leaders of the Renovated Church later repented their action and their congregations returned to the Russian Orthodox Patriarchate.

❖ Living Church; Renewed Church; Renovationist Church

RENOVATED CHURCH OF CHRIST

Fr Michael Collin, a priest of the ROMAN CATHOLIC CHURCH who had been ordained in 1933 in Lille, France, created the Renovated Church of Christ. Within two years of his ordination Michael

Collin had a mystical experience in which he was, apparently, consecrated as a bishop. This was followed by another mystical happening, in 1950, through which Collin claimed that he had received universal jurisdiction, in a manner similar to St Paul's Damascene experience. Collin set up headquarters in a farmhouse at Clemery, Lorraine, which he called *Le Petit Vatican de Marie Co-Rédemptrice* and by 1960 he was declaring that he was Pope Clement XV, whose mission it was to bring about the renovation of the Church; he also claimed to be part of the final secret of Fátima, which at that time had not been revealed. The Roman Catholic Church placed Collin under interdict in 1961. In 1965, in order to ensure that he had a valid apostolic succession that would stand up to scrutiny, Collin received an additional consecration, within the OLD CATHOLIC (CHURCH) Succession of Archbishop Vilatte.

Meanwhile, in the 1940s, a young Canadian member of the Order of St John of God in Montreal, Jean-Gaston Tremblay (later known as Fr John of the Trinity), was also receiving visions in which he was instructed to establish a community of *New Apostles* for the age to come when the present civilization is destroyed. In 1958 a monastery, with a strong Marian emphasis, was organized, its rule of life based on that allegedly given by the Blessed Virgin Mary at La Salette in 1846. Known as the Order of the Magnificat of the Mother of God, there are now mission houses in Canada, the USA, Europe, the West Indies and South America; it has attracted priests, religious brothers and sisters, and disciples, who can be married or single people who live in community, as well as tertiaries, who are men and women who live outside community life but retain firm links with it. Tremblay became aware of Pope Clement XV's mission and activities and he sent a priest to France to live amongst Pope Clement's followers; a little later Pope Clement agreed to ordain Jean-Gaston Tremblay and consecrate him as a bishop.

In 1968, Bishop Tremblay received further visions, claiming that he had been chosen as the universal shepherd of the holy Church and was to adopt the name of Gregory XVII. Although Pope Clement confirmed this revelation, this was not well received by some of his followers. With Clement's death in 1974, the group at Clemery declined. The Canadian community announced that papal authority was now passed to Tremblay as Pope Gregory XVII (*a fact that was apparently ignored when another Pope Gregory XVII, Clement Dominguez Gómez, was crowned pope in Seville, Spain, in 1978 as head of 'The One, Holy, Catholic, Apostolic and Palmarian Church'*).

The Renovated Church of Christ, which is also known as the Catholic Church of the Apostles of the Latter Times, is autonomous and independent. It aims to provide religious teaching for adults and children and to preserve the deposit of faith. It also seeks to return to the purity and simplicity of the early Christian Church and accepts the beliefs and practices of the pre-Vatican II Roman Catholic Church, with the exception of the ordination of women to the priesthood, which the Renovated Church of Christ practises. Considerable emphasis is placed on the importance of the Virgin Mary and upon the practice of the perpetual adoration of the Blessed Sacrament. The Church and the Order are to be found throughout North and Latin

America, the Caribbean, Europe and Africa, with headquarters maintained in Canada, at St Jovité, Quebec.

Pope Clement XV was also responsible for the formation of another group, that of the Church of St Joseph, which had originally been founded by Fr Henry Lovett as part of the Catholic traditionalist movement. In 1970 Lovett met a fellow traditionalist, Fr John Higgins, in Rome and both became convinced of Clement XV's claims. Higgins was consecrated bishop by Clement XV, after which he returned to the USA to head this single, independent parish of St Joseph in Cicero, Illinois. Clement XV died in 1974, since when the faithful of the Cicero parish consider there to be no legitimate pope as they do not accept the validity of the Roman Catholic incumbent in Rome.

❖ Catholic Church of the Apostles of the Latter Times; Renewed Church of Jesus

RE-ORGANIZED CHURCH OF JESUS CHRIST OF LATTER-DAY SAINTS

This must not be confused with the Church of Jesus Christ of Latter-Day Saints, *which has its headquarters in Salt Lake City, Utah.*

This American Church, based in Independence, Missouri, claims to be the original successor of the Church of Jesus Christ of Latter-Day Saints that was founded by Joseph Smith in 1830. Following Smith's death in 1844 there was a time of turmoil when the leadership question was being fought over. Those who held to the principle of succession through lineal descent, as outlined in Joseph Smith's *Book of Doctrine and Covenants*, came together in Beloit, Wisconsin, in 1852 to form the New Organization. The remaining Mormons accepted the leadership of Brigham Young and are now centred in Salt Lake City, Utah. Joseph Smith's son agreed to become president of the New Organization, which was renamed as the Re-organized Church of Jesus Christ of Latter-Day Saints in 1860.

The Church has a more conventionally Christian doctrinal position than the parent Church, and while it still accepts both the *Book of Mormon* and the *Book of Doctrine and Covenants*, both written by Joseph Smith, it does not regard all parts of his *Pearl of Great Price* to be inspired. The Church also affirms the doctrines of faith in God, baptism by immersion and the laying on of hands for the gift of the Holy Spirit and believes that life after death is a system of reward, or punishment, with the reward being graded according to how a person conducted life on earth. Tithing and voluntary contributions are used to maintain the Church in its many avenues of work, such as education and foreign missions, which are conducted in many parts of the world but do not include door-to-door witnessing. Since 1984 it has been possible for women to be ordained to the priesthood within the Church. The Church clearly rejects polygamy, the sealing of marriages for eternity, marriage by proxy to people who are dead, and baptism of the dead.

The policy of an hereditary leader was maintained until the 1990s, when no descendant of Joseph Smith could be found who was willing to accept the role. In 1996 a non-lineal candidate was selected as first president for the first time. This presidency is composed of three high priests and a quorum of twelve apostles. Bishops are appointed to take care of the financial dealings of the

Church but for all questions of doctrine, and for legislative matters, the ultimate church authority is a delegate conference that meets biennially at Independence, Missouri, which is the present headquarters of the Church, from where the church expects Christ to reign for a thousand years after his second coming (REVELATION 20).

REPUBLICAN METHODIST CHURCH

This American Church had a brief career, arising in the eighteenth century as a protest group led by a Methodist minister, the Reverend James O'Kelly of Virginia, who broke away from the METHODIST EPISCOPAL CHURCH in protest against the arbitrary and absolute power of the first American Methodist bishop, Francis Asbury.

The protest was aimed directly at the appointment of ministers to their congregations by the bishop. O'Kelly set up the Republican Methodist Church, which was anti-episcopal and reflected the post-revolutionary wave of democratic thought that was then common in the country. By 1794 O'Kelly and his followers had decided to reject sectarian labels and wanted to be known simply as Christians, and as such they later became absorbed into a group that was known as the CHRISTIAN CHURCH, a body that had been formed in 1833 as a result of a general conference of various Churches calling themselves Christian, which was held in Portsmouth, New Hampshire, in 1819.

The Christian Church was non-creedal and held to the view that the Bible was the sole source of doctrine and faith; open communion and baptism by immersion were both practised. The Christian Church united with the CONGREGATIONAL CHURCH in America in 1931, to form the CONGREGATIONAL AND CHRISTIAN CHURCHES, and some thirty years later this denomination became part of the UNITED CHURCH OF CHRIST, a liberal-minded Church with an active social programme.

RESTORED APOSTOLIC MISSIONARY CHURCH

With the deaths of all but one of the British apostles of the CATHOLIC APOSTOLIC CHURCH during the nineteenth century, a debate arose in 1860 about the appointment of new apostles to fill the posts left by these deaths. The Church excommunicated Bishop Friedrich W. Schwartz of Hamburg in 1862 for proposing that new apostles should be elected and for actually electing a young priest, named Preutz (Preuss), to this position, a calling that was rejected by the remaining British apostles. A schism in the German arm of the Church followed, involving around five hundred of its members. Schwartz was sent to the Netherlands, arriving in Amsterdam in September 1863.

Before his arrival in the city three evangelists, named Nijersam, Hubner and Allihn, had been sent ahead from Hamburg to prepare the way, but falling into financial difficulties they were forced to go, leaving Schwartz to carry on the work alone. The Apostle Schwartz had to contend with considerable opposition, especially from a hostile priest named Voorhoeve who issued a pamphlet condemning Schwartz's work, which by then was believed to include some healings. To make matters worse, further financial difficulties arose. Despite many setbacks a church was nevertheless fashioned out of a disused chicory warehouse (it came to be known as the Chicory Church), which was consecrated in 1874 and officially identified as the Chapel of the Apostolic Mission. Several congregations were established in the Netherlands before Schwartz's death in 1895, and by then the Church had been renamed as the Restored Apostolic Missionary Church; up to this time these congregations were in unity with the Catholic Apostolic Church in Hamburg.

After Schwartz's death, Apostle Fritz Krebs in Hamburg came to the conclusion that he could discern the will of the Spirit and this led to a disagreement within the Dutch congregations about the apostles that had been selected, and a split developed. Those who supported Krebs' discerning became organized as the Restored Apostolic Church in the Unity of the Apostles, while the others became the Restored Apostolic Mission Church, with its headquarters in Amsterdam. This Church now has 10 congregations with a committed membership of around 700 adults.

❖ Restored Apostolic Mission Church

REVELATION 20

Then I saw an angel coming down from Heaven with the key of the abyss and a great chain in his hands. He seized the dragon, that serpent of old, the Devil or Satan, and chained him up for a thousand years; he threw him into the abyss, shutting and sealing it over him, that he should seduce the nations no more till the thousand years were over. After that he must be let loose for a short while.

The second coming of Jesus Christ to earth is interpreted in several ways.

AMILLENNIALISM (also AMILLENARIANISM; AMILLENARIANISTS; AMILLENIALISTS)

Amillennialists do not believe in a millennium at all, but see the teaching in Revelation 20 as referring to the whole period between Christ's ministry on earth and his second coming.

MILLENARIANISM (also MILLENARIANISTS)

A belief in the thousand–year period of time when Christ will reign on earth over a perfect world. This belief is derived from a literal understanding of the passage in Revelation 20.

❖ Chiliasm; Chiliasts

POSTMILLENNIALISM (also POSTMILLENARIANISM; POSTMILLENARIANS; POSTMILLENIALISTS)

A belief that Christ's return to earth will take place after a millennium – a period of one thousand years – during which there will be a restoration of the true Church and worldwide revival; this is seen as a *golden age* on earth, which will be achieved through evangelization.

PREMILLENNIALISM (also PREMILLENARIANISM; PREMILLENARIANS; PREMILLENIALISTS)

A belief that holds that the state of the world is so bad that when Christ returns the dead will rise and that true Christian believers still alive at that time will be caught up into the air to meet him; this is known as the *Rapture*, after which they will reign with Christ on earth for a period of one thousand years.

ROMAN CATHOLIC CHURCH (also ROMAN CATHOLIC; ROMAN CATHOLICISM)

To be Roman Catholic means to be in communion with the Church of Rome and to accept the leadership of the Pope; this applies both to members of the EASTERN CATHOLIC CHURCHES, who are often pejoratively described as Uniats, as well as to western-rite Roman Catholics.

The Roman Catholic Church believes itself to be the Church founded by Jesus Christ, who gave authority to the apostle Peter, who in turn passed on this special ministry and responsibility to successive Bishops of Rome throughout the centuries. This apostolic succession is an unbroken and authoritative transmission of the mission and powers conferred by Christ on St Peter and the apostles, and from them to those who are validly ordained and consecrated in the threefold ministry of bishops, priests and deacons.

The spiritual life of the Church is maintained and nurtured through the seven sacraments, which convey sanctifying grace. These sacraments are baptism, confirmation, penance (or reconciliation), Eucharist (Mass), marriage, ordination and anointing of the sick. This sacramental life of the Church is supplemented by other practices, such as the divine office, devotion to the Blessed Virgin Mary through the recitation of the rosary, veneration of the saints, the stations of the cross and other services such as the benediction of the Blessed Sacrament. The Eucharist (Mass) is the central liturgical rite of the Church and in its celebration the elements of bread and wine are believed to become, by transubstantiation, the body and blood of Christ. The Mass is understood to be a propitiatory and bloodless renewal of the sacrifice on Calvary.

Roman Catholicism, together with Eastern Orthodoxy, affirms the basis of Christian belief and polity to be both scripture and tradition. In the early years of the Church the mysteries of the Trinity and the incarnation had to be determined through the ecumenical councils, which dealt with heresies such as Arianism, Apollinarianism, Nestorianism, Eutychianism, MONOTHELITISM and Iconoclasm.

In the Middle Ages the concerns concentrated upon the relation of God and mankind through grace and the sacraments, after which the Church faced demands for reform in the sixteenth century, prompting the Council of Trent (1545–63) which marked the high point of the Counter-Reformation. The Church then turned its attention to its own structure and government, and to the role of the Blessed Virgin Mary in the economy of salvation, which led to the defining of the dogma of her Immaculate Conception (1854) and of her Assumption (1950); during the First Vatican Council, in 1869–70, the dogma of papal infallibility was declared. More recently, Vatican II has been an occasion for a complete rethinking of the Church and its mission. It was the first time ever that non-Roman Catholic observers (or separated brethren) were invited to attend and this emphasized the ecumenical aim of the Council. Furthermore, the presence of *periti*, or theological experts, as advisers to the council fathers underlined the Church's recognition of new movements of theological thought that had to be addressed and assessed.

Religious life, which in the Middle Ages

had been largely confined to some old Orders of monks, friars, canons and enclosed nuns, has since the Reformation led to a great blossoming of new Orders and congregations devoted to addressing all the needs of humanity. More recently, the encouragement and burgeoning of the lay movements and secular institutes, throughout the Roman Catholic world in particular, has been a response by the Church to the concerns of the world in the twentieth and twenty-first centuries.

ROMANIAN ORTHODOX CHURCH

Romania arose from the Roman province of Dacia, its inhabitants said to be the descendants of the veterans of Trajan. According to some sources St Andrew the apostle preached and evangelized in the country that lay between the Danube and the Black Sea (*Pontus Euxinus*), later called *Dobrudgea* and known from ancient sources as *Scythia*. It is also understood that St Nicetas of Remesiana (*c.* 335 – *c.* 414) was the principal evangelist of the country and that by the fourth century a see had been established at Tomi (now Constanța). The early religious history of Dacia is obscure, but threads of Christianity may have been brought in by convert soldiers, colonists and their slaves who went to Dacia from Rome, and by Christian prisoners brought to the area by the Goths in the third century.

The Bulgarians conquered Romania in the ninth century, bringing Romanian Christianity gradually within the orbit of Constantinople's ecclesiastical control. The practice of worship in the Romanian Church then acquired an eastern character; until this time the liturgical language of the Church had been Latin.

The Reformation of the sixteenth century in Europe saw CALVINISM make great gains amongst both ROMAN CATHOLIC and EASTERN ORTHODOX faithful, but the advances made by PROTESTANTISM were halted at the end of that century when the Austrians drove out the Turks in 1687 and the ROMAN CATHOLIC Jesuits arrived to re-inforce the efforts being made to halt the country's slide into Calvinism. The Church was not granted any acknowledgement in Transylvania in the post-Reformation settlement. By an act of union made in 1698 a proportion of the Romanian Orthodox clergy and laity accepted papal jurisdiction and became Byzantine-rite Catholics.

The Romanian Orthodox Church declared itself to be autocephalous in 1856 and this was recognized by the Ecumenical Patriarch of Constantinople in 1885. The Patriarchate of Romania was established in 1925; its first patriarch, Miron Cristea, died in 1939. The Romanian Orthodox Church appears to have flourished and prospered under communism, but the Romanian Byzantine-rite Catholics were persecuted, forced to worship in Orthodox churches, with many of their own churches handed over to Orthodox clerics, and constantly monitored by the state. New legislation has appeared since the collapse of communism, which guarantees religious freedom and largely releases the Church from state control.

The Romanian Orthodox Church, whose patriarch is known as His Beatitude, provides for clergy training in several seminaries and two university theological institutes with opportunities for existing clergy to extend their education. A vigorous rebuilding and repair programme is currently in progress in the country to remedy the effects of war and neglect endured during the twentieth century. An agreement has now been reached between the Orthodox Church and the Romanian Byzantine-rite Catholics for the return of church property confiscated during communist rule.

ROMANIAN ORTHODOX CHURCH OF AMERICA

This official Romanian Orthodox presence in North America dates from 1929 when the ROMANIAN ORTHODOX CHURCH created a diocese and elected its bishop, Polycarp Morusca, who settled in Grass Lake, Michigan; until the creation of this diocese there had been only two parishes in North America to provide spiritual care for Romanian immigrants. The first of these had been established in Canada, at Regina, Saskatchewan, in 1902, and the second was created in 1904 in the USA, at St Mary's Church in Cleveland, Ohio. The RUSSIAN ORTHODOX CHURCH provided oversight for both of these parishes on behalf of the Romanian Church.

Bishop Morusca left the USA and returned to Romania at the outbreak of the Second World War, but he was forcibly retired by the Romanian authorities and never returned to his American diocese. His place was taken by Bishop Andrei Moldovan, who had been the parish priest at the parish of Akron, Ohio, and who had gone to Romania for the purpose of being consecrated as bishop without first having been elected by the American faithful through a diocesan congress. When he returned to the USA, Bishop Andrei was rejected by as many as 48 parishes. Those that chose to remain within his episcopal jurisdiction constituted themselves as the Romanian Orthodox Missionary Episcopate in the United States, Canada and South America.

The headquarters of the Church is in Detroit, Michigan, from where the 10 parishes, with around 4,000 members in the USA, Canada and Venezuela, are supervised.

❖ Romanian Orthodox Missionary Archdiocese in America & Canada; Romanian Orthodox Missionary Episcopate

ROMANIAN ORTHODOX EPISCOPATE OF AMERICA

Two parishes for Romanian immigrants to Canada and the USA were established at the start of the twentieth century, in Regina, Saskatchewan, and in Cleveland, Ohio. The Romanian Orthodox Church in America burgeoned with the settlement of large numbers of Romanian immigrants who were arriving in North America. A dispute developed when the first bishop returned to Romania and was replaced, in 1950, by Bishop Andrei Moldovan. This election had not been ratified, or endorsed, by any diocesan congress and, as a result of the dispute, 48 of these Romanian parishes left the jurisdiction of the Patriarch of Bucharest. A year later the breakaway group elected Valerian D. Trifa as bishop and he was able to bring the administratively self-governing Romanian Orthodox Episcopate of America under the protection of the Russian Orthodox Greek Catholic Church of America, which is now known as the ORTHODOX CHURCH IN AMERICA. Bishop Trifa retired to Portugal in 1984, where he died some three years later. Bishop Nathaniel Popp, an American ex-Romanian ROMAN CATHOLIC priest who had converted to Orthodoxy in 1968, succeeded him.

A Church congress and the episcopal council, both of which are presided over by the bishop and constituted by delegates from the parishes, govern the

Church, which is represented in parishes across the USA and Canada as well as in South America and Europe.

RONGA-TSONGA PRESBYTERIAN CHURCH

A Church founded by Swiss missionaries to Mozambique in 1881, when it was a Portuguese colony. The missionary efforts were directed at the Tsonga and Shangaan peoples who live north-west of the capital city, Maputo (Lourenço Marques).

The Church now has over 1,000 congregations with an adult membership of 43,000 for whom native-born clergy minister in the REFORMED tradition.

❖ Presbyterian Church of Mozambique

ROWITES

The Rowites were followers in Scotland of John McLeod Campbell (1800–72). After studying theology at the universities of Glasgow and Edinburgh, Campbell was licensed as a minister of the CHURCH OF SCOTLAND in 1821 and was appointed as minister to Row (now Rhu) in Dumbartonshire, near the Firth of Clyde, some four years later.

It was not long before Campbell was accused of preaching heresy and in 1830 the Dumbarton presbytery ejected him. Campbell had been preaching the doctrine of universal atonement and pardon through Christ's death and that assurance is 'of the essence of faith and necessary to salvation'. Since he had been deposed by the general assembly of the Church of Scotland, despite his pleas, Campbell continued to preach as an independent minister to congregations in the Scottish Highlands, and to an independent congregation in Glasgow, from 1833–59.

Campbell retired to Roseneath in 1870 and died two years later. His theological expertise was recognized by the University of Glasgow, which awarded him the degree of doctor of divinity in 1868.

RUSSIAN CATHOLIC CHURCH

This Byzantine-rite Church is in communion with Rome. The Liturgy is usually said in the vernacular, although Church Slavonic, the liturgical language used by the RUSSIAN ORTHODOX CHURCH, may also be used, and there is also provision for the use of the Latin Rite for Catholics in Russia.

The Council of Florence (1438–45) was an attempt at reunion between the Greek and Latin Churches and was attended by Isidore, the Metropolitan of Kiev, who signed the *Decree of Union* against the instructions given to him. Upon his return to Russia, Isidore was deposed and imprisoned, but eventually escaped and fled to Rome.

During the years after the Council of Florence there were few ROMAN CATHOLICS under Russian rule until after the partition of Poland (1772–95). In the nineteenth century a small number of Orthodox Christians came under the influence of the philosopher and theologian Vladimir Solovyov, who began a movement in favour of those Russians who had converted to Rome being enabled to retain their own distinctively Eastern rite. *Suc'ı a situation was then considered to be legally impossible in Russia where a Byzantine Christian had to be a member of the Orthodox Church; this pertained even after Tsar Nicholas II issued an edict of religious tolerance in 1905.*

Solovyov, himself, became a Roman Catholic in 1896, making a profession of faith before a Catholic Byzantine-Rite priest, Fr Nicholas Tolstoy, in Moscow. Groups of Russian Catholics of the Byzantine rite, which enjoyed the moral protection of some influential people, were formed throughout the country. In 1908 a decree from the Vatican secretariat of state appointed Fr Zerchaninov as administrator of the Russian Catholics and commended the use of the Byzantine-Slavonic Rite, which was to be followed without any Latin modifications; Pope St Pius X (1903–14) later confirmed this commendation.

At the time of the Russian Revolution in 1917, some members of the Byzantine-rite Catholic community wanted to take up the religious life. Under Anna Abrikosova a religious community for young women under simple vows was organized, along the lines of the Dominican Third Order. Anna was married to Vladimir Abrikosov and after taking vows of chastity they both entered the Church, Vladimir ordained as a priest and his wife becoming Mother Catherine in her small religious community.

The Russian Catholic Church faced many problems during the years of upheaval encompassing the Revolution and the First World War. It appointed as its first exarch (an office similar to that of a provincial bishop in the western Church), Leonid Feodorov, who as a young man had been involved in Solovyov's circle in St Petersburg before travelling to the West where he was ordained as a Roman Catholic priest. He was arrested in 1913 in St Petersburg for being a Byzantine Catholic priest and for his association with the leader of the Ukrainian Byzantine Catholic Church, and sent into internal exile in Tobolsk until 1917. Feodorov was again arrested in 1923, this time by the Bolsheviks, for being a Christian and with many other clergy and laity was sent to a prison camp in Siberia. In 1935 Leonid Feodorov died as a result of his considerable sufferings and in June 2001 Pope John Paul II beatified him during his historic visit to Ukraine.

The small Byzantine-rite Catholic community was scattered during these troubled times, with many of its members facing imprisonment and execution. Around 2,500 left Russia, settling in many parts of the world, in North and South America, Europe, and the Far East. Those who had gone to the Far East, where they opened schools in Harbin and Shanghai, were sent from these areas in the face of the Japanese invasion of Manchuria and the rise of Chinese communism; they sought new homes in Hong Kong and Australia, others in Argentina and Los Angeles. To provide the clergy for an apostolate amongst the scattered communities of the diaspora, the Russicum, a Pontifical Russian College, was established in Rome in 1929.

With the collapse of communism in Russia in 1991 the structures of the Church are being restored. New dioceses are now to be established with their centres at Moscow and Saratov, on the Volga River, and at Novosibirsk and Irkutsk for western and eastern Siberia. Some of these moves have not found favour with the Russian Orthodox Church. Reliable statistics as to the strength of the Russian Catholic Church are difficult to acquire, but some conservative estimates suggest that there are currently some 212 parishes and 300 priests, many of them foreigners.

❖ Russian Catholics of the Byzantine Rite

RUSSIAN ORTHODOX CHURCH

According to tradition St Andrew, who was known as the *First Called*, stood on the Kievan hills during his travels and evangelization and blessed the site of the future city of Kiev, but it was not until 988 that the first known baptism, that of St Vladimir, is recorded. His grandmother, Princess Olga, who was regent between 945 and 964, had been converted and baptized in Constantinople. Her son, Svyatoslav, refused to convert for fear of the ridicule that he felt would follow if he allowed himself to be baptized, and it fell to St Vladimir to accept baptism. *(It has been said that this may have been prompted by Vladimir's desire to marry Anna, the Christian sister of the Byzantine emperor.)* With Christianity proclaimed the official faith of the realm in 988, Vladimir ordered all citizens to be baptized, a command that was taken up enthusiastically by the urban classes but only slowly accepted by the lower classes and rural dwellers.

In the pre-Tartar period of Russian history the Russian Church was one of the metropolitanates of the Patriarch of Constantinople. Until 1051, its metropolitan was chosen by Constantinople from amongst the Greek clergy, but this changed with the installation of Metropolitan Hilarion, a native born Russian, in the primatial see. During the tenth and eleventh centuries an extensive building programme was undertaken and monasticism was introduced by St Andrew of the Caves, a monk of Mt Athos, when the Monastery of the Caves was established in Kiev. His successor, St Theodosius (d. 1074) consolidated this work and introduced a monastic rule of life with an emphasis on poverty and humility, which was taken from the monastery of the Stadium at Constantinople.

The twelfth century saw the start of a period of feudal divisions and the Russian Orthodox Church became the focus of unity for the Russian people. Divided principalities began to unite around Moscow in the fourteenth century and Metropolitan Jonas (1448–71), by sheer force of personality and authority, was able to help end the feudal discords and preserve a state of unity. In 1448, five years before the fall of Constantinople to the Turks, the Russian Church became independent and a council of Russian bishops elected Jonas as the Metropolitan of Moscow and All Russia. During the fifteenth century the Russian state gathered strength and the Church increased in stature and authority, its importance emphasized when the Metropolitan of Moscow was elevated to the rank of patriarch.

A thorough revision of the Church's service books and rites was undertaken during the seventeenth century, bringing them into line with the ideas of the other ancient patriarchates, a revision largely undertaken by Patriarch Nikhon and from which the OLD BELIEVERS schism was derived. Under Peter I (the Great) the patriarchate was abolished and a collective supreme administration of the Church, known as the holy and governing synod, was established. This remained the supreme church body for nearly two hundred years, a period during which a programme of religious education, church building and missionary work was undertaken.

Following the abdication of Tsar Nicholas II in 1917, an all-Russian church council met in Moscow and a programme of church reform was started. Provision was made for the restoration of the patriarchate, but this was subsequently abolished in 1925. The Church suffered initially under the Soviet state, but by the outbreak of the Second World War the anti-religious posturing was eased when Stalin sought the Church's aid in providing him with material help for the war effort. In 1943, a rapprochement was struck between Church and State in a *patriotic union*, but in reality the Church remained firmly under state control despite the patriarchate being again restored. Further difficulties arose under President Khrushchev and thousands of churches were closed, for ideological reasons, throughout the Soviet Union. Since 1997, with the passing of a new *Freedom of Conscience and Religious Association* bill, a period of security for the Church seems assured.

The Church is now vigorous, with 128 dioceses and many parishes. Theological education is provided at several academies, 26 seminaries and 2 Orthodox universities as well as at many icon-painting schools. A youth programme has united many young people and involved them in various social services, in restoration work in monasteries and churches and in making contact with young people around the world.

RUSSIAN ORTHODOX CHURCH OUTSIDE RUSSIA

In the period following the 1917 Russian Revolution the Russian Orthodox Church experienced some initial freedom, underlined when a *Sobor*, or synod of the Church, met in Moscow and voted for the restoration of the patriarchate, which had been discontinued under Tsar Peter the Great over two hundred years before. Basil Ivanovitch Belavin (1866–1925), known as Metropolitan Tikhon of Moscow, was elected as patriarch. Barely two years later the Soviet government revealed its opposition to the very continuance of the Church. Clergy salaries were discontinued, clergy education was forbidden, the legal status of marriages was made dependent on validation by a civil ceremony, and the registration of births and deaths was handed over to civil bureaux. Patriarch Tikhon and the *Sobor* denounced this interference in the running of the Church; any such resistance was met with imprisonment, suppression or even execution.

In 1920 Patriarch Tikhon, foreseeing the trouble that undoubtedly lay ahead for the Church, issued a decree permitting Russian Orthodox bishops to establish temporary independent organizations that could be put into operation should relations with the patriarchate become impossible. In time, millions of exiled Russians were in need of a supervised religious life and bishops of the Church, now living outside of Russia, applied the conditions of Tikhon's decree.

In 1921 the Patriarchate of Serbia invited the exiles to assemble a council at Sremski-Karlovci (Karlovtzy) in Yugoslavia, at which a temporary ecclesiastical administration for Russian Orthodox exiles could be created. As a result, control was vested in a synod of bishops, who were to meet annually at Karlovtzy, and an administrative board, composed of representatives of both clergy and laity, was established.

There was an attempt during the Second World War to broker an understanding that was begun in 1935 between the Russian Orthodox Church Outside Russia and the Russian Orthodox Greek Catholic Church of America, but this attempt had failed by 1940. The synods at Karlovtzy met regularly in the inter-war period, but the immense number of immigrants and refugees who fled to the

USA after the war made it necessary for the synod to move its headquarters, first to Munich and later to New York. With the dispersal of so many Russian immigrants many new dioceses were established around the world that persist to this day. There is an estimated adult membership of some 200,000, mainly to be found throughout the USA and Canada, and in Europe, South America and Australia.

❖ Russian Orthodox Church Abroad; Russian Orthodox Church in Exile

S

SABBATIANS

A fourth-century sect of followers of Sabbatius, who was a NOVATIANIST and as such objected to those who had apostatized being readmitted to the Church. The Sabbatians were distinctive in their strict application of the *Quartodeciman Rule*. This required the observance of Easter to be kept on the same day as the Jewish Passover, which was kept on the fourteenth day of the month of Nisan, regardless what day of the week it fell upon, whereas the EASTERN ORTHODOX CHURCH observed Easter on the Sunday following the fourteenth day.

SABELLIANS

Followers of Sabellius, a presbyter, who lived in Pentapolis in Cyrenaica (in modern-day Libya) in the third century, according to St Basil (330–79), but who may also have been a citizen of Rome. Sabellius was influential in promoting the heresy of the MONARCHIANS in Rome, having gone there towards the end of the pontificate of Pope St Zephyrinus (199–217). St Hippolytus opposed this heretical teaching and Sabellius was excommunicated in *c.* 220 by Pope St Callistus (217–222).

The Monarchian doctrine proposed by Sabellius concerned the notion that God was revealed at one time under the mode of the Father, then, at another time, under the mode of the Son and at yet another time under the mode of the Holy Spirit. In spite of their excommunication the Monarchians in Rome survived and tried to set up their own Church and bishop. Sabellius returned to Cyrenaica, where he founded a school. By 257, after his death, the doctrines he proposed were flourishing and causing a division amongst the Christian population which was, in part, settled by a synod assembled by Pope St Dionysius (259–68), who also wrote *Against the Sabellians* in *c.* 262.

❖ Patripassians

SALVADORAN LUTHERAN SYNOD

The first LUTHERAN congregation in El Salvador was begun in 1947 and by 1952 it had become part of the mission outreach programme of the LUTHERAN CHURCH – MISSOURI SYNOD. The Church formally joined the Lutheran World Federation in the mid-1980s.

Until 1982 only two ordained pastors had served the Church; of three others who were intending to serve, one was murdered and the other two fled the country during its long civil war. A massive growth in church planting is now underway, with members involved in programmes concerned with evangelization, preaching, education and social work. The Church operates various health care ministries, with dispensaries set up to serve those in need. The education of the young is catered for through a network of kindergarten and primary schools. Training for leadership in the Church is provided for in the recently established faculties of theology and science in the Lutheran University of El Salvador. Agricultural assistance and relief programmes for the poor and for displaced persons also continue.

The Salvadoran Lutheran Synod was at the forefront of efforts to deal with recent natural disasters in the country, such as the consequences of Hurricane Mitch in 1998 and the earthquakes at the start of 2001. There are currently some 76 congregations in the country and an innovative *sister parish* programme has been formed to deepen commitment to peace and justice issues, to provide support for small community-based development projects and to forge links with PROTESTANT congregations in North America and Europe. The headquarters of the Church is in San Salvador.

SALVATION AND DELIVERANCE CHURCH

This Church should not be confused with the SALVATION AND DELIVERANCE FULL GOSPEL CHURCH, which was formed in Chicago, Illinois, in 1983 (see next entry).

This very active American Church was first formed in 1975 as a healing, or deliverance, ministry within the AFRICAN METHODIST EPISCOPAL CHURCH by William Brown, an ex-ROMAN CATHOLIC who converted to METHODISM and became a minister in that Church.

In pursuit of his vision for extending the deliverance ministry along more international and inter-racial lines, William Brown withdrew during the 1980s from the African Methodist Episcopal Church. The work has now been extended to over 40 countries and has current affiliations with Churches in Haiti, Jamaica, Nigeria, Liberia, India and Canada. The Church has established an important drug rehabilitation centre in Harlem, New York, as part of its deliverance ministry, and it also supports elementary schools, schools for the retarded and Bible colleges.

SALVATION AND DELIVERANCE FULL GOSPEL CHURCH

This Church should not be confused with the SALVATION AND DELIVERANCE CHURCH (see previous entry).

This American Church was founded in Chicago, Illinois, in 1983 by Pastors Curtis and Linda Stennis in response to a spiritual experience that prompted them to initiate this multi-faceted work.

The Church expanded readily, and by 1986 it had taken possession of the former Simon Peter Lutheran Church Cathedral in Chicago. A desire to expand its work led Linda Stennis to form the *Women Moving Forward for God Ministries* in 1990. This was designed to enable and empower women and families in the workplace and in society. A media ministry was established in 1993, with the radio outreach programme known as *God Always Keeps His Promises* (GAKHP); this was soon expanded into a television outreach ministry. The radio outreach extended from Chicago to the southern states, and by the year 2000 its own website was launched. The public are asked to provide their personal prayer requests through these media outlets.

Other ministries have been established, including a youth ministry involving dance, Sunday schools, drama groups and a monthly youth fellowship. The outreach ministries work with the needy and homeless, as well as those requiring nursing, and also provide support through a telephone ministry.

SALVATION ARMY

The Salvation Army is an international PROTESTANT sect, which carries out both a religious mission and a social service for the underprivileged. It was founded by a METHODIST NEW CONNEXION minister, William Booth (1829–1912), who was given to preaching out-of-doors where he felt he could reach those who were unable, or unwilling, to attend a conventional church. Booth left the Methodist ministry and started evangelistic and social work in East London, where there was much poverty and neglect, making his first foundation, the Christian Mission in Whitechapel, in 1865. When many of his converts complained that they had not been made welcome in Methodist and ANGLICAN circles, Booth urged these converts to become the manpower he needed for the rapidly expanding outreach programme, which from 1872 included *Food for Millions* shops providing cheap meals for the poor. The title *Salvation Army* was adopted in 1878 and two years later, following the introduction of uniforms, the work of the Army spread throughout Britain and the USA. During the 1880s the witness of the Salvation Army extended into other parts of Europe, including Iceland, to Australia, India and South Africa.

The basic unit of the Salvation Army is the corps, which meets in citadels to be found in many cities. The corps' members, or soldiers, sign the sixteen *Articles of War*, which are directed against all vices, including the use of tobacco and alcohol, and undertake unqualified obedience to the Army. Each corps is under the direction of an officer, who may hold any rank from lieutenant to brigadier. To become an officer a candidate undergoes a period of residential training, after which further studies allow for progression through the ranks. Salvation Army officers may perform marriages, preach and serve as military chaplains. From 1929 the highest rank, that of general, which had been held by William Booth's son, Bramwell, was decided by an election taken within the high council, which was made up of territory commanders and leading officers.

The Salvation Army's doctrine is found in the *Articles of War*, which express the Army's ARMINIAN theology and uncompromising belief in the Bible as being the only rule of faith and practice. There is a full belief in the Trinity, in universal redemption, the importance of human free will and the validity of the post-conversion sanctification experience. The Army rejects baptism and the Lord's Supper, the latter because it has been the source of so much bitter strife; Christianity is regarded as a spiritual, not a ceremonial religion. Although children are not baptized, a *Dedication of Children* service is provided. Funerals are intended to be joyful occasions, when the deceased soldier is thought of as having been promoted to glory.

The well-publicized social work undertaken by the Army is based on the view that the improvement of a person's social well-being will be both physically and spiritually uplifting. Members are heavily involved with rescue missions, especially amongst the homeless, alcoholics, and criminals and their families. Soup kitchens and workers' hostels are manned along with night shelters, hospitals, schools and community centres for people of all ages. There has always been a strong association between the Salvation Army and music, their hymn-playing marching bands a colourful part of street life in most towns and cities, with the female members in their distinctive bonnets (now almost a thing of the past – see below), the polished brass instruments and colourful banners decorated with the emblems of blood and fire, representing the blood of Christ and the power of the Holy Spirit.

Two groups separated from the mainstream Salvation Army. The first to do so was the AMERICAN RESCUE WORKERS, founded in 1882, which was followed by the VOLUNTEERS OF AMERICA, which was founded in 1896 by Ballington Booth and his wife, Maud. These groups are both engaged in social work but, unlike the Salvation Army, they observe the sacraments of baptism and the Lord's Supper.

The classical Salvation Army black straw bonnet for women is now an optional item of dress for which a felt, brimmed hat with the Salvation Army badge may be substituted. Many Salvationists have a great attachment to their distinctive bonnets and continue to wear them.

❖ Salvationists

SAMAVESAM OF TELUGU BAPTIST CHURCHES

This Indian BAPTIST Church was started when missionaries of the Triennial Convention (a missionary organization that evolved into the AMERICAN BAPTIST CHURCHES IN THE USA) began their work in Andhra Pradesh in 1836, amongst the Telugu-speaking people. Two years later, in 1838, the Reverend Samuel Day, a founder missionary, created the Telugu Baptist Mission in Madras. In 1844 he organized the Church in Nellore, the present-day headquarters of the Church in Andhra Pradesh.

As part of their evangelical ministry the early missionaries at Ramapatnam, near Nellore in the coastal region a little north of Madras, started the Telugu Baptist Theological Seminary in 1869. The provision of the seminary was essential for providing trained pastors and leaders for the growing Baptist community. Attention was also paid to the provision of an educational ministry, with its principal emphasis upon primary and secondary schools, but with the passage of time its more ambitious plans of creating Bible schools, vocational schools and teacher training colleges proved to be very expensive and many such enterprises were closed and handed over to the Indian government.

The Telugu Baptist mission also opened hospitals, dispensaries and training facilities for nurses, all of these maintained wholly by mission funds because the target patients were poor and had to receive free treatment. Some of the Telugu students were selected and sponsored for training in the medical and nursing courses provided by the Christian Medical College at Vellore, west of Madras, and after graduation they were employed at the mission hospitals. This undertaking was also to prove burdensomely expensive and yet again these facilities were closed, or handed over to the Indian government. The Telugu Baptist Convention was formed in 1897, to be followed by the formation of a joint council that began operations in 1941. With the coming of Indian independence in 1947 all foreigners were asked to leave India. The Telugu Baptist Church faced many resultant difficulties. At this point it changed its name to the Samavesam of Telugu Baptist Churches (STBC). A new constitution was drawn up and a general council was formed. There was much progress made and the Telugu Baptists are now financing and building their own churches. There are now over 1,600 congregations serving an adult membership in excess of 856,000.

SCHMIEDELEUT (HUTTERITE)

The Schmiedeleut HUTTERITE group, which migrated to Bon Homme County, South Dakota, in 1874, took its name from its leader, a blacksmith named Michael Waldner, who because of his occupation was known as Schmied-Michael (German 'Schmiede' – blacksmith). Other colonies were founded in South Dakota, with later expansion during the twentieth century into Manitoba, Canada. By 1974 there were 91 colonies of this conservative group, all closely united, with its headquarters at Tabor in Bon Homme County. Although conservative in outlook, the Schmiedeleut Hutterites have now abandoned the general use of hooks and eyes in favour of buttons for fastening their clothes. At worship services the minister is the first to enter the gathering place; in some of the Hutterite groups the minister will follow after his congregation has entered.

SCHWENCKFELDIANS

Followers of Caspar von Ossig Schwenckfeld (1489–1561), a Silesian aristocrat who had studied at the universities of Cologne and Frankfurt-on-the-Oder and served in the courts of several Silesian dukes. Although he had been raised as a Roman Catholic, by 1521 Schwenckfeld had become a public adherent of the PROTESTANT Reformation although differing from protestantism over the Lord's Supper, Christology and church order. It was this deviation from orthodox protestant views that led Schwenckfeld into conflict with the Reformers Martin Luther, Ulrich Zwingli and Martin Bucer, as well as with the ROMAN CATHOLIC CHURCH.

Schwenckfeld understood the bread and wine used at the Lord's Supper to be no more than symbols of the body and blood of Christ and he aimed to free Christianity from dogma, believing that a formal church organization was superfluous. Differences of opinion between Schwenckfeld and Luther forced the former to move from Silesia to Strasbourg in 1529; he was later banished from the city in 1533. This period of persecution from LUTHERAN preachers, who condemned his writings and his *Great Confession*, led to a time of wandering for Schwenckfeld; the *Great Confession* was also condemned during a convention, led by Philipp Melanchthon (1497–1560), which was held at Schmalcalden in 1540. This repudiation by the Lutherans led Schwenckfeld to withdraw from the Lutheran Church. Having established a community of worshippers, known as the *Confessors of the Glory of Christ*, he died at Ulm, near Augsburg, in December 1561.

His followers continued to propagate Schwenckfeld's writings and they flourished in groups spread throughout Silesia, Swabia and Prussia, especially in the town of Goldberg in the north of Germany, until in 1720, at the insistence of the Holy Roman Emperor Charles VI (1711–42), the Jesuits started a forceful mission against the groups. This resulted in the emigration of most of the followers, first to Saxony and then to Holland and England. Under the Prussian King Frederick the Great (1740–86), the colony of Schwenckfeldians who had once lived in Silesia was restored in 1742; the group remained there until 1826, by which time most of the remaining members had emigrated to America where they settled in eastern Pennsylvania.

Descendants of this group still exist in south-eastern Pennsylvania. The members still hold to the view that their theology, which is decidedly Christocentric, should be derived entirely from the Bible. Christ's divinity is understood to be progressive, so that his human nature became more and more divine without losing its human identity. The sacraments are retained only in a symbolic sense, and while baptism of infants is discarded as unnecessary, it is thought to be legitimate, although still unnecessary, for adults to receive it. The Lord's Supper is observed as an open communion in which the bread and wine are still regarded merely as symbols of Christ's body and blood. Schwenckfeldian church services are extempore and non-liturgical.

The polity of the Church is congregational, and each congregation is self-supporting, conducting its affairs through local, or district, conferences. A general conference, through which the planning of educational and mission programmes is undertaken, meets twice a year and consists of delegates from the congregations in Pennsylvania.

❖ Confessors of the Glory of Christ

SCOTTISH CONGREGATIONAL CHURCH

Congregationalism can be traced back to Martin Luther, and to a certain extent to John Calvin. According to this viewpoint, the spiritual power of the Church lies within the local church, or congregation. Each community is responsible for itself, not only in matters of discipline and order, but also in doctrine, and each local church is markedly autonomous. Congregationalists refuse, therefore, to recognize hierarchical regimes, but only admit to a federation of local churches.

In the British Isles there were those living during the reign of Elizabeth I (1533–1603) who would not recognize the Anglican state Church and who favoured, instead, the *gathered church* principle. One of the more vocal leaders of this movement, whose members became known as Separatists (also Brownists), was Robert Browne and it was these Separatists who became the forerunners of the Congregationalists.

In Scotland, it was through the preaching of James Morison (1816–93), a minister of the United Secession Church, that a large number of ministers and laity left the Church of Scotland to form a number of independent groups, or churches. Morison had openly challenged Calvinism and was suspended from his duties in 1841 because he preached that Jesus Christ had made atonement for all, and not just for the *elect*. By 1843, these smaller groups, or churches, had combined to form the Evangelical Union in Kilmarnock, where Morison's preaching had attracted many followers. Towards the close of the nineteenth century the similarity of views held by the Evangelical Union and those held by the Congregational Union of England and Wales (formed 1832) persuaded them to unite, which they did in 1897.

Congregationalism has always been a keen supporter of ecumenism and in Scotland, from the 1960s, there were many attempts to form mergers between the Congregational Union and other Scottish denominations, although in general these efforts went unrewarded. Since the 1980s consideration has been given to forming a union with the UNITED REFORMED CHURCH (URC), following the successful union that took place between most of the Congregational Churches in England and Wales with the Presbyterian Church of England to form the URC in 1972. Those Congregational Churches of England and Wales that did not join the URC formed themselves into the Congregational Federation.

In 1993, the Congregational Union changed its constitution and became the Scottish Congregational Church (aka Congregational Church of Scotland). However, not all individual congregations were in agreement with this move, and about thirty of them elected to retain their congregational principle; these eventually joined the Congregational Federation in 1994.

Members of the Scottish Congregational Church affirm the autonomy of each local church and insist upon the separation of church and state. They maintain the REFORMED tradition, with its emphasis upon the authority of the Bible in the ordering of faith and practice. The Church adopts the priesthood of all believers and does not therefore recognize the existence of a hierarchy within any local church, or association of churches. Most Congregational churches now practise infant baptism, by sprinkling, using the Trinitarian formula, although some congregations prefer the tradition of the believer's baptism. At the very heart of every local Congregational church is the concept of the *gathered* and covenanted fellowship of Christians. Clergy are ordained by a laying on of hands by ministers and church representatives during the singing of the *Hymn to the Holy Spirit (Veni Creator)*.

❖ Congregational Church of Scotland

SCOTTISH EPISCOPAL CHURCH

This Church, which is part of the ANGLICAN COMMUNION, has seven dioceses, the bishops of which elect one of their number as *Primus*.

The Scottish Episcopal Church derived from the reformed CHURCH OF SCOTLAND (est. 1560), which was disestablished and disendowed in 1689 when William of Orange arrived in Britain and required an oath of allegiance to be taken by all clergy. The Scottish bishops refused this, on the grounds that they had already sworn such an oath for King James. King William then set up the PRESBYTERIAN CHURCH to replace the Episcopal Church, the clergy of which were evicted. The Episcopalian clergy were outlawed after the 1745 uprising, with the exception of those *qualified* chapels that had agreed to the use of the English Prayer Book.

The disestablished Episcopal Church persevered until the passing of the penal statutes, which remained in force from 1746–93. These statutes, which were imposed for political reasons, made it illegal for Episcopalians to own any chapels or churches, and no Episcopalian priest was allowed either to conduct public services or provide any ministry to a group in excess of five in number; the penalties for disobedience were imprisonment or banishment. In 1784, the Scottish Episcopal Church, or Non-Juring Church (NONJURORS), managed to consecrate the first bishop for the American Episcopal Church, Samuel Seabury of Connecticut, in an upstairs room in Aberdeen. Seabury was unable to swear an oath of allegiance to the British crown, a prerequisite for episcopal consecration in England, and so he sought consecration in the Scottish Episcopal Church.

From 1792, with the revocation of the penal statutes, the Church began to grow steadily with a strong burst of activity during the Victorian era at the time that the Tractarians were publishing their *Tracts for the Times* (1833–41). (*Tractarianism was an attempt to persuade the members of the ANGLICAN COMMUNION of the Catholic principles upon which they thought the Church depended, and featured the work of such men as John Keble (1792–1866), Edward Pusey (1800–82) and John Henry Newman (1801–90), amongst others.*)

The Scottish Episcopal Church is episcopally led, but governed synodically. Since 1982 there has been a general synod of the Church, an elected body that meets annually and is made up of about 180 elected members. The Church makes use of the liturgies of 1929, 1970 and 1982, and the Eucharistic prayers, which include a distinct *epiclesis* (a prayer invoking the descent of the Holy Spirit upon the bread and wine to effect their consecration) in addition to the usual words of consecration. The Church supports two retirement homes, one in Edinburgh and the other at Newport-on-Tay in Fife, as well as retreat and conference centres in Scotland.

SE-BAPTISTS

This was a name that was occasionally given to the followers of John Smyth, or Smith, (d. 1612) who had been ordained in the CHURCH OF ENGLAND by the Bishop of Lincoln and appointed as a lecturer at Lincoln Cathedral in 1600, a post that he lost two years later on account of his unorthodox views.

For a short while Smyth was pastor to a group of BROWNISTS in Gainsborough, Lincolnshire, but in order to escape persecution for his SEPARATIST views he, and most of his congregation, fled to Amsterdam in 1607. While there, Smyth became convinced that the *Church* was any gathered company of believers who could gain membership by a believer's baptism. Smyth then baptized himself (hence the soubriquet Se-Baptists from the Latin '*se baptizare*' – to baptize oneself) and proceeded to baptize others from his congregation, including Thomas Helwys, a friend from his Lincoln days who later returned to England and founded there what was probably the first General Baptist Church.

By 1609 Smyth was in America, where he acquired a bakehouse from a Mennonite, Jan Munter, and opened the first Baptist Church in America, the members of which he styled The Brethren of the Separation of the Second English Church at Amsterdam. By the time of his death, in 1612, it was clear that John Smyth was becoming increasingly influenced by MENNONITE beliefs. Helwys and some of his congregation established the Baptist Church in Great Britain in Newgate Street, London. Although they practised believer's baptism, it was not administered by total immersion but by a Mennonite-style of affusion.

SECOND CUMBERLAND PRESBYTERIAN CHURCH IN AMERICA

In the nineteenth century, following the American Civil War (1861–5), ministers of the CUMBERLAND PRESBYTERIAN CHURCH wanted to evangelize African-Americans in the southern states, especially amongst the slave population. A move was made in 1869 to establish the Colored Cumberland Presbyterian Church for black members of the Church and this later became known as the Second Cumberland Presbyterian Church in America.

The Church grew and established synods in Alabama, Tennessee, Kentucky and Texas. A review of both doctrine and polity was undertaken and a new *Confession of Faith* was produced in 1984.

The doctrinal position of the Church follows that of the *WESTMINSTER CONFESSION of Faith* with some reservations, for example they hold that there are no eternal reprobates and that Christ died for all mankind, and not for the *elect* alone. There has recently been a revision of the doctrinal position of the Church and a new *Confession of Faith* was issued in 1984.

The Church has care of over 143 congregations with over 6,000 adult members spread throughout the southern States; there is also an affiliated presbytery in Liberia. A move to reunite with the parent Church was made in 1991, but this was defeated.

❖ Colored Cumberland Presbyterian Church; Second Cumberland Presbyterian Church in the United States

SEEKERS

This group should not be confused with an American occult group of the same name.

The Seekers were a seventeenth-century English SEPARATIST, PURITAN group who were so-named because of their claim that they were *seeking* the true Church, scripture, ministry and sacraments. This, they believed, would be a Church of apostolic power that God would establish by ordaining new apostles, or prophets, as its founders. In this way, they repudiated the doctrines, organization and ceremonies of the visible contemporary Church. It is also possible that this group held millenarian views (REVELATION 20). The sect may have been called *Seekers* for the first time by John Murton in his work *Truth's Champion*, which was published in 1617.

The Seekers held to the views put forward by two Germans, Caspar von Ossig-Schwenkfeld (1489–1561) from Silesia (SCHWENKFELDIANS) and Sebastian Franck (1499–1542), from Swabia, and by a Dutchman, Dirck Coornheert (1522–90). They seem to have attracted a large following in northern England and in Bristol, but from 1652 the group was absorbed by the Quakers (RELIGIOUS SOCIETY OF FRIENDS). Persecution in England sent many followers to America where a group settled in Rhode Island under the guidance of Roger Williams who taught Seeker ideas and preached on the notion of absolute religious freedom for all. Roger Williams founded the earliest Baptist Church at Providence, Rhode Island, in 1639.

Seeker views and ideas were also taught by Bartholomew Legat(e) (c. 1575–1612), a cloth merchant who traded in Holland and

who was eventually burnt at the stake, in Smithfield, London, for espousing the heresy of Arianism.

❖ Legatine-Arians; Scattered Flock

SEPARATE BAPTISTS IN CHRIST

Separate Baptists first arrived in America in 1695 as part of the SEPARATIST groups that left England to escape persecution. These seventeenth-century refugees were independent Christians who wanted to separate from the established CHURCH OF ENGLAND, which they regarded as debased, in order to form a purer Church. They had been members of the PARTICULAR BAPTISTS, or the REGULAR BAPTISTS, but left those groups over disputes concerning the criteria for membership, refusing to associate with others who did not insist that a rebirth experience was essential, a matter that was of the greatest importance to them.

The doctrinal position of the Separate Baptists is mildly CALVINISTIC. Because of their custom of accepting for membership those who had been baptized but not immersed, even including infants, other Baptist groups would not accept them. Nevertheless, a union was effected towards the close of the eighteenth century and the start of the nineteenth between the Regular and Separatist Baptists. Those Separate Baptists who would not accept this union retained their independence and formed the General Association of Separatist Baptists.

Separate Baptists do not acknowledge any creed, but they affirm the infallibility of the Bible and believe in the Trinity; foot-washing, the Lord's Supper and baptism by immersion are recognized as ordinances but the Calvinistic notions of predetermined election, reprobation and fatality are rejected.

Church polity is congregational, with support for Sunday schools and an active home mission programme. The Church has at present 101 congregations and over 10,000 adult members.

❖ General Association of Separate Baptists; General Association of Separatist Baptists

SEPARATIST (also SEPARATISTS)

These were members of a small group, formed at the end of the sixteenth century, who took PURITANISM to its logical conclusion. They wished to separate themselves from the national Church, which they considered to be tainted. Unlike the Puritans, who considered themselves still to be Anglican and who could effect reforms within that Church, the Separatists formed autonomous congregations whose members were united with each other and with Christ by a covenant; these congregations appointed their own clergy, who had no authority over other congregations and also submitted to none other.

Agents of both Queen Elizabeth I and King James I and VI persecuted the Separatists. The movement was associated with such people as Robert Browne, whose followers, the BROWNISTS, considered any kind of ordination to be an abomination and the whole church system rotten. Separatism, or Brownism as it is sometimes called, was illegal under the Commonwealth and Protectorate in England (1649–59). It became acceptable, and widespread for a short time before being declared illegal again under the Clarendon Code, a series of statutes enacted between 1661 and

1665 and aimed at removing from any civil or ecclesiastical office anyone who was at variance with the liturgy and doctrines of the established CHURCH OF ENGLAND.

SERBIAN ORTHODOX CHURCH

Organized Christianity had reached the Slavic lands from both Rome and Constantinople by the middle of the fourth century, but under the influence of Sts Cyril (826–69) and Methodius (*c.* 815–85) there was a gradual increase of influence from Constantinople during the ninth century. Stephan I Nemanja, who brought the various chieftains, or *Zupani*, together into a single state in the twelfth century, united the Serbs and established himself as their king. Abdicating in 1196 in favour of his son, Stephen II, he took himself off to become a monk at Mt Athos, taking the name of Simeon; his wife followed contemporary custom by entering a convent as a nun. Stephen was canonized in 1216 as St Simeon. Stephen's other son, Sava, had gone as a young man of 17 to live in the monastic settlement of Mt Athos, in northern Greece, and father and son together founded a monastery there for Serbian monks, which they named *Khilandari* and which is still in existence.

Sava and several other monks returned to Serbia where they found Christianity to be in a muddled condition, mixed with paganism and under the control of very few, and mostly ignorant, clergy. Sava, who was later canonized, set up a monastery at Studenica from where his monks could create daughter foundations and begin to evangelize different parts of the country. When Constantinople fell to the Crusaders, Sava was sent by his brother, Stephen II, to Nicaea to be consecrated as bishop by the Patriarch of Constantinople, who had taken refuge there. Until this time the southern Serbs had wavered in their ecclesiastical allegiance between Rome and Constantinople but with Sava's return to Serbia, and his appointment as a metropolitan of the Church in 1219, a unity was established between the various Serbian principalities in support of Constantinople.

On his return journey to Serbia, Sava had made a detour to Mt Athos where he was able to recruit some monks who were brought back to Serbia to help Christianize the country. In 1346–7, under King Stephen III Dushan (1308–55), a synod was held at Uskub that proclaimed the Church to be autocephalous and elevated the Metropolitan of Pec to become the first patriarch. From 1389, after the Turkish victory at Kossovo Polje (*the field of blackbirds*) until 1815, Serbia was under Turkish rule and the Church experienced severe persecution, but with the release of this control in the nineteenth century it underwent a revival. A measure of internal autonomy was granted in 1832 when the Serbian Orthodox Church was allowed the right to elect its own metropolitan and bishops.

The Serbian Orthodox faithful were divided into four small Orthodox Churches at the time of the outbreak of the First World War, those of Karlovtsy, Bosnia-Herzegovina, Montenegro and Czernovitz. By August 1920 these had been united in the revived Patriarchate of Pec, a move that was subsequently recognized by Patriarch Meletios IV of Constantinople. The Church and its clergy now began to enjoy many privileges, but these were swept aside by the communists after the Second World War. Since the collapse of communism, a new constitution has been adopted (1992) in which provision is made for the Church and the state to be kept separate so that the Church is free to conduct its own religious affairs. Consequently, while there is no official state religion in the country, preferential treatment has been given to the Serbian Orthodox Church. In 2001 a draft law was drawn up by which the name 'National Church', a title by which the Serbian Orthodox Church was officially known, is no longer to be used and in its place the name 'Traditional Church' was suggested; the legal status in Serbia of the ROMAN CATHOLIC and PROTESTANT Churches, together with the Jewish and Islamic communities, will now be guaranteed under the new law.

The head of the Church is its patriarch, who is the Archbishop of Pec and Metropolitan of Belgrade-Karlovci, with his ecclesiastical see in Belgrade. He is assisted by several bishops, or metropolitans, and several *eparchies*, or ecclesiastical provinces, outside of the country that are responsible for the diaspora. The Church is now estimated to have some 8 million adherents with about 70,000 of these living in the USA and Canada. There are in total 32 dioceses, including 4 in North America, and 4 seminaries for the training of clergy.

SEVENTH-DAY ADVENTIST CHURCH (also SEVENTH-DAY ADVENTISTS)

William Miller (1782–1849), an American ex-army captain and Baptist preacher who was licensed in 1833, had studied the scriptures at length and calculated that Jesus Christ would return to earth at some time between 1843 and 1844, signalling that the end of the world was at hand (REVELATION 20). When the deadline passed, a more confident prediction was made that it would occur on 22 October 1844. When this date also passed without incident it became known as the *Great Disappointment.*

Many people who had become followers of Miller became disillusioned and left the movement that had, until then, been gaining in momentum. One who left to seek clearer evidence from the scriptures was Hiram Edison, who concluded that the year 1844 only marked the beginning of a period of investigative judgement in heaven and that once this work was completed Christ would return visibly to earth. Other ADVENTISTS alleged that the reason why the second coming had not eventuated was because of the failure of members to observe the seventh day as the sabbath. This conclusion was confirmed by visions that Ellen Gould White (1827–1915) of Maine had been receiving. A prolific writer, she came to be regarded as God-inspired.

The early Adventists were found chiefly in the New England states, but by 1855 they had begun to move westwards, establishing their headquarters at Battle Creek, Michigan. By 1860 the growing movement had chosen to be called Seventh-Day Adventist and within a few years its 125 churches and 3,500 members had become officially recognized as a Church. The work of the Church was confined to America at the start, but in 1874 their first missionary, J. N. Andrews, left for Switzerland. The missionary work expanded, with workers sent to Africa (1879), Russia (1886), the Pacific Islands (1890) and present-day Ghana, Matabeleland, South Africa and South America (1894), followed two years later when missionaries were sent to Japan. This vigorous proselytism is linked to the belief that the Advent, or second coming, will occur when the gospel has been proclaimed throughout the world.

Part of the success of the missionary work was due to extensive publishing enterprises, which still continue. Their leading paper, *Review and Herald*, is one of the oldest continuously published religious periodicals in the USA, having been started by Ellen Gould White and her husband, James White, in Paris, Maine, in 1850. A strong emphasis has been placed upon education, which is offered through the fifteen colleges and universities as well as the many primary and secondary schools that the Church maintains. Health and healthy lifestyles are promoted through many medical colleges and hospital facilities throughout the country.

The Seventh-Day Adventist Church believes in the observance of the seventh day of the week as the sabbath, and that after Christ's return to earth there will be a millennium, or thousand-year reign, during which the righteous dead will be raised and, together with the righteous living, will spend the millennium in heaven. Satan will rule on earth for the millennium, but at the end of this period Christ and his saints will descend to destroy the wicked with fire before creating a new earth with a New Jerusalem at its centre. Members do not believe in the innate immortality of the soul but they hold that the dead await resurrection in an unconscious state. They affirm the inspired nature of the Bible, the Trinity and a belief that salvation is achieved by Jesus Christ's atonement. Baptism of believers is preceded by a period of instruction and public assent to the commitment being prepared for, and is followed by immersion. The Holy Communion, celebrated four times a year and preceded by foot-washing, uses unleavened bread and unfermented wine as symbols of the body and blood of Christ.

The Church insists upon the proper care of the body, and to that end the members abstain from foods that are forbidden in the Old Testament; these include pork and pork products, such as ham and bacon, and shellfish of any kind. Smoking is forbidden as is the taking of drugs and alcohol and members are discouraged from wearing immodest clothing, cosmetics and jewellery.

In 1903 the headquarters of the Church moved from Battle Creek to Washington, DC, and moved again, in 1989, to Silver Springs, Maryland. The Church is represented in 208 countries throughout the USA and the world at large and is still involved in missionary work, conducting ethnic home missions as well as relief agencies and other social welfare programmes amongst the poor and the disadvantaged. A general conference meets every four years, attended by delegates from local conferences.

SEVENTH-DAY BAPTIST CHURCH

This denomination is not to be confused with the SEVENTH DAY BAPTIST CHURCH (GERMAN) *– (see next entry).*

This evangelical denomination is distinctive in that it insists that the seventh day of the week – Saturday – is the true Christian sabbath and must be observed as such. The first Church was organized in London in 1617, at Millyard, Goodman's Fields, under the leadership of John Trask; another congregation was founded at Nutton, Gloucestershire, in 1640. The Nutton congregation differed from that founded in London in that it initially held both Saturday and Sunday worship services, gradually giving way to Saturday worship as the dominant form. By 1700, there were about fifteen congregations scattered throughout England.

An English immigrant to America in 1664, the Reverend Stephen Mumford of the Bell Lane Seventh-Day Baptist Church in London, joined the Baptist Church at Newport, Rhode Island, which had been founded by Dr John Clark, upon his arrival. Mumford raised the issue of the Seventh-Day observance with other Baptists and despite some opposition he was able to found the first Seventh-Day Baptist Church at Newport in 1671. As they arrived to settle in America, other Sabbatarian Baptists joined him and new foundations were made, including one in Philadelphia in the 1680s and another at Piscataway, New Jersey, in 1705.

The members of the Church insist on a belief in salvation through faith in Christ, baptism by immersion of believers and the right of every member to interpret the Bible for himself. The ordinances observed are those of the Lord's Supper and baptism, with open communion practised two to four times a year. The churches are organized administratively through the annual general conference, which has its headquarters at Janesville, Wisconsin, having moved there from Plainfield, New Jersey, in 1982. The Church is very active in the mission field and affiliated Seventh-Day Baptists are found in some twenty countries throughout the world. A Spanish-speaking congregation was organized in 1978 at Collingwood, near Melbourne, Australia, which led to a demand for an English-speaking congregation to be formed, which has now been satisfied; other groups have since been organized in New South Wales and Queensland.

❖ Sabbatarian Baptists; Seventh Day Baptist General Conference USA and Canada;

SEVENTH DAY BAPTIST CHURCH (GERMAN)

This denomination is not to be confused with the Seventh-Day Baptist Church *(see previous entry).*

Having heard of William Penn's work in Pennsylvania, a group of German Separatist immigrants to America in the seventeenth century travelled to Germantown, Pennsylvania, in order to escape the persecution they faced in their own country. One of these organized a commune known as the Woman in the Wilderness, at Wissahickon Creek in Germantown in 1694. When a German immigrant from the Palatinate, Johann Conrad Beissel, came to the area in 1720, however, he found that it had closed down.

Beissel moved on to Lancaster County, Pennsylvania, and formed a settlement there. He became a Sabbatarian Baptist in 1728 and worked in close collaboration with Peter Becker (1687–1758), the founder of a Brethren group at Germantown. Beissel and Becker parted company in 1732, when the former founded a semi-monastic community at Ephrata, Pennsylvania, which was known as the Ephrata Society. The community observed strict celibacy, the sexes sleeping separately, and sharing goods in common. By 1764 the work of Johann Beissel had begun to decline. A group of German Seventh Day Baptists settled at Snow Hill, Pennsylvania, and organized a Sabbatarian Society there in 1800. It was from this group that other congregations were organized, amounting to five groups in all by 1900.

This small denomination is still in existence. Its members affirm the divine inspiration of the scriptures and hold to an orthodox belief in the Trinity. They practise baptism by triple immersion, with the receiver kneeling in a bath of water, foot-washing, the Lord's Supper, the anointing of the sick and the blessing of infants. Saturday is observed as the sabbath day and ordination is by personal request of the ordinand and not by congregational election. Members of this Church are non-combatants in time of war. There is a small mission programme, but no educational or charitable work is undertaken. The administration of the Church is ordered through an annual general conference.

SEVENTH-DAY CHRISTIAN CONFERENCE

A small American ADVENTIST-type Church, which was founded in 1934 in New York City, whose members observe the seventh day as the sabbath and accept the Bible in its entirety as the only rule of life.

The Church observes three ordinances, those of baptism by immersion, the Lord's Supper and what is termed *Fellowship*. The members regard war as immoral and register as conscientious objectors in time of enlistment. The few congregations still in existence are always led by males, who can become bishops, pastors and elders. There are two congregations of the Church, one in New York City and the other in Montclair, New Jersey, and four affiliated congregations in Jamaica. An earlier mission in Panama seems now to have closed down.

SHAKERS

The denomination, known familiarly as the Shakers, was an early branch of the Quakers (RELIGIOUS SOCIETY OF FRIENDS) whose members were much influenced by a Quaker group known as the *French Prophets*, or *Shaking Quakers*, who had been much given to prophetic visions, trembling and ritualistic dancing. This group had arisen in England, in Bolton and Manchester, in 1747 and was led initially by a tailor and his wife, James and Jane Wardley. The Wardleys were succeeded as leader by Ann Lee (1736–84), a factory worker from Manchester who had married Abraham Standerin in 1762, by whom she had four children who all died in infancy. This maternal loss had a profound effect upon Ann's view of marriage and led her to regard celibacy as the holy state.

Ann Lee, or Mother Lee as she came to be called, had joined this Quaker fringe group in 1758 whereupon she received a prophetic vision declaring that she had been possessed by the second person of the Trinity and was the *female* principle in Christ, Jesus being the *male* principle. As such, the prophesied second coming of Christ was now complete and mankind had only to await the arrival of the millennium, the thousand-year period of blessedness that was to follow (REVELATION 20). In conversation it was reported that should she fail to be addressed as *Mother*, Ann Lee would exclaim 'I am Ann the Word.' On account of persecution Mother Ann was persuaded to take her group to America and she left Manchester in 1774, together with six men and two women, settling at Watervliet, near Albany, New York. The Wardleys, until then still members of the English group, did not travel with her but entered an almshouse, where they later died.

Once settled in America, Ann Lee set about preaching and spreading her message, which she coupled with faith healing, for she had now come to the belief that sin was the cause of disease. Many communities were founded, peopled by like-minded members who patiently awaited the imminent coming of the millennium. The movement prospered and in time the leadership passed to Joseph Meacham and Lucy Wright.

The Shakers were noted for their vigorous worship, which included dancing, barking, ecstatic shouting and trances; these were seen as evidence of the presence of the Holy Spirit. The members also believed Ann Lee to be God's revelation to humanity and, though they observed celibacy themselves, did not condemn or disapprove of marriage *per se*. They also practised open confession of sins, communal possession of goods and pacifism; the latter attracted a considerable amount of opprobrium at the time of their arrival in America and has been a matter of discussion at many different times since.

Shakers lived daily lives of great simplicity, adopting the wearing of a uniform dress style and taking their meals in common, with alcohol and smoking discouraged. This simplicity of style extended to the creation of Shaker houses and furnishings and their beautiful designs, particularly of furniture, remain much sought after and copied.

Shakers encouraged separation from the world and achieved this by organizing the followers into large *families* of upwards of 90 people, who were governed hierarchically. Now almost defunct, the Shakers decided in 1965 to accept no new members, but at least one group is known recently to have broken this rule.

❖ Alethians; Millennial Church; United Society for Believers in Christ's Second Coming

SHILOH TRUST

A retired American businessman, Eugene Crosby Monroe (1880–1961), who was an ordained minister in the APOSTOLIC CHURCH, formed the Shiloh Trust on his farm near Sherman, Texas. A self-supporting, PENTECOSTAL commune was established there, supporting itself through the production and marketing of various foodstuffs. By the time of Monroe's death the Shiloh Trust had begun a successful business. The group holds very similar beliefs to those of the Apostolic Church. In 1968 the headquarters moved to Sulphur Springs, Arkansas.

SIALKOT CHURCH COUNCIL

This Church was established in 1854 through the efforts of Scottish PRESBYTERIAN missionaries at Sialkot, about 50 km east of Gujranwala, an industrial city in the Punjab province of India. It had formerly belonged to the United Church of North India and Pakistan.

SILESIAN EVANGELICAL CHURCH OF THE AUGSBURG CONFESSION IN THE CZECH REPUBLIC

A Polish-speaking LUTHERAN Church originating through the spread of Lutheranism in the mid-sixteenth century. It is to be found in the Tesin (in Silesia), Karvina and Ostrava border areas of Moravia and Slovakia, with the majority of members living in the Beskyd valleys of Tesin, where many are employed in the iron industry and others in the coal and steel industries in the Ostrava-Karvina regions.

The Church is divided into five administrative units, or *Seniorates*, and has a supreme legislative body in the triennial synod that elects the church council to serve for a period of six years. The Church established a missionary body known as the *Christian Community*, which works with children and young people, and the *Silesian Diaconia*, which helps to provide aid for senior citizens, the lonely and abandoned and those physically and mentally disabled, through a network of some seventeen centres. The Church is also responsible, through its *Evangelical Society* for producing many publications, including the monthly *People's Friend* and *The Evangelical Calendar*, together with various theological and educational periodicals. In the field of education the Church is active in the department of catechetics in the pedagogical faculty of the University of Ostrava. There is a current adult membership of about 40,000 and the Church is a member of the Lutheran World Federation, which it joined in 1956.

SIMALUNGUN PROTESTANT CHRISTIAN CHURCH

There was considerable LUTHERAN missionary activity amongst the Dayak people of Borneo and the Batak people of Sumatra during the nineteenth century, conducted by the Rhenish Missions that had been founded in Barmen, Germany, in 1828. This activity led ultimately to the formation of the Simalungun Protestant Christian Church (GKPS) in 1903.

The GKPS maintains the Lutheran tradition and through the Lutheran World Federation, which it joined in 1967, it has been able to develop several community projects amongst rural communities; farming is the main source of income for the Simalungun people. One of these projects involves bringing clean water to small villages, partly funded by the villages themselves and partly by the Lutheran World Federation Department for Mission and Development. Another important health programme was started at Seribudolok, west of the GKPS headquarters at Pematangsiantar in north Sumatra, Indonesia.

SIX PRINCIPLE BAPTISTS

This is an American Church of ARMINIAN Baptists, who separated in 1652 from the first BAPTIST CHURCH that was established in the seventeenth century at Providence, Rhode Island, by Roger Williams (1600–83).

The majority of members who joined the division held Arminian views and affirmed the six principles, as listed in Hebrews 6:1–2, as their creed. These principles are: repentance, faith, baptism, the laying on of hands, the resurrection of the dead and the final judgement. The imposition of hands is performed during the reception of a new member into a congregation and is seen as a sign of the reception of the gifts of the Holy Spirit.

Despite an initial growth in membership and the formation of congregations in Rhode Island, Massachusetts and Pennsylvania, the number of members has now fallen away dramatically; the current estimated membership is only a little in excess of one hundred and limited to Rhode Island. The polity of the Church is congregational and the conference is located at North Kingstown, Rhode Island.

❖ General Six Principle Baptists

SLAVIC PENTECOSTAL CHURCH

A small, PENTECOSTAL Church in Australia that is linked to the United Pentecostal Church of Australia, also known as the *Jesus Only Church*. It is a ONENESS Pentecostal group that teaches the deity of Jesus Christ and the Holy Spirit but regards them only as modes in which God reveals himself, and not as distinct persons of the Trinity. Members affirm the necessity for baptism in the name of Jesus Christ alone, and hold to the belief of Christ's premillennial return to earth (REVELATION 20). Baptism of the Holy Spirit, as evidenced by *glossolalia*, or speaking in tongues, and foot-washing are observed by its small congregations.

SOCIAL BRETHREN

This small American denomination, which was organized in Saline County, Illinois, has its origins in the aftermath of the American Civil War (1861–5). It was founded formally in 1867, when several PRESBYTERIAN and METHODIST clergy, and some laity, came together with the aim of seeking reconciliation amongst Christians in America over the question of slavery, holding that all those who believed in Christ should have fellowship with each other regardless of the position that each affirmed over the slavery issue.

The members of this Church affirm the sufficiency of the scriptures in all matters of faith and believe that they contain all that is necessary for salvation. Members observe only two ordinances, those of baptism, by any mode, and the Lord's Supper. The polity is best described as loosely congregational and the Church is organized on the basis of fellowships, of which there are three that meet annually. There is also an annual general assembly at which the leader, or moderator, is elected.

SOCIETY OF BROTHERS (HUTTERITE)

The Society of Brothers was formed in Germany in 1920. The leader, Eberhard Arnold, who had been a member of both the Christian Socialist Movement and the Student Christian Movement, centred his preaching around the text of the Sermon on the Mount. Members gathered at Sannerz Farm in 1920, where they supported the commune through farming while they studied the writings of the ANABAPTISTS and HUTTERITES. In 1931 a merger was made with Hutterite groups in the USA and Canada. After the death of Eberhard Arnold in 1935, members of the group, harassed in the years leading up to the Second World War by the Gestapo, who objected to the pacifism espoused by the society, began to move abroad, settling in England, Paraguay, Uruguay and the USA. The first settlement in the USA, called Woodcrest, was made at Rifton, New York, where a light industry business, Community Playthings, was set up with an emphasis on toy making. In 1955 the Hutterite colony from Forest River, North Dakota, joined them at Woodcrest. This period was one of great expansion, but in the early 1960s disputes broke out between the Hutterites and the Society of Brothers. By 1962 the communes had been much reduced.

The Society is run along mainly Hutterite lines, maintaining Anabaptist beliefs, but has modernized over the years, the members now wearing modern dress and mixing in the world at large. Prayer meetings, called *Gemeindestunde*, are held once or twice a week. The communes, known as *Hofs*, are governed by a chief servant – *der Vorsteher* – with the help of elders, stewards, witness brothers and housemothers.

SOCIETY OF ST PIUS X

This is one of several traditionalist ROMAN CATHOLIC groups that came into being in the wake of the reforms suggested by the Second Vatican Council (1962–5). The Society's founder was Archbishop Marcel Lefebvre (1905–91), a member of the Holy Ghost Fathers who had been appointed as Archbishop of Dakar by Pope Pius XII. In the face of his perception of his Order's acceptance of the liberalism of the Second Vatican Council, the archbishop resigned in 1968 with the intention of retiring from public life.

However, in response to the growing need expressed by some theological students for a traditional Roman Catholic training for the priesthood, Lefebvre opened a seminary, the *Fraternité Sacerdotale de Saint Pius X* in 1969, which was attached to the University of Fribourg. The seminary soon moved to Écône, in the canton of Valais in Switzerland, where a full traditional seminary curriculum, disregarding the Vatican reforms, could be pursued. News of this seminary, which at the start had the approval of the local Roman Catholic bishops, soon spread and in 1975 this approval was withdrawn. When, in 1976, Lefebvre prepared to ordain some thirteen of the seminary graduates he incurred the displeasure of Pope Paul VI and was suspended from celebrating the Mass. Undeterred by this turn of events, Lefebvre hoped for a commission of traditional Roman Catholics to be formed, from which he would be able to consecrate some traditionally minded bishops to serve those members of the Society worldwide, but this hope was soon dashed. In 1988, Lefebvre informed the Pope that he would consecrate four auxiliary bishops, assisted by Castro Meyer of Brazil; the participants in this ceremony were all excommunicated by Rome.

Members of the Society of St Pius X, popularly known as Lefebvrists, who currently number some 150,000 members spread throughout the world, do not think of themselves as being in schism because they continue to recognize papal authority, but not the reforms of the Second Vatican Council. The Vatican Commission *Ecclesia Dei* has confirmed that it has been entrusted with the care of those who wish to return to full communion with Rome and there have also been rumours of the provision of a personal prelature for the Lefebvrists.

❖ Lefebvrists; Lefebvrites

SOCINIANISM

A sixteenth-century movement that derived its name from Laelius Socinus (*or* Sozzini, *or* Suzzini), a lawyer from Siena, Italy, and his nephew, Faustus Socinus (1539–1604). The elder Socinus had developed anti-Trinitarian views, which were expanded upon by his nephew. Laelius was motivated by his attempt to restore primitive Christianity and to denounce what he called 'the idolatry of Rome'. His quest forced Laelius to travel widely, through Switzerland, France, England, Holland, Germany, Austria, Bohemia and Poland, before finally dying in Zürich.

Faustus, his nephew, although originally a member of the ROMAN CATHOLIC CHURCH, had gone to Basle in Switzerland in 1574 where he became a CALVINIST, but he developed strong views, which are best described as UNITARIAN, based on his reading of the scriptures. He left Basle for Poland in 1578, where he spent the rest of his life. Faustus held that the miracles in the Bible, and Christ's resurrection, proved the truth of Christianity – that Christ existed to bring mankind to the knowledge of God and that imitation of Christ's life would effect salvation. Baptism was recognized as the outward expression of a person's acknowledgement of Christ as their Lord and for this reason it was restricted to adults. The Lord's Supper was considered to be a commemorative feast only. While the supernatural character of Christ is not denied altogether, it goes further than Arianism, a heresy that maintained Christ's divinity but denied that he is coequal with the father.

Many of these views were being circulated in Poland amongst members of the REFORMED Churches. Faustus led his group, known as Socinians, to Rakow, north-east of Krakow, and with the help of his friends and followers produced the *Racovian Catechism*, which was first published in 1605; as it was not a binding doctrinal statement it underwent many subsequent and major revisions. As time went by the Socinians became more rationalistic and came to regard Jesus Christ as 'the best of men'. Under the devout Roman Catholic Polish king, Sigismund III Vasa (1566–1632) the group was severely persecuted, and finally expelled from Poland from 1648–68; in 1658 the Polish parliament passed the death sentence for adherents to the *Racovian Confession*. Many Socinians sought refuge in Transylvania, a country where anti-Trinitarian views were much in evidence and where, in the second half of the sixteenth century, LUTHERANS, Roman Catholics, Reformed Churchmen and Unitarians, as the Socinians came to be called, were granted equal status before the law. Others of the group went to Germany (Silesia and Prussia), the Netherlands and England.

The influence of the Socinians is evident in the history of the seventeenth and eighteenth centuries in Europe and they exerted considerable influence on Christian Humanists, Calvinists and English PRESBYTERIANS; Socinian ideas also came to flourish amongst the New England PURITANS in America.

SOUTHCOTTIANS

This ADVENTIST group was organized by followers of Joanna Southcott (1750–1814), who was born in Gittisham, Devon, the daughter of a tenant farmer. Originally associated with the Wesleyan METHODISTS, Southcott began to have visions in the 1790s, which she wrote down in verse and prose. At a Bible class in 1792 she declared herself to be 'the Lamb's wife', promptly had a fit and had to be removed from the room. Southcott gradually became convinced of her prophetic gifts and the importance of her messages, which were generally within a Christian context and centred upon Christ's second coming (REVELATION 20), and was also given to speculation about the meaning of the 'woman clothed with the sun' (Rev. 12:1), who would give birth to a son. Her major impact was in England at the start of the nineteenth century and the prophecies were published in several pamphlets, attracting many disciples.

Southcott had found a small seal, bearing the initials 'I. C.' with two stars upon it, and this she adopted as her own, interpreting the initials as those of Jesus Christ. Around 1802 she met William Sharp, a wealthy engraver, who became one of her disciples and may have financed the establishment of the first Southcottian chapel at Southwark, London, which was headed by a West Country dissenting minister, William Tozer. Southcott taught that eternal salvation was to be limited to only 144,000 followers and that the overthrow of Satan would be accomplished when people renounced him and were 'sealed as of the Lord'. This *sealing* consisted of receiving a square piece of paper, in the middle of which a circle was drawn within which were written the following words: 'The Sealed of the Lord, the Elect and Precious, Man's redemption to inherit the Tree of Life, to be made Heirs of God and Joint Heirs with Jesus Christ.' The document was then folded and sealed with wax, bearing Southcott's appropriated I. C. monogram, with its two stars. It has been said that Joanna Southcott issued at least 10,000 of these certificates, one of which was later found in the possession of a murderess called Mary Bateman.

In 1814, at the age of 64, Southcott wrote a letter to the newspaper, the London *Times*, and to every bishop and member of parliament announcing that she was soon to become the 'mother of Shiloh' (Gen. 49:10) as she had been told in a revelation that not only was she 'the Woman' (identified in Rev. 2), but that she was about to prepare for the birth of a son she identified with Shiloh. Southcott began, indeed, to show signs of pregnancy and it is said that some nine doctors who examined her were convinced that she was pregnant and that her child would be born on Christmas Day, 1814. Equally convinced, her followers presented Southcott with a crib, embossed in gold, for the expected child. On the appointed day, however, it became apparent that Joanna Southcott was dying and her last instruction allegedly requested that her dead body was to be kept warm for four days, after which it was to be opened. Two days later Joanna Southcott died and an autopsy revealed no foetus.

As part of her legacy, Joanna Southcott also left a corded and nailed box, about the size of a coffin and weighing 156 pounds, with the instructions that it was to be opened only in the presence of all the bishops at a time of national crisis. The box would appear to have been opened in 1928, with only one bishop present, revealing nothing of interest beyond an old night cap, a flintlock pistol and some unimportant papers. This story, however, has been challenged.

In 1866 the future Mabel Barltrop was born, who later declared herself to be the soul child who had been conceived and born of Joanna Southcott. Convinced that she had heard the Lord say that she was Christ's bride, Mabel Barltrop, the widow of a CHURCH OF ENGLAND clergyman, went to Albany Road, Bedford, in 1906 where some properties had been bought and set aside by those who believed Bedford to be the site of the original garden of Eden and the centre of the world's land mass. It was here that the Panacea Society, which was to be responsible for the sealed box and the best interests of Southcottian legacies and wealth, was to be established. The Panacea Society was organized in Albany Road by Mabel Barltrop, who had begun to take dictation from a spirit voice; a voice she continued to hear until her death in 1943. The spirit voice told her that the Godhead was not, in fact, composed of Father, Son and Holy Ghost, but of father, mother, son and daughter. A sort of middle-class commune was established at Albany Road and the Panacea Society flourished, with an especially vigorous growth in the 1930s. The Society still maintains a chapel on Albany Road, where services involve a reading from the *Book of Common Prayer* and from some of the communications granted to Mabel. A sum of money was recently raised by the Panacea Society when many of the gifts and legacies of past members were auctioned, the proceeds distributed to worthy charities including the Bedford Hospital and the Bedford Child Development Centre. Following the death of Joanna Southcott, in 1814, many of her followers, unhappy with the new leadership, joined the CHRISTIAN ISRAELITE CHURCH and the HOUSE OF DAVID.

SOUTHERN BAPTIST CONVENTION

This is the largest BAPTIST Church in the USA, having a current adult membership in excess of 15 million. The Church had its origins in 1845, when some three hundred Baptist congregations in the southern states organized themselves as a separate group from the Northern Baptists over the question of slavery and also over the issue of the need felt by the Southern group to have a more centralized organization than was the case with the Northern Baptists.

At the time of the split between these groups the acting board of foreign missions of the Baptists in America was located in Boston and was therefore much influenced by the abolition of the slavery movement. The board concluded, in the early 1840s, that it would not accept as missionaries those who were slaveholders. It was also the 'Brethren of the North' who first suggested separation, and this was accomplished in May 1845, when the Southern Baptist Convention (SBC) was established, forming its own foreign and mission boards.

The Church is noted for its heavy emphasis on evangelism and missionary work, combined with a tradition in its ministry of commitment to the common people. To these ends, the SBC subscribes to the *New Hampshire Confession* of 1833, which underwent revision in 1925 to produce the statement known as the *Baptist Faith and Message*. This statement is largely a document of consensus that has been described as being 'for the general institution and guidance of our own people' and 'having no authority over the conscience', since the Church does not accept binding creedal statements. There was a further revision of the document in 1963, which underlined the Church's position within the REFORMED theological tradition.

The Bible is recognized as the sole source of faith and practice and is held to be divinely inspired, but there is a difference of opinion between the members over the question of its inerrancy. SBC members accept the need for regeneration and baptism by immersion. The Church has a vigorous independent spirit and maintains a sense of religious liberty that is supported by the institutional separation of church and state in the USA. The polity of the Church is congregational, with members from the state conventions sending *messengers* to the annual national convention. This oversees the work of the various boards and commissions, seminaries and publishing programmes. Many colleges and universities are sponsored and supported by the Church, as well as orphanages, hospitals and retirement homes. The Church is also vigorous abroad in its missionary outreach, maintaining some 400 missionaries in 130 countries; there are also many home missions conducted in the USA.

The SBC has not been committed to ecumenical work, and though it belongs to the Baptist World Alliance, it is not a member of the World Council of Churches. The headquarters of the SBC is in Nashville, Tennessee.

SOUTHERN METHODIST CHURCH

In 1939, in the USA, a merger of the METHODIST EPISCOPAL CHURCH (MEC) with the Methodist Episcopal Church (South) was promoted and this eventually led to the formation of the METHODIST CHURCH. Not all church members were happy about this development, which brought about a shift in their doctrinal position and a perceived move towards centralized control, and they formed themselves into a separate group. The seceders met in convention at Columbia, South Carolina, to form what they saw as a continuation of the Methodist Episcopal Church (South), but they were faced with litigation in 1945 that prevented both their use of the denominational name and the retention of church property, and they adopted instead the name of Southern Methodist Church.

The Church fully subscribes to the 25 Methodist Episcopal *Articles of Religion*, with the added belief in the doctrine of prevenient grace, by which is meant that grace is available to all. The members furthermore affirm the witness of the Spirit, Christian perfection, the evangelization of the world and the creation story as told in Genesis; they also believe in premillennialism (REVELATION 20).

The polity of this all-white Church is congregational, with conferences, both annual and general, that elect a president for a period of four years. It has a vigorous mission outreach programme, currently working in Cameroon, Cyprus, Ethiopia, Zimbabwe, Italy, Peru, Mexico and Venezuela. The headquarters of the Church is in Orangeburg, South Carolina.

SPANISH EVANGELICAL CHURCH

In the Spain of 1868, with the proclamation of religious toleration written into the country's constitution, the way was opened for official PROTESTANT activity to begin. Various proselytizing attempts had previously been made by some PLYMOUTH BRETHREN from England, who began to hold house meetings as early as 1836, while other groups attempted to introduce evangelistic outreach programmes from Gibraltar and formed groups in Granada and Málaga.

The Spanish Evangelical Church (SEC) was officially formed around 1868, but in 1880 a split developed within the Church and the Spanish Reformed Episcopal Church came into existence. The SEC's first bishop was consecrated by three bishops from the CHURCH OF IRELAND, establishing important links between the Church and the ANGLICAN COMMUNION.

The SEC is essentially within the REFORMED tradition and may be best described as CONGREGATIONAL/PRESBYTERIAN, with its 35 congregations and pastoral care for around 8,400 adult members. The Church maintains a witness through the practice of open-air missions.

SPIRIT OF JESUS CHRIST

This indigenous Church in Japan owes its foundation to Murai Jun (born 1897), the second son of a METHODIST minister. Murai read theology at the Methodist-affiliated Aoyama Gakuin in Tokyo, but dropped out of the course, following an incident in which he was tempted to commit suicide; he went on to have a mystical experience of the presence of the Holy Spirit, began to talk in tongues (*glossolalia*) and was prompted to evangelize.

Murai eventually became the pastor of the Japan Bible Church in Nishisugamo (Tokyo); in 1949 this Church became the Japan Assembly of God. In 1941 he visited the True Jesus Church in Taiwan, a PENTECOSTAL Church that had been founded in Peking in 1917 by Paul Wei. While in Taiwan, Murai made the decision to leave his congregation and found a new Church, one which would be concerned with the recovery of an apostolic faith that he thought was missing from the mission-based Church to which he belonged. At the same time his wife, Suwa, had a revelation that the name of the new Church would be the Spirit of Jesus Church.

Murai and his followers were subject to criticism on account of the Church's growing emphasis upon speaking in tongues, and upon the very emotional healing services that Murai conducted, which stemmed from his experience of Pentecostal Christianity. He also introduced foot-washing of newly received members, baptism for the dead, sabbath worship and the doctrine of the second coming of Christ (REVELATION 20). All these emphases Murai justified by appeals to various biblical texts.

The Spirit of Jesus Church places little value on educational activities. It focuses attention on both sabbath and Sunday worship, which possibly derives from the influence of SEVENTH-DAY ADVENTIST missionaries in the Far East who were working in the area at the start of the twentieth century. In the course of the services, conducted by both male and female pastors, emphasis is placed upon the worldly benefits of religion and upon physical healing, which is available to all church members. It is customary for those who seek healing to approach the pulpit towards the end of the service, when special prayers are recited; the supplicants may then be anointed with oil, which comes from a small flask kept beside the pulpit Bible. Pastors are trained to develop an enthusiastic, evangelistic style and they frequently appeal to members of their congregations to destroy pagan idols and abstain from pagan rituals. Each pastor is responsible for his local church, in which no member of the laity plays any part. The congregations are represented at an annual conference, presided over by the bishop, who may be of either sex and who symbolizes the authority of the Church. It is the bishop's function to officiate at an annual celebration of the Lord's Supper during the conference and to conduct the funerals of pastors and the dedication of any new church buildings.

The success of this Church, like that of others in Japan, may be in part due to its recognition of the religious needs of its members and its substitution of Christian practices for the more traditional Japanese religious customs. As an example, ancestor worship was substituted for by baptism of the dead, citing 1 Corinthians 15:15–19 as justification for the custom.

This is now one of the largest of the mission-founded Japanese Churches and it sends missionaries to the USA and to Brazil. It is a thriving body, with 470 congregations and over 350,000 committed adult members.

STANDARD CHURCHES OF AMERICA

The Standard Churches of America was founded and incorporated in 1919 in Waterton, New York, by the Reverend Ralph Horner (1854–1921), an ex-METHODIST evangelist from the Montreal Conference of the Methodist Church, Canada.

Horner was a keen evangelist, but it has been alleged that this was at the expense of his pastoral duties. He was discharged from the ministry in Canada in 1895, whereupon he founded the Holiness Movement Church. Under his leadership, this Church experienced considerable growth in Canada, the USA (New York), Ireland, Egypt and China. When Horner was asked to retire because of his age, although he was still relatively young, being only 67 years old at the time of his death, he was unhappy at the prospect. He left the Holiness Movement Church only to found the Standard Churches of America.

The Standard Church of America is Methodist in doctrine, but it places a greater emphasis upon evangelism. With an episcopal polity, the Church is administered through four annual conferences, which are responsible for appointing pastors to the 70 congregations that serve an adult membership of 6,000. The headquarters of the Church is in Canada, at Brookville, Ontario.

STAUFFER MENNONITE CHURCH

This small American group of Mennonites, with its headquarters at Ephrata, Pennsylvania, was organized in 1845 by Jacob Stauffer, a minister of the MENNONITE CHURCH, together with a colleague from the OLD ORDER (WENGER) MENNONITES, Joseph Wenger. The group came into being at Stauffer's church in Groffdale, Pennsylvania, formed because of a disagreement concerning the application of the *ban*, which required that any member placed under it could have no further communication with either the Church, or any of its members, even if they were of the same family. The separating group felt that the imposition of this *ban* was becoming lax and they sought a return to older, stricter ways.

The small group that emerged is noted for its conservatism. Members do not involve themselves in local politics and neither is any value set upon education, charitable works or missionary initiatives. There was a schism within the group in 1916, when the son of a Mennonite bishop, Aaron Sensenig, married a young woman from outside the Mennonite community, into which she was received for a short time. Her subsequent departure from the Church caused the *ban* to be applied to her. The issue of the strictness of the *ban* once more split the Church. Those who inclined towards a more lenient application of the rule, led by Sensenig's son and John A. Weaver, together formed a new congregation that later became known as the WEAVER MENNONITES.

STUNDISTS

The Stundists were a Russian evangelical sect originating in present-day Odesa (formerly Odessa, Ukraine) in the mid-nineteenth century amongst a group of Bible students. It was started when German REFORMED missionaries conducted devotional Bible study and prayer meetings for both Russians and German settlers. The Bible classes lasted for one hour and these followers came to be called Stundists, taken either from the German *Stunde* – an hour, or from the Russian *Studinsty* – a devotional hour. The movement, which broke with most of the Reformed tradition, was organized in 1862 by the son of one of the German pastors, Karl Bohnekämper. Sacraments were rejected, even baptism to begin with, although this was later brought back into use, as were all church holidays. The Stundists also refused to accept an ordained clergy, since they believed in the priesthood of all believers.

Splits occurred within the group and by 1871 it had separated into different divisions and was being persecuted by both the Russian state and the RUSSIAN ORTHODOX CHURCH. Stundists were refused permission to open and maintain their own churches and were liable to arrest and imprisonment should as few as three members meet together for worship, but despite this the movement continued to spread widely. In more recent times, the Stundists came increasingly under BAPTIST influence, which Church's views were considered to be similar. This attachment allowed the opportunity for worship and the union was formalized in 1944, with the creation of the All-Union of Evangelical Christian-Baptists (AUCECB), an amalgamation of Christians which included not only the Stundists but also the PENTECOSTALS (since 1945–7) and the MENNONITES (since 1963).

The AUCECB has been seen as part of an attempt by the State to drive all PROTESTANT traditions into a single body, making state control easier to maintain. The Union underwent a schism in the 1960s on account of the Soviet government's anti-religious campaign, which led to the formation of the Council of Churches of Evangelical Christians-Baptists, whose members remained critical of the state's policies and of the harassment and imprisonment of some of its leaders. The formation of this Council was a protest against what was seen as the AUCECB's accommodation to the restrictions imposed by the state. As recently as 1975, it remained an illegal and underground movement and many of its members, especially young people, were imprisoned.

❖ Stundo-Baptists

SWADDLERS

This was a nickname applied originally to Wesleyans, and later addressed to Dissenters and PROTESTANTS by ROMAN CATHOLICS.

The term Swaddlers was applied, allegedly, to Wesleyan Methodists because, according to Robert Southey (1774–1843), in his *Life of Wesley* (1820 – *Volume II*), a Roman Catholic layman happened to hear a Christmas Day sermon given by a Wesleyan, John Cennick (1718–55), based upon Luke 2:12, in a vernacular translation that would not have been familiar to Roman Catholics at that time.

This vernacular text read: 'And this will be a sign for you; you will find a babe wrapped in swaddling clothes and lying in a manger.' The unnamed Roman Catholic found the use of the word 'swaddling' to be such a novelty that he nicknamed John Cennick a *Swaddler* and the expression is said to have been used as a scornful soubriquet for many years.

SWEDENBORGIANS (also SWEDENBORGIAN)

This Church does not hold a conventional Trinitarian view of theology.

Swedenborgians are believers in the religious doctrines taught by Emmanuel Swedenborg (1688–1772), a Swedish scientist, theologian and mystic who wrote many books, including *On the New Jerusalem and its Heavenly Doctrine* and *The True Christian Religion containing the Universal Theology of the New Church.* These works were influential in suggesting the names of two Swedenborgian groups, the Church of the New Jerusalem and the New Church, although the name 'Swedenborgian' commonly persists. Swedenborg did not, in fact, create either Church and it was his followers who were responsible for founding the Swedenborgian movement in England. Two of these enthusiastic followers were ANGLICAN clergymen, Thomas Hartley of Winwick, Northamptonshire and John Clowes of St John's, Manchester, who translated much of Swedenborg's writings from the original Latin in which they were written. By 1782 a society had been formed in Manchester for the purpose of publishing and circulating these writings and this led to many members of other Churches, including John Wesley, being inspired by Swedenborg's thoughts, although they were not usually prompted to leave their own Churches.

In 1787 the formal organization of the New Church occurred, in London, through the efforts of a METHODIST, Robert Hindmarsh, who was chosen by lot to officiate at the inaugural meeting held in a chapel at Eastcheap. By 1789, after other Swedenborgian societies and groups had been formed, the first general conference met at Great Eastcheap. The movement grew, and at the start of the twentieth century the Church in Great Britain had 45 ministers, 70 societies and in excess of 6,000 adult members. Today, the numbers have fallen and there are currently some 36 congregations, with less than 2,000 adult members in the UK.

Other Swedenborgian Churches are still in existence in other parts of the world, throughout Europe and the USA, in Australia and New Zealand and with a growing interest from Africa and Asia; these include the GENERAL CONVENTION OF THE NEW JERUSALEM IN THE USA, the GENERAL CHURCH OF THE NEW JERUSALEM and the LORD'S NEW CHURCH.

❖ Church of the New Jerusalem; General Conference of the New Church

SWEDISH MISSION COVENANT CHURCH

Until 1951 every Swedish citizen was considered to be *de facto* a member of the national, or state, Church of Sweden, which is based upon LUTHERAN creeds.

During the nineteenth century there was a strong spiritual revival felt throughout Sweden where, for more than 100 years, a prohibition had existed that prevented a gathering in a private home for Bible reading and prayers unless a priest was present. At the time of the revival this prohibition was abolished.

The revival led to the formation of several groups, which included the Swedish Evangelical Mission, also known as the Evangelical National Foundation, formed in 1865, the Baptist Union of Sweden, formed in 1848 and the Swedish Mission Covenant Church, formed in 1878. The Swedish Mission Covenant Church (MCCS) was promoted by two former priests of the Church of Sweden, P. P. Waldenström and A. J. Ekman, who, having studied the New Testament rigorously, saw in it the model of a Church in which all the members professed the Christian faith and in which the Lord's Supper was a celebration for believers rather than a citizen's duty.

The MCCS does not subscribe to any particular creed and regards the Holy Spirit as the only mentor for faith and doctrine; members are accorded the right to read and interpret the scriptures in their own way, under the guidance of the Holy Spirit. To become a member of the MCCS only a confession of faith in Christ is required. The MCCS has been involved in ecumenical dialogue with the Church of Sweden since 1965 and a report was generated and published in 1975 that made many suggestions for practical co-operation at local level.

Today, the MCCS is strongest in rural areas and despite a slow decline in the rate of growth, it still has over 1,000 congregations ministering to a membership in excess of 77,000 believers.

❖ Mission Covenant Church of Sweden

SYRIAN CATHOLIC CHURCH

The Syrian Catholic Church is descended from those Syrian Christians who did not accept the MONOPHYSITE heresy, which denied the Council of Chalcedon's (451) definition that Jesus Christ has two natures, divine and human. The Monophysite heresy was preached throughout the Middle East by the heretical Bishop of Edessa, Jacob Baradeus, after whom his followers came to be known as JACOBITES.

There were some unsuccessful attempts made by ROMAN CATHOLIC Dominican and Franciscan missionaries during the thirteenth century to convert the Jacobites, but it was not until the seventeenth century that success followed the efforts of the Capuchin Franciscans and Jesuits in Aleppo and led to large numbers of conversions to Rome. Such was the volume of conversions that in 1656 a Syrian Catholic priest, Andrew Akhidjan, was elected as Bishop of Aleppo; the Jacobites persecuted this Catholic community. In 1782–3 a Syrian Catholic convert, Michael Jarweh, was nominated as Patriarch of Antioch, but he was forced to flee by the Jacobites and escaped to Baghdad and then to a Maronite monastery at Sharfeh, in Lebanon, where he established a permanent patriarchate-in-exile. The patriarchate was later moved to Aleppo and is now settled in Beirut.

There are about 30,000 members of the Syrian Catholic Church living in the Middle East and the USA. The Church celebrates the *Liturgy of St James* in Syriac, a language akin to Aramaic, with many prayers and readings in local languages such as Arabic, Turkish and Kurdish.

SYRIAN ORTHODOX CHURCH

The Syrian Orthodox Church is in the MONOPHYSITE tradition, which originated when the Church, amongst others, refused to accept the conclusion of the Council of Chalcedon (451) that Jesus Christ had two natures, divine and human, maintaining instead that in Christ there is only the divine nature.

Sometimes known as the JACOBITE Church, it took this name from Jacob Baradeus, the sixth-century Monophysite Bishop of Edessa who wore very unkempt clothes as part of his disguise as a beggar, adopted for the purpose of avoiding arrest. Baradeus evangelized, ordained and consecrated many clergy within the Monophysite tradition throughout the Middle East for some 37 years.

Over the centuries, the Church's history has been one of conflict with various enemies, including Islam. By the start of the twentieth century, its members having endured massacres at the hands of the Turks, the survivors began to emigrate to other parts of the Middle East as well as to the USA, different parts of Europe and Australia.

The doctrinal position of the Church is the same as that held by other ORIENTAL ORTHODOX CHURCHES, those EASTERN ORTHODOX CHURCHES that also reject the Council of Chalcedon's Christology of the two natures of Jesus Christ. The Syrian Orthodox Church uses the *Liturgy of St James* and celebrates in Syriac; other local languages may be used for various prayers and readings. There is a current membership of some 3 million, presided over by the Patriarch of Antioch who resides in Damascus, in Syria. The Church became a member of the World Council of Churches in 1960, largely through the efforts of its late patriarch, Mar Ignatius Jacob III.

❖ Syrian Jacobite Church

SYRO-MALABARESE CHURCH

This large body of EASTERN CATHOLICS in south-west India is derived from some Chaldean Catholics who had been established in the area, probably from the time of St Thomas the Apostle's missionary work in the first century and that of Chaldean missions in the following centuries. Portuguese colonists, who arrived in India at the end of the fifteenth century, mistakenly thought that these Christians were Nestorian heretics because they celebrated the Chaldean, or East Syrian, Liturgy in Syrian and they were thought to be in need of being latinized.

With the death of their last Chaldean-rite bishop, Mar Abraham, in 1597, the Malabarese were determined to have a native bishop, an aim that was thwarted by the Portuguese, who were deeply suspicious of anything that was not Latin rite. The Synod of Diamper was convened in 1599, by the Archbishop of Goa, with its aim 'to purify all the Churches from the heresy and errors which they hold'. This was, quite naturally, deeply offensive to the Malabarese Christians. A schism followed and the troubles were partly healed through the efforts of Carmelite friars, sent to the area by Pope Alexander VII. Although over half of the schismatic parishes had returned to the ROMAN CATHOLIC CHURCH by 1662, the pleas for a native hierarchy went unheeded. Finally, in 1896, Pope Leo XIII agreed to appoint three Indian bishops to vicariates at Trichur, Ernakulam and Changanacheri; a fourth, at Kottayam, was added in 1911.

The Divine Liturgy used by the Syro-Malabarese Church is that of the Chaldean rite, the *Liturgy of the Holy Apostles Mar Addai and Mar Mari*, but there have been many attempts at revision and reform of the text to bring it into line with modern Indian culture. The revisions of 1962, 1986 and 1989 have not been well received and many liturgical practices are still being debated. The 3 million members of this Church are now under the pastoral care of the major Archbishop of Ernakulam-Angamaly.

❖ St Thomas Christians

SYRO-MALANKARESE CHURCH

This small EASTERN CATHOLIC CHURCH in India grew out of an early CHALDEAN CATHOLIC (CHURCH) community that was targeted for latinization by Portuguese colonists who had been in occupation on the south-west coast of the country since 1498, in the mistaken belief that these Eastern-rite Catholics were Nestorian heretics.

Schism from the ROMAN CATHOLIC CHURCH, dissensions and legal wrangles continued until the end of the eighteenth century. It was not until 1926 that a synod of these disaffected schismatics, who by then had become JACOBITES (members of the SYRIAN ORTHODOX CHURCH), authorized Mar Ivanios, the Jacobite Metropolitan of Bethany, to seek reunion with Rome. This move was welcomed by Pope Pius XI, and in 1930 Mar Ivanios, his suffragan bishop, Mar Theophilos, and other church officials were received into the Roman Catholic Church. In order to distinguish these Catholics from others in the region they were designated as members of the Syro-Malankara Church. Pope Pius XI established a Malankarese hierarchy, with Mar Ivanios appointed as Archbishop of Trivandrum and Mar Theophilos as Suffragan Bishop of Thiruvalla, Kerala.

The Church observes the Antiochene rite, and while it enjoys administrative autonomy, it has accepted some Roman Catholic canon laws and customs. There are now three dioceses, with those of Trivandrum and Thiruvalla joined by the suffragan diocese at Sultan Battery, which was established in 1978. The Church has a current membership of about 300,000 faithful, who are served by 500 priests and around 1,200 male and female religious.

❖ Malankarese Christians; Syro-Malankarese of the Antiochene Rite

T

TABORITES

Members of a militant HUSSITE reform group in southern Bohemia that came together after the execution of John Huss, the Czech reformer who went to the stake in 1415 for heresy. In their extreme Bible-based approach, the members were strongly anti-ROMAN CATHOLIC, rejecting the distinction between priests and laity as well as transubstantiation, purgatory, relics and saints. The use of Latin in Church services was proscribed, replaced by Czech, all clergy were permitted to marry and all the sacraments, other than baptism and the Eucharist, were rejected. They were also ultra-nationalistic and aimed for social reform, which fitted in with their message concerning the imminence of Christ's second coming, a time held to be preceded by a period of turmoil (REVELATION 20). Social anarchy broke out in 1419 when thousands of the disaffected population of landless labourers, inner-city dwellers and other citizens attended open air rallies that were held on mountain tops; these mountain tops were named *Tabor* and were thought to be where the second coming of Christ would be accomplished. The leaders of the Taborites calculated that this would occur between 10–14 February 1420, and taught that members of their group would be the only ones to survive the destruction of the world by fire. Christ's failure to appear on the expected dates was explained away by claiming that he had, indeed, come to earth, but in secrecy.

The Taborites remained united as a group under the military leadership of John Zizka *the One-Eyed*, and formed a short-lived alliance with the moderate CALIXTINES whom they rescued during an armed skirmish with the imperial army near Prague. The alliance failed upon the death of Zizka in 1424. *(It has been said that Zizka may have invented the forerunner of the military tank by putting armour around a wagon, which was loaded with small cannons.)*

Led by Andrew Procopius the Great, who was also known as *The Shaven*, or *The Holy* because he had been a monk, the Taborites were defeated by the Calixtines, who had united with the Roman Catholic Czech nobility in 1434, at the battle of Lipany (now Lippau) near Prague. The Czech nobility, although at one time sympathetic to Hussite religious reforms, felt threatened by the Taborites' social agenda, which included, for example, the unwelcome suggestion that peasants should refuse to pay rent to landowners on the grounds that the last days were at hand. Procopius was killed and the Taborite movement was annihilated.

TAIWAN LUTHERAN CHURCH

The former island of Formosa (now Taiwan) became the refuge for many mainland Chinese in the wake of the communist revolution in 1949. By 1951, the Taiwan Lutheran Church (TLC) had been established by Chinese LUTHERANS who had moved to the island.

An immigrant medical lay preacher, Dr C. A. Chin, began to bring together many factory workers at his home, in Kaohsiung, for Bible study and this led to the formation of a Lutheran congregation. Dr Chin, who was later ordained, saw his congregation grow into the Taiwan Lutheran Church, with large congregations in Taipei and Koahsiung, at opposite ends of the island, together with small congregations and mission stations in the central part of Taiwan. The Church has introduced a support ministry for university students at Taipei, Taiching and Tainan, and the Taiwan Leprosy Relief Association, which provides programmes dealing with the prevention, treatment and support of sufferers and their families. Other medical work has extended to the provision of a large medical care facility at Kaohsiung and the Christian Hospital, established in Chiayi in 1962 through the missionary work of Dr Marcy Ditmansan, which also provides mission outreach for factory workers from Thailand and the Philippines who work on the island.

Education for future clergy is provided at the inter-Lutheran theological training centre of the China Lutheran Seminary in Hsinchu. The Taiwan Lutheran Church joined the Lutheran World Federation in 1960 and currently has about forty congregations, all overseen by a president.

TEMPLE SOCIETY

Christian Hoffmann (1815–85) was the founder of the Temple Society, which was formed in Württemberg, Germany, in 1853. Hoffman believed that the second coming and the establishment of Christ's kingdom in Jerusalem were imminent (REVELATION 20). Others joined him, with the intention of settling in the Holy Land but they were frustrated because of the political situation there. They remained in Germany and formed a commune at Kirschenhardthof, which they organized along theocratic lines.

Hoffmann's understanding of Christianity was very firmly seen from an Old Testament viewpoint. He decried a belief in the Trinity and did not hold that either Christ or the Holy Spirit was divine. Instead, he believed that the incarnation was the expression of God's creative thought put into the mind and body of Christ and that through his resurrection Christ became man-made-God. Hoffmann understood this to show the potential that man could achieve.

In 1866 migrants introduced the Temple Society into the USA, and before his death in 1885 Hoffmann also saw three colonies established in Palestine. The numbers have dwindled but the Temple Society still maintains headquarters in Jerusalem and at Santa Barbara, California.

❖ Friends of the Temple; Jerusalem Friends

THEE ORTHODOX CATHOLIC OLD ROMAN CHURCH

Thee (*sic*) Orthodox Catholic Old Roman

Church was founded in the USA in the 1970s by Peter Charles Caine Brown (aka William C. Brown), who had been consecrated in 1973 by three bishops, taking the name of Archbishop Simon Peter; according to some accounts he was ordained priest the following day by one of the consecrating bishops. The Church has its headquarters in Chicago, Illinois, but no up-to-date statistics of membership are currently available.

THEOPHILANTHROPISTS

This group did not hold a conventional Trinitarian view of theology.

A short-lived sect, formed in France in the eighteenth century at the time of the French Revolution and during the rule of the Directory, that was designed to be without dogma. The tenets of belief were set out in a pamphlet, *Manuel des Théophilanthropes*, written by J. B. Chemin-Dupontes, and called for a belief in God, virtue and immortality. After a meeting in Paris in 1797, it was agreed that the sect should be given the use of the Cathedral of Notre Dame as well as of ten other Paris churches.

With the re-establishment of ROMAN CATHOLICISM by the Concordat of 1801, which was followed by the restoration of churches to Roman Catholic use in 1802, the movement began to falter. An attempt to revive it was made in the late-nineteenth century, but it proved ineffectual.

TODAY CHURCH

Bud and Carmen Moshier formed this American group in Dallas, Texas, in 1969; it was originally known as the *Academy of Mind Dynamics*. Bud Moshier was a southern BAPTIST minister who later became influenced by NEW AGE ideas. He preached that man's problems come directly from his having lost sight of his spiritual beginnings and that he must return to his roots. A programme of lectures, also made available on tape in order to reach a wider audience, was backed up with various publications and a weekly periodical that aimed to show how to achieve this.

TRADITIONAL ANGLICAN COMMUNION

The Traditional Anglican Communion is an international organization embracing groups from the CONTINUING CHURCH throughout the world. The foundation dates from the *Affirmation of St Louis* (1977), when the need to uphold traditional ANGLICAN beliefs and practices was affirmed, and many traditionalist congregations and new jurisdictions were established.

By 1992, in the face of the tolerated changes taking place and accepted within the ANGLICAN COMMUNION, such as the ordination of women, many jurisdictions, such as the ANGLICAN CATHOLIC CHURCH, and the Anglican Catholic Churches of Canada, Australia, New Zealand, Hong Kong and Central America, were created; together they formed the Traditional Anglican Communion, with Archbishop Louis W. Falk, of the ANGLICAN CHURCH IN AMERICA, elected as its primate.

To this list has now been added the Traditional Anglican Church (England), the Church of Ireland (Traditional Rite), the Anglican Church in Southern Africa (Traditional Rite), the Orthodox Church of Pakistan (Anglican) and the Church of Torres Strait.

TRADITIONAL PROTESTANT EPISCOPAL CHURCH

This small, traditional and conservative Church was formed in 1986, when the head of the United Episcopal Church of America, Bishop Charles Edward Morley, disbanded that Church to form the Traditional Protestant Episcopal Church (TPEC). The TPEC arose partly on account of a reaction against what some laity and clergy saw as a growing Anglo-Catholicism in the United Episcopal Church, which they thought was inappropriate, but also because some members were seeking a more traditional Anglican home.

Liturgical practice of the TPEC may best be described as *Low Church*. The Bible is considered to be inerrant and is used in the King James' version, along with the *1928 Book of Common Prayer*. A missionary body, the Diocese of the Advent, has been created to provide a structure for missionary activity across the USA and Canada. This single diocese facilitates work that can be undertaken for those parishes that have left other Anglican jurisdictions but wish to maintain their PROTESTANT identity, and also to help to form new congregations. At present the Church is not part of the ANGLICAN COMMUNION.

TRASKITES

The PURITAN sect which later became absorbed into the SEVENTH-DAY BAPTIST CHURCH movement was founded in England in the seventeenth century by the Somerset-born John Traske, who worked initially as 'a school master in a gentleman's house' until the death of his first wife after only a few years of marriage. Traske then took up preaching and applied to James Montague, Bishop of Bath and Wells, for ordination but this was at first refused. His persistence was rewarded in 1611, when he was ordained into the CHURCH OF ENGLAND. He then embarked upon a career as a wandering preacher; although licensed to preach by the Church, Traske took his message into unlicensed premises, which earned for him a spell in London's infamous Newgate Gaol. After his release, Traske remained undeterred. He remarried and set about forming congregations that were sympathetic to a literal understanding of the Bible and separate from the Church of England. He believed that the Old Testament was not only a history of ancient Israel, but was the source of many truths that God revealed to his own people and that the instructions it contained were to be obeyed.

One of Traske's companions in his work, a tailor named Hamlet Jackson, interested himself in the dietary laws outlined in the Old Testament, concluded that these were also applicable to Christians and the congregations began to avoid 'unclean meat' (Lev. 11). Jackson had also concluded that the seventh day sabbath (Saturday) should be observed, but Traske continued to observe the conventional Christian Sunday until Jackson received a mystical experience. This convinced Traske of the need to observe the biblical sabbath, to which the congregations gave ready assent.

For Traske, the consequences of these actions were serious and in 1618 he was again imprisoned, along with some of his followers, for being a member of a Judaizing sect. *(Even while in prison, Traske managed to conduct a Jewish Passover Seder ritual.)* Traske was summoned to the court of Star Chamber, which found him guilty of 'detraction and scandal' upon the king, and of a serious attempt to 'divert His Majesty's subjects from their Obedience'. He was sentenced in 1618, receiving the severe punishment of imprisonment for life, a whipping and a fine of £1,000. He was defrocked and set in a pillory, with one ear nailed to it, and was branded on the forehead with the letter 'J' because he had 'broached Jewish opinions'.

Traske recanted his heretical views and was released, after which he began to associate with the BAPTISTS, who were then being led by Henry Jessey, but he died soon afterwards.

TRIDENTINE CATHOLIC CHURCH – TRADITIONAL CATHOLIC ARCHDIOCESE IN AMERICA

This is an independent, western-style Catholic Church, which was founded in the USA in 1976 by Fr Leonard J. Curreri, a former priest of the Traditional Catholic Church. This had been founded for Hungarian immigrants in Quebec, Canada, in 1965 by Archbishop Csernohorsky-Fehervary. Leonard Curreri, together with two other priests, went to New York to found a mission in the USA; this mission was renamed the Tridentine Catholic Church. In the 1970s, Curreri accepted consecration, as bishop, from some independent Catholic and EASTERN ORTHODOX sources. By 1991, the Church had changed its name to its present form.

Doctrinally and liturgically, the Church follows pre-Vatican II norms, but an acknowledgement of papal infallibility is not insisted upon. The moral position adopted is largely that of the ROMAN CATHOLIC CHURCH and clerical celibacy is usual. The Church is very small, consisting of 4 clergy and around 100 members, with its headquarters in Brooklyn, New York.

TRIUMPH THE CHURCH AND KINGDOM OF GOD IN CHRIST CHURCH

This black PENTECOSTAL Church was founded in the USA in 1902 by Elder D. Smith, who five years earlier had received a religious experience that inspired him to found the Church. The Church places considerable emphasis upon the experience of the fire-baptism, which is similar to the baptism of the Holy Spirit but without the *glossolalia*, or speaking in tongues; it is experienced as a sense of being overpowered by the Holy Spirit.

The head of the Church, who is called the chief bishop, oversees the work of subordinate bishops and other officials who care for 500 churches with an adult membership of 45,000. The headquarters of the Church, originally in Baton Rouge, Louisiana, is currently located in Atlanta, Georgia.

TRUE JESUS CHURCH

This Church does not hold a conventional Trinitarian view of theology.

The True Jesus Church (TJC) had its beginnings in Beijing, China, in 1917 when three members of the Apostolic Faith Movement, Paul Wei, Ling-Shen Chang and Barnabas Chang, had a revelation concerning the truth about salvation and how it may be achieved. The message of the TJC spread throughout China, by means of missionaries and gospel newsletters, and then to Taiwan and south-east Asia during the 1920s and to Hawaii in 1930. Having established headquarters in Nanjing, China, in 1926, a year later it relocated to Shanghai. When mainland China was taken over by the communists in 1949, the TJC moved again, to Taiwan. The International Assembly of the True Jesus Church was held there in 1975 and attracted many delegates from around the world. In 1985 the headquarters was moved to Los Angeles and centres for the co-ordination of missions in the USA, Europe, SE Asia and NE Asia were established.

The name of the Church came from one of the early revelations received by the founders in Beijing in 1917. The TJC teaches that for salvation a person, and that may include infants, must be baptized with natural, living water by full immersion with the head facing downwards; this rite is administered in the 'Name of the Lord Jesus Christ' alone and the baptizer must have received not only the baptism of water, but also the baptism of the Holy Spirit. Foot-washing is regarded as a sacrament and must be performed, by a church member, for all newly baptized members in the name of the Lord Jesus Christ alone. Where possible, the officiating member should be ordained, or must at least have received the baptism of water and that of the Holy Spirit. Baptism of the Holy Spirit is considered a prerequisite for entering heaven and is evidenced by *glossolalia*, or speaking in tongues. Holy Communion is regarded as a commemorative meal and consists of unleavened bread and grape juice, while the observance of the sabbath on the seventh day of the week completes the requirements necessary for salvation. The Church maintains that on the last day Jesus Christ will descend from heaven and will judge everyone, with eternal life awarded to the righteous and eternal damnation to the wicked (REVELATION 20). The TJC is active in 21 countries, including the USA, Canada, the UK, Russia, Korea, Malaysia, New Zealand, Australia, India and the Philippines.

TWENTIETH CENTURY CHURCH OF GOD

This ADVENTIST-type Church was founded in the USA in 1974 by Al Carrozzo, following his disagreement with Garner Ted Armstrong, the son of the founder of the WORLDWIDE CHURCH OF GOD, in which Church Carrozzo had held an executive position. Leaving the World Wide Church of God and travelling widely within the USA, Carrozzo employed many forms of media to spread his message, making use of radio broadcasts, audiotapes and published literature in an attempt to reunite in his Church those people who had left the Worldwide Church of God. The principal emphases of the Twentieth Century Church of God are focused on spiritual growth, prayer, Christian living and reconciliation, all set in the context of the familiar Worldwide Church of God doctrinal position.

TWO-SEED-IN-THE-SPIRIT PREDESTINARIAN BAPTISTS

The doctrine of the Two-Seed-in-the-Spirit Church was first spread in America in the late eighteenth and early nineteenth centuries through the evangelizing of a BAPTIST preacher, Elder Daniel Parker. Parker took a text from Genesis 3:15, 'I will put enmity between you and the woman, and between your seed and her seed', and argued that Abel and Cain represented the two seeds, either one of which is carried by every member of the human race. Abel's seed is of God and Adam, while Cain's seed is of Satan. Every baby is predestined, born with one seed or the other. Since the seed is in the spirit, not the flesh, nothing can be done about it, and since nothing can be done, then missions were to be regarded as useless. This argument explains why these Baptists protested against both missions and Sunday schools and were opposed to the METHODIST and ARMINIAN doctrine. The Church, which is now almost defunct, observes the Lord's Supper and the practice of foot-washing.

U

UKRAINIAN CATHOLIC CHURCH

Sometimes the name Ruthenians is applied to those Byzantine-rite Catholics who are found mainly in Poland, Czechoslovakia, Hungary, Ukraine and elsewhere in Europe as well as in the Americas and Australia.

Modern-day Ruthenians of the diaspora in the USA are styled as members of the Byzantine Catholic Church, with their own hierarchy.

The Ukrainian Catholics, or Ruthenians, are descendants of those people who had been converted at the time when St Vladimir, the apostle of the Russians and the Ruthenians, made his capital at Kiev, 'the God-protected Mother of Russian Cities', in the tenth century. It remained the centre of religious life in this region until the Tartars pillaged the city in 1240.

By 1320, the see had moved from Kiev to Vladimir and then to Moscow. Isidore was appointed as Metropolitan of Moscow by the Byzantine patriarch, Joseph II, who favoured reunion with Rome (and, in fact, died as a Roman Catholic in Florence). Metropolitan Isidore and another Russian bishop attended the Council of Florence (1438–45), when Rome sought reunion with the Greek Church after the *Great Schism* in 1054, and these two bishops signed the decree of union (1439) which resulted in Isidore's deposition and imprisonment by the Tsar in 1441 for disobeying his specific instructions about the question of reunion with Rome (see below). Isidore managed to escape to Rome where he resigned his post. Although a temporary reunion with Rome had been effected by the Council of Florence, a definitive union was achieved at Brest-Litovsk in 1596 when Metropolitan Michael Ragoza of Kiev and the Bishops of Vladimir, Lutsk, Polotsk, Pinsk and Kholm agreed to join the Roman Communion on condition that their traditional rites be preserved intact. The Bishops of Lvov (now Lviv) and Peremysl opposed the decision to reunite and delayed their affirmation of Union until the end of the seventeenth and start of the eighteenth centuries.

The partition of Poland (1772–95) brought almost all of Ukraine under Russian influence and orthodoxy. Under Catherine II, Nicholas I and Alexander I of Russia, the Ruthenian episcopal sees were reduced to three, the monasteries were closed and parishes were handed over to the Orthodox Church. The Ruthenians continued to flourish in western Ukraine, which became part of the Austrian empire. After the Russian *Edict of Toleration* of 1905, around

500,000 Ukrainians returned to Roman Catholicism and the Ukrainian Catholic Church was able to reorganize under the leadership of Metropolitan Andrei Szeptyckyj of Lvov, especially after the greater part of its territory had been divided between Czechoslovakia and Poland following the end of the First World War. The Soviet Union occupied the western Ukraine after the Second World War and the Ruthenian, or Ukrainian, Church was singled out for persecution. The Church was closed down and its clergy were imprisoned. It went underground and became known as the Church of the Catacombs, emerging some fifty years later, after the collapse of the Soviet Union and the establishment of the Ukrainian state. With the advent of independence in 1991, the 3.5 million Ruthenian Catholics seized control of their church buildings. The Church was reorganized by the Vatican into some thirteen new dioceses and is now to be found throughout parts of western Europe as well as in North and South America and Australia. In 2002 the Vatican announced the creation of a new Ukrainian jurisdiction, the exarchate of Donetsk-Kharkiv, which is to be headed by the newly elected bishop, Stephan Meniok, a Ukrainian who had entered the Redemptorist Order in 1975 when the Ukrainian Catholic Church was still illegal. At the end of June 2002, permission was given for the opening of a Catholic University at Lviv, in western Ukraine, the first to be opened on former Soviet territory. Pope John Paul II blessed the cornerstone of the new building during his visit to the city in 2001.

The Ukrainian Catholic Liturgy is Byzantine, with Latin modifications and with the *filioque* clause added to the creed. No hot water is added to the chalice before Holy Communion and the sacred vessels are left on the altar until the conclusion of the Liturgy. The doors of the iconostasis are left open during the entire Liturgy, in contrast to the practice in the Orthodox Church, and a sequence of liturgical colours of vestments is observed.

There are many stories concerning Isidore, but some may be apocryphal. It is said that he was given the task of attending the Council of Florence by the Grand Duke of Muscovy, Basil II, and ordered to return to Moscow with the 'rights of Divine Law and the constitution of the Holy (Orthodox) Church uninjured'. Despite this, Isidore signed the Union decree. On his way back to Moscow, Isidore received news that he had been made a cardinal by Rome. His reception in Moscow was understandably frigid and his imprisonment understandable, but it is suggested that Basil II aided Isidore's escape. He was subsequently sent by Rome as papal legate to Constantinople and was present there at the time that this city was captured by the Turks in 1453. Isidore narrowly escaped death by dressing up a corpse in his cardinal's robes. The Turks beheaded the corpse and paraded it through the streets while Isidore escaped to Asia Minor dressed as a slave. He was able to flee the country and return to Rome, where he died in 1463.

❖ Little Russians; Ruthenians

UKRAINIAN ORTHODOX CHURCH

Ukrainian Orthodox believers are represented within three jurisdictions, each answering to a different hierarchy. These are: 1) The Ukrainian Autocephalous Orthodox Church; 2) The Ukrainian Orthodox Church, Moscow Patriarchate; and 3) The Ukrainian Orthodox Church, Kiev Patriarchate.

The Ukrainian Orthodox Church developed from the preaching of St Andrew the apostle and his disciples. The kingdom of Ukraine became officially Orthodox in the year 988, when its sovereign, Olga's grandson St Vladimir (Volodymyr) was baptized according to the Byzantine rite by the Bishop of Chersonesus (now Sevastopol), on the Black Sea; this brought the country within the jurisdiction of Constantinople. St Vladimir ensured that the people of his country were brought into Byzantine Christianity, and churches were built throughout the region. By the eleventh century a strong Church had emerged, bishops were appointed and monastic communities were formed, including the famous Monastery of the Caves that was founded at Kiev in 1050. The primate of the Church, the Metropolitan of Kiev, came within the patriarchal jurisdiction of Constantinople and he exercised wide local administrative jurisdiction as the Constantinopolitan patriarch's exarch in Rus-Ukraine. However, in 1686, without the knowledge and assent of the Metropolitan of Kiev, Constantinople placed the Ukrainian Orthodox Church under the control of the Patriarch of Moscow.

With this integration with Moscow the independence of the Ukrainian Church was lost and it was not until the fall of the tsarist empire in 1917–20 that Ukrainian ecclesiastical independence was returned. In October 1921, the first All-Ukrainian synod was held in Kiev and the Ukrainian Autocephalous Orthodox Church came into existence. The Church now has in the region of 1,200 parishes and is headed by the Patriarch of Kiev and All Ukraine, Mefodiy (Kudryakov). The policy of the Church favours the unification of all three Ukrainian bodies.

The Ukrainian Orthodox Church (Moscow Patriarchate) is an exarchate of the Russian Orthodox Church and comprises the majority of Orthodox believers in Ukraine. The Ukrainian Orthodox Church (Kiev Patriarchate) came into existence in 1992.

UNION OF EVANGELICAL CHRISTIAN-BAPTISTS OF THE RUSSIAN FEDERATION

This voluntary association, which now has around 1,200 congregations in its membership, was formed in 1944 as a union between Evangelical Christians and members of the Baptist Church. After the Russian Revolution of 1917 there was a period of religious freedom in the country, but this was closely followed by a time of religious suppression that began in 1929. After the Second World War the government in Russia began to make concessions to the various Churches and about half of the then-known Pentecostal congregations, known collectively as the Christians of Evangelical Faith, joined the All-Union Council of Evangelical Christians and Baptists; some left in 1970 to form the Pentecostal Union of United Churches.

❖ All-Union Council of Evangelical Christians and Baptists; Euro-Asiatic Federation of Evangelical Christians-Baptists

UNION OF THE ARMENIAN EVANGELICAL CHURCHES IN THE NEAR EAST

The arrival in Constantinople (now Istanbul) in 1831 of William Goodall, a member of the American Board of Commissioners for Foreign Missions, signalled the start of the first permanent Protestant mission to work amongst the Armenians. The claim made by the mission, that the aim of this effort was to stimulate interest in the traditional Armenian Orthodox Church amongst the people of the country rather than to convert Armenians to protestantism, was not believed and in 1846 the Armenian Patriarch of Constantinople became alarmed and excommunicated all those who had followed the missionaries. In the same year the first ARMENIAN EVANGELICAL CHURCH was organized.

The following year saw the Turkish authorities recognize the semi-autonomous status of the protestant community but trouble in the area, which led to Turkish massacres, forced many members of the Church to flee to Lebanon, where they founded the Union of Armenian Evangelical Churches in the Near East for the various protestant Churches involved in 1918.

The Union is the second largest protestant community in Lebanon and it places considerable emphasis upon its educational programme for primary and secondary schools; it has further responsibility for the Haigazian University in Beirut, which was founded as the Haigazian College in 1955. At present the Union has 5 congregations, providing care for over 2,000 adult members, and is represented in Liberia, Syria, Iran, Egypt, Turkey, Greece and Austria. The headquarters of the Union is in Beirut, Lebanon.

UNITARIANISM (also UNITARIAN)

Unitarianism is not considered to be a conventional Christian denomination.

This is a system of religious thought that denies the Trinity and affirms a belief that it is possible to create a religious community without insistence upon doctrinal agreements. It evolved from a teaching alleged to be based upon scriptural authority and has now become heavily rationalized. Unitarianism had its roots in the Reformation and was established in the sixteenth and seventeenth centuries in Poland, Hungary and England; in the mid-eighteenth century it found its way across the Atlantic to America, as part of a reaction to contemporary revivalism.

Apart from a denial of the Trinity, Unitarianism does not acknowledge the divinity of Jesus Christ, man's fall, the atonement, the infallibility of the Bible or eternal punishment in hell, together with most other conventional doctrines. Today, it is a creedless movement that stresses the legitimacy of many forms of divine revelation and affirms man's essential goodness. As a worldwide movement it has been prominent in its support of issues concerning social justice.

UNITAS FRATRUM

This group, which is also known as the Bohemian Brethren, was to be the spiritual ancestor of the MORAVIAN CHURCH. It appeared in the fifteenth century, in the present-day Czech Republic, as a group of Utraquists (CALIXTINES) led by Brother Gregory, a nephew of the Archbishop of Prague, John Rokycana. In 1467 they separated from their parent body in order to follow more closely the teachings of Peter Chelcicky (*c.* 1390–1460), the founder of the CHELCIC BRETHREN, which advocated social reconstruction and unwordliness.

As followers of Peter Chelcicky, the Brethren rejected oaths and military service and tried to live a simple and unworldly Christian life. The group was organized as a Church by Lukas of Prague (d. 1528) during the sixteenth century.

Lukas, who saw a strong growth of the Church during his stewardship, stood implacably against any form of union with the LUTHERANS, but after his death the leadership passed into the hands of pro-Lutherans. The Holy Roman Emperor, Ferdinand I, attempted to repress the Unitas Fratrum in 1547 and this prompted many of the Brethren to leave Moravia and go to Poland, where they joined the CALVINIST movement in 1555. Twenty years later, those Brethren who had remained in Moravia were given the right to their religious freedom by Emperor Maximilian II (1527–76). In 1620, at the battle of the White Mountain, Moravia and Bohemia (later Czechoslovakia) lost their independence and the Brethren were forced into exile.

A remnant of these exiled Brethren, who had travelled as far as Saxony in the east of Germany, received an offer of help from Count Zinzendorf to settle on his lands and they established a community there, at Herrnhut, in 1721. Zinzendorf invited the Brethren to hold a communion service at his estate chapel on 17 August 1727, where the congregation is said to have received a massive outpouring of the Holy Spirit, and this is taken as the foundation date of the Moravian Church.

❖ Bohemian Brethren; Moravian Brethren

UNITED BRETHREN IN CHRIST

The Church was started as a PIETIST revival in America in the mid-to-late eighteenth century, amongst German speakers in Pennsylvania, Maryland and Virginia. In 1752 a minister of the Reformed Church of Holland, Michael Schlatter, asked for a German pastor, Philip William Otterbein, to come out from Germany to help with the American colonies. Otterbein, together with Martin Boehm who had been born into a MENNONITE family and had been selected by his people to be their preacher, preached at an interdenominational meeting, held in Isaac Long's barn near Lancaster, Pennsylvania, on Pentecost Sunday in 1767. Otterbein was so impressed by Boehm's preaching that he is said to have embraced the diminutive Boehm and exclaimed 'Wir sind Brüder' (We are brothers), and from this meeting the United Brethren stemmed. Otterbein preached at further meetings, usually held in groves and barns, for the immigrant German-speaking communities of Baltimore, Maryland, and it became evident, following a conference held there in 1789, that there was a growing need to unify the work and make co-ordinated plans for the future. Further conferences, in 1791 and 1800, declared the official name of the denomination to be Church of the United Brethren and Otterbein and Boehme, by then old men, were elected as bishops, or superintendents, of the Church. In 1815 a *Confession of Faith* was proposed, a concise statement of the principal doctrinal beliefs published in 1817.

Missionary work was undertaken from the earliest years of the Church, and in 1853 a thirty-wagon caravan of about a hundred people moved west into Oregon to plant the first congregation in that part of the USA; two years later a mission was established in Sierra Leone, Africa. By the end of the nineteenth century, division within the Church was inevitable when Bishop Milton Wright, the father of the pioneering aeronautical Wright brothers, walked out of the 1889 Conference claiming that the 1815 *Confession of Faith* was being abandoned, along with the 1841 Constitution, which had, among other matters, pronounced against membership of secret societies, a proscription now being eased. Bishop Wright and his small group of followers formed the Church of the United Brethren in Christ (Old Constitution); the other branch of the Church was thereafter known as the Church of the United Brethren in Christ (New Constitution). Wright's group lost most of their property to the New Constitution group through various court actions and had to reorganize themselves, moving their headquarters to Huntington, Indiana, in 1897. Further building programmes erected Huntington College (founded 1897), which remains the only college of this denomination, providing a liberal arts undergraduate course as well as a graduate school of Christian ministries for the training of United Brethren ministers; a new international headquarters was built in 1976. The New Constitution group established its headquarters at Dayton, Ohio, and became known as the Liberal United Brethren. They united with the Evangelical Association in 1946 to form the EVANGELICAL UNITED BRETHREN CHURCH, which in 1968 united with the METHODIST CHURCH to form the UNITED METHODIST CHURCH (USA).

The work of the United Brethren in Christ Church is extensive, including family and youth ministries, evangelism, publishing, a ministry for single people and senior citizens, and the provision of Sunday School curricula. Its home mission work is currently concerned with establishing Hispanic churches in Southern California and Arizona, as well as a Chinese and Jamaican church in New York City and a Latin American ministry in Los Angeles, California. Foreign missions have taken members to many parts of the world, including China, Thailand, Hong Kong, India, Jamaica, Honduras, Mexico and Sierra Leone.

❖ Church of the United Brethren in Christ (New Constitution); Church of the United Brethren in Christ (Old Constitution); Evangelical United Brethren Church

UNITED CHRISTIAN CHURCH

The United Christian Church, a small American denomination with only 400 adult members distributed between 10 congregations, was founded in the mid-nineteenth century as part of a schism from the group that became the UNITED BRETHREN IN CHRIST. The schism arose over a disagreement concerning the bearing of arms, the practice of infant baptism, human slavery and membership of secret societies. It also opposed the parent Church's position on the issue of 'man's depravity' – a doctrine that recognizes man's sinfulness after the Fall, by which the human will is held in bondage and unable to turn to God. In 1857 those who could not affirm this doctrine formed the United Christian Church, under the leadership of George W. Hoffman.

The Church had no formal organization until 1877, when at a meeting in Campbelltown, Pennsylvania, it adopted a *Confession of Faith*; the following year the present name was approved. The work of the Church includes a prison ministry and support for the aged, a foreign mission to Jamaica and co-operative support of the United Brethren in Christ's work in Japan. An annual conference currently legislates for this small body.

❖ Hoffmanites

UNITED CHURCH OF CANADA

At the close of the nineteenth century in Canada there were talks about forming a merger, or union, between the METHODIST CHURCH and the PRESBYTERIAN CHURCH. In 1902 the Congregational Union of Canada felt ready to participate in these talks and an ecumenical plan of union, called the Basis of Union, which was considered acceptable to the General Council of Union Churches, was presented. The Basis of Union, which was formally effected in 1925, sought to affirm the best traditions in REFORMED theology and polity. The Union affirmed a position midway between CALVINISM and ARMINIANISM, allowing for considerable latitude in such matters as predestination, election and the availability of God's free grace to everybody. Not all Presbyterian congregations felt that they could affirm the 1925 merger that formed the United Church of Canada (UCC) and they remained outside, forming the Presbyterian Church in Canada. In 1968 the Canada Conference of the Evangelical United Brethren had also joined the UCC.

The government of the UCC is by means of a biennial church council, which elects the moderator who serves a two-year period in office. Nationally, the UCC is divided into 11 geographical conferences, and sub-divided into 93 presbyteries, with local churches administered by an official board. Evangelism, social service work and a missionary outreach programme are undertaken by various boards, centralized in Toronto, Ontario.

The headquarters of this very large PROTESTANT denomination, with around 1,960 congregations, is in Etobicoke, Ontario, from where the work is currently co-ordinated. The UCC is in fraternal association with the World Alliance of Reformed Churches and Methodist world bodies and is a member of the World Council of Churches.

UNITED CHURCH OF CHRIST

The United Church of Christ was formed in the United States as a result of a merger between the EVANGELICAL AND REFORMED CHURCH and the General Council of CONGREGATIONAL-CHRISTIAN CHURCHES; each of the merging groups had themselves been formed as a result of earlier unions.

Congregationalism is a product of the SEPARATIST movement in England, while the Evangelical and REFORMED Church was a fusion of two German CALVINIST groups in 1934 that drew its membership from the descendants of German immigrants in Pennsylvania and the midwestern states. Where Congregationalism emphasizes the complete autonomy of the local congregation, the Evangelical and Reformed Church operated a modified presbyterian polity. Furthermore, the Congregationalists do not require any adherence to creeds or declarations of faith, whereas the opposite holds true of the Evangelical and Reformed Church, which upholds Luther's *Small Catechism* (1529), the *Augsburg Confession* (1530) and the *Heidelberg Confession* (1563). The union came about after a series of negotiations had taken place that began in 1942 and ended with the final merger in 1957. A small minority of the Congregational-Christian Churches refused to join the merger and some of them organized a NATIONAL ASSOCIATION OF CONGREGATIONAL-CHRISTIAN CHURCHES, while others joined the fundamentalist Conservative-Congregational Churches Conference.

The constitution of the United Church of Christ, which was affirmed in 1961, provides for a general synod to be its principal policy-making body. A *Statement of Faith* confirms the role of the scriptures as the word of God and affirms the importance of the creeds of the ecumenical councils (Apostles', Nicene and Athanasian) as well as the *Confessions*. The highest representative body of the Church is the general synod, which meets biennially, composed of delegates elected by local conferences of churches throughout a geographical area; these local conferences are made up associations, in which the local churches in an area are combined, and they meet annually.

UNITED CHURCH OF CHRIST IN JAPAN

This is the largest PROTESTANT Church in Japan and it came into existence during the mid-nineteenth century at the time when Japan was opening itself to western trade and influence. American missionaries, representing the PRESBYTERIAN, PROTESTANT EPISCOPAL and DUTCH REFORMED Churches involved themselves initially with developing hospitals and schools and providing dictionaries and translations of the Bible. The first permanent Baptist mission was established in Yokohama in 1872, and in 1877 some Presbyterian and CHURCH OF CHRIST groups merged to form the United Church of Christ in Japan. The Japanese government in 1940 insisted upon the union of the different Christian denominations into one body, or Kyodan, and those who were unwilling to join it ceased to exist officially.

This arrangement was abolished following the Second World War and Japan received an influx of American Protestant missionaries. The United Church of Christ in Japan continued in strength, despite the existence of many independent BAPTIST, Presbyterian and LUTHERAN missions that had developed in response to General MacArthur's call for '1,000 missionaries' to go to Japan from the USA.

The United Church of Christ in Japan, with its headquarters in Tokyo, now has 1,707 churches and an adult membership of around 128,000.

UNITED CHURCH OF CHRIST IN THE MARSHALL ISLANDS

This Church, which is the largest within the PROTESTANT and REFORMED tradition in these Pacific Islands, with over half the population belonging to it, was formed in the 1850s as a result of the missionary work of members of the American Board of Commissioners for Foreign Missions. It is presently constituted as a union of the CONGREGATIONAL with the Evangelical and Reformed Churches. The headquarters of the Church is at Majuro.

UNITED CHURCH OF CHRIST IN THE PHILIPPINES

After several centuries of Spanish rule the Philippines were annexed by the USA in the 1890s, and with this came the arrival of American PROTESTANT missionaries, who were responsible for the conversion of many nominal ROMAN CATHOLIC islanders to various protestant denominations. A series of unions between these various groups followed and the United Church of Christ in the Philippines emerged, with a current membership of around 580,000 believers who are cared for in 2,486 congregations. The headquarters of the Church is in Manila.

UNITED CHURCH OF CHRIST IN ZIMBABWE

This small, independent PROTESTANT Church owes its formation, in 1892–3, to the missionary work of the American Board of Commissioners for Foreign Missions. Now self-governing, the Church entered a global partnership with the New Hampshire Conference of the United Church of Christ (USA) in 1996, to promote friendship, or *Ukama*, between the congregations in Zimbabwe and New Hampshire.

The general synod is the governing body of the Church and is presided over by a president, who is elected for a term of four years. Members of the synod are elected by each congregation, each of which is part of one of several conferences. all headed by a conference minister who is also elected every four years.

The work of the Church is under the control of seven national ministries, each overseen by a president and an executive council. These national ministries include *Ruwadzano*, a fellowship concerned with the rights of women and children and the care of the elderly, the Christian Youth Fellowship, which cares for the needs of young people, and the Volunteer's council, which is a men's guild that works with the people to direct their voluntary services for the Church and the community. Other ministries include an educational council, responsible for several high and junior high schools, as well as a horticultural training college, a (mission) station council and a medical council, which oversees the work in several major hospitals, clinics and rural health outposts. The current membership of the Church stands at around 10,000, distributed in 160 congregations.

UNITED CHURCH OF ZAMBIA

The United Church of Zambia is one of the largest PROTESTANT denominations in the country, with an adult membership of around 300,000. The Church places its foundation at 1884, but its origins are earlier. The work of the non-denominational London Missionary Society in the mid-nineteenth century was not very successful and gave way to the Paris Mission in 1879; the first permanent Paris Mission station was established in the country in 1885.

The various missionary teams, apart from those from London and Paris, included personnel from the METHODIST Missionary Society and the Scottish Presbyterian Church who came to work in Zambia and opened many churches. In 1965, these agreed to unite and to form the United Church of Zambia. The Church has responsibility for 1,200 congregations, composed mainly of Lozi and Bemba speakers. There are still many foreign missionaries in Zambia, helping the indigenous clergy to serve this growing Church.

UNITED CONGREGATIONAL CHURCH OF SOUTHERN AFRICA

This Church has its foundations in the early days of the history of Cape Colony when the British arrived, in 1795, and took over possession of the colony from the Dutch who had been settled there since 1652. The first missionaries, from the London Missionary Society, arrived in the British Cape Colony on 31 March 1799 and established a permanent missionary station at Bethelsdorp, in the south-east of the Colony. Many of the early missionaries played prominent parts in the establishment of congregations and in the translation of the Bible into Setswana (Tswana). The famous missionary-explorer, David Livingstone, was the son-in-law of Robert Moffat who went to South Africa in 1817, settling at Kuruman where he established early congregations.

From 1820 onwards, groups of English, Scottish and Welsh CONGREGATIONALISTS came to the colony and created fellowships that mirrored their own congregations back in Britain. American missionaries began to arrive from 1835 and one of these, David Lindley, was the first to establish a mission in the area that is now Durban, where he worked amongst the Boers.

The United Congregational Church of Southern Africa (UCCSA) arose in 1967 from a union of several missionary initiatives, including the Congregational Union of South Africa, the Bantu Congregational Church and the American Board Mission and in 1972 the CHRISTIAN CHURCH (DISCIPLES OF CHRIST). Congregationalists in Southern Africa were notable for being amongst the first denominations to ordain women, from the 1930s onwards. The UCCSA is very active ecumenically and places considerable emphasis upon the biblical principle of *covenant*, in which individuals, and groups, of God's people respond to divine revelation. The Church, being Congregationalist, also emphasizes the importance of local church autonomy and affirms the REFORMED tradition of CALVINISM.

The headquarters of the UCCSA, in Johannesburg, has responsibility for over 2,500 congregations and around 244,000 adult members.

UNITED EVANGELICAL LUTHERAN CHURCH IN INDIA

The Church is composed of many member LUTHERAN Churches, whose representatives agreed to form a single United Church body in 1975; this title was amended in 1988, with each member Church retaining its autonomy. The United Church was then able to function developmentally and ecumenically for all of its member Churches, making for greater efficiency and use of available resources, especially in the field of mission development in India.

The member Churches that united in 1975 include the following (membership statistics are taken from the Lutheran World Federation, Geneva, 1996):

Andhra Evangelical Lutheran Church

Founded in 1842 through the work of J. C. F. Heyer at Guntur, Hyderabad, the Andhra Evangelical Lutheran Church later became an important centre for general and higher education under Lutheran auspices. The work is carried out largely in Andhra Pradesh, among the Telugu-speaking people. There are approximately 400,000 members.

Arcot Lutheran Church

A Tamil-speaking Church that originated through the work of the Danish Missionary Society, which took over the work of the former Leipzig missionary, the Reverend Ochs, in 1864, as well as some of the mission work undertaken by the English BAPTISTS, in 1882. The Danish Lutheran Church established centres in Chennai (Madras), Bangalore and South Arcot. It has approximately 33,000 members.

Evangelical Lutheran Church in Madhya Pradesh

This Church was founded by the Swedish Evangelical National Mission (SEM), which sent its missionaries to the Central Provinces (later Madhya Pradesh) in 1877 to work among the Gonds, or forest people. Their work later included missions to the caste Hindus. The Church was formally established in 1923 and assumed its present name in 1949. The Church is heavily involved in community health programmes and provides children's homes, a school for the blind and other educational facilities. There are 11,402 members.

Gossner Evangelical Lutheran Church in Chotanagpur and Assam

This Church arose through the missionary efforts of the Gossner Missionary Society, which was founded by a German, ex-ROMAN CATHOLIC priest, Fr Johannes Gossner. The Society sent missionaries to North India in 1845 to work among the Adivasi people and a base was established at Ranchi, north-west of Calcutta. The mission supports education, with the Gossner Theological College at Ranchi, as well as health and developmental projects. This Church has 354,432 members.

India Evangelical Lutheran Church

This Church was founded by four German missionaries who had been sent to India by the Leipzig Mission at the end of the nineteenth century, but who left its employ to work for the LUTHERAN CHURCH – MISSOURI SYNOD in 1895. The Church was formally organized in 1958 and supports many schools, including schools for the handicapped, and a teacher training institute. The headquarters of the Church is at Vellore, west of Chennai (Madras), in Tamil Nadu. There are 56,493 members.

Jeypore Evangelical Lutheran Church

The foundations of this Church were laid in 1845 by missionaries sent from Germany by the Schleswig-Holstein Evangelical Lutheran Missionary Society, who began work in the Rajahmundry area, east of Hyderabad. In 1882 two missionaries, Pohl and Bothman, moved their activities further north-east, but because of early difficulties, not only with language but later with the internment of Germans during both world wars, the mission was eventually handed over to the Americans. In 1950 the India Church constitution was adopted and a seminary at Kotapad was founded for the training of lay leaders and future pastors. The Church now has 140,000 members.

Northern Evangelical Lutheran Church.

This Church came into being in 1867 through the work of a Danish missionary, Hans Peter Boerresen, and a Norwegian missionary, Carl Olsen Skrefsrud, who had left the German Gossner Missionary Society. The two men worked among the primitive tribes in western Bengal, known as Santals, and in this work they were supported by the Scandinavian Lutherans. Mission stations and colonies were established and a Church was formally organized in 1953, with a missionary superintendent in charge. By 1958 a native Indian had been elected as president of the Church, assisted by an all-Indian board of trustees. The Church now has 72,000 members.

South Andhra Lutheran Church.

This Church owes its origin to the work of a missionary from Leipzig, August Mylius, who belonged to the Hermannsburg Evangelical Lutheran Mission and was sent to India in 1865. Mylius established mission stations at Nayadupet and Gudur, where schools for boys and girls were also started. Internment of the German missionaries at the outbreak of the First World War in 1914 led to the mission work eventually being taken over by the American Lutheran Church. The South Andhra Lutheran Church was organized finally in 1945 with an emphasis upon self-support and autonomy. There is co-operation between this Church and the Andhra Evangelical Lutherans in the maintenance of the Luthergiri seminary at Rajahmundry. There are now 28,022 members.

Tamil Evangelical Lutheran Church

This Church was begun by two German missionaries, Ziegenbalg and Ploetschau, from Pulsnitz near Dresden, who went to India under the patronage of the Lutheran Danish king and made for the Danish settlement of Tranquebar in 1705. Ziegenbalg quickly mastered the Tamil language and began a translation of the Bible into Tamil, a work that was completed in 1725 by Benjamin Schultz, with the assistance of J. E. Gruendler. A substantial Lutheran community grew up around Tranquebar and other centres. The work of the mission eventually passed into the hands of the ANGLICANS of the Church Missionary Society; by 1874 the Church of Sweden Mission had taken over responsibility for the Tamil mission field. Following the creation of a separate Swedish diocese, in 1919 the Church was formally established, adopting the episcopal form of polity. The first native Indian bishop was consecrated to succeed the last Swedish bishop in 1956. There are now some 103,093 members.

❖ United Evangelical Lutheran Churches in India

UNITED EVANGELICAL LUTHERAN CHURCH OF NAMIBIA

The Church came into existence as the result of a union made in 1971 between two independent and separate LUTHERAN Churches. These were the Evangelical Lutheran Church in South West Africa and the Evangelical Lutheran Ovambokavango Church.

The Evangelical Lutheran Church was formed in 1842 by the Rhenish Missionary Society (German Lutherans), who responded to a request from the London Missionary Society. The Finnish Mission Society also sent workers into the area and they founded the Evangelical Lutheran Ovambokavango Church in 1870. This Church became autonomous in 1954 and experienced rapid growth up to the time of the 1971 union that gave the newly formed body the name of the United Evangelical Lutheran Church of Namibia; this now has an adult membership of around 229,000 distributed amongst 600 churches. The headquarters of the Church is in the capital, Windhoek.

Provision for the white, German-speaking Lutheran community was made in the separate German Evangelical Lutheran Church. When, in 1975, this group reluctantly agreed to join the United Evangelical Church of Namibia, their acceptance was refused and they remain separate. This Lutheran group has its headquarters in Cape Town, South Africa, and forms one of the four synods of the United Evangelical Lutheran Church of South Africa, which caters for white, German-speaking Lutherans.

UNITED FREE CHURCH OF SCOTLAND

When the *Disruption* of 1843 occurred in Scotland over the issue of the freedom of the CHURCH OF SCOTLAND to govern itself, about one third of the clergy left to form the FREE CHURCH OF SCOTLAND. In 1900 this body joined with the UNITED PRESBYTERIAN CHURCH (SCOTLAND) to form the United Free Church of Scotland.

The two uniting Churches were responding to moves to try and soften the CALVINIST doctrines and to make changes to public worship with the introduction of music and hymns. In 1929 there was a large reunion of many members of the United Free Church of Scotland with what was left of the Church of Scotland, to form one of the largest PROTESTANT Churches in the English-speaking world. Those who chose not to join the reunion remained as the United Free Church of Scotland, which functions within the REFORMED tradition and today has 73 congregations and in excess of 7,000 members.

❖ United Free Church (Continuing)

UNITED FREE CHURCH OF THE FALKLAND ISLANDS

The Falkland Islanders are mostly ANGLICAN, members of the United Free Church's five congregations, which are currently composed of some 450 mixed LUTHERANS and BAPTISTS. The first colonial chaplain arrived in the capital, Stanley, in 1845 and the organization of the United Free Church is said to date from 1872. The Church is in the evangelical Christian tradition, with two worship services on Sunday and a broadcast service in the evening sent out by the Falkland Islands broadcasting station. The main place of worship, called the Tabernacle, was shipped out from Great Britain by the Victorian BAPTIST preacher, Charles Haddon Spurgeon (1834–92). It took its name from that of Spurgeon's own church at Elephant and Castle in London, the still extant Metropolitan Tabernacle.

UNITED FREE METHODIST CHURCHES

This now defunct Church was formed in England in 1857 by a union of the WESLEYAN METHODIST ASSOCIATION, the WESLEYAN REFORM UNION and the Protestant Methodists.

In 1827 the ministers and trustees of the Brunswick METHODIST Chapel in Leeds expressed a wish to install an organ for use during Sunday worship. Many members and local preachers objected to this on the grounds that artificial music was 'of the devil', and dishonoured God. The minister of the chapel, in the face of this refusal, referred the matter to the president of conference, Dr Jabez Bunting (1779–1858). Bunting had become a Methodist minister in 1799 and had risen meteorically through the ranks of the Church, becoming the conference's secretary and elected four times as its president. He had, however, a tendency to centralism and ministerial dominance, and dissent and secession inevitably followed. A positive decision regarding the organ was made and it was duly installed, leading to the disaffection of many, who left to form the Protestant Methodists. It has been said that the organ cost a thousand pounds and also lost a thousand souls.

The Wesleyan Methodist Association arose within the Methodist community in 1834, when Dr Samuel Warren was appointed as head of a committee to explore the possibility of setting up a theological college. Many of Warren's plans were overruled by Dr Bunting and when Warren complained about this he was rebuked, suspended and finally expelled, taking with him another thousand Church members who together formed the Wesleyan Methodist Association.

The largest group of disaffected Methodists who left on account of Dr Bunting's style of Church government formed the Wesleyan Reform Union when, in 1849, some circulars, or *Fly-Sheets*, highly critical of Bunting and calling for the reform of the Church, were published and circulated. Three ministers stood accused and were expelled from the Church, gaining a large wave of sympathy from much of the membership, and this time a hundred thousand left, many of them to form the Wesleyan Reform Union. Some of these Wesleyan Reformers joined together in forming the United Methodist Free Churches in 1857. The remainder of the Wesleyan Reform Union established an autonomous Church in 1859, which continues in Great Britain to the present time.

The United Methodist Free Churches united in 1907 with the METHODIST NEW CONNEXION and the BIBLE CHRISTIANS to form the United Methodist Church. In 1932 this body united with the PRIMITIVE METHODIST CHURCH to form the METHODIST CHURCH OF GREAT BRITAIN.

UNITED FREE WILL BAPTISTS

Established in the USA in 1901, this Church is independent of what became of the NATIONAL ASSOCIATION OF FREE WILL BAPTISTS and is represented by 750 congregations spread throughout North Carolina, Florida, Louisiana, Georgia, Mississippi and Texas.

As the Church's title implies, these Baptists are ARMINIAN and emphasize that salvation, which is for everyone who believes in Jesus Christ as their personal saviour, is achieved by grace alone and not by works. The members of the Church believe in the Trinity, in the Bible's inerrancy as the word of God, in the perseverance of those who are saved and in the resurrection of the body to eternal life for those who are good and to eternal damnation for those who are wicked and unrepentant. The Church also professes a belief in Christ's second coming (REVELATION 20) and sees its mission as preaching the gospel throughout the world.

The Church observes the Gospel ordinances of baptism by immersion, the Lord's Supper and foot-washing. In the area of Church polity, however, it is best described as being a modified congregational-type, in that though each local church is autonomous, these local churches are organized voluntarily into quarterly, annual and general conferences, which decide on questions of doctrine. The headquarters of the United Free Will Baptists is at Kingston, North Carolina.

❖ United Free Will Baptist Church (Colored)

UNITED HOLY CHURCH OF AMERICA, INC.

Founded in the USA in 1886, this PENTECOSTAL Church developed from a HOLINESS revival meeting held by the Reverend Isaac Cheshier at Method, a suburb of Raleigh, the capital of North

Carolina. From 1900 onwards the name of the Church underwent several changes, adopting its present title in 1916. In 1976, however, there was a loss of around half the membership when a disagreement between two bishops developed. This resulted in the loss of one bishop, James Alexander Forbes, and the Southern District congregations, which a year later led to the founding of the Original United Holy Church International.

Doctrinally, the United Holy Church of America, Inc. affirms the orthodox view of the Trinity, the inerrancy of the Bible and its message of man's redemption through Christ, and the premillennial second coming of Christ (REVELATION 20). The Church observes the ordinances of baptism by immersion, the Lord's Supper and foot-washing. In common with other Pentecostal Holiness groups, the members of this Church seek out the three experiences of justification or being born again, sanctification and baptism of the Holy Spirit, the evidence for which is taken to be *glossolalia*, or speaking in tongues. The Church is very active abroad, and has established missions in Great Britain, Liberia, Trinidad and South Africa.

❖ Holy Church of North Carolina; Holy Church of North Carolina and Virginia; United Holy Church of America

UNITED HOUSE OF PRAYER FOR ALL PEOPLE OF THE CHURCH ON THE ROCK OF THE APOSTOLIC FAITH

An American denomination that dates its foundation to 1919 when Bishop Marcelino Manoel de Graça (1882–1960), who was also known as Sweet Daddy Grace, built his first House of Prayer, with his own hands, at West Wareham, Massachusetts. During the depression years (1929–34), he continued to build churches in areas stricken with poverty and unemployment. His charitable work amongst the poor was legendary and attracted a considerable amount of attention and publicity.

The United House of Prayer was incorporated as a Church within the PENTECOSTAL tradition in 1927 and as such affirms the apostolic faith, holds an orthodox view of the Trinity and observes the ordinances of baptism in water for repentance; (*it has been alleged that in 1998 this was administered to some 2000 converts in one ceremony by means of a fire hose*).

With Sweet Daddy Grace's death in 1960, his successor, Bishop Walter McCollough, continued to build new Houses of Prayer as well as erecting housing for the elderly and the poor. McCollough also introduced a scholarship scheme for more than one thousand students. The building work continued unabated, financed by the Church with no recourse to mortgages or government grants. The Church has a current adult membership estimated at some 25,000; during the years of the depression this is estimated to have risen to more than one million. The headquarters of the Church is in Washington, DC.

❖ United House of Prayer for All People

UNITED METHODIST CHURCH (UK)

This Church is not to be confused with the UNITED METHODIST CHURCH (USA).

The United Methodist Church (UMC) came into existence in 1907 with the merger of three small METHODIST groups, the METHODIST NEW CONNEXION, the BIBLE CHRISTIANS and the UNITED FREE METHODIST CHURCHES.

This last named group was itself formed by a union of three further Methodist groups, the Protestant Methodists, the Wesleyan Methodist Association and the Wesleyan Reformers. In 1932, the UMC united with others, to form the METHODIST CHURCH OF GREAT BRITAIN.

UNITED METHODIST CHURCH (USA)

The United Methodist Church (UMC) is the third largest denomination in the USA, behind the ROMAN CATHOLIC and the Southern Baptist Churches. It was formed in 1968 after a succession of unions, between 1939 and 1946, between five American Churches within the METHODIST traditions.

In general, the members of the Church affirm the Wesleyan *Twenty-Five Articles of Religion* (1784), the *Minutes of the British Wesleyan Conference*, which had settled many doctrinal concerns, John Wesley's *Sermons* and his *Explanatory Notes on the New Testament*. The *Articles of Religion* places the UMC within the REFORMED tradition. Baptism, for both young and adult alike, is administered by sprinkling and Holy Communion is open to all Christians. The polity of the Church is episcopal and it is administered through a four-yearly general conference made up of equal numbers of clerical and lay representatives who are delegated by the annual conferences that are distributed across the country. Through these conferences the bishops and district superintendents assign ministers to their circuits. It is the work of the general conference to make decisions for the Church and these are published in the *Discipline*, or Church rule book.

Mission work abroad is found in most countries and is directed by the board of global ministries. In order to provide a co-ordinated response to emergencies and natural disasters there is a United Methodist committee on relief, which is directed by the board of global ministries. The United Methodist Church, which has a current adult membership of around 8.5 million distributed amongst some 36,000 churches and under the care of 53,600 clergy, is very active ecumenically.

UNITED MISSIONARY CHURCH

The origin of this American Church, which merged with the MISSIONARY CHURCH ASSOCIATION in 1969 to form the MISSIONARY CHURCH, lay in an evangelistic movement that arose during the nineteenth century in some MENNONITE groups, many of which underwent several name changes and mergers. In 1947 one such group, the Mennonite Brethren in Christ, changed its name to the United Missionary Church.

Despite its Mennonite background, the United Missionary Church did not have any residual Mennonite connections and its members remained very evangelical in their preaching within the Wesleyan-ARMINIAN, HOLINESS tradition. Their belief in the Trinity was quite orthodox as was their faith in the divinity of Jesus Christ, his atonement, redemption and premillennial return to earth (REVELATION 20). The Bible was regarded as the inspired word of God. The group practised baptism by immersion and a policy of open communion. Foreign mission work was extensive throughout Africa, India, South America, Egypt, Japan and Mexico. The administration of the Church was organized through three-yearly general conferences, general boards and various annual district and local conferences that were held amongst the member congregations. Leading up to the

1969 merger there was a great deal of close co-operation with both the Missionary Church Association and the Christian and Missionary Alliance.

UNITED NATIVE AFRICAN CHURCH

The United African Church was formed as a breakaway group from the Anglican Church, which had been established in Nigeria by the Church Missionary Society in 1842. The schism arose when, in 1891, a European bishop was appointed to replace its African-born bishop and it continues to the present day. The Church remains within the Anglican tradition, although not in communion with the Church of England, and has a current adult membership of about 17,000 and some 300 churches. Growth within the Church has begun to spread into neighbouring Benin.

UNITED PENTECOSTAL CHURCH INTERNATIONAL

An American Church formed in 1945 at St Louis, Missouri, by the merger of two Pentecostal groups, the Pentecostal Church, Inc. and the Pentecostal Assemblies of Jesus Christ, both of which derived, through a contorted series of splits, from the Pentecostal Assemblies of the World, Inc. The Church is firmly within the Pentecostal and Oneness tradition and, as such, rejects the doctrine of the Trinity as inadequate. The Church identifies Jesus Christ with Jehovah, the God of the Old Testament.

The Church practises foot-washing, Holy Communion and divine healing. Its members are expected to refrain from joining secret societies and to avoid mixed bathing and worldly amusements, which include the theatre and television, with women further enjoined to wear their hair long. The members are, in general, pacifists and they are forbidden to take human life for any reason.

The Church, with its headquarters at Hazelwood, Missouri, has a current total worldwide membership of 2 million and maintains a presence in 136 countries including the USA and Canada. The congregations are autonomous, each electing its own pastors and leaders and owning its own property. There is an annual general conference, when the work of the Church is co-ordinated, led by the general superintendent and other executive members of the general board. The Church endorses the work of at least seven Bible colleges, a children's home, a ministry for alcohol and drug dependency and a prison and military chaplaincy.

UNITED PRESBYTERIAN CHURCH (SCOTLAND)

This Church, which no longer exists in Scotland as such, was formed in 1847 through the union of the United Secession Church and the Relief Church. The union was a difficult one to forge, since the United Secession Church was ecclesiastically strict whereas the Relief Church was notable for its evangelical and lax approach to doctrine.

In 1900 the United Presbyterian Church united with the Free Church of Scotland, which had been formed as a result of the *Disruption* in 1843 that split the Church of Scotland.

UNITED PRESBYTERIAN CHURCH IN THE UNITED STATES OF AMERICA

The United Presbyterian Church in the United States of America came into existence as a result of a merger made in 1958 between the PRESBYTERIAN CHURCH IN AMERICA and the United Presbyterian Church of North America that had itself been formed by an earlier union between two Presbyterian bodies. The newly-formed Church then united in 1983 with yet another Presbyterian body to form the PRESBYTERIAN CHURCH (USA).

UNITED PRESBYTERIAN CHURCH OF BRAZIL

This relatively small Brazilian PROTESTANT denomination was founded in 1978, when many members, finding themselves in disagreement with the Presbyterian Church of Brazil (IPB)'s policies, were consequently expelled from the IPB during the country's military dictatorship of the 1960s. The United Presbyterian Church of Brazil (IPU) is heavily committed to human rights issues and deals with questions of social justice. The Church is ecumenically involved with many other protestant Churches and also with the ROMAN CATHOLIC CHURCH.

As one of its major doctrinal standards, the IPU adopted the *Book of Confessions* (1967). This Confession was published during the merger negotiations between two American Presbyterian groups and its stated position, concerning reconciliation in society and encouragement to promote peace, may lie at the base of the Church's commitment to social issues. The IPU also affirms the 1934 protestant declaration known as the *Barmen Declaration*. The headquarters of the IPU, which has over 20,000 adult members distributed in about 60 congregations, is at Vitória, on the coast north of Rio de Janeiro.

UNITED PROTESTANT CHURCH OF BELGIUM

At the time of Belgium's independence from French rule in 1830, there were only a few thousand PROTESTANT Christians in Belgium and it was thought that the most expedient course of action was to unite these to form the Evangelical Protestant Church of Belgium. In 1969, a union between the Evangelical Protestant Church of Belgium and the UNITED METHODIST CHURCH (USA) was undertaken and this formed the United Protestant Church of Belgium.

UNITED PROTESTANT CHURCH OF CURAÇAO

The United Protestant Church of Curaçao was one of the three PROTESTANT Churches that united in 1968 to form the UNITED PROTESTANT CHURCH OF NETHERLANDS ANTILLES. The Church claims its origin to coincide with the arrival of Dutch colonists in 1650 who brought with them the DUTCH REFORMED CHURCH (NHK). By the start of the nineteenth century the NHK in Curaçao, Aruba and Bonaire, just off the Venezuelan coast, evolved into the three Protestant Churches, of Curaçao, Aruba and Bonaire respectively.

The Church was originally conceived as a merger of the REFORMED and LUTHERAN tradition, but the services are now in the Reformed tradition only. At the beginning only the Dutch language was used in worship, but the Church now uses English and Papiamento, an amalgam of Portuguese, Dutch, Spanish and English. The doctrinal position of these uniting Churches was identical to that of the REFORMED CHURCHES IN THE NETHERLANDS and the DUTCH REFORMED CHURCH. Infant and believer's baptisms are administered and the Lord's Supper is celebrated, by either male or female ministers, on a monthly basis.

This is the largest protestant Church in the group of islands, with an adult membership of around 3,700. The headquarters of the Church is in Willemstad.

❖ Protestant Church of Curaçao

UNITED PROTESTANT CHURCH OF NETHERLANDS ANTILLES

This Church was formed in 1968 when three PROTESTANT Churches, which had been formed in the nineteenth century by the NETHERLANDS REFORMED CHURCHES, adopted a revised church order and united together. These were the UNITED PROTESTANT CHURCH OF CURAÇAO, the PROTESTANT CHURCH IN ARUBA and the PROTESTANT CHURCH IN BONAIRE.

UNITED REFORMED CHURCH

The negotiations that eventually resulted in the formation of the United Reformed Church (URC) were begun in 1945 and involved representatives from the CONGREGATIONAL CHURCH in England and the PRESBYTERIAN CHURCH of England. The successful outcome of these talks was realized in 1972, and nine years later some of the CHURCHES OF CHRIST IN GREAT BRITAIN AND IRELAND also opted to join the union. Not all Congregationalists wanted the union and they remained outside, while some others refused to vote on the issue; a group of Presbyterians from the Channel Islands declined to join the union and were later accepted into the CHURCH OF SCOTLAND.

The union of some of the Churches of Christ with the other two Churches meant that the *Book of Services* (published 1980) had to be revised, particularly in the provision for the baptism of infants. Members of the Church of Christ hold to a believer's baptism, and the *Book of Services* now contains a service for the blessing of children, and for the dedication of parents. The ordination of a minister to serve a URC congregation involves an affirmation of conventional doctrine, such as the Trinity, and the place of the scriptures as containing 'all doctrine required for eternal salvation through faith in Jesus Christ'. After the singing of the *Veni Creator* the ordination prayer is read, while ministers and church representatives place their hands on the ordinand's head.

The URC has twelve provinces, each with a moderator, and its overseas missions are conducted through the Council for World Missions (founded 1977). At present there are 1,800 places of worship for around 117,900 adult members.

UNITED SECESSION CHURCH

The United Secession Church, which is no longer in existence, was formed in 1820 when two groups from within the Secession Church in Scotland agreed to unite. The Secession Church had arisen in 1733 when a PRESBYTERIAN minister, Ebenezer Erskine (1680–1754), was appointed to a congregation in Stirling, where he preached against clerical patronage, or the right of a patron to nominate for appointment a minister without reference to the parish. Erskine, together with three supporters, was suspended by the general assembly of the CHURCH OF SCOTLAND. Attempts to effect reconciliation were made, but were unsuccessful. In 1737, Ralph, Ebenezer's brother, joined Erskine and his supporters and they formed themselves into a presbytery, an action that led to their formal deposition by the Church of Scotland in 1740.

The Secession Church having been founded, a split began to form in 1747 over the question of whether it was lawful for newly elected burghers to take the 'Burgess Oath'. The text of the oath contained the words: 'I protest before God and your lordships that I profess and allow with my heart the true religion presently professed within this realm and authorised by the laws thereof; I shall abide threat and defend the same to my life's end, renouncing the Roman religion called Papistry.'

Erskine and the others maintained that there was no inconsistency in the members, known as Seceders, taking this oath because the established religion was still the true religion, in spite of its faults. Those who upheld the oath were known as *Burghers*, while those who opposed it were known as *Anti-Burghers*. Further splits within these breakaway groups appeared towards the end of the eighteenth and start of the nineteenth centuries. By 1820 some of these groups had reunited to form the United Secession Church that, in 1847, united with the RELIEF CHURCH to form the UNITED PRESBYTERIAN CHURCH (SCOTLAND). Some Anti-Burghers joined the FREE CHURCH OF SCOTLAND in 1852, while others continued as the ORIGINAL SECESSION CHURCH.

UNITED SEVENTH-DAY BRETHREN

The single congregation of this American Church that is known still to exist could best be described as ADVENTIST. It was formed in 1947 when several independent congregations decided to unite in order to make their evangelization more effective, especially in the promotion of sabbath day observance, and to seek fellowship with like-minded individuals. The uniting congregations retained their autonomy.

The doctrinal position of the Church affirms a belief in the Bible as the inspired word of God, but denies the immortality of the soul. The members believe that there is one God and that Jesus Christ is his Son, born of a virgin, who died, was resurrected and ascended to heaven. In keeping with the sabbatarian stance Church members avoid what have been declared to be 'unclean meats'.

UNITED WESLEYAN METHODIST CHURCH OF AMERICA

This small, American denomination, with some 550 members and its headquarters in New York, had its origins in 1905 with the arrival in America of immigrants from the West Indies who wished to maintain the style of METHODISM imported from Great Britain to which they had become accustomed in their homeland. The polity of the Church is non-episcopal and its principal administrative body is the biennial general conference.

UNITED ZION CHURCH

When Bishop Matthias Brinser of the BRETHREN IN CHRIST CHURCH was expelled from that body in 1855 for building, and holding services in, a separate meeting house, he and some fifty others organized the United Zion's Children, which in 1954 became incorporated in the USA as the United Zion Church.

Doctrinally, there are no major differences between the two Churches. Plain, simple clothing is worn and the women members are expected to keep their heads covered during church services. The polity of the United Zion Church is congregational, with its clergy classified as bishops, ministers and deacons.

In 1967, the Brethren in Christ Church – River Brethren passed a resolution seeking forgiveness from the United Zion Church for the wrong it may have done them in 1855, a resolution which was accepted in the following year. This has led to co-operation between the Churches in mission work and in higher education, especially in the work of Messiah College of Grantham, Pennsylvania, (founded 1909).

There is an annual general conference, to which representatives from individual churches are sent, and district conferences that are arranged to deal with the administration of the Church. The membership has been declining over the years, and several congregations have ceased to meet.

❖ Brinsers; United Zion's Children

UNITING CHURCH OF AUSTRALIA

An Australian Church, that was formed in 1977 when the METHODIST Church of Australia, the CONGREGATIONAL Union of Australia and the PRESBYTERIAN Church of Australia agreed to merge and to form a new denomination. The use of the word *Uniting* in the title of the Church is deliberate, in the hope that further and wider union, embracing ANGLICANS, BAPTISTS and LUTHERANS, might be accomplished in the future.

The negotiations about a union were started as early as the start of the twentieth century, with a vote taken by all three Churches in 1918. While most of the Methodists and Congregationalists were in favour of the union, only 60 per cent of the Presbyterians were, and this opposition to the proposed union had to be respected. Another attempt to form a united Church was made in 1951, and once again it failed to attract sufficient support from the Presbyterians; this was repeated again and with the same result in 1972. A fresh vote, taken in 1973, was successful in attracting enough support for the union to take place, with those Presbyterians who declined to join the rest forming the Presbyterian Church of Australia Continuing.

The doctrinal basis of the Uniting Church of Australia affirms the Apostles' and Nicene creeds, and the Bible is accepted as the inspired word of God. Baptism, for both children and adults, is administered either by sprinkling, or pouring, while the Lord's Supper is celebrated regularly, ranging in frequency from monthly to quarterly. These sacraments are administered by ordained ministers, who may be male or female and who may wear an *ecumenical alb*, or white robe, when conducting services.

The Uniting Church of Australia is broadly based, with some congregations being more liturgically inclined than others, who may be more evangelical. The use of an ecumenical lectionary with a three-year cycle has had a unifying effect. This is the third largest denomination in Australia, with its headquarters in Sydney, New South Wales, surpassed only in size by the ROMAN CATHOLIC CHURCH and the ANGLICAN CHURCH OF AUSTRALIA.

UNITY OF THE BRETHREN

The Unity of the Brethren Church was formed in America by descendants of Moravians, not of those who had fled in the face of persecution during the eighteenth century, but of those who were part of a wave of immigration to Texas in the middle of the nineteenth century.

These immigrants were organized by the Reverends A. Chumsky and H. Juren into the Evangelical Union of the Bohemian and Moravian Brethren in North America. In 1919 they were joined by an independent group and renamed as the Evangelical Unity of Czech-Moravian Brethren in North America; in 1962 the present, shortened name was adopted.

The present 26 congregations provide fellowship for over 2,500 members, who follow a doctrine similar to that of the MORAVIAN CHURCH IN AMERICA. The Church, which is now considered to be in slow decline, is administered through a biennial synod of clergy and lay delegates that meets on the 6 July, the anniversary of the execution of John Huss in 1415.

❖ Evangelical Unity of the Czech-Moravian Brethren in North America

UNITY SCHOOL OF CHRISTIANITY

An American husband and wife, Charles and Myrtle Fillmore, who both suffered from tuberculosis and believed themselves to have been cured after attending a New Thought lecture, formed the Society of Silent Help towards the end of the 1880s, a NEW AGE prayer group offering help for those requesting assistance; this work was also known as *Unity*. The teaching of the Unity group is very similar to that of other New Age groups, but unlike most, it lays great stress on reincarnation (Fillmore believed himself to be a reincarnation of St Paul) and the position of Jesus as the Christ. Fillmore regarded his movement as *Scientific Christianity* and his writings, heavily influenced by the Christian Gospels, contain elements from other religions, such as Hinduism. These writings, and those of other Unity leaders, remain the chief source of teaching within the group. The movement proved to be popular. A settlement, Unity Farm, was established in 1920 a few miles from Kansas City, Missouri, at a place known as Lee's Summit. This became one of the largest religious centres in the USA, offering conference facilities and operating a mail order service for the distribution of Unity literature. The Society of Silent Help grew into a 24–hour intercessory prayer facility, changing its name to Silent Unity; a radio station, known as Unity Radio, was also set up. There has been steady growth within the group, with many congregations established, which are supervised by the Association of Unity Churches. Ministers are trained at the School of Ministerial and Religious Studies. Unity centres have also been founded outside of the USA.

UNIVERSAL CHRISTIAN SPIRITUAL FAITH AND CHURCHES FOR ALL NATIONS

This American ONENESS, PENTECOSTAL Church was formed from a union made in 1952 between three similar groups, including the NATIONAL DAVID SPIRITUAL TEMPLE OF CHRIST CHURCH UNION (INC.) USA (NDSTCCU), which had been founded in 1932 in Kansas City, Missouri, by the Reverend Dr David William Short, an ex-BAPTIST preacher. Before the merger of these groups, Short had founded the St David Orthodox Christian Spiritual Seminary at Des Moines, Iowa, in 1949.

The NDSTCCU is now in rapid decline, having only 20 congregations and an adult membership of around 5,000; in earlier days, before the 1952 merger, there had been a membership of nearly 41,000 distributed between 66 congregations.

UNIVERSAL CHURCH OF THE KINGDOM OF GOD

This large, and growing, indigenous Brazilian Church is found throughout the country and in a further thirty countries worldwide, where its wealth enables it to buy radio and TV stations as well as to embark upon immense building programmes.

Bishop Edir Macedo Bezerra, who offers faith-healing opportunities that attract generous donations from the faithful, founded the Church in 1977; in 1995 these donations were estimated to be in the region of $15 million weekly. The message preached is that faith can cure almost any condition, from nearsightedness to cancer and AIDS. More controversially, the Church attracted some bad publicity in 1995 when a bishop of the Church, Sérgio von Helde, struck and kicked at a statue of Our Lady of Aparecida, a Black Madonna, on television. Pious ROMAN CATHOLICS venerate this statue throughout Brazil and it caused a religious uproar that prompted the Attorney General of Brazil to launch an investigation into the Church's finances; as a result the Church's founder and leader deposed von Helde.

The mother Church of this PENTECOSTAL denomination in São Paulo is described as the largest evangelical temple in the world. It is from there that the 10,000 congregations are administered.

UNIVERSAL INDUSTRIAL CHURCH OF THE NEW WORLD COMFORTER

An American, Allen Moonan, started the movement, which is more usually known as the One World Family, or as Messiah's World Crusade, believing that through a psychic message he claimed to have received in 1947 while on an astral trip to another planet, God had appointed him as a messiah and charged him with putting right the world's wrongs. Various attempts to form a commune for his followers failed, but by 1969 a group had been established at Larkspur, Marin County, California; this later moved to the university city of Berkeley. Moonan attracted bad publicity when, in 1968, he was arrested on a drugs offence; his followers were mainly *flower children*, members of *Flower Power* groups that arose in California during the 1960s and did much to spread a drug culture amongst the young.

Believing themselves to be directed, through Moonan, by *higher beings* that are variously named as the angels of the Bible, or as beings inside flying saucers, members seek to unite the world into *One Family*.

❖ Messiah's World Crusade; One World Family

USAGERS

The Usagers were a group of NONJURORS who, in 1719, accepted the Communion service drawn up by Bishops Jeremy Collier (1650–1726) and Thomas Brett (1667–1744), assisted by a young priest (later bishop) Thomas Deacon (1697–1753). The additions, or *usages*, which were inserted into the text of the service were drawn from earlier Christian liturgies as well as from the 1549 *Book of Common Prayer*.

The four additions were: 1) the use of the mixed chalice; 2) prayers for the dead; 3) the invocation of the Holy Spirit, or epiclesis, upon the Eucharistic elements; 4) a prayer of oblation of the consecrated Eucharistic elements.

The first two *usages* were considered by Thomas Brett to be of less importance than the other two, but they were nevertheless incorporated into the text of the Eucharistic service that was authorized for use by Bishop Collier in March 1719. The new service book also contained other offices, for example for the administration of the sacrament of confirmation. The use of chrism and the sign of the cross were restored and provision was made for anointing the sick. There was a reunion between the Usagers and the Non-Usagers in April 1732, when an instrument of union was signed in London.

V

VIENNA COMMUNITY CHURCH

This Church, which has been described as international, inter-racial, inter-denominational and ecumenical, originated within the English-speaking community in Vienna, Austria, in 1957 at a meeting held in the American International School, when a constitution was adopted and a board elected.

The Church is very active, catering especially for English-speaking Christians. A Sunday School programme has been organized and members also participate in *Project Centipede*, a programme initiated to support orphanages and schools in Romania.

VIETNAMESE EVANGELICAL CHURCH IN AUSTRALIA

This is a small evangelical Church that was established initially in Sydney, NSW, in 1978. From very small beginnings within the Vietnamese immigrant community in the city the Church soon spread and other congregations have been formed in New South Wales, Victoria, South Australia, Queensland, Western Australia, the Australian Capital Territory (ACT), Tasmania and also in New Zealand. The membership is still quite small, but the Church provides, through its members, support for Christians living in Vietnam. The work of the Church is co-ordinated by means of an annual conference.

VOICE OF ELIJAH, INC.

The founders of this American group, Carl and Sandra Parks, were inspired to form the Voice of Elijah, Inc. in 1970 at Spokane, Washington, DC. The members, who believe that the second coming of Christ to earth is imminent (REVELATION 20), claim that they have received a message from Jesus about how to prepare the world for this event. People must choose to follow God, and war, poverty, racism and immorality can be eliminated on earth by working towards the plan for mankind that has been given by Jesus. This is an evangelistic group with many centres throughout the USA.

VOLUNTEERS OF AMERICA

This is a Christian-based, social welfare organization that began in the USA in 1896 in the Bowery District of New York City. Its founders were Ballington and Maud Booth, the son and daughter-in-law of William Booth, the British founder of the SALVATION ARMY. When Ballington Booth died his widow, Maud, succeeded him as commander-in-chief from 1940–8, and in turn their son, Charles Brandon Booth, succeeded her.

From the very start its members have been dedicated to going wherever a need presents itself. Initially, the work was concerned with the poor, and day-crèches and summer camps were organized for the children from impoverished families as well as accommodation for the single homeless. At the start of the twentieth century the Volunteers initiated a system of halfway houses for released prisoners, a work that has now flourished and is today expressed in an extensive prison ministry.

The Great Depression in America, in the late 1920s and early 1930s, was a time of great unemployment and financial ruin. Volunteers worked to help the homeless and unemployed, work that continues today. Programmes to reach drug abusers and those who are alcohol dependent have been undertaken, but none of this work is allowed to be at the expense of the main work of the Volunteers in providing spiritual help through counselling, Bible study classes, the distribution of religious literature and the holding of non-denominational religious services. Missions and Volunteer centres are to be found throughout the USA. The headquarters is at Metairie, Louisiana.

The Volunteers differ from the Salvation Army in that they are more democratic, observe both baptism and the Lord's Supper and place less emphasis upon sanctification and the tradition of HOLINESS.

WALDENSIAN CHURCH

The Waldensians began as a reform movement in twelfth-century France, organized by Peter Waldo, a rich merchant from Lyons who had become convinced that his prosperity had been gained at the expense of his soul. He decided to seek the apostolic life, sold his possessions and began to wander the country, preaching as he went. Waldo's wife, unhappy about this reversal in her life, complained to the archbishop who forbade Waldo's unauthorized preaching, but he was undeterred.

Gathering some like-minded followers, who were mainly poor people who earned for the group the popular name of *Poor Men of Lyons*, Waldo took to the road and preached the restoration of the Church to make it as Christ had intended. This irritated the ecclesiastical authorities who objected to Waldo's lack of training and his use of translations of parts of the New Testament into the Provençal language. His appeal for authorization to preach having been refused by the Archbishop of Lyons, Waldo appealed to Pope Alexander III (1159–81), but with no success even though Alexander was impressed by Waldo's voluntary poverty.

By 1184, Pope Lucius III had placed the Waldensians under a ban and it was this action that prompted Waldo and his followers to persevere in their preaching, much of it considered heretical by the Church. Waldo taught that there was a priesthood of all believers and that any good Christian man or woman could preach, absolve from sin and administer the sacraments. He also denounced the doctrine of purgatory and the practice of indulgences and refused to recognize the ministry of unworthy priests. The Waldensians also refused to recognize the authority of the secular courts because this entailed the taking of oaths, to which they were strongly opposed. The movement spread rapidly to Spain, northern France, Flanders, southern Germany and southern Italy, and even reached Poland and Hungary. Rome's response was active persecution, and even the execution, of its members. By the end of the thirteenth century many Waldensians had returned to the ROMAN CATHOLIC CHURCH and by the end of the fifteenth century the movement was confined to the French and Italian valleys of the Cottian Alps. In the middle of the nineteenth century, through the *Statute of Emancipation* (1848), the Waldensians received full civil rights in Italy, as well as financial support from fellow

PROTESTANTS in Great Britain and the USA.

The Waldensians were a religious and cultural force in Italy, founding theological colleges in Florence and Rome. The nineteenth century saw the movement of Waldensians from Italy, to Uruguay (1856) where they established a Waldensian Church, and to the USA, where a congregation was founded in the 1890s. This American foundation developed into the First Waldensian Church in 1951, but is now rather diminished in numbers. Small Waldensian groups were also established in Missouri, Texas and Utah and an important community was set up around Valdese, in Burke County, North Carolina.

The supreme governing body of the Church is the annual synod, which meets in Torre Pellice, Italy, and which elects a moderator to govern the Church for a period of seven years; an executive board of seven members assists the moderator. The Church has responsibility for schools, orphanages, homes for the elderly, hospitals and mission support in Africa. There has been some co-operation between Waldensians and the METHODIST CHURCH to the extent that clergy and church members are mutually recognized.

❖ Evangelical Waldensian Church; Poor Men of Lyons; Vaudois; Waldenses; Waldensians

WALWORTH JUMPERS

An English sect founded at the end of the nineteenth century by Mary Ann Girling, a sailor's wife from Suffolk. After the death of eight of her ten children Mary turned to religion for comfort, joining her local METHODIST CHURCH and in time becoming one of its leading preachers. She claimed to have been named as a messenger by Christ himself, through a vision, but for a while she stayed with the Methodists. A second vision commanded her to spread the message of Christ and the imminence of his second coming (REVELATION 20). After more visions, with Christ telling her to leave her husband and remaining children, Mary began her evangelical mission in 1868, leaving Suffolk and going to live in the Walworth area of London, where she attracted many followers. The message she preached was one of immortality for those without sin, which could be achieved only through celibacy; the family break-ups that followed made *Sister* Girling unpopular. Their enthusiastic physical activities during meetings, which included much leaping and throwing themselves around, gave the members of the sect the local name of Walworth Jumpers.

In 1871, after a visit home to Suffolk, *Mother* Girling, as she had now become, met a wealthy woman, Miss Julia Wood, who became a convert and bought for the group a house in the Battersea district of London. Miss Wood, who had visited the SHAKER communities in the USA, enthusiastically embraced her new life and when Mother had another vision, this time telling her that a house in Hampshire, New Forest Lodge at Hordle, was waiting for her to take her followers there in readiness for Christ's second coming, Miss Wood provided money for part-payment of the house; the rest was mortgaged to Mother Girling. Believing that they were divinely directed the group went to Hordle and took occupation of New Forest Lodge, an estate with 30 acres of land.

With even minimal care this could have

provided the group with a comfortable living, but Mother Girling was no manager. Unable to delegate, she insisted on taking full command of the enterprise and it failed dismally, leading eventually to the foreclosure of the mortgage and eviction for Mother and her dwindling group. Miss Wood, now declared insane by doctors brought in by her nephew, left the sect and spent many years in a lunatic asylum. Worse still, some of the members died. Although this was not supposed to happen as they had led the prescribed celibate life inside the group, Mother claimed that they had stopped believing and had therefore ceased to be immortal. With the group's fortunes at their lowest ebb, Mother metamorphosed into the *God-Mother*, dressing in a white robe with blue ribbons and wearing a wreath of china *immortelles*. She walked around barefoot, showing on her feet and hands the stigmata, the marks of the crucifixion, claiming that she was greater than the Holy Ghost and that she was the returned Christ, come back in female form. The Bible was to be ignored as it was only 'the dead letter of God' and superseded now by her own message which, by her way of thinking, made her even greater than God.

In 1886 Mary Girling became terminally ill and died in great agony; she is buried in the cemetery at Hordle. By then her sect had almost died out and it did not long survive her.

❖ Girlingites; Jumpers

WAY OF THE CROSS OF CHRIST

An American ONENESS, PENTECOSTAL Church that was founded by Henry C. Brooks, an independent black Pentecostal minister, in 1927. The members of this Church had previously been part of the CHURCH OF OUR LORD JESUS CHRIST OF THE APOSTOLIC FAITH, INC. (COLJCAF). A disagreement arose about the authoritarian style of Church polity that existed within the COLJCAF and this prompted the formation of independent Pentecostal congregations by Brooks in the eastern USA. The Church currently has 48 congregations, with about 50,000 adult members who are headed by a presiding bishop, assisted by 12 other bishops. The Church has also undertaken mission support in Ghana and Liberia.

WEAVER MENNONITES

A very small American group of MENNONITES, formed around 1916 by two members of the STAUFFER MENNONITE CHURCH, Sensenig and John A. Weaver, over a disagreement about the strict imposition of the *ban*, an instruction to the members of the Church to shun wrongdoing members, when this was applied to Sensenig's wife. Although she was not a member of the Mennonite Church before her marriage, she was received into the Church but later left, at which point the *ban* was imposed. Sensenig and Weaver, believing that a less rigid application of the rule was called for, left to form a new community, known as the Weaver Mennonites, in New Holland, Pennsylvania. The Church has only a single congregation, with around sixty members.

WELSH CALVINIST METHODISTS

The Welsh Calvinist Methodists at one time attracted the disparaging nickname JUMPERS *because of the enthusiastic behaviour of some of its members, who were given to groaning, shouting, singing aloud and jumping to the point of exhaustion as part of an evangelical movement that preceded the arrival in Wales of Methodism.*

The Welsh Calvinist Methodists were partly established in Wales by Thomas Charles in 1811, and later completed, in 1864, when the first general assembly of the Church was held. Doctrinally, the Church adopted a *Confession of Faith* in 1823, which was closely modelled along the lines of the *Westminster Confession*, and a presbyterian polity was agreed upon.

The Church was notable for the quality of some outstanding preachers, including Daniel Rowlands and Howell Harris (1714–73), a Welshman who remained a member of the Church of England despite his enthusiasm for an evangelical style of preaching. The form of Methodism that finally reached Wales, through the ministry of George Whitefield (1714–70) was Calvinist, unlike the Arminian form introduced by John Wesley in England. The Church today, with over a thousand congregations, has been renamed as the Presbyterian Church of Wales and has its headquarters in Brecon.

❖ Jumpers; Presbyterian Church of Wales

WESLEYAN CHURCH

This must not be confused with the Wesleyan Church that was founded in Great Britain and in 1932 became part of the Methodist Church of Great Britain.

An American Church within the Holiness tradition which was formed in 1968 as a result of a merger between the Wesleyan Methodist Church and the Pilgrim Holiness Church; the latter had been formed by the union of several holiness groups.

The Church is administered through a modified episcopal type of polity, by means of a board of general superintendents. Each local church is established within one of two General Conferences, either that of North America, or the Philippines. The general superintendents are elected by the General Conference for a four–year tenure. The day-to-day work of the Church is coordinated through a general board of administration.

WESLEYAN METHODIST ASSOCIATION

A group of British Methodists, formed in 1836, which later merged with the Protestant Methodists (founded Leeds 1827). This newly formed group later united with most members of the Wesleyan Reform Union to form the United Free Methodist Churches in 1857. In 1907, another merger with two other groups led to the formation of the United Methodist Church (UK).

WESLEYAN METHODIST CHURCH

The Wesleyan Methodist Church was formed in the USA, in Utica, New York, in 1843 when some Methodist ministers and laity left the Methodist Episcopal Church in protest against that Church's growing liberalism, especially concerning issues such as slavery and the ownership of slaves by church members, with some disquiet also being expressed at the time about the episcopal style of church government.

As a result some 22 ministers and around 6000 laity withdrew from the Church and formed the Wesleyan Methodist Church, which reiterated its uncompromising stand against the use of alcohol and tobacco, the joining of secret societies and the wearing of fashionable, but worldly, dress. The new group also argued in favour of the teaching of the doctrine of entire sanctification for its members. The Church was administered through annual conferences, to which lay delegates were sent, when a president was elected. The witness of the Church was not limited to the USA, but was established in Australia in 1945.

The Church in the USA formed a merger in 1968 with the PILGRIM HOLINESS CHURCH to form the WESLEYAN CHURCH. Other Wesleyan Methodist Churches can be found in Canada, Great Britain and forty other countries worldwide.

WESLEYAN REFORM UNION

In 1849, those members of the Wesleyan Reformers in Great Britain who would not accede to the union between the METHODIST groups that later formed the UNITED FREE METHODIST CHURCHES (1857), were constituted as the Wesleyan Reform Union.

The disagreement was over the question of polity. The non-acceding Methodists wanted an autonomous form of church government, with each church having the right to administer its own affairs. The Wesleyan Reform Union continues today, with over 2,000 adult members worshipping mainly in the Midlands and Northern England.

❖ Wesleyan Reformers

WEST AFRICAN METHODIST CHURCH IN SIERRA LEONE

Granville Sharp, a member of the CLAPHAM SECT, was responsible for the founding of Sierra Leone in 1787, as a haven for freed African slaves. The foundations of the West African Methodist Church were laid in 1792, with the arrival in Sierra Leone of a Briton, Thomas Clarkson, together with 1100 freed black slaves from Nova Scotia, Canada, to settle in the area as part of the anti-slavery programme of the METHODIST CHURCH. When a Wesleyan missionary from Great Britain, George Warren, arrived in Sierra Leone in 1811, he found that the inhabitants, who had brought their religious affiliations with them from Nova Scotia, had already established the basis of a Methodist congregation. The formal foundation of the Church has been set at 1844 when the Sierra Leone Conference was established. This became actively involved in evangelism, education, agriculture, health concerns, female training centres and the provision of clean water systems.

The West African Methodist Church is the smallest numerically of the Methodist groups in Sierra Leone; others include the large UNITED METHODIST CHURCH (UK) (founded 1850) and the WESLEYAN METHODIST CHURCH.

WESTMINSTER CONFESSION

A creedal statement adhered to by CALVINISTS, composed for the PRESBYTERIAN CHURCH in 1643–6 by order of Parliament during the Interregnum. This statement remains the doctrinal basis of the Presbyterian Church in Scotland.

WISCONSIN EVANGELICAL LUTHERAN SYNOD

Some German immigrants, who had arrived in Wisconsin some ten years earlier, founded this conservative American Lutheran Church in Milwaukee in 1850, in response to a call for pastoral care. In 1917 this synod, along with two other theologically conservative synods, those of Michigan and Minnesota, joined the Lutheran Synodical Conference and were later also federated as a joint synod. The synods merged to form one body known then as the Evangelical Lutheran Joint Synod of Wisconsin and Other States; by 1959 the present name had been adopted.

The synod is uncompromising in its interpretation of doctrine and the Lutheran *Confessions* and will not undertake any form of co-operation with other Lutheran groups unless there is total agreement on doctrine and practice. This policy even extends to a ban on praying with other groups as this is thought to involve compliance with their doctrinal position.

The Church is divided into twelve geographical districts, which all send delegates to the biennial synod meetings. Each congregation is, for the most part, autonomous. An extensive network of schools is maintained, providing an education ranging from parochial to college degree level. Membership of secret Lodges and movements such as the Boy Scouts is forbidden to all church members, and pastors of the Church are not permitted to become military chaplains. The synod supports an extensive home mission programme, especially amongst Native Americans and Hispanic groups. Overseas missions are at present undertaken in Latin and South America, Europe, the Far East and Africa. There are currently 1,225 congregations and about 320,000 adult members, excluding those living outside the USA; the headquarters is in Milwaukee, Wisconsin.

WORLDWIDE CHURCH OF GOD

The American denomination known as the Worldwide Church of God was founded originally as the Radio Church of God by Herbert W. Armstrong (1892–1986). As a young man, Armstrong had a conversion experience that led him to a study of the Bible, from which he drew and acted upon his own conclusions. In 1931 he was ordained into the ministry of the Oregon Conference of the Churches of God, a sabbatarian group that he had joined in 1927, becoming an active member. After his ordination, Armstrong started to deliver a series of lectures in and around Eugene, Oregon, and in 1934 he launched the radio programme known as *The World Tomorrow* and produced a small publication called *The Plain Truth*.

By the late-1930s Armstrong's activities led to his being obliged to leave his ministry in the Church of God and he founded his own group, which adopted its present name in 1968. Moving to Pasadena, California, in 1947, Armstrong launched the Ambassador College as a training ground for ministers of his Church. Still operating as the Radio Church of God, the message was broadcast around the world; in the 1960s a television ministry supplemented this.

Armstrong denied many tenets of evangelical Christianity, such as the Trinity, the person of the Holy Spirit and the full deity of Jesus Christ. He also taught British Israelism, which was a belief suggested by a Scotsman, John Wilson, in 1840 that the dispersed *Lost Ten Tribes of Israel* had migrated to Europe and that the prophecies in the Bible about the tribes of Ephraim and Manasseh refer directly to Great Britain and the USA. By promoting these ideas Armstrong was able to apply certain prophecies to Great

Britain, the USA and, later, to the European Community, especially those about the End Time (REVELATION 20). He affirmed that Jesus Christ's return to earth was imminent and that true believers would be the rulers of the world during the millennium, a time when others would be given the opportunity to be saved, with destruction, rather than hell, as the fate of the unsaved. Armstrong also taught that the Bible is literally true, including the account of the creation in Genesis, and required of the members that they avoid sin, keep the Jewish dietary laws, provide money for the Church through tithing, refuse conventional medical treatment, use no cosmetics and give up the celebration of birthdays and the Christian feasts of Easter and Christmas.

Although initially very successful in attracting members, church growth declined during the 1970s and disagreements broke out from within its ranks. Armstrong and his son, Garner Ted, fell out with the result that the younger Armstrong left the Church, taking with him about 1,000 followers; in 1978 he formed the Church of God International.

Herbert W. Armstrong died in 1986, which ran contrary to the commonly held belief that he would be around to see Christ's return to earth and receive his reward. Just prior to his death, Armstrong appointed a successor, Joseph W. Tkach (pronounced Ta-cotch), who made important doctrinal changes that included the abandonment of the teaching of British Israelism. Tithing was also made voluntary, the Trinity was reinstated and the observance of the sabbath as the day of worship was to be considered traditional, rather than imperative. These changes, which were continued after the death of Tkach in 1995 by his son, Joseph Tkach Jnr, caused many to leave the Church and found new groups. These were mainly dedicated to teaching various forms of Armstrong-ism and drew thousands away from the Church. Today, the Worldwide Church of God is largely an evangelical Church in which believer's baptism and Holy Communion are celebrated. The priesthood is all male and women are not admitted on the premis that this is not sanctioned in the New Testament. The stringent rules about an acceptable lifestyle have been moderated and while the taking of drugs is still strictly proscribed, the use of alcohol is permitted in small quantities and tobacco is only discouraged, but not forbidden.

There have been moves to reform the Church from within, to return it to its former beliefs, and a small schism resulted in the formation of the Worldwide Church of God Restored, but little encouragement was received. The headquarters of the Church is in Pasadena, California.

Z

ZILLERTHAL EVANGELICALS

The Zillerthal Evangelicals were a group of PROTESTANTS who lived in Zillerthal, a valley in the Austrian Tyrol, in the nineteenth century and who seceded from the ROMAN CATHOLIC CHURCH in 1829. They were persuaded to leave their Church by the enthusiastic evangelical teaching of two brothers from Mairhofen, called Stainer.

The Archbishop of Salzburg, Frederick Schwarzenberg (1809–85), and the Roman Catholic authorities were alarmed and tried to persuade these protestant converts to return to the Roman Catholic Church, using alternate methods of gentle persuasion and harassment, but all to no avail. The Tyrol had always been tolerant of protestantism but, seeking to avoid possible trouble, the group left Zillerthal in 1837 and travelled north in six wagons, to form a colony at Erdmannsdorf in Silesia, on land granted to them by King Frederick William III of Prussia (1797–1840), who had been made sympathetic to their cause following the visit of one of his court preachers, named Strauss, to Zillerthal and his description of their difficult position.

ZION CHRISTIAN CHURCH

This large South African denomination was founded in 1914 and is in the PENTECOSTAL tradition, being derived from the Apostolic Faith Mission that was founded in 1908 as a Pentecostal breakaway from the DUTCH REFORMED CHURCH. The emphasis of the Church is upon a ministry of healing and deliverance, provided through confessions, purification rites and exorcisms. Baptisms are conducted in flowing rivers and worship services are ritualistic, accompanied by singing, dancing, clapping of the hands and the wearing of special garments, usually of green and yellow.

The Zion Christian Church is one of the largest of the 2,500 Zion bodies in South Africa, none of which is recognized by the government as being registered for grants of land for building places of worship.

ZION'S ORDER OF THE SONS OF LEVI

An ex-minister of the CHURCH OF JESUS CHRIST OF LATTER-DAY SAINTS, Mark Kilgore, who, having left that group to join the AARONIC ORDER, moved to live in Bicknell, Utah, where he came under the influence of a local sawmill owner named Taylor. Taylor successfully persuaded Kilgore that they should join together and found yet another religious group; this they called Zion's Order of the Sons of Levi. A commune was opened at Mansfield, Missouri, in 1953. Most of the teaching coming from the group is centred on more than 650 revelations that Mark Kilgour claims to have received since 1951, the bulk of which revolve around the running of the group. Members believe that the site of their commune is the place referred to in Isaiah 2:2 as the place where Zion will be built anew. An effort to get others to join them in this work does not seem to have met with great success.

ZWICKAU PROPHETS

Martin Luther (1483–1546) gave this label to three early sixteenth-century German ANABAPTIST reformers, Nicholas Storch (d. 1530), Thomas Drechsel and Marcus Stübner. Their doctrines included the rejection of both infant baptism and a professional clergy, since these reformers considered all men to be equal and under the direct influence of the Holy Spirit. They also preached the imminence of Christ's return to earth and the value of revelation through dreams and visions (REVELATION 20).

It was while the three reformers were in their native town of Zwickau that they may have influenced Thomas Münzer (*c.* 1490–1525), a preacher in the LUTHERAN CHURCH. Münzer angered the church authorities by teaching what they considered to be subversive doctrines, for which he was banned from the city by the civil authorities who recognized the dangers in teaching the equality of all men and insisting that all goods should be held in common.

Storch and his companions went to Wittenberg in 1521, where their preaching attracted many followers and impressed Philipp Melanchthon (1497–1560), the protestant reformer, who was Professor of Greek at the University of Wittenberg. However, their teaching about Christ's second coming (REVELATION 20) and their criticism of the Wittenberg liturgy led to the expulsion of the Zwickau Prophets from that city in 1522. Beyond this point little is known of the group except that Storch died in 1525.

Thomas Münzer, meanwhile, went to Bohemia and subsequently to Allstedt where he married a former nun. He eventually became involved in the peasant's revolt in Germany (1524–6), his teachings influencing the peasants in their demands for reform, and he was finally apprehended and executed.

❖ Storchites

ZWINGLIANS

Followers of Ulrich Zwingli (1484–1531), a leader of PROTESTANTISM in Switzerland who, having been elected as people's preacher at the Old Minster in Zürich in 1518, attracted much attention through his sermons and denunciations.

Having learnt from Erasmus, Zwingli was clearly a humanist but, unlike Martin Luther, he had little respect for the past and the traditional ways of worship. To Zwingli, everything connected with public worship had to be authorized explicitly by the scriptures. In the course of his Zürich lectures on the New Testament, given in 1519, Zwingli attacked purgatory, the invocation of the saints and monasticism. He called for freedom from papal and episcopal control for believers. He further taught that the Holy Mass should be abolished, papal authority rejected and clerical celibacy likewise consigned to oblivion, appealing to the Bible as the sole source of truth.

Zwingli married in 1524 and there followed a period of great development in his distinctive Eucharistic teaching. He did not accept any kind of Real Presence in the Eucharist, unlike Luther, who was accused of teaching that this Real Presence was there by *impanation*, a sort of embodiment of Christ's presence in the sacred elements of the Eucharist. An attempt to resolve the differences between the Lutheran theologians, represented by Martin Luther, Philipp Melanchthon and others and the Swiss and Strasbourg theologians, represented by Zwingli, Martin Bucer and others, at the Marburg Colloquy in 1529 failed to settle the question of the nature of the Lord's Supper. This was the fifteenth and last Article to be discussed, with general agreement achieved on the other fourteen, which dealt with such matters as the Trinity, Christology and justification by faith. Towards the end of his life Zwingli seems to have moved away from his earlier belief that the Eucharist was a mere memorial and towards a belief in the doctrine of spiritual presence.

Zwingli had the support of the city council of Zürich and steps were taken to abolish images, pictures, relics and organs from the city churches; the altars, too, were stripped of any ornamentation. Unlike Luther, Zwingli sought to abolish hymns, as being unscriptural, and preferred that they should be replaced by metrical versions of the psalms. Zwingli was killed during the battle of Kappel in 1531, an altercation between Zürich and the Catholic cantons.

ALTERNATIVE NAMES

Alternative name	*See entry*
Abelians	Abelites
Abelonians	Abelites
Abyssinian Church	Ethiopian Orthodox Church
Acacians	Homoeans
Adelphians	Euchites
Adoptionists	Monarchians
Advent Christian Association	Advent Christian Church
Advent Christian General Conference of America	Advent Christian Church
Aetians	Exoucontians
African Reformed Church in Zimbabwe	Reformed Church in Zimbabwe
African Union and First Colored Methodist Protestant Church of America or Elsewhere	African Union First Colored Methodist Protestant Church
African Union Methodist Protestant Church	African Union First Coloured Methodist Protestant Church
African Universal Church and Commercial League	African Universal Church
Aglipayan Church	Philippine Independent Church
Agonistici	Circumcellions
Agonistics	Circumcellions
Albigenses	Albigensians
Alethians	Shakers
All-One-God-Faith, Inc.	All-One-Faith-in-One-God-State Inc.
All-Union Council of Evangelical Christians and Baptists	Union of Evangelical Christian-Baptists of the Russian Federation
Allegheny Conference	Allegheny Wesleyan Methodist Connection
Alogians	Alogi
Alumbrados	Illuminati
Amana Community of Inspirationists	Amana Church Society
Aminadab	Religious Society of Friends

Alternative name	*See entry*
Amminadab	Religious Society of Friends
Amis de l'Homme	Friends of Man
American Bible Churches	American Evangelical Christian Church
American Millennial Adventists	Evangelical Adventists
Ancient Oriental Churches	Oriental Orthodox Churches
Angel of the Lord Philanthropic Association	Friends of Man
Anglican Church in Aotearoa, New Zealand and Polynesia	New Zealand, Anglican Church in
Anglican Church of Papua New Guinea	Papua New Guinea, Anglican Province of
Anomoeans	Exoucontians
Anti-Mission Baptists	Primitive Baptists – Moderates
Apostolic Brethren	Apostolici
Apostolic Faith Mission of Portland, Oregon	Apostolic Faith (Oregon)
Apostolic Service Church	Old Catholic Orthodox Church
Apostolics	Apotactics
Apotactites	Apotactics
Armenian Church	Armenian Apostolic Church
Army of the Eternal, The	Friends of Man
Assyrian Church	Assyrian Church of the East
Australasian Christian Fellowship of Apostolic Faith	Church of Jesus Christ End Time Revival
Autocephalous Orthodox Church of Poland	Polish Orthodox Church
Awakenists	New Awakening
(BC America)	Conservative Baptist Association of America
Bali Christian Protestant Church	Protestant Christian Church of Bali
Baptist Bible Union	General Association of Regular Baptist Churches
Baptist Unitarians	Christian Church
Barclayites	Barclayans
Basel Church	Basel Christian Church of Malaysia
Batak Protestant Christian Church	Batak Christian Protestant Church
Behmenists	Philadelphians
Bekennende Kirche	Confessing Church
Belarusian Catholics	Belarusian Uniat Catholic Church
Belarusian Greek Catholics	Belarusian Uniat Catholic Church
Believers	Plymouth Brethren
Bereans	Barclayans
Bethel Assembly	Bethel Baptist Assembly, Inc.
Bethel Ministerial Association	Bethel Baptist Assembly, Inc.
Bible Communists	Oneida Community
Bible Methodist Connection of Tennessee	Bible Methodist Church

Alternative name	*See entry*
Bickertonite Organization, The	Church of Jesus Christ (Bickertonite)
Bickertonites	Church of Jesus Christ (Bickertonite)
Black Jews	Church of God and Saints of Christ
Black Stockings	Cooneyites
Bohemian Brethren	Unitas Fratrum
Borneo Basel Self-Established Church	Basel Christian Church of Malaysia
Brethren of the Covenant	Melchiorites
Brethren of the Free Spirit	Amalricians
Brinsers	United Zion Church
Brothers of Christ	Christadelphians
Brüdergemeinde	Mennonite Brethren Church of North America
Bryanites	Bible Christians
Byelo-Russian Byzantine Catholic Church	Belarusian Uniat Catholic Church
Byelo-Russian Autocephalous Orthodox Church	Belarusian Autocephalic Orthodox Church
Byelo-Russian Orthodox Church	Belarusian Orthodox Church
Caianites	Cainites
Calvary Pentecostal Church, Inc	Calvary Pentecostal Church
Cataphrygians	Montanists
Cathars	Albigensians
Catholic Church of the Apostles of the Latter Times	Renovated Church of Christ
Charismatic Episcopal Church	Charismatic Episcopal Church of North America
Chiliasm	Millenarianists
Chiliasts	Millenarianists
Chinese Christian Three-Self Patriotic Church	Chinese Christian Three-Self Movement
Christ Foundation Church	Meserete Kristos Church
Christ is the Foundation Church	Meserete Kristos Church
Christian Catholic Apostolic Church	Christian Catholic Church
Christian Community Church, The	Christian Catholic Church
Christian Faith Band	Church of God (Apostolic)
Christian Growth Ministries	Discipleship Movement
Christian Marching Church of Central Africa	God Bless Christian Marching Church
Christian Workers for Fellowship	Church of the Living God
Christians	Plymouth Brethren
Christians of St John	Mandaeans
Church Equality Baptists	American Baptist Association
Church of God (Bishop Poteat)	Church of God (House of Prayer)
Church of God (Huntsville)	Church of God (World Headquarters)

Alternative name	*See entry*
Church of God of All Nations	Church of God (Jerusalem Acres)
Church of God of the Abrahamic Faith	Church of God General Conference (Abrahamic Faith)
Church of God General Conference	Church of God General Conference (Abrahamic Faith)
Church of God in Christ Jesus	Church of God General Conference (Abrahamic Faith)
Church of God Reformation Movement	Church of God (Anderson)
Church of Greece	Greek Orthodox Church
Church of Jesus Christ of Latter-Day Saints (Strangite)	Church of Jesus Christ (Strangite)
Church of Laestadius	Apostolic Lutheran Church of America
Church of Sobantu	Church of England in South Africa
Church of the Agapemone	Agapemonites
Church of the Full Gospel, Inc	Evangelical Baptist Church
Church of the Initiates	Bwiti
Church of the Kingdom of God, The	Friends of Man
Church of the Lord (Aladura or Praying)	Aladura International Church, UK and Overseas
Church of the New Jerusalem	Swedenborgians
Church of the United Brethren in Christ (New Constitution)	United Brethren in Christ
Church of the United Brethren in Christ (Old Constitution)	United Brethren in Christ
Churches of God in Ireland	God's Apostolic Church
Churches of God in North America (General Eldership)	Churches of God General Conference
Churches of God in the Fellowship of the Son of God, the Lord Jesus Christ	Churches of God in the British Isles and Overseas (Needed Truth)
Clementines	Petite Église
Colored Cumberland Presbyterian Church	Second Cumberland Presbyterian Church in America
Community Churches	American Evangelical Lutheran Church
Confessional Church	Confessing Church
Confessors of the Glory of Christ	Schwenckfeldians
Congregational Church of Scotland	Scottish Congregational Church
Conservative Amish Mennonite Church	Conservative Mennonite Conference
Convention, The	General Convention of the New Jerusalem in the USA
Convulsionists	Convulsionaries
Covenanters	Melchiorites
Crypto-Calvinists	Philippists
Cumberland Presbyterian Church in America	Cumberland Presbyterian Church

Alternative name	*See entry*
Cyranists	Jansenism
Czechoslovak Church	Czechoslovak Hussite Church
Damnation Army	Cooneyites
Dancers	Molokan Spiritual Christians
Defenseless Mennonite Brethren of Christ in North America	Fellowship of Evangelical Bible Churches
Dippers	Cooneyites
Disciples of Christ	Christian Church (Disciples of Christ)
Donkey Church	Bantu Methodist Church
Door, The	Potter's House
Duck River Baptists	Duck River (and Kindred) Association of Baptists
Dukhobors	Doukhobors
Dunkers	Church of the Brethren
Eastern Church	Eastern Orthodox Church
Ebenezer Society	Amana Church Society
Elder Michaux Church of God	Gospel Spreading Church
Elim Foursquare Gospel Alliance	Elim Pentecostal Church
Elim Missionary Assemblies	Elim Assemblies
Enlightened Ones	Illuminati
Esikoiet	Apostolic Lutheran (Church of the First Born)
Estonian Evangelical Lutheran Church Abroad	Estonian Evangelical Church in Exile
Ethiopian Orthodox Tewahedo Church	Ethiopian Orthodox Church
Ethiopian Overcoming Holy Church of God	Apostolic Overcoming Holy Church of God
Etoism	Christian Fellowship Church
Euro-Asiatic Federation of Evangelical Christians-Baptists	Union of Evangelical Christian-Baptists of the Russian Federation
Evangelical Christian Churches	American Evangelical Lutheran Church
Evangelical Church Mekane Yesus	Ethiopian Evangelical Church Mekane Yesus
Evangelical Church of Bohemian Brethren	Evangelical Church of Czech Brethren
Evangelical Church of Egypt	Coptic Evangelical Church
Evangelical Church of Egypt, Synod of the Nile	Coptic Evangelical Church
Evangelical Covenant Church	Evangelical Covenant Church of America
Evangelical Lutheran Church in Denmark	Church of Denmark
Evangelical Lutheran Church in Oldenburg	Lutheran Church of Oldenburg
Evangelical Lutheran Church of Finland	Finland, Church of

Alternative name	*See entry*
Evangelical Lutheran Church of Iceland	Iceland, National Church of
Evangelical Mennonite Brethren Conference	Fellowship of Evangelical Bible Churches
Evangelical United Brethren Church	United Brethren in Christ
Evangelical Unity of the Czech-Moravian Brethren in North America	Unity of the Brethren
Evangelical Waldensian Church	Waldensian Church
Evangelistic Association	International Church of the Four Square Gospel
Evangelistic Missionary Alliance	Bethel Baptist Assembly, Inc.
Family, The	Children of God
Family of Love, The	Children of God
Family of Love	Familists
Federation of Latvian Evangelical Lutheran Church in America	Latvian Evangelical Lutheran Church in America
Fellowship of Evangelical Bible Christians	Fellowship of Evangelical Bible Churches
Fellowship of Grace Brethren Churches	Brethren Church (Grace Group)
Filipino Assemblies of God	Philippino Assemblies of the First Born
Filochois	Petite Église
Finnish Apostolic Lutheran Church of America	Apostolic Lutheran Church of America
Fire-Baptized Holiness Church of God	Fire Baptized Holiness Church of God of the Americas
First Born Laestadians	Apostolic Lutheran (Church of the First Born)
Fora	Lesotho Evangelical Church
Fraternitas Rosae Crucis	Church of Illumination
Free Will Baptists	National Association of Free Will Baptists
French Prophets	Camisards
Friends, The	Religious Society of Friends
Friends of the Temple	Temple Society
General Association of Separate Baptists	Separate Baptists in Christ
General Association of Separatist Baptists	Separate Baptists in Christ
General Conference of Mennonite Brethren Churches	Mennonite Brethren Church of North America
General Conference of the Evangelical Baptist Church	Evangelical Baptist Church
General Conference of the New Church	Swedenborgians
General Six Principle Baptists	Six Principle Baptists
German Baptist Brethren	Church of the Brethren
German Christians	Faith Movement of German Christians
German-Christian Church	Faith Movement of German Christians

Alternative name	*See entry*
Gichtelians	Angelic Brethren
Girlingites	Walworth Jumpers
Glassites	Glasites
Go-Preachers	Cooneyites
Gospel Harvesters Evangelical Association	Gospel Harvester Churches
Greek Archdiocese of North & South America	Greek Orthodox Archdiocese of North and South America
Greek Catholic Church	Greek Eastern-rite Catholics
Greek Church, The	Greek Orthodox Church
Gregorian Church	Armenian Apostolic Church
Hackney Phalanx	Clapton Sect
Hard Shell Baptists	Primitive Baptists – Moderates
Harmonists	Harmony Society
Harris Church	Harrist Church (Ivory Coast)
Head-less	Acephalites
Heavenly Christianity Church	Celestial Church of Christ
Hicksites	Hicksite Quakers
High Attainers	Ranters
Hinschites	Hinschite Evangelical Church
Hoffmanites	United Christian Church
Holy Apostolic and Catholic Church of the East	Assyrian Church of the East
Holy Church of North Carolina	United Holy Church of America, Inc.
Holy Church of North Carolina and Virginia	United Holy Church of America, Inc.
Holy Greek Orthodox Archdiocese of Vasiloupolis	Greek Orthodox Archdiocese of Vasiloupolis
Holy Orthodox Archdiocese of Vasiloupolis	Greek Orthodox Archdiocese of Vasiloupolis
Holy Orthodox Church of Japan	Japan Orthodox Church
Hussite Church of the Czech Republic	Czechoslovak Hussite Church
Hutterian Brethren	Hutterites
Hydroparastatae	Aquarians
Hypsistians	Hypsistarians
Illuminati	Alumbrados
Illumines	Petite Église
Independent Episcopal Church	African Orthodox Church
Independent Methodist Connexion	Independent Methodist Church
Independent Pentecostal Churches	Independent Assemblies of God, International
Independents	Brownists
Indian Orthodox Church	Malankara Orthodox Syrian Church

Alternative name	*See entry*
International Communion of the Charismatic Episcopal Church	Charismatic Episcopal Church of North America
Italo-Greek Church	Italo-Albanian Catholic Church
Italo-Greek-Albanian Church	Italo-Albanian Catholic Church
Irvingites	Catholic Apostolic Church
Jerusalem Friends	Temple Society
Jesus Army	Jesus Fellowship Church
Jesus Fellowship Army	Jesus Fellowship Church
Jesus Freaks	Jesus Movement
Jesus Revolution	Jesus Movement
Jesus Way, The	Cooneyites
Jumpers	Molokan Spiritual Christians
Jumpers	Walworth Jumpers
Jumpers	Welsh Calvinist Methodists
Kenya African Church	African Church
Kilhamites	Methodist New Connexion
Kirisuto Kyodai-Dan	Christian Brotherhood Church
La Puerta	Potter's House
Lakher Independent Evangelical Church	Mara Evangelical Church
Lampetians	Euchites
Landmarker Baptists	American Baptist Association
Landmarkers	American Baptist Association
Leapers	Molokan Spiritual Christians
Lefebvrists	Society of St Pius X
Lefebvrites	Society of St Pius X
Legatine Arians	Seekers
Lesser Eastern Churches	Oriental Orthodox Churches
Little Congregation, The	Evangelical Mennonite Church
Little Russians	Ukrainian Catholic Church
Living Church	Renovated Church
Living Water Christian Church (*sic*)	Living Waters Christian Fellowship
Lord's New Church Which is Nova Hierosolyma	Lord's New Church, The
Louisets	Petite Église
Lumpa (Visible Salvation) Church	Lumpa Church
Lusitanian Church, Catholic, Apostolic, Evangelical	Lusitanian Church
Luxmore Needed Truth	Churches of God in the British Isles and Overseas (Needed Truth)
Macedonians	Pneumatomachi

Alternative name	*See entry*
Malankara Orthodox Syrian Church – Catholicate of the East	Malankara Orthodox Syrian Church
Malankarese Christians	Syro-Malankarese Church
Mar Thoma Syrian Church of Malabar	Mar Thoma Syrian Church
Marathonians	Pneumatomachi
Megiddo Mission	Megiddo Church
Melchites	Melkites
Messalians	Euchites
Messiah's World Crusade	Universal Industrial Church of the New World Comforter
Methodist Church in Tonga	Free Wesleyan Church of Tonga
Metropolia	Orthodox Church in America
Millennial Church	Shakers
Millennial Dawn Students	Millennial Dawnists
Millennial Dawnists and International Bible Students	Jehovah's Witnesses
Ministers and Churches of the Lord Jesus Christ	Church of Jesus Christ End Time Revival
Mission Covenant Church of Sweden	Swedish Mission Covenant Church
Modalists	Monarchians
Monotheletism	Monothelitism
Moravian Brethren	Moravian Church
Moravian Brethren	Unitas Fratrum
Morisonians	Evangelical Union
Mormons	Church of Jesus Christ of Latter-Day Saints
Mummyjums	Pilgrims
Nameless House Church, The	Cooneyites
Nasoraeans	Mandaeans
National Church of Czechoslovakia	Czechoslovak Hussite Church
National Church of Denmark	Church of Denmark
National Council of Congregational Churches	Congregational-Christian Churches
National Fellowship of Brethren Churches	Brethren Church (Grace Group)
Nazarites	Free Methodist Church of North America
Nestorian Church	Assyrian Church of the East
Netherlands Free Reformed Churches	Netherlands Reformed Churches
Neu Teufer	Church of the Brethren
New and Latter House of Israel	Jezreelites
New Beginnings Church of Jesus Christ	New Beginnings
New Beginnings Fellowship	New Beginnings
New Church	General Church of the New Jerusalem
New Itinerancy, The	Methodist New Connexion
New Methodists, The	Methodist New Connexion

Alternative name	*See entry*
New Testament Church, The	Cooneyites
Nias Protestant Christian Church	Nias Christian Protestant Church
Nicolaites	Nicolaitans
Non-Chalcedonian Churches	Oriental Orthodox Churches
Non-Denominational Church, The	Cooneyites
(Non-Papal Catholic) Evangelical Orthodox (Catholic) Church in America	Evangelical Orthodox (Catholic) Church in America (Non-Papal Catholic)
North American Baptist General Conference	North American Baptist Conference
Norwegian Synod of the American Evangelical Lutheran Church	Evangelical Lutheran Synod
Old Apostolic Lutheran Church	Apostolic Lutheran (Church of the First Born)
Old Catholic Episcopal Church	Old Catholic Church (Anglican Rite)
Old Landmarkers	American Baptist Association
Old Order (Black Bumper) Mennonites – Weaverland Conference	Old Order (Horning) Mennonites – Weaverland Conference
Old Order Dunkers	Old German Baptist Brethren (Old Order Dunkers)
Old Ritualists	Old Believers
Old School Baptists	Primitive Baptists – Moderates
One World Family	Universal Industrial Church of the New World Comforter
Order of St Germain	Liberal Catholic Church, Order of St Germain
Order of St Germain Ecclesia Catholica Liberalis	Liberal Catholic Church, Order of St Germain
Oriental Malankara Orthodox Syrian Church of India	Malankara Orthodox Syrian Church
Orthodox Christian Church	Eastern Orthodox Church
Orthodox Church in Japan	Japan Orthodox Church
Orthodox Church of Poland	Polish Orthodox Church
Orthodox Syrian Church of the East	Malankara Orthodox Syrian Church
Ortlibenses	Ortlibarii
Ortlibians	Ortlibarii
Palaioemerologitai	Old Calendarists
Patarelli	Patarines
Patarins	Patarines
Patripassians	Monarchians
Patripassians	Sabellians
Peculiar People, The	Plumstead Peculiars
Peculiars	Plumstead Peculiars

Alternative name	*See entry*
Pentecostal Church of God International	Pentecostal Church of God (of America)
Pentecostal Free Will Baptist Church, Inc.	Pentecostal Free Will Baptist Church
People's Church, The	Iceland, National Church of
Pepuzians	Montanists
Perfectibilists	Illuminati
Perfectionists	Oneida Community
Philadelphists	Philadelphians
Philanthropic Association of the Friends of Man, The	Friends of Man
Philomarianites	Collyridians
Phrygians	Montanists
Pikarti	Picards
Pilgrims	Cooneyites
Pneumatomachians	Pneumatomachi
Polish National Catholic Church of America and Poland	Polish National Catholic Church of America
Poor Men of Lyons	Waldensian Church
Portuguese Episcopal Church	Lusitanian Church
Praise Chapel, Grace Chapel	Potter's House
Presbyterian Church in Liberia	Presbytery of Liberia in West Africa
Presbyterian Church of Mozambique	Ronga-Tsonga Presbyterian Church
Presbyterian Church of Singapore and Malaysia	Chinese Christian Church
Presbyterian Church of Wales	Welsh Calvinist Methodists
Primitive Baptists – Regular	Primitive Baptists – Moderates
Protestant Church in Sabah	Basel Christian Church of Malaysia
Protestant Church of Curaçao	United Protestant Church of Curaçao
Protestant Orthodox Western Church	Evangelical Orthodox (Catholic) Church in America (Non-Papal Catholic)
Quaker Methodists	Bible Christians
Quakers	Religious Society of Friends
Radio Church of God	Gospel Spreading Church
Ranters	Primitive Methodist Church
Rappites	Harmony Society
Reformed Evangelical Church	Evangelical Presbyterian Church of Australia
Reformed Presbyterian Church	Macmillanites
Reidites	Cooneyites
Religious Libertines	Ranters
Religious Society of Friends (General Conference)	Hicksite Quakers
Remonstrant Brotherhood	Dutch Remonstrant Brotherhood

Alternative name	*See entry*
Remonstrant Reformed Congregation	Dutch Remonstrant Brotherhood
Renewed Church	Renovated Church
Renewed Church of Jesus	Renovated Church of Christ
Renewed Church of the Brethren	Moravian Church
Renewed Unitas Fratrum	Moravian Church
Renovationist Church	Renovated Church
Renunciators	Apostolici
Restored Apostolic Mission Church	Restored Apostolic Missionary Church
Rhynsbergers	Collegiants
River Brethren	Brethren in Christ Church
Romanian Orthodox Missionary Arch-Diocese in America and Canada	Romanian Orthodox Church of America
Romanian Orthodox Missionary Episcopate	Romanian Orthodox Church of America
Rosicrucians	Illuminati
Russellites	Jehovah's Witnesses
Russian Catholics of the Byzantine Rite	Russian Catholic Church
Russian Exarchate in Western Europe	Orthodox Church, Archdiocese of France and Western Europe
Russian Greek Catholic Church	Orthodox Church in America
Russian Orthodox Church Abroad	Russian Orthodox Church Outside Russia
Russian Orthodox Church in Exile	Russian Orthodox Church Outside Russia
Ruthenians	Ukrainian Catholic Church
Sabbatarian Baptists	Seventh-Day Baptist Church
Sabellians	Monarchians
Sabians	Mandaeans
St Thomas Christians	Syro-Malabarese Church
Saints	Plymouth Brethren
Salvationists	Salvation Army
Sandemanians	Glasites
Scandinavian Assemblies of God in the USA, Canada and Foreign Lands	Independent Assemblies of God, International
Scandinavian Free Baptist Society	Independent Baptist Church of America
Scandinavian Independent Baptist Denomination in the United States of America	Independent Baptist Church of America
Scattered Flock	Seekers
Schwarzenau Brethren	Church of the Brethren
Schwenkfeldians	Schwenckfeldians
Second Cumberland Presbyterian Church in the United States	Second Cumberland Presbyterian Church in America
Secret Sect, The	Cooneyites
Seventh Day Baptist General Conference USA and Canada	Seventh-Day Baptist Church

Alternative name	*See entry*
Skippers	Molokan Spiritual Christians
Society of Dependants	Cokelers
Society of Friends	Religious Society of Friends
Spirit Fighters	Doukhbors
Spirit Fighters	Pneumatomachi
Spiritual Food Church	Ling Liang Chinese Church
Spiritual Food Church of Indonesia	Ling Liang Chinese Church
Spiritual Food Worldwide Evangelical Mission	Ling Liang Chinese Church
Starkyites	Agapemonites
Steadfast, or Constant, Molokans	Molokan Spiritual Christians
Stevenists	Petite Église
Storchites	Zwickau Prophets
Strict Baptists	Gospel Standard Strict Baptist Churches
Stundo-Baptists	Stundists
Swedenborgians	General Church of the New Jerusalem
Swedenborgians	General Convention of the New Jerusalem in the USA
Swedish Evangelical Mission Covenant Church of America	Evangelical Covenant Church of America
Swedish Independent Baptist Church	Independent Baptist Church of America
Synergists	Philippists
Synod of United Original Seceders	Original Secession Church
Syrian Indian Church of the Patriarch of Antioch	Malankara Syrian Orthodox Church
Syrian Jacobite Church	Syrian Orthodox Church
Syrian Orthodox Church of the Patriarch of Antioch	Malankara Syrian Orthodox Church
Syro-Malankarese of the Antiochene Rite	Syro-Malankarese Church
Testimony, The	Cooneyites
Themistians	Agnoetae
Thomasites	Christadelphians
Tramp Preachers	Cooneyites
True Church of Jesus Christ (Cutlerite)	Church of Jesus Christ (Cutlerite)
True Holland Reformed Church	Christian Reformed Church
True Levellers	Diggers
Truth, The	Cooneyites
Tunkers	Church of the Brethren
Two-by-Two Preachers (2x2 Preachers)	Cooneyites
Ultraquists	Calixtines
Utraquists	Calixtines
Uniat Churches	Eastern Catholic Churches

Alternative name	*See entry*
United Evangelical Lutheran Churches in India	United Evangelical Lutheran Church in India
United Free Church (Continuing)	United Free Church of Scotland
United Free Will Baptist Church (Colored)	United Free Will Baptists
United Holy Church of America	United Holy Church of America, Inc.
United House of Prayer for All People	United House of Prayer for All People of the Church on the Rock of the Apostolic Faith
United Mennonite Brethren of North America	Fellowship of Evangelical Bible Christians
United Society for Believers in Christ's Second Coming	Shakers
United Zion's Children	United Zion Church
Utraquists	Calixtines
Vaudois	Waldensian Church
Victory Chapel, the Christian Fellowship	Potter's House
Waldenses	Waldensian Church
Waldensians	Waldensian Church
Watch Tower and Tract Society	Jehovah's Witnesses
Way, The	Cooneyites
Wee Frees	Free Church of Scotland
Wesleyan Reformers	Wesleyan Reform Union
Western Laestadians	Apostolic Lutheran (Church of the First Born)
Winebrennerians	Churches of God General Conference
Wycliffites	Hussites
Zion's Watch Tower	Jehovah's Witnesses